A Pentecostal Commentary on
ROMANS

The Pentecostal Old and New Testament Commentaries

Series Preface

Over the last century, the Pentecostal movement has transformed the face of global Christianity. Nevertheless, Pentecostal voices continue to be underrepresented in biblical scholarship. Therefore, we would like to introduce *The Pentecostal Old and New Testament Commentaries*. The Pentecostal authors of this series come to the text with a high view of Scripture; however, we desire to say more than has already been said by non-Pentecostals. Thus, the contributors to this series have been charged with the task of articulating a truly Pentecostal perspective on every verse of the Bible.

This grand vision began in the heart of our series founder, Eun Chul Kim. He spent nearly a decade tirelessly advocating for this Pentecostal commentary and recruiting authors. However, like so many of God's servants, it was not given to him to see the fulfillment of the promise. On September 22, 2018, Kim succumbed to cancer, but his vision continues.

The commentaries themselves target the educated layperson, Pentecostal pastor, and student of the Bible and focus their attention on the exegesis and translation of the Greek (NA28) and Hebrew (BHS and BHQ) texts. In keeping with the diversity that characterizes Pentecostals and Charismatics themselves, we have left the authors with a great deal of liberty regarding their approaches. As the editors, we highly value academic freedom. Consequently, although all the authors identify as Pentecostals and greatly esteem the authority of Scripture, we have not required them to espouse any particular theological viewpoints or to take any prescribed theological positions. Accordingly, each author is responsible for what he or she has written and not the editors. Although the approaches of the various authors vary widely, two things have been deemed essential: a rigorously critical approach and a distinctively Pentecostal contribution. This combination will certainly profit Pentecostal believers whether in the pew, the pulpit, or the classroom.

It is our sincere prayer that God will use this commentary series to encourage Pentecostals everywhere to read the Bible *as Pentecostals*.

CHRISTOPHER L. CARTER—New Testament Editor
DAVID C. HYMES—Old Testament Editor

A Pentecostal Commentary on
ROMANS

Introduction, Translation, and Commentary

Glen W. Menzies

Foreword by Doug Clay

THE PENTECOSTAL OLD AND NEW TESTAMENT COMMENTARIES

WIPF & STOCK · Eugene, Oregon

A PENTECOSTAL COMMENTARY ON ROMANS
Introduction, Translation, and Commentary

Copyright © 2025 Glen W. Menzies. All rights reserved. Except for brief quotations in critical publications or reviews, no part of this book may be reproduced in any manner without prior written permission from the publisher. Write: Permissions, Wipf and Stock Publishers, 199 W. 8th Ave., Suite 3, Eugene, OR 97401.

Wipf & Stock
An Imprint of Wipf and Stock Publishers
199 W. 8th Ave., Suite 3
Eugene, OR 97401

www.wipfandstock.com

PAPERBACK ISBN: 978-1-5326-1024-0
HARDCOVER ISBN: 978-1-5326-1026-4
EBOOK ISBN: 978-1-5326-1025-7

VERSION NUMBER 04/18/25

Permissions:

Cartoon Features Syndicate

To my sons, Sam and Lucas,
who are following in Abraham's footsteps of faith (Rom 4:12)

CONTENTS

Foreword by Doug Clay	xi
Preface	xiii
Abbreviations and Sigla	xvii

INTRODUCTION — 1

Romans: Paul's *Magnum Opus*	1
The Occasion of Paul's Writing	2
The Origins of the Jewish and Christian Communities in Rome	6
Paul's Own Situation When He Wrote Romans	11
Paul's Identity and the Date of Romans	12
Slavery in Roman Society	15
The Reformation Heritage	18
The New Perspective on Paul	21
The New-Perspective Adjacent Scholar John M. G. Barclay	24
The Ending of Romans	28

ROMANS 1 — 30

Translation: Rom 1:1–7	30
Excursus: Calling in the New Testament	37
Excursus: "The Gospel" or "Paul's Gospel"?	38
Translation: Rom 1:8–13	42
Translation: Rom 1:14–17	44
Excursus: The Language of Righteousness and Justification	50
Translation: Rom 1:18–32	69

ROMANS 2 — 79

Translation: Rom 2:1–11	79
Translation: Rom 2:12–29	85
Excursus: "O Man"	90
Excursus: The Law and the Lawless	92

ROMANS 3 — 97

Translation: Rom 3:1–8 — 97
Translation: Rom 3:9–20 — 99
Translation: Rom 3:21–31 — 103
Excursus: Works of the Law — 111
Excursus: The Faith in Christ/Faithfulness of Christ Debate — 114

ROMANS 4 — 117

Translation: Rom 4:1–15 — 117
Translation: Rom 4:16–25 — 123
Excursus: Paul's Concepts of Sin and Transgression — 125

ROMANS 5 — 132

Translation: Rom 5:1–11 — 132
Translation: Rom 5:12–14 — 135
Translation: Rom 5:15–21 — 144
Excursus: Paul Reads Genesis — 147

ROMANS 6 — 155

Translation: Rom 6:1–11 — 155
Translation: Rom 6:12–23 — 158

ROMANS 7 — 163

Translation: Rom 7:1–6 — 163
Translation: Rom 7:7–25 — 165
Excursus: The Puzzle of Romans 7:7–25 — 170
Excursus: Paul's Use of the Word "Flesh" — 178

ROMANS 8 — 183

Translation: Rom 8:1–8 — 183
Translation: Rom 8:9–17 — 185
Translation: Rom 8:18–25 — 189
Translation: Rom 8:26–30 — 191
Translation: Rom 8:31–39 — 197
Excursus: The Indispensable Spirit — 199
Excursus: The New Order of the Latter Rain and Romans — 210

A SHORT ROMANS 9 — 214

Translation: Rom 9:1–5 — 214
Translation: Rom 9:6–13 — 217
Translation: Rom 9:14–29 — 220

A LONG ROMANS 10 — 227
Translation: Rom 9:30—10:4 — 227
Translation: Rom 10:5–13 — 235
Translation: Rom 10:14–21 — 238

ROMANS 11 — 243
Translation: Rom 11:1–10 — 243
Translation: Rom 11:11–24 — 247
Translation: Rom 11:25–36 — 254
Excursus: Guidance from Israel's History — 264
Excursus: All Israel will be saved — 271
Excursus: Dispensationalism — 286

ROMANS 12 — 305
Translation: Rom 12:1–21 — 305
Excursus: Rom 12:6 and "The Analogy of Faith" — 325

ROMANS 13 — 334
Translation: Rom 13:1–7 — 334
Excursus: The Governing Authorities — 338
Excursus: The Impact of Rom 13:1–7 on Western History — 345
Translation: Rom 13:8–14 — 360

A LONG ROMANS 14 — 363
Translation: Rom 14:1—15:6 — 363
Excursus: The Weak and the Strong — 371

A SHORT ROMANS 15 — 386
Translation: Rom 15:7–21 — 386
Translation: Rom 15:22–33 — 392

DOXOLOGY — 396
Translation: Rom 16:25–27 — 396

ROMANS 16 — 400
Translation: Rom 16:1–16 — 400
Excursus: The Women of Romans 16 — 415
Translation: Rom 16:17–19 — 429
Translation: Rom 16:20 — 431
Translation: Rom 16:21–23 — 431
Translation: Rom 16:24 — 439

Appendix 1: The Ending of Romans	441
Appendix 2: Comments on 1 Cor 14:34–35 and 1 Tim 2:11–15	448
Bibliography	461
Name Index	471
Ancient and Medieval Sources Index	477

FOREWORD

Dr. Glen Menzies belongs to a legacy of Pentecostal scholarship. His father and brother have contributed works that have and continue to shape the hearts and minds of Assemblies of God students. They have exercised academic leadership at multiple Pentecostal schools. The Menzies name remains highly respected in academia and in our movement.

Glen Menzies lives out this legacy in his own way. For almost three decades, he taught with excellence at one of our Assembly of God universities. He led the ministry college at the university in preparing credentialed ministers. Dr. Menzies earned a reputation for the breadth of his expertise in New Testament studies, theology, church history, and biblical languages.

Dr. Menzies has demonstrated an unwavering commitment to Pentecostalism, and to the Assemblies of God in particular. He has faithfully served his local church, his ministry network, and a host of pastors who continue to look to Dr. Menzies as a trusted guide. He has also helped the cause of Pentecostal scholarship in the Assemblies of God by his own contributions and his encouragement of other scholars.

This commentary represents the culmination of a lifetime of biblical study and scholarship. Dr. Menzies doesn't just take the reader through the book of Romans verse by verse. He explains, thoroughly, the background to what is being read as well as the ways of reading and applying those passages historically. Dr. Menzies focuses on how Pentecostals read Romans, what they have done with various texts and, in his own judgment, what they should be doing with them.

Readers will not find this commentary a quick read. Dr. Menzies weaves together his wealth of knowledge in church history, biblical languages, and theology throughout the book. The reader will receive the benefit of learning to read a biblical text deeply through that contribution.

Like many commentaries, you may not agree with everything, but you cannot disagree with the heart of the author in producing a work for the benefit of Pentecostals. He writes to help us think deeply about the meaning of Scripture. He writes so that we will understand Paul well, to have this letter inscribed on our hearts. Dr. Menzies writes to exalt Jesus who represents the faithfulness of God in Romans.

I am grateful for the contribution of this book, and others like it, to the Pentecostal movement. Thank you to Dr. Menzies for providing us with one more source, written with Pentecostals in mind, for appreciating Paul's words.

Rev. Doug Clay
General Superintendent
Assemblies of God-USA

PREFACE

This commentary appears in the series Pentecostal Old and New Testament Commentaries. While this series title might seem self-explanatory, the term "Pentecostal" requires some unpacking, certainly more than it would have needed sixty years ago when I was a young boy. At that time my family considered itself to be "Pentecostal," a term unadorned by qualifiers. Today, I often call myself a "classical Pentecostal," using a term surprisingly coined by a Benedictine monk, Dr. Kilian McDonnell. I count Father Kilian, who is now 103 years of age, as a friend. He created this term to distinguish Pentecostals hailing from denominations who traced their heritage back to the Azusa Street Revival of 1906 from their more recent relatives, Charismatics (or "Neo-Pentecostals," as they were sometimes called at the time), a grouping that includes Roman Catholics and mainline Protestants. Over the past three decades the situation has grown even more complex with Third-Wave evangelicals and "Renewalists" entering the picture, not to mention Neocharismatics (a very vague grouping that seems to include most any Spirit movement that does not fit neatly elsewhere).

This commentary, and the series of which it is a part, is aimed at the whole range of Pentecostals, Charismatics, and others described above. I call this "Pentecostalism broadly conceived." Although the situation has improved greatly in recent years, Pentecostalism broadly conceived has historically suffered from a lack of biblical scholarship tailored to its special questions and requirements. While the target audience of this commentary is Pentecostals, I hope it will also be of use to other branches of the Christian family.

I want to make clear that there is no unified Pentecostal view of Romans. Not only is this commentary unable to present a pristine Pentecostal viewpoint someone might imagine, I do not even claim to present what is typical in the Pentecostal world, however that might be assessed. What I claim is that I am a life-long Pentecostal and therefore I present an authentic Pentecostal perspective. However, it is only one perspective of many. I have been an Assemblies of God minister for nearly forty-five years, and I taught Bible and theology at an Assemblies of God university for twenty-seven years.

In recent years a hermeneutical tendency has emerged contending that every theological tradition is entitled to its own version of the truth. The idea is that communities contribute to the production of meaning, so that a Catholic reading of Romans, a Lutheran reading of Romans, a Reformed reading of Romans, a Wesleyan reading of Romans, and a Pentecostal reading of Romans, etc., may all be equally true. I do not accept this viewpoint. While each of these readings may authentically reflect the mainstream views of their respective traditions, they cannot all also reflect the meaning intended by the Apostle Paul. Since I am not infallible, and since I deny the existence of some special Pentecostal truth that differs from what is true for other Christian traditions, this implies that I have almost certainly misunderstood some of what Paul intended to teach. Interpretations cannot both disagree and simultaneously all be correct. If I knew the ways in which I have misinterpreted Paul, I would certainly correct those errors. Unfortunately, I do not.

For many decades—fortunately now long past—it was considered important to build an unscalable wall between biblical studies and theology. According to this notion, commentaries should focus on narrow technical issues of history, lexicology, grammar, rhetoric, etc., and not intrude into discussions of meaning or significance. While this is a book of biblical scholarship, I consider ascertaining the meaning intended by Paul to be my primary task. He meant his letter to the Romans to teach theology and therefore it is necessary for this commentary to discuss theology.

In a related vein, I also hope to present how both correct and incorrect interpretations of Romans have shaped important theological discussions over the centuries. However, such discussions of the history of interpretation could overwhelm my central goal of interpreting Paul's words, so these will necessarily be limited.

Several different styles of commentaries are available in the public marketplace. Some are highly technical; this is not one of those. Some record in encyclopedic fashion the positions of major interpreters on every conceivable topic; this commentary also does not do that. In fact, the views of relatively few contemporary scholars will be mentioned. Some commentaries are storehouses of aphorisms and anecdotes selected for use in preaching. Again, while it contains great material for use in preaching, this is not a "homiletical" commentary it that sense.

I should also add that this is a commentary on the Greek text of the New Testament; it is not a commentary on an English translation. Furthermore, all biblical quotations, unless otherwise stipulated, are my own translations.

The goal of this commentary is simply to explain the meaning of Romans to the best of my ability to the non-specialist. While there is quite a bit of Greek in this book, and a lesser amount of Hebrew, these Greek and Hebrew words are always transliterated into English letters, and they are translated. When such words are discussed, they will usually be presented in their "lexical form"—the form used to look up the word in a dictionary—to make it easier for the reader to find them in one of the standard study tools.

My approach is to try to reduce the barrier posed by the biblical languages, not to accentuate that barrier. To say this differently, Greek and Hebrew function as impenetrable blinders through which the typical English-speaking reader tries to view the biblical text. An equally problematic approach would be to ignore the biblical languages altogether and treat some English translation as God's divine revelation. Instead, my goal is to allow the reader to "get behind" the blinders the Greek and Hebrew pose almost as if they themselves were able to read these biblical languages. While English translations help penetrate the blinders, they also mask the many interpretive decisions the translators have made for the reader. By burying these decisions, these translations are a two-edged sword that both cuts for the reader and cuts against her. In contrast, a good commentary explains to the reader the options that were open to the translator and lets the reader decide.

Let me offer an example. In my translation, the first part of Rom 14:23 reads: "But the person making distinctions, if he should eat, he is condemned, for his action is not from faith." In contrast, the RSV translates, "But he who has doubts is condemned, if he eats, because he does not act from faith." Why do I translate "the person making distinctions" where the RSV translates "he who has doubts"? Both translate the words *ho diakrinomenos*. Both are possible translations of the definite article ("the") plus the participle of the verb *diakrinō*. (I will add that although both meanings are possible, the meaning "to make distinctions" is far more common.)

My translation focuses on the larger controversy Paul addresses. It is between those who make distinctions about which foods and drinks are appropriate to consume and those who will eat or drink anything. The RSV takes a different path by focusing more on faith or its absence. It understands "he who doubts" to be the person who lacks faith. I will also add that in this verse I think Paul makes a play-on-words. The verb *diakrinō* ("to make distinctions") and the verb *katakrinō* ("to condemn") are both built on the same root (*krinō*), and they sound alike. Both the translators of the RSV and I interpret the text within the context Paul addresses. However, we end up making different choices.

While it is possible to read a commentary by starting at the beginning and reading straight through to the end as a person would read a novel, most commentaries are used more like a reference book or an encyclopedia. Short sections are read as the need arises. This is a legitimate way to read a commentary, but such choppy reading can also obscure larger themes. One way I have accommodated this reality is to include excursuses on major topics. These excursuses focus on major issues raised in Romans and aim to present a more synthetic discussion. While many commentaries contain excursuses, few offer as many and as detailed excursuses as this commentary. I consider this to be a feature, not a bug.

At the end of this long adventure, I would like to thank Michael A. Stone, Timothy Dresselhaus, and Kean Salzer for reading manuscript drafts and offering invaluable comments and corrections. I also owe my brother, Robert P. Menzies, profound thanks for an ongoing dialogue about many issues raised in this book and for reading in advance portions of it.

As a last thought, I hope the reader will find this commentary edifying. I believe the Bible to be the word of God and a blessing to all who read it. But it is an even greater blessing when people read it and understand it well. This commentary is offered to help achieve that goal.

Glen Menzies
All Saints' Day (November 1), 2024

ABBREVIATIONS AND SIGLA

//	parallel text (in the gospels), e.g., Matt 24:1–3//Mark 13:1–2//Luke 21:5–6
[. . . .]	text that is not original
ad loc.	*ad locum* ("at the place," e.g., at the scriptural reference)
BAG	Bauer, Walter, et al. (i.e., Walter Bauer, William F. Arndt, and F. Wilbur Gingrich). *A Greek-English Lexicon of the New Testament and Other Early Christian Literature.*
BDB	Brown, Francis et al. *The Brown-Driver-Briggs Hebrew and English Lexicon.*
Bl-D-F	Blass, Friedrich, et al. (i.e., F. Blass, A. Debrunner, and Robert W. Funk) *A Greek Grammar of the New Testament and Other Early Christian Literature*
Bl-D-R	F. Blass, A. Debrunner, and F. Rehkopf, *Grammatik der neutestamentlichen Griechisch*
CIJ	Frey, *Corpus Inscriptionum Iudaicarum*
CIL	*Corpus Inscriptionum Latinarum*
e.g.	*exemplum gratia* ("the favor of an example)" or *exempli gratia* (the favor of examples")
i.e.	*id est* ("it is" or "that is")
IGR	*Inscriptiones Graecae ad Res Romanas Pertinentes*, edited by René Cagnat
ILS	*Inscriptiones Latinae Selectae*, edited by Hermann Dessau
JIWE	*Jewish Inscriptions of Western Europe*
KJV	King James Version of the Bible
LW	Luther's Works
MPG	*Patrologia Graeca*. Edited by J. P. Migne. 167 vols. Paris: 1857–1886.

MPL		*Patrologia Latina*. Edited by J. P. Migne. 217 vols. Paris: 1857–1864.
n.		note
NIV		New International Version of the Bible
pl.		plural
RSV		Revised Standard Version of the Bible
sing.		singular
s.v.		*sub verbo* ("under the word"; often used to cite dictionary or encyclopedia articles)
TDNT		*Theological Dictionary of the New Testament*, edited by Gerhard Kittel
vs.		verse
vss.		verses

INTRODUCTION

Romans: Paul's *Magnum Opus*

Few would argue against the proposition that Paul's letter to the Romans is his *magnum opus*. While it is the longest of his letters, at least the longest of his surviving letters, it is not a particularly long book as books go. *Magnum* can mean "big," but it can also mean "great," in the sense of being important, and Romans is an exceedingly important book. The impact it has made is literally incalculable, for it is impossible to imagine how Christianity would have developed without it and how its shape would now appear absent this book. This is especially true in Western Christianity due to the great rupture that tore the West apart in the sixteenth century largely over the interpretation of this book. This wound may not be quite as bloody and raw today as it once was, but it is also a wound that remains unhealed.

However, Romans is not the most accessible of Paul's letters. Raymond Brown once wisely suggested that the beginning student of Paul should not start with Romans, even though it is the most important of his letters, but rather with 1 Corinthians, which he considered "easier to follow and more immediately applicable."[1] This very lack of accessibility and more theoretical nature heightens the importance of a commentary to help guide those who find Romans difficult. I myself find Romans difficult but perhaps the results of my struggle to comprehend Paul's soaring theological affirmations and compressed argumentation can help others as they find their way to a better understanding of this great book.

One challenge is the elliptical nature of much of Paul's writing. Paul is a thinker who recognizes the many ways his ideas connect with each other. A very linear thinker moves from one idea to the next showing how the first supports the second, and the second idea supports the third, which

---

1. Brown, *Introduction*, 559.

supports the fourth, and so on. But this is difficult when a first idea supports two or three different ideas that flow in different directions from it. Paul will move from one idea to the next and then to the next, but he will also later return to that first idea and explore how it supports another different line of argumentation (e.g., Paul discusses justification or "right standing" in 3:21—4:25 and then again in 9:30—10:13). When he discusses similar topics from slightly different angles, Paul has often been accused of offering contradictory ideas—for instance, are works important or not?—but we must always assume that a problem of interpretation is our own, not Paul's. It is an arrogant commentator who chooses to blame the author when sufficient clarity has not been attained.

Many commentaries have been written on Romans. In my opinion, the best of them do not belabor technical minutiae but instead expose the reader to the commentator's own struggles with the big issues raised by the text. That was certainly true of Luther. His commentary was written as his revolutionary ideas were being formulated and stirring his soul, and the implications of his discoveries came out forcefully. The same was true of Barth's *Römerbrief*, as the young pastor at Safenwil called out the Modernists' arrogant and simplistic substitution of universal human experience for the Word of God that always smashes human pretentions. I do not make similar claims of greatness for this commentary, but I do hope my own struggle will help others better understand this ancient document and lead to a profound internalization of what Paul saw as God's plan for the transformation of the entire world.

The style in which commentaries are written varies a great deal. Some present comments as a series of running glosses embedded within the text. Others present detailed lexicographic and grammatical observations in one section, more general comments in another section, and summaries of the argumentation in another section.

This commentary will start with observations on introductory matters. Then the body of the commentary will offer a fresh translation, interspersed with general comments and a series of excursuses. These excursuses will comprise a larger portion of the commentary than is usual, and they will provide opportunities to wrestle with the most momentous issues raised in Romans.

The Occasion of Paul's Writing

All of Paul's letters can be described as "occasional letters." This means that they are written in response to specific situations. They are not manifestos for a general audience.

When considering the occasion for the writing of one of Paul's letters, it is the recipients' context that first comes to mind. For instance, 1 Corinthians was written in response to reports from "Chloe's people" of quarreling among the Corinthian believers (1 Cor 1:11) and to answer questions raised in a letter probably delivered by Stephanas, Fortunatus, and Achaicus (16.:17). Paul's successive answers were marked by the phrase *peri de* ("now concerning") (1 Cor 7:1; 7:25; 8:1; 12:1; 16:1; 16:12).[2]

Romans is also an occasional letter, although a greater part of the "occasion" is defined by Paul's own situation rather than the situation of his recipients. In this, it is unusual among Paul's letters. He has never been to Rome, although he knows some about the history of the proclamation of Jesus as Messiah there, probably through both personal contact with Prisca and Aquila when they lived in the Aegean world (in Corinth and in Ephesus)[3] and probably through subsequent letters from them. However, he does not know the situation in Rome nearly as intimately as places where he has lived and ministered. Rom 16:17–19 suggests that knowledge of the Roman believers' obedience is widely known, but Paul couples his gratefulness for this good news with warnings, suggesting he has also heard of disagreements. Paul's lack of detailed knowledge about the situation works to the advantage of the contemporary reader since Paul must explain his ideas more thoroughly than would be the case otherwise. He can make fewer assumptions about what the Christ followers in Rome know and what they believe.

Paul wrote his letter for three main reasons. First, he wanted to ask for help getting to Spain. Paul wrote from the vicinity of Corinth,[4] while he was on his Third Missionary Journey, or what might be better called his "First Fundraising Journey."[5] He explains that after he has finished collecting money for the saints in Jerusalem and then journeyed to Jerusalem to deliver these funds, he plans to travel the furthest west he has ever gone, to

---

2. In 1 Thessalonians Paul also uses *peri de* to mark off serial answers to questions he has been asked. These occur in 4:9 and 5:1, with a very similar formulation also in 4:13.

3. See Acts 18.

4. This may be surmised from his report about fundraising in Macedonia and Achaia (where Corinth is located) coupled with his commendation of Phoebe, a deacon of the church at Cenchraea, one of the ports near Corinth. It seems likely that Phoebe carried Paul's letter to Rome and in line with ancient practice was charged with explaining anything in the letter its recipients found confusing.

5. Rather than focusing on planting new churches as he had during his first two missionary journeys, on this journey Paul checks on previously planted churches, strengthens them, and raises money from them to help with the serious financial needs of the church in Jerusalem.

Spain (15:24, 28). In fact, at this point he has apparently never been further west than Illyricum (15:19), which was northwest of Greece, in the present-day Balkans. *En route* to Spain, he planned to stop at Rome, and he hoped that the believers there would contribute to the next leg of his journey. So, in part, he wrote Romans to ask for assistance.

The second reason Paul wrote his epistle was to defend his message, or to be more precise, what he sometimes calls "my gospel." He calls it "my gospel" three times: in Rom 2:16; in Rom 16:25; and in 2 Tim 2:8. Another three times he calls it "our gospel," probably because he is politely including his travelling companions and fellow ministers Silvanus or Timothy: in 2 Cor 4:3 (Timothy); in 1 Thess 1:5 (Silvanus and Timothy); and in 2 Thess 2:14 (Silvanus and Timothy). *For more about this, see the excursus titled "'The Gospel' or 'Paul's Gospel.'"*

Paul knows that his gospel is controversial and that some people in Rome either oppose it or at least have deep reservations about it. It would be very helpful to know how Paul had learned of these reservations harbored in Rome, but the details about this are unclear.

One reasonable conjecture is that Paul's primary source for what was happening in Rome was the couple Prisca (Priscilla) and Aquila. Not only had they worked with Paul in Corinth and Ephesus and had lived previously in Rome, but it is possible that they moved back to Rome specifically to prepare for a planned visit to Rome by Paul.[6] *For more about this, see the excursus titled "Women of Romans 16."*

Today, the word "gospel" is often used as a shorthand term referring to "the central message about Christ which all believers shared." By the end of the first century, it does eventually come to mean this, but in the middle of the first century it did not mean this yet. Not every Christian accepted Paul's gospel.

A central element of Paul's gospel was the inclusion of gentiles within the family of faith, and in certain quarters—apparently including groups in Rome—this was controversial. In Gal 3:8 Paul makes the connection between "the gospel" and the gentiles especially clear: "The scripture, foreseeing that God would pronounce gentiles upright from their faith, announced the gospel beforehand to Abraham, saying, 'In you shall all the gentiles be blessed.'"

The third reason Paul wrote Romans was to bring together quarreling house churches. However, the word "quarreling" may not be correct since

---

6. The idea that Prisca and Aquila returned to Rome in anticipation of a visit by Paul apparently originated with Otto Michel (*Brief an die Römer* 341). See Bruce, *Paul: Apostle of the Heart Set Free*, 388.

this word would assume these house churches spoke to one another, and perhaps they did not.

Romans is unusual in its opening salutation as Paul does not address his letter to "the church at Rome" or some similar formulation.[7] Instead, he addresses it more generally "to all God's beloved in Rome, called to be saints." One must ask why he departs from his normal pattern. He uses the term *ekklēsia* ("church") five times elsewhere in Romans, so the term itself is not problematic. He refers to the church that meets in the house of Prisca and Aquila (16:5). He mentions the church of Cenchreae in which Phoebe served as a deacon (16:1).[8] He also somewhat enigmatically refers to "the whole church" (16:23)—perhaps meaning the whole church of Corinth, or perhaps the whole church of Cenchreae—that sends its greetings to Rome. He mentions "all the churches of the Gentiles" (16:4) and "all the churches of Christ" (16:16).

The most likely explanation for Paul's avoidance of the phrase "the church at Rome" is that the Christians of Rome were not organized as a unified church. This seems especially likely if Robert Jewett's theory that most of the clusters of greetings found in chapter 16 are largely addressed to house- and tenement-church leaders and that these clusters reflect at least five such *ekklēsiai*.[9] It is possible that the Roman believers were organized into house and tenement churches for reasons of convenience such as disparate geographic locations or social networks, but in view of Paul's reluctance to call them collectively a "church," it appears the house and tenement churches were aligned in separate factions. The number of these factions is unclear, although probably it was fewer than a faction for every house or tenement church, and perhaps there are as few as two factions.

Our limited evidence suggests that much, although probably not all, of the division was between Jewish believers and gentile believers. The disagreements noted in chapter 14 point in this direction, disagreements over which foods were acceptable to eat and whether certain days should be honored over others. Also, the fact that Paul directs some comments specifically to Jewish believers (2:17–24; 3:9; 4:1; 7:1, 4) and other comments directly to gentile believers (11:13) may also reflect fault lines and tension separating these groups. He speaks directly to Jewish believers more often than to

---

7. Usually Paul addressed his letters to "the church of God which is in Corinth" (1 Cor 1:2) or "the churches of Galatia" (Gal 1:2) or the like. That Paul surprisingly does not call the entirety of Roman Christianity a "church" (*ekklēsia*) is pointed out by Lampe, *From Paul to Valentinus*, 359.

8. Cenchreae was a port city of Corinth, something like what we would call as "suburb" today.

9. Jewett, *Romans*, 65.

gentile believers likely because he is aware that the Jewish faction has been more critical of his ministry.

The Origins of the Jewish and Christian Communities in Rome

The first followers of Jesus in Judea were Jews. Similarly, the first followers of Jesus in Rome were Jews. Thus, it is impossible to tell the story of the first Christians in Rome without first telling the story of Rome's early Jewish community.

When Paul wrote Romans, there had been a Jewish presence in the city of Rome for over a century-and-a-half.[10] However, the presence of Jewish individuals is different from the presence of a Jewish community, which developed later. While a small network of Jewish families may have existed earlier, the Alexandrian Jew Philo connects the formation of Rome's Jewish community with an influx of Jewish slaves, probably the result of the Roman general Pompey's conquest of Judea in 63 BC.[11] Although they arrived in Italy as slaves, many became *liberti* ("freed slaves") and moved to a section of Rome located west of the Tiber river. Then in accordance with Roman law, their children, as the children of freed slaves, became freeborn citizens of Rome.

Philo had reason to know about these matters. In AD 38 he led a delegation of Jews from Alexandria to Rome to protest their mistreatment before the Emperor Gaius Caligula. It is also evident that this Alexandrian delegation consulted with the local Jewish community when it arrived in Rome. In Philo's account of his overtures to Gaius, written a few years after the events took place, Philo explains that the emperor's predecessor Augustus

---

10. Samuele Rocca points to epigraphic evidence for a Jewish presence in Rome "in the second half of the second century B.C.E." Rocca, "In the Beginning," 8–9. See also Rocca, *In the Shadow of the Caesars*, 16–17. He also suggests that the first Jewish residents of Rome likely lived in the "crowded lower-class" Subura neighborhood of Rome, where most foreigners were housed. Rocca, *In the Shadow of the Caesars*, 19.

11. Rocca agrees in part with Philo's assessment. He thinks Philo overemphasizes slavery and underplays the migration of unemployed laborers seeking jobs. He also believes Philo conflates two waves of immigration due to slavery. The first came in the wake of Pompey's conquest, but there was also a second wave of slaves taken captive in 53–51 BC by C. Cassius Longinus, the *quaestor* of Crassus in Syria. It is Rocca's conjecture that the slaves taken in these two waves likely lived in the Subura district of Rome where most foreigners lived. Rocca, "In the Beginning," 8. Rocca, *In the Shadow of the Caesars*, 12–13, 20–21, 26–27.

had treated Jews benevolently. In particular, he discusses Augustus's treatment of the Jews living in Rome. By Augustus' time—he ruled from 27 BC to AD 14—the Jewish community was well developed and clearly identified with a specific location:

> How then did he [Caesar Augustus] show his approval? He was aware that the great section of Rome on the other side of the Tiber is occupied and inhabited by Jews, most of whom were Roman citizens emancipated. For having been brought as captives to Italy they were liberated by their owners and were not forced to violate any of their native institutions. He knew therefore that they have houses of prayer and meet together in them, particularly on the sacred sabbaths when they receive as a body a training in their ancestral philosophy. He knew too that they collect money for sacred purposes from their first-fruits and send them to Jerusalem by persons who would offer the sacrifices. Yet nevertheless he neither ejected them from Rome nor deprived them of their Roman citizenship because they were careful to preserve their Jewish citizenship also, nor took any violent measures against the houses of prayer, nor prevented them from meeting to receive instructions in the laws, nor opposed their offerings of the first-fruits.[12]

Archaeological research has shown, in harmony with Philo's description, that the earliest Jewish community in Rome—as opposed to isolated Jewish residents—was centered in an area called *Transtiberim*, Latin for "across the Tiber."[13] This was designated Region XIV in Augustus' reorganization of Rome into fourteen administrative districts. Interestingly, the northern portion of Transtiberim included the Vatican hill. This region, excluding Vatican City, is now known as Trastevere (pronounced tras-TEV-er-ay). In Italian, the Tiber River is called the "Tevere," and Trastevere is

---

12. Philo, *Embassy to Gaius* 23 (155–57). Josephus indicates there were Jewish communities in both Puteoli (the Greek name is *Dikaearcheia*) and Rome during Augustus's rule. He relates a story about an impostor who claimed to be Alexander, the son of Herod the Great. He made his way to Puteoli and then to Rome, where he was hailed by the Jewish communities of both places. His undoing was Augustus's unwillingness to believe Herod was wrong about his son being dead. Josephus tells the same story in both *Jewish War*, 2.104 (ii.7) and *Antiquities*, 17.324–31 (xii.1).

13. Rocca notes that in the Augustan period at least four and probably five synagogues are known to have existed in *Transtiberim*: the Synagogue of the Hebrews; the Synagogue of the Augustesians; the Synagogue of the Agrippesians; the Synagogue of the Volumnesians, and probably the Synagogue of the Herodians. Rocca, *In the Shadow of the Caesars*, 24–25.

a contraction of "trans-Tevere," meaning "across the Tiber River" just like *Transtiberim* in Latin. For both names, the center of Rome is the implied point of reference. At a point to the west of the center of the city, the Tiber zigs to the east and then zags back west, leaving Trastevere close to the city to its east yet separated from most of the city by the Tiber. Interestingly, this area is still the center of Jewish life in Rome 2,100 years later, and sometimes today Trastevere is called "the Jewish Quarter" of Rome.

The evidence that the first Christians in Rome were Jews is well documented,[14] and in the first century they lived primarily in the *Transtiberim* section of Rome, although some may also have lived along the Appian Way in the *Campus Martius* ("Field of Mars") north of the city proper.[15]

Peter Lampe suggests that the connection between *Transtiberim* and the emerging Christian population may explain why Nero used the Christians as scapegoats after the Great Roman Fire of AD 64. Tacitus summarizes the ravages inflicted by the fire: "Rome is divided into fourteen regions, among which only four remained intact. Three were burned to the ground, and of the other seven there were only a few houses left, which were severely damaged and half-burnt."[16] Lampe argues that one of the regions that survived must have been *Transtiberim*, since it was protected from the rest of the city by the Tiber. When the Christians survived relatively unscathed, they became easy targets for Nero's demagoguery.[17] Of course, there were also many Jews in *Transtiberim*, but they were better known, older as a community, and less vulnerable than the Christians.

Another factor sparing the Jews may have been the influence of Poppaea Sabina, Nero's second wife, whom the Jewish historian Flavius Josephus describes as a "Godfearer" (*theosebēs*).[18] While the exact meaning of this term is debated, two things are clear about it: Poppaea continued to be a gentile who had not converted to Judaism; and she was associated in some way with the Jewish community, probably as an admirer.

We do not know how Christianity came to Rome, and we do not know when it arrived. Probably it was sometime in the 40s of the first century, and it likely did not arrive as the result of an organized mission. Paul does not seem aware of any such mission or of missionaries who brought Christianity to the Empire's capital, with the possible exceptions of Andronicus and

---

14. See Lampe, *Paul to Valentinus*, 11–16.
15. Lampe, *Paul to Valentinus*, 19–47.
16. Tacitus, *Annals*, 15.40.
17. Lampe, *Paul to Valentinus*, 47.
18. Josephus, *Antiquities* 20.195.

Junia (Rom 16:7). They seem to be a married couple who minister together, and since they were "in Christ" before Paul, which is to say, quite early, they likely became converts to the faith in the East prior to Christianity's expansion into the West. They had been imprisoned for the faith, perhaps in Rome during the disturbances that led to Claudius's edict of exile for some Jewish—likely Jewish Christian—leaders (see below). The fact that Paul calls them "apostles" might indicate that they had a pioneering role in spreading the faith, but exactly what Paul implies by use of that term is unclear. *For more detail about Andronicus and Junia, see the excursus "The Women of Romans 16."*

The extensive list of people Paul greets in Romans 16:3–16 mentions numerous people with backgrounds in the East who ultimately migrated to Rome. But the East was a vast area. Since the earliest Christians were Jews living in Israel, of particular interest are Roman Jews with personal connections to Judea. One tantalizing possibility is raised by the mention in Rom 16:10 of "Aristobulus's people," which is probably a reference to his household, including slaves. This household apparently contained Christian believers. Since Aristobulus is a name firmly connected with the Herod family, this Aristobulus may have brought Jewish-Christian slaves with him when he moved from Israel to Rome.[19] Similarly, Paul mentions a Jewish-Christian named Herodion, which may be a shortened form of Herodianus. Paul apparently knows of him but does not know him personally. His name may indicate that he also is a slave connected with the Herod family.

Another intriguing figure is Epaenetus, with whom Paul likely spent time in Ephesus. The apostle describes him as "the first fruit of Asia." Whether that means he was the first Christian convert in Asia or the first Pauline convert in Asia is unclear, but in either case he became a Christian rather early. However, he was not Jewish and therefore is unlikely to have spearheaded the establishment of Christianity in Rome.

Prisca and Aquila are also extremely interesting figures. Since they were exiled from Rome under Claudius (Acts 18:2), it is likely they were already Christians in AD 49, which is quite early. But, if they were exposed to Christianity in Rome, this means they did not bring the faith to that great city.

Extensive tradition and archaeological evidence connect Peter with Roman Christianity, and both he and Paul died martyrs' deaths during the reign of Nero. But Peter must have arrived in Rome after Paul's letter was written because Paul makes no mention of him despite seemingly mentioning every Christian in Rome he knew or knew of in his letter's final chapter.

---

19. On this possibility, see Lampe, *Paul to Valentinus*, 165.

Since it is unclear when Christianity first came to Rome, it is also unclear when problems first developed between the Jewish Christians and the Jews who did not worship Jesus. But problems clearly arose. The Roman historian Suetonius gives the following report concerning the year AD 49 or thereabouts: "Since the Jews constantly made disturbances at the instigation of Chrestus, he [the Emperor Claudius] expelled them from Rome."[20] "Chrestus" is probably a mistaken spelling of *Christos*, "Christ."[21] Apparently, the disturbances Suetonius mentions were over disputes about the role of Jesus Christ in the lives of Roman Jews. Similarly, Acts 18:2 reports that Priscilla and Aquila had come to Corinth because Aquila was a Jew, and Claudius had expelled Jews from Rome. It may be inferred from these brief accounts that it was mainly Jewish Christian leaders who were expelled from Rome. In addition, it is unlikely that those who had obtained Roman citizenship would have been subject to expulsion.[22] Such expulsions usually applied to *peregrini* ("foreigners"). Regardless of how many Jewish Christians were expelled, their potent message had provoked conflict.[23]

The Roman tradition was that when an Emperor died, any expulsions he had ordered were canceled. The emperor Claudius died in AD 54 and that meant the exiled Jewish Christian leaders could go home. By the time Paul writes Romans—probably in AD 57 or 58—the exiles Priscilla and Aquilla have already returned to Rome where a house-church met in their home.

But when the Jewish Christian leaders returned to Rome after the end of their exile, were they able to resume the leadership roles they had previously enjoyed? One theory is that in the absence of Jewish leaders, new gentile leaders had stepped up. When the Jewish leaders returned, the gentile leaders were unwilling to step aside for the Jewish leaders to resume the *status quo ante*. Instead, some house-churches met under gentile leadership and other

20. Suetonius, *Lives of the Caesars*, Claudius 25.4

21. Part of the problem may have been that *Christos*, a Greek word that meant something like "smeared one," seemed an improbable name if a person did not know about the Israelite custom of anointing kings. The Greek word *Chrēstos*, meaning "useful," "pleasant," or "good" would have seemed a more likely name. *Chrestus* simply replaces the masculine singular Greek ending of *Chrēstos* with the masculine singular Latin ending.

22. Keener, *Romans*, 12.

23. There may have been a prelude to this expulsion. The second and third century historian Cassius Dio (*Roman History* 60.6.6) reports that the emperor did not expel the Judeans because of their great numbers; he prohibited them from assembling, while permitting them to maintain their ancestral way of life. Dio may have gotten the matter wrong—he is not always reliable—or he may have noted an earlier event.

house-churches met under Jewish leadership. It is also probable that as gentile believers emerged, they did not remain as rooted in the Jewish stronghold "across the Tiber" as did the Jewish Christian community. Two (or more) distinct communities began to emerge. It is also possible the gentile believers did not want to be associated with the Jewish believers who had been exiled due to continuing stigma as troublemakers, even after their return.

Paul's Own Situation When He Wrote Romans

Paul reports the most salient points of his situation in Rom 15:15–32. He has reached time for a transition in his ministry. Until this time, he has effectively proclaimed his gospel from Jerusalem in the East to "as far around as Illyricum" in the West (15:19). Now, he has run out of "room" (*topos*) for ministry "in these regions" (15:23), and he seeks a new field, Spain.

The choice of Spain as his new mission field implies that he had chosen to leapfrog over Rome and all of Italy as he expanded his ministry to the west. He apologizes for not having visited Rome sooner, and the explanation he gives might be seen as a half-apology for choosing not to minister among the Romans in a more extended manner. But his explanation might also be understood as reassurance that he does not plan to barge in and try to take over. Paul writes carefully because he does not really know how the believers in Rome will react to the news that he plans to visit.

Paul insists his policy is to avoid building "on someone else's foundation" (Rom 15:20). This resembles what he writes in 2 Cor 10:15–16. There he explains he does not want "to boast in the labors of others." He also expresses his desire "that we may proclaim the gospel in lands beyond you, so as not to boast in another person's record (*kanōn*) of accomplishments achieved" (2 Cor 10:13).

He briefly describes his plans to deliver "funds contributed for the poor among the saints in Jerusalem" (Rom 15:26), which must take place prior to his trip west to Rome and then Spain. These funds had been collected by the (gentile) churches of Macedonia and Achaia.

One wonders how the Christians of Rome responded to Paul's description of this project. Were the Jewish believers grateful for this act of benevolence and solidarity with their brothers and sisters in Jerusalem? Might they even have seen it as a partial fulfillment of the eschatological vision of riches from the gentiles flowing to Jerusalem? As Isa 60:5 (LXX) says, "Then you shall see and fear and be amazed in your heart that the wealth of the sea and of the gentiles and of the peoples shall come back to you."

And how might the gentile believers of Rome process this? They have been excluded—certainly not willfully but excluded nonetheless—from this contribution of the gentiles to the poor of the saints of Jerusalem. Might they harbor a bit of resentment that this "apostle to the gentiles" is not their apostle and their representative?

Might both groups, the Jewish and the gentile followers of Jesus, wonder at the fact that Paul has worked so hard to foster unity between his gentile churches and the Jewish believers in Jerusalem? Might they also be embarrassed that this extraordinary effort to link gentile with Jew is taking place in the East while in Rome Jewish believers and gentile believers are having difficulty getting along with their fellow saints in the same city?

Paul's Identity and the Date of Romans

If it had been Paul's habit to do two things differently, life would be much simpler for contemporary interpreters. If he had written using his full trinomen ("triple name") rather than simply giving the single name "Paulos," it is likely we would know more about who he was. So often the insights of prosopography (the study of names and family relationships) reveal a great deal about an ancient person's background and social networks.

As a Roman citizen, he surely would have had a trinomen. This name might also reveal how a Jew (reflecting one kind of citizenship), who was also a citizen of Tarsus, had also been born a Roman citizen.[24] In all likelihood his Roman citizenship was inherited from an ancestor who had provided outstanding service to Rome. If Paul's full name were known, we might be able to discover who this ancestor was and the nature of his service.

But the Christians of the New Testament appear to have avoided use of trinomina, apparently since possession and use of such names projected elite status incompatible with the egalitarian nature of Christian fellowship. A similar dynamic caused the early Pentecostals of the Azusa Street Revival to avoid using titles, even the church title Reverend or common titles such as Mister, in favor of Brother Jones or Sister Smith. They also eschewed wearing neckties, since these were seen as tokens of white-collar elitism. For more on Paul's name see the comments on Rom 1:1.

---

24. In Acts 21:39 Paul announces he is a citizen of Tarsus. In Acts 22:28 Paul claims to have been born a Roman citizen.

Paul's other lamentable habit is that he does not date his letters. Letters were often dated in the ancient Roman world, whether written formally or informally, but often they were not dated as well.

Since Paul sends greetings from Erastus "the Treasurer [*oikonomos*] of the city [of Corinth]," one might hope to locate a *terminus a quo* for the writing of the letter. Unfortunately, it is not known when Erastus served in this capacity. There is an inscription crediting an *aedile* ("public works commissioner" or "Treasurer") named Erastus with providing a public pavement, but it is unclear if this inscription reflects a first- or second-century context.[25] For more about this, see the comments concerning Rom 16:23.

Since Paul did not date his letter and since Romans mentions nothing external to Paul's own career that is datable, the only avenue for dating this letter is through the relative chronology of events in Paul's life gathered from his letters and the book of Acts. The most clearly dateable event of Paul's career is his trial before Gallio the proconsul of Achaia while in Corinth on his second missionary journey (Acts 18:12). Due to an inscription discovered at Delphi, which mentions Gallio serving as a proconsul at the time, we may calculate the date of this event with considerable precision. The inscription was written in late spring or early summer of the year AD 52, and it reflects observations that Gallio had made to the Emperor Claudius a short time earlier, probably in an official report.

Jerome Murphy-O'Connor points out that Gallio was the brother of Seneca, the famous Stoic philosopher, and that Seneca mentions in one of his letters that his brother did not serve out the full term of his office as proconsul of Achaia:[26]

> When, in Achaia, he began to feel feverish, he immediately took ship, claiming that it was not a malady of the body but of the place (*Letters*, 104:1).

Murphy-O'Connor reasons that Gallio's proconsulship probably began 1 July, 51 and was scheduled to run through 30 June, 52, although he did not complete his assignment. Since the seas were regularly closed from November through March due to the likelihood of winter storms, Gallio probably left Corinth sometime before the end of October, 51. While it is conceivable that he left in the spring of 52, after the seas reopened, this

---

25. According to Friesen the largely intact inscription reads: "[. . .]erastus pro aedilit[at]e | s(ua) p(ecunia) stravit;" "[. . .]erastus, in return for his aedileship, paved (this) at his own expense." Friesen, "Wrong Erastus," 236–45.

26. See Murphy-O'Connor's extended discussion of Gallio in *St. Paul's Corinth: Texts and Archaeology*, 149–60.

would not leave much time for Gallio to submit his report and for Claudius to comment on it by early summer. Likely then Paul stood trial before Gallio in the late summer or early autumn of 51.

Rom 15:23–25 makes clear that Paul wrote Romans as he was wrapping up the phase of his ministry that has come to be known as his third missionary journey. It is impossible to calculate with certainty how much time passed between Paul's trial before Gallio and the final stages of his third missionary journey, but it seems that at least four and more probably five years must have passed. Acts 18:18 reports that after his trial before Gallio, he stayed in Corinth "many days longer." He then traveled to Antioch, where he spent "some time" (Acts 18:23). At the beginning of his third missionary journey, Paul "went through the region of Galatia and Phrygia, strengthening the disciples" (Acts 18:23), but the duration of this ministry is not given. To this must be added the three years Paul ministered in Ephesus (Acts 20:31).

Acts 20:16 informs us that Paul's aim was to reach Jerusalem with the offering the gentile churches had raised "by Pentecost." If five years had passed from his trial before Gallio in the late summer or early autumn of 51, and since Pentecost occurs in the late spring, he would likely have been aiming to arrive in Jerusalem by the Pentecost of 57 or 58.

We might also try to estimate the date when Paul wrote Romans by calculating from the date of his death, although a substantial amount of conjecture is required for this. The great fire of Rome occurred in July of 64, and we know that Nero scapegoated the Christians to deflect blame from himself for this great tragedy. Likely Paul was beheaded either in the second half of 64 or the beginning of 65 to bolster Nero's posturing.

As Acts concludes, Paul has already spent two years in Rome under house arrest (Acts 28:30). Following his house arrest, a certain amount of time must be calculated for the show trial that would have inevitably preceded Paul's execution. Additionally, prior to his house arrest in Rome, he had spent two years incarcerated in Caesarea Maritima (Acts 24:24–27), as well as an indeterminate time under arrest in Jerusalem.

In addition, following his incarceration at Caesarea, his voyage to Rome was beset by multiple mishaps. At first, they lost a lot of time due to poor winds (Acts 27:7, 9). Then a gale struck, and the sailors threw out the ship's tackle to lighten the load (Acts 27:14, 19). Driven helplessly by the wind, they were unable to steer without tackle, and they suffered for lack of food (Acts 27:21). Finally, after fourteen days, they were shipwrecked (Acts 27:27, 33, 41). After swimming to land, they discovered they were on the island of Malta (Acts 27:43–44; 28: 1). They then had to wait three months to catch another ship bound for Rome (Acts 28:11).

From his arrival in Jerusalem to deliver the offering from the gentile churches until the book of Acts closes, at least five but more probably six years must have passed. If the traditions are true that Paul was released from Roman custody, succeeded in traveling to Spain, and then was rearrested and returned to Rome—traditions I doubt to be true—a substantial amount of additional time would also have to be included in the calculation.

If Paul was only imprisoned once, calculating back from the time of his probable death, he could possibly have written Romans as late as 59 but more probably in AD 58. If he was imprisoned twice, Romans would need to have been written earlier, perhaps in AD 56. While sometime between AD 56 and 59 is possible, I suspect that Romans was written in the early months of either AD 57 or 58, with AD 58 being more likely.

Slavery in Roman Society

Discussions of Roman slavery can easily become very complex; nevertheless, some consideration of this topic is necessary since slavery and social status permeated every aspect of Roman society. Discussion of these matters is also necessary because Roman slavery differed in important respects from the better-known patterns of modern slavery that existed in the English-speaking world until well into the nineteenth century.

MALE SLAVE (LATIN "SERVUS") AND FEMALE SLAVE (LATIN "SERVA" OR "ANCILLA")

The most basic idea connected with slavery was that the slave was property. While slaves had some rights, they could not become citizens and they could not assume Roman names, particularly the *nomen gentilicium*. To assume such a name would imply full personhood, and slaves were considered mere property. Slaves had single names, roughly equivalent to the Roman *praenomen* (more-or-less a "first name"), although sometimes they listed this name followed by the name of their master with "Servus" (i.e., "slave") or simply "S" appended.

People became slaves in various ways: through captivity in battle; through debt, i.e., being sold to compensate an unpaid creditor; or being born into slavery as children of slaves. Under some conditions slavery could also be imposed as a criminal sentence. A slave could never become a "freeborn" person. Even if a person had been born free and then fallen into slavery, that freeborn status was permanently erased. Although a slave was property, she could own property herself. In fact, slaves were often encouraged to accumulate a measure of wealth so they could buy their freedom.

FREEDMAN (LATIN "LIBERTUS") AND FREEDWOMAN (LATIN "LIBERTA")

Freedmen and freedwomen (i.e., freed slaves) were no longer slaves, and at least in some contexts they could become citizens. While they were not property, they were not entirely free of their previous masters, who were now referred to as "patrons." It did not matter if the patron had freed the slave without compensation or in exchange for payment: the freedman remained obligated to express gratitude to his patron for the rest of his life. One problem for a freedman or freedwoman was that the continuing obligations owed to his or her patron was a pediment to travel. If the patron moved, the freed slave could certainly move with the patron. However, the freed slave could not easily choose to move at will.

In certain ways manumission resembled adoption. An important similarity is that the freed slave took the name of his patron much as the adopted son took the name of the person adopting him. The freedman usually assumed the *praenomen* and *nomen gentilicium* of his patron followed by the initial letter of the patron's praenomen and the letter "L" (for *Libertus*) and finally, his old slave name was tacked on at the end. Thus, when the orator Marcus Tullius Cicero freed his slave Tiro, the newly minted freedman became Marcus Tullius M(arci) L(ibertus) Tiro.[27]

The children of *liberti* (the plural of *libertus*) were freeborn, marking an end to the familial descent into slavery. Also, freedmen often became wealthy, and freedmen often lived significantly more prosperous lives than the plebeian ("working class") freeborn.

FREEBORN MAN (LATIN "LIBER") AND FREEBORN WOMAN (LATIN "LIBERA")

The freeborn man or woman is the easiest station to explain. This person was free, not bound to any master or patron. During the first century most freeborn were not Roman citizens, although universal citizenship was granted to the freeborn during the second century.

---

27. This example is borrowed from Binns, "Roman Personal Names."

NAMES USED AMONG CHRISTIANS

There was a strong egalitarian impulse within first-century Christianity. One way this was demonstrated is by the nearly universal use of single-word names in Paul's letters.[28] Since slaves had only one name, even the freeborn who possessed full *trinomina* ("three-name names") in Christian circles went by single names. This demonstrated that before God they were all on the same level.

SOME STATISTICS

Peter Lampe estimates that when Romans was written roughly forty percent of Italy's population were slaves. He is unable similarly to estimate the percentage of Rome's population that was enslaved.[29] In Paul's greetings to people in Rome found in Rom 16:3–16, twenty-four believers are named. For many of these people it is not possible to determine if they are, on the one hand slaves or freed slaves, or on the other hand, freeborn. Lampe concludes that for only thirteen of these people can a reasonable secure determination of their status be determined. Of these thirteen, four are freeborn and nine are either slaves or freed slaves. This means that over two-thirds of the Christian leaders Paul greets have a background in slavery. When Paul starts his letter by calling himself "a slave of Jesus Christ," this is no flippant comment. The audience to which he writes understand very deeply what slavery implies.

One of the most remarkable testimonies of Christian love I have ever encountered is found in a letter written about forty years after Paul wrote Romans. This letter was written from Rome to Corinth—precisely the reverse of Paul's letter from Corinth to Rome. In *1 Clement*, the earliest document included in the collection known as the Apostolic Fathers, the author (presumably Clement) writes:

> We know that many among us have had themselves imprisoned, that they might ransom others. Many have sold

---

28. An exception is "Jesus who is called Justus," mentioned in Col 4:11. This pattern is also generally the case throughout the whole of the New Testament, although there are exceptions particularly in Acts: "Joseph who is called Barsabbas and surnamed Justus," mentioned in Acts 1:23; "Joseph who is surnamed Barnabas," mentioned in Acts 4:36; "Simeon who is called Niger," mentioned in Acts 13:1; and "John surnamed Mark," mentioned in Acts 12:12 and 15:37.

29. Lampe, *From Paul to Valentinus*, 172.

themselves into slavery, and with the price received for themselves have fed others.[30]

Being slaves of Christ, these saints chose to become slaves of men in the service of their Master.

The Reformation Heritage

It is hard to overstate the impact of the Protestant Reformation on the interpretation of Romans. Because the way the Reformers read Romans impacted their theology so greatly, the course of the Reformation cannot be traced accurately or unleashed from the interpretation of this book.

But if the interpretation of Romans is crucial to any account of the Reformation, in a similar way the shadow of the Reformation lies over the interpretation of Romans even today, constantly shading and coloring it. For this reason, some account of the Reformation's impact on the interpretation of Romans is necessary in an honest commentary aimed at a Pentecostal/Charismatic audience, which is largely but not entirely located within the Protestant theological tradition.

It is widely believed that the central theological issue of the Reformation was "justification," yet when one lists specific hot-button issues in the early sixteenth century—indulgences, the veneration of relics, pilgrimages, penance, purgatory, etc.—most had to do not with entry into the Christian life, but rather matters of sin committed by adult Christians. In the Europe of the sixteenth century, except among the Radical Reformers (Anabaptists), baptism was agreed upon as the point of entry into the Christian faith, and almost all baptisms were administered to infants. It is difficult to untangle justification and sanctification, but since so many hot-button issues involved post-baptismal sin, there is a strong argument that the central issue of the Reformation was sanctification, not justification.

However, this may be beside the point since Romans has so much to say about both topics. Romans 4 is the central New Testament locus for discussions of justification by faith. Romans 5 is the central New Testament locus for discussions of the nature of sin and death, the fall of Adam, and the vindication and life that are available through Jesus Christ. Romans 6 and 7 deal with the struggle with sin every person faces, and Romans 8 deals with the crucial importance of the Holy Spirit in the life of the believer. It is no wonder that Romans featured so prominently in Reformation debates!

---

30. *1 Clement* 55.2.

It is also not widely recognized that a central point of disagreement between Protestants and Catholics during the Reformation was the relationship between justification and sanctification, and this is a disagreement that continues to this day. When Protestants speak of a person's "salvation," this certainly includes his or her justification, but it includes little to no actual sanctification.[31] In contrast, for Catholics everyone who is justified is also fully sanctified; everyone who is sanctified is also justified.[32]

For Catholics an act of (mortal) sin removes one's sanctification and her justification as well.[33] The person who has committed a mortal sin, which has not been absolved by a priest, and then dies is likely headed for hell. (This is only "likely" because in Catholic theology God always retains the privilege to extend extra mercy as he wills.) This idea that individual acts of sin change one's eternal destiny is not so different from what was often taught in many Pentecostal churches fifty years ago. Many people committed sins each week, felt they had lost their salvation, and then "got saved" every Sunday night. As Pentecostals have increasingly understood humanity's root problem to be the principle of sin rather than specific sins, they have also concluded that the death of Christ provides forgiveness for sins committed after conversion as well as before that moment. Because of this changed perspective, this pattern of repeated salvation experiences has nearly disappeared.

Today, Catholics emphasize the guilt arising from specific sinful acts more than most Pentecostals and evangelicals do. And these differing approaches to sin create some confusion when these heirs of the Protestant Reformation talk with Catholics. For Pentecostals and evangelicals, if a person is "a Christian" then she is headed for her eternal reward. If she is not headed for an eternal reward, then she is not a Christian. For Catholics, a person becomes a Christian at baptism, and he does not relinquish that

---

31. Some Protestants will speak of "positional sanctification" taking place at the moment of salvation, but they distinguish this from "actual sanctification."

32. In this regard *Catechism of the Catholic Church* §1989 quotes the "Decree on Justification," which Session 6 of the Council of Trent issued in January of 1547 (cited in Denzinger-Schönmetzer, *Enchiridion Symbolorum* 1528): "Justification is not only the remission of sins, but also the sanctification and renewal of the interior man." While Catholic theology regards sanctification and justification as occurring together, it also speaks of the possibility of growth in both. When certain individuals grow so greatly in justice and sanctity that they far exceed what makes them worthy of salvation, the church may formally declare them to be "saints," normally after they have died.

33. Mortal sins are not just matters everyone considers serious, like murder or adultery. Not attending weekly mass on a festival day (generally Saturday or Sunday) is also considered a mortal sin and removes a person from a state of grace.

status unless he does something extreme such as convert to another religion or renounce his Christianity. Through, on the one hand, committing mortal sins and, on the other hand, making confession and receiving absolution from a priest, a person may toggle back and forth between "being in a state of grace" and "not being in a state of grace" all the while remaining "a Christian." Furthermore, there is no doctrine of "assurance of salvation" in Catholicism; even the pope cannot be sure of receiving an eternal reward at the final judgment.

Because in Catholic theology all who are justified are also sanctified, those whom Christ justifies are worthy of salvation (i.e., an eternal life of blessing). Because they are worthy, God saves them. The Reformers famously rejected the notion that those whom Christ saves are in themselves worthy of salvation. Instead, Christ's "alien righteousness" or "passive righteousness" is imputed (reckoned) to the believer.[34] Actual righteousness is not imparted. (The Reformers also taught that faith in Christ brings the non-imputation of a person's sins to his or her account.) Thus, in Protestant theology there is a great distinction between how a justified person appears in the sight of God (*coram Deo*, literally "before God"), i.e., as righteous, and how that person appears in his own sight and in the sight of other human beings (*coram hominibus*, literally "before men"), i.e., as a sinner. This is the theological basis of the famous Reformation slogan *simul justus et peccator* ("At the same time justified and a sinner"). Those who have been justified understand that God considers them clean and holy on the basis of Christ's righteousness even though they know that by nature they are scoundrels.

Implied by this slogan ("At the same time justified and a sinner") is a distinction between justification and sanctification. Justification turns on how the believer appears in the sight of God (*coram Deo*) when he or she comes to faith, while sanctification starts with one's awareness of the vast chasm between his lack of holiness and the holiness of God. Sanctification is then one's attempt in cooperation with God to achieve movement from one's current waywardness and rebellion toward the holiness of God.

While Catholics believed that all who were justified were also sanctified, the Reformers believed that sanctification begins at justification but is like the acorn to the oak; it develops gradually. As the Genevan theologian Francis Turretin explains, "Although we may be of the opinion that these two benefits [i.e., justification and sanctification] must be distinguished and

---

34. This righteousness is "alien" because it does not come from the person to whom it is credited. It is "passive" because the individual credited with it does nothing to earn or merit it.

never confused . . . they are never to be torn asunder."³⁵ In the same way, while works are never the basis for justification, as the justified person progresses in actual sanctification, good works will emerge. Furthermore, while a person can contribute nothing to his justification, that person must cooperate with the Holy Spirit in the production of good works. This premise is reflected in the oft-repeated Protestant slogan "Faith alone is what justifies, but the faith that justifies is not alone."³⁶

The New Perspective on Paul

Today it is inconceivable to write a commentary on Romans without discussing "the New Perspective on Paul," as it has come to be called. There are many disagreements about what this phrase means, but whatever it means, discussion of it has dominated Pauline studies for more than four decades.

This phrase—"new perspective on Paul"—was coined by Krister Stendahl in 1963,³⁷ and then later, in 1978, was given its present-day meaning by N. T. Wright.³⁸ The pivotal idea is that Protestant interpreters have largely misunderstood Paul. Another key point is that Judaism has often been misrepresented by New Testament scholars.

Despite the importance of the years 1963 and 1978 for this topic, the beginning of the New Perspective really should be placed in 1977. In that year E. P. Sanders published his groundbreaking work, *Paul and Palestinian Judaism*. Since then, a coterie of scholars including Sanders and Wright, as well as James D. G. Dunn, Richard B. Hays, and many lesser luminaries has emerged who give voice to similar, but by no means identical, themes. These scholars have argued that Martin Luther misunderstood Paul and became not so much an interpreter of Paul as someone who projected his own issues onto the texts that lay before him. Sensing "works-righteousness" in the Catholic church of his day, Luther imposed the dynamics of his own

---

35. Franciscus Turrettinus, *Institutio Theologiae elenchticae*, Editio nova (Utrecht and Amsterdam: 1701), XVII, i, 15 as cited and translated in Heppe, *Reformed Dogmatics*, 566.

36. The Latin form of this slogan is "Fides sola est quae justificat; fides quae justificat non est sola." This is a slightly altered form of the title of a poem by Richard Crashaw, published in 1648 in his collection of poems titled *Steps to the Temple*. The full title was *Fides sola est quae justificat; fides quae justificat non est sine spe et dilectione*. See Grosart, *Complete Works of Richard Crashaw*, 2.209.

37. Krister Stendahl, "Apostle Paul and the Introspective Conscious," 199–215.

38. Wright, "Paul of History and the Apostle of Faith," 61–88; for Wright's perspective on who coined the term, see Wright, *Justification*, 28.

struggle with the Catholic church upon his reading of Paul. The *eisegesis* (reading an interpretation *into* the text rather than extracting an interpretation from it) that resulted from Luther's projection launched Protestant theology on an errant trajectory from which it still has not recovered. In fact, the shadow Luther has cast on subsequent interpretation of Paul is so great that today most Protestants read Paul through a lens crafted by Luther, whether they realize it or not.

For some, Luther's basic mistake was to explain Paul's gospel in largely individualistic terms. Luther understood Paul to focus on the salvation of the individual: Jesus as my savior or yours. Many have argued that this was a great mistake: the great sweep of salvation-history that Paul discusses has to do with groups of people: Jews, and gentiles. Moreover, Paul's focus is not so much on individual expressions of faith but rather on the faithfulness of Jesus. See the related excursus: "The Faith in Christ/Faithfulness of Christ Debate."

Sanders claimed Luther had not only misunderstood Paul, he had also badly mischaracterized Judaism. As Luther saw it, Jews believed keeping the Torah (Law of Moses) was a way to earn entry into the ranks of the righteous and ultimately—at least for those Jews who believed in an afterlife—to receive an eternal reward.

This Protestant presentation of Judaism did not square with what Sanders thought he knew about the subject. The famous phrase he used to characterize Judaism was "covenantal nomism." Central to Judaism was membership in the chosen "people of Israel," who had a relationship with God defined by a series of covenants, the most prominent of which was the Mosaic covenant. Entry into this people often happened by birth, but it could also happen by conversion, and a non-Jew who converted could hardly be said to have earned salvation based on her scrupulous observance of Torah, since she had not to this point in life been living as a Jew. Similarly, an eight-day-old male, who was thought to become part of the people of Israel at circumcision, could hardly have earned his way in.

The Torah did serve as a kind of marker, but it was a marker for those who were already within the people of God. By observing the requirements of the Torah, one demonstrated his or her continuing affirmation of the Mosaic covenant and the importance of one's status within the people of Israel. Neglect of the Torah might be understood to announce just the opposite. Torah observance was not about entering the people of God, but rather a way of maintaining one's place within the people of God. Moreover, in Sanders's view, to observe the Torah could never mean keeping every provision perfectly. Built into the Torah were provisions for atonement, i.e., the removal of guilt, and for divine forgiveness. Much of the sacrificial system would be unnecessary, were there no need for the atonement of sin.

To summarize Sanders's central point: ancient Judaism was, and its modern successor remains, a religion of divine grace, not a religion of works-righteousness achieved by individual effort. People enter both the covenant and the people of Israel because God has chosen them. And similarly, only God could accomplish any eschatological reward his people might possibly hope to receive. Thus, in the end, at the *eschaton* ("the end"), salvation is accomplished exclusively by divine grace. Consequently, either Paul misrepresents Judaism or interpreters such as Luther have misunderstood Paul.

It seems presumptuous for modern interpreters of Paul to claim they understand ancient Judaism more accurately than did Paul, who had firsthand participatory knowledge. In my judgment, the "Old Perspective," i.e., Luther and his exegetical relatives, may have gotten some things wrong, but it did not misunderstand Paul completely. Therefore, this commentary will incorporate insights from both the New Perspective and the Old Perspective.

Over the years, in addition to receiving numerous plaudits, there have also been many criticisms of the New Perspective. I would like to mention one of these, offered by the immensely important scholar of Judaism, Jacob Neusner. This is not the official title of his critique, but I think of it somewhat fancifully as "A Different Perspective on the New Perspective." Neusner offered this assessment in a very negative review of one of Sanders's books, *Jewish Law from Jesus to the Mishnah: Five Studies*. The actual title of this review is "Mr. Sanders's Pharisees and Mine," and it was published in the *Bulletin for Biblical Research* in 1992.

In this review, Neusner has many complaints about Sanders's work, but perhaps the most radical criticism—radical in the sense that it strikes at the "root" of the matter—is that in his view Sanders attempts to turn ancient Judaism into a variant form of the modern liberal Protestantism Prof. Sanders himself embraces. In other words, Neusner accuses Sanders of the same kind of projection Sanders had charged Luther with. He suggests that Judaism does not need this sort of defense and that although Sanders is fighting against one kind of anti-Semitism found in Luther's interpretation of Paul, in the end Sanders simply introduces another kind of anti-Semitism in its place. Neusner concludes by saying, "With friends like Sanders, Judaism hardly needs any enemies."

This is a fair warning: Every interpreter needs to be careful not to project his own views onto the author he interprets. In this commentary, I am subject to Paul's ideas; he is not subject to mine.

The New-Perspective Adjacent Scholar John M. G. Barclay

Before moving on entirely from the topic of the New Perspective, I'd like to examine briefly the work of John M. G. Barclay, and in particular his book *Paul and the Gift*. He should not be counted as a New Perspective scholar., but perhaps he is New-Perspective adjacent. Barclay's contributions are more recent than those of the leading New Perspective scholars and in important ways move beyond their core ideas. However, since the argument advanced in *Paul and the Gift* includes a careful critique of the central thesis of E. P. Sanders's *Paul and Palestinian Judaism*, I think it is fitting to discuss his work alongside the New Perspective scholars.

The central point of E. P. Sanders's work is that a great deal of Christian scholarship has misconstrued Judaism as a religion centered on righteousness achieved through works, when in fact Judaism is, and in Paul's time was, a religion of grace. He asserts this because Judaism understands obeying the Law, not as a means of entering the covenant, but a way of affirming continuing identification with the people of God, who had been chosen by God. Whether a male child who is circumcised on his eighth day of life or a proselyte who becomes a Jew much later, no one enters Judaism based on his great record of Torah observance. For Sanders, the fact that inclusion in God's people comes *prior* to any works, implies that grace is the fundamental dynamic of Judaism.

Barclay thinks that although Sanders was onto something, the situation is more complex than he suggests. To help analyze what "grace" might mean, Barclay turns to the insights of anthropology, which over the past century has made intensive study of gifts and gift-giving.[39] While the anthropological analysis of gift-giving covers a very wide spectrum, the conceptions of grace found within Judaism and within Paul's writings certainly can be included within the bounds of this area of study.

Barclay acknowledges that the dynamics surrounding gift-giving can be somewhat messy.[40] Nevertheless, he identifies six concepts (or dimensions) that help clarify what is involved. Each of these concepts is sometimes

---

39. Barclay considers Marcel Mauss to be the seminal figure in this initiative. His essay "Essai sur le Don: Forme et raison de l'échange dans les sociétés archaïques" was marked as published in 1923–24, but it was actually published in 1925. Barclay considers the best English translation of this essay to be by W. D. Halle, published with the title *The Gift*.

40. He states this in more elegant, academic language: "'Gift' is neither a single phenomenon nor a stable category." Barclay, *Paul and the Gift* 11.

in play, but rarely or never are all six involved in the same situation. To simplify matters, I will only discuss three of these six concepts. They are 1) Priority, 2) Incongruity, and 3) Non-Circularity.

Each of these concepts can be "perfected." Perfecting "refers to the tendency to draw out a concept to its endpoint or extreme, whether for definitional clarity or for rhetorical or ideological advantage."[41] Barclay borrows this term from the literary theorist Kenneth Burke.[42]

Sanders presents Judaism as a religion of grace because one enters the covenant *prior* to having performed any works. Using this mode of analysis, he emphasizes the concept of Priority. This is a legitimate dimension of grace in Judaism, but it may also not present the whole story.

To explain the two other concepts, Incongruity and Non-Circularity, it will be necessary first to explore some striking differences between ancient and modern attitudes about gift-giving. While Barclay reviews the ideas of many ancient sources, perhaps the first-century AD philosopher Seneca proves to be most insightful. As Seneca explains things, the very fabric of society is formed by interlocking connections formed through gift-giving and commerce. Gift-giving involves the reciprocity of counter-gift-giving, through social debt and obligation, and through gratitude. While gift-giving should be distinguished from its "sordid" counterpart of commercial transactions, both create the connections necessary to the full functioning of society.[43] Commerce involve legally binding obligations; gift-giving is less formal and more personal.

Barclay notes that in the ancient world the primary goal of gift-giving is to create or to sustain enduring relationships. This means that gift-giving entails obligations, the nature of which are determined by many factors including the relative social status of the giver and the receiver, the relative wealth of the giver and receiver, and relationships that precede the gift. Sometimes the obligation is not material; it does not require a counter-gift. Often, it involves only gratitude, but gratitude expressed in a visible manner. However, obligation is often relieved by giving a counter-gift, sometimes of greater value than the original gift. This sort of giving was considered meritorious and a way to elevate an existing bond. Of course, the counter-gift might also be reciprocated, continuing the cycle of gift-giving.

Particularly when gifts are substantial, the selection of the recipient is important. It is important to create ties with people who are worthy and

---

41. Barclay, *Paul and the Gift*, 67.

42. Barclay, *Paul and the Gift*, 67.

43. Seneca expresses his views in his seven book *De Beneficiis*, which Barclay summarizes. See Barclay, *Paul and the Gift*, 45–51.

whose social status is recognized. Those who are considered ungrateful will likely not be given gifts, and they will to some degree become excluded from the ties that bind society together.

It is also true that gifts were not given to strangers or to people at random. Such people are not known to be worthy. It would be inviting trouble to create ties with those about whom nothing is known. Instead, gifts should be reserved for relatives, friends, or those already in one's social network (or perhaps adjacent to one's social network but of slightly higher social status). The net effect is that while gifts are voluntary—this is what distinguishes them from the payments involved in commercial transactions—there is an expectation of a return, although its exact form will be unknown.

In the ancient world, gifts sometimes were not accepted. When people felt unable to bear the obligation that accepting a gift might entail, they would politely refuse the gift. This might be done to avoid the shame of appearing ungrateful if they felt unable to offer an appropriate counter-gift. Someone might also refuse a gift if for some reason she did not want to create or strengthen ties with the giver.

While there are some similarities to gift-giving in the modern West—I think of the obligation someone often feels to return the favor of an invitation to dinner—there are also substantial differences. Barclay summarizes Seneca's perspective, presenting it as a general summary of ancient attitudes toward gift-giving:

> Seneca *never* idealizes the one-way, unreciprocated gift. While he figures the return in unusual ways (primarily as gratitude itself), he retains the unanimous ancient assumption that the point of gifts is to create social ties; thus, *the proper expression of gift is reciprocal exchange.*[44]

As a result, Barclay contends that the modern concepts of the "pure gift" and "altruism" were completely foreign to ancient thinking. He also demonstrates how Immanuel Kant's "universal ethical ideal" severed the moral value of an act from either real or anticipated outcomes of that act and contributed to the modern notion of altruism.[45]

Barclay contends that awareness of ancient attitudes toward gift-giving should impact how interpreters understand Paul's use of the word "grace," especially as it relates to God's great gift of the sacrifice of his son.

Barclay highlights the extraordinary nature of Paul's message through use of his concept of Incongruity. While ancient gift-giving focused on the

---

44. Barclay, *Paul and the Gift*, 50–51. The italics are Barclay's.
45. Barclay, *Paul and the Gift*, 57–59.

congruity of selective giving to appropriate recipients, Paul claims God's great gift is freely offered without regard to the recipients' worth. The gift is offered without regard to one's ethnicity, social status, wealth, reputation, goodness, influence, or any other marker of worth. In the ancient world, this was completely alien to the standard understanding of gift-giving.

We have already established that using Barclay's concept of Priority (earlier offered by Sanders) Judaism is a religion of grace. But is it also a religion of grace in the same sense as Paul's Christianity was when examined through the dimension of Incongruity? Apparently not always. This suggests that it is important to be more precise. It is not enough to say something is characterized by grace. One must specify in what way grace is operative. As Barclay will further elucidate, there were various forms of Judaism that exhibited grace in different ways, as evaluated by Barclay's six concepts.[46]

If the concept of Incongruity was generally absent in antiquity, equally absent were gifts offered according to Barclay's concept of Non-Circularity. Non-Circularity means there is no expectation of something given back in return. In the modern world, many institutions hand out prizes or scholarship to deserving people (i.e., people of worth, defined in various ways). But generally, there is no expectation of a counter-gift or another type of return. Often a person is required to accept the prize or scholarship, but usually that is the only requirement. This expectation (or might we say non-expectation of return) accords with the modern notion of altruism as the foundation of a "pure gift," as opposed to some kind of manipulative transaction. This way of thinking was foreign to the ancients.

But here is where Barclay's examination of Paul's writings (particularly Galatians and Romans) gets tricky.

> Paul . . . combines two features that appear paradoxical only to us. On the one hand, he perfects the incongruity of the gift, its donation to those unfitting to be its recipients; on the other, he presumes its strongly obliging character, reorienting the allegiances of those to whom it is given. Here it is crucial to remind ourselves that a perfection of gift in one dimension does not entail the perfection of every other: Paul perfects the incongruity of the gift (given to the unworthy) but he does *not* perfect its non-circularity (expecting nothing in return). The divine gift in Christ was *unconditioned* (based on no prior

---

46. Barclay analyzes five different collections of Jewish literature from around the time of Paul, and he finds elements of grace in each of them, even though the way grace is understood in these collections differs considerably. See Barclay, *Paul and the Gift*, 194–328.

conditions) but it is not *unconditional* (carrying no subsequent demands).[47]

According to Barclay, the reception of the Spirit that marks the beginning of one's new life in Christ is utterly transformative, making possible what previously had been impossible. While Paul insists that no one is worthy prior to faith and the transformation that comes with it, through the power of the Spirit the new Christian comes alive and attains worth in the eyes of God, even while remaining in a mortal body and struggling with sin. Barclay prefers to describe this dual dynamic with the slogan *simul mortuus et vivens* ("at the same time dead and alive") rather than with the Lutheran slogan *simul iustus et paccator* ("at the same time just and a sinner").[48]

If Barclay is right, and I think he is, then traditional Christian theology remains correct in maintaining that salvation is offered as a free gift. It is entirely the work of God, and the recipient adds nothing to it. It is received on a purely voluntary basis; no coercion is involved. However, this is what Barclay adds to the traditional presentation: conversion begins a new relationship—as gifts in the ancient world were intended to do—that presumes the recipient's allegiance and obligation to the bestower of this wonderful gift.

The striking idea that divine grace is *unconditioned* but not *unconditional* explains Paul's expectation that Christ-followers will produce good works and will even be judged on the basis of their works in the final judgment. This insight helps explain difficult passages such as Rom 2:5–11 and 1 Cor 3:12–15. Furthermore, a fresh examination of Paul's theology in this light holds promise of bringing greater clarity and perhaps even a measure of reconciliation to both controversies between Protestants and Catholics and controversies within Protestantism that are rooted in conflicting interpretations of Paul.

The Ending of Romans

The way Romans ends is perplexing. Various forms of the final chapters of Romans exist in the manuscript tradition, but none is without difficulties. Some of this material, even what is traditionally printed in modern Bibles, may not have originally been part of the letter. (In my analysis only one verse, Rom 16:24 is not original, although some additional material is not in its original location.) While there are a few problems determining what represents Paul's original text in the earlier parts of Romans, these difficulties

---

47. Barclay, *Paul and the Gift*, 500. The italics are Barclay's.
48. Barclay, *Paul and the Gift*, 502.

are modest compared with the tangles and challenges posed by the various forms of the text that come after 14:23, the last verse of chapter 14 in modern printed Bibles.

For those readers interested in the intricacies of the text critical arguments about what constituted the original form of the letter, please consult Appendix 1: "The Ending of Romans." To keep from overwhelming the general reader, here I will simply outline the conclusions detailed in this appendix.

The most important manuscript of the Pauline Corpus (*Corpus Paulinum*) is P^{46}. This papyrus is early (late second century to early third century), and it did not simply contain a book or two, but rather a collection of Paul's writings (including Hebrews but without 2 Thessalonians, Philemon, and the Pastoral Epistles). It is the single manuscript that probably stands closest to the archetype (original manuscript) of the *Corpus Paulinum* (the original collection of Paul's letters). Not surprisingly, it also likely retains the original form of the ending of Romans, which deviates slightly from the order of material that has become traditional to print in modern editions of the New Testament. The translation included with this commentary will follow the order of P^{46}. This is not simply because of the authority of this important manuscript, but because of the cumulative weight of the text critical evidence.

There are three units of text. First, the great bulk of Romans appears in 1:1—15:33. This is followed by a short doxology containing the material traditionally known as 16:25-27. Finally comes 16:1-23. The first sixteen of these verses are comprised of greetings. The next four verses contain ethical exhortations concluding with a grace benediction in vs. 20. Then vss. 21-23 function as a postscript.

The only verse entirely omitted, as opposed to being relocated, is 16:24, which does not appear in the earliest and best manuscripts.

ROMANS 1

TRANSLATION: ROM 1:1–7

OPENING GREETING

¹Paul, a slave of Christ Jesus, called to be an apostle, set apart for good news from God, ²which he promised beforehand through his apostles in the holy scriptures ³concerning his son, the one born of the seed of David in the natural, ⁴the one powerfully marked by his resurrection from the dead as son of God according to the Spirit of Holiness, Jesus Christ our Lord. ⁵Through him we have received grace and apostleship for the obedience of faith among all the gentiles for the sake of his name, ⁶among whom you are also called people of Jesus Christ. ⁷To all God's beloved in Rome, called to be saints, grace to you and peace from God our Father and Lord Jesus Christ.

COMMENTARY

Vss. 1–7: It was customary for Roman letters to begin with an opening greeting that followed a particular convention. The opening greeting began by stating the name of the writer(s), moved on to mention the recipient(s), and finally employed the formulaic greeting *chairein*, which can loosely be translated "greetings." A good example of this standard opening salutation is found in Acts 15:23: "The brothers, both apostles and elders [i.e., those writing the letter], to those brothers among the gentiles in Antioch, Syria, and Cilicia [i.e., the recipients], greetings [the formulaic greeting]." However, Paul habitually gives this convention a Christian spin by substituting the word *charis* ("grace"; vs. 7) for the conventional *chairein*. In addition, as a good Jew he also often adds, as he does here, *eirēnē* ("peace"), a translation of *shalom*, the standard greeting in the Hebrew-speaking world.

Some consider vss. 2–6 to reflect elements of an early creed which Paul has appropriated for his opening.[1] If so, it is likely Paul thought these elements would be received sympathetically by the Roman believers to whom he writes.

The Greek of vss. 1–7 makes up one long very complex sentence. Since rendering it literally would result in a run-on sentence, which is a *faux pas* in English grammar, I have broken the translation up into shorter sentences.

Vs. 1: Although while growing up he had used his Hebrew name *Sha'ul*, ("Saul"), he later adopted the name *Paulos*, with which begins his letter. This was how he was known among the various Christian communities of the day, but it was not his complete, formal Roman name.

As a Roman citizen,[2] Paul would have had at least two, probably three, and possibly four names. He certainly would have had a *praenomen* (roughly equal to a first name) and a *nomen gentilicium* (the name of his *gens* ["clan"]). In addition, a *cognomem* was usually added as a third name, and in very rare and special cases a fourth part called the *agnomen* could be added. This *agnomen* was usually an honorific title. The *cognomem* could either designate a family within a *gens* ("clan"), or it could be a personal name.

Since Paul was a Jew, he would not have come from a family of extensive Roman lineage. Instead, it is likely either that an ancestor rendered important service to a high Roman official and was subsequently rewarded with Roman citizenship or an ancestor had been adopted by a Roman citizen. Acts 22:28 tells us that Paul was born a Roman citizen; Roman citizenship was not something he acquired. If an ancestor was adopted by a Roman patron, it would have been customary for the adopted son to assume the *nomen gentilicium* or the *cognomen* of his patron, or possibly both.

The Latin name Paulus (or Paullus) means "small," and it was used as both a *praenomen* and as a *cognomen*. There was no *gens* Paulus, so it was not used as a *nomem gentilicium*. Beginning with the church father Jerome, some have theorized that Paul claimed the *cognomen* of Sergius Paulus as a way of honoring him. According to Acts 13:6–12, this proconsul of Cyprus converted to Christianity under Paul's influence. It is also possible that Sergius Paulus chose to honor Paul by adopting him, although if Paul had already been born a Roman citizen, this is not how he obtained his citizenship. These scenarios are highly speculative, but it is intriguing that Acts relates that "Saul was also called Paul" (Acts 13:9) immediately after the

---

1. See for example, Jefford, *Apostolic Fathers*, 62–63.

2. In Acts 22:25–28 Paul claims to be a Roman citizen, and the whole narrative of him being sent to stand trial before Caesar (Acts 25–28) is based on the premise of his Roman citizenship.

name Sergius Paulus is mentioned in Acts 13:7.³ From this point in the Acts narrative, Paul replaces Saul as the name designating him, except where events prior to this moment are recalled. Unfortunately, even if Paulus was Paul's *cognomen*, his *nomen gentilicium* remains unknown and this makes it difficult to determine if he is mentioned in any secular literature from the Roman world.

Paul calls himself "a servant of Christ Jesus." Several Greek words are sometime translated as "servant." The word used here, *doulos*, is often translated "slave," and this is the better translation here. Paul's introduction of himself as a slave in the extremely class-conscious world of the Roman Empire shows he rejects the value system of that world. Beyond this striking way of introducing himself, he never mentions his Roman citizenship anywhere in the letter. He is willing to recognize the status of others, in 16:23 calling Gaius the "host" or "patron" of both himself and "the whole church" and recognizing Erastus as "the city treasurer" (of Corinth). Nevertheless, he is unwilling to boast of his own secular status.

Paul then moves on to describe himself as "a called apostle set apart for good news from God." One wonders how Paul's claim to apostleship was received by the believers in Rome. Did they accept that someone who had not been taught directly by Jesus could hold such a title? They would not have been surprised to hear that Paul made this claim since some living in Rome had known Paul in the East. But not being surprised by his claim and accepting his claim are not the same thing. Archaeological evidence and later calendars of the saints make it certain that eventually Paul would be revered as a sainted martyr claimed by the Roman community, but the first reaction of the Roman Christians might not have been so warm.

This phrase *euangelion theou* is usually translated "the gospel of God," but here it does not have a definite article. A possible translation is "a favorable announcement from God." It is unclear what the believers in Rome

---

3. The *praenomen* of Sergius Paulus is not known for certain, but it may have been Lucius. According to Inscription 5926 recorded in Dessau, *ILS*, Vol. 2, Part 1, an L. Sergius Paulus was appointed by the Emperor Claudius to serve as a member of the governing board overseeing the water coming into Rome from the Tiber River and the aqueducts. This is the sort of honor that might well have been conferred on a former proconsul/consul. In an inscription from Cyprus (Cagnat, *IGR* 930) a proconsul (*anthypatos*) named Paulos is mentioned. Since Paulus was not the name of a *gens*, Paulos must have been his cognomen. In addition, there was a Sergia *gens* so perhaps Sergius Paulus is the individual mentioned here. Whatever his name, this proconsul served in the tenth year of someone's *imperium*. If that emperor was *Claudius*, it would mean this Paulos served as proconsul in the year AD 50, which fits the timeline of Paul's encounter with Sergius Paulus mentioned in Acts 22. For a helpful discussion, see Mitford, "Inscriptions from Roman Cyprus," 201–4.

would have understood by this expression. *See more about the word* euange-lion *in the excursus titled "'The Gospel' or 'Paul's Gospel.'"*

In contrast to his reticence to claim secular honors, Paul is not shy about claiming the title of "apostle." Furthermore, he clearly links this title with a "calling" to that role, which came through a direct encounter with Jesus. Paul's conversion and calling are depicted as the result of a direct encounter with Jesus in Acts 9, and Paul himself claims as much in 1 Cor 9:1: "Am I not an apostle? Have I not seen Jesus our Lord?" Here in vs. 1 he also states he has been "set apart" to advance the gospel, which seems to be a special aspect of his particular apostolic calling. *For more on "calling," see the excursus titled "Calling in the New Testament."*

The Greek word *apostolos* was an old word by Paul's time, appearing in secular Greek as early as Herodotus. Taken very literally, it means "a sent person," and is usually considered an equivalent to the Hebrew *shaliach*, which also means "a sent person." The Hebrew *shaliach* does not appear in the Old Testament, although it does occur occasionally in the Talmud. Similarly, the Greek *apostolos* does not appear in the LXX.[4] Of course, *apostolos* appears frequently in the New Testament.

It is likely that Jesus used *sheluchim* (the plural of *shaliach*) or a similar Semitic word in his teaching to refer to his students whom he sent out. Luke 6:13 recounts that Jesus "called his disciples, and chose from them twelve, whom he named apostles." And, of course, both Matthew's and Luke's Gospels record the "sending out" of the Twelve (Matt. 10:5–23; Luke 9:1–6). Similarly, Luke's Gospel also records Jesus "sending out" the Seventy (Luke 10:1–12).

In the New Testament the word "apostle" is used in a variety of ways. Epaphroditus is an agent or "apostle" of the church at Philippi, sent to care for Paul when he had fallen ill (Phil 2:25). "Apostles of churches" are mentioned in 2 Cor 8:23. They apparently represent churches and act as their agents. With one exception (Acts 14:14), the book of Acts uses the word "apostle" to refer exclusively to members of the Twelve.[5] However, in Paul's

---

4. *Apostolos* does appear once in Origen's *Hexapla* in an asterisked passage (3 Kingdoms 14:6), marking where there was no equivalent to the Hebrew of 1Kings 14:1–20, prompting Origen therefore to supply what was missing from other Greek translations of the Hebrew.

5. Some regard this one exception (where Barnabas and Paul are identified as apostles) to be a later emendation of the text because in Acts 15 Paul and Barnabas come "to the apostles," a somewhat awkward formulation if Paul and Barnabas are counted among the apostles. Also, granting this one exception, elsewhere Acts portrays the apostles as empowered to speak for the church of Jerusalem suggesting that a connection to Jerusalem was important. In Acts 14:14 a few manuscripts omit the words "the apostles."

famous catalogue of resurrection appearances found in 1 Corinthians 15, he seems to distinguish "the Twelve" (vs. 4) from "all the apostles" (vs. 7). Some believe that the Seventy, who were sent out, served as a secondary network of apostles. When Andronicus and Junia are described as apostles in Rom 16:7, what kind of apostles might they be? "Apostles of churches" or members of the Seventy?

In 1 Cor 15:8 Paul seems to agree with the view expressed in Acts 1:21–22, that being a witness to the resurrection of Jesus is a prerequisite for being an apostle of Jesus Christ. When describing himself as such a witness, Paul calls himself "one untimely born," to use the euphemistic wording of the RSV. The word he uses is a grim one: *ektrōma*, which refers to a stillbirth. Throughout this passage Paul is self-deprecating, and associating himself with this uncomfortable image is part of his rhetorical strategy. Rather than being born unnaturally early as the word *ektrōma* would normally imply, he became a witness of the resurrection unnaturally late. He employs the adverbial phrase "last of all" to introduce this reference to his encounter with the risen Jesus. It is unclear whether this phrase implies that Paul's experience was the last direct, physical human encounter with the risen Lord to occur before the close of this age and thus that he is the last apostle—a maximalist interpretation—or simply that this encounter was the last entry on Paul's list of resurrection appearances—a minimalist interpretation. Which of these interpretations is correct cannot be decided based on grammar alone. In either case, by calling himself "last" Paul continues his pattern of self-deprecation.

Paul's next sentence (in 1 Cor 15:9) is even more modest and begins with the causal conjunction *gar* ("for" or "because") linking his approaching discussion of apostleship to the preceding discussion of resurrection appearances: "For I am the least of the apostles, who is not worthy to be called an apostle . . . ."

As is evident in this passage, Paul recognizes the unusual, even odd, nature of his apostleship. Nevertheless, he will not back away from defending what he believes God has given him. In Corinth he encountered criticism that he was not so eloquent as others who falsely claimed apostleship (2 Cor 11:6, 13) and that he lacked the résumé of "apostles" who boasted of letters of recommendation, perhaps issued by the leaders in Jerusalem (2 Cor 3:1). Nevertheless, he insists "I am not inferior to these 'super-apostles'" (2 Cor 11:5). This is clearly a swipe at their arrogant claims. Furthermore, Paul understands apostles to have an extremely important place in God's plan, so false claims of apostleship were no trivial matter. In Eph. 2:19–20 he says that "the household of God is built on the foundation of the apostles and the [New Testament] prophets."

In Rom 11:13 Paul describes himself as "an apostle of the gentiles," and similarly he speaks in Rom 15:15-16 of "the grace given me by God to be a minister of Christ Jesus to the gentiles." Paul's ministry to the gentiles came "from God," but it could also be described as a strategic division of labor, a division acknowledged by the leaders in Jerusalem. In Gal 2:7 he notes that the Jerusalem circle "saw that I had been entrusted with the gospel to the uncircumcised, just as Peter had been entrusted with the gospel to the circumcised."

Vss. 2-4: For Paul the resurrection of Jesus marked the beginning of a new era of salvation. However, the gospel that announced this new era of salvation had already been promised long before by the OT prophets. The verb used here, *proepangellō*, ("promised beforehand") is related to the noun *euangelion* ("gospel" or "good news").

In continuity with Israel's history Jesus was born of the seed of David, and like Israel's kings was regarded as an adopted "son of God."[6] However, unlike any previous son of David/son of God, in the spiritual sphere he was marked out powerfully as God's son when God raised him from the dead. The phrase "Spirit of Holiness" indicates that Paul is not speaking of the anthropological spirit, but rather the Spirit of God.

The verb *horizō* ("to mark") that appears in vs. 4 echoes the verb *aphorizō* ("to set apart") that appears in vs. 1. However, this is also the only place in all his letters that Paul uses *horizō*. This verb could also be translated "declared" rather than "marked." Some scholars, most notably James D. G. Dunn, have argued that *horizō* here means "to designate." Dunn believes Christ was designated" at his resurrection as the son of God by the Spirit of Holiness, a status he did not previously enjoy. Because the term "son of God" was a messianic title, this means that Jesus also became the

---

6. In Old Testament studies, a key hypothesis of the Scandinavian "myth and ritual" school, of which Sigmund Mowinckel was the most prominent representative, was that the Israelite monarchy was legitimated in part by the annual observance of "The Enthronement of Yahweh" including an "adoption ceremony" in which the king (re)enacted his adoption as son of God. The key text for Mowinckel's thesis was Ps. 2:7: "He said to me, 'You are my son. Today I have begotten you.'" Thus, through this annual celebration the title "son of God" became roughly synonymous with the title "king," and eventually became a messianic title.

Mowinckel wrote extensively on the Psalms, but his most important work dealing with the title "son of God" was *He That Cometh: The Messiah Concept in the Old Testament and Later Judaism*, published in 1951 in Norwegian and then published in an English translation in 1954. In this work he discusses the annual festival of the Enthronement of Yahweh and the adoption of the king.

Anointed One of the Lord at his resurrection. Dunn's position is one form of "adoptionist" Christology.[7]

However, this whole line of argumentation cannot be correct. The gospels suggest that Jesus accepted his messianic status during his earthly ministry, even if he did not advertise it broadly. Additionally, they argue that he was crucified as a king (the point of the title "Anointed One" or Messiah), even if this was done in a mocking way. Furthermore, Paul clearly notes Christ's preexistence in heaven and his exalted status prior to his incarnation. 2 Cor 8:9 reads: "For you know the grace of our Lord Jesus Christ, that although being rich, for your sakes he became poor in order that you might become rich through that poverty." Christ left the riches of heaven to become impoverished in this world.

Similarly, the great Christ hymn in Philippians 2, although probably pre-Pauline in origin, was clearly affirmed by Paul. As Phil 2:6–7 tells us, "though he [Christ] was in the form of God, he did not consider equality with God something to be grasped, but emptied himself, taking the form of a slave, being born and being found in the likeness of men . . . ."

The resurrection of Jesus marked him, publicly announced his role as Messiah and Son of God, a messianic title. Paul saw this as the hinge on which an extraordinary transition in salvation-history turned.

The word "powerfully" does not translate an adverb in the Greek but rather a preposition and a noun, *en dynamei* ("in power"). However, "marked in power" and "powerfully marked" mean the same thing.

Vs. 5: The phrase "obedience of faith" occurs only here and in 16:26, functioning as an *inclusio* bookending the major arguments of the letter.[8] The genitive is best understood either as a "genitive of explanation," specifying a specific type of obedience, or as a "genitive of apposition," stating that faith is obedience.[9] Judaism valued obedience to God and Paul is eager to show he does not promote disobedience, but his gospel promotes an obedience based on faith rather than scrupulous conformity to codes defining

---

7. Paul uses the word *huiothesia*, which can be translated either "adoption" or "sonship" to speak of the position of believers with respect to God, but he never uses this term to speak of Christ's relationship to God. Christ is God's son, but he is not God's adopted son.

8. Notice that I argue for relocating 16:25–27 to the end of chapter 15, rather than its traditional location. However, this does not preclude "obedience of faith" from functioning as a bookend since Paul's arguments largely conclude with chapter 15. Chapter 16 is chiefly devoted to greetings and a farewell.

9. On the genitive of explanation, see Smyth, *Greek Grammar* §1322. On the genitive of apposition, see Bl-D-F §167.

ritual practice. Both Jews and gentiles can obey God through faith. A similar expression "obey the gospel" is found in Rom 10:16 and 2 Thess 1:8.

Vs. 7: As has already been noted in "The Occasion of Paul's Writing" above, Paul does not address his letter to "the church in Rome," as might be expected. Instead, he addresses it rather vaguely to "all God's beloved in Rome, called to be saints." This likely suggests that the Christians in Rome did not worship together as a unified community.

In all Paul's letters the word "grace" appears in his opening greeting, and in ten of Paul's thirteen letters (all except the pastoral letters) his opening greeting contains the phrase "grace to you." Furthermore, in all Paul's letters his opening greeting contains the word "peace," and in every letter except for 1 Thessalonians, his opening greeting contains the phrase "peace from God." These statistics demonstrate the very formulaic nature of Paul's opening greetings.

Excursus: Calling in the New Testament

The word "calling" (*klētos* in Greek) is often overused in contemporary Christian church life. Much of this is due to an extremely popular but misguided teaching initiated by Martin Luther. Based on 1 Cor 7:17–24, and especially a single verse found within that passage, vs. 20, Luther taught that everyone has a calling, a vocation assigned by God. In fact, the word "vocation" comes from *vocatio*, the Latin word for "calling." Today many accountants, plumbers, carpenters, bankers, etc. who never darken the door of a church speak easily of their "vocation," not realizing the term is rooted in the idea of divine calling.

The point of 1 Cor 7:17–24 is that if a person is married and becomes a Christian, she does not have to become single. If she is single and becomes a Christian, she does not need to get married. If a person is a slave and becomes a Christian, he does not have to figure out how to be freed. If he is free and becomes a Christian, he does not have to be enslaved. As vs. 20 says, "Each one in the calling [at the time] in which he was called [to be a Christian], in this let him remain." Paul is not discussing God's plan for how a person should make his living. He simply teaches that a person does not have to change everything about his life when becoming a Christian. God has accepted that person as he or she is. In contrast, Luther mistakenly concluded Paul was teaching that every person is called by God into some profession.

In fact, Paul does teach that every believer is "called," but that calling is to follow Christ; it has nothing to do with one's profession. Most occurrences of the word "calling" in the New Testament refer to a person being called to follow Christ. As an example of this principle that all believers are "called" to follow Christ, Paul addresses Romans to "all God's beloved in Rome, [who are] called to be saints."

In a related vein, in Rom 9:7 and 12 Paul describes the patriarchs Isaac and Jacob as being called. This, of course, was before the advent of Jesus, and describes them as being called to be part of God's chosen people. I consider this to be a special subset of the first way "calling" or "called" is used in the New Testament.

There is a second way in which the word "called" is used in the New Testament. Apostles of Christ are consistently "called" by Christ, and this calling makes that person an agent of Christ. This is why Paul describes himself as being a "called" apostle. He has been authorized to transact business on Christ's behalf. In the New Testament other church leaders—pastors, deacons, elders, overseers, etc.—are not described as being "called" in this way.[10]

Excursus: "The Gospel" or "Paul's Gospel"?

Today the meaning of the term "the gospel" seems uncontroversial and nearly self-evident. But a great deal of controversy has swirled around this term over the past three decades. The debate is not over what it came to mean by the end of the first century. By that time, it was a summary term for the common Christian heritage of salvation in Christ Jesus. The debate concerns what "the gospel" (*to euangelion*) meant when it was first used in Christian discourse.

The church did not invent the term; that much is clear. It was used infrequently in secular Greek beginning with Homer.[11] In its plural form

---

10. Some who want to connect calling with a wider range of ministries point to what are often described as "call narratives" associated with the onset of prophetic activity of various Old Testament prophets. However, neither the noun "call" nor the verb "to call" normally figure in these narratives. In the one such narrative in which the verb "call" (MT *qara'*; LXX *kaleō*) figures prominently, 1Sam 3:2–9, the Lord calls *to* Samuel and the point is that young Samuel learns to recognize the voice of God, not that he receives a call into prophetic ministry as a profession.

11. Steve Mason, *Josephus, Judea, and Christian Origins*, 285–86.

it was used occasionally in imperial inscriptions beginning in 9 BC.[12] Generally it meant "news" or an "announcement."

But later the word acquired a special sense in Christian circles. By the end of the first century in 1 Clement and into the early second century in the *Epistle of Barnabas* and the letters of Ignatius, "the gospel" clearly refers to the common witness of the church about salvation through Jesus Christ. And this has remained its normal meaning in church use ever since.

Furthermore, many scholars claim "the gospel" was part of vocabulary of the Jesus movement from the outset.[13] Both the Gospels of Matthew and Mark regularly employ the term and place it on the lips of Jesus. Mark's Gospel famously opens with the title: "The beginning of the gospel of Jesus Christ the son of God."[14] However, the Gospels of Luke and John avoid the noun (although not its cognate verb). It is also important to note that what Paul calls "the gospel" goes beyond Jesus's teaching about the kingdom of God. Although a follower of Jesus, Paul is not content merely to restate the teaching of Jesus his Master. Paul's gospel focuses more on the meaning of the death and resurrection of Jesus than on his teaching.

At times, when *euangelion* appears in a saying of Jesus, it has a distinctly cosmopolitan flavor. Mark 13:10 says: "And first it is necessary for the gospel to be preached for all nations." And Mark 14:9 alludes to a time ". . . when the gospel is preached in the whole world . . . ."

But if Jesus used the term, from where did he get it? The standard explanation is that the source is Isa 52:7, although that precise word does not appear in the LXX of that verse. Instead, a participle (a verbal form) appears. Both the Hebrew of the MT and the Greek of the LXX usually employ the verbs, *basar* and *euangelizō* respectively, rather than the related nouns (*besarah* and *euangelion* or *euangelia*). To quantify this a bit, the Hebrew noun *besrah* occurs six times and the related verb *basar* occurs twenty-one times and the noun-to-verb ratio is the LXX is similar. In fact, in the entirety of the LXX the noun *euangelion* appears only once (at 2 Sam 4:10) and there

---

12. According to Koester, an imperial inscription from Priene, dated 9 BCE, reads: "The birthday of the god was the beginning of the *euaggelia* through him." Helmut Koester, *Introduction to the New Testament* 2:92.

13. Important proponents of this viewpoint include Gerhard Friedrich and Helmut Koester. See Friedrich, "euangelion." *TDNT*, 2:727–29 and Koester, *Ancient Christian Gospels*, 6.

14. This famous heading is the primary reason the word *euangelion* came to designate a genre, and therefore why we speak of the "Gospels" of Matthew, Mark, Luke, and John.

in the plural form.[15] A feminine noun (*euangelia*) that means roughly the same thing, but which never appears in the New Testament, appears in the LXX five times.

In the one place where *euangelion* appears in the LXX the word refers to "news," but not to "good news"—at least not "good news" in the assessment of David. When a man gleefully reported to him that Saul was dead, David killed the messenger as his reward for passing on this "news."

The cumulative picture provided by these data from the Old Testament is that neither *besrah* nor *euangelion* had yet crystalized into technical terms. Both referred rather blandly to some sort of "announcement" or "news." Nevertheless, it seems clear that sometime in the first century "the gospel" (*to euangelion*) did achieve a clear technical meaning; it had become a shorthand term summing up the church's message of salvation through Jesus Christ.

Luke's Gospel suggests that the basic contours of the church's early proclamation were guided by Jesus in post-resurrection appearances. Luke 24:13–35 presents Jesus explaining how his death and resurrection were foretold in the Old Testament. Then in Luke 24:44–49 Jesus, when speaking to the Eleven, "opened their minds to understand the scriptures." Speaking further, he outlined the basic message: "Thus it is written, that the Christ should suffer and on the third day rise from the dead, and that repentance and forgiveness of sins should be preached in his name to all nations, beginning from Jerusalem" (Luke 24: 46–47). While the word "gospel" is not used in this passage, Paul would have recognized in this summary much, although perhaps not all, of his gospel.

Helmut Koester, Gerhard Friederich, and others have contended that the term "the gospel" was the church's "common property" from its start.[16] But is this correct? What are we to make of Paul's somewhat proprietary claim that the message he proclaims is "my gospel" (Rom 2:16; 16:25; 2 Tim 2:8), or "our gospel," when he includes a traveling companion as a sort of co-author? (For specific examples, see 2 Cor 2:3 apparently including Timothy; 1 Thess 1:5 apparently including Silvanus and Timothy; and 2 Thess 2:14 including Silvanus and Timothy again.)

According to Koester and Friederich, when Paul identifies the gospel as "his," he simply refers to his own distinctive presentation of a gospel common to all Christian churches. In contrast, Steve Mason contends that

---

15. In the Hebrew of the MT the noun is singular: *besrah*.

16. The expression "common property" comes from Friedrich, s.v. *euangelion*. *TDNT* 2:727.

Paul's proprietary claims are more robust and that he claims the gospel as "something peculiar to [himself] and his assemblies."[17]

In Galatians 1:6 Paul takes offense at the prospect of a "different gospel" (*heteron euangelion*) than the one he delivered to churches of Galatia. The exact situation is unclear. Had the teachers Paul criticizes already called their message "gospel" prior to coming to Galatia? After arriving in Galatia, had these teachers appropriated the word "gospel" they learned Paul had previously used? Or did some in the Galatian churches themselves characterize the new teaching as a "different gospel," implying it was an equally acceptable (or even better) option? Or, finally, was it Paul himself who labelled the new teaching a "different gospel" to drive home the point that it was contrary to the gospel he had taught when in Galatia?

The same phrase, a "different gospel" (*heteron euangelion*) also appears in 2 Cor 11:4, although there it is part of a triple formula of "another Jesus" (*allon Iēsoun*), a "different Spirit" (*pneuma heteron*), and a "different gospel" (*heteron euangelion*). While there are some similarities between Paul's opponents in Galatia and his opponents in Corinth, they are likely different people teaching somewhat different ideas. While certainty is impossible, the fact that Paul uses the same phrase—a "different gospel"—to characterize theological aberrations from his message in two separate venues suggests that the phrase "different gospel" is likely Paul's own coinage.

Returning to Galatians 1, Paul there makes a second point against his opponents. He says in vss. 11–12 that his gospel is not "according to man" (*kata anthrōpon*). He was not taught it, and he did not receive it from a merely human source. It came "through revelation from Jesus Christ" (*di' apokalypseōs Iēsou Christou*), a revelation which he alone experienced.

Koester minimizes this claim in light of 1 Cor 15:1–11. Key to Koester's analysis is the language of vs. 3, where Paul writes: "I delivered to you as of first importance what I also received, that Christ died for our sins . . . ." As Koester understands the matter, the verbs *paradidōmi* ("to deliver") and *paralambanō* ("to receive") indicate that Paul passed on the tradition he had received from his predecessors in the faith concerning the details of the gospel. These words probably reflect the Hebrew verbs *masar* ("to deliver") and *qibel* ("to receive"), so often used by the rabbis to describe the transmission of earlier teaching. As a Pharisee and a rabbi, Paul certainly would have been familiar with such language.

---

17. Mason, *Josephus, Judea, and Christian Origins*, 293.

An implication of Koester's theory is that, in contrast to Paul's explicit testimony in Galatians 1, whatever insight Paul received about the gospel, it did not come from God unmediated by those who preceded him. Therefore, it also could not have been uniquely his possession. Instead, it was earlier than Paul, having already become the shared property of the primitive Jerusalem church.

In response to Koester's theory, Mason makes two important points. First, in 1 Cor 15:3 Paul acknowledges he "received" the content of the gospel, but he does not say from whom he received it. Paul's testimony in Gal 1:12 suggests he received it directly from Christ, not from the Jerusalem circle that preceded him in the faith. Second, the likelihood that Paul received the gospel message from Christ himself is heightened by Paul's own use of the verb *paralambanō* ("to receive") in Gal 1:12, where he explicitly and adamantly denies receiving this tradition from man.

An obstacle to Mason's theory is what Paul says in Gal 2:7, a verse that apparently reports on the decision of the so-called Jerusalem Council described in Act 15. Paul states: "[The leaders in Jerusalem] saw that I had been entrusted with "the gospel of the uncircumcision" (*euaggelion tēs akrobystias*) just as Peter [had been entrusted with a message] "of the circumcision (*tēs peritomēs*)."[18] Was that message also described as a "gospel"? While Paul does not specifically use the full phrase "gospel of the circumcision," the concept may be implied. However, even if the word "gospel" was associated with Peter's message, it is unclear exactly how that word was understood.

TRANSLATION: ROM 1:8–13

THE THANKSGIVING

[8]First, I thank my God through Jesus Christ for all of you because your faith is being broadcast to the whole world. [9]For God is my witness, by whom I offer sacrifice within my spirit for the gospel of his son, as unceasingly I make mention of you [10]always in my prayers, asking if, somehow, I might at last find the right path in the will of God to come to you. [11]For I long to see you in order that I may contribute some spiritual gift to solidify you, [12]that is, to encourage you in unity both through your faith in each other and also

---

18. Acts 15:7 also records Peter using the term "gospel" approvingly at the Council of Jerusalem.

through my faith. ¹³I do not want you to be ignorant of the fact, brothers [and sisters], that I have often planned to come to you (but until now I have been prevented), in order that I might have some fruit both among you and among the rest of the gentiles.

COMMENTARY

Vss. 8–13: "The Thanksgiving" is a regular feature of Paul's letters. It always immediately follows the opening salutation, and in it Paul seemingly prays to God in written form. Usually, he thanks God for those to whom he is writing, as is the case here, and reports about his prayers to God for them, which also is the case here. Often, in the Thanksgiving Paul also previews a topic or two that he will discuss in the body of his letter. Paul's regret that he has not been able to visit Rome earlier is mentioned here, and this will be discussed at greater length in chapter 15. However, the major themes of this letter are not previewed.

In his Thanksgivings, Paul also usually makes some reference to eschatology (e.g., mentioning the second coming of Jesus). Surprisingly, he does not do that here.

Vs. 11: My translation includes the words "contribute some spiritual gift." The phrase "spiritual gift" (*charisma pneumatikon*) is ambiguous, but it may well refer to an oral gift of the Spirit. That is what Paul means in 1 Corinthians 14 when he discusses *pneumatika* (the plural of *pneumatikon*). The verb *metadidōmi* might mean either "to impart" or "to contribute," but elsewhere Paul uses it exclusively in the sense of "contribute" (Rom 12:8; Eph 4:28; 1 Thess 2:8). The question is whether, on the one hand, Paul will install in the Romans a gift for them to exercise, perhaps through the laying on of hands, or on the other hand, he will share the benefit of a gift he exercises. Based on his use of the verb elsewhere, the latter option is to be preferred.[19] In any case, Paul is not referencing the reception of the Spirit experienced at conversion.

Vs. 12: The clause "to encourage you in unity" perhaps hints at a lack of unity in Rome.

Vs. 13: Paul's stated desire to "have some fruit both among you and among the rest of the gentiles" has puzzled many. Does he mean that he wants to make gentile converts in Rome, or is the "fruit" he envisions strengthening and teaching those who have already professed faith in

---

19. For a more extensive discussion of this issue, see Robert P. Menzies, "Subsequence in the Pauline Epistles," 356–62; Fee, *God's Empowering Presence*, 487; and E. Earl Ellis, "'Spiritual Gifts' in the Pauline Community," 128.

Christ? The more natural reading would be the latter, that the reference is to people expected to read his letter.

If he means he wants to strengthen those who are already Christians, this statement might conceivably imply Paul is writing to an entirely gentile audience in Rome, and so he wants to have fruit among both those gentiles in Rome and gentiles outside of Rome. But his statement does not need to be read quite so narrowly. Paul is the "apostle to the gentiles," and as part of God's commission for him to minister primarily to gentiles, he would naturally desire to extend that ministry to gentiles in Rome, the predominately gentile capital of the empire that spanned the limits of his ministry. However, his special interest in ministering to the gentiles of Rome does not mean his letter is intended only for gentiles. Paul's intense interest in the place of Jews in God's eternal plan, as reflected in the body of his letter, makes this evident.

TRANSLATION: ROM 1:14–17

OBLIGATED TO SPREAD THE GOSPEL

¹⁴I am under obligation to both Greeks and to barbarians, to both the wise and to those without understanding, ¹⁵so my desire is to proclaim the gospel also to you who are in Rome, ¹⁶because I am not ashamed of the gospel, for it is the power of God for salvation, to everyone who believes, to the Jew first and also to the Greek. ¹⁷For the righteousness of God is being revealed in it from one declaration of faith to the next, as it is written, "The person who is made right by faith will live."

COMMENTARY

Vss. 14–15: Paul's argument in these verses and the two that follow is quite compressed. He begins by noting his special obligation to "Greeks and barbarians," a way of expressing *ethnē* ("gentiles"). "Barbarians" would refer to those from outside the Graeco-Roman world that centered around the Mediterranean, what the Romans referred to as *mare nostrum* ("our sea"). Barbarians were literally outliers, coming generally from lands to the north.

Often Paul simply uses "Greeks" (*hellēnes*) as an alternative designation for gentiles. The number of barbarians Paul ministered to must have been much smaller than the number of Greeks, since any such barbarians must have learned to speak Greek, there being no evidence Paul knew any barbarian languages.

The parallelism between "Greeks and barbarians," on the one hand, and "the wise and those without understanding," on the other hand, suggests that Paul is invoking the standard stereotype associating Greeks with learning evidenced by philosophy, the first ancient universities such as Plato's Academy and Aristotle's Lyceum, and the poetry of Homer and Hesiod. In contrast, there was no similar academic tradition associated with the barbarians. But perhaps "Greek and barbarians" and "the wise and those without understanding" are best understood as merisms, the mentioning of extremes to indicate the whole. (Merism is a precise subcategory of synecdoche.) In other words, Paul claims he is under obligation to every kind of gentile. This helps to clarify why, as vs. 15 indicates, he desires to proclaim the gospel in Rome. He is obligated to proclaim the gospel to Roman gentiles just as he is obligated to proclaim the gospel to every other type of gentile.

The clause "to proclaim the gospel also to you who are in Rome" could be translated differently: "to evangelize also you who are in Rome." However, this might suggest Paul does not believe his intended readers are Christ-followers, a suggestion that does not ring true. Two other possibilities come to mind. First, while in general "you [pl.]" in this letter refers to God's beloved in Rome who are called to be saints (1:7), here Paul may refer to the unsaved inhabitants of Rome with whom the saints mingle. Second, he may her use the verb "evangelize" (*euangelizō*) with a deferent nuance than is normal for him. Rather than implying his evangelization will make them Christ-followers, he may indicate he plans to introduce those who already follow Christ to his distinctive theology, i.e., his "gospel." In light of his discussion of the gospel that follows, this second option seems more likely.

But it is also worth noting that nowhere in his letter does Paul call what the Roman believers have already received "the gospel." What they have received is "instruction" (*didachē*). In 6:17 he mentions "the pattern [literally "type"] of instruction you were provided." In 16:17 it is "the instruction you were taught."[20]

Vs. 16: This verse implies there is a special connection between the gospel Paul proclaims and the inclusion of gentiles in God's program of salvation. This is because it is for "everyone who believes," a proposition some of Paul's past opponents have denied. Were there also Jewish believers in Rome who denied gentiles could be saved if they remained gentiles? It is certainly possible, if not probable.

Paul also asserts that he is "not ashamed" of the gospel. This raises the obvious question: Have people been telling Paul he should be ashamed

---

20. I should credit Steve Mason with pointing me in this direction. Mason, *Josephus, Judea, and Christian Origins*, 321.

of his gospel? Probably. However, as Craig Keener points out, this could be an example of litotes, an ironic understatement in which an affirmative is expressed by the contradiction of its negative.[21] To state the same sentiment without using litotes, Paul might have said: "I am wonderfully proud of the gospel...." Nevertheless, I am inclined to believe that some, probably including some in Rome, regard Paul's gospel as shameful. While they are willing to accept Jesus as the Messiah of Israel, they consider the gospel Paul proclaims to be a betrayal of their Jewish faith and their Israelite heritage.

When Paul says the gospel is "the power of God for salvation," he employs metonymy, the association of one thing with another related thing. Metonymy is often used to avoid excessive wordiness. Here "the power of God for salvation" is shorthand for "the message God uses to activate the change necessary to result in reconciliation with God and eternal salvation." God's power (*dynamis*) is his power to transform, and this power is mediated through the gospel.

Paul's use of the expression "power of God" calls to mind 1 Cor 1:18 where he uses the same expression. There he says, "the word of the cross" is the "power of God," but of course "the word of the cross" and "the gospel" are two ways of referring to the same thing.

This verse contains the first of three occurrences of the formula "to the Jew first and also to the Greek" in Romans (a formula that occurs nowhere else in Paul's letters or in the rest of the NT). Jews and Greeks are frequently mentioned together elsewhere, but this precise formula is distinctive to Romans, occurring here and in 2:9 and 2:10.

In each of the three occurrences of this phrase, the emphasis is on equal inclusion and God's impartiality. That the Jew is first is more of an honorific designation of seniority than a substantial one. I am inclined to liken it to the honor of being an elder brother rather than a younger brother, but this illustration is imperfect since in the ancient world the elder brother often was afforded greater inheritance rights. Nevertheless, there is a sense in which Israel was God's firstborn (see Exod 4:22).

Vs. 17: In this verse Paul links his gospel with "the righteousness of God." Paul's gospel, and indeed Paul himself, came to be closely associated with teaching about righteousness. Roughly forty years after he sent his letter to Rome, a leader in Rome eulogized Paul with the vivid comment that he had "taught righteousness to the world."[22]

Paul asserts that the "righteousness of God" is being revealed. This might be construed to mean that "God's righteous way" or "God's righteous

---

21. Keener, *Romans*, 26.
22. *1 Clement* 5.7.

plan" is being revealed since his righteous character is seen through this activity, i.e., through the gospel. Paul will go on to argue that God's righteous activity should already have been apparent through his gracious activity in creation, but apart from God's special revelation of himself to Israel, it was not. In the face of this reality, the gospel constitutes a new revelation.

The verb "revealed" (*apokalyptō*) is important in Paul's letters and throughout the NT because it refers to matters that have previously been hidden but now are "unveiled." This verb is in the present tense, suggesting this revelation is an ongoing process. This onset of revelation marked the beginning of a new era, which Paul has already linked to the resurrection of Christ. While it would be wrong to suggest that prior to the resurrection nothing was known of God's righteousness, it has now been revealed in a fresh new way. Furthermore, that "God's righteousness is being revealed" should be paired with Paul's contention that "God's wrath is being revealed" in vs. 18. They are flip sides of the same coin.

Luther famously concluded that the phrase "righteousness of God" meant "the righteousness that comes from God" and is imputed to those who believe in Christ. Here the Greek *dikaiosunē theou* (literally "righteousness of God") is ambiguous and could imply a "genitive of source" meaning "righteousness from God." Interestingly, in Phil 3:9 Paul wrote *tēn ek theou dikaiosunē* (literally "the righteousness from God") which is unambiguous, and the wording in Phil 3:9 encouraged Luther to translate Rom 1:17 similarly. However, that sword cuts both ways. N.T. Wright argues in the opposite direction of Luther, suggesting that if Paul wanted to make clear that this righteousness was from God, he would have employed the same phrasing he used in Philippians.

I agree with Wright that it is more likely "righteousness of God" here refers to the personal character of God himself as exhibited through the gospel. This distinctive plan highlights God's impartiality and fairness in new and unexpected ways. *For more about this and related issues, see the excursus "The Language of Righteousness and Justification."*

The phrase *ek pisteōs eis pistin* (literally "from faith to faith") is something of a conundrum. What does "from faith to faith" mean? Does it reflect an idiom? If this construction used a noun that regularly occurs in a sequence, such as the word "day," the meaning would be clear: "from day to day," as in the LXX of Judg 11:40. Even though faith is not so obviously sequenced, it is possible this means "from one declaration of faith to the next." Or it may imply ascending levels of faith: "by one level of faith to the next." Citing the similar expression in 2 Cor 2:16 (". . . to one a fragrance from death to death [*ek thanatou eis thanaton*], to the other a fragrance from life to life [*ek zōēs eis zōēn*]."), Keener suggests this means "the gospel is a matter of faith from start to finish."[23]

Only slightly further removed grammatically is the expression *kath' hyperbolēn eis hyperbolēn* [literally, "according to excess into excess"] of 2 Cor 4:17. This probably means something like "exceeding excess."

Another issue is that *pistis* can mean "faithfulness" rather than subjective "faith." If this is the meaning of *pistis* here, it likely refers to God's "faithfulness" rather than the individual's faith: "from one instance of [God's] faithfulness to the next."

Another approach is to give the two references to faith different meanings. Liddell-Scott lists a possible meaning of *pistis* as "assurance" or "guarantee."[24] Therefore a possible translation is "the righteousness of God is revealed in [the gospel] by faith for the purpose of assurance." While this translation makes a certain amount of sense, it also seems overly subtle, and I doubt that Paul's readers would have ferreted out such a meaning.

If this phrase means "from one declaration of faith to the next," as I consider most likely, these words underline that declarations of subjective faith in Christ (i.e., conversions) time and time again demonstrate God's righteousness and his faithfulness to his covenant obligations.

After making his great statement connecting the gospel with God's power, Paul then quotes Hab 2:4 to buttress his contention that this gospel is linked to faith. He words this quotation as, "The righteous person will live by faith (*ek pisteōs*)," which differs slightly from the texts of both the MT and the LXX. The MT, as well as *4Q82Minor Prophets*ᵍ, reads "by his faith" (*be'emunato/b'mwntw*),[25] while the LXX reads "by my faithfulness" (*ek pisteōs mou*). We do not know how Paul's copy of Habakkuk read, but it is possible he knew of the discrepancy and simply omitted the questionable possessive pronoun as a result.

In the context of Habakkuk, either "by his faith" or "by my faithfulness" makes sense. The book pictures the life of civilians in either Israel or Judah during the rise of the Chaldeans, circa 612 BC. These people in the land are defenseless in the face of a military onslaught, and they are likened to fish dragged up by fishermen with nets or hooked and yanked out of the water. The Chaldean soldiers laugh and gloat as they catch their prey, just like fishermen when landing a fish. They are self-satisfied: "Their strength is their god" (Hab 1:11). And perhaps most troubling of all is that the Lord claims he

---

23. Keener, *Romans*, 29.

24. Liddell-Scott, *Greek-English Lexicon*, s.v. "pistis," II.1.

25. These texts are the same except that the MT text includes vowel pointing while the Dead Sea Scroll text does not.

is the one who has raised up these Chaldean warriors! (Hab 1:6). Two great plaintive questions to God precede Hab 2:4: "How long, O Lord, will I cry out for help, and you will not hear?" (Hab 1:2); and "Why are you silent when the wicked swallow up those more righteous than they?" (Hab 1:13).

The prophet stations himself on the rampart waiting for the Lord to answer him (Hab 2:1), and then he receives a vision. He is told to record the vision, and he is given some context for it: "The vision is yet for a set time, it gives birth to the end, and does not lie; if it dawdles, wait for it, for it will come and not delay forever" (Hab 2:3). Attitudes are also important: "Behold the presumptuous person [or "puffed up person"], his soul is not right within him, but the righteous person will live by his faith/by my faithfulness" (Hab 2:4). It is not clear if the presumptuous person refers to the Chaldean warriors, to those who do not wait for the vision to play out, or to both. The rest of chapter 2 then discusses how the arrogant and wicked will receive just comeuppances.

Within the context of Habakkuk, "by his faith" makes the most sense. The text encourages continued hopeful waiting for the Lord's salvation. But "by my faithfulness" also makes sense. The basis for continued hopeful waiting is trust in the Lord's faithfulness to his promises.

Another exegetical question regarding Rom 1:17 (and Hab 2:4) concerns whether *ek pisteōs* is more closely connected with *ho dikaios* ("the righteous person") or with *zēsetai* ("will live"). Is it that this person is "made righteous by faith," as opposed to "made righteous by works"? Or is it that the person who has already been declared righteous will conduct his life so that he lives "by faith"? The Habakkuk text suggests that the former option is more likely. In Habakkuk, the righteous person is contrasted with the presumptuous or arrogant person who ignores God. It is belief in God's faithfulness to his promises that distinguishes him from the puffed up or presumptuous person who disregards them.

Another important issue is what *dikaios* means. It is usually translated "the righteous" or "the righteous person." It can, however, convey other shades of meaning. It might mean "the person in the right" or the person who has been "made right." I have translated this key clause "the person who is made right by faith will live."

In Romans 4 Abraham, the great model of faith, is presented as someone who believed God's promises even though they seemed impossible. There, Paul also reports that Abraham was declared righteous (or "in right relationship") before obeying God's directive to be circumcised. Since Paul focuses on Abraham's subjective faith in chapter 4, he is also probably focusing on subjective faith here in chapter 1.

Excursus: The Language of Righteousness and Justification

PAUL'S USE OF THE *DIK-* WORDS

It has long been recognized that the Greek words *dikaiosynē* (traditionally translated "righteousness" or "justice"), *dikaioō* (traditionally translated "to justify"), and *dikaios* (traditionally translated "righteous" or "just"), as a word group play an important role in Romans. For convenience sometimes these words are lumped into a category called "the *dik-* words."

The English equivalents for these *dik-* words" come in two families: words based on "right"; and words based on "just." But there is diversity even within these family groupings. To be "right" or to be "in the right" means one thing, and "to be righteous" means something else. While a person can be "morally right," more often we think of "right" meaning "factually correct." Being factually correct is quite different from being "righteous."

The "just" family of English words comes from a very similar-sounding group of Latin words from which they were derived (e.g., justice comes from *iustitia*), all of which ultimately are related to the Latin word *ius* ("what is allowed," "law").[26]

However, to think of "just" and "justice" exclusively in terms of legal enactments would be misleading. There was another Latin word for "law", *lex*, that more precisely specified formal legal declarations. To highlight the difference, *ius* is more general and more abstract. When a person goes to school to study "law," he or she is studying *ius*, the theory of law, not *lex*, although the study of *ius* may involve studying many *leges* (the plural of *lex*; i.e., many specific laws).

What happens in a courtroom is *ius*. It is a search for justice, often involving the application of *leges*, specific laws, but also more. A sense of fairness is crucial. Surprisingly, *lex* is the word used by the Vulgate to designate the Law of Moses, which at least in part mischaracterizes the Hebrew word *torah*. *Torah* means "instruction" and much of the *torah*, such as the entire book of Genesis, is instructive but does not consist of codified rules. The Latin *lex*, even more than the Greek *nomos*, (over)emphasizes the law codes and statutes within the *torah* and therefore is misleading.

---

26. This impact of Latin on English is testimony to the influence of the Latin Vulgate, which was Europe's standard Bible for well over a millennium.

So, when Paul uses the *dik-* words, should we think in terms of being "right" and rectifying what has gone wrong, or should we think of "justice" and "fairness"? It is a complicated issue.

N.T. WRIGHT AND SPEECH-ACT THEORY

In recent years N. T. Wright has argued that Paul's use of the *dik-* words has been misconstrued by thinking of them primarily in terms of elevated character and morality. To understand these words accurately, he argues, we must consider the milieu from which they come: the world of lawsuits and courtrooms. When a judge rules in favor of someone, the judge does not pronounce that person morally virtuous. Instead, the judge proclaims a new legal status for that person; he is declared to be "in the right" and absolved from the legal action (whether criminal or civil) brought against him. The judge's words do not merely describe something; they create a new reality by clearing the defendant.

Wright's point invokes an important distinction made in contemporary Speech-Act theory. While people often think the only function of language is to describe things, in fact, language often functions in other ways. When a man romantically coos compliments into the ear of a woman, what is happening is not primarily description but rather a way of indicating affection.[27] Similarly, when a minister pronounces a couple "man and wife," these individuals move from the status of unmarried to married. In much the same way in criminal court, when a judge or jury pronounces a verdict, the status of the accused changes. A new reality has been created. At that moment, in the eyes of both the law and society, she becomes either guilty or not guilty.[28] In the jargon of Speech-Act theory, the intended effects of verdicts are called "illocutions" and the actual changes in status that result are called "perlocutions."

---

27. The "later" Ludwig Wittgenstein spoke about the diverse ways people use language with the term "language games." Just as different games have different rules, when used for different purposes language plays by different rules.

28. In U.S. courts, as in most of the West, defendants are never found "innocent," but rather may be found "not guilty" of the specific charges levelled against them. They may be guilt of other charges, or they may in fact have committed the crime of which they are accused, but in court an insufficient case of their guilt has been presented.

According to Wright, this perspective is important to keep in mind when a modern interpreter studies what Paul means by "justification." As in any case before any judge, the Great Judge does not convey to the repentant sinner a morally elevated character. Instead, God declares the charges levied against her to be either supported by the facts or unfounded. When the verdict goes the defendant's way, this justified person is declared to be "in the right," not somehow made righteous or virtuous. From this moment on, the defendant enjoys a new status—pronounced "in the right" before the public—but he is neither made morally better by this verdict nor declared to be a good person. The charge against him is dismissed and can no longer be pursued.

So, what are we to make of Wright's approach? Is Wright's analysis of the *dik-* words correct? Even more importantly, are the implications that flow from his lexical study and his application of Speech-Act theory correct?

He certainly has some points in his favor. Wright's approach yields a nifty solution to a passage that has troubled many. Rom 5:7 reads: "A person will almost never die for some *dikaios* ["righteous person" according to the traditional translation], although perhaps for a good person someone might even dare to die." We normally consider a "righteous" person to be better than a "good" person. But if this is the case, then Rom 5:7 makes no sense. However, if *dikaios* simply means something like "cleared by the judge" then the comparison makes perfect sense: "A person will almost never die for someone cleared of a crime, but for a good person someone might even dare to die." This is because a cleared person might or might not be a good person. In fact, this point calls to mind the ridiculous moral posturing of Big Jule in the Broadway musical "Guys and Dolls." In his dopey manner this thug brags, ". . . I've gone straight, as has been proved by my record: Thirty-three arrests and no convictions!" He was legally in the clear, but not necessarily a paragon of virtue.

While below I will quibble with aspects of Wright's presentation, I affirm his central thesis that "justification" means that when God pronounces sinners *dikaios* ("in right standing"), he clears them of the charges that stand against them. This is a thoroughly Protestant interpretation because it rejects the Catholic notion that God imparts righteousness to them therefore making them worthy of salvation. While it avoids the traditional Reformation language of the imputation of Christ's "alien righteousness" to the believer, it gets to fundamentally the same place using the insights of modern Speech-Act theory.

I also think it is important to acknowledge that, despite Wright's protests, in some places *dikaiosynē* is used to note elevated character, at least in some person's mind if not in reality. An example is the LXX text of Deut 9:5:

> It is not because of your righteousness or because of the holiness of your heart you are going in to inherit their land, but because of the ungodliness of these nations and in order that his covenant might stand, the Lord will destroy them before your face.

Probably this passage should be translated, "It is not because of your *claim of* righteousness or because of *your claim of* the holiness of your heart . . . ," because surely this is what the author intended to express. Whether they are in fact righteous or holy remains unadjudicated. Rather the ungodliness of the nations about to be destroyed is emphasized. Nevertheless, what is claimed, rightly or wrongly, is a measure of elevated character. In this particular case, Wright's analysis does not work well.

SPEECH-ACT THEORY AND FALSE CLAIMS OF JUSTIFICATION

By leveraging the tools of Speech-Act theory Wright has advanced the discussion surrounding Paul's perspective on justification. However, perhaps this course can be pursued even further to reveal an important distinction between intended justification and accomplished justification. In an attack on the theology of those in Galatia who promoted the circumcision of gentile believers, Paul uses the verb *dikaiaō* in a way that is instructive: "You have been severed from Christ; whoever of you has been justified by the Law [*en nomō dikaiousthe*], you have fallen away from grace" (Gal 5:4). Perhaps scare quotes should be placed around the words "justified by the Law" since Paul clearly believes that no such thing has occurred.

To say this in a gauzier, more academic way: Paul reveals the illocutionary force (intentionality) associated with such circumcisions. The claim is "We have been justified by the Law." Paul contends, however, that such claims are a mirage. What has actually been accomplished (the perlocution) is that those circumcised gentiles have not been justified by the Law, but in fact, have nullified the grace of justification they had previously received through Christ.

This illustrates an ambiguity inherent in both the English verb "to justify" and in the Greek word *dikaiaō*. Both verbs can be used to claim a moral or legal basis for some action when no such basis objectively exists, and these verbs can also be used to describe an objective moral or legal truth.

THE *DIK-* WORDS AND ABRAHAM

Wright's theory brings at the same time both an advantage and a disadvantage: He ties the meaning of the *dik-* words closely to legal and courtroom imagery. While in some passages in Romans this is an advantage, this does not seem to be the case in Romans 4 where the *dik-* words nevertheless figure prominently. There Paul holds up Abraham as someone to whom *dikaiosynē* was reckoned based on his faith, even though the Law of Moses had not yet been given and Genesis 15 does not picture a courtroom setting. (Gen 22:1 describes Abraham being "tested," but that comes much later in his life.) In Genesis 15 the *dik-* words seem to describe the development of a right relationship with God rather than a public declaration of an upright status after prevailing in court. Abraham believes God, and that becomes the basis for a special relationship.

However, rather than embodying a counterargument to Wright's analysis of how the *dik-* words function, this divergence should be seen as a reinforcement of Paul's contention that the Law is not the way to either righteousness or to life. Abraham was declared *dikaios* without obedience to the Law, and in this way, he becomes a model for the gentiles of Paul's day. In other words, Paul argues that the equivalent of a courtroom decision can be obtain in a non-judicial setting.

This suggests that even in contexts where Abraham is not in view the *dik-* words function with bivalent force. That is, they involve both the Great Judge declaring a person to be "in the right" and they also underscore that this same person is in right relationship with God. In fact, these dynamics are often two sides of the same coin. Before the Law came, Abraham might be declared to be in right relationship with God without also having been acquitted in court, so to speak. But it is hard to see how a later figure, someone living in the shadow of the Law of Moses, could be acquitted by the Great Judge and continue to remain in a wrong relationship with him.

THE ONE WHO CLEARS THE UNGODLY

Of course, perhaps the largest question raised by any theory of justification is this: How can defendants so obviously in the wrong be cleared of charges when they are brought to trial? Rom 4:5 highlights this conundrum by describing God as "the one who justifies/clears the ungodly (*ton dikaiounta ton asebē*)." Muslims would say such a statement implies God is an immoral, bad judge.

One answer sometimes proposed is that God simply "pardons" sin. The language of "pardon" calls to mind a line from the well-known hymn "Great is Thy Faithfulness": ". . . *pardon* from sin and a grace that endureth . . . ." So, is it within God's prerogative simply to pardon sin? Perhaps. There are two verbs in the Hebrew OT that conceivably imply pardoning: *salach*; and *chanan*.

The first of these, *salach*, means "to pardon" or "to forgive." While "to pardon" and "to forgive" are similar, the meanings of these English words also differ substantially. Usually, we think of "pardoning" in a legal context and "forgiving" in an interpersonal context, although when we say, "Pardon me," the line between the two is blurred. Still, pardoning is generally more formal and official than forgiving.

In the American legal system, pardon occurs when a chief executive (a state governor or the President of the United States) clears a person of the charges against him. Sometimes there is a question about whether the convicted person was guilty, or whether the punishment assigned was appropriate for the crime. At other times, the person is obviously guilty but is cleared, nonetheless. Perhaps the most famous example of the latter was when President Gerald Ford pardoned former President Richard Nixon to put an end to a grave national trauma.

The Hebrew verb *salach* is always used only when God is the active agent.[29] This certainly makes it special and distinguishes what the word implies from the normal forgiveness humans extend to one another. In Leviticus and Numbers, and nowhere else, *salach* occurs closely linked to the verb *kipper* (the *pi'el* of *kapar*). In the *qal* stem, *kapar* means "to cover." In the *pi'el*, it means "to make atonement for."[30] The linkage of *salach* and

---

29. See BDB, s.v. "salach."

30. To those unfamiliar with Hebrew stems, this comment may seem opaque. There are seven stems in Hebrew and specific Hebrew verbs often appear in several (although not all seven) of them. Some stems make a normally active verb passive. Others make a verb causative ("to come" can become "to cause to come," i.e., "to

kipper happens ten times in Leviticus and twice in Numbers, and in each of these cases, *salach* is found in the *nip'al* stem, making it passive. In fact, in each case, a "divine passive" is implied. Usually, a priest is said to make atonement, but the implication is that God pardons as a result.

The translators of the LXX apparently had trouble rendering *salach* into serviceable Greek. While the most common word they used was *aphiēmi* (literally to "to release from"), they also used *aphaireō* ("to take up from", e.g., Exod 34:9), *katharizō* ("to cleanse"; e.g., Num 30:5 [30:6 in the LXX], 30:9, 13), *euilateuō* ("to be merciful"—expressing the action of a god, e.g., Deut 29:19; Ps 103:3 [LXX 102:3]), *hilateuō* ("to be gracious"— expressing the action of a god, e.g., Dan 9:19), *hilaskomai* ("appease" when used of a god, "pardon" when used of a human, e.g., 2 Kgs 5:18; 24:4; Ps 25:11 [LXX 24:11]; Lam 3:42; 2 Chr 6:30), and *exilaskomai* ("propitiate" or "expiate" when used of a god, "atone for" when used of a human, e.g., Num 15:28). In 1 Kgs 8:30, 34, 36, 39, 50; Jer 5:7; 31:34 [LXX 38:34]; 35:3[LXX 43:3], 50:20 [LXX 27:20], Amos 7:2; 2 Chr 6:21, 25, 27, 39, and 7:14, *salach* is translated with a clause meaning "to be merciful [*hileōs*]." In Jer 33:8 [LXX 40:8] it is rendered "I will not remember their sins [*mē mnēsthēsomai hamartiōn autōn*]."

The second Hebrew verb that expressed something like "pardon" was *chanan* ("to show favor or mercy"; "to request favor or mercy"). (*Chen* is the Hebrew noun for "favor" or "grace.") Unlike *salach*, *chanan* is used to indicate the actions of both people and God. The Greek verb corresponding to *chanan* is *eleeō* and its later form *eleaō* ("to pity, to show mercy"). This verb appears a couple of times in Romans. Similarly, the noun "mercy" (*eleos*) appears three times. In Rom 9:16; 11:31; and 15:9 God's mercy is presented as benevolent response to people who have been disobedient.

The Old Testament depicts Yahweh as both gracious and merciful, but his wrath is also vividly portrayed. Furthermore, the existence of a sacrificial system implied that forgiveness came with a cost. The fact that the verb *salach* is reserved only for God and is never used of a human suggests that divine pardon differs not just in scale but in kind from human forgiveness.

People sometimes act as if God ought to be a good sport and just overlook human weaknesses. "My neighbors think I'm a good guy; God ought to as well." Such thinking diminishes both the problem and the solution. Pardon is a possibility, but only on God's terms. The fact that atonement is

---

bring"). Still other stem changes can make a verb more intensive ("to massacre" rather than "to kill"). Some stem changes defy any systematic explanation.

often connected with pardon suggests that the idea of God waving away sin is an inadequate view of divine pardon.

CHRIST AND JUSTIFICATION

Many will be surprised to learn that Christ is never the subject of the verb *dikaioō* ("to justify"). To say this differently, Christ is never the one doing the justifying. Furthermore, when *dikaioō* occurs in the passive voice, Christ is never presented as the agent doing the justifying.[31] (In Greek the normal way to express agency is to use *hypo* with the genitive, and this construction does not occur when describing Christ's role in justification.)

While Paul may not consider Christ the one who justifies, he and other NT authors attribute to Christ a judicial role. 2 Cor 5:10 mentions "the judgment seat [*bēma*] of Christ" before which all must give an account of what has been done "in the body." 2 Tim 4:8 calls Christ "the righteous judge," and 2 Tim 4:1 asserts Christ Jesus is "to judge [*krinein*] the living and the dead." In a non-Pauline context, Acts 10:42 calls Christ "the judge [*kritēs*] of the living and the dead." Similarly, James 5:9 proclaims, in a passage about the second coming of Christ, "the Judge is standing at the doors." In these passages it may be that Christ is considered an agent of God's role as judge, so that when Christ judges, God judges through him.

In some sentences, God, used in an absolute sense (i.e., God the Father when expressed in trinitarian terms), is the grammatical subject of the verb "to justify" (e.g., Rom 3:30; 8:30, 33; Gal 3:8), and frequently God is implied to be the one justifying through use of the "divine passive" (e.g., Rom 3:20, 28; 4:2; 5:1).[32] Justification may be pictured as a public event, much like the public announcement of a verdict at the end of a trial, but justification also happens "before God," picturing him as a presiding judge (Gal 3:11) before whom those accused stand.

---

31. In Gal 2:17 Paul writes, "But if, seeking to be justified in Christ . . . ." This could be translated "But if, seeking to be justified by Christ . . . ," but is seems better to understand it as a divine passive with God as the agent with "in Christ" serving as shorthand for "by faith in Christ," the longer expression that appears in the preceding verse and is also linked to justification.

32. The divine passive is frequent in the NT. It was a way of avoiding the direct mention of God, apparently to reverence him. For instance, to say "the heavens were opened" means "God opened the heavens," but this passive construction avoids mentioning God.

So, to summarize, Jesus Christ does not justify directly; this is the work of God (the Father). But this is not the totality of the matter. Paul also explains that justification happens "by faith" (Rom 3:28) or "through faith" (Gal 2:16), and "by [God's] grace" (Rom 3:24). Furthermore, Paul clearly connects Jesus to God's justification of sinners. This connection is expressed potently through the language of sacrifice. Believers are justified "at the price of [Christ's] blood" (Rom 5:9). Justification comes "through the redemption (*apolytrōsis*) that is in Christ Jesus" (Rom 3:24). Furthermore, God put Jesus forth as a mercy-seat offering (*hilastērion*) to expiate sin (Rom 3:25).[33]

Even though it is very important, redemption as a mercy-seat offering is not the only ministry of Jesus. Paul explains Christ's work in other ways that do not use sacrificial language. In Rom 8:32–34 he describes the intercession of Christ, which likely refers to something more forceful than simply pleading on behalf of those who stand before "the one who justifies"; in Roman law an *intercessio* could refer to the veto of a magistrate's decision. The point is not that Christ vetoes God's judgments, but rather that in Roman law it was legitimate for a judge's verdict to be influenced by outside voices in a way modern justice in the West generally avoids (at least publicly).

In addition, Christ's followers are said to die to sin with him and rise into newness of life with him (Rom 6:4). Similarly, they also die "with Christ away from the elemental spirits of the universe" (Col 2:20). Paul also explains that God sent his son to buy those enslaved to the Law that they might receive sonship (Gal 4:4–5). While these passages speak powerfully about benefits Christ brings to those who believe in him, they do not mention justification.

GENTILES AND SACRIFICE

One wonders how the gentiles to whom Paul writes would have understood the connection he makes between justification and sacrifice. They came from a world steeped in sacrifice, so the general idea would not have repelled them. But the workings of the Jerusalem temple, the Levites and Aaronic priesthood, not to mention the diverse sacrifices themselves and the complexity of the rules surrounding them, must have been baffling.

---

33. Some prefer to translate *hilastērion* as "propitiation" (i.e., "appeasement"), but according to this verse God sets forth Christ Jesus as a *hilastērion*. If this means "propitiation," the God would be appeasing himself, which makes little sense.

Why did Paul explain justification in this way? Evidently, he considered the two concepts inseparable.

Marcion, the second-century figure who claimed to be an avid follower of Paul, famously jettisoned the Old Testament as the scripture of the "synagogues" he founded. To him it was important that the Christian faith not be expressed in too Jewish a form. But Marcion misunderstood Paul because his hero would never have rejected the Old Testament. While gentiles did not have to become Jews outwardly to worship the Messiah of Israel, they did have to learn some elements of Israel's history and accept the Old Testament as their Bible too, if they were to understand Paul's gospel. Paul did not proclaim one message for Jews and another message for gentiles. Neither did he suggest that Jews and gentiles were blessed independently of each other. The gentiles were an integral part of the gospel he presented to Jews, just as Israel was an integral part of the gospel he presented to gentiles. This is because it was a single, unitary gospel. Paul was willing to tailor his manner of living and his manner of presentation to his audience—to the Jew he became a Jew, and to the gentile he became a gentile (1 Cor 9:19–23)—but the foundation of his gospel remained the same. It had to since he had received it from Christ.

THE RIGHTEOUSNESS OF GOD

We will return to the matter of how God, a righteous judge, can justly clear the unrighteous. But first, we must consider what Paul says about "the righteousness of God" (*dikaiosunē theou*).

Traditionally, there have been two approaches to understanding this expression. The older (pre-Reformation) understanding was that "the righteousness of God" was a testimony to the supremely elevated moral status of God. This was a very straightforward interpretation.

However, Martin Luther did not find such affirmations about God's righteousness to be comforting. To him, they highlighted the huge contrast between his own failings and God's faultless moral virtue, miring him in guilt and shame. However, Luther found great comfort when he realized that *dikaiosynē theou* could be translated "the righteousness *from* God" rather than "God's [personal] righteousness." This spoke of righteousness conveyed from God to the believer, and it gave him hope. For this reason and others, he rejected the more traditional interpretation.

Neither of the two passages that most strongly support Luther's interpretation comes from Romans. They are Phil 3:9 and 2 Cor 5:21. In Phil 3:9 Paul mentions his desire to have a "righteousness that comes from God" (*tēn ek theou dikaiosunēn*) in contrast to a "righteousness of my own from the Law." Unlike in Rom 1:17, where the text could be translated as either "righteousness of God" or "righteousness from God," in Phil 3:9 the construction is unambiguous: God is the source of the righteousness Paul mentions.[34]

In 2 Cor 5:21 Paul explains that God made Christ, who knew no sin, to become sin "for us" in order that "in him [Christ] we might become the righteousness of God." This verse could be interpreted to imply that the removal of our unrighteousness effectuated righteousness in "us" (i.e., Paul's fellow Christians and himself). However, in this verse the little phrase "in him [Christ]" is crucial. It is by incorporation into Christ that believers "become the righteousness of God." Although those who follow Luther like to claim this verse, it seems more supportive of a "union with Christ" theology than the imputation of Christ's alien righteousness.[35] It also is likely this verse teaches that Christ became not "sin" but rather "a sin offering" for us. For more about this possibility, see the discussion near the end of this excursus.

While Rom 1:17 was dear to Luther as the passage he believed placed "the [alien] righteousness of God" at the center of the gospel, Rom 10:3 is more supportive of his theology. There Paul writes, "For by ignoring God's righteousness and seeking to establish their own, they [i.e., unbelieving Jews] did not submit to the righteousness of God." Does this mean that they did not submit to the righteous judgment of God? This would accord with the pre-Reformation view. Or does it mean that they did not submit to the righteousness that comes from God? This would reflect Luther's view.

---

34. Wright acknowledges that in this verse Paul speaks of righteousness that comes from God. However, he suggests that this passage makes it less likely Paul meant "righteous from God" in Rom 1:17 when discussing what is revealed in the gospel. According to Wright, Paul could easily have used in Rom 1:17 the construction found here in Phil 3:9, if he wanted to indicate righteousness transferred from God to the believer.

35. I do not want to deny the importance of the "Finnish School" of interpretation of Luther that moves "union with Christ" to the center of Luther's soteriology. Whether or not this is the best way to interpret Luther is not the point under discussion. Whatever the merits of this view, Luther as understood by the Finns is not the Luther that has cast such a long shadow over Protestant theology.

In addition to the traditional (pre-Reformation) approach to understanding the *dikaiosynē* of God and Luther's innovation, N.T. Wright has added a third option (or perhaps a modification of the first option). He thinks Luther got the matter wrong: *dikaiosunē theou* ("righteousness of God") does not mean righteousness imputed to the believer from, and by, God. But Wright does not fully embrace the traditional view either. While *dikaiosynē theou* might also refer to other aspects of God's elevated moral status, primarily it refers to his fairness, his exemplary conduct as the judge of all the earth. God is impartial. God is *dikaios* ("just") because he fulfills his role as judge properly. That is the central point. For Wright, the *dik*–words must be interpreted within a legal framework, and he concludes that the *dikaiosynē* of God speaks of God's fairness and his faithfulness to the covenant (Israel's legal framework). In fact, the reason that Paul's gospel highlights the righteousness of God is to explain why the inclusion of the gentiles in salvation is so important. Were God to exclude the gentiles from his promises, he would not be faithful to his own *dikaiosynē* or fairness.

Another point, which I think is perhaps more my own than Wright's, is that functionally "the righteousness of God" means "God's righteous plan." This is because God's righteous character is revealed primarily through his actions toward humanity. As Paul understands things, God's righteousness is seen most clearly though the life, death, and resurrection of Jesus and their implications for humanity, the story of which lies at the center of "the gospel."

Wright's denial that *dikaiosynē theou* means "the righteousness received from God" has irritated many of his Protestant friends. However, Wright also gores the ox of his Catholic friends by denying that when God justifies a repentant sinner, he makes that person just and therefore worthy of salvation, as Catholic theology proclaims. Wright contends that God clears the charges, but this does not transform the sinner into someone worthy of salvation. (Again, justification changes one's legal status but does not change a person's character.) In a sense, Wright affirms the Protestant slogan *simul iustus et peccator* ("At the same time justified and a sinner"), so long as we recognize that "justified" means "cleared of the charges."

It is in Wright's presentation of God's personal righteousness that he seems to slide off the track. In my view, he errs by downplaying the biblical presentations of God as an advocate and an interested party in human affairs. Yes, God is the great judge of all the earth, but this description does not exhaust his relationship to humanity. He is not aloof. He is not a disinterested arbiter of truth.

In certain ways, the debate about how God exercises his role as judge mirrors the debate about divine *apatheia* ("passionlessness"). For many centuries God was portrayed in the Aristotelean mode as a being so changeless that he could not experience emotion or be impacted by the desires or pleas of the creatures he had created. For many, this traditional characterization was blown up by Jürgen Moltmann's *The Crucified God*, which highlighted that God's central revelation of who he was came through divine suffering on a cross. How could a passionless God be most fully revealed in Christ's passion?

God can be a righteous judge without being disinterested. In fact, his righteousness requires radical engagement with humanity and an orientation in their favor. Rom 5:17 speaks of "the gift of *dikaiosynē*." If receiving *dikaiosynē* simply means being cleared by God as he properly fulfills his role as judge, why is it called a "gift." When a fair verdict is rendered, this is not usually considered a gift from the judge. However, if being cleared of charges is the result of divine advocacy, speaking of his involvement as a "gift" makes perfect sense. (Of course, this "gift" language also makes sense with Luther's interpretation. If righteousness comes to the believer from God, then it might properly be called a gift.)

Rom 4:3 famously quotes Gen 15:6: "Abraham believed God and it was reckoned to him as *dikaiosynē*." Here *dikaiosynē* seems to mean "right relationship with God" since Abraham was not on trial. In Paul's account of salvation history, Adam and Eve encountered a special law decreed by God in the Garden of Eden and they trespassed. But from Eden to Moses there was no law, and consequently, there was no possibility of "trespass." Therefore, God's justification did not involve clearing Abraham of a charge brought against him. Instead, it seems, it was a gift given to him by God, and at its center was a special and ongoing relationship.

In several places (Rom 4:13; 9:31–32; 10:4–5; Gal 2:19–21; 3:21–22; Phil 3:9) Paul contrasts the attempt to base one's righteousness on the Law of Moses with the righteousness, right standing, or right relationship that comes from faith. One of Paul's key points is that God reckoned Abraham as *dikaios* long before there was a Law of Moses. This makes it impossible to connect this legal status or relationship with God too closely with the Law.

Another problem with Wright's approach involves a lexical consideration. He emphasizes that the *dik–* words reflect the background of a court of law. He makes a strong point if the meaning of these words is determined entirely by the usage of these words in the Greek world. However, often the meanings of words found in the New Testament are colored by their earlier usage in the LXX, the Bible of both the Greek-speaking, first-century synagogue and the Greek-speaking, first-century church. The LXX was a translation into Greek of the books of the Hebrew Bible (with a few other books added), and sometimes the Greek words used in it reflected not just their Greek meanings but rather the meanings of the underlying Hebrew words.

Two terms from the Hebrew Bible are often translated into English as "righteousness" or "justice": *tsedeqah*; and *mishpat*. The basic meanings of the feminine noun *tsedeqah* and its masculine noun counterpart *tsedeq* are "rightness" or "righteousness." When things are ordered in *tsedeqah*, they are rightly ordered. While this word can refer to the blessing that results when courts function properly, it is not primarily a legal term. It is frequently used to refer to the leadership of effective and virtuous kings and the positive results of that leadership. And perhaps most commonly *tsedeqah* refers to upright ethical conduct in any person, whatever his role in society.

Mishpat, on the other hand, is related to the word *shophet*, the primary Hebrew word for a "judge." In Hebrew, the book of Judges is called *Shophtim* (the plural of *shophet*). A *mishpat* most commonly means a "judgment," usually a judgment of a court or a judge, and most commonly a correct judgment.[36] Sometimes, however, the meaning includes the larger justice that prevails when judges judge justly.

Since as Wright has pointed out, the Greek word *dikaiosynē* is drawn from the world of judges and the courtroom, one might expect the LXX routinely to translate the Hebrew *mishpat* with the Greek *dikaiosynē*. However, that is not what we find. Far and away the most common word used to translate *mishpat* in the LXX is *krisis*, which usually means "a decision" or "a judgment," often of a court. The Hebrew word routinely translated by *dikaiosynē* is *tsedeqah*, which is not as closely connected to courts of law. Indicative of this is the fact that seven times the Hebrew word *tsedeqah* is translated not by the Greek *dikaiosynē* but rather by *eleēmosynē* ("mercy").[37] Given the LXX's imperfect correlation between *dikaiosynē* and *tsedeqah*, the connection between *tsedeqah* and ethical behavior, and the demonstrable impact of the LXX on Paul's thinking and vocabulary, Wright's account of Paul's use of the *dik–* words and his description of justification in Paul deserve further scrutiny.

---

36. Often the "judge" who issues the *mishpat* is God himself.

37. The specific occurrences are Deut 6:25, Psalm 24:5 (23:5 in the LXX), Psalm 33:5 (32:5 in the LXX), Psalm 103:6 (102:6 in the LXX), Isa 1:27, Isa 28:17, and Isa 56:16.

One other quibble about Wright's analysis does not concern the entire *dik–* family of words, but rather only the verb *dikaioō*, usually translated "to justify," but according to Wright more properly translated "to decide in one's favor." In several places in the LXX, *dikaioō* translates the Hebrew verb *riv*. This verb usually means "to advocate" for someone or "to take someone's side." In Isa 1:17 the Hebrew verb *riv* and the Greek word *dikaioō* are used to exhort people "to plead the case of the widow." Similarly, in Isa 50:8 we find: "He who takes my side is near. Who will contend with me?"

Perhaps most interestingly of all, Mic 7:9 depicts God as both a judge and an advocate at the same time: "I will bear the wrath of the LORD because I have sinned against him until he pleads (*riyv/dikaioō*) my cause and executes judgment for me. He will bring me forth to the light; I will behold his righteousness (*dikaiosunē/tsedeqah*)." This passage also suggests that God is an aggrieved party in this lawsuit. He is not disinterested in his service as judge.

According to the norms of the contemporary West, the roles of the judge and the advocate are strictly isolated from each other. The same person cannot serve as both judge and advocate. But the norms of Jewish justice with which Paul was raised did not isolate these roles so clearly. The pursuit of *tsedeqah* required a good judge to be sensitive to the plight of the widow and the orphan and to protect the interests of the poor against the predations of the rich. In this sense, blindfolded Lady Justice would not have been a fitting image for Israelite or second-temple Jewish justice, nor would the maxim "equal justice under the law" have been an entirely apt slogan. This does not mean that impartial justice was not valued. However, the overwhelming concern was that judges would favor the rich and powerful to the disadvantage of the poor and powerless, not the other way around. First and foremost, a good judge was to be an advocate for *tsedeqah* itself, not for one of the parties in the lawsuit.

Wright is correct in stating that when a judge declared someone to be in the right, that did not confer greater moral virtue upon that person. It also did not amount to a judgment that he or she was a good person. But since judging involved advocacy for *tsedeqah*, the judge could also serve partly as an advocate, and thus "justification" could be recognized as a gift. And considering matters of sin, since sin is an offense against God, God could himself be one of the aggrieved parties.

Wright has pointed to two important components of God's righteousness: his impartiality; and his faithfulness to the covenant.[38] I have argued for a third component: his commitment to *tsedeqah* ("righteousness") itself, perhaps best understood as "basic fairness." It seems we are left with two quite different, but hopefully not incommensurate, pictures: a great Judge who with righteousness renders proper verdicts; and a God who justifies (*dikaioō*) the unrighteous based on the sacrifice of Jesus Christ.

So, how are these competing images to be brought into harmony? It is important not to interpret the phrase "God's righteousness" too one-dimensionally. Yes, the *dik-* words have been shaped by the world of lawsuits and courts, but the Hebrew words *tsedeqah* and *riv* have also shaped Paul's concept of *dikaiosynē*, and this adds *advocacy* to the impartiality at the core of God's righteousness. God may be an impartial judge, but he is not an uninvolved judge.

Giving his Son to be sacrificed is the ultimate proof of God's involvement. And this involvement is essential to his justifying work. Contemporary Christians in the West are uncomfortable discussing sacrifice since it seems primitive and alien. But sacrifice was widespread among the religions of the Roman world and the Ancient Near East, and the modern interpreter of Paul must recognize sacrifice was not only common but endemic. By Paul's time, sacrifice generally involved animals, grain, or libations of various sorts. But earlier it had often involved human sacrifice, usually the sacrifice of children.

HUMAN SACRIFICE

Archaeologists of the Ancient Near East have discovered many examples of "foundation deposits," the bodies of infants or small children. These young victims were often placed in clay containers and buried in the foundation of newly constructed houses—usually beneath a doorway—killed as an offering in the hope of currying divine favor. Because the killing of the innocent was considered detestable, the Old Testament contains clear prohibitions of human sacrifice (Deut 18:10; 19:10–11; Jer 7:31; Ezek 23:36–39). Despite these proscriptions, child sacrifice to Molech appears to have been an ongoing problem (Lev 18:21; 20:2–5; Jer 32:35), as was child sacrifice to Baal (Jer 19:4–6; 32:35). Horribly, the sacrifices to Molech involved offering up the children "by fire" (Lev 18:21; Deut 12:31). Children were considered precious,

---

38. Perhaps he has argued for additional components as well. His writings are so voluminous, it is hard to know for sure.

even though *ipso facto* today their sacrifice seems bizarre. By giving up something of great value, the sacrifice became more powerful. It is also probable that the gruesome nature of these sacrifices added to the personal suffering of the parents and thus to the perceived power of the sacrifice.

The religions of the Ancient Near East were largely fertility religions and sacrifices were often inducements encouraging the god(s) to make the crops fertile, the livestock fertile, and one's own family and clan fertile. Giving a child to the god(s) was a plea for them to send large harvests and abundant offspring in return.

The lure of human sacrifice was so great that kings of Israel adopted the practice. Both Ahaz (2 Kgs 16:2–3; 2 Chr 28:1–3) and Manasseh (2 Kgs 21:6) sacrificed sons. Anticipating Paul's identification of pagan gods with demons in 1 Cor 10:20–21, Psa 106:37 says, "They sacrificed their sons and their daughters to demons (MT *le-shēdim*; LXX *tois daimoniois*)."

Part of the scandal of the cross is that it involves human sacrifice, although in an inversion of the normal way it had usually been practiced. God did not execute his son, but he allowed his Son to die at the hands of wicked people, and as we have seen, his Son's death is presented as a sacrifice. Normally a person would sacrifice his son or daughter as a gift offered to a god. But in a spectacular reversal, in this case it is God whose Son was offered up and the benefit accrued to the people. What a tremendous gift!

COMMENTS ON TRANSLATION

The complexities outlined in the preceding discussion hint at the difficulties associated with the choice of English approximations to the *dik-* words. Originally, I had hoped to translate the *dik-* words with a great degree of consistency. As my study progressed, however, I realized that complete consistency would eliminate the differing nuance Paul gives these words in different contexts. In the end, I chose to honor nuance over consistency.

The choices I have settled upon are hardly revolutionary, and they are open to criticism. In some contexts, it seems best to translate *dikaiosynē* with "righteousness" and *dikaios* with "righteous," particularly when they describe God. At other times a simple "right" seems the better translation. When Paul discusses Abraham in Romans 4, I understand the *dik-* words to describe a "right relationship" with God, since there is no legal or courtroom context in view. At other times, I have sometimes translated *dikaiosynē* with "right standing" and *dikaios* with "cleared," "in right standing," or "upright." The verb *dikaioō* (traditionally rendered "to justify") is sometimes translated "made right," and at other times "declared to be in the right." In addition, I sometimes surround my translations with "air quotes" when a note of irony is in the air.

TWO FINAL THOUGHTS

Over the centuries many theories of atonement have been proposed, including the "fishhook" theory, *Christus Victor*, Anselm's satisfaction theory, Abelard's moral influence theory, and Luther's penal substitution. Of these, generally evangelicals (including Pentecostals and many Charismatics) affirm *Christus Victor*, Anselm's satisfaction theory, and Luther's penal substitution theory. However, Paul's language about the sacrificial death of Jesus suggests Luther's penal substitution may not be the best way of explaining the significance of Christ's death—at least when expounding on Paul's writings. This is because Paul never says Christ died "in place of" (Greek *anti*) those who receive his benefits. Instead, he consistently says that Christ gave himself or died "for" (Greek *hyper*) them (Rom 5:8; 1 Cor 1:13; 2 Cor 5:14; Gal 2:20; Eph 5:2, 25), or "for" (*hyper*) "their sins" (1 Cor 15:3). Paul's language indicates that Christ died "on behalf of" or "for the sake of" others, not specifically that he was a substitute victim standing in their place.

Other New Testament authors echo the language of Isa 53:12 that the servant "bore the sin of many," understanding Jesus to fulfill the rule of the servant (Heb 9:28; 1 Pet 2:24). Paul does not do this, although through different wording he clearly maintains that on the cross Jesus dealt with the sin of humanity. Nevertheless, it is not the same thing to say Jesus dealt with the sinner's sin as to say that Jesus died in place of the sinner.

So, we may conclude with Paul that Christ died on our behalf so that we might live, as Paul affirms in Rom 6:8 and 1 Thess 5:10. And we may further conclude that his death served to avert the spiritual death toward which we were heading. Nevertheless, we must also recognize that this language of substitution goes a step beyond what Paul says, even if it is built on Pauline ideas. For this reason, I have come to prefer a version of Anselm's satisfaction theory to Luther's penal substitution theory.[39]

---

39. A full discussion of the satisfaction theory of the atonement is not possible here. It was first articulated at the end of the eleventh century in Anselm's work *Cur Deus Homo?* ("Why the God-Man?"). The New Testament portrays Christ's death as a ransom payment, but it does not make clear to whom that ransom was paid. A key innovation of Anselm's theory was that the ransom was paid to the requirements of God's righteous nature, rather than to Satan, as in earlier atonement theories. In

Given the fact that Paul never says Christ died "in our place" (*anth' hēmōn*),⁴⁰ I have often wondered why Luther ever developed his penal substitution theory of the atonement. Likely 1 Pet 2:24 was a factor, but I also I think two other factors may have been at work.

First, in places where the Greek text speaks of Christ dying "for" (*hyper*) others (e.g., Rom 5:6; 1 Cor 1:13), the Vulgate translates the Greek preposition *hyper* with the Latin preposition *pro*. Unlike *hyper*, *pro* can mean both "for" and "in place of."⁴¹ This may have suggested to him that *hyper* could also convey both meanings, which was incorrect.

Second, the LXX text of the beginning of Isa 53:12 may have influenced him. It reads: "Therefore, he inherited many and he divided the plunder of the strong, in whose place [*anth' hōn*] his soul was delivered unto death, and he was reckoned among the lawless." But this raises a hermeneutical question: Are contemporary interpreters of Paul justified in attributing to him interpretations of Old Testament scriptures which seem plausible but which he himself never clearly articulated? Luther may well have read Paul this way, or he may have read Paul's writings through the lens of 1 Peter, but for a modern interpreter of Paul to presume either possibility relies more on conjecture than careful interpretation of the Apostle.⁴²

Another concluding thought covers similar ground. It concerns Paul's famous statement in 2 Cor 5:21: "For our sake he [God] made him who did not know sin to be sin (or "a sin offering") in order that in him we might become the righteousness of God." The vivid language Paul uses—contrasting the bare word "sin" with "righteousness"—grabs the reader's attention. But we should probably understand the second reference to *hamartia* in this verse, not as a reference to "sin" but rather as a reference to "a sin offering"

---

addition, there are several variations of this theory, and few today would embrace Anselm's theory fully in its original form. The essence of the theory is contained in the familiar words of Ellis J. Crum's song "He Paid a Debt," the key words of which are: "He paid a debt He did not owe, I owed a debt I could not pay. I needed someone to wash my sins away." An infinite offense required an infinite ransom, which humanity could not provide. Because the offences were committed by humans, it was necessary that a human provide the ransom. This necessitated the incarnation of a God-Man, one who was both infinite and human. Thus, Anselm's *Cur Deus Homo?* explains both the incarnation and the atonement.

40. Before words that begin with a rough breathing (i.e., an "h" sound), the word *anti* changes form to *anth'*.

41. *Oxford Classical Dictionary*, s.v. *pro*.

42. Thanks to Timothy Dresselhaus for pushing me to consider more deeply the place of Isa 53 in Lutheran explanations of the atonement.

paralleling the language of Rom 3:25. The sinless Son of God was offered as a sacrifice "for us" even in our sinful state. Although this verse is often used to support a doctrine of substitutionary atonement, to say that Jesus was offered as a sacrifice "on our behalf" or "for our sake" is not quite the same as saying he was offered as a sacrifice "in our place." We were never meant to serve as sacrifices because in our fallen state, we were the problem, not the solution.

TRANSLATION: ROM 1:18–32

THE CONSEQUENCES OF SUPPRESSING THE TRUTH

[18]For the wrath of God is being revealed from heaven against all irreverence and wrongdoing of people who by doing wrong suppress the truth [19]because that God can be known is plain to them, for God has demonstrated it to them. [20]For, from the creation of the world, his invisible attributes, both his eternal power and deity, concepts seen by means of the things that have been made, are made evident, to render them without excuse, [21]since discerning God, they did not glorify [him] as God or thank [him], but rather they were futile in their inquiries and their senseless hearts were darkened. [22]Claiming to be wise, they became foolish,[23]and they traded away the glory of the immortal God for likenesses of images of mortal humans and birds and quadrupeds and reptiles.

[24]And so, God handed them over to the desires of their hearts for the impurity of dishonoring their bodies among themselves. [25]These traded away the truth of God for falsehood and reverenced and worshiped the creation instead of the Creator, who is blessed forever. Amen.

[26]On account of this, God handed them over to passion for dishonor, and their females traded away the natural function for the unnatural, [27]and likewise the males, giving up the natural function with the female, were enflamed in their desire for each other, males being used by males in obscene ways, they themselves receiving the necessary repayment for their deviancy.

[28]And, as they did not accept having God in their thoughts, God handed them over to an unacceptable mind, to do unseemly things, [29]being filled with every wrongdoing, with evil, with greed, with vice. They are full of envy, murder, quarrelling, deceit, maliciousness. They are gossips, [30]slanderers, God-haters, insolent, arrogant, boasters, innovators in evil, heedless

of parents, ³¹thoughtless, faithless, heartless, merciless. ³²Although they know the just decree of God—that those who do such things are worthy of death—they not only practice these things but also collectively approve those who do them.

COMMENTARY

Vss. 18–25: During the High Middle Ages, far and away the most popular biblical text for preaching was Rom 1:20: "For, from the creation of the world, his invisible attributes, both his eternal power and deity, being understood by means of the things that have been made, are made evident . . . ." This was the inspiration for the famous "Five Ways" of Thomas Aquinas, his so-called proofs for the existence of God. All these proofs began with observation of the created world and used that observation to demonstrate God's existence. Framed simply, the existence of created things implied the existence of a Creator.

According to Aquinas, when we examine the world around us using our senses, "seeing" is more persuasive than "hearing." On the one hand, believing Christian doctrines through reading or hearing Scripture (i.e., through "special revelation") can be likened to "hearing." On the other hand, working through the demonstration of a "proof" based on examination of the world about us apart from Scripture, can be likened to "seeing." What is learned about God through examining nature is often called "natural revelation." According to Aquinas, both the special revelation of Scripture, on the one hand, and on the other hand, the proofs, based as they are on natural revelation, lead to the truth that God exists. Furthermore, just as seeing is more persuasive than hearing, the proofs are more persuasive than the proclamation of Scripture and therefore in a sense they are superior.[43] However, in another sense, Aquinas thought the proofs were not superior, for many ideas contained in the special revelation of Scripture (such as that God exists as Father, as Son, and as the Holy Spirit) can never be proved by natural revelation.

In Aquinas's view, the proofs for the existence of God were particularly useful for apologetics and evangelism. If a person is discussing the existence of God with a person who accords Scripture no authority, arguing that Scripture says God exists is not very persuasive. However, if, as Rom 1:19–20 suggests, nature itself declares that God exists, this affords a better line of argumentation and can lead the doubter to develop believing faith. But do these verses really teach that nature reveals such knowledge?

---

43. Aquinas, *Summa Theologiae* II, q. 4, art. 8, ad 2.

Not according to the Swiss theologian Karl Barth. In December 1918 Barth published the first edition of his famous *Römerbrief* (*Epistle to the Romans*),[44] in which he strongly denied this interpretation. Barth contended that context matters and that this whole section of Romans is controlled by the declaration in 1:18 that "the wrath of God is being revealed." Accordingly, the entire passage concludes that because of wickedness and the suppression of truth, the evidence that is available to people through nature is always ignored and never leads them to an appropriate knowledge of, or relationship with, God. Instead, it renders them "without excuse." As it is sometimes put, because of an inherited sinful nature, people looking at nature receive enough "light" to damn them, but not enough light for them to be saved. What unregenerate people see when viewing the wonders of creation is by itself unable to overcome their built-in suppression of the truth; it never leads them to true knowledge of God.

In Barth's analysis, rather than being a shining promise that people can find God through their own faculties, Rom 1:18–25 is an announcement that apart from the gospel, people are doomed. Stated another way: "We cannot find God; God must find us." This idea is commonly articulated in Pentecostal and Charismatic churches. While the name Karl Barth is not often mentioned among Pentecostals and Charismatics, this same basic insight expressed in Barth's *Epistle to the Romans* is widely embraced.

This Barthian reading of Rom 1:18–25 does not mean that believers already enlightened by God's grace cannot recognize that the existence of creation implies the existence of a Creator; in fact, this is explicitly taught in scripture (e.g., Ps. 19:1–6). But Barth taught that apart from special revelation, apart from God taking the lead and his Word first encountering a person, that person is lost. In this fallen world, people simply cannot find God on their own.

The teaching of Aquinas was in the background of Barth's thinking, but his more immediate targets were the proponents of theological Modernism, which had become an important force in the central Europe of his time. Friedrich Schleiermacher is considered the founding father of theological Modernism, although when Barth published his commentary on Romans, Schleiermacher had been dead for more than eight decades.

Schleiermacher's theology of "the fatherhood of God and the brotherhood of Man" was built squarely on the Modernist idea that the "universal experience" of humanity was the starting point of human knowledge.

---

44. Despite when it was released, it bore the publication date of 1919. A second edition, which was thoroughly revised and expanded, came out in 1922, and an English translation was published in 1933.

Truth was found by looking inside oneself. Descartes had pioneered the self-awareness of the ego as the foundation of knowledge, but he was a rationalist and understood this self-knowledge exclusively in terms of reason. Schleiermacher added universally experienced feelings as a source of self-knowledge.

According to Schleiermacher and his followers, sooner or later, everyone becomes aware of how tenuous life is. Everyone needs food and water, air, warmth (but not too much warmth), and the proper operation of gravity and the planets to survive. Everyone is dependent on things over which they have little or no control. This leads to "a feeling of dependence." In fact, each is aware of his *absolute* dependence on things outside of himself. Each person also recognizes that his neighbors—in fact, the whole of humanity—are also in the same situation. They too are absolutely dependent. But it is logically impossible for everything in the universe to be dependent on other things or beings. There must be at least one being that is self-existent and not dependent on anything else, or nothing at all could exist. The commonly used name for such a being is "God." Recognition that they depend on the one necessary self-existent being makes them recognize "the Fatherhood of God." Recognition of their commonality as dependent beings leads every human to awareness of "the brotherhood of Man."

This approach to religion completely bypassed the need for Jesus Christ and the special revelation found in the gospel. Modernism was built upon the adequacy of the universal experience and universal reason of mankind for answering spiritual questions. Barth considered this way of approaching the truth an idol, and he believed Romans 1 condemned rather than supported the Modernist approach.

Biblical studies and theology are usually considered separate disciplines, and often they compete. Therefore, it is surprising that Barth's *Römerbrief*, which in form is a work of *biblical studies*, is nevertheless often considered the most important *theological* work of the twentieth century. Barth's commentary marked the start of the challenge to theological Modernism known as Neo-Orthodoxy. Ultimately, Neo-Orthodoxy vanquished its foe, Modernism (but not its foe's descendants).

Unfortunately, when surveying the history of theology, a pattern becomes apparent. There is a recurring trend within the theological academy to replace special revelation or, to put a finer point on it, the gospel that Paul proclaimed, with other supposed sources of knowledge about God. In 1 Cor 1:18–25, Paul contrasted "the wisdom of the world" with "the foolishness of what we preach," which is to say Paul's gospel. In both Rom 1:17 and 1 Cor 1:21 Paul insists it is only the gospel that has the power to save.

Vs. 18: "The wrath of God is being revealed from heaven": The word "wrath" often conjures puzzlement and can be unsettling. I remember being amused by a comic in the "Pepper . . . and Salt" series that appears regularly in *The Wall Street Journal*. It depicted Zeus (or perhaps Thor) holding a lightning bolt and lying on a psychiatrist's couch. This god explained to the doctor, "I have wrath issues."[45] What makes it funny is that we associate "wrath" with God or a god, while we typically use the word "anger" with humans. A human lying on the couch would have said, "I have anger issues."

However, when we think of wrath, it seems to imply something so extreme that humans are incapable of it. But the Greek word *orgē* does not necessarily imply association with a god or an over-the-top mode of anger. Ernst Käsemann warns that wrath should not be interpreted "psychologically," which of course is how the comic uses the term.[46] Instead, in this verse *orgē* is an eschatological term implying "a visitation of punishment" in line with the many prophetic announcements of judgment in the Old Testament; it is not a fit of rage.

Although *orgē* is an eschatological term, it does not relate exclusively to the future. The final judgment is being stored up for the "day of wrath" (2:5), which will also be "revealed"—Paul uses the same Greek verb *apokalyptō* there as in this verse—but the eschatological climax described in 2:5 reaches back from the future to the present day. Paul says God's judgment is already underway. He indicates this by placing the verb "revealed" (*apokalyptō*) in the present tense. This indicates an ongoing process that has already begun.

As mentioned in the comment to vs. 17, the word *apokalyptō* ("to reveal") usually means "to unveil what previously has been hidden." As in vs. 17, this verb is also in the present tense, suggesting a current, ongoing process. With these two verses standing back-to-back and both using the verb *apokalyptō*, it is hard to avoid the implication that the revelation of the "righteousness of God" and the revelation of "God's wrath" are linked. The gospel may be "good news," but it is accompanied by an announcement of judgment currently in process. In fact, the chance to avoid this judgment is a central feature of the gospel.

Paul's double use of the verb *apokalyptō* ("to reveal") in Rom 1:17–18, as he describes the gospel he proclaims, leads to a second point. Like Jesus's proclamation of the kingdom of God, Paul's gospel is an "apocalyptic" message, not only in the sense that something previously hidden is being disclosed, but also in that it announces a divine intervention to solve problems that are beyond human ability. The kind of hope offered by human methods

---

45. "Pepper . . . and Salt," *Wall Street Journal*, Feb. 1, 2023, A14.
46. Käsemann, *Romans*, 60.

is based on pious activity and gradual moral improvement. But Paul rejects such conceits, announcing that the only hope for mankind is for God to break in from outside of human history and completely rebuild everything anew.

By the beginning of the first century, a belief in two ages had emerged within Judaism: *ha'olam hazeh* ("this age" or "this world") and *ha'olam habba'* ("the age to come" or "the world to come"). The latter expression is found in the final chapter of the "parables" of Enoch (1 Enoch 71:15). In 4 Ezra 7:48–50 an angel explains: "[Because] an evil heart has grown up in us . . . the Most High has made not one world but two." Similarly, in 4 Ezra 8:1 the angel says: "The Most High has made this world for the sake of many, but the world to come for the sake of few." Similarly, in the *Apocalypse of Baruch* 15:7, it is affirmed that this coming world will appear on account of "the righteous ones."[47]

Jesus also used the expressions "this age" and "the age to come." Matt 12:32 records Jesus saying, "whoever should speak against the Holy Spirit, it will not be forgiven him either in this age or in the coming age." See also Mark 10:30, Luke 18:30, and Luke 20:34–36.

Paul understands the coming of Jesus into this world to have marked the beginning of the pivot from this age to the coming age of eschatological blessing and judgment. As I understand it, this transition from old to new will be completed with his second coming.

Vs. 19: In my rendering, the words "that God can be known" translate *tou theou* ("of God") plus *to gnōston*, which could mean either "what is known of God" or "the knowability of God." Philo, the early first century Jewish scholar from Alexandria used *gnōston* in the first sense, so this usage is often reflected in translations of this verse. However, in context the second meaning makes more sense. Rather than using the rather awkward formulation "the knowability of God," I have rendered this "that God can be known." Paul's point is not that what can be known about God is already known by all, but rather that people are aware of the simple fact that God can be known. This is evident because God has demonstrated it to all who care to consider the matter. Despite the fact that God is knowable, most choose to suppress this truth and instead create their own substitutes for God.

The verb *phaneroō* ("to demonstrate," "to make evident") often takes a direct object, but there is none here. The English verb "demonstrate" requires a direct object, so the direct object "it" has been supplied. "It" refers to "that God can be known."

Vs. 20: The phrase "from the creation of the world" (*apo ktiseōs kosmou*) has two possible meanings. It might mean "*since* the creation of the

---

47. For more on this see Ladd, *Theology of the New Testament*, 43.

world," or it might mean "*by* the creation of the world." Does this phrase answer the question, "Since when?" or does it answer the question, "How would I know?" While the first option ("since") seems more likely, both are possible.

The clause "to render them without excuse" (*eis to einai autous anapologētous*) is a purpose clause, a fact that offends many and causes them to try to obscure this. God intended that those who suppress the truth and ignore that knowledge of God is available to them would be "without excuse," and liable to judgment, apart from the grace of the gospel. Often translations wrongly convert this clause into a result clause: "so they are left without excuse."

The word *anapologētos* ("without excuse") is used here of those who have ignored evidences of a Creator found in nature, but this also foreshadows the word's use in 2:1, where hypocrisy renders smug self-righteousness empty. Paul does not explicitly spell this out, but chapter 1 seems most directly targeted against the unbelieving gentile, whereas chapter 2 seems directed against the Jew who refuses to believe he or she needs the salvation made possible by Jesus.

The word *noumena* ("concepts") literally means "things being thought" or "things in the mind." Paul is arguing that *aorata* (the neuter plural of the substantival adjective *aoratos*; "invisible things") are seen, but not directly. They are seen by implication through the material evidences God has wrought through his acts of creation. Paul's argument is the basis for all the classical *a posteriori* arguments for the existence of God, such as Thomas Aquinas's "Five Ways."[48] The fault with these arguments for the existence of God is that, as Paul himself argues, by themselves they will not lead to belief in God, even though they should. Instead, they fail because of the fallen nature of humanity, leaving unbelievers without a defense before the great Judge. For Paul, the gospel, which mediates the power of God, is the only effective path to knowledge of God and to salvation.

This does not mean that God's revelation of himself in nature is worthless. To the mind enlightened by God's grace, "The heavens declare the glory of God," as Ps 19:1 declares. But what appears obvious to the believer, is not so obvious to the unbeliever. By itself, observation of nature will not lead the unbeliever to God and a proper relationship to him.

Vs. 21: "Discerning God" translates *gnontes ton theon*. While this could be translated to imply a more robust knowledge, the thrust of Paul's

---

48. *A posteriori* arguments take data gathered by the senses into account. These arguments differ from *a priori* arguments that use pure reason alone and do not depend on sensory data. Literally, *a posteriori* means "from behind" and *a priori* means "from the front."

argument is that apart from the gospel people universally suppress the truth, leaving them with a vague awareness that is not pursued.[49]

The failure to glorify God that Paul describes in this verse stands in marked contrast to Abraham's encounter with God which he commemorated by building an altar (Gen 12:7). In 4:20 Paul says that Abraham, who came from a background filled with idolatry, "gave glory to God." Rather than refusing to glorify God and instead choosing idolatry like the bulk of humanity, Abraham receives a special revelation of God and turns from idolatry to belief in God and glorification of him.

"Their senseless hearts were darkened": While in the OT the heart sometimes represents the seat of emotions, quite often it represents the seat of thought. (I know of no place where the "brain" is referenced this way.) This means that "senseless heart" is an oxymoron; what is supposed to function sensibly does not, due to being darkened. The metaphor is slightly mixed since "darkened" assumes the image of "seeing," while the main image is "thinking."

Vs. 22: "Claiming to be wise, they became foolish": This is a core tenet of Paul's diagnosis of the human condition without the gospel. Two or three years earlier he had written 1 Cor 1:18–25, which includes the similar statement, "For since in the wisdom of God, the world did not know God through its wisdom, God was pleased through the foolishness of what we preach to save those who believe" (1 Cor 1:21).

Vss. 23–28: These six verses are filled with two sets of repeated verbs. First, *allassō* appears in vs. 23 and *metallassō* in vss. 25 and 26. I have translated these as "traded away," attempting to capture the sense of "making a poor exchange" or "squandering" in each instance. These exchanges are self-inflicted wounds.

In vss. 24, 26, and 28 the verb *paradidōmi* appears, each time with God as the verb's subject. In each instance I have translated *paradidōmi* as "to hand over," although "surrendered" is another possible translation. Normally this verb is used to explain one person handing over something to another person. However, in these verses God hands people over to three moral deformations: "the desires of their heart for the impurity of dishonoring their bodies"; "passion for dishonor"; and "an unacceptable mind." What is pictured in each case is the loss of God's benevolent oversight to destructive compulsion and domination. Even though these choices are destructive, God honors human agency, at least in the immediate timeframe.

It has already been argued that "the wrath of God" mentioned in vs. 18 should not be understood psychologically as some sort of divine rage.

---

49. On "discerning" as a possible translation, see Liddell and Scott, *Greek-English Lexicon*, s.v. "gignōskō."

Instead, the word implies judgment. While 2:5 mentions a future "day of wrath" on which this wrath will be fully revealed, the present tense of the verb *apokalyptō* ("to reveal") in vs. 18 suggests that this revelation of divine judgment has already begun. From one perspective, humans darken their minds and destroy themselves through wickedness. From another vantage, this "handing over" of people to their own destructive impulses can be described as divine wrath or divine judgment.

The inferential conjunction *dio* in vs. 24, which I have translated "and so," can mean "therefore," assuming evidence already laid out is the basis for the coming remarks, which seems the case here.

Vs. 25 contains Paul's classic description of idolatry: worshiping the creation rather than the Creator. In vs. 22 he has already noted the worship of mortal human beings, birds, quadrupeds, and reptiles. But rather than merely listing examples of things people worship, this verse describes the principle of idolatry: anything that is created or that flows out of this created universe is derivative and therefore less than God himself, who alone is worthy of worship. Money, power, fame, beauty, one's own sexuality, and even the entire universe are all inferior to God. Yet people seem to have an almost limitless capacity to find obsessions and erect idols. Often, they project quasi-divine attributes onto their idols. Today it is common to hear someone say, "The universe wants . . . ." rather than "God wants . . . ." Needing to find order and purpose in something, but not wanting to acknowledge God, they project the power to order and plan onto "the universe." Recognizing a strong but invisible power in *libido*, they worship their own sexuality and sexual experiences, rather than the God who is the designer of all positive human interaction.

Some have tried to portray the clear descriptions in vss. 23-25 of homosexual activity, both male homosexuality and lesbianism, as condemnations of homosexual prostitution but not condemnation of consensual homosexual activity. However, an honest reading of the text quickly reveals such portrayals as tendentious and dishonest.

Paul does not deny the essential humanity of homosexuals or God's concern for them. By saying that God has handed them over to unrighteousness, he does not imply that there is no hope for redemption or transformation. In 1 Cor 6:9-11 Paul explains that "the unrighteous will not inherit the kingdom of God," explicitly including *malakoi* (literally "the soft," but functionally meaning "the passive partners in homosexual activity") and *arsenokoitai* (literally "men who bed other men" and perhaps functionally meaning "the active partners in homosexual activity"). But he goes on and explains, "And these some of you were. But you were washed, you were sanctified, you were justified in the name of the Lord Jesus Christ and in the Spirit of our God."

Vs. 28: The Greek of this verse contains a play on words that I have attempted, perhaps badly, to mimic in English. The word *dokimazō* ("to accept," "to judge acceptable") is cognate with *adokimon* ("unacceptable"). Perhaps the play on words might also be mimicked by stating, "They did not approve of having God in their thoughts" and "God handed them over to an unapproved mind." In either case, the point is that because these people do not recognize or approve of God, the minds they used to slight God will themselves be displayed as defective.

Vss. 29–32: Paul does not single out only homosexual behavior. Vss. 29–31 list seventeen sins that often characterize those whom God has handed over to an unacceptable mind. This "sin list" can be divided into four parts: 1) the initial part in which the sins are all in the dative case; 2) a second part, beginning with "They are full of" and the sins being listed in the genitive case; 3) a third part (beginning at the start of vs. 30) in which kinds of sinners are mentioned, each being placed in the accusative plural; and 4) a subset of the third grouping, starting with the last sin of vs. 30 and extending through vs. 31, in which each sin begins with an alpha privative (similar to the function of "a" in "amoral"), which I have attempted to capture by translating with English words ending in -less.

Vs. 32: In this verse Paul describes people who do things "worthy of death." The Old Testament prescribed capital punishment for certain "abominations," including male homosexual practice (Lev 20:13). But Paul is incensed by more than this behavior. The gentiles Paul has in view "not only" do such things, they also publicly defend this behavior. Paul frequently uses the expression *ou monon* ("not only") found here as well as in Rom 9:24; 13:5, but often as part of the slightly longer phrase *ou monon de* (found in Rom 5:3; 5:11; 8:23; 9:10).

Paul never approves of sin, but he is especially annoyed when people collectively approve and endorse the sin of others. Often people will acknowledge what they are doing is wrong but claim they have difficulty overcoming temptation. When they deny that their behavior is wrong, this amplifies the problem. And if they *collectively* deny that some sinful behavior is wrong, this takes things to a whole new level. An example is Paul's outrage at the perverse pride the Corinthian believers took in accepting a man who was sleeping with his father's wife (1 Cor 5:2).

In this verse Paul uses the verb *syneudokeō*. If he had used *eudokeō*, it would have implied approval and endorsement. But by prefixing this word with *syn*, Paul describes *collective* approval and endorsement. Such outrages result from the exercise of "unacceptable" minds.

ROMANS 2

TRANSLATION: ROM 2:1–11

GOD'S JUDGMENT ON HYPOCRITES

¹And so, you are without excuse, O Man, everyone who judges! For when you judge the other person, you condemn yourself. For you, the one judging, practice the same things. ²And we know that the judgment of God is correct against those who do such things. ³Consider this, O Man, the one judging those who practice such things while doing the same: Do you think you will escape the judgment of God? ⁴Or, do you think wrongly about the abundance of his kindness, his forbearance, and his patience, being unaware that the goodness of God is for leading you to repentance? ⁵Considering things according to your extremely hard and impenitent heart, you are storing up for yourself wrath in the Day of Wrath, and the revelation of the righteous judgment of God, ⁶who will repay each according to his [or her] works: ⁷glory, honor, and immortality to those who by the steadiness of their good works seek eternal life ⁸and wrath and fury for those who by quarrelling and not believing the truth, instead are persuaded by evil. ⁹There will be trouble and distress for every person promoting evil, for the Jew first and also for the Greek. ¹⁰But [there will be] glory, honor, and peace to everyone doing good, to the Jew first and also to the Greek. ¹¹For there is no favoritism with God.

COMMENTARY

Vss. 1–11: In this passage Paul turns from his denunciation of gentile immorality in chapter 1 that would have been well received by Paul's Jewish audience, to a moral discussion much more challenging to his Jewish audience.

Paul begins by noting the widespread tendency of people to condemn in others what they excuse for themselves. He then turns to consider God's perspective on such hypocrisy and concludes by asserting God's avoidance of favoritism. The group that might have claimed a favored status before God would have been the Jewish believers of Rome, not the gentile believers.

Käsemann describes vss. 7–10 as "hymnic," apparently suggesting that Paul uses well-known verbiage either from the Jewish community or from the Christian community.[1] If so, he certainly has not used traditional language without putting his own stamp on it. The Pauline phrase "to the Jew first and also to the Greek" (or, perhaps "for the Jew first and also for the Greek") appears twice.

Noting the paucity of verbs in these verses, Käsemann takes this as a marker of liturgical language. He also describes these verses as "highly stylized rhetorically."[2] That this is hymnic material redeployed by Paul may be right, although if so, the hymnic material likely begins in vs. 6, with the original hymn asserting "God will repay . . . ," or the like, rather than "who will repay . . . ."

Vs. 1: The inferential conjunction *dio*, which I have translated "and so," suggests that what follows is self-evident. This conjunction can mean "therefore" and point to preceding comments as the basis for what is about to be stated, as it does in 1:24. Here, however, a new argument begins which is not based on the argument of 1:18–32.

The vocative address "O Man" (*ō anthrōpe*) of a generalized and anonymous figure occurs three times in Romans (at 2:1, 2:3, and 9:20), twice in this chapter. Of these three occurrences, only this one adds the qualifier "everyone" (*pas*). Although it is only an unproven conjecture, I suspect the Vulgate translation of this as *o homo omnis* ("every man") is the inspiration for title of the late fifteenth-century morality play "Everyman." *For more about this, see the excursus titled "O Man."*

Normally, I translate the word *anthrōpos* as "person" or "human being"—it does not mean "male"—but in light of the possibility that this passage has had an important influence on English literature, I have chosen to translate *ō anthrōpe* in the three places it occurs with the traditional "O Man."

Paul's charge that all are hypocrites is a bracing rebuke, but it is hard to deny. As he points out, every person is "without excuse" (*anapologētos*) when faced with this charge. Whereas the argument of 1:18–32 pointed to the wonders of creation as objective evidence for God and his invisible

---

1. Käsemann, *Romans*, 59.
2. Käsemann, *Romans*, 59.

attributes, here Paul begins an indictment of every human based on subjective evidence. A quotation of C.S. Lewis is apt:

> There is one thing, and only one, in the whole universe which we know more about than we could learn from external observation. That one thing is Man. We do not merely observe men, we are men. In this case we have, so to speak, inside information; we are in the know. And because of that, we know that men find themselves under a moral law, which they did not make, and cannot quite forget even when they try, and which they know they ought to obey.[3]

For Lewis, it is not the specifics of this internal law that are important, but rather that every person has an internal moral code which she cannot escape. Even in a high-security prison, with a population of prisoners convicted of heinous crimes, inmates struggle with moral sentiments such as blame, guilt, and regret. Having broken some laws, one might think they would scoff at all laws. But this is not the case. They get angry when others treat them unfairly, and they feel guilty or regretful when they do what they would not like done to themselves, even if they suppress outward evidence of such feelings.

A similar quotation decorates the tombstone of the great eighteenth-century philosopher Immanuel Kant. Taken from the Conclusion of his *Critique of Practical Reason*, in translation from the German, it reads: "Two things fill the mind with ever new and increasing admiration and awe the oftener and the more steadily we reflect on them: the starry heavens above and the moral law within."

Kant's "starry heavens above" echoes Paul's argument in 1:18–32 that creation points to its Creator. His reference to "the moral law within" was likely generated, at least in part, in response to 2:1–11. But Paul and Kant head in somewhat different directions.

For Kant, the moral law within was the application of universal reason to moral decision-making, what he called "the categorical imperative." Put negatively, the thrust of the categorical imperative is that people should never do what they would not always find acceptable if others did the same thing. Put more simply, this means: Never be a hypocrite, doing yourself what you do not approve in others. If people think logically, and if they recognize that any moral system worthy of the name must be universally applicable, which is to say, it must apply to every person equally, then actions are only right if a person determines that every other person in the world

---

3. Lewis, *Mere Christianity*, 23.

would be justified in acting in the same way. For instance, if lying is immoral when someone else does it, then it is never morally acceptable for you to lie. However, this grand idea is not exactly Paul's point.

Paul's claim is that every person is a hypocrite, guilty of things we condemn in others. Furthermore, deep down we all know we are hypocrites. But the problem is not just bad behavior; it is that people are so greatly inclined to appoint themselves as judges over others. When they do this, in effect they usurp the place of God, the one before whom every human being must give an account. There is a dual problem: People both condemn themselves in their hearts as hypocrites, and they arrogantly elevate themselves as judges over others. As a result, all stand condemned before God.

Another problem with Kant's moral philosophy is that he assumes everyone thinks the same way. That is the meaning of "universal reason." However, the prevailing viewpoint in this postmodern age (or post-postmodern age) is that people do not all think alike, so there is no such thing as universal reason. Kant's analysis is trapped in his time in a way that Paul's argument is not. Paul recognizes that no one lives up to her own code of what is right, but different people may condemn themselves in different ways over different issues. Furthermore, because of this self-condemnation and the judgmentalism associated with it, everyone invites divine punishment. On the one hand we show ourselves to be immoral, and on the other hand we show ourselves to overstep the bounds of whatever morality we claim.

Vss. 2–3: Having explained in vs. 1 why everyone stands condemned, in these verses Paul points out that God is the one properly vested with the right to judge. Also, notice that in vs. 3 the generalized address "O Man" reappears.

Vss. 4–5: Paul challenges the person who considers herself to be righteous to ask whether or not she is thinking wrongly, using the verb *kataphroneō*. He suggests that some rely on God's "abundance" (*ploutos*; literally "wealth") of "kindness" (*chrēstotēs*, which could also be translated "goodness"), "forbearance" (*anochē*), and "patience" (*makrothymia*; literally "long to emotion" or "longsuffering," an English expression that now seems a bit dated).

God is gracious, but that does not mean he has lax standards of morality. He is patient, but that does not mean that a day of judgment is not coming. In 1:18 Paul explained that God's wrath, his judgment, is already being revealed. But this current revelation of wrath is only partial and an anticipation of the full revelation of his wrath that will take place on the future Day of Wrath.

Vss. 5–11: In the history of Protestant interpretation this passage has been regarded as problematic since it can be read as an endorsement of "works-righteousness," the bugaboo of Reformation theology. However, as N. T. Wright repeatedly points out, Paul is a proponent of good works, and in this passage and in others he links good works with salvation. The solution that Wright proposes is a double judgment. In this life, a proleptic judgment—one offered in advance of the final verdict—is based entirely on faith. Ultimately, there will be a final verdict based on works. In a way that seems inscrutable to many, these two judgments will always return the same result.[4]

Wright's analysis is helpful, but greater clarity is provided by John M. G. Barclay's contention that divine grace and the salvation received through this grace comprise an *unconditioned* gift (i.e., apart from any sort of worth, be it ethnicity, pedigree, class, accomplishments, etc.). When a person exercises faith in Jesus, the Holy Spirit is imparted and a transformation begins. Different aspects of this transformation are described in chapters 5, 6, and 8, but a notable part is the emergence of new life through the Spirit. With this new life, what was formerly impossible becomes possible. While this salvation constitutes an *unconditioned* gift, God's bestowal of the gift of his Son's death "for us" is not *unconditional*.[5] As was the normal pattern of gift-giving in the ancient world, giving a gift creates a new relationship—here a new relationship between God and the recipient of his grace—and it implies obligations. One obligation is allegiance. Another is to live in the new life the Spirit's transformation allows. This is why Paul can speak of an eschatological judgment based on one's works. A transformed life will result in good works. *For a fuller exploration of Barclay's thought, see "The New-Perspective Adjacent Scholar John M. G. Barclay" in the introductory material of this commentary.*

In passages such as Rom 3:20 and Phil 3:9, Paul sets faith firmly against works in the context of how people pursue righteousness. Any attempt to demonstrate one's own righteousness and thus to receive justification as a reward is doomed to failure. However, faith and works are not opposed when viewed retrospectively. The person of faith will also be a person of works. And the person who attempts to be righteous without faith will

---

4. Wright simultaneously maintains two things: 1) God's final judgment of human beings will assess the totality of their lives; and 2) those who are "in Christ" will at this final judgment be vindicated as part of God's faithfulness to his covenant. See Wright, *Paul and the Faithfulness of God*, esp. 936–44.

5. To say a gift is "unconditioned," means it is given without regard to a person's worth, status, or previous behavior. However, to say a gift is "unconditional" means it entails no obligations. Barclay contends rightly that Paul does not view the gift of salvation as being "unconditional." The gift of salvation comes with the expectation of allegiance and obedience.

never accomplish what is pleasing to God. As it is often put: "It is therefore faith alone which justifies, and yet the faith which justifies is not alone."[6]

Why does Paul emphasize the role of works in God's judgment, especially at this early point in laying out the logic of his gospel? Those who objected to his gospel usually did so by associating it with "lawlessness," and by its supposed gratuitous acceptance of lawless and wicked gentiles. This, Paul's opponents contended, besmirched God's righteous character. In anticipation of this charge, Paul eagerly emphasizes that his gospel affirms both God's righteousness and the importance of good works.

Vss. 6–10 contain only one finite verb, *apodōsei* ("he will repay"; from *apodidōmi*) in vs. 6. Those five verses also contain five participles. Because English requires more finite verbs to be readable than does Greek, I have added a couple, translating them as futures in keeping with the future tense of *apodōsei*.

Vs. 7: "Glory, honor, and immortality" (*aphtharsia*; literally, "incorruptibility") are promised to those who seek "eternal life" (*zoēn aiōnion*). Since "immortality" and "eternal life" mean essentially the same thing, the point is that what is sought after will be found when sought through "the steadfastness of their good works." One wonders if Paul considers "the steadfastness of their good works" to be another way of saying "faithfulness." In vs. 10 the third member of the triad, "immortality" is replaced by "peace."

Vs. 8: In this verse a single group is described in logically contrapositive ways: those who are unpersuaded by the truth; and those who are persuaded by evil. They are quarrelsome and will inherit divine "wrath" and "fury." In the following verse, this recompense is reframed as "trouble" and "distress."

Vss. 9–11: These verses recapitulate what has already been written in vss. 7–8, but they add the important point that the same dynamics—blessing and wrath—are operative for both Jews and Greeks, showing God's impartiality. As already expressed, the formula "to the Jew first and also to the Greek," puts Jews in the position of historical priority and honor, but also indicates that there is no functional distinction between the two groups.

In vs. 9 the word translated "person" is literally "soul" (*psychē*). The use of *psychē* as a metonym for "person" was so common that the words had almost become synonyms, although this usage had roots in Gen 2:7: "... and the man became a living soul [MT *nephesh*; LXX *psychē*]."

The statement in vs. 11 that God shows no partiality is echoed by Peter's statement in Acts 10:34. In addition, James 2:9 suggests that the Law itself prohibits partiality: "But if you show partiality, you commit sin, and

---

6. This essential point was made by John Calvin in 1547. Calvin, *Acts of the Council of Trent with the Antidote*, Canon 11. See also p. 21, note 36.

are convicted by the law as transgressors." This probably is a reference to Deut. 16:19: "You shall not pervert justice; you shall not show partiality; and you shall not take a bribe, for a bribe blinds the eyes of the wise and subverts the cause of the righteous."

TRANSLATION: ROM 2:12–29

"JEWS IN WHAT IS HIDDEN" FULFILL THE PURPOSE OF THE LAW

[12]For as many as sin without the Law, will also perish without the Law, and as many as sin with the Law, will be judged through the Law. [13]For it is not the hearers of the Law who are right before God, but rather the doers of the Law will be made right. [14]For when gentiles, who by nature do not have the advantages of the Law, do the things of the Law, although being without the Law, for themselves they are the Law. [15]Such people demonstrate the work of the Law written in their hearts (testifying alongside their conscience even in the midst of thoughts that alternately reproach or defend), [16]as will become evident on the day when, according to my gospel, God judges people's secrets through Jesus Christ.

[17]But if you call yourself a Jew and you lean upon the Law and boast in God, [18]and you know his will and you weigh distinctions, being instructed from the Law, [19]and being convinced that you yourself are a guide to the blind, light to those in darkness, [20]a babysitter of the unthinking, a teacher of children, having the profile of knowledge and truth in the Law, [21]then do you, the one teaching the other person, not teach yourself? The one preaching not to steal, do you steal? [22]The one saying not to commit adultery, do you commit adultery? The one loathing idols, do you plunder temples? [23]You who boasts in the Law, do you dishonor God through transgressing the Law? [24]"For on account of you the name of God is blasphemed by the Gentiles," just as it is written.

[25]On the one hand, circumcision helps if you observe the Law, but on the other hand, if you are a transgressor of the Law, your circumcision has become uncircumcision. [26]Therefore, if the uncircumcised man keeps the just decrees of the Law, will not his uncircumcision be reckoned as circumcision? [27]And the physically uncircumcised man who completes the purpose of the Law, will judge you, the one transgressing the Law while you have the letter and circumcision. [28]For it is not the Jew in appearance who is the real one nor the circumcision in the flesh that is real, [29]but the Jew in

what is hidden, and the circumcision of the heart, in the Spirit not in the letter. This person's praise comes not from people but from God.

COMMENTARY

Vss. 12–16: This passage does not teach that gentiles can recognize the truth on their own. Paul here talks about gentiles who have been transformed by Christ without any in-depth understanding of the Mosaic Law. They live in faith while loving and worshipping God. These are attitudes and behaviors which the Law of Moses is meant to inculcate.

Vs. 13: The expression "doers of the Law" (*'oseh hatorah*) is common in rabbinic Judaism. In the context here, Paul clearly does not mean fulfilling the explicit legal requirements of the Pentateuchal Law codes. Instead, he means fulfilling the divine desires and purposes communicated in the Pentateuch. "Torah" is a wider concept than law codes; its fundamental meaning is "instruction."

Vs. 14: The translation "the advantages of the Law" is not literal, but it is accurate. Literally the Greek says, "the things of the Law," but here Paul is referring to the advantages which Jews have but gentiles do not, advantages that come from the Law. When Paul speaks of gentiles not having these advantages "by nature," he simply means "in the ordinary course of things." In other places Paul also uses the word *physis* ("nature") to mean something like "what is observable" or "what is customary," rather than "based on the physical order." For instance, when he asks, "Does not nature itself teach you that when a male has long hair it is a disgrace to him?" (1 Cor 11:14), he is talking about generally observable behavior, not biology. If left ungroomed, men will grow as much hair on their heads as women and more hair than women on the rest of their bodies.

The translation "for themselves they are the Law" makes a couple of assumptions. The key question is this: Does *nomos* ("law") refer to the Mosaic Law or instead some other law or principle? Since Paul usually means the Mosaic Law when he uses *nomos*, that seems the preferable interpretation, if the context allows for it.

In a few verses (in vs. 29) Paul will refer to "the Jew in what is hidden" or "the Jew in secret," i.e., the person who does not outwardly behave as a Jew. Therefore, he seems convinced that believing gentiles have internalized the essence of the Law of Moses. This means what God has already done in them is a signpost for their continuing spiritual life in the days and years ahead. Their own experience is a testimony that God's plan has been revealed to gentiles as well as to Jews. Paul's argument here is not so very different from his argument in Gal 3:2 posed through the rhetorical question: "Did you receive the Spirit by works of the Law or by hearing with faith?" He asks the Galatians why they would want to follow the Law of Moses like Jews when God has already begun to guide them through his Holy Spirit. Here in Romans 2 Paul speaks of this internal witness as a kind of "Law" within them; in Galatians 3, Paul identifies this internal witness as "the Spirit." In Romans 8, Paul will also discuss the role of the Spirit in the lives of the Roman believers.

While Paul here likely refers to the Mosaic Law, it is possible that Paul alludes to a passage from Aristotle's *Politics*. Aristotle argues that "for men of pre-eminent virtue there is no law—they are themselves a law [*autoi gar eisi nomos*]."[7] Given this, perhaps Paul's Roman readers would not have found the idea of such internal regulation to be utterly strange.

Vs. 15: In this verse Paul mentions Law that is "on the heart" or "in the heart," echoing the language of Jer 31:33, a verse from a passage that promises a new covenant. In Rom 11:27 Paul will also use language drawn from this same verse in Jeremiah. There his point is that the promised new covenant is superior to the covenant given at Sinai. In this verse, he presumes that gentile believers participate in that promised new covenant.

Paul also mentions the word "conscience," but he distinguishes between the Law written inwardly and conscience. They are different, but they work together. Conscience's role is not tightly defined. The description "even in the midst of thoughts that alternately reproach or defend" is exceedingly loose. This makes it difficult to determine if Paul conceives of conscience as an arbiter between such thoughts, the author of such thoughts, or something else entirely. In 1 Cor 8:12 Paul indicates that one's conscience can be "beaten up" or "wounded," and that it can be "weak." Therefore, it seems that conscience is neither innate nor impervious to outside influence. In the middle of the first century AD conscience had not yet become a major topic in any of the philosophical schools, although by the beginning of the next century it would become an established element of Stoic vocabulary. In Paul's day, conscience was mainly featured in popular literature, and its contours had not yet been well established.

This verse contains the only occurrence in Paul's letters of the phrase "work of the Law" in the singular. This phrase has a positive connotation whereas he uses the plural "works of the Law" negatively.

Vs. 16: The *krupta* ("hidden things") in people's hearts will be revealed on the day of judgment. This reflects one of Paul's complaints about his former life as a Jew relying on external regulations without accompanying

---

7. Aristotle, *Politics* 3.13.

faith: hypocrisy thrives in such an environment. He also mentions "hidden" or "secret" things in 1 Cor 4:5 ("[The Lord] will bring to light the things hidden in darkness and will disclose the decisions of the heart") and in 1 Cor 14:25 ("the secrets of his heart become apparent; and so, falling on his face, he will worship God declaring that God is really in your midst").

Vss. 17–24: These verses constitute a diatribe, i.e., an argument with a hypothetical opponent in debate. They drip with sarcasm, every bit as much as the classic putdown found in 1 Cor 4:8–13. This attack is not aimed at believing Jews who accept believing gentiles into the community of believers. But it is also not aimed at the larger Jewish community that rejects Jesus. It is aimed at believing Jews who nonetheless refuse to accept believing gentiles as their equals in the Lord.

Vs. 17: The verbs *eponomazē* (from *eponomazō* "to call" or "to name") and *epanapauē* (from *epanapauomai* "to rely on" or "to hope on") sound very similar. This assonance is an artistic flourish that is evident in Greek but does not come through in English translation. The expression "boast in God" may be an allusion to the Song of Hannah (specifically 1 Sam 2:10 in the LXX).

Vs. 21–22: These verses mention three specific sins: stealing; adultery; and idolatry. The sins of adultery and idolatry are often linked in the Old Testament, since unfaithfulness to a wife is often likened to unfaithfulness to Yahweh, the God of Israel (e.g., Exod 34:15–16; Deut 4:12–18, and the whole book of Hosea). In Matt 16:4 while speaking with Pharisees and Sadducees, Jesus speaks of "an evil and adulterous generation." He does not mean that these Pharisees and Sadducees are promiscuous, but rather that they are prone to idolatry.

Although Paul seems to direct his comments in vss. 17–24 against self-righteous Jews who do not live outwardly sinful lives, he knows that what faces outward often bears little resemblance to what is inside. Nevertheless, when Paul discusses stealing, he probably is not referring to armed robbery or burglary, which are overt and visible if one is caught. He likely has in mind shorting customers when weighing out goods or misleading customers about the quality of items, theft that can be plausibly defended as accidental. These are the more common sins of the hypocrite. In the charge of adultery, Paul may have in mind coveting another man's wife (Exod 20:17) or lust (Matt 5:27–29).

Paul's question, "Do you plunder temples?" is perplexing. It is reasonable to ask, Would Paul's Jewish audience generally admit to plundering temples? Most would probably never set foot in pagan temples, and they would certainly not plunder the Jerusalem temple. The word *hieron*, often translated "temple," and here fashioned into the verb of Paul's question, literally means "holy place" or "holy thing." Is Paul asking if the Jews to whom he speaks ever destroy what is holy? If so, then Paul's question not only makes sense, but it is very revealing of the situation at Rome.

If the believing Jews to whom Paul writes have been tearing down gentile believers or gentile house churches, is this not a sacrilege of what is holy? Paul regularly teaches that the body of Christ, both his physical body and the church, are now God's temple (see 1 Cor 3:16 and 2 Cor 6:16). In 1 Cor 3:17 Paul warns, "If someone destroys God's temple, God will destroy that person."

Another interesting possibility has been proposed by my friend Michael A. Stone. He suggests that some Jewish believers at Rome craved the virtues associated with certain pagan gods, whether that be wisdom in warfare (Athena/Juno), beauty (Aphrodite/Venus), luck and prosperity (Tyche/Fortuna), etc. By coopting the values pagan temples idealized, metaphorically they "robbed temples."[8]

Vs. 24: The scriptural quotation in this verse is from the LXX of Isa 52:5. Paul's point is that there is a long history of Jews dishonoring their God. The mere appearance of Jewish identity does not make a person righteous.

Vss. 25–29: In this passage Paul makes his point through three important contrasts: physical circumcision versus circumcision of the heart; the Jew in outward appearance versus the Jew in what is hidden; and the Spirt versus the letter. In each case, what is inward is more important than what is outward.

Vs. 27: In the clause "while [*dia*] you have the letter and circumcision," the use of *dia* is unusual. Lexically it might mean "because you have the letter and circumcision," but Paul does not seem to be blaming these things. Instead, he suggests they make little practical difference. On the possibility of *dia* meaning "while," see Bl-D-F §223.3.

Vs. 29: Paul's use of the expression "Jew in what is hidden" to refer to the gentile believer is a serious blow to the Dispensationalist principle that the Bible always distinguishes between the church and Israel (God's two separate peoples). Here Paul suggests that believing gentiles become what we might call *spiritual Israel*. To call a gentile a "Jew in what is hidden" resembles what Paul says in Rom 11:17–24, where he speaks of gentiles, represented by the image of branches of the wild olive tree, being grafted into the domesticated olive tree, which represents Israel.

---

8. Private email from Michael A. Stone dated Nov. 21, 2023.

Excursus: "O Man"

IN ROMANS AND THE REST OF THE NT

Three times in Romans (at 2:1, 2:3, and 9:20) we find the curious expression "O Man" (*ō anthrōpe*). In the Greek, the particle "O" that precedes the noun emphasizes that "Man" occurs in the vocative case, indicating that Man is being directly addressed. I have capitalized "Man" here to indicate that the word is used generically to refer not to a particular man, but rather to mankind, or more precisely, to every human individual. The RSV inserts an entire clause not found in the Greek to make the same point: "O man, *whoever you are*."

Beyond the three occurrences we have just discussed, the word "O" ("ō" in Greek) is found one additional time in Romans (at 11:33), but there it seems to function not as a sign of the vocative but rather as an interjection, that is, a word that provides emphasis but otherwise has no grammatical function in its sentence: "O the depth of riches . . . ." To say this differently, "O" is not a sign of the vocative here because "the depth of riches" is not being directly addressed. Instead, this is an interjection expressing amazement. Paul is amazed at God's wisdom, and "O" simply adds emotion to the words that follow.

Paul is not the only NT author to use "O" (ō in Greek). In total ō occurs 17 times in the Greek New Testament, not counting the three times the letter appears simply to represent the final letter of the Greek alphabet (in the expression "Alpha and Omega").

IMPACT ON ENGLISH GRAMMAR

The way "O" is used in Romans and elsewhere in the NT has had an impact on the development of English grammar. The English words "O" and "Oh" probably both derive from the Greek usage being described here. This impact was mediated through the Latin translations of the Bible, especially the Vulgate. Based on the Greek, in Romans 2:1, 2:3, and 9:20 the Vulgate simply inserts "o" before "homo," its rendering of "man." Early English Bibles continued this pattern of retaining the word "O," thus the now familiar "O Man." In a later development, the English word "Oh" appeared as a variant spelling of "O."

In modern English vocatives are not used much outside of prayers and worship songs. But in those contexts, they are quite common, with "O" and "Oh" often being used indiscriminately and interchangeably. However, some have argued that "O" should be used where a vocative is indicated, and "Oh" should be used only as an interjection. Thus, it would be, "O Lord thou art great!" or "Bless the Lord, O my soul!" And it would be "Oh, how wonderful are your works, O Lord." While this might be an admirable principle for English usage, Greek usage is not so consistent. As already stated, the Greek of Rom 9:20 uses ō as an interjection, "O the depths of riches . . . ."

IMPACT ON ENGLISH LITERATURE

It is my opinion that Rom 2:1 has also had an important impact on English literature (probably through the intermediaries of Latin and Dutch). I speak of the medieval morality play *The Summoning of Everyman*, or as it is more commonly called, *Everyman*. While some have dated this work to as early as the ninth century, the scholarly consensus is now that it is an early sixteenth century work, and that it not an original English composition but rather a translation of the fifteenth-century Dutch work *Den Spyeghel der Salicheyt van Elckerlijc* ("The Mirror of the Salvation of Everyman"). In both versions, the protagonist faces the prospect of his own death by exploring how he might invest his resources and efforts in this life to achieve a reward in the next life. The NT parables of the Rich Young Man (Matt 19:16–30//Mark 10:17–31//Luke 18:18–30) and the Talents (Matt 25:14–30) are notable influences.

However, I think the work's name reflects the language of Rom 2:1. In the Greek, that verse contains the words *ō anthrōpe pas ho krinōn*. These five words present a bit of an exegetical challenge: With what is the word *pas* ("every") most closely connected, what precedes or what follows? Is it, "O Every Man, the one judging . . ." or "O Man, everyone judging . . ."? The Latin Vulgate seems to favor the first option when it converts the participial clause of the Greek into a relative clause: "O Every Man, who judges . . . ." When read this way, the direct address implied by the vocative seems to regard "Every Man" as a name. It is quite easy to imagine a creative author collapsing this into a one-word name "Everyman," and then making him the protagonist of his morality play. In a very real sense, in the beginning of Romans 2 Paul himself addresses Everyman.

Excursus: The Law and the Lawless

THE "LAW"

There is no doubt that the Greek word *nomos* (usually translated "law") is an important word in Romans. Almost automatically people from the modern West think of *nomos* as legal regulation. But for the ancient Greeks *nomos* was a broader term than the modern English term "law." It was common to relegate "nature" (*physis*) and "law" or "custom" (*nomos*) to separate realms. Nature described what was common among all peoples regardless of their nationality. Law or custom described what was variable and peculiar to one people group and not to others. *Nomos* ("law" or "custom") therefore encompassed much more than formal governmental edicts. Matters of convention such as dress and social organization fell under the heading of *nomos*.

Similarly, *torah*, the Hebrew word so often translated by *nomos* in the LXX, had a broad meaning within Judaism. It could refer to the five books of Moses even though only a minority of this material contains regulations, much more being devoted to narrative, prayer, or worship. The Psalms repeatedly celebrate the Lord's *torah* (e.g., Ps. 1:2; Ps. 19:7; Ps. 119:18), which is pictured as conveying wisdom and suggests that more than legal codes are in mind. Thus, the word "instruction" is often a better translation of *torah* than "law."

The Pharisees of Paul's day—and remember that he had once been one of them—spoke of two *toroth* (the plural of *torah*): the written *torah*; and the oral *torah*. The written *torah* was Scripture; the oral *torah* was divine revelation Moses shared orally with Joshua, who passed it on to the elders of Israel, who then passed it on to the next generation, who also passed it on as well (*m.Aboth* 1.1). Thus, the oral tradition was thought to have been transmitted from one generation to the next and what was implicit in it was elaborated and made more explicit in a cascade extending to Paul's own day and beyond it. This theory clearly indicates that for the Pharisees *torah* involved much more than simply the books of Moses. It also involved wisdom unrelated to legislation or judicial pronouncements.

In the first century AD many Jews regarded their community possession of the *torah* and living their lives regulated by the *torah* as the chief boundary markers that distinguished them from the gentiles. *Torah* meant a Jewish way of life, which in the eyes of a Greek would have been understood as Jewish custom. Thus, both *nomos* and *torah* could embrace the notion of custom. This fluidity of meaning is probably why the LXX typically translates *torah* with *nomos*, and we should avoid thinking of *nomos* too narrowly.

In Romans 1 Paul contends revelation is given to all—Jew and gentile alike—through the abundant evidence of a creator reflected in the world around us, which is his handiwork. But this evidence does not lead people to honor God or to give him thanks. Instead, this general revelation only reveals the darkness of their hearts and their refusal to see the truth, thus condemning them to the consequences of this refusal.

However, some commentators read the next chapter as taking this blanket condemnation back, for in Rom 2:14 Paul writes: "When gentiles, who by nature do not have the Law, do the things of the Law . . . ." Does Paul here suggest that some pagans have hearts that are not so darkened to keep them from discerning the truth evident in the natural world? Does he suggest that on the basis of this revelation in nature they are able to live morally and uprightly before God? Not at all.

The gentiles Paul discusses in 2:14 are believers in Christ, not run-of-the-mill gentiles. In fact, they are the gentile believers (alongside Jewish believers) to whom Paul has sent his letter. The rhetorical power of Paul's argument rests on the contrast between the blanket condemnation of the wicked gentile world pictured in chapter 1 and those gentiles who do the things of the Law pictured in chapter 2. This contrast highlights what an extraordinary thing these gentile believers represent.

When Paul says that gentiles by nature do not possess the Law [of Moses], he is articulating the conventional Jewish view of the situation in which the Law of Moses was the unique possession of Israel. If these gentiles did possess the Law [of Moses], this would be unexpected, even unnatural (but not wrong).

However, many gentiles were aware of the Law of Moses, even if they did not know it in any detail. In fact, Isa 66:19 suggests that God's "glory" will be dispersed throughout the gentile world as Israel is dispersed among the nations. Thus, even the disaster of the diaspora served to bring about God's ultimate purposes.

Within Judaism God's glory has often been closely linked with the *torah*. At Mt. Sinai, after the great sin of the golden calf and Moses' destruction of the original tablets written by the finger of God, the great prophet ascended the mountain again. When in the company of the Lord once again, Moses makes a request: "Show me your glory!" (Exod 33:18). In response, he is commanded to cut new stone tablets, and the Lord promises to write on them again. Since the tablets reflect the core of the Law, the association of God's glory with the Law is quite natural.

When Paul says that gentiles "do [*poieō*] the things of the Law," he implies that they were living in a manner Jews found commendable and God-honoring. This does not require that these gentiles lived this way with no knowledge of the Scriptures (i.e., the Old Testament), of Jewish worship, or of Jewish behavioral norms. But these gentiles had not converted to Judaism, or they would no longer have been gentiles. Almost certainly Paul is speaking of gentile Christ-followers, so they would have become acquainted to some degree with the scriptures through their worship, and it is also likely they understood the legal and ritual obligations of Israel's covenant to be Jewish custom but not their own custom.

A sizeable number of commentators have disagreed with the analysis just outlined. They argue that the word *physei* ("by nature") does not modify the verb "have," as I have done, but rather the verb "do" (*poieō*), leading to the translation, "[they] by nature do the things of the Law." While grammatically this is possible, rhetorically it is problematic because it confuses the standard Greek distinction between *physis* ("nature") and *nomos* ("law/custom"). It is not a problem to imply that Jews normally (i.e., "by nature") have the Law. But it is a violation of the *physis/nomos* divide to imply that based on what is built in (*physis*) people follow certain customs (*nomos*).

Interestingly, in extant literary Greek the precise phrase Paul uses in 2:14 *ta tou nomou* ("the things of the law") occurs only once prior to its appearance in Paul's epistle. Plato's *Gorgias* (483, a, 4) contrasts *ta tēs physeōs* ("the things of nature") with *ta tou nomou* (which in this text should be translated "the things of custom").

Paul implies, but does not specifically state, that the gentile followers of Jesus in Rome were creating a new identity and a new custom. They constitute "a custom of their own (*heautois eisin nomos*)." Perhaps we see here the first glimmer of a notion that would later develop more fully of gentile Christians as "a third race," not Jewish, not gentile, but something new.

THE LAWLESS

Many find it surprising to learn that in the first century AD Greek was the most commonly used language in Rome. Latin had its place in governmental and military circles, but Greek was the language of everyday life. Greek was the standard language of worship for Roman Christians up through the end of the second century, and this likely was true in the synagogue as well, although some Hebrew may also have been incorporated. This was the diaspora after all.

The standard Bible (Old Testament) in use was the Old Greek or LXX. The translation of the LXX from the Hebrew began in the third century BC and is associated with the Jewish community of Alexandria, Egypt. Some of the decisions made by the translators had important and long-lasting repercussions. One of the most important was the practice of translating general Hebrew words for the wicked or morally obtuse (e.g. *rashaʿ, pashaʿ*) with *anomos* ("lawbreaker" or "lawless"). This word is made up of two parts, the so-called "alpha privative," which negates, and *nomos*, meaning "law" or "custom." As this word is used in the LXX, it generally means "contrary to law/custom" or "lawbreaker." This word is an adjective, although it is most often used substantivally, which is to say, more-or-less as a noun. An associated adverb (*anomōs*) appears once in the LXX in 2 Maccabees, a book originally composed in Greek. Paul uses this adverb twice in Rom 2:12, the only places in the New Testament where this adverb occurs.

Paul uses *anomōs* in a way that differs from its use in the LXX and the use of the related adjective (*anomos*) in the LXX. In Romans it does not mean "in a manner contrary to law/custom" but rather "lawlessly" or "without the Law." Paul points out that the gentiles "by nature"—meaning roughly "by common experience"—are without Jewish law or custom, i.e. they are without the Law of Moses. Paul knows that gentiles are not without any sort of law or custom at all.

At many points the New Testament makes clear that the place of the Law of Moses was a flashpoint between Jewish and gentile followers of Jesus. An associated idea was the image of God as the great Judge, who righteously pronounces judgment at the last day. Jewish believers worried that marginalizing the Law of Moses would efface the role and status of God as the righteous Judge.

Paul has no interest in minimizing God's role as judge. He is just as unwilling to impugn God's righteousness. The project he undertakes in his epistle to the Romans is to explain how gentile believers in Jesus Christ, whom some Jews consider *anomos*, might be saved by the righteous and omniscient Judge.

An associated issue is what Paul depicts as widespread Jewish pride in keeping the Law. Many Jews believed their practice of the statutes, commands, and ordinances of the Law gave them an elevated moral status, especially when compared with the gentiles surrounding them. Paul regards the Law as holy and spiritual (Rom 7:12, 14), but it can also be used to establish a righteousness of one's own rather than "the righteousness of God" (Rom 10:3). It can make people feel they are deserving of God's gifts. This was despite Moses's teaching that the Lord led Israel into the promised land "not because of your righteousness" but rather to punish the godlessness of the current inhabitants and "that his covenant might stand" (Deut 9:5). Being chosen is a gift; it is not earned. So, if God chooses to extend his favor to gentiles as well as Jews, that is his right.

ROMANS 3

TRANSLATION: ROM 3:1–8

JEWS HAVE ADVANTAGES

¹What then is the advantage of the Jew? Or, of what benefit is circumcision? ²Much in every way! First, they were entrusted with the sayings of God. ³Of course, even if some were unfaithful, does their unfaithfulness nullify the faithfulness of God? ⁴Absolutely not! Let God be true, even if "every human is a liar!" as it is written:

> So that you may be proved right in your sayings,
>
> and you will be victorious when you judge.

⁵But if our wickedness highlights the righteousness of God, what shall we say? Is not God, the one bringing wrath, wicked? (I say this from a human perspective.) ⁶Absolutely not! [If that were the case,] then how could God judge the world? ⁷"But if God's truth abounds to his glory by my false dealing, why am I still judged as sinful?" ⁸Is this not just how we are mocked, and how some say we say that we should do evil things in order that good things may come? Of these people, condemnation is just.

COMMENTARY

Vss. 1–8: Since in the previous section of text (2:12–29) Paul has argued that believing gentiles become "Jews in what is hidden," this raises the question of whether there is any benefit to being a Jew. Paul answers this question with a resounding "Yes!" but then in vss. 9–20 he also insists God shows no partiality.

In this passage Paul also asserts that when God condemns sin, it brings him glory since this displays the high standards of his own righteousness; he could not demand righteousness from others if he were not righteous himself. However, some have suggested that if God receives glory whether his people sin or do not sin, why not just live a lax life and sin? Paul rejects this suggestion completely.

Vs. 2: Paul gives a short list of advantages to being a Jew. He gives a longer list in 9:4–5. He uses the expression "sayings of God" rather than "the Law," which is his more usual verbiage, because he wants to match (roughly) a phrase from the scriptural passage he intends to quote.

Vs. 3: The words "unfaithful," "unfaithfulness," and "faithfulness" could also be translated as "disloyal," "disloyalty," and "loyalty." Each of these words translates a form of *pistis* ("faith," "loyalty," or "allegiance") or a related word. The point is that even if some Jews were disloyal to God, he will not be disloyal to them.[1]

Vs. 4: "Absolutely not!" (*mē genoito*): This expression is common in Paul's writings, and it reflects an old formula. This is the first occurrence of this expression in the Pauline corpus, which occurs ten times in Romans (3:4, 6, 31; 6:2, 15; 7:7, 13; 9:14; and 11:1, 11). It also occurs in 1 Cor 6:15; Gal 2:17; Gal 3:21; and Gal 6:14. Paul very rarely uses the optative mood, but the verb *genoito* is in the optative. The fact that it is a traditional formula explains this deviation from his normal avoidance of the optative.

The clause "as it is written" probably refers to the lines that follow, even though what immediately precedes the clause is also a quotation. The preceding quotation is from Ps 115:2 in the LXX (Ps 116:11 in the English and in the MT). The quotation that follows is from Ps 50:6 in the LXX (Ps 51:4 in the English and Ps 51:6 in the MT). These quotations affirm the absolute trustworthiness of God. What I have translated "that you may be proved right" (an aorist passive subjunctive of *dikaioō*) is often translated "that you may be justified." It is quite unusual to speak of God as this verse and Ps 50:6 (LXX) do. They seem to picture God himself being on trial.

Vs. 5: The expression *ti eroumen* ("what shall we say?") is similar to a fuller expression that appears six times in Romans. For more about this, see the comment on 3:9.

Vs. 6: "Absolutely not!" appears here again, as it did in vs. 4. Paul emphatically rejects any hint that God is wicked.

It is possible to argue that literally this verse asks, "How will God judge the world?" not how *could* he do this. This is because the verb is future imperfect in form. If Paul were writing classical Greek, this argument would

---

1. Bates, *Salvation by Allegiance Alone*, 80.

be compelling. In classical Greek a potential optative would have been used to express "how could God do this?" But Paul is writing Hellenistic Greek, which has simplified the grammar and virtually eliminated the use of optative forms. Therefore, Paul must use the future indicative to express a future potential possibility.[2]

Vss. 7–8: I have put the question, "But if God's truth abounds to his glory by my false dealing, why am I still judged as sinful?" in quotation marks. Because Paul is engaging in a diatribe, a somewhat artificial debate with an opponent of his own creation, perhaps this is not necessary. However, vs. 8 suggests that Paul has heard this very question raised by people who challenge his teaching. He gives voice to this question so that he can dismiss it as being completely unworthy.

TRANSLATION: ROM 3:9–20

BUT GOD IS IMPARTIAL

⁹What shall we say then? Are we [Jews] better off? Not at all! For previously we advanced the argument that both Jews and Greeks all are under the power of sin, ¹⁰as it is written,

> There is no righteous person, not one.
> ¹¹There is no person of understanding,
> There is no one who seeks after God.
> ¹²All turn away from him,
> and immediately they become corrupt.
> There is no one doing good, not even one.
> ¹³Their throat is an open grave,
> they deceive with their tongues,
> the venom of asps is under their lips.
> ¹⁴Their mouth is filled with cursing and bitterness.
> ¹⁵Their feet are quick to shed blood.
> ¹⁶Destruction and misery lie in their paths,
> ¹⁷and they do not know the way of peace.
> ¹⁸There is no fear of God before their eyes.

¹⁹We know that what the Law says, it says to those accused by the Law, in order that every mouth might be gagged, and the entire world might

---

2. Bl-D-F §385.

become answerable to God ²⁰since by works of the Law no human being will be cleared when standing before him, for through the Law only comes identification of sin.

COMMENTARY

Vss. 9–20: This passage is dominated by a *catena* (Latin for "chain") of quotations or paraphrases from the Old Testament. *Catena* are sometimes also called *florilegia* (singular *florilegium*, Latin for "a collection of flowers" i.e., a collection of special texts). These quotations or paraphrases are linked by catchwords that relate one passage to the next. A sequence of references to parts of the body is the main device for stringing these passages together.

The point of these texts is that Israel often sinned, and therefore Jews should not be automatically regarded as more virtuous than gentiles. The Law of Moses identifies what is sinful, but piling up "works of the Law" does not clear a person when judged by God.

Vs. 9: The full question "What shall we say then?" (*Ti oun eroumen*) does not appear here. Instead, the Greek provides an abridged form of it "What therefore?" (*ti oun*), which I have expanded. The full form of the expression appears six times in Romans, at 4:1, 6:1, 7:7, 8:31, 9:14, and 9:30, plus near matches in 3:5 and 9:19. Oddly, despite the full expression's frequent use in Romans, it appears in none of Paul's other letters. Paul uses this expression not so much to make transitions as to refocus his argument. It does not mark the beginning of a completely new topic as does *peri de* ("now concerning") in 1 Corinthians. Rather, it sometimes means more-or-less "so, the point I have been moving toward is . . . ."

Paul follows, "What shall we say then?" with a second question: "Are we better off? This is a partial restatement of the question that opens chapter 3: "What then is the advantage of the Jew?" In this verse the word "Jew" is omitted, but it is implied.

One might think Paul's answer to this question, *ou pantōs*, should be translated, "Not completely." However, his use of the expression elsewhere suggests that "not at all" is his meaning. In 1 Cor 5:9–10 Paul references his famous "previous letter," demonstrating that 1 Corinthians was not the first letter he wrote to the Corinthians. He says, "I wrote you in my letter not to interact with immoral people, not at all (*ou pantōs*) meaning the immoral of this world . . . ." In 1 Cor 16:12 his use of the phrase is similar although the order of the words (*pantōs ouk*) is reversed.

Although the Jews have been blessed by receiving "the sayings of God" (vs. 3), they, like the gentiles, are held under the power of sin. Some might ask: Is Paul talking out of both sides of his mouth? Do the Jews have an advantage or do they not?

I think an anecdote from my own life might illustrate Paul's perspective. About a decade ago I was teaching at a university one of my sons attended, and he registered for a course with me. He took the same exams as everyone else in the course, which were objective in nature, and he wrote the same papers as all the other students. These papers were graded by a teaching assistant, so other than overseeing the process, I took no part in grading the papers. Also, he got no special tutoring in the course. Considering these factors, my son had no objective advantage over his peers. However, my son knew how I think very well. Over the years we had talked about many things relevant to the course. Did that give him an advantage? Of course it did, and he received an "A" as his course grade. So, which is it? Did he have an advantage or not? The answer is both, depending on the perspective. I think this is essentially Paul's point. Based on external criteria, the Jews have no advantage over gentiles, but how can a national history of focusing on divine values not have a subjective impact?

Vss. 10–12: The biblical material Paul cites is a paraphrase of Ps 14:1–3 (= Ps 53:2–4). In the LXX the equivalent references are Ps 13:1–3 (=Ps 52:2–4).[3] Paul's use of the word *dikaios* may come from the LXX of Eccl 7:20. It is important to point out the crucial role of Psalm 14 in the argument Paul lays out in Romans.

Vss. 13–18: This text in these verses matches the LXX text of Ps. 13:3 perfectly. However, there is a problem. The equivalent psalm in the MT is Psalm 14, but there is no equivalent in the MT of that psalm to Paul's long quotation in Rom 3:13–18. Most scholars believe that sometime in the Christian era the Greek of Rom 3:13–18 was incorporated into LXX manuscripts of Ps 13:3, building Paul's quotation of Ps 13:1 (=Rom 3:10–12). Paul's quotation is actually a catena ("chain") of quotations from various portions of scripture, as the comments below indicate.

Vs. 13: The first two strophes of Paul's quote match the LXX text of Ps 5:10 exactly. In the English and MT, the equivalent text is Ps 5:9. The third strophe is an exact quotation of the LXX text of Ps 139:4. The equivalent text in English is Ps 140:3. In the MT it is Ps 140:4.

---

3. Psalm 14 and Psalm 53 are nearly identical. Psalms is divided into five books, each of which was probably collected independently prior to being joined together into a single collection of Psalms. These earlier collections probably served as the hymnals the various courses of Levites used when singing in the Jerusalem temple. Apparently, the same psalm was appreciated and used by two different courses of Levites and was gathered into both Book 1 and Book 2 of the Psalter.

Vs. 14: Here Paul quotes the LXX text of Ps. 9:28 exactly. The equivalent text in the English and the MT is Ps 10:7.

Vss. 15–17: In these verses Paul paraphrases the LXX text of Isa 59:7–8.

Vs. 18: The text Paul writes in this verse exactly matches the LXX of Ps 35:2, except that where Paul writes "their eyes" the LXX has "his eyes." The equivalent English passage is Ps 36:1. In the MT it is Ps 36:2.

Vs. 19: "To those accused by the Law": the construction *tois en tō nomō* (literally "to those in the Law" or "to those . . . by the Law") never appears in Greek literature before Paul, and after Paul only in Christian literature, usually quoting him. Therefore, it seems to be his coinage. Eusebius understands this to mean that the Law speaks only to the wicked: "to those [accused] by the Law," since those who are not lawbreakers have no need of the Law. This interpretation fits the context well and probably is correct.

Paul's contention that *every* mouth will be gagged and the *whole world* held accountable suggested to Origen (and many others after him) that in this verse the word *nomos* ("law") did not refer exclusively to the Law of Moses but rather also included natural law.[4] To him the point is that every person is a lawbreaker; only the specific law code that is broken—Law of Moses or law of nature—varies.

Barth takes a different tack. He understands *tois en tō nomō* to be equivalent to Paul's more common formulation *hypo nomon* ("under [the] Law"). In other words, Paul here suggests that the Law of Moses condemns the faithlessness of Jews, not the sinfulness of both Jews and gentiles. As Barth sees it, the gentiles already stand condemned. When the Law of Moses also condemns faithless Jews, they are added to the gentiles, in order that "every mouth might be gagged, and the entire world might become answerable to God."

It is at this point in his commentary where Barth deploys the controversial image of "the empty canal" that highlights by its absence the water no longer flowing in it. In Barth's view Israelite religion once was vibrant and filled with faith in God. He pictures the Judaism in Paul's day as ritualistic and devoid of true religious value, like a dry riverbed that no longer contains water. It brings to mind what used to flow, not what currently flows.[5]

---

4. Reasoner suggests Origen included natural law. *Romans in Full Circle*, 23–24. In a modern affirmation of this view, Koester says Paul argues "both Jew and gentiles possess full knowledge of God and the law. The law of nature which is given to the gentiles (Rom 2:12–16) is thus entirely equivalent to the law of the Bible." Koester, *History and Literature*, 140.

5. Barth, *Epistle to the Romans*, 87–88.

Barth's image has been widely denounced as antisemitic, and I think it misses Paul's point. Paul is not contrasting the vibrancy of earlier Israelite religion with the dead Judaism of his present day. Instead, Paul argues that "works of the Law" unaccompanied by faith have never pleased God either in the past or in the present. Paul himself is an example of a vibrant Judaism enlivened by faith.

Despite Barth's unfortunate imagery, I think he is probably correct that 3:9–20 is directed at Jews who hold themselves to be superior to gentiles simply because of their identity as Jews.

Vs. 20: In this verse the important phrase "works of the Law" first appears. *For a fuller discussion of this phrase, see the excursus titled "Works of the Law."*

According to my translation Paul writes, "through the Law only comes identification of sin." The Greek word translated "identification" is *epignōsis*. Most translations render this word "knowledge," but since *gnosis* by itself means "knowledge," what then is the force of the prefix *epi* (which often means "on" or when prefixed to a verb serves to intensify it)? Here I think it transforms the basic word, making it mean something like "recognition" or "identification." Paul's point is that the Law identifies sin; it points out the problem. But it provides no solution to the problem of sin.

TRANSLATION: ROM 3:21–31

JESUS, THE GREAT SIN OFFERING

[21] But now, the righteousness of God has been manifested apart from the Law, although it is testified to by the Law and the Prophets. [22] This righteousness of God is shown through the faithfulness of Jesus Christ for those who believe. For there is no distinction. [23] For all have sinned and do not measure up to the glory of God, [24] being cleared freely by his grace through the redemption found in Jesus Christ, [25] whom God set forth as a mercy seat sacrifice through faith in his blood. This was to show the evidence of his righteousness in light of the withholding of past sin offerings. [26] God being longsuffering, this was to show the evidence of his righteousness at the present time, in order to be righteous himself as well as the one declaring the individual upright by the faithfulness of Jesus.

[27] Then where is boasting? It is excluded. Through which law? The law of works? Certainly not, rather through the law of faith. [28] For we reckon a person to be justified by faith without works of the Law. [29] Or is God the God of the Jews only? Is he not also the God of the gentiles? Yes, also of the

gentiles. ³⁰Since God is one, he will declare the circumcised upright by faith and the uncircumcised upright through faith. ³¹We do not nullify the Law through faith. Certainly not. Rather, we uphold the Law.

COMMENTARY

Vss. 21–31: This passage contains the most complete discussion of "God's righteousness" found in Romans, or for that matter all of Paul's writings. In this passage he argues that Jesus Christ not only manifests God's righteousness without relying on the Law of Moses, he also manifests God's righteousness more widely since faith in Jesus has been made available to both Jews and gentiles. If the Mosaic Law is not the only way God has demonstrated his righteousness, then the Law is not so essential as some Jews suppose. This means that Jews have no right to boast of superiority over gentiles.

Some of Paul's opponents, and perhaps some in Rome, have accused Paul of being lax about God's righteous standards, i.e., his righteousness. But Paul will have none of this. He insists the God's righteousness lies at the center of his gospel. Jesus Christ and his sacrificial death are the ultimate manifestation of God's righteousness expressed through his righteous plan, also known as "the gospel."

This passage further suggests something about the nature of God's righteousness: He upholds his standards, but in a merciful way. While God could have exacted punishment for past sins, especially since sin offerings for these sins had been neglected, instead he chose to "set forth" his son (vs. 25) as a perpetual sin offering, making up for the omission of neglected sin offerings and demonstrating his righteousness.

These verses are very densely argued. Steps in Paul's argument seem to have been omitted, perhaps because Paul thought these steps would be obvious to his readers. The problem is that they are not so obvious to modern readers. Part of the problem is the precise meanings of four words: *hilastērion* (vs. 25); *paresis* (vs. 25); *hamartēma* (vs. 25); and *anochē* (vs. 26). The meanings of these words will be addressed below in comments to vs. 25 and to vs. 26.

Vs. 21: Paul's statement that the righteousness of God is testified to "by the Law and the Prophets" uses a construction used only of animate beings, i.e., use of the preposition *hypo* with its associated noun or nouns in the genitive case. (If something is accomplished by means of an inanimate object, another construction is required.) This means that Paul is personifying both "the Law" and "the Prophets." This is not without parallel. 4 Maccabees 22:9 reads: "And should someone be naturally stingy, he is ruled by the Law [*hypo tou nomou*] through reason, so that he neither gleans his crop nor gleans his vines."⁶ Here too the Law is personified and exercises agency.

Vs. 22: This verse has been a primary battleground in the Faith in Christ/Faithfulness of Christ debate. *See the excursus "Faith in Christ/Faithfulness of Christ Debate" for more details.* This verse argues that those believing in Christ experience God's righteousness through "the faithfulness of Jesus Christ," not through the Law.

Vs. 23: In this verse we find one of those great declarations that make Romans such an important and powerful landmark of the Christian faith. Although this declaration is famous, it is also widely misunderstood. Often translated, "For all have sinned and come short of the glory of God," many understand that assessment to be roughly equivalent either to "Nobody's perfect" or to "I'm only human." As a result, this verse is understood as an excuse for a measure of sin in one's life with the implication that God "grades on the curve." The implication is that if a person does not depart from the norm by sinning excessively, she is safe. However, Paul's point is almost diametrically the opposite of this. *Sin condemns everyone.* It is intolerable. Most pointedly, it affects Jew and gentile alike. Fortunately, this is not the end of the story. While all stand condemned, redemption is also available to all.

Vs. 24: The decision whether to translate *dikaioō* "cleared" or "justified" is a difficult one. Does it refer to the imputation of Christ's righteousness to the individual who receives it passively (the Reformation understanding)? Or does it refer to God the righteous judge finding in favor of the individual and announcing his verdict of "not guilty"? *For more on this, see the excursus "The Language of Righteousness and Justification."*

The important word *apolytrōsis* ("redemption") appears in Romans only here and at 8:23, where it speaks of "the redemption of our body." The word describes the release of someone when a ransom is paid, in this case the ransom payment being the death of Jesus on the cross. While the New Testament is clear that Christ's death constituted a ransom, to whom the payment was made is never clarified. The fathers of the early church generally assumed the payment was made to Satan, but in the West following the publication of Anselm's *Cur Deus Homo?* (Why the God-Man?) sometime in the 1090s, most came to regard the payment as being made to satisfy the just requirements of God's righteous nature. In the East, the whole notion of ransom is downplayed to the point of elimination.

Vs. 25: The images in this passage are drawn from the sacrificial practice in the temple, particularly the sin offering described in Lev 4:27–35 and the Day of Atonement ritual described in Lev 16. The word *hilastērion*

---

6. 4 Maccabees likely was composed later than Romans.

appears in Lev 16:13 (LXX), and *hamartēma* appears in Lev 4:29 (LXX). In both passages young goats are offered as sacrifices for the atonement of sins.

This raises the question of whether these words mean the same thing in Romans 3 as in Leviticus. In Lev 16:13, *hilastērion* refers to the "mercy seat" (Hebrew *kapporet*), a kind of cover to the ark of the covenant. This is the consistent meaning of the word throughout the LXX.[7] Consequently, many exegetes, extending back as early as Origen, take this tack. Others translate it more abstractly as "propitiation" or "expiation," relying for this meaning largely on the use of the related adjective *hilastērios* in Josephus, *Antiquities* 16.182 and on the meaning of the cognate verb *hilaskomai*. As a reminder, the word "propitiation" refers to "averting God's anger." "Expiation" refers to "the removal of defilement."

In 4 Macc 17:22, the famous story of a mother who is martyred along with her seven sons is commemorated in this way: "And through the blood of those devout people and the propitiation (*hilastērion*) of their death, divine providence preserved Israel that had previously been mistreated." If this passage refers to a "mercy seat," it does so metaphorically, considering the place of the martyrdom as spiritually equivalent to the mercy seat covering the ark.

As mentioned above, the adjective *hilastērios* appears in Josephus, *Ant* 16.182, where it refers to a *hilastērion mnēma* ("propitiatory monument"). Josephus tells the colorful tale of Herod, after hearing that his predecessor Hyrcanus had found items of great value in King David's tomb, decided to plunder the tomb again, seeing if Hyrcanus had overlooked anything of value. However, when two of Herod's guards attempted to enter a chamber deep within the bowels of the tomb, they were consumed by fire. Fearing greatly because of this apparent act of divine judgment, Herod built his "propitiatory monument" of white stone "at the mouth of the sepulcher." Josephus suggests that Herod built this monument to avert the judgment and wrath of God, or to state this differently, to propitiate God. However, it is also true that the Herod of this story would not have built the monument if his guards had not died. So, the monument was intended both to commemorate a sacrifice and to avert continuing wrath from God.

Those who suggest translating *hilastērion* either "propitiation" or "expiation" focus on the way the cognate verb *hilaskomai* is used. This verb appears twice in the NT, in Luke 18:13 and in Heb 2:17. In Luke a penitent tax collector uses an aorist passive imperative form of the verb. This is often translated, "Be merciful!" but literally it means "Be propitiated" or perhaps

---

7. This presumes the generally observed pattern of not including 4 Maccabees among the books of the LXX.

"Let your anger be assuaged." The Hebrews text describes Jesus either "making expiation" or "making a [sin] offering" for the sins of the people. In the context, both translations make sense.

In various passages of the LXX the verb *hilaskomai* translates three different Hebrew verbs: *nacham* ("to be merciful"; Exod 32:14); *salach* ("to forgive"; 2 Kgs 5:18, 24:4; 2 Chr 6:30; Ps 24:11 [25:11]; Lam 3:42); and *kaphar* ("to cover" or "to forgive"; Ps 64:4 [65:4]; 77:38 [78:38]). This evidence suggests that the LXX translators thought the basic sense of *hilaskomai* involved forgiveness, not propitiation.

One great difficulty with understanding *hilastērion* to mean "propitiation" is that the logic of God "setting forth" or "presenting" a propitiation to avert his own wrath seems rather convoluted. It makes better sense to understand God proposing an alternative "mercy seat sacrifice" or "forgiveness sacrifice" to make up for the many sin offerings that individuals had not made over the years. These offerings were supposed to take place whenever a "person of the land," i.e., a regular Israelite as opposed to a high ("anointed") priest or a high-ranking political leader, committed a sin *akousiōs* ("involuntarily").[8] (This word is apparently a biform of *aekousiōs*, which combines the alpha privative (*a-*) with *ekousiōs* ["voluntarily"]).

In general, a sin seems to have been regarded as "involuntary" whenever it was anything short of formal, public blasphemy ("the sin of the high hand"; Num 15:30–31). This understanding is out of line with modern sensibilities, so this can be hard for modern readers to grasp. For instance, except under very unusual circumstances, today theft is regarded as voluntary, while according to the standard Jewish interpretation of Paul's day, it would have been regarded as involuntary. In contrast, when Jesus was charged with a capital offense by the Sanhedrin[9] (Matt 26:59//Mark 14:55), no doubt he was officially alleged to have committed a "sin of the high hand"—formal blasphemy.

Another important word in this verse is the noun *hamartēma*, which occurs in the plural (*hamartēmata*). This word is related to the more common feminine noun *hamartia*, which is usually translated "sin." Like its more common counterpart, *hamartēma* also sometimes means "sin."

---

8. More costly sacrifices were required of high ("anointed") priests and political leaders (Lev 4:3–12, 22–26).

9. The word "sanhedrin," which is the name of a tractate of the Talmud and functions as a loan-word in Hebrew and Aramaic documents meaning "council," is a corruption of the Greek word *synedrion* ("council").

But both *hamartēma* and *hamartia* can mean "sin offering."[10] In the key verse Lev 4:29 (LXX) the sin offering is called the *hamartēma*. Similarly, in Rom 3:25 I believe the plural form of this word is used with the meaning "sin offerings."

Because of the way Paul links them in this verse, we will need to consider the meaning of the word *paresis* ("withholding" or "passing over") in conjunction with the meaning of *hamartēma*. The noun *paresis* is related to the verb *pariēmi*, which literally means "to go by." It can carry various shades of meaning, generally describing some measure of non-functioning or abeyance. The second half of vs. 25 is often translated something like the following: "This was to demonstrate [God's] righteousness because of the passing over of former sins . . . ," rendering *paresis* "passing over." I propose a distinct alternative: "This was to demonstrate his righteousness in light of the withholding of past sin offerings." In this translation *paresis* is rendered "withholding." In the traditional translation, God is the agent of *paresis*; in my alternative translation people are the agents of *paresis*. They have neglected to offer sin offerings.

There are four main reasons I prefer this interpretation to the more traditional one. First, it is hard for me to understand how Paul could with a blanket statement suggest that God simply "passed over" all sins that had transpired prior to the appearance of Jesus Christ. How then should the great flood be understood with its destruction of life as a judgment for "wickedness" (Gen 6:5)? How about the destruction of Sodom and Gomorrah (Gen 19:24–26)? Or for that matter how about the litany of groups of Israelites whom God destroyed for sinful behavior that Paul recounts as a warning in 1 Corinthians 10? These groups include the Israelite worship of the golden calf and the slaughter of 3,000 in response (Exod 32:28), the worship of the Baal of Peor and the ensuing plague in which 24,000 died (Num 25:9), Nadab and Abihu who offered strange fire before the Lord (Lev 10:1–2) and those who died with them, apparently 23,000 in number (Num 26:61–62), and the instigators led by Korah who rebelled against Moses and were then swallowed up when "the ground opened up its mouth" (Num 16:32).

Second, Rom 3:21–26 is filled with sacrificial imagery and language. While every interpreter will understand that Paul portrays Jesus's death as a redemptive sacrifice, reading *hamartēmata* as "sin offerings" rather than "sins" continues and underlines this emphasis on sacrifice.

---

10. In Rom 8:3 I believe *hamartia* means "a sin offering." There Paul uses the idiom so often used in the LXX, *peri hamartias* ("as a sin offering"), which is a dead giveaway of what he intends.

Third, it is important to remember that the Jewish believers to whom Paul writes were all diaspora Jews. While every adult male Jew in the diaspora was supposed to pay a half-shekel annual tax for the upkeep of the temple in lieu of visiting the temple for the three great high holidays, this still left them without full access to the sacrificial system. Specifically, they would have had no opportunity to make individual sin offerings, i.e., to atone for the failures that were uniquely their own. Paul is not brutal, but he makes clear that "those who know the Law" (Rom 7:1) also know that they have broken it and failed to atone for their sins.

Fourth, in this passage Paul also offers hope that the mass of sin offerings neglected over the years is not a burden of doom. God has provided an alternative way of meeting the requirement of sin (mercy-seat) offerings. This is through the blood of Jesus Christ. The traditional interpretation of this passage claims that God simply "passed over" past sins.[11] The interpretation contended for here suggests that these sins were not ignored; they have been redeemed by the sacrificial death of Christ. This makes the entire argument of vss. 21–26 more coherent.

Some may object that it is awkward to speak of "sin offerings that happened beforehand" (*progegononta*) when the point is that these offerings did not actually occur. However, this participle has likely become a "frozen form," simply meaning "past" regardless of the actual or hypothetical nature of the events under discussion. The verb *proginomai* (alternate form *progignomai*) only appears in the NT in this one passage, and it only appears in the LXX three times, and in those cases only in the Apocrypha, i.e., the later books originally written in Greek (2 Macc 14:3; 15:8; Wis 19:13).

Vs. 26: The verbiage I have translated "God being longsuffering" literally reads, "in the longsuffering of God." However, this phrase employs a circumstantial dative, so the translation is apt. The larger question is whether it should be construed with what precedes it (vs. 25), or with what follows (the remainder of vs. 26). I have chosen the latter course, although without great conviction.

The word *anochē* refers to holding something back. It is used with a wide variety of nuances; it can mean a "truce," "delay," "longsuffering," "forbearance," even "permission." In the context, it probably refers to God's "forbearance" or his "longsuffering."

The phrase "the evidence of his righteousness" that appeared in vs. 25 is repeated in this verse, but with the added qualification "at the present time." Whereas vs. 25 discusses the evidence of God's righteousness in light

---

11. Timothy Dresselhaus calls the theory that God simply passed over past sins "the divine mulligan."

of the withholding sin offerings in the wake of repeated sins, matters which relate to the past, in this verse the focus is on the evidence of God's righteousness in the present. While the repetition of this phrase seems awkward, the repletion is deliberate. In one fell swoop God deals with the past and the present through the sacrifice of his son. This assertion of God's present righteousness is amplified at the end of the verse by Paul's magnificent announcement of God's intention to be shown righteous himself and also to declare those he judges upright.

While the name Jesus appears in this verse rather than Christ, the dynamics surrounding the phrase *ek pisteōs Iēsou* are identical to those in the Faith in Christ/Faithfulness of Christ controversy. (*For more about this, see the excursus called "The Faith in Christ/Faithfulness of Christ Debate."*) The final part of the verse could be translated either "by faith in Jesus" (the more traditional translation) or "by the faithfulness of Jesus" (reflecting the newer approach).

Vs. 27: The primary puzzle of this verse is how to translate the word *nomos*, which in most contexts is rendered "Law" or "law." In contrast, many (most?) scholars here translate it "principle." Daniel Fuller notes Charles Hodge and other covenant theologians contend that in this verse the phrase *dia nomou pisteōs* means through "the principle of justification by faith alone," which seems a creative if not wild translation.[12] However, when Paul uses *nomos* he usually intends the Law of Moses, and that is not impossible in this verse. Sometimes when Paul refers to the Law, he means the regulations of the written Law, the regulations specified in the Oral Law, or "works of the Law," which he views negatively. At other times, he means "the books of Moses" or God's "instruction" in a general sense, which he views as positive and enlightening. That is why he so often quotes scripture, including the books of Moses. When he refers in this verse to "[the Law] of works," this is probably an alternative way of expressing "works of the Law." When he writes, "the Law of faith," he probably means "the Law, when it presents faith." Paul might characterize Genesis 15 as "the Law of faith," in as much as that passage presents Abraham's faith as a model.

Vss. 28–29: In these verses Paul makes clear that "works of the Law" are the exclusive purview of Jews. That is why a righteous Judge cannot issue verdicts based on such "works of the Law." To do so would exclude gentiles from his impartial and righteous judgment.

Vs. 30: Perhaps to nail down his argument that faith is taught in the Law and therefore the Law is not a problem when used properly, Paul cites in abbreviated form, the *Shema'*, the central confession of Judaism: "God is

---

12. Fuller, *Gospel and Law*, xi.

one." If there is only one God then that God must be the God of both the Jews and the gentiles. How could the gentiles possibly have another God? Some might think there are other gods, but this cannot possibly be correct. There is one God for both, and he dispenses justice with an even hand.

Paul's distinction between *ek pisteōs* ("by faith") and *dia tēs pisteōs* ("through [their] faith") is murky and maybe constitutes an attempt at humor, sort of like pretending there is a difference between a "to-may-to" and a "to-mah-to."

Vs. 31: Clearly Paul has been accused in some quarters of nullifying or overturning the Law. He rejects this adamantly, while at the same time maintaining opposition to misuse of the Law. When he supports the Law, he primarily has the Law as generalized divine instruction in mind.

Excursus: Works of the Law

The phrase "works of the Law" appears eight times in Paul's epistles, twice in Romans and six times in Galatians (Rom 3:20; 3:28; Gal 2:16 [three times]; 3:2; 3:5; and 3:10). The singular construction *to ergon tou nomou* ("the work of the Law") also appears once in the Pauline corpus, in Rom 2:15, and there it bears a positive connotation. In addition, the form *ta tou nomon* ("the things of the Law"), which could possibly be construed as "the works of the Law" appears once, in Rom. 2:14. The Hebrew form of "works of Law" (*m'sy twrh*) appears in *4QMMT* C 27,[13] and the very similar "works of the Law" (*m'sy htwrh*) appears in *4QFlor* (4Q174) 1.7,[14] both Dead Sea Scrolls documents.

---

13. The document known as 4QMMT, or MMT for short, is both untitled and anonymous. It gets the 4Q part of its name from the fact that fragments from six manuscripts of this document were found in Cave 4 at Khirbet Qumran. MMT is an abbreviation of *miqtsat ma'asey haTorah*, "some works of the Law" or perhaps "select precepts of the Law," one of the more striking phrases found in this document. In the Hebrew of the Dead Sea Scrolls, vowels are not printed.

14. *4QFlor* is an abbreviation for *4QFlorilegium*. Again, the 4Q portion of the name refers to Cave 4 at Khirbet Qumran, where the text was found. A florilegium is a chain of quotations from earlier documents, in this case the Old Testament. While 4QFlor probably mentions "works of the Law," a few scholars deny this. One of the letters in this phrase is unclear, and it is possible the phrase is "works of thanksgiving" (*m'sy htwdh*). Since the word *torah* ("Law") is approximately thirty times as common in the Old Testament as the word *todah* ("thanksgiving"), the likelihood is that the phrase is "works of the Law."

In Paul's letters, the word "work" (*ergon*) is a neutral term. There are good works and bad works, and the word is usually qualified in some way, sometimes with an adjective (e.g., "good" or "evil"), sometimes with a phrase (e.g., "works of the Law"). Often *ergon* is contrasted with or paired with something else: "in word and deed" (Rom 15:18); "works" or "faith" (Rom 3:27); "works" or "grace" (Rom 11:6); "works" or "calling" (Rom 9:12). Sometimes the quality of works is left uncharacterized because the point is that these works will be assayed in a future judgment (e.g., Rom 2:6). The phrase "work of God" appears in Rom 14:20. Similarly, the phrase "the work of the Lord" appears in 1 Cor 15:58 and 16:10. The Corinthian believers are said to be Paul's "work" (1 Cor 9:1).

When Paul uses the expression "works of the Law," he refers to a type of activity that at best is ineffective in obtaining at the final judgment a favorable verdict from God. But beyond not accomplishing this goal, Paul treats "works of the Law" as truly harmful because they lead to false hope, and they prevent an accurate understanding of God. He also implies that "works of the Law" constitute a "[Law] of works", which is contrary to the "law of faith" (Rom 3:27).

In some sense, "works of the Law" is a technical term, but what type of technical term is it, and what does it specify? Is it general? Is any effort to curry favor with God a work of the Law? Or does the phrase name a specific set of actions? In the document 4QMMT, mentioned above, it appears that "works of the Law" designate a specific set of exercises designed to produce righteousness.

This document dates from about 150 BC and takes the form of a letter from a leader of the Dead Sea Community—possibly the man they call The Teacher of Righteousness—to a potential ally who is a man of great authority since he leads people, possibly the greater part of Israel. The author disapproves of the current teachings of this powerful recipient, but he hopes to persuade him to change course. In lines 26–27 of the document, the author writes this: "Indeed we have sent you select works of the Law according to our decision, for your welfare and the welfare of your people." These "works of the Law" seem to be a code of conduct that the author believes, if followed, will result in greater righteousness for the recipient and his people. The specific wording of the letter exhorts that, if the recipient accepts the counsel offered, "this will be reckoned as righteousness to you, since you will be doing what is righteous and good in His [i.e., God's] eyes, for your own welfare and for the welfare of Israel" (lines 31–32).

Does this letter, written by a Dead Sea sectarian (probably an Essene) about a century before Paul writes Romans, tell us anything helpful about what Paul might mean by "works of the Law"? The Jewish believers to whom Paul writes are surely not Dead Sea sectarians or Essenes. Moreover, since Sadducees did not believe in resurrection or an afterlife, the followers of the risen Jesus in Rome are not likely to have been Sadducees. In the 50s of the first century, the Zealots were not yet an organized movement, and there was no practical way to exhibit zealotry in Rome, so Paul's audience would not have included Zealots. The Jewish believers to whom Paul writes are either Messianists who no longer identified with any of the main branches of Judaism—as was the case with Paul—or they are Jewish Christian Pharisees, perhaps not too different from those mentioned in Acts 15:5.

It is likely that the phrase "works of the Law" resonated with Jewish Christian Pharisees, whether they were overtly aligned with Phariseeism or were merely influenced by the ideas of Phariseeism. After the First Jewish War (AD 66–74), Phariseeism is better described as Rabbinic Judaism, but these are two phases of the same movement. Rabbinic Judaism expressed its belief in two forms of the Law passed down from Moses: the written Law; and the oral Law. In fact, the Mishnah, the earlier of the two parts of the Talmud, is essential written "oral Law," as oxymoronic as that sounds.

The Mishnah was not considered a commentary on the Pentateuch, as is sometimes suggested; it was regarded as a path separate from the written Law. It was a path transmitting divine Law from one generation to the next in oral form.[15] Oral Law could supplement although not contradict the written Law. Furthermore, a central strategy for avoiding sinful behavior was the construction of "a fence" around the Law, i.e., adding rules that are more rigorous than the statutes articulated in the written Law.[16] While these ideas were probably still somewhat inchoate in the middle of the first century, it is likely that the phrase "works of the Law" reflects an early form of that "fence" meant to keep people from even getting close to violating the written statutes. Because of the ambiguity caused by having two Laws, one oral and one written, "works of the Law" may well have referred to a mode of living directed by the extra-scrupulous standards of the oral Law as it was understood at the time.

---

15. This understanding of the oral Law is explicitly affirmed in *m.Abot* 1:1.

16. *M.Abot* 1.1. In a sense, this passage, which is part of the oral Law, defends the need for the entire framework of the oral Law.

We are handicapped since no documents written by a first-century Pharisee have survived (unless Paul himself is counted). But if the dynamics reflected in 4QMMT are any guide, "works of the Law" constituted a set of behavioral norms and following it was considered not only prudent but righteous in God's eyes.

Of course, Paul disagrees with this approach entirely. God looks on the heart. Following codes of external behavior will never lead to true righteousness. For this reason, the phrase "works of the Law" is always negative in Paul's letters while the bare word "works" is not.

Excursus: The Faith in Christ/Faithfulness of Christ Debate

For roughly thirty years there has been a controversy in New Testament Studies that is not completely separate from the larger New Perspective on Paul/Old Perspective on Paul debate, but it can also be discussed in a self-contained way. This controversy is usually called the *Pistis Christou* ("Faith of Christ") debate, but it can also be called the "Faith in Christ/Faithfulness of Christ" debate.[17] This is because it centers on how a handful of texts in Paul's letters ought to be translated.

Genitive relationships in Greek, such as the *pistis Christou* ("faith of Christ") example under discussion, are often translated into English by linking words using the preposition "of." These genitive relationships are also often ambiguous regarding the meaning the author intends to convey. This leaves much for the reader to ferret out based on factors such as context and congruity with other ideas expressed by the author.

This debate is adjacent to the New Perspective on Paul controversy in this way: Those who choose to translate the Greek phrase *pistis Christou*, or similar constructions, as "the faithfulness of Christ" generally also embrace the New Perspective on Paul. Similarly, those who embrace the New Perspective on Paul will likely, at least sometimes, translate *pistis Christou* as "the faithfulness of Christ." In contrast, those who reject the New Perspective will generally translate *pistis Christou* as "faith of Christ" or even "faith in

---

17. In Greek there are two similar words: *pistos*, which means "faithfulness"; and *pistis*, which can mean either "faith" or "faithfulness." In the New Testament the word *pistis* occurs much more frequently than *pistos*.

Christ." However, the *Pistis Christou* debate is largely a matter of translation, and it is not as deeply intertwined with questions about Reformation theology and the character of first-century Judaism as is the New Perspective controversy.

When Paul intends to indicate a subjective "faith in Christ," i.e., a personal belief in and reliance upon Christ for salvation or for strength, he sometimes uses less ambiguous constructions such as *tēs eis Christon pisteōs hymōn* (literally "your [pl.] in Christ faith") found in Col 2:5, or *hēmeis eis Christon Iēsoun episteusamen* (literally "we believed in Christ Jesus") as found in Gal 2:16.

But Paul does not always use these unambiguous phrases. When Paul uses the ambiguous *pistis Christou*, it has been traditional also to translate this phrase as reflecting a subjective faith in Christ like the unambiguous counterparts. However, over the past three decades many scholars have argued these passages speak not about the believer's faith in Christ but rather about the faithfulness of Christ, i.e., his actions, not the believer's inward thoughts and commitments.

Most occurrences of the phrase *pistis Christou* occur not in Romans but rather elsewhere in Paul's epistles. However, one very important occurrence is in Rom 3:22. If this verse and the preceding verse are translated in the traditional manner, the result will be something like this:

> But now, the righteousness of God has been manifested apart
> from the Law, although it is testified to by the Law and the
> Prophets. This righteousness of God is available through faith
> in Jesus Christ [*pisteōs Iēsou Christou*] to those who believe.
> For there is no distinction . . . .

In contrast, a translation understanding *pistis Christou* to mean "the faithfulness of Christ" will result in approximately the following:

> But now, the righteousness of God has been manifested apart
> from the Law, although it is testified to by the Law and the
> Prophets. This righteousness of God is shown through the
> faithfulness of Jesus Christ to those who believe. For there is
> no distinction . . . .

The problem with the first option is that it seems redundant: God's righteousness comes "through faith in Jesus Christ" to "those who believe." Are not "those who believe" exactly those who experience God's righteousness "through faith in Jesus Christ"? The second translation solves this problem by implying that the experience of God's righteousness comes through two things: 1) "the faithfulness of Christ"; and 2) through belief in Christ.

In this passage at least, the "faithfulness of Christ" approach seems superior.

On a related note, Matthew W. Bates has demonstrated that the first century historian Flavius Josephus (among others) often uses the word *pistis* to mean "allegiance" or "loyalty." In fact, he states that this usage is so common space limits him to providing only a few examples.[18] In a letter, King Ptolemy of Egypt speak of the loyalty (*pistis*) required of those who will serve in his court.[19] Similarly, King Antiochus of Syria praises the allegiance (*pistis*) of the Jews who continued to serve him during a time of revolt.[20] However, as Bates explains things, understanding *pistis* to imply "loyalty" or "allegiance," does not only mean that Christ was radically loyal to God the Father. It also means that the believer's *pistis* implies more than mental assent. It describes a radical "allegiance" to Christ.

---

18. Bates, *Salvation by Allegiance Alone*, 80.

19. Josephus, *Antiquities* 12.47; Bates, *Salvation by Allegiance Alone*, 80.

20. Josephus, *Antiquities* 12.147; Bates, *Salvation by Allegiance Alone*, 80. These are my selections from Bates's already limited store of examples.

ROMANS 4

TRANSLATION: ROM 4:1–15

FOLLOWING IN ABRAHAM'S FOOSTEPS OF FAITH

¹What shall we say then that Abraham, our forefather in the natural, discovered? ²For if Abraham was put in right relationship [with God] by his works, he has grounds for boasting (but not before God). ³For what does the Scripture say? Abraham believed God and it [his faith] was reckoned to him as [establishing] a right relationship. ⁴But the wage is not reckoned by the worker to be a favor, but rather to be something owed. ⁵It is not to the person working but instead to the person believing the one who clears the ungodly, that his faith is reckoned as [establishing] a right relationship. ⁶And it is just as David says about the blessedness of the person to whom God reckons a right relationship apart from works:

> ⁷Blessed are they whose transgressions have been forgiven
> and whose sins have been covered.
> ⁸Blessed is the man to whom the Lord does not reckon his sin.

⁹So, is this blessing only on those of the circumcision, or is it also on those of the uncircumcision? For we say, "To Abraham, his faith was reckoned as [establishing] a right relationship." ¹⁰How then was it reckoned? To a circumcised person or to an uncircumcised person? ¹¹He received the sign of circumcision which was a seal of his right relationship by faith while uncircumcised, in order to be the father of all who believe during uncircumcision, in order for a right relationship to be reckoned to them also, ¹²and the father of circumcision, not by circumcision only but also by following in the ordered footsteps of faith of our father Abraham, while he was uncircumcised.

¹³The promise to Abraham (or, should I say, to his seed) that the world was to be his inheritance did not come through the Law but rather through the right relationship of faith. ¹⁴For if they are heirs by the Law, faith has been emptied out and the promise is nullified. ¹⁵The Law brings wrath, but where there is no Law, neither is there transgression.

COMMENTARY

Vss. 1–8: This passage is an example of *midrash haggadah* ("the creative retelling of an Old Testament story"), that is common in rabbinic literature. In his discussion Paul explores Abraham's story from a different angle than was customary. The focus of the story is not on Abraham's character but rather on how he came to have a special relationship with God, what the *dik-* words that appear throughout this passage imply was a "right relationship." *For more about these dik- words, see the excursus titled "The Language of Righteousness and Justification."*

Paul continues to pursue some of the same themes as he had in chapter 3, but now through the lens of Abraham's experience. He opens this passage by asking what Abraham discovered. Paul presumes Abraham was a lawless idolater before his first encounter with God, which is described in Gen 12:1–3, having come from a region devoted to polytheism and idolatry. As the narrative of Genesis unfolds, Abraham gradually develops into the iconic patriarch of God's people. This transformation did not happen because Abraham was special or because he earned God's blessing. He just believed God when God made extravagant promises. Abraham's special relationship was granted as a favor, not the result of some obligation.

Paul then links Abraham's situation to a psalm of David through the word "to reckon," a catchword common to Gen 15:6 and Ps 32:2 (lexical form *chashav* in Hebrew, *logizomai* in Greek). This psalm describes the non-reckoning or non-imputation of sin as a blessing.

Vs. 1: In the previous chapter, Paul has been discussing how there is only one God and therefore this one God must be the God of both Jews and gentiles. This is the case even though gentiles did not receive the Law as Israel did. While Paul insists that he upholds the Law, he also insists that God sometimes declares people to be in right relationship with him apart from the Law. God is bigger than the Law of Moses.

This passage begins with the question Paul uses repeatedly in Romans: "What shall we say then?" (*For more on this, consult the comment to 3:9.*) However, unlike several of the other instances where Paul deploys this question in a general way, in this verse Paul directs the question to a specific issue: what Abraham discovered. As is his practice in Romans, this question does not mark a sharp transition but rather refocuses his argument. Paul will continue to discuss the relationship of believing Jews to believing gentiles and how people are brought into right relationship with God, but now reframed in terms of Abraham.

The two key exegetical questions of this verse are 1) how to understand the infinitive *heurēkenai* (lexical form *heuriskō*, "to find" or "to discover"), and 2) whether "Abraham" is its subject or object, either of which is grammatically possible. Bafflingly, some translations simply ignore the infinitive altogether, treating it as if it were not there.

The most straightforward way to translate the verse is this: "What shall we say then Abraham, our forefather according to the flesh, discovered?" This translation assumes "Abraham" to be the subject of *heurēkenai*. A difficulty with this translation is that it is not obvious what Abraham discovered.

An alternative would be to translate the verse: "What shall we say then? Have we found Abraham to be our forefather according to the flesh?" This assumes that "Abraham" is the object of *heurēkenai*. It also requires that the subject of the infinitive be supplied. However, since "we" is the subject of the preceding clause, Paul might readily have presumed his readers would supply "we" as the subject of the infinitive as well. Taking the verse this way, Paul does not offhandedly refer to Abraham as "our forefather according to the flesh." Instead, he asks the question: Is Abraham our forefather *according to the flesh*, or is he perhaps our forefather some other way? While either alternative makes sense, the first option is the more natural way to read the Greek and is more likely to represent what Paul intended.

If Paul refers to "Abraham, *our* forefather according to the flesh," as I think he does, at this point Paul is primarily addressing fellow Jews. He is also suggesting that they put themselves in Abraham's shoes and contemplate his story afresh.

Vss. 2–4: The word "boasting" picks up the "boasting" of 3:27. That Abraham had nothing about which to boast before God apparently is part of what he discovered. When Paul suggests Abraham may have had something to boast about, "but not before God," he alludes to Abraham's successes. Abraham became rather wealthy quickly, and he was even able to field a small army (Gen 14:14). By his efforts, he had achieved things about which a man might easily boast (if he did not attribute them to God's blessing). But Abraham could hardly hold his trophies up to God and boast of them. God had directed him to Canaan, where there was great opportunity, and he had given him the land. In Isa 41:8 God calls Abraham "my beloved" (Hebrew *'ohavi*), an insightful observation of the relationship portrayed in Genesis.

Gen 15:6, which Paul quotes in vs. 3, is a very important verse and rather central to Israel's history and self-awareness. Despite its importance, not all Jews understood it the same way. 1 Macc 2:52, alludes to Gen 15:6 and asks, "Was not Abraham found faithful in temptation, and was it not counted to him as righteousness?" Rather than affirming that "Abraham believed the Lord," or "Abraham believed in the Lord," as Gen 15:6 says, 1 Maccabees suggests Abraham was faithful when tested and therefore deserved to be counted as righteous.[1] Of course, this interpretation defies the chronology presented in Genesis. Abraham is blessed in chapters 12, 13, 15, and 17 before his great testing in chapter 22.

In contrast, Paul understands the Genesis 15 narrative to teach that God's blessing of Abraham was gracious, although Genesis 15 does not explicitly mention grace. It does, however, describe God making a promise to Abraham: "Do not fear, Abram. I will protect you. Your reward (*ho misthos sou* in the LXX) will be very great" (Gen 15:1). In Rom 4:4 Paul latches onto the word *misthos* to make his point. The word *misthos* is ambiguous in that it can mean either "wages" or "reward." However, in the Genesis narrative God asks nothing of Abraham. As Abraham believes God's promises, God graciously blesses him.

Vs. 5: The grammar of this verse is tangled but grammatically correct. To make it better conform to standard English style, I have converted the main clause into a dependent clause.

Perhaps the most interesting question raised by this verse relates to the description of God as "the one who clears the ungodly" or "the one who justifies the ungodly." Does this mean Abraham believed in God, who it turns out happens to clear the ungodly? Or does it mean Abraham believed God to be the kind of God whose nature it is to clear the ungodly? In other words, did Abraham's belief mean he thought the Lord was different from the vindictive and immoral gods of Mesopotamia he had known of earlier in his life? Yes, he thought the Lord was different. A person does not trust without some assessment of the character of whomever is being trusted. Abraham concluded that God was trustworthy, so he believed.

Vss. 6–8: Paul's quotation is an exact match to Ps 31:1–2 in the LXX (Ps 32:1–2 in the English). The catchword linking this psalm to Gen 15:6 is "to reckon" (lexical form *chashav* in Hebrew, *logizomai* in Greek). For the Reformers this quotation was extremely important since they understood it to teach the non-imputation of sin, in addition to the doctrine of the

---

1. Ps 106:30–31 describes the actions of Phineas as being reckoned to him as righteousness. In addition, 1 Clem 31:2 and 32:3 seem to allude to Romans 4 and Genesis 15.

imputation of Christ's alien righteousness. Because this psalm describes the removal of the condemnation of sin as a "blessing," Paul concludes it teaches God's gift of proper standing apart from works.

Vss. 9–12: The midrash continues. Paul pivots back and forth between discussing grace versus works of the Law and discussing circumcision and uncircumcision because these discussions are linked. The latter subject is the focus of this paragraph. In it, he argues that Abraham is the father of both the circumcised and the uncircumcised.

Vss. 9–10: Paul begins by asking if the "blessing" of Ps 32:2 applies only to the circumcised or also to the uncircumcised. Since he considers Ps 32:2 and Gen 15:6 to be connected, he answers his question about Ps 32:2 by an examination of Genesis 15. Paul asks, when God reckoned a right relationship to Abraham, was he circumcised or still uncircumcised? Since Abraham does not receive the sign of circumcision until Genesis 17, in Genesis 15 he clearly was still uncircumcised.

Vss. 11–12: The grammatical construction of these verses is very complex, and they are filled with rich insight.

Paul refers to the "sign" (Greek *sēmeion*) of circumcision. The word "sign" is a reference to Gen 17:11 where the phrase "sign of the covenant" appears. There circumcision is described as such a sign, which Abraham "received."

Paul's phrase "seal of his right relationship by faith" does not seem intended to recall a specific biblical text. But seals were widely used in the ancient world, mainly to seal documents but also to seal containers of goods such as wine. The point of the seal was to indicate that the contents had not been tampered with, and therefore were genuine. By calling the sign of circumcision a "seal of his right relationship by faith," Paul asserts that God gave Abraham circumcision as an indicator that the relationship between them was genuine and that it derived from faith. I consider the genitive construction "by faith" (*tēs pisteōs*) to be "a genitive of source," specifying that this new relationship came from faith, or by way of faith. "Furthermore, Paul emphasizes that this sign and seal were given while Abraham was uncircumcised: Faith came first and then circumcision followed. How Paul describes Abraham's circumcision is not far from the expression "an outward sign of an inward work of grace," which is common in many Protestant circles and has roots at least as early as the eleventh century.[2]

---

2. This formulation is rooted in the Latin expression *sacramentum est invisibilis gratiae visibilis forma* ("A sacrament is the visible form of an invisible grace"), which is widely attributed to Augustine but never with a specific citation. It likely was first misattributed to the great bishop of Hippo by the eleventh-century theologian Berengar of Tours. See Kornelis, "Peter Lombard and the Holy Eucharist," 9.

The expression "during uncircumcision" translates *di' akrobystias*. When the preposition *dia* is used with a noun in the genitive case to indicate a measure of time, it refers to "uninterrupted duration," which "during" captures nicely.[3]

In vs. 12 Paul stipulates that following Abraham's example of being circumcised does not by itself make Abraham one's father. One must also follow in his "footsteps of faith." Just as there is an orderly sequence to footsteps, Abraham's faith was expressed in proper order. The participle *tois stoichousin* is from the verb from *stoicheō*, which means "to put in a prescribed order," such as reciting the letters of an alphabet in proper order. Paul's point is probably not so much getting the order properly sequenced as avoiding missing any steps. In this way he takes a swipe at empty ritualism, i.e., practicing circumcision without accompanying faith. The result is that Abraham is the father of two kinds of people: believing gentiles; and Jews who combine their circumcision with faith.

Vss. 13–14: When Paul writes of "the promise to Abraham or to his seed" as the text reads literally, the reference to "his seed" appears to be a qualification for the sake of accuracy. The promise of "the world" is given to Abraham, but it will in fact be received by his descendants. This justifies the paraphrastic translation "(or, should I say, to his seed)."

This verse echoes the promise given in Gen 13:15: "All the land which you see, I will give it to you and to your descendants forever." Both the phrase *kol ha'arets* in the MT and the phrase *pasan tēn gēn* in the LXX are ambiguous: They can mean either "all the land" or "all the earth [i.e., the whole world]." This phrase is limited by "which you see," but it is not clear if this means "all this land only to the horizon" or "all the earth," specifically the earth at which you are looking. Similarly in Gen 12:7 and Gen 15:7 *ha'arets haz'ot* and *tēn gēn tautēn* are ambiguous. Both phrases could mean either "this land" or "this earth."

The extent of the land promised is described differently elsewhere: Gen 15:18–21 sets outer boundaries of "the river of Egypt"—probably the Wadi el-Arish—and the Euphrates; and Gen 17:8 limits its extent to the land of Canaan.

But Paul understands the promise of Gen 13:15 in maximal terms. This is indicated by his use of the word *kosmos* ("world" or "universe") rather than the ambiguous *gē* found in the LXX version of Gen 13:15. Whether he knew a Greek text with different wording than the LXX that has come down to us or whether he modified the wording based on his understanding of the Hebrew is unclear. Whatever the case, Paul understood the smaller

---

3. Smyth, *Greek Grammar* §1685 (b).

areas defined in Gen 15:18–21 and 17:8 as promises that came to pass in a timeframe closer to Abraham's day, while the vision for his seed to inherit the whole earth remained a more distant eschatological promise.

Of course, the promise of the land is tied in Paul's mind to the people who live on the land. Were these the people of the land of Israel, or were these people covering the entire face of the earth? The apostle to the gentiles clearly embraced the latter alternative.

While the extent of the land promised is important to Paul, what is more important is how the promise came, namely, "through the right relationship of faith." As extravagant as God's promises were to Abraham, he believed them. The implication, of course, to those who would receive Paul's letter is similar: As extravagant as God's promises may seem, you should believe them, as you follow in Abraham's footsteps of faith.

Vs. 15: The verb *katergazomai* usually means "to work" or "to accomplish." I have translated it "brings" with the idea that bringing something into play is essentially the same as accomplishing that thing. Paul's point is that the Law has no ability to forestall divine judgment. By identifying trespasses, the Law promotes judgment. *For a more detailed discussion of this verse, see the excursus "Paul's Concepts of Sin and Transgression."*

TRANSLATION: ROM 4:16–25

THE GOD WHO BRINGS THE DEAD TO LIFE

[16]For this reason it is by faith, in order according to grace to be a firm promise to every descendant, not only the one [descending] by the Law but also to the one [descending] by the faith of Abraham, who is the father of us all, [17]as it is written, "I will make you a father of many nations/gentiles." When in his presence, he believed God to be the kind who brings the dead to life and calls the things that do not exist into existence. [18]With hope against hope he believed in [the promise] he would become a father of many nations/gentiles, as had been said. [19]And although not weakening in faith, he considered his own body already dead, being around one hundred years old, as well as the deadness of Sarah's womb. [20]He did not waver in unbelief about the promise of God, but rather was strengthened in his faith by giving glory to God [21]and was fully convinced God was able to do what he had promised. [22]That is why his faith was reckoned to him as [establishing] a right relationship. [23]But, "it was reckoned to him" was not written because of Abraham alone, [24]but also on our account, the ones to whom it will be reckoned, who believe on the one

who raised Jesus our Lord from the dead, ²⁵who was handed over on account of our trespasses and raised up for our vindication.

COMMENTARY

Vss. 16–25: These verses explain the central message of the gospel, first by explaining Abraham's faith and then by explaining how faith affects Abraham's descendants who follow him by exercising faith, specifically faith in Jesus Christ. The theme of promise, discussed in vs. 13, is further extended and to it is added the theme of hope.

Vss. 16–17: The great pastoral concern of Paul's career was to promote unity between Jewish believers and gentile believers. His claim that Abraham "is the father of us all" encapsulates this message of unity. To some Jewish believers this may have seemed offensive, watering down their distinctive identity as Abraham's descendants. But Paul must insist that gentiles also can become children of Abraham, not by physical descent, but rather by emulating his exercise of faith. In fact, his position was that even Jews were not true children of Abraham without following in his footsteps of faith (vs. 12).

Since Abraham knew nothing about Jesus, some may wonder how Paul connects Abraham's faith with the faith in Jesus that Paul proclaims. Paul explains that Abraham's faith required belief in the kind of God who "brings the dead to life and calls things that do not exist into existence." In Abraham's case dead reproductive organs brought forth Isaac. In the case of Jesus, his dead body was raised to new life. In both cases God brought entirely new realities into existence.

In the translation the words "the kind who" is an attempt to express something the grammar of the verse implies. The clauses that literally read "bringing the dead to life" and "calling the things that do not exist into existence" function as one large attributive adjective, modifying "God." These clauses therefore describe aspects of God's character.

Vss. 18–19: The expression "hope against hope" (*elpida ep' elpidi*) is probably meant to convey "extreme hope," even "desperate hope." But this was not just a wish for something that seemed impossible. It was a hope founded on a promise from God. In this sense, Abraham's hope is hard to distinguish from his faith.

Many translations describe the "barrenness of Sarah's womb"—no doubt in sensitivity to post-menopausal women—but this euphemism obscures Paul's point. The Greek literally reads, "the deadness of Sarah's womb." Paul draws a straight line between the deadness of Sarah's womb, which nevertheless gave birth, and the dead body of Jesus, which God raised to newness of life.

Vss. 20–22: The nature of Abraham's belief is described in two ways: It was belief in God's promise; and it was belief that God was able to do the seemingly impossible thing he had promised. When Paul writes that the patriarch "was strengthened in his faith by giving glory to God," he is referring to the altar Abraham built at Bethel (Gen 12:8) and revisited (Gen 13:3–4).

Wright makes the important observation that Paul depicts Abraham's faith as the complete inverse of the suppression of truth described in Rom 1:18, which was accompanied by exchanging "the glory of the immortal God" for mere images (1:23).[4] In effect, Abraham, who came from a background of idol worship, exchanged those idol images for worship of the true God and gave glory to him. God helped him to think clearly, contrary to the general pattern of fallen humanity. Note, however, that this clear thinking did not come apart from special revelation: God initiated this process by speaking to Abraham in a unique and personal way (Gen 12:1–3).

Vss. 23–25: In these verses Paul insists that God's interaction with Abraham was not only for his benefit but that his story might be passed on to Paul and his contemporaries. Paul highlights that faith can be reckoned as right standing before God in the present day. Such faith will involve belief in God's promises (including that those in Christ will be raised from the dead along with him), belief that God is able to do what seems impossible (such as raise the dead to new life), and ascribing glory to the one true God rather than the many substitutes others worship.

While it is somewhat unusual for the preposition *dia* to express purpose, as it seems to here "for our vindication," it is not unprecedented. This is one of only two occurrences of *dikaiōsis* ("vindication") in the New Testament. The other is in Rom 5:18.

Excursus: Paul's Concepts of Sin and Transgression

Paul's letters reveal a particular schema or framework of salvation history which helps explain his understanding of the Law and of sin. He derived this framework, at least in part, from the way certain words are used in the Bible he usually read, which was a Greek Old Testament similar to the Septuagint (LXX) modern scholars know.

---

4. Wright, *Paul and the Faithfulness of God*, 1122.

In Romans, Paul uses the noun *parabasis* ("transgression") three times (in 2:23; 4:15; and 5:14) and the similar noun *paraptōma* ("trespass") nine times (in 4:25; 5:15 [twice], 16, 17, 18, 20; 11:11, 12). He does not use *parabainō*, the cognate verb of *parabasis*.

In Genesis the LXX never uses *parabasis*, its cognate verb *parabainō* ("to transgress"), or the similar noun *paraptōma*. The cognate verb of *paraptoma*, which is *parapiptō* ("to transgress"), is never used by Paul and does not occur in the LXX of Genesis either. What these words have in common is that they imply the violation of a stated law, so it is hardly surprising they do not appear in the narratives of Genesis, which all take place prior to the giving of the Law at Mount Sinai. One might expect one or more of these words to appear in Genesis 3, the account of "the fall of Adam," but that chapter never characterizes the actions of Adam or Eve with any of these words, even though the first humans violated a specific command issued by God. Instead, the narrative conveys the depth of the offense simply by relating the story, and through the curses the snake, the woman, and Adam receive.

In contrast, the LXX of Genesis regularly uses both the noun *hamartia* (usually translated "sin") and its cognate verb *hamartanō* (usually translated "to sin"). These words can describe an offense against another person even if a formal law is not violated. We all are familiar with the acts of others that we think are rude, objectionable, or offensive, but which do not warrant bringing to the attention of the police or courts of law. They are not crimes or violations of any official law. More importantly, while an offense against a fellow human being might also constitute an offense against God, such an offense against some other person is not necessarily a sin against God. I may inadvertently embarrass someone, and she may take great offense at this, but does such a thing always constitute an offense against God? "Sin" and "to sin" are rather vague and general terms, and perhaps *hamartia*—which is often translated "missing the mark"—could be translated "offensive behavior" and *hamartanō* "to behave offensively."[5]

Interestingly, the first time "sin" is mentioned in the Bible (in Gen 4:7, using the noun *chata't* in the MT and the verb *hamartanō* in the LXX), it is personified, or more accurately "animalized." Sin is depicted as a vicious beast that is crouching and waiting to pounce. Paul extends and amplifies this image in Romans 5, presenting sin as the residue of Adam's fall that persists in all his offspring. This force is thoroughly personified and is said to "reign in death." Genesis' image of a crouching beast ready to pounce also

---

5. Wright discusses some of these distinctions. Wright, *Paul and the Faithfulness of God*, 859.

reappears in 1 Pet 5:8, which reports that "the devil prowls as a roaring lion seeking someone to devour."

This complete avoidance of notions of "trespass" or "transgression" in Genesis, coupled with the book's free use of the idea of "sin," informs Paul's *schema* of salvation history. This contrast provides a backdrop to his account of the differing situations of humanity before the giving of the Law and humanity in the era that followed. In 4:15 Paul writes: "Law promotes wrath, but where there is no Law, neither is there transgression." In chapter 1 Paul describes floridly how "the wrath of God is being revealed from heaven," a thought filled out in 2:5 where he describes this wrath being "stored up" for a coming day of judgment. The watershed point of transition between the period when no transgressions are assessed and the period in which transgressions are counted is the moment when the Law is given to Moses.[6]

One might argue, based on Gal 3:19, that transgressions predate the giving of the Law: "Why therefore the Law? It was delivered thanks to transgressions [the plural of *parabasis*] . . . ." However, such an analysis would miss the essential point: While technically they were not "transgressions" until after the Law was given, the reason for the giving of the Law was to highlight the actions that offended God and will henceforth be prohibited and penalized.

The logic of the argument that the giving of the Law was a key dividing line is straightforward and clear with respect to Israelites/Jews. They received the Law. But Paul's great declaration in Rom 1:18 that God's wrath is being revealed, a revelation which seems already to have begun in some proleptic way, appears in a passage aimed squarely at gentiles. Was the giving of the Law also a critical dividing line for these peoples to whom the Law had not been given? If so, why?

Paul does not explain his views about this in any detail, but perhaps we can presume he shared the view expressed in Isa 66:19:

> I will set a sign among them [the Israelites], and I will send refugees to the gentiles/nations, to Tarshish, and Libya, and Lud, and Meshech, and Tubal, and Greece and to the far-off islands who have not heard my name or seen my glory, and they will announce my glory to the gentiles/nations.

---

6. One wonders how Paul understood the story of Noah and the flood recounted in Genesis 6–9, which describes punishment for "the wickedness of people" (Gen. 6:5). Neither Noah nor the ark is mentioned in the entire Pauline corpus.

The worldwide Jewish diaspora may have seemed a great calamity, but it had the silver lining of spreading the Mosaic Law throughout the world. While the gentiles had not taken upon themselves the yoke of the Law in the same way as the Israelites, knowledge of the Law conveyed the basic principles of ethical monotheism, and it differentiated between what pleased God and what displeased him. Thus, while the Law was not given to the gentiles in a single moment, as it was to Israel, it had been given. It had spread gradually with the diaspora. Consequently, Paul can argue the giving of the Law served as a salvation-historical dividing line for the gentiles as well as for the Jews.

How does Paul's explanation of trespass square with his statement in 5:13 that before the Law came sin was already in the world? As mentioned above, the words *hamartia* ("sin," or perhaps "bad behavior") and *hamartanō* ("to sin," or perhaps "to behave badly") appear regularly in Genesis, so this is what we should expect Paul to report.

But 5:13 continues in a way that might suggest little difference between sin and trespass, despite what I have argued so far. According to the conventional translation, this verse reads: "Sin is not counted when there is no Law." But this translation is incorrect. It should be translated, "Sin is not *recognized* when there is no Law." While *elogeō* means "account to" or "impute to" the one other time it is used in the NT (Phlm 18), there the verb is an imperative and it describes to whom something is imputed. However, in Rom 5:13 "sin" is the subject, and *ellogeitai* is middle/passive in form, here functioning as a passive.[7] While this verb is usually translated as if a quasi-financial transaction is being described, with God the great accountant keeping score, the context implies that "sin is not recognized" *by humans* when there is no Law. The purpose of the Law is to point out more clearly to people when they disappoint God.

Some might object, "But surely we recognize when we are being wronged, even without the Law of Moses!" Yes, we may feel wronged, but what one person considers wrong another person considers right. Today many Christians who argue for traditional sexual values are labeled homophobic, transphobic, or intolerant in some other way, and what they consider vices are celebrated as virtues by others. Apart from God's revelation of his values, humans often construct moral codes on their own that bear

---

7. In secular Greek, this verb *elogeō* is normally used in contexts discussing financial transactions or in contexts where something is measured (e.g., *IG* IX,1 61, line 37, an inscription from AD 138 dealing with measurements of land mass). It can mean "to recognize," "to consider", or "to count."

little resemblance to what God reveals as his will. Thus, the proper extent of sin "is not *recognized* when there is no Law."

Another point of possible objection to a clear distinction between sin and trespass might be based on Rom 3:25, which refers to past sins that God "had passed over," as this verse is traditionally translated. This might suggest that before the giving of the Law people were not held accountable for either sins or trespasses. Again, however, I translate this material differently. I do not think Rom 3:23–25 refers to "sins" but rather "sin offerings." In addition, I do not believe it is God who "passes over" these sin offerings, but rather that individual Jews have "withheld" sin offerings that were owed. When God offered his son Jesus as a sin offering, this fulfilled the obligations incurred by this past neglect and it also made any future sin offerings unnecessary. *For a more complete discussion, see the commentary on Rom 3:21–26.*

The relationship of sin and trespass may be explored from a different angle. While every trespass is a sin, which is to say, an incident of bad or offensive behavior, not every sin is a trespass. There are many ways to behave offensively without breaking a specific commandment. This means that sin is a greater problem than trespasses because it casts a wider net.

The Law speaks clearly about the penalties appropriate for many kinds of trespass. There is not the same clarity about what punishment is due for many other types of sin. But this does not mean such sin carries no repercussions. As Paul explains in the Rom 5:14: "But death reigned from Adam until Moses, even over those who did not sin in like manner to the trespass [*parabasis*] of Adam." Two important points emerge from this statement. First, Paul is willing to state what Genesis 3 does not: Adam trespassed against a specific commandment of God. He was therefore a lawbreaker.

Second, sin distorted—maybe it is not too much to say "destroyed"— the order of the world God had created. Adam and Eve sabotaged the idyllic quality of the paradise God had made for them. (The word the LXX uses to translate the Hebrew word *gan* ["garden"] is *paradeisos*, the word from which our English word "paradise" is derived.)[8] An obvious consequence of this was that Adam and Eve and all their offspring became mortal, subject to death.

Paul pictures the trespass of Adam and Eve as unique. They violated a specific command given only to them, and so from the moment of their expulsion from the Garden until the giving of the Law at Mt. Sinai, similar trespasses were not possible. Why does Paul make this point? He wants to highlight that there was both an up-side and a down-side to the giving of

---

8. Ultimately this word is of Persian origin, so it is a loan word in Greek just as in English (through the Greek).

the Law. The up-side was that it revealed to Israel much about what pleased God and what displeased him. The down-side was that it held the Israelites responsible before God in a new and somewhat oppressive way. The Law was not a way for the people of Israel to demonstrate their righteousness. Instead, it set a standard that revealed their unrighteousness.

But someone might quibble: Is it not true that something akin to transgression is implied by the great flood (Genesis 6–8) and by the destruction of Sodom and Gomorrah (Genesis 19)? God certainly held responsible those who had offended him and his moral standards. In fact, he destroyed them as a consequence of their sin. So how can Paul say, "Where there is no Law, neither is there transgression" (Rom 4:15)?

However, in both the flood narrative and in the story of Sodom and Gomorrah, sinners destroy themselves before God adds an objective finality to what was already an inward truth. This is especially evident in Gen 6:12–13:

> And God saw the earth, and look, it was destroyed [a *nipʿal* perfect of the Hebrew verb *shachat*], for all flesh had destroyed [a *hipʿil* perfect of *shachat*] his way on the earth. And God said to Noah, "The end of all flesh has come before me for the earth has been filled with violence through them, and look, I am destroying [a *hipʿil* participle of *shachat*] the earth.

The point is often missed that God's formal and outward destruction followed an earlier, internal destruction that humans had already inflicted on themselves. Translators often label what is destroyed by humans as "corrupted," reserving the word "destroyed" for the devastation God first contemplates and later executes. This obscures the fact that the same Hebrew verb (*shachat*) is used all three times, although with somewhat different lexical inflections. In the LXX of Gen 6:12–13 the same Greek verb (*kataphtheirō*) is also used in each instance.

This conjunction of self-inflicted destruction with divine judgment echoes how Paul describes the state of the gentile world in Romans 1. God's wrath is depicted as both coming from God and what happens when God "hands over" the wicked to the fruit of their wickedness. This wickedness suppresses the truth and brings self-imposed destruction on those who practice it.

Those from a Wesleyan background will likely notice both similarity to, and difference from, John Wesley's understanding of sin. He famously defined sin as "a violation of a known law." That formulation summarizes how I understand Paul's definition of a "trespass," if the caveat is added that the "known law" under consideration is the Law of Moses. In contrast, I do not think Wesley's formulation fully explains Paul's understanding of "sin," which is a broader concept than "trespass." Perhaps Wesleyan readers will accept this discussion as a refinement of Wesley's basic impulse.

ROMANS 5

TRANSLATION: ROM 5:1–11

FORMER ENEMIES NOW RECONCILED TO GOD

¹Therefore, having been made right by faith, we have peace with God through our Lord Jesus Christ, ²through whom we have also obtained access to this place of favor in which we stand, and we rejoice in hope of beholding the glory of God. ³Not only this, but we also rejoice in troubles, knowing that trouble promotes endurance, ⁴and endurance promotes character, and character promotes hope. ⁵And hope does not disappoint, for the love of God has been poured out into our hearts through the Holy Spirit which has been given to us. ⁶For we were still weak—yet at that very time—Christ died for the ungodly. ⁷A person will almost never die for some exonerated person, although perhaps for a good person someone might even dare to die. ⁸But God has demonstrated his love for us, for while we were still sinners Christ died for us. ⁹Now having been made right by his blood, how much more will we be saved from wrath through him. ¹⁰And if being enemies, we were reconciled to God through the death of his son, how much more, having been reconciled, will we be saved by his life. ¹¹And not only this, but we also take delight in God through our Lord Jesus Christ, through whom now we have received our reconciliation.

COMMENTARY

Vss. 1–11: Paul begins this passage by celebrating the blessings both he and the Roman believers have received, which have come through faith, and which include peace with God. They are also full of delight because of their hope of experiencing the glory of God. This hope is not just a vaporous wish, but a realistic expectation. They also delight in their sufferings because of the moral development to be achieved through them. In addition, God's love which has been poured into their hearts by the Holy Spirit keeps them from being disappointed by suffering.

After discussing the outrageously loving death of Christ, who "died for us" even "while we were sinners," Paul amplifies what having peace with God means: having been enemies of God, "we were reconciled to God by the death of his son," and furthermore, "we shall be saved by his [resurrection] life."

Vs. 2: The translation "this place of favor" is a not strictly literal rendering of *eis tēn charin* ("in grace"), but the image of standing "in favor" or "in grace" implies standing in a place. The traditional translation of *kauchometha* is "we boast," but if the image is one of beholding the divine essence, then perhaps words expressing inward emotion such as "we take delight" make better sense here. The same verb will be repeated in the following verse.

Paul's reference to "the glory of God" provokes a little surprise since the expression more commonly found in scripture is "the glory of the Lord." That being said, "the glory of God" appears in the great declaration of Ps 19:1: "The heavens declare the glory of God!"

"Glory" (Hebrew *kavod*, Greek *doxa*) recalls the revelation of divine glory in the cloud (Exod 16:10) as the Lord miraculously provided manna and quail for his hungry people in the wilderness. It also recalls the glory that covered Mt. Sinai along with the cloud, a glory which appeared as "a consuming fire" (Exod 24:16–17). Similarly, Deut. 5:24 connects God's "glory and his greatness" with the giving of the ten commandments. Exod 40:35 reports that the glory of the Lord filled the tabernacle so that Moses was unable to enter the Tent of Meeting. Num 14:10 reports that "all Israel" beheld the "glory of the Lord" at the Tent of Meeting.

While these events from Israel's history frame the resonance of the word "glory," Paul's focus is not on the past but rather the future. The psalmist cries out with the eschatological hope, "May your glory cover the whole earth!" (Ps 57:5, 11). This too is Paul's hope.

Vs. 3: "Not only this": Paul frequently uses the expression *ou monon de* ("and not only") found here as well as in Rom 5:11; 8:23; 9:10, and sometimes as part of the slightly shorter phrase *ou monon* (found in Rom 1:32; 9:24; 13:5). The point is that what follows will augment what has already been expressed.

Paul has already stated that "we rejoice in the hope of beholding the glory of God." His readers would surely have concurred with this. More surprising is Paul's claim that "we also rejoice in troubles" because we grow through such experiences. No doubt some would prefer not to experience such opportunities for growth. But Paul is confident that God is in control and that he has his people's best interests in mind. This will be explained more clearly in Rom 8:28.

Vs. 5: To this point Paul has written very little about the Holy Spirit. He mentioned "the Spirit of holiness" in 1:4, his own spirit in 1:9. In 2:29 he describes "the circumcision of the heart," which is accomplished by the Spirit not by the letter. This will be his only reference to the Spirit in this chapter, followed by not a single mention in chapter 6, and only one in chapter 7, before the explosion of discussion about the Spirit in chapter 8.

This verse states not just that the Holy Spirit pours out "love" (*agapē*) into the hearts of believers, but this love which the Spirit pours out comes from God. While the construction is likely a genitive of source ("love from God"), it also suggests that this love is beyond merely human affections and desires. In Gal 5:22–23 "love" (there also *agape* in Greek) heads the list of virtues Paul calls "the fruit of the Spirit."

The verb "to pour out" (*ekchynō*; in classical usage *echeō*) appears in the LXX of Joel 2:28 (Joel 3:1 in the LXX), where God says, "my Spirit will be poured out on all flesh." The use of this verb to describe the pouring out of the Spirit is echoed in Acts 2:17 and 2:18, and in Acts 10:45 "the gift of the Holy Spirit" is said to be poured out. In Titus 3:5–6 Paul similarly refers to ". . . the renewal of the Holy Spirit, which he [God] richly *poured out* on us through Jesus Christ our savior." Throughout the Bible the Holy Spirit is often depicted using images of wind, breath, or liquids such as anointing oil, rather than solid objects. The point is likely that the Spirit flows unpredictably and is beyond human control.

In this verse, however, it is "love" which is poured out, albeit "through the Holy Spirit." Surely this image of liquid love has been impacted by its association with the Spirit.

Vs. 6: In his expression "while we were weak," Paul lumps together and personifies the entire human race. He means, "while the human race was helpless." This collective discussion of humanity's history will permeate the remainder of the chapter.

The adverb of time *eti* ("still" or "yet") appears twice in this verse. It is difficult to understand the exact force. Often the sentence is translated something like, "For while we were still weak—at the right time—Christ died for the ungodly," While such a translation conveys the general point Paul is trying to make, it does not do justice to the double use of *eti*. An alternative is this: "For we were still [*eti*] weak—yet [*eti*] at that very time—Christ died for the ungodly."

Vs. 7: This is a key verse in the argument that *dikaios*, which has traditionally been translated "righteous," does not mean "morally virtuous" but rather "cleared" or "exonerated." The logic of the verse requires that a "good" (*agathos*) man must be better than a man who is *dikaios*. For more about this, see the excursus titled "The Language of Righteousness and Justification."

Vs. 8: "For while we were still sinners": this clause is very similar to the clause from vs. 6: "For we were still weak," and in fact it explains the nature of this weakness. Similarly, the clauses that follow in these two verses are parallel. Vs. 6 states that "Christ died for the ungodly." This verse drives home who those ungodly people were: "Christ died for us."

A larger point is that as sinners "we"—Paul, the Romans, and ultimately modern readers of Paul's letter—were alienated from God and unable to find him on our own or address this alienation. We could not first clean ourselves up to prepare properly for repairing our broken relationship with Gd. No, he had to find us first and both initiate and complete our healing.

Vs. 9: In this verse Christ's death is noted by the metonym "blood." Paul invokes an *a fortiori* argument (a *Qal vaChomer* argument using rabbinic terminology) and argues from the greater—having been made right by Christ's blood—to the lesser—we will be saved from wrath through Christ.[1] Implicit in the argument is the notion that if God has declared us to be in the right, we will not be subject to wrath.

Vs. 10: In this verse another *a fortiori* argument is presented paralleling the one in the preceding verse: If we were enemies of God but have been reconciled to him through Christ's death, how much more will we be saved (from eternal death and punishment?) by his life. Implicit in this argument is the notion that being reconciled to God is a more difficult proposition than being rescued from death and damnation.

Vs. 11: The capstone of Paul's argument in these verses is that former enemies of God now take delight in him!

TRANSLATION: ROM 5:12–14

SIN AND DEATH ARE UNIVERSAL

[12]Therefore, just as through one person sin entered the world, and death [entered] through sin, so also it [sin] spread to all people, inasmuch as all sinned. [13]For until the Law came, sin was in the world, but sin is not

---

1. In Latin *a fortiori* means "from the stronger," implying "to the weaker." Paul here suggests that Christ dying to be able to declare those who trust in him "upright" is a more difficult task than shielding these same people from wrath. If he has done the more difficult thing, then we can be assured he will do the easier thing. In Hebrew, *Qal* means "easy" and *Chomer* means "difficult" and *Qal vaChomer* arguments are equivalent to *a fortiori* arguments.

recognized when there is no Law. ¹⁴But death reigned from Adam until Moses, even over those who did not sin in like manner to the trespass of Adam, who is a type of the coming one.

COMMENTARY

Vs. 12: If asked what the most controversial verse in Romans is, I would judge it either to be this verse or 11:26. Historically, this verse has been more fraught, but at the present 11:26 generates more heated discussion.

Before addressing the meaning of this verse, two preliminary issues must be addressed. The first is a text critical problem. Does *ho thanatos* ("death") appear once or twice?[2] We are told, ". . . death entered through sin." There is no textual problem here. But in the clause that follows, *ho thanatos* ("death") may or may not appear. Does this verse read, "And in this way *death* spread to all people." Or does it read, "And in this way *it* spread to all people"? The second option, the one without "death," is found only in "western" manuscripts. The Nestle-Aland and United Bible Society texts print a second "death," but Bruce Metzger's *Textual Commentary* reports that the decision about whether to print *ho thanatos* in this location was a close call. While the weight of external (i.e., manuscript) evidence favors printing the second "death," it is easier to explain why that word would have been added than it is to explain why it might have been removed. If the verb *diēlthen* ("spread" or "passed on") did not have an explicit subject, copyists might have been tempted to supply one. In contrast, why would an explicit subject have been removed? The geographic concentration of texts supporting *ho thanatos* being limited to the West, as opposed to a wider distribution, also raises questions about this variant.[3]

This is one textual question that makes a significant difference. If there is no explicit subject expressed, then it is at least as likely that *hē hamartia* ("sin") should be considered the verb's subject as *ho thanatos*. And that, in fact, did happen when this verse was translated into Latin. The *Vetus Latina* (Old Latin) is not a single text but a stream of Latin translations that were used in the Western Church prior to when the Vulgate superseded this stream and in the late fifth century became the standard Latin translation.

---

2. While *thanatos* is preceded by the definite article, it does not mean "the death." The force of the article is to identify death as an abstract concept.

3. If the reading of the western manuscripts were shorter than the alternative, the reading would be more persuasive, since by this characteristic the reading would qualify as a so-called "western non-interpolation," a term popularized by J. F. A. Hort. Instead, it appears to be an expansion of the text typical of western manuscripts.

The Old Latin text was preferred by Ambrose, the anonymous figure called Ambrosiaster, and Augustine, three individuals whose interpretation of Rom 5:12 marked a key pivot in the theology of the western church. For instance, in his *Against Two Letters of the Pelagians*, Augustine argues that "sin" spread to all people rather than "death":

> For where the apostle says, "By one man sin entered into the world, and death by sin, and so passed upon all men," they [the Pelagians] will have it there understood not that "sin" passed over, but "death." What, then, is the meaning of what follows, "Wherein all have sinned"?[4]

The second exegetical crux is alluded to at the end of the quotation just cited. How should *eph' hō pantes hēmarton* be translated? (*Eph' hō pantes hēmarton* is the Greek corresponding to "wherein all have sinned" in the quotation.) The two traditional options are "in which all sinned" and "in whom all sinned," both of which make grammatical sense. More recently other options have also been proposed.

Leaving aside these more recent options for the moment and providing the opportunity to select between the two traditional variables at the verse's end, vs. 12 reads: "Therefore, just as through one person sin entered the world, and death [entered] through sin, so also it [sin] spread to all people, *in which all sinned* [or] *in whom all sinned*."

Historically the Eastern church has preferred "in which all sinned," assuming that "death," the subject of the preceding clause, is being referenced. Nevertheless, it is not entirely clear what sinning "in death" would mean. Does "death" here refer to physical mortality? Or does it refer to being in a condition of spiritual death? Or perhaps it might refer to both?

In a sense, the Western church had its decision made for it by those who translated the New Testament into Latin. Both the Old Latin and the Vulgate opted to translate *eph' hō* with *en quo* ("in whom"), implying "in Adam." Whereas in the Greek *eph' hō* could refer back either to "death" or to "Adam," both of which are masculine, in Latin *en quo* could only refer back to "Adam."[5] This is because *quo* is masculine and *mors* ("death") is feminine.

It was the prolific writer Augustine who standardized the idea in Western theology that all Adam's descendants sin "in him." As Augustine

---

4. Augustine, *Against Two Letters of the Pelagians* 4.7. See also Augustine, *On the Merits and Forgiveness of Sins, and On the Baptism of Infants* 3.1, where his quotation of Rom 5:12 shows a second "death" does not appear in his text. In contrast, the Vulgate clearly includes the word *mors* ("death") a second time in this verse.

5. Theoretically, *en quo* could also refer back to the neuter word *peccatum* ("sin"), but this would result in the nonsensical "in sin all sinned."

read the text, it did not suggest that each and every descendant of Adam made moral decisions that must be regarded as sinful; it is that in some way they all participated in Adam's sin of eating the forbidden fruit in the Garden. When Adam sinned, his descendants were reckoned to have sinned too. The famous *McGuffey Reader* that introduced the alphabet to many young Americans in the late 19th and early 20th centuries, introduced the letter "A" with this couplet: "In Adam's fall/We sinned all." This distills Augustine's interpretation of Rom 5:12 very succinctly.

However influential Augustine's teaching became, he was not the originator of this exegesis. His thought was shaped by the earlier figures, Ambrosiaster and Ambrose. "Ambrosiaster" is a name coined for an anonymous figure who lived in Rome and "flourished" in the latter part of Damasus's pontificate (the early 380s).[6] This means Ambrosiaster was roughly half a century younger than Augustine. Not surprisingly given the difference in ages, Ambrosiaster's influence on Augustine came through his writing, not through personal contact.

Ambrosiaster's most famous line is "in Adam all sinned as in a lump."[7] His inspiration for this image of a lump was likely Rom 9:21 or 11:16, where Paul uses the "lump" (Greek *phyrama*) as a metaphor. In Rom 9:21 the potter's right to do whatever he wants with a lump is likened to God's right to do whatever he wants with his creation. In Rom 11:16 the larger lump of dough is likened to the smaller portion taken from it as a first fruits offering.

Ambrosiaster's influence on Augustine is apparent, not only in the impact of the idea that all sin "in Adam," but even in the latter's use of the word "lump" (Latin *massa*) to characterize fallen humanity. In *Diverse Questions to Simplicianus*, Augustine writes, "For from Adam there is one lump/mass of sinners and wicked people."[8] And in *The City of God*, he writes, "Hence the whole lump/mass of the human race is condemned; for he who at first

---

6. Hunter, *Ambrosiaster*, 6–7.

7. The Latin is *in Adam omnes peccasse quasi in massa* (*Commentary on the Pauline Epistles: Romans*, ad. loc.). This Latin word *massa* comes from the Greek word *maza* and has nothing to do with the later Latin word also spelled *massa*, that becomes the name for the kind of church service called a "mass" in English. This second word is something of a mistake derived from the words *Ite, massa est*, often spoken at the conclusion of the service. This formula originally assumed the word *concio* "congregation" as the subject of *massa est*, giving the meaning, "Go, [the congregation] has been sent." People erroneously came to believe that *massa* was a noun and that these words meant, "Go, the mass is ended." In this way, *massa* did become a noun. See Liberman, "Missionary Imposition."

8. The Latin is *Una est enim ex Adam massa peccatorum et impiorum* (Augustine, *De Diversis Quaestionibus ad Simplicianum*, 1.2.19).

gave entrance to sin has been punished with all his posterity who were in him as in a root, so that no one is exempt from this just and due punishment, unless delivered by mercy and undeserved grace."[9]

The guidance of Ambrose, bishop of Milan, was even more important in Augustine's formation. It was through the impact of Ambrose's preaching that Augustine became a Christian, and it was Ambrose who baptized his young convert. In his funeral sermon *On the Death of His Brother Satyrus* Ambrose summarizes Western theology pithily: "In Adam I fell, in Adam I was cast out of Paradise, in Adam I died."[10] It is not hard to draw a straight line between the bishop of Milan and the man who later would become the bishop of Hippo.

The more vexing question is how to relate these ideas to the earlier theology of the church, which generally understood the *eph' hō* of Rom 5:12 to mean, "in death all sinned." Early on, less attention had been paid to the relationship between Adam and his offspring. For instance, the second-century figure Irenaeus focused on inheritance of the physical corruption of death rather than moral or spiritual corruption. He was impressed with the symmetry of fall and redemption, picturing redemption as a great reversal. He writes, "as the human race fell into bondage to death by means of a virgin [Eve], so is it rescued by a virgin [Mary],"[11] and "the sin of the first created man receives amendment by the correction of the First-begotten . . . those bonds being unloosed by which we had been fast bound to death."[12]

However, the spiritual dimension was highlighted by some Eastern fathers. The fourth century bishop and theologian, Gregory of Nazianzus writes, "[As an heir of Adam] I had a share in the image, and I did not keep it."[13] But all was not lost, for "He [Christ] shared in my flesh in order both that the image might be saved, and that flesh might be made immortal."[14]

As Gregory understood it, the means of rescuing that image of God was through baptism, as he explains:

---

9. The Latin is *Hinc est uniuersa generis humani massa damnata; quoniam, qui hoc primus admisit, cum ea quae in illo fuerat radicata sua stirpe punitus est, ut nullus ab hoc iusto debitoque supplicio nisi misericordi et indebita gratia liberetur* (Augustine, *De civitate Dei* 21.12).

10. The Latin is *Lapsus sum in Adam, de paradiso ejectus in Adam, mortuus in Adam* (Ambrose, *On the Death of His Brother Satyrus* 2.6).

11. Irenaeus, *Against All Heresies* 5.19.

12. Irenaeus, *Against All Heresies* 5.19.

13. Gregory of Nazianzus, *Oration 38*, 13.

14. Gregory of Nazianzus, *Oration 38*, 13.

> . . . just as He [God] gave existence to those who did not exist, so [by instituting baptism] He gave new creation to those who did exist, both a diviner and loftier form than the first, which is to those who are beginning life a seal, and to those who are more mature in age both a gift and a restoration of the image which had fallen through sin.[15]

Gregory depicts God as only meting out discipline reluctantly and redemptively. Even Adam's expulsion from the Garden was a "mercy" (*philanthrōpia*) rather than a punishment (*timōria*), as it is usually envisioned. Had God not "cut off" sin and blocked Adam from continuing access to the Tree of Life, evil might have become eternal and a never-ending obstacle to complete redemption of the fallen world.[16]

Beginning in the middle of the twentieth century a significant reassessment has taken hold concerning how to interpret the *eph' hō* of Rom 5:12. Rather than translating it 1) "in which" with "death" as the presumed antecedent as later became typical in the Eastern church, or 2) "in whom" with "Adam" as the presumed antecedent as is typical in the Western church, it has become common 3) to consider *eph' hō* an idiom. Previously, scholars had tried to translate the two constituent words of this phrase each according to their individual meanings. By regarding the phrase as an idiom, this newer approach chooses instead to translate the whole unit (*eph' hō*) as one complex and to explore its meaning against the backdrop of how it is used in other passages.

Herbert Smyth, in his magisterial grammar of classical Greek, suggests that the phrase *eph' hō* can introduce a proviso, meaning "on condition that" or "for the purpose of."[17] However, he also notes that according to the normal classical pattern, when this phrase is used as a proviso, it normally appears accompanied by the infinitive or the future indicative, which is not the case in Rom 5:12. However, since *Koinē* Greek often ignores such stylistic niceties, the "proviso" theory may still be an option, with the translation "if indeed all people sin" catching the proper nuance. This would result in vs. 12 reading: "Therefore, just as through one person sin entered the world, and death [entered] through sin, so also it [sin] spread to all people, *if indeed all people sinned.*"

C.F.D. Moule offers another option. He claims this phrase "in II Cor. v. 4 and Rom. v.12 [the verse that presently concerns us] almost certainly

---

15. Gregory of Nazianzus, *Oration 40 (Oration on Holy Baptism)*, 7.
16. Gregory of Nazianzus, *Oration 38*, 12.
17. Smyth, *Greek Grammar*, §2279.

means *inasmuch as*."[18] Moule's hypothesis would result in translating 2 Cor 5:4: "For being weighted down in this tent [i.e., "this physical body"] we cry out, inasmuch as we do not want to disrobe but rather to put on more clothing...." The verse that presently concerns us, Rom 5:12, would read: "Therefore, just as through one person sin entered the world, and death [entered] through sin, so also it [sin] spread to all people, *inasmuch as all people sinned*."

In Rom 6:21 a similar construction occurs, but with the relative pronoun in the plural: *eph' hois*. Moule is not as convinced that "inasmuch as" is the correct translation for this passage, but I believe it is a perfectly plausible translation in this passage as well.[19]

A third alternative is presented by Friedrich Blass, Albert Debrunner, and Robert W. Funk, who suggest the translation "for the reason that, because." Just as with Moule's suggestion, this translation makes sense in each New Testament instance where *eph' hō* occurs. However, there are differences of nuance. In Rom 6:21 Paul asks his readers a rhetorical question. Which translation is better turns on whether the apostle is noting a relevant situation or if he is making a causal connection between one thing and another. The first is a more tactful approach: "... what fruit do you have then, inasmuch as now you are ashamed?" With the second approach, he would hammer the point home more directly and forcefully: "... what fruit do you have then since now you are ashamed?" The implied answer in both cases is "None at all," but the nuances differ. If we take the lead of Blass, Debrunner, and Funk, then Rom 5:12 would read: "Therefore, just as through one person sin entered the world, and death [entered] through sin, so also it [sin] spread to all people, *because all people sin*."

So, of the several possibilities for translating *eph' hō* which is the strongest? As my translation reflects, I believe the Moule option ("inasmuch as") has strong lexicological merit and fits the context best. The discussion below will explain this in greater detail.

Vss. 13–14: Paul understands Genesis 3 to teach that death results from sin. Furthermore, the rest of Genesis teaches that sin has been ever-present since Adam and Eve, and consequently, death is ever-present as well.

Traditionally the final portion of v. 13 has been translated something like this: "... but sin is not charged when there is no Law." The implication is that God is the one doing the charging. However, I contend that this

---

18. Moule is undecided whether this is also its meaning in Phil 4:10, or if in that verse it might mean "with regard to which." He is also not completely certain the phrase means "inasmuch as" in Phil 3:12, but he regards it as a possibility.

19. Moule, *Idiom-Book*, 132.

translation is wrong. I render it as follows: "... but sin is not *recognized* when there is no Law." The subject of the middle-passive form *ellogeitai* (from *en* + *logeō* or *en* + *logaō*) is *hamartia* ("sin"). The key question is this: Who is the implied agent of this passive verb? I contend it is humanity, not God.

The chief argument for the traditional view rests on the use of *ellogeō* in Phlm 18, where Paul directs Philemon that if Onesimus has wronged him in any way, or if Onesimus owes him anything, "charge that to me." No doubt the verb means "to charge to an account" in this particular context. But this verb is only rarely used. Besides in Rom 5:13, the word only occurs this once in Philemon in the whole of the New Testament, and it does not occur at all in the LXX.

Herbert Preisker claims *ellogeō* was formed from the phrase *en logō tithenai* ("to lay to account"), understanding the word *logos* to designate a financial logbook.[20] But the word *logos* can mean many other things, and only rarely is used in the New Testament with this financial meaning (it is used this way in Matt 18:23 and 25:19, for example), and it is never used in this way in Paul's letters. Often *logos* is associated with what is plainly indicated or reasonable (e.g., a "word" or a "message," even "reason" itself), so *en logō tithenai* might well mean "to make apparent," as might the verb *ellogeō*. While we cannot make words mean whatever we want them to mean, the context in which a word appears must always guide how that word is understood.

Paul has already argued in Rom 4:15 that "where there is no Law, neither is there transgression." But the point he makes in vss. 12–14 is that, unlike transgression, sin was in the world prior to the giving of the Law. In fact, "death reigned from Adam until Moses," giving mute testimony to the presence and destructive power of sin. This is because death is a consequence of sin.

When the Law was given, the contours of sin became clearly identified and sin came to be "recognized." That was the fundamental power of the Law. However, Paul will go on to suggest that this function of making sin recognizable also turned the Law into a source of condemnation. The Law highlighted sin, but it offered no cure for the problem sin presented, a problem that long predated Moses and the promulgation of the Law at Sinai.

While sin and death are linked in Paul's argument, in my view sin has the logical priority. Sin entered the world, and then "death [entered] through sin." Nowhere does Paul suggest that death is prior to, or independent of, sin. Paul's focus is on sin, which "spread to all people," as has been made manifest "inasmuch as all sinned."

---

20. Herbert Preisker, *TDNT*, s.v., "elogeō" (2:516–17).

Despite the priority of sin, Paul repeatedly hammers home the awful and universal power of death. In both vss. 14 and 17 Paul says, "death reigned." Then in vs. 21 he says, "sin reigned in death," or perhaps "sin reigned by means of death."

This interpretation bears similarities to Augustine's, but there are differences. According to Augustine, Paul plainly states that all Adam's posterity sinned when the primal father ate the forbidden fruit. According to my interpretation Paul is not quite so specific. Yes, sin enters the world in the Garden of Eden, and yes, it spreads to all people, who demonstrate sin's spread by sinning themselves. But no moral culpability is attached to Adam's descendants for his original sin. Sin is pictured more as a genetic disease which is transmitted from one generation to the next. Sin spreads universally, and as a result, death spreads universally as well.

In what seems to be a departure from the main thrust of his argument, Paul also says Adam was a *typos* ("type," "pattern") of "the coming one," by which he clearly means Jesus Christ. He does not make completely clear why this is the case. Was it that both Adam and Christ bore the image of God? Was it more simply that both have had tremendous effects on "many" or "all"?

In many places throughout his letters, Paul refers to those who are "in Christ." However, bracketing for the moment Augustine's interpretation of the *eph' hō* of vs. 12, which is hotly debated, 1 Cor 15:22 is the only place in his writings where Paul explicitly speaks of people being "in Adam": "For as in Adam all die, so also in Christ all will be made alive." (In 1 Corinthians 15 the topic of discussion is death and resurrection, not sin and its connection to death.) It is conceivable that Rom 5:12–21 could presume a similar correlation of "in Christ" with "in Adam," particularly if the *eph' hō* of vs. 12 is translated "in whom," meaning "in Adam." But there are reasons to think this is not the case. Instead, repeatedly this passage explains effects that come "through" (*dia*) the one person [Adam] (vss. 12, 16, 18) or "through" (*dia*) the one person [Christ] (vss. 17, 18) rather than positing the culpability of all humanity "in" Adam, the first father.

The theological implications are clear. If all people are a single mass united with Adam, they would share his guilt with him. If, however, they have somehow been infected by Adam's sin and then confirm and propagate this infection through their own sins, they condemn themselves through their own behavior rather than through an association with their primal father.

TRANSLATION: ROM 5:15–21

GRACE WILL OVERCOME SIN AND DEATH

¹⁵But the gracious gift is not like the trespass. For if by the trespass of one many died, how much more will the grace of God, that is, the gift by the grace of one person, Jesus Christ, abound to many. ¹⁶And the gift is not as the sinning of one person. For, on the one hand, the judgment stemming from one individual leads to condemnation, but on the other hand, the gracious gift stemming from many trespasses leads to right standing. ¹⁷For if by the one trespass, death reigned through the one person, how much more will those receiving the abundance of grace and the gift of right standing, come to reign in life through the one person, Jesus Christ.

¹⁸So therefore, as through one trespass all people were led into condemnation, so also through one upright act all people are led to the vindication that brings life. ¹⁹As through the disobedience of one person many were proclaimed sinners, so also through the obedience of one, many will be proclaimed upright. ²⁰The Law came in alongside in order that the trespass might increase. But where sin increased, grace increased even more, ²¹so that just as sin reigned in death, grace might reign through right standing leading to eternal life, through Jesus Christ our Lord.

COMMENTARY

Vss. 15–21: In these verses Paul makes a series of parallels and contrasts between the trespass of Adam and the grace of God manifest through Jesus Christ. Paul uses both the words "trespass" and "sin," but with an important difference. While all trespasses are sins, not all sins are trespasses, since a "trespass" (= "transgression") involves the violation of a known law decreed by God (Rom 4:15), of which there were none between Adam and Moses. In these verses, the word "trespass" refers primarily to Adam's violation of God's commandment in the Garden, although in vs. 20 this "trespass" is said to increase, aided by the Law. Paul considers violations of the Law of Moses to be "trespasses" like Adam's.

Vs. 15: "Gracious gift": this translates the Greek word *charisma*, which means a "gift," but which is also related to the word *charis*, which means "grace." The connection is made explicit by Paul's reference to "the grace of God" in the following sentence. Furthermore, the grace wrought by Jesus Christ will abound "much more" (*pollō mallon*) than the death wrought by Adam. Adam is referred to "the one" and Jesus Christ as "the one person."

In this way, Paul shows both a contrast—their relative power—and a parallel—that each number only one—between Adam and Christ.

Vs. 16: This verse makes two contrasts: the sinning of one person is contrasted with "many trespasses," which in reality is a metonym for "many trespassers"; and "condemnation" is contrasted with "right standing." The word *dikaiōma* is sometimes translated "justification," but outside of this chapter Paul uses it in the sense of a "just decree" or a "just requirement" of the Law. That sense is difficult to maintain in this verse and in vs. 18, although clearly some scribe or scribes tried. A few manuscripts append *zōēs* ("of life") to *dikaiōma*, resulting in "a decree of life." This is a partial assimilation to the phrase at the end of vs. 18: *dikaiōsin zōēs* ("vindication [that brings] life"), and certainly this variant is not original. Keeping these factors in mind, the best translation is "right standing."

Vs. 17: This verse presents another *a fortiori* ["from the stronger" to the weaker] (Rabbinic *Qal vaChomer* ["easy and difficult"]) argument. If death reigned as a result of one trespass by one person, "how much more" will those graced and gifted by Christ reign in life through him. Although Paul does not make the point explicitly, probably the royal connotations of the title Christ ("anointed one," i.e., "one designated as king") underlines this argument. Boiled down to the simplest terms, "Adam" means "human being" and "Christ" means "king." Thus, the idea that Jesus the Messiah provokes the reign of grace is more intuitively obvious and more compelling than that the first human being provoked a kingdom of death.

In the excursus called "The Language of Righteousness and Justification" I have already discussed the significance of Paul calling "righteousness"/"right standing" a gift. It is not just a judicial decree by an uninvolved and uncaring God. Toward the end of the first century, when a leader in Rome traditionally identified as Clement, lists "the gifts of God," he includes "splendor in righteousness."[21]

The expression "reign in life" means "to reign in the Age-to-Come," which will be characterized by resurrection life. In a sense too, Paul implies that the present age is an age of death. Certainly, death is universally experienced in this age.

Vs. 18: This verse begins with the first of eight occurrences of *ara oun* ("so therefore") in Romans. In the New Testament this construction only occurs in Paul's letters, and eight of the twelve occurrences are in Romans (5:18, 7:3, 7:25, 8:12, 9:16, 9:18, 14:12, and 14:19).

The centerpiece of this verse is the contrast between "one trespass," that of Adam, and "one upright act," that of Christ.

---

21. *1 Clem.* 35:1–2.

A secondary contrast juxtaposes the consequences of those acts: the one act leading "all people" to condemnation; the other leading "all people" to vindication. While at first glance "all people" seems all-inclusive—an observation that some New Perspective advocates use to suggest universalistic implications for Paul's teaching—such a sweeping generalization misinterprets Paul. A presumption of his argument is that the "all people" of the first group is shorthand for "all people whose identity is defined by Adam" and the "all people" of the second group is shorthand for "all people whose identity is defined by Christ." Since Paul's entire missionary career presupposes that the identities of most people are not defined by Christ, to interpret this text in too sweeping a fashion would be to misread it.

Paul's use of the noun *dikaiōma*, here as in vs. 16, differs from the normal way he uses the word. Usually, it is abstract, meaning "a just decree." Here it is more concrete, meaning a "just" or "upright" act, congruent with God's will, as otherwise expressed in the Law.

Vs. 19: This verse contrasts the divergent verdicts proclaimed due to the disobedience of the one person and the obedience of the other: condemnation, and an upright status.

Vs. 20: The verb of this verse's first clause, an aorist of *pareiserchomai*, is often translated "came in." However, that treats it as precisely equivalent to *eiserchomai*. A better translation is "came in alongside" since *para* means "alongside."[22] This verb can suggest surreptitiously mixing in with others, and that is likely why Paul uses it here. The Law which outwardly appears to oppose sin and transgression, in fact was sin's secret ally. It came in alongside "that the trespass might increase." In other words, it snuck in not just to identify behavior that was contrary to God's will but also as a plant positioned to reinforce the havoc created by Adam's trespass, as covert forces assist an army in battle.

In vs. 13 Paul has argued that sin is not recognized when there is no Law. Here he asserts that the Law not only pointed out the presence of sin by bringing sin into clearer focus, it *increased* trespass and sin. Paul may have in mind the common urge to push against boundaries whenever they are asserted. It is more likely, however, that by converting unrecognized sins into transgressions known to violate God's decrees, the Law increases the culpability of the sinner. He uses "sin" as a metonym for that culpability. However, God's grace is so abundant that even after the Law reinforced the trespass of Adam thereby increasing the extent of the problem of sin, God's grace increased even more. As Paul says in 2 Cor 4:15: ". . . as grace extends

---

22. See Wright, *Paul and the Faithfulness of God*, 890.

through more and more people, may it increase their thanksgiving to the glory of God."

This verse contains the first occurrence of a typically Pauline contrast between "Law" and "grace." Similar contrasts occur in Rom 6:14, 15; Gal 2:21; and Gal 5:4. John 1:17 also contains a similar contrast.

Vs. 21: This increase in grace will result in a new era ruled by grace, as sin had ruled, "in an era defined by death" (*en tō thanatō*). In this new era, grace will reign "through being declared in right standing" (*dia dikaiosunēs*), and it will result in eternal life through the resurrection power of our Lord Jesus Christ.

Excursus: Paul Reads Genesis

This excursus is probably best seen as a collection of smaller excursuses. What unites them to some degree is that each provides a separate window into how Genesis impacts Paul's letter to the Romans. First, we will explore the rabbinic technique of *midrash*, which Paul frequently employs. Next, we will examine the "open" nature of Genesis 1–3, which invites the reader to fill in ambiguities it intentionally leaves exposed, including the relationship of sexuality to sin. Then in a short section, we will examine how Paul relates what Genesis says about Adam to the career of Jesus, since Romans 5 posits a series of similarities and contrasts between the two. Finally, we will examine a sea change in how the fathers of the ancient and medieval church interpreted Genesis 1–3. The key transition came with the exegesis of the fifth century bishop Augustine of Hippo. The modern scholar Elaine Pagels has focused considerable attention on this matter.

A MIDRASH ON GENESIS 2–3

Rom 5:12–21 is *midrash* on Genesis 2–3. It is not the only midrash in Romans. Chapter 4 contains an extended *midrash* on Abraham's interactions with God as described in Genesis 15 and 17, and chapters 9–11 contain a discussion of the meaning of Israel's history with repeated references to biblical passages, in what might loosely be described as a *midrash*, or perhaps better as a series of *midrashim*.

The noun *midrash* is cognate with the Hebrew verb *darash*, which means "to seek," and it denotes a kind of interpretation that is common in rabbinic literature. It involves considering a biblical narrative creatively or in a light that diverges from the most obvious or conventional interpretation. Often, *midrash* involves retelling a biblical story from a unique vantage. The Jewish Studies scholar Tzvee Zahavy has characterized *midrash* as "fancy interpretation," as compared with *pshat* ("regular interpretation"). Objections to the characterization of this passage as a *midrash* include the non-rabbinic context in which it appears—an effete quibble considering Paul's Jewish upbringing and education—and that the passage does not exactly retell Genesis 3. However, even if a person would deny that Rom 5:12–21 is a *midrash*, there is no denying it constitutes a creative interpretation of Genesis 3.

It is important to note that Paul presumes the literal existence of Adam and Eve. If he had interpreted it allegorically as did his contemporary, the Alexandrian Jew Philo, the gnostics of the second century AD, or for that matter the church father Origen, it would not qualify as *midrash* or *midrash*-like.[23] *Midrash* does not deny the fabric of the literal narrative; it merely suggests additional insights the narrative may offer.

QUESTIONS RAISED BY GENESIS 1–3

Genesis 3 is one of the greatest pieces of literature in the Bible. And that is part of the interpreter's problem. Some kinds of writing, e.g., a contract, seek to make everything clear and eliminate ambiguities. This explains why such writing is not considered literature. Literature is more open-ended, leaving important judgments unclear and thereby inviting the reader to speculate and draw conclusions about what is meant.[24] This open-endedness makes literature such as Genesis 3 extremely interesting to read and reread and reread again, and it invites debate about how it should be interpreted. These debates about the meaning of Genesis 3 have now continued for millennia.

---

23. Philo believed Adam represented "mind" and Eve represented "sensation." While there was diversity among the various gnostic groups, generally for them Adam and Eve represent the *psychē* ("soul") and *pneuma* ("spirit") of humans and their "pneumato-psychodynamics," to use the expression coined by Elaine Pagels (cf. Pagels, "Adam and Eve and the Serpent," p.3). Origen believed Adam and Eve represented themselves, but not within the created world but rather in heaven prior to creation, with their disobedience, whatever it was, leading to the creation of the world as we know it as an environment for human rehabilitation.

24. The Italian novelist and literary critic Umberto Eco introduced this important distinction between "open" and "closed" works in 1962 with the publication of his book *Opera aperta*, which was translated into English as *The Open Work* in 1989.

One question Genesis 3 presents is whether Adam was created mortal or immortal. The question is hinted at in the previous chapter. If Adam and Eve were created immortal, what possibility might the Tree of Life have represented? And yet the specter of death is raised when Adam is warned not to eat from the Tree of the Knowledge of Good and of Evil: "In the day you eat of it, you shall surely die" (Gen 2:17).

What does this potential consequence imply? Is it that Adam was originally formed immortal but can have that immortality revoked (a dynamic presumably shared by his helper Eve when she makes her appearance)? Or does it mean Adam and Eve were created as mortals who could have their lives immediately cut short, as if the fruit they might eat were poisonous? Whatever the potential outcome, it will happen "in the day you eat from it." Does this refer to immediate death or to death drawn out over a longer horizon? The latter interpretation appears in the book of *Jubilees*, which considers the "day" mentioned here to be 1,000 years, based on Ps. 90:4.[25]

Of course, as the story progresses, the snake contradicts the warning of the Lord God, saying to the woman, "You [pl.] will not surely die. For God knows that in the day you [pl.][26] eat from it, your [pl.] eyes will be opened, and you [pl.] will be as God, knowing good and evil" (Gen 3:4–5). Vs. 7 then reports that, in fact, the eyes of both were opened, as the snake had promised, although somewhat mysteriously the first thing they notice is that they are naked. This reference to nakedness draws the reader's attention back to Gen 2:25, where it is stated: "It happened that the two of them were naked, the man and his woman, and they were not ashamed." The implication is that the opening of their eyes resulting from their new moral awareness brought with it a sense of personal shame. The mention of nakedness also adds a sexual element to the story.

The Hebrew of 2:25 contains a play on words, which is not possible to match either in Greek or in English. The word "naked" (in Hebrew *'arummim*, a plural form of the singular *'arum*) sounds identical to the word *'arum* ("subtle" or "crafty") that occurs in the very next verse (3:1), where

---

25. That a day in God's sight is as 1,000 years is echoed in 2 Pet 3:8. According to *Jubilees* 4:30, when Adam died "he lacked seventy years from one thousand years, for a thousand years are like one day in the testimony of heaven and therefore it was written concerning the tree of knowledge, 'In the day you eat from it you will die.' Therefore, he did not complete the years of this day because he died in it."

26. The presence of the plural "you" in the clause "in the day you eat from it" shows that the snake put it in the woman's mind to take her husband along with her in disobedience. In contrast, the second person forms in God's command (Gen 2:16–17) had been "you" singulars.

it describes the snake.[27] Furthermore, the snake is not just "crafty," he is "craftier than any other animal of the field which the Lord God made."

What is the point of this play on words? Perhaps it is simply a display of literary artistry without great significance. However, the nakedness of the first couple might be seen as defenselessness or vulnerability, which the snake exploits through his craftiness and subtle words. After they defy God's command, the first couple choose to mask their nakedness by making aprons of fig leaves (Gen 3:7)[28] and by hiding (Gen 3:8). This seems to be an etiological explanation for the universal pattern of humans clothing themselves, and points to the continuation of shame in the subsequent generations of the human family.

There are at least two possible ways of viewing the newly awakened shame of Adam and Eve. The first takes their shame at face value: They had no shame when they were innocent, but after having disobeyed God's command they had something to hide. The second suggests that after eating the forbidden fruit, "their eyes were opened" and they became more inwardly aware. This new awareness included their potential for moral failure. The human tendency to guard one's inner life and what is private, and to segregate it from what is on public display is a hallmark of fallen humanity. Of course, these two ways of viewing shame are not mutually exclusive.

The craftiness of the snake is twofold. It cleverly exploits the selfish desires of Adam and his wife to be like God, with no boundaries imposed on them whatsoever. Secondly, the snake's craftiness also drove a wedge between, on the one hand, what God had actually said, and, on the other hand, the dishonorable motivations Adam and his wife thought lay behind God's prohibition.

After eating the forbidden fruit, neither Adam nor Eve keels over and dies on the spot. So, was the snake telling the truth and God lying? God had said, "In the day you eat of it . . . ." A reader could understand the first couple reaching this conclusion.

But if the reader presumes that God does not lie, she may conclude that a kind of death did occur, not immediate death, but the forfeiture of immortality and a transition to the mortal state. At the conclusion of chapter 3

---

27. While the words sound alike, there is a slight difference in the Hebrew vowel pointing, and they come from different Hebrew roots. Still, the proximity of these homophones is striking.

28. These aprons of fig leaves are later replaced by "garments" of skins made by God himself (Gen 3:21). Since leather requires the death of an animal, some have seen here the first reference to a death in Genesis.

this mortal status is then confirmed when Adam and Eve are removed from Eden "lest they eat of the Tree of Life" and reclaim immortality.

Another way to interpret the story, and still maintain God's truthfulness, is to interpret the death that Adam and his wife experience as immediate but spiritual in nature.[29] This death involved the loss of the close fellowship they had previously enjoyed with God. Their later expulsion from the Garden and from God's presence was then a public display of their recent alienation from God. However, the concluding line of the curse upon Adam (Gen 3:17-19) seems to require Adam's physical death, whether or not that also includes a spiritual aspect: "You are dust, and to dust you will return."

A second question raised by Genesis 3 is whether there was a sexual component to the disobedience of Adam and Eve. An associated issue is how procreation fits into the larger narrative of Genesis 1-3.

Augustine famously regarded the disobedience of Adam and Eve somehow to be sexual in nature since it resulted in the perpetual struggle of their offspring to tame unruly sexual urges. In his personal life, especially before his conversion, Augustine struggled with sexual desires that he willed to control but felt unable to master. This losing battle lay behind his famous line: "You command continence; grant what you command and command whatever you want" (*Confessions* 10.29).[30] This plea to God elicited bitter criticism from Pelagius and ignited the Pelagian controversy.

But Augustine also thought sexual union and reproduction were willed by God from the beginning. Genesis 1 discusses various forms of plant and animal life reproducing "according to their kind." After declaring these creatures good, God blesses them and commands: "Be fruitful and multiply" (Gen 1:22). The finale of God's creation is to create Adam (Human Being), both male and female. Adam too is commanded, "Be fruitful and multiply" (Gen 1:28).[31] Genesis 2 then pictures the creation of the woman

---

29. A death that is only spiritual and not physical seems contradicted by the curse God pronounced upon Adam: "You are dust and to dust you will return" (Gen 3:19).

30. Augustine based his plea to God on the words of Wisdom 8:3: "As I knew that no one can be continent except God grants it, and this very thing is part of wisdom, to know whose gift this is."

31. Some would object to using the first creation narrative (Gen 1:1—2:4a) to interpret what follows. However, this misses two key points. First, whatever sources were used to construct the version of Genesis we have received, it is the knit together text that constitutes the book of Genesis. Second, before the modern era, no one—certainly not Paul—read Genesis after dividing it into pieces this way.

from one of Adam's sides, leaving the remainder male, and clarifying how sexual union and reproduction would be possible.[32]

Augustine imagined sexual intimacy before "the fall" differed markedly from what came to prevail in a postlapsarian world. As he envisioned it, having many saints in the world was always part of God's plan, but this plan required Adam and Eve to reproduce and not remain alone in Eden. According to the bishop of Hippo, this reproduction was to be accomplished "without the shame of lust" and without passions that refuse to serve the will. Prior to the distortions introduced by sin, the bodily members involved in procreation would have been as under control of the will as are a person's feet or hands.[33]

ROM 5:12–21: PAUL'S NARRATIVE STRATEGY

The overarching strategy of Rom 5:12–21 is to compare the ways in which the actions of both Adam and Jesus have produced consequences "for all people" (*eis pantas anthrōpous*), in the wording used twice in 5:18. Adam brought "condemnation" and "death," but Jesus the Messiah brings "life" and "acquittal." Incorporated as part of this strategy is the theme that "death reigned," which is mentioned in both v. 14 and v. 17. This is contrasted with the goal that through Jesus Christ "grace might reign" (v. 21) and that those who receive grace might also reign (v.17). Another prominent feature is the repeated contrast between "one" and "many" (v. 15 twice, v. 16, v. 19 twice) or between "one" and "all" (v. 12, v. 18 twice). In addition, "Law" creeps into Paul's line of reasoning, first in v. 13 and then in v. 20. Thought to be an opponent of sin, the Law surreptitiously comes alongside sin and functions as its ally. As this summary suggests, the flow of the argument is dense.

A complicating factor is that Paul frequently expects his readers to fill in unstated steps in the logical progression of his arguments. This is not a criticism. It is common for literature to omit parts of arguments to avoid becoming tedious, especially when the omitted steps can easily be filled in.

---

32. The traditional translation "rib" or "rib-bone" is probably overly specific. The splitting of an originally united couple into separate halves approximates the story Aristophanes recounts in Plato's *Symposium* 189c–193e of eight-limbed beings who are each separated by Zeus into two four-limbed individuals. These individuals thereafter seek to recombine with the other half from which they were divided. Both Genesis and the *Symposium* highlight the innate human longing for sexual (re)union and intimacy.

33. This is all carefully explained in Augustine, *City of God*, 14.23.

Unfortunately, sometimes the omissions that were obvious to a letter's original recipients are not so obvious to contemporary readers.

Some of Paul's logic is based on his interpretation of Genesis 1–3. Although he does not completely retell the story found in Genesis 2 and 3, he telegraphs enough to his readers for them to understand the highlights of his midrashic retelling of the story. Paul's argument suggests several distinctive features of what he understood Genesis to teach. It taught that Adam was created immortal. It taught that God's prohibition of eating from the Tree of Knowledge in Gen 2:17 was a law similar in kind to the decrees found in the Law later given to Moses. It taught Adam and Eve's disregard of that prohibition to be a "trespass," even though Genesis does not use that terminology. Furthermore, Genesis taught that the death pronounced on Adam and Eve involved both an immediate fall from physical immortality to mortality and an immediate spiritual death. Consequently, the offspring of the primal pair are in need of both physical and spiritual healing.

THE OBSERVATION OF ELAINE PAGELS

In a very perceptive article written in 1985, which was later expanded into a book, Elaine Pagels describes how Augustine's exegesis of Genesis 1–3 was a radical departure from the exegesis that had prevailed before his time, and how it redirected the course of subsequent theology in the West.[34] As she explains the earlier view, "Many Christian converts of the first four centuries regarded the proclamation of *autexousia*—the moral freedom to rule oneself—as virtually synonymous with 'the gospel.'" This moral freedom to rule himself was given in creation in addition to the other gifts he received at that time of dominion over the earth and over the animals.

In support of her argument, Pagels cites Gregory of Nyssa, who was about one generation younger than Augustine:

> Preeminent among all [the gifts man is given] is the fact that we are free from any necessity, and not in bondage to any power, but have decision in our own power as we please; for virtue is a voluntary thing, subject to no dominion. Whatever is the result of compulsion and force cannot be virtue.[35]

---

34. Pagels, "Politics of Paradise."; Pagels, *Adam, Eve, and the Serpent*.

35. Gregory of Nyssa, *De hominis opificio* ("On the Creation of Mankind") 4.1, cited in Pagels, "Politics of Paradise," 68.

John Chrysostom, the patriarch of Constantinople who was roughly contemporaneous with Augustine but died at a much younger age, takes this even further. He anchors the freedom to rule oneself in "the image of God" in which mankind was created. When considering the meaning of the "image," he concludes: "The image of government (*tēs archēs eikona*) is what is meant; and as there is no one in the heaven superior to God, so there is no one on earth superior to humankind."[36]

As a younger man, Augustine argued much the same way as did Gregory and Chrysostom, but his thinking changed as he grew older.[37] In the mature Augustine's account of the lives of Adam and Eve, it was the desire for *autexousia* ("freedom to rule oneself") that was the cause of Adam's fall, not the essence of God's image in which he was created. The freedom to rule oneself implied a desire to be free of God's sovereignty. This desire gave force to the subtle temptation of the snake.

Furthermore, Adam was never actually free to rule himself, nor is any person. As Augustine explains: "[M]an has been naturally so created that it is advantageous for him to be submissive, but disastrous for him to follow his own will, and not the will of his creator."[38] Thus, claims of *autoexousia* are an illusion, for no human will ever usurp the place of God. But even worse, Augustine found himself to be damaged—to have the image of God within him marred—just as Adam had been damaged through his sin. "For we all were in that one man, since all of us were that one man who fell into sin through the woman who was made from him."[39]

Far from being a celebration of human freedom as earlier interpreters had considered it, Augustine declared Genesis 1–3 to be a story of human bondage. While neither Augustine nor his predecessors may completely understand Paul or Romans, Augustine raised issues that even today interpreters of the Apostle cannot ignore.

---

36. Chrysostom, *Homilia ad populum Antiochium* ("Homily to the People of Antioch") 7.3, cited in Pagels, "Politics of Paradise," 68.

37. Pagels, "Politics of Paradise," 77–78.

38. Augustine of Hippo, *De civitate Dei* ("City of God") 14.2, cited in Pagels, "Politics of Paradise," 78–79.

39. Augustine of Hippo, *De civitate Dei* ("City of God") 13.14, cited in Pagels, "Politics of Paradise," 80.

ROMANS 6

TRANSLATION: ROM 6:1–11

DEAD TO SIN, LIVING FOR GOD

¹What shall we say then? Shall we remain in sin so grace may increase? ²Absolutely not! We who have died to sin—how shall we still live in it? ³Or are you unaware that as many of us as were baptized into Christ Jesus, we were baptized into his death. ⁴Therefore, we were buried with him through baptism into death, so that just as Christ was raised from the dead through the glory of the Father, so also we might walk in newness of life. ⁵For if we have become engrafted [in him] in the likeness of his death, we will also be [engrafted in him] in resurrection. ⁶This we know, that our old self was crucified so the body of sin might cease to function, to serve us no longer in sin, ⁷for the person who dies has been cleared from [charges of] sin. ⁸But if we have died with Christ, we believe we will also live with him. ⁹Knowing that Christ was raised from the dead, [we also know] he is no longer mortal; death no longer rules him. ¹⁰For [the death] he died, he died to sin once and for all. [The life] he lives, he lives for God. ¹¹So also reckon yourselves to be, on the one hand, dead to sin, and on the other hand, living for God in Christ Jesus.

COMMENTARY

Vss. 1–11: In these verses Paul explains how both the death of Christ and his resurrection serve as models for the believer to emulate. Through baptism "into his death" believers crucify their old selves and die to sin. And through identification with his resurrection, believers are able to "walk in newness of life." Conversion involves a new way of thinking, and those who follow Christ in baptism should reckon themselves to be dead to sin and alive to God.

Vs. 1: *Ti oun eroumen* ("What shall we say then?"): This exact wording is found in 4:1, 6:1, 7:7, 8:31, 9:14, (close in 9:19), and 9:30. (For more about this, consult the comment on 3:9.) This expression does not mark the beginning of a completely new topic. Instead, it refocuses the previous topic to explore a new aspect of it.

Vs. 2: Some discussion of the grammar of this verse is necessary. The verse begins with an expression that is very characteristic of Paul: "Absolutely not!" (*mē genoito*). (For more about this expression, see the note on Rom 3:4.)

The following sentence is unusual in two ways. First, it seems to have two main clauses that are not joined by a conjunction. The technical term for this is asyndeton. Furthermore, the "we" of the second clause "calls back" to the "we" of the first clause, a literary device known as anaphora. In any case, I have indicated the loose coupling of these clauses by means of a dash.

Second, if the clause I have translated "we who have died to sin" were translated following strict rules of classical grammar, it would read, "we, whoever we are, have died to sin." In Classical Greek indefinite relative pronouns, such as *hoitines* (the word used here) would mean "whoever." However, in *Koinē* Greek (also called "Hellenistic Greek"), they are sometimes used as if they were relative pronouns. Therefore, in this verse, *hoitines* functions as if it were *tines*, meaning "who."

Vss. 3–4: Paul's question, "Are you unaware?" raises the issue of what has been taught in Rome about the meaning of baptism. Acts 18:25–26 suggests that Priscilla (Prisca) and Aquila, who at this point have again become residents of Rome, had a good understanding of Christian baptism even when they previously lived in the East. Paul's question may only be a rhetorical flourish used to highlight the importance of what he is about to say, but it is also possible that some gentiles in Rome emphasized divine grace in such a way that it obscured the importance of personal transformation.

These verses link the meaning of baptism with the death of Christ, baptism becoming a personal participation in Christ's death through a ritual reenactment of it. A linkage with the resurrection of Christ is also mentioned, although the exact association is left vague.

Immersion is the standard mode of baptism described in the New Testament, whatever one may say about the later baptismal practices that developed from it. Through use of the verb *synthaptō* ("to bury with"), Paul pictures immersion into the water as a symbolic burial and a symbolic reenactment of Christ's death. While burial is the image in vs. 4, in vs. 6 it will become crucifixion.

Paul may also imply that reemerging from the water is a symbol of resurrection, but the focus of his comments is not on the *moment* of transformation, the rising. Instead, he focuses on *continually walking* in new life implied by conversion. This new life is analogous to Christ's post-resurrection life.

Vs. 5: The adjective "engrafted" (*symphytos*) is more customarily translated "united," which is not wrong, but which minimizes the botanical roots of the word. The related verb *symphyō* primarily means "to grow with," although in a medical context it can also mean "to reunite the edges of a wound." In a botanical context it often pictures the intertwining of branches.

Vs. 6: In the Greek, "our old self" is literally our old "person" (*anthrōpos*). For Paul, coming to faith is not a minor attitude adjustment. It is the destruction of one's old identity and its replacement with a new one. While here Paul describes conversion by the death of the old self, elsewhere he can describe conversion in terms of the birth of something new. In Titus 3:5 he writes, "[God] saved us through the washing of rebirth [or perhaps "regeneration" or "re-creation"]."

The purpose of crucifying the old person is so "the body of sin" might "cease to function" (*katargeō*). Paul clearly does not desire for the bodies of the Roman believers not to function at all; he does not desire their physical death. Quite to the contrary, he longs for spiritual sin and death to be disassociated from the physical body. To express this differently, his phrase "the body of sin" is a way of referring to the sinful activities and desires of the body. This resembles his reference to "this body of death" in Rom 7:24.

Paul's image is both striking and powerful. Mankind is trapped in sin and death, and the only escape from death is for the "body of sin" and the "body of death" themselves to die—through participation in the crucifixion of Christ. Paul's imagery is reflected in that great hymn "Crown Him with Many Crowns," which contains these magnificent words: "Who died eternal life to bring, and lives that death may die."[1]

Vs. 7: The word "cleared" is sometimes translated "freed." Since the Greek verb *dikaioō* is drawn primarily from the courtroom, perhaps "cleared" is preferable. The point is that when the accused dies, any charges of sin become moot.

Vs. 8: If a Christ follower has been engrafted into Christ, as vs. 5 says, that person will not only participate in Christ's death but also in his resurrection.

---

1. Verse 2 of "Crown Him with Many Crowns," lyrics by Matthew Bridges and Godfrey Thring (1851). The "many crowns" of the title is an allusion to Rev 19:12.

Vs. 9: "[Christ] is no longer mortal": Literally, the Greek says, "he no longer dies," but the meaning is more abstract, that "he is no longer subject to death." When Paul writes, "death no longer rules him," he implies that death rules all who are not engrafted into Christ. Paul is writing to Roman believers who remember being ruled by death. But, if believers will be raised up as Jesus was, then they too are no longer mortal, and they are no longer ruled by death.

Vs. 10: The Greek translated "the death he died" literally reads "that which he died," but of course he died a "death."[2] Paul's statement "he [Christ] died to sin" parallels the statement of vs. 2: "we who have died to sin." But there is a difference! We have renounced the sin which previously defined our lives. By his death Christ also renounced sin, but his was not what previously had defined his life. By his death he renounced our sin for us as a result of our being engrafted into him. And his death renounced this sin "once and for all" (*hapax*). Unlike animal and grain sacrifices that needed to be repeated continually, the death of Christ accomplished its purpose fully for all time. Furthermore, the new life that follows the crucifixion of the old life is to be lived "for God," understanding the dative case of *tō theō* as a "dative of advantage."[3]

Vs. 11: This verse provides a summary of the argument of vss. 1–10: The believer should consider herself both dead to sin and living for God. In the words of the seventeenth-century Puritan John Owen, "Be killing sin or it will be killing you." This also echoes the slogan championed by John M. G. Barclay, *simul mortuus et vivens* ("at the same time dead and alive").

TRANSLATION: ROM 6:12–23

FROM SLAVES OF SIN TO SLAVES OF RIGHTEOUSNESS

[12]Therefore, do not let sin reign anymore in your mortal body to obey its passions. [13]And do not surrender your members to sin as weapons of wickedness, but rather surrender yourselves to God as the living coming back from the dead and your members to God as weapons of righteousness. [14]For sin will not rule you, for you are not under the Law but under grace.

---

2. The relative pronoun *ho* is a neuter. Here it stands in place of "death," despite the fact that *thanatos* is masculine. See Bl-D-F §154.

3. Two common uses of the dative case are to express advantage and disadvantage. 1 Cor 6:13 provides a good example of a "dative of advantage": *ta brōmata tē koilia*, "Food is for [the benefit] of the stomach." Matt 23:31 provides a good example of "the dative of disadvantage": *martyreite heautois*, "You testify against yourselves."

¹⁵What shall we say then? Let us sin because we are not under the Law but under grace? Absolutely not! ¹⁶Do you not know that to whatever you surrender yourselves in obedience as slaves, you are slaves of what you obey: of sin leading to death; or of obedience leading to righteousness? ¹⁷Thanks be to God that you who were slaves of sin obeyed from the heart the type of teaching you were provided, ¹⁸and having been set free from sin, have become slaves of righteousness. ¹⁹I speak in a down-to-earth manner because of the [strength] of your fleshly desires, for just as you surrendered your members as slaves to impurity and lawlessness leading to anarchy, so now you will surrender your members as slaves to righteousness leading to holiness. ²⁰When you were slaves of sin you were free from righteousness. ²¹What fruit did you have then, inasmuch as you are now ashamed? For the end result of those things is death. ²²But now after being freed from sin and becoming slaves to God, you have your fruit in holiness, the end result of which is eternal life. ²³For the wages of sin is death, but the gracious gift of God is eternal life in Christ Jesus our Lord.

COMMENTARY

Vss. 12–14: In these verses, and through the end of the chapter, Paul continues to anthropomorphize sin, treating it as a willful adversary plotting against God's allies. This suggests he has in mind the story of God's encounter with Cain in Gen 4:6–7, the first time in the Bible that sin is personified. In fact, the beginning of vs. 14 ("sin will not rule you") paraphrases the end of Gen 4:7 ("you will rule it [sin]").[4]

Vs. 12: The language of this verse echoes vs. 9 but whereas that earlier verse spoke of Christ, this verse addresses Roman believers. In vs. 9 Paul declared that after his resurrection death could no longer "rule" (*kyrieuō*) over Christ. In this verse, believers are exhorted not to let sin "reign" (*basileuō*) over them "anymore."[5] In vs. 9, because of his resurrection, Christ is said no longer to be "mortal" (literally "to die"; *apothnēskō*). In this verse the body of the believer is described as "mortal," using the adjective *thnētos*.

Vs. 13: Paul points out that one's members (i.e., body parts) may be deployed either as "weapons of wickedness" or as "weapons of righteousness."

---

4. When reading the Old Testament, Paul usually follows the LXX, but not always. His understanding of God's encounter with Cain comports well with the MT, but not with the LXX, which in these verses translated a corrupt text.

5. There is not a specific Greek word behind "anymore"; it is an implication of Paul's use of *mē* ("not") with the third person imperative of *basileuō* ("to reign"). Bl-D-F §337 (1).

This image differs some from the way he uses "weapons of righteousness" in 2 Cor 6:7, where "the word of truth" and "the power of God" are pictured as weapons wielded in the right hand and the left.

The basic meaning of the verb *paristēmi* is "to present," but in military contexts it can mean either "to surrender" or "to come over" to another side. In view of the image of weaponry Paul has deployed, "surrender" seems a better fit than "present."

Vss. 14–15: These verses contain two of the five places where Paul contrasts "Law" and "grace," three of which are in Romans. (For more on this contrast, see the comment on Rom 5:20.) The expression "under Law" or "under the Law" is also typically Pauline. "Under Law"/"under the Law" occurs in Rom 3:21, these two verses, 1 Cor 9:20, Gal 3:23, Gal 4:4, 5, 21, and Gal 5:18. The parallel expression "under grace" occurs only in these two verses and nowhere else in the Bible.

Usually the expression "under the Law" is explained spatially (i.e., literally meaning "under") and then this meaning is extended metaphorically. It is associated with the image of the "yoke of the Law" or "the yoke of the *mitzvot* ['commandments']" resting on a person's shoulders. An example is *m.Aboth* 3.5, "Whosoever takes upon himself the yoke [obligations] of the Law, from him shall be removed the yoke of government [oppression] and the yoke of worldly affairs."[6] According to this theory, even when a yoke is not specifically mentioned, "under the Law" retains an association with yoking. Whether or not this is the correct explanation for the origin of "under the Law" as normally used in Judaism, the expression certainly implied that the Law had binding authority.

"What shall we say then?": Literally the Greek simply says, "What then?" but this is likely an abridged form of the longer question. (For more about this, see the comment to Rom 3:9.)

"Let us sin because we are not under the Law but under grace?": This is often translated "Shall we sin . . . ," but it takes the exact same form as the so-called "hortatory subjunctive" ("Let us . . . ."), and I think it is a hypothetical exhortation to sin embedded within a question. In vs. 14 Paul has elevated grace over Law. Then in vs. 15 he asks what should be said in light of this principle, illustrating his question by throwing out a possible example of what might be said. The supposed justification for sinning is the very idea Paul has just asserted: The believer is "not under Law but under grace."

It seems Paul has been accused of making this argument—that being under grace justifies continuing to sin—and in response he tries to dispose of this accusation once and for all. In any case, after raising this

---

6. The translation is from Jastrow, *Dictionary*, s.v. "ol."

hypothetical, he completely dismisses it with his strong denial, "Absolutely not!" This same form of denial occurs ten times in Romans. (For more about this, see the comment to Rom 3:4.)

Vs. 16: Apparently Paul's critics accuse him of promoting disobedience, and therefore he counters by promoting "obedience," even though this twists his argument to suggest somewhat artlessly that the goal is to be "[the slave of] obedience leading to life." Can "obedience" be a master? One would have expected a more symmetrical contrast between being "[the slave of] sin leading to death" and "[the slave of] righteousness leading to life," but this is not what he writes. Nevertheless, Paul's point is clear. It is obedience to God that leads to life.

Vss. 17–18: The word "type" (Greek *typos*) means "pattern." Paul does not know exactly what the Roman believers have been taught, and doubtless not all have received precisely the same teaching. Nevertheless, he is aware of the basic pattern of teaching at Rome, and he generally approves of it, although he clearly has trouble with some things that have been taught there. The most foundational truth is that through this teaching they have been freed from slavery to sin and become slaves of righteousness.

Vs. 19: The phrase "in a down-to-earth manner" translates the neuter adjective *anthrōpinon* (literally "in a human manner"). Paul's point is that he is trying to communicate effectively with every-day people, not scholars or religious experts.

He further clarifies that he is doing so because of "the strength [literally "weakness," *astheneia*] of your fleshly desires [*sarx*]." In contrast to English, Greek embraces double negatives, and Paul uses the negative concept "weakness" rather than the positive "strength" as well as the negative "flesh" rather than the positive "Spirit." Therefore, this phrase should be translated either "because of the strength of your fleshly desires" or "because of the weakness of your spiritual discernment." Since Paul is aware of the deeply sinful pasts of many of the Roman believers, he is especially worried about the allure of the "flesh." Therefore, I think the former translational option is better.

While the word "flesh" (*sarx*) has already appeared in Romans four times prior to this verse, it will appear again three times in chapter 7 leading into chapter 8 where it appears thirteen times! While the central thrust of this chapter is that sin is put to death in the believer (vs. 2) and therefore "sin will not rule you" (vs. 14), the problem of the flesh remains. This matter will be discussed at greater length in the two chapters that follow. *For a lengthier discussion of what Paul means by "flesh," see the excursus titled "Paul's Use of the Word 'Flesh.'"*

In this context Paul is clearly addressing gentile believers since he uses the word "lawlessness" (*anomia*), a common trope Jews associated with gentiles. The word "lawlessness" only occurs three times in Romans, two of which are in this verse. The other occurrence is found in 4:17 in a quotation from the LXX. What I have translated "anarchy" in this verse literally reads "greater lawlessness," suggesting that lawlessness has a tendency to spiral out of control. By using the word "anarchy," I have followed the suggestion of Robert Jewett.[7] While "anarchy" may not be the precise concept Paul has in mind, it cannot be far off the mark.

The verb "surrender" (*paristēmi*) occurs twice in this verse, but the forms are inflected differently. The first occurrence is clearly an aorist indicative ("you surrendered") but the form of the second occurrence (*parastēsate*) is difficult to determine since it defies the standard conventions. Most scholars treat it as an aorist imperative even though it deviates from the normal imperative pattern, which would be *parastēte*. It more closely resembles the future indicative (which normally would be *parastēsete*), although it differs slightly from that form as well. Nevertheless, I have chosen to treat it as a future indicative ("you will surrender"). If this is a future form, it expresses Paul's confidence that the Roman believers will continue on the good path they have started.

Vss. 20–22: In these verses Paul contrasts slavery to sin with slavery to God. The final result of the former is death, and the final result of the latter is eternal life. This contrast is also expressed by the images of being "free from righteousness" and being "freed from sin."

The clause "inasmuch as you are now ashamed" incorporates the expression *eph' hois*, which is identical to the controversial phrase *eph' hō* in Rom 5:12 except that the relative pronoun is plural. For this reason, I have followed the pattern of my translation in 5:12 with the translation here.

Rather than "inasmuch as," the phrase *eph' hois* could plausibly be translated "about which" or "because." The past lawlessness of the gentile believers has not borne any positive fruit. Moreover, it has resulted in them "being ashamed." How carefully does Paul bring this fact up? Does he gently say, "inasmuch as you are now ashamed"? Or does he in a matter-of-fact manner say, "about which you are now ashamed?" or "because you are now ashamed?" I have opted for the first option.

Vs. 23: This verse contains one of the great summary statements of Paul's gospel. The Greek word translated "gracious gift" is *charisma*; eternal life is freely given by grace, much as the gifts of the Spirit discussed in Rom 12:6–8 and in 1 Corinthians 12 are given graciously to the church.

---

7. Jewett, *Romans*, 413.

ROMANS 7

TRANSLATION: ROM 7:1–6

DEAD TO THE LAW

¹Or do you not know, brothers [and sisters]—for I am speaking to those who know the Law—that the Law rules the individual for as long as he or she lives? ²For the married woman has been bound to her husband by law, but if the husband should die, she is released from the law pertaining to her husband. ³So while the husband lives, she is called an adulteress if she becomes wife to another man, but if the husband dies, she is free from the law, not being an adulteress when becoming wife to another man.

⁴So also, my brothers, you too have been put to death to the Law through the body of Christ, in order to belong to another, to one raised from the dead, in order that we may bear fruit for God. ⁵For when we were in the flesh, the sinful passions were energized in our members through the Law, bearing the fruit of death. ⁶But now we have been released from the Law, dying to what held us back, in order that we might serve in the new age of the Spirit and not in the old age of the written code.

COMMENTARY

Vss. 1–4: In these verses Paul's comments are directed to "those who know the Law": Jewish believers. He then describes how the death of a woman's husband frees her from the bond of marriage stipulated by the Law so that she can marry another man. Furthermore, Paul contends that the situation of the newly freed widow is like their own situation with respect to the Law.

Paul's argument presumes a word which is never mentioned but nevertheless is implied. That word is "yoke" (*'ol* in Hebrew; *zugos* or *zeugos* in

Greek; *iugum* in Latin). The central act in the Roman marriage rite was the *conjunx manoram* (Latin for "the yoking together of the hands"), also called the *conjunx dextarum* ("the yoking together of the right hands").[1] In this ceremony the officiant would take one hand of the prospective bride and one hand of the prospective groom and join them together, often wrapping the clasped hands with a stole (a long narrow strip of cloth). A vestige of this ceremony survives in the English word "conjugal," which means "relating to marriage." Yoking, as it relates to marriage, is also presumed in Paul's admonition not to be "unequally yoked" (*heterozugeō*)—married to someone who is not a Christian—in 2 Cor 6:14. (Paul may allude to the "yoke" while not specifically mentioning it since the Jews of Rome may not have married employing the Roman rite.)

In the Old Testament the "yoke" is also a common image of hard labor or slavery since yoked animals served more-or-less as slaves of their masters (e.g., 1 Kgs 12:11; Isa 14:25). The yoke also became connected with the Law of Moses, although the exact mechanism and the timing is somewhat obscure. Today, when a Jewish boy has his *bar mitzvah*, making him a "son of the commandment," as the phrase literally means, he takes upon himself the "yoke" of the commandments. This implies that he has become an adult who is responsible for his actions. While the *bar mitzvah* rite likely was not yet practiced in Paul's day, the underlying ideas were present. Acts 15:10 records Peter speaking of "putting a yoke on the necks of the disciples," apparently a reference to requiring gentiles to observe the Law of Moses. Similarly, in Gal 5:1 Paul exhorts Galatian gentiles not "to submit again to a yoke of slavery." First, they were enslaved to sin. Paul fears they are about to become gentile slaves of the Law of Moses that was never given to the gentiles.

The upshot of this is that Paul is telling the Jewish believers of Rome that their relationship to the Law of Moses is like the relationship of a widow to her dead husband. It may be part of their history, but the Law does not limit their future. In fact, they now belong to another, to Jesus Christ!

Vss. 5–6: "When we were in the flesh" refers to the past before being "in the Spirit." This is one instance that demonstrates "the flesh" cannot simply be equated with "the body," for both Paul and his Roman audience are still alive and living a bodily existence. "In the flesh" means something like "merely in the flesh," which is to say, without the Holy Spirit's presence.

---

1. Although *iugum* ("yoke") and *conjunx* ("yoking" or "spouse") do not look much alike, they are related. In Latin "i" and "j" are the same letter. The noun *iugum* leads to the verb *iungo* ("to yoke together"). Prefixing *con* (=*cum*) and adding an adjectival ending, leads to the adjective *conjunctus* ("joined with"). From there, it is a short step to *conjunx* ("yoking" or "spouse").

What I have translated "sinful passions" literally reads "passions of sin." The construction is probably a "genitive of source" indicating that these passions originate with sin.

In vs. 4 Paul told his readers they "have been put to death to the Law," a point he repeats in vs. 6 by calling the Law "that which held us back." This death to the Law is also marked by reception of the Spirit, and consequently entrance into a "new age of the Spirit" rather than the "old age of the written code." The implication is that for Jews this "old age of the written code" can also be called being "in the flesh" (vs. 5). The Law may be "spiritual," as Paul will say in vs. 14, but without the Spirit animating one's life, it is reduced to a fleshly guide or (by identifying faithless acts as transgressions) even made an executioner.

These verses divide the Jewish believer's life into two eras, separated by the moment of their coming to faith. Paul calls the earlier phase being "in the flesh" and "the old age of the written code." What comes after is "the new age of the Spirit." His description in vss. 7–25 of a life tormented by the inability to do what is right is likely a retrospective foray into the struggles of the earlier era.

TRANSLATION: ROM 7:7–25

A DIGRESSION: THE LAW BECAME A TOOL OF SIN

⁷What shall we say then? The Law is sin? Absolutely not! But I did not recognize sin except through the Law: I would have not known what it was to covet if the Law did not say, "Thou shalt not covet." ⁸But Sin, seizing a beachhead through the commandment, promoted in me every covetous desire. For apart from the Law Sin is dead. ⁹At one time I was alive without the Law, but when the commandment came, Sin sprang to life ¹⁰and I died, and the commandment [supposedly] leading to life, I discovered, leads to death. ¹¹For Sin, seizing a beachhead through the commandment, deceived me, and through the commandment killed me. ¹²So, the Law is holy, and the commandment is holy and righteous and good.

¹³So, did the good [intended] for me become death? Absolutely not! But Sin, in order that it might be seen to be sin, through the good [intended] for me accomplished death, in order that through the commandment Sin might become supremely sinful.

¹⁴We know that the Law is spiritual, but I am fleshly, sold as a slave under the power of Sin. ¹⁵For I do not know what I am doing. I do what I do not want, but [instead] I do what I hate. ¹⁶But if I do what I do not want [to

do], I agree with the Law that it is good. ⁱ⁷But at this point, I am no longer doing this, but rather the Sin that lives inside of me. ¹⁸For I know that good does not live in me, that is in my flesh. For the desire is present with me, but actually doing good is not. ¹⁹For I do not do the good which I want, but the evil which I do not want, this I do. ²⁰And if I do what I do not want to do, I am no longer doing this but rather the Sin living within me. ²¹So I discover the pattern, by my desiring to do good, that evil is present with me. ²²For I take delight in the Law of God with my inner self, ²³but I see another pattern in my members battling against the Law of my mind and taking me captive by the pattern of Sin in my members. ²⁴I am a tormented person. Who will rescue me from this this body of death? ²⁵Thanks be to God through Jesus Christ our Lord! For I myself serve as a slave, on the one hand, to the Law of God with my mind, and on the other hand, to the Law of Sin with my flesh.

COMMENTARY

Vss. 7–12: Once again Paul uses the question, "What shall we say then?" (*Ti oun eroumen?*) to refocus his argument. The exact direction he wants to go is indicated by a possible response, framed as a question: "The Law is sin?" He has told his readers both that sin leads to death (5:12–14) and that sinful passions were energized by the Law (vs. 5). This raises the natural question: How are sin and the Law related? But Paul raises this possibility that the Law is sin only to dismiss it most emphatically.

The clause "I would not have known" is translated as if its verb were a subjunctive, even though it is in the indicative mood. The justification for this is that the form is a pluperfect, and Greek pluperfects have no subjunctive forms. Furthermore, the context seems to require an English subjunctive.

In vs. 5 Paul has already mentioned the Law's power to energize sinful passions. By mentioning the Law's awakening of covetousness within, he reinforces this connection.

"Apart from the Law Sin is dead" (vs. 8): This is not a statement about salvation-history, i.e., hypothetically relating to the period when there was no Law. Instead, it is an experiential statement relating to a typical Jewish childhood prior to taking on the yoke of the Law. Similarly, Paul's reference to being "alive without the Law" describes the innocence of youth. Using the terminology of those who practice "believer's baptism," Paul refers to a time prior to "the age of accountability." To those from a Reformed background who assert that Adam's progeny are born not with just a predisposition to sin but are actually born guilty, this interpretation will likely be unacceptable.

For the Jew who transitions from childhood's lack of accountability to adulthood and becomes bound to the Law, Sin springs to life and that individual receives a deathblow under the burden of Sin. What Paul says here is quite scandalous to Jewish ears. According to Deuteronomy 30 Moses presented the Law to Israel as the way to "life," exhorting them to "choose life" (Deut 30:19). But Paul suggests that the experience of every Jew as he or she becomes an adult is very much the reverse of what Moses seems to promise.

Paul does not accuse Moses of teaching error. His point is that a simplistic reading of Deuteronomy does not square with the experience many Jews hold in common. The Law of Moses points beyond the commandments it contains to God's plan for the redemption of all humanity. It points to the Messiah, to life in him, and to life in the Spirit.

As argued in the excursus "The Puzzle of Rom 7:7-25," these verses do not properly constitute autobiography, but rather role-playing by Paul of the typical Jew's experience. In Phil 3:4-6 (and elsewhere), Paul implies that his pre-Christian struggle was not with a sense of helplessness and guilt, but rather with a case of spiritual blindness. There he describes how he mistakenly felt "blameless according to righteousness by the Law," even though he later came to realize that such self-righteousness was "refuse" or "garbage" in comparison with Christ (Phil 3:8). Similarly, in 2 Cor 3:14-18 Paul describes the resistance to the gospel of his Jewish kinsmen with the words, "a veil lies over their hearts"—another way of describing spiritual blindness. If there is anything in Rom 7:7-25 that similarly points toward spiritual blindness, it is found in vs. 11: "For Sin . . . deceived me." Sin is villainized, complete with evil intentions and cunning.

In vs. 12 Paul calls the Law "holy" and the commandment "holy, righteous, and good." There is probably no significance to "the commandment" receiving a longer list of commendations than "the Law." Most notable is that, despite the holiness of the Law, it is regularly used as a tool of Sin.

Vs. 13: The phrase "the good [intended] for me" appears twice in this verse, differing only by the case is which "the good" (*to agathon*) appears. "The good [intended] for me" is another way of referring to the Law. The great puzzle Paul explores is how something meant to produce unalloyed good instead contributed to evil and accomplished death.

Sin continues to be personified. Here Paul presents Sin as arrogantly self-aggrandizing. It wants to be recognized for what it is, and its interest in producing death is to become—probably "in the minds of others," should be assumed—supremely sinful. Sin exploits the Law, substituting its own purposes for those purposes for which God created the Law. Yet surprisingly, both the existence of Sin itself and its exploitation of the Law were foreseen by God and play a role in his plan for ultimate redemption of the entire cosmos.

Vs. 14: In contrast to Paul's triumphant declaration in chapter 6 that believers no longer must live in slavery to Sin, here Paul describes himself (or the person whose role he is playing) as both fleshly and a person who has been sold as a slave to Sin. This is despite the spiritual nature of the Law, in which he had placed his trust. He has been unable to utilize the Law effectively, so while in theory the Law promised life, in practice trying to follow it led to death. As N. T. Wright summarizes Paul's argument: "There wasn't anything wrong with Torah [Law], but only with the people to whom it was given."[2]

"Under the power of Sin": The preposition *hypo* (literally "under") is here used with the accusative case, so it does not express agency ("sold by") as it would if used with the genitive. But *hypo* with the accusative can express subjection to someone's dominion, as it does here.

Vss. 15–16: In these verses Paul expresses a lack of psychological integrity; his will and his desires conflict. What is worse, his own judgment about what is good agrees with the judgments of the Law, thereby condemning his actual behavior. In this way he damns himself and is unable to live with any sort of equanimity or personal wholeness.

Vss. 17–20: The dissonance between what Paul wants to do and what he does is so great that he feels he has lost control of his actions. Sin has become the agent, in place of his mind or self. This is not Paul's way of denying responsibility for these actions. Far from it. This is an expression of how out-of-control life has become.

"But at this point" (vs. 17) translates *nuni* (literally "now"). It marks the present point in the progression of an evolving—or better, a devolving—narrative.

"I know that good does not live in me" (vs. 18): This is often translated, "I know that no good lives in me," but this is incorrect. The position of the negative *ouk* shows that the verb "lives" is being negated, not the adjective "good."

Vss. 17 and 20 are very similar, and they bracket the argument of the intervening verses.

Vss. 21–24: In these verses the English words "pattern" and "Law" both translate the same Greek word: *nomos*, which elsewhere I have usually translated "Law." Where I have translated *nomos* as "Law," I believe it refers to the Law of Moses. Where I have translated *nomos* as "pattern," it refers to a pattern Paul (or the character he portrays) has observed. This pattern is

---

2. Wright, *Paul and the Faithfulness of God*, 507

that whenever he tries to do good, he inevitably becomes aware that evil is "present in him" or "present with him." The grammar does not make clear which meaning is to be favored.

When I have translated *nomos* as "pattern," this does not exclude the possibility that it also refers to the negative consequences of the Law of Moses when it is being exploited by Sin. Paul often uses words with such polyvalent meanings. *For a more extensive discussion of these matters, see the excursus titled "The Puzzle of Rom 7:7–25."*

In vs. 24 Paul vividly describes himself (or the person he portrays) as "a tormented person." This is followed by a cry of desperation: "Who will rescue me from this this body of death?" The expression "body of death" is surprising; one might have expected Paul's complaint to be about his "flesh" or even "his body of flesh," since "the flesh" is his usual designation for life devoid of the Spirit. "Body of death" indicates the person to whom the body belongs is headed for death, and of course Paul's cry to be rescued indicates much the same.

Vs. 25: This verse is extraordinarily puzzling. The first part of the verse, "Thanks be to God through Jesus Christ our Lord!" seems completely out of place. However, no significant manuscript evidence points to a textual dislocation. Nevertheless, it is so awkwardly located that I am suspicious that a marginal note has accidentally crept into the epistle's text itself. If such a thing happened, it must have occurred very early in the transmission of the text to leave no manuscript evidence that it was not originally there.

Many have suggested that this expression of thanksgiving is an oblique answer to the cry of desperation found in vs. 24: "Who will rescue me from this this body of death?" The answer is that God, through Jesus Christ, will come to the rescue.

Michael A. Stone has suggested a creative solution to this problem that combines elements of the alternatives just presented. His theory is that this is not a marginal note that crept into the text but rather a momentary interruption of Paul's role-play as a typical Jew struggling under the burden of the Law.[3] *See the excursus titled "The Puzzle of Romans 7:7–25" for a fuller account of this role-playing theory.* This is the Spirit-enlivened, triumphant Paul intruding on his own (written) performance, thanking God that he does not presently find himself in the fix he has been describing while in character. It is like a spontaneous "Hallelujah" that erupts in a distracting manner during a gripping portion of Sunday morning sermon. It is real, but it also defies certain conventions. This written eruption is both an expression

---

3. Michael A. Stone conveyed this idea to me in a personal email dated January 15, 2024.

of thanksgiving and a declaration from Paul that Jesus Christ is the rescuer needed! Then, in the second half of the verse Paul once again assumes the guise of a typical Jew and quickly brings his role-playing to a close with the desperate cry of a disintegrating self: "For I myself serve as a slave, on the one hand, to the Law of God with my mind, and on the other hand, to the Law of Sin with my flesh."

Excursus: The Puzzle of Romans 7:7–25

THE INTRUSIVE CHARACTER OF ROM 7:7–25

Rom 7:7–25 is both puzzling and controversial. At least to modern readers, Paul's rhetorical strategy is opaque, and consequently the theological implications of what he writes are unclear. This lack of clarity has produced several different theological paradigms based on the various ways this passage is interpreted. With such variety of perspectives comes controversy.

Following Paul's triumphant assertion at the end of chapter 6 of the twin victories of freedom from sin and sanctification leading to eternal life, the first six verses of chapter 7 provide an interlude, the main point of which is to differentiate the old age of the written code from the new age of the Spirit. Then Rom 7:7–25 seems to rehearse the same issues discussed in chapter 6 but with far less optimism. In fact, whereas chapter 6 had proclaimed new-found freedom from slavery to sin, chapter 7 seems to reassert that same slavery when Paul cries out in vs. 14, "I am fleshly, sold as a slave under the power of sin."

Also perplexing is the unusually abrupt transition from the end of chapter 7 to the beginning of chapter 8, particularly since the flow of Paul's argument seems to be interrupted at that point. Rom 7:7–25 rests as uneasily ahead of chapter 8 as it does behind chapter 6 and 7:1–6. This suggests it is best to consider Rom 7:7–25 as an extended digression aiming to make an important point but also deviating from the flow of Paul's main argument.

WHAT KIND OF NARRATIVE IS ROM 7:7–25?

Paul writes in the first person throughout much of chapter 7, particularly in vss. 7 and following. Naturally, this has led many to assume Paul is engaging in autobiography. He describes a war between "the law [or "pattern"] of his mind"—whatever that may be—and another "law [or "pattern"] of his members," the precise meaning of which is also unclear. The latter "law" seems to prevail, leading him to captivity by "the Law of Sin."

Could it be that the normal Christian life is a constant struggle with "the members" and their desires generally triumphing over what the "inner self" (*ton esō anthrōpon*; vs. 22) desires? If so, the chances of achieving a holy life seem quite remote.

This dark prospect has led some to posit that Paul describes a situation where he is regenerate but not yet "sanctified," and therefore unable to live a victorious Christian life. The theory of such a state, saved but unable to live triumphantly, is the foundation of Wesleyan Holiness theology. The cure for this unhappy state is an experience of "entire sanctification" which is separate from the experience of conversion. The term "entire sanctification" comes from 1 Thess 5:23: "And the very God of peace sanctify you wholly; and I pray God your whole spirit and soul and body be preserved blameless unto the coming of our Lord Jesus Christ" (KJV). John Calvin and the tradition that followed in his wake had taught that sanctification was a gradual process, and this process would never be completed until a person's "glorification" in heaven. But John Wesley thought Paul's prayer that the Thessalonians would be sanctified "wholly" meant that entire sanctification is available in this life. Furthermore, the picture Rom 7:7–25 provides of a soul torn between divergent impulses illustrates the predicament of the saved, but not yet sanctified, person.

Unlike Wesley, others have concluded that, while Paul is writing autobiography, Rom 7:7–25 is a sort of flashback to his pre-conversion life. He struggles so greatly because he is unregenerate.

A difficulty with viewing this chapter as a glimpse into Paul's life prior to faith in Christ is that it paints a picture sharply different from the portrait of his pre-Christian life found in Phil 3:4–6. There Paul describes himself as confident, zealous, and "blameless according to righteousness by the Law." The implication in Philippians is that Paul's spiritual problem was blindness, not an overwhelming sense of guilt; he was smug and did not realize how far from God he stood. In the Acts 9 account of Paul's conversion, his physical blindness and the scales that fall from his eyes seem to be literal manifestations of his spiritual blindness.

Still another approach to Romans 7 understands Paul's first-person presentation not as autobiography but rather as role-playing: Paul is acting out the story of someone else. Could he be dramatizing the history of Israel, including both before-the-giving-of-the-Law and since-the-giving-of-the-Law phases? Could he be acting out the plight of the stereotypical unconverted Jew who struggles with impossible demands of the Law?

So many options have been proposed.

PLACING ROMANS 7 IN CONTEXT

At least the last half of chapter 6, and perhaps the whole of it, is directed to gentile believers. This is made most apparent by Paul's use of the word "lawlessness" (*anomia*) twice in vs. 19. This is significant because *anomia* is the special problem of the gentiles. But beyond this, in all of chapter 6 the word "Law" only appears twice (in vs. 14 and in vs. 15), and in both places it occurs in an expression that excludes the Law rather than emphasizing it: "not under the Law but under grace." In chapter 6, Paul is certainly not addressing people preoccupied with the Law.

This all shifts in chapter 7. Paul begins the chapter by identifying his target audience: "I am speaking to those who know the Law" (vs. 1). And this statement contains the first of the chapter's 23 references to *nomos* ("Law"). In this chapter Paul is addressing people for whom "the Law" is a central issue: Jewish believers.

Also of significance is the paucity of the word "Spirit" (*pneuma*) in chapter six (where it does not occur at all) and in chapter seven (where it occurs once). The single occurrence of "Spirit" in chapter 7 is in vs. 6, not in vss. 7–25 where the gut-wrenching struggle of the conflicted soul is so vividly described. This single occurrence of "Spirit" in two chapters is followed by an explosion of 21 occurrences in chapter 8. This total for chapter 8 is more than all the occurrences in all the other chapters of Romans put together, which total 13. To put this differently, excluding chapter 8, the word *pneuma* (Spirit") occurs on average less than once per chapter, but in chapter 8 it occurs 21 times.

Thus, it is fair to say that chapter 8 highlights the Spirit and the Spirit's role in much the same way as chapter 7 highlights the Law and its role. The single occurrence of *pneuma* in chapter 7 (in vs. 6) serves to contrast two eras: life under "the written code"; and life in "the new age of the Spirit." In a sense, this verse underscores the larger contrast between chapters 7 and 8.

Another contextual clue about the meaning of Rom 7:7–25 is the way the first six verses of chapter 7 frame the transition from a life dominated by "the flesh" to a new reality (7:5). Vs. 6 describes the Law as "what held us back," a hindrance from which both Paul and his (Jewish) Roman readers have been "released." These two periods of before and after can also be described as "the old age of the written code" and "the new age of the Spirit."

Having framed the contrast between before and after so starkly, when Paul then depicts a life of torment as he does in vss. 7–25, we should perhaps take his earlier division of time into two periods as a clue to his rhetorical strategy. Although he does not announce what he is doing in vss. 7–25 as clearly as one might like, it does seem that in vss. 5 and 6 he has signaled he could head into a deeper exploration of one of those periods.

WHAT DOES PAUL MEAN BY "MEMBERS"?

Sometimes when Paul explains his theology, he exhibits a philosophical bent. In this chapter he makes a rather sharp distinction between, on the one hand, "the inner self" or "the mind," and, on the other hand, "the members" or "the passions of the members." This is very close to the distinction modern philosophers often make between "reason," which takes place in a mysterious entity called "the mind"—not to be confused with the physical organ called "the brain"—and sensations, which are apprehended through the senses and provoke what knowledge we have of the physical world.

Paul is rather confident about the ability of the "inner self"/"mind" to assess God's Law as God intended. In contrast, he fears that the "members"—body parts, through which sensations are experienced—and the passions of these members are vulnerable to attack. In Paul's discussion, Sin is personified (which is why I am capitalizing it) and is the agent of such attacks. As in Gen 4:7, at the conclusion of the story of Cain and Abel, Sin is crouching at the door, and "its desire is for you." All Sin needs is a foothold or beachhead from which to spring.

The Greek word *aphormē* (which I have translated "beachhead") is often translated "opportunity," and it certainly can mean that, but it is a word primarily used in military contexts. It designates a base from which an attack is mounted. According to Paul, "the commandment" provides just such a beachhead.

Although the commandment is of divine origin and it was intended to clarify which behaviors please God and which behaviors displease him, Paul explains that the commandment also provides a beachhead for Sin's attack. By setting boundaries, the commandment *ipso facto* raises the question, "Am I willing to honor such boundaries?" Just as in the Garden the snake used God's commandment as a beachhead for doubt and disobedience, so too the commandments contained in the Law of Moses provide beachheads for doubt and disobedience among those who "know the Law."

In a sense, Paul suggests that the drama of the Garden is reenacted on a regular basis in the lives of his fellow Jews.

WHAT DOES PAUL MEAN BY *NOMOS*?

Some Pauline scholars contend that Paul believed gentiles had Roman law and Jews had the Law of Moses, so when writing to the Romans, Paul addressed the general *principle of law* in order to be relevant to both groups. Although some truly gifted scholars take this position, it strikes me as extremely unlikely. I believe in almost every place where Paul uses the word *nomos*, he means "the Law of Moses." Therefore, I think it is important to try to understand Paul's use of *nomos* in this way, wherever it is at all possible.

With that caveat out in the open, I should also point out that three of the places where many interpreters consider it impossible for *nomos* to mean "the Law of Moses" occur in Romans chapter 7, so this issue is not irrelevant to the topic at hand.

If *nomos* does not mean "the Law of Moses," then what might it mean? The claim is often made that Paul sometimes uses *nomos* to express roughly what the English word "principle" means. Another suggestion is that in some cases *nomos* is best translated "pattern."

This last suggestion calls to mind a quirk of the English word "law" that is often overlooked. "Law" can be used in two distinct ways. First and most obviously, it means a decree by some acknowledged authority, maybe a congress, a parliament, or an emperor. This is the most common way we use the word.

But sometimes "law" is used of patterns we observe. When we speak of the "laws of nature," we are not speaking of legislation or edicts, but rather what appear to be immutable patterns. The "law of gravity" always seems to be in effect. Because of the overwhelming uniformity of this pattern, we call it a law.

The historian Henry of Huntingdon relates an apocryphal tale about King Canute I of England, Denmark, and Norway. To modestly illustrate that even his great power was limited, King Canute set his throne near the edge of the sea at low tide and commanded the tide not to rise. But of course, it did rise, drenching Canute's throne and his royal robes with seawater. There are human decrees that may be called "laws," and then there are also forces that lie beyond human control, which we also sometimes call "laws." This tale illustrates the two quite different meanings of the word "law" and their respective domains.

However, someone might quibble, "We call such things as gravity 'law' because God or Mother Nature or some other great power has decreed these rules and nature always follows them." Fair enough. But people often believe more strongly in these constant patterns than in whatever authority might have decreed them. Many who strongly affirm the laws of nature claim not to believe in God or Mother Nature or any ordering intelligence.

As already mentioned, three of the places where *nomos* may not refer to the Law of Moses occur in Romans 7, and two of these places are in the same verse. Consider the following: "So I discover the *law*, by my desiring to do good, that evil is present with me" (Rom 7:21). In this verse, the italicized word *law* makes more sense if it means "pattern" or "principle" than "Law of Moses." Here Paul is describing a dynamic he observes regularly.

As the role-playing Paul looks inward, his character finds himself conflicted. He lacks integrity, in the sense of a unified approach to life. Instead, he finds within himself a consistent pattern of dueling impulses. The part of himself he considers good condemns another part, which he recognizes to be evil. This evil part is either "in him" or "with him"; the grammar is ambiguous about which is implied.

Also consider vs. 23: ". . . but I see another *law* in my members battling against the Law of my mind and taking me captive by the *law* of Sin in my members." The word *nomos* occurs three times in this verse, but in the second occurrence it likely means "the Law of Moses." For Paul, it is not his mind that is the "beachhead" for Sin's attacks but rather his "members." So, it is the first and third occurrences of *nomos* that are at issue. The two phrases are similar but not identical. In the first instance, a "law" is said to be "in my members." In the other instance, "the law of Sin" is said to be "in my members."

In both cases the translation "pattern" or "principle" could be substituted for the italicized word *law* and the verse would make sense. But could the italicized word *law* also mean "the Law of Moses"? Could Paul imply that the passions of his members are stirred up by the limitations the Law of Moses imposes and produce doubt about God's character and disobedience to his command? Could it be that "the law of Sin" is "the law of Moses" when viewed from a certain perspective? This would mean that "the Law of my understanding" and "the law in my members"/"the law of sin in my members" both refer to "the Law of Moses" but viewed from different vantages.

If this is the case, and I think it is, this does not mean that the italicized *law* in the two places it occurs in this verse cannot also mean "pattern" or "principle." The technical term for a word carrying two meanings at the same time is "polyvalence." Paul often uses words like a poet, and such a polyvalent use of *nomos* is quite in keeping with Paul's normal style.

The net result is this: while there is one Law, it is appropriated in two different ways. Its claims are reasonably appropriated by the mind and judged to be valid, but through the sensual desires of the body, the Law gives Sin a beachhead and encourages rebellion against God. It is Eden all over again. By limiting the individual's options in a way she does not welcome, the Law provokes mistrust of God.

QUESTIONS THAT GET IN THE WAY

When approached solely from a literary perspective, Romans 7 contains difficult puzzles. However, the interpretation of this chapter has also been burdened further by questions—understandable questions—imposed from beyond the context of Romans. Systematic theology by its very nature seeks to answer the questions thoughtful Christians ask. The problem is that when this happens sometimes biblical texts are interrogated for answers to questions that have nothing to do with the argument the author presents.

Interpreters often approach Romans 7 as if it is an essay on sanctification, which I do not think it is. They also often ask how much of the conquest of sin stems from human effort cooperating with divine grace and how much depends entirely on the work of God with no human effort involved. The following illustration may help illustrate how this question has sometimes played out.

When John Wesley sailed for America to do missionary work in Georgia, he encountered a group of Moravians (members of the *Unitas Fratrum* ["Unity of the Brothers"]) sailing aboard the same ship. These Moravians belonged to a community at the village of Herrnhut, located in the Germanic state of Saxony. This community had been founded thirteen years earlier on land donated by Count Nicolas Ludwig von Zinzendorf. Martin Luther had been from Saxony, and the impact of Luther's theology on the Moravians was quite strong. While Luther had argued that people were saved entirely by grace alone—human works had no role in achieving their justification—the Moravians extended this dynamic to sanctification as well. Human effort was unnecessary and irrelevant in the pursuit of a sanctified life.

When Wesley encountered the Moravians *en route* to Georgia, he was both greatly attracted to their strong Christian faith and greatly dismayed by their theology of sanctification. Wesley agreed with them that justification came by grace through faith, but he also believed that the converted individual needed to struggle against sin. He was amazed at what he called the "quietism" of the Moravians. They believed that if God gave them the gift of actual righteousness and holiness, then they would be righteous and holy. If he did not, they did not believe that any human struggle, even in cooperation with divine grace, could accomplish such a spiritual triumph.[4]

While the Moravians' tolerance of immoral living bothered Wesley greatly, the Moravians had an impact on the father of Methodism. He later developed his doctrine of "entire sanctification," by which God empowers the believer to become free from the compulsion to sin. Wesley never denied that human cooperation was a necessary component of sanctification, but he did acknowledge that without this experience of entire sanctification a person might be a Christian believer and still struggle greatly with sin.

UNRAVELLING THE PUZZLE OF ROMANS 7

This question of how human effort contributes to sanctification is an important one, but Romans 7 provides no answer because it is not addressing the struggles of a person who has already come to faith in Christ. The chapter, especially from vs. 7 on, is preoccupied with the struggle to obey the Law of Moses. It suggests the Law indicts this individual but provides no power to obey. The Law cannot overcome the attacks launched by Sin.

---

4. The careful work of John M. G. Barclay can help explain the conflicting views of the Moravians and Wesley. The Moravians, like Luther, recognized Paul taught that salvation was a free gift. Salvation was not conditioned on any prior deeds, worth, or status, what Barclay calls the perfection of Priority. But they also thought that for a gift to be free it must also be perfected in what Barclay calls Non-Circularity. Luther and the Moravians believed accepting the free gift of salvation did not result in any sort of obligation. In contrast, Wesley believed that salvation involves an obligation of allegiance and submission. In effect, Wesley denied that the divine gift of salvation was perfected in Non-Circularity. In addition, Wesley believed the gift of the Holy Spirit that accompanies salvation changes a person and overcomes one's prior enslavement to sin, allowing the individual to live a sanctified life. This, I believe, was also Paul's perspective. *For more about Barclay's thought see the Introduction to this commentary in the section titled "The New-Perspective Adjacent Scholar John M. G. Barclay."*

In fact, one's "members" provide a beachhead from which Sin's attacks are viciously deployed.

The absence of the word "Spirit" (*pneuma*) also suggests that the torment described in vss. 7–25 are not the cries of a regenerate person. In these verses, Paul assumes the role of a Jew who has not yet come to faith in Christ and who does not yet "have the Spirit of Christ" (Rom 8:9). As Paul explains things, it is the Spirit who enables the believer to overcome the onslaughts of Sin, and to fulfill the just requirements of the Law, although not through strict observance of the letter of the Law (vs. 6).

I would suggest that vss. 7–25 do not constitute autobiography in the way that Phil 3:4–6 does. I suspect Paul came to believe he had been even more deluded than most Jews without faith in Christ. He was so spiritually blind that his superficial conformity to the outward demands of the Law kept him from recognizing deep inward failures. It takes a more spiritually aware person to agonize over a conflicted self as is depicted in vss. 7–25 than the self-righteous person described in Phil 3:4–6. But Paul knew many Jews who reported just such dynamics, and he chooses to remind the believing Jews of Rome of the troubles they had left behind.

This does not mean that believing Jews, like believing gentiles, will not have continuing struggles with sin. But they will no longer struggle with sin powerlessly. Chapter 8 will describe a continuing struggle against "the flesh," but this struggle will be energized by "the Spirit." This struggle is not fought alone. It also seems true that Paul makes a distinction between being "in the flesh" (vs. 5), which means not having the Spirit in one's life, and the believer's struggle between living "according to the flesh" and living "according to the Spirit," which is an ongoing battle.

Excursus: Paul's Use of the Word "Flesh"

THE COMPLEX WAY PAUL USES *SARX*

If one were to divide authors into two camps, one consisting of those like scientists or contract lawyers who try to use words very precisely and uniformly, and another consisting of those like poets who use words in more flexible and fluid ways to engage the emotions and to captivate one's readers, Paul lies firmly in the second camp. By using the same word in multiple ways Paul keeps his readers engaged and on edge, lest they lose the thread of his argument. While in some respects this is a virtue, it also makes life difficult for the person trying to interpret him precisely.

One of Paul's most troubling words is *sarx*, which is usually translated "flesh." Unfortunately, this single-word, gloss-style translation obscures as much as it helps. It can allow the translator or interpreter to avoid making difficult decisions about Paul's specific meaning in specific contexts. What is most certain is that he uses the word in multiple ways and with multiple meanings.

Listing the specific ways Paul uses *sarx* is especially challenging since one meaning often shades into another. Nevertheless, I will try to describe Paul's varied uses of this word to help clarify this complex and difficult matter. I will also try to give one or more examples illustrating each usage.

I would like to propose eight ways Paul uses *sarx*. They are:

1. as a synonym for one's personal "body";
2. to indicate the unity of one's kindred or tribe;
3. to indicate humanity (as opposed to supernatural beings);
4. to indicate the standards of this world in contrast to the standards of the spiritual world;
5. to indicate a naturalistic worldview, in contrast to a worldview that includes spiritual dimensions beyond the natural;
6. as shorthand for inappropriate desires or conduct;
7. to name the self in rebellion against God; and
8. personified as an agent of evil.

I have ordered these eight usages on a continuum ranging from the most concrete and specific (one's body) to the most metaphysical (a personified agent of evil). These eight usages could also be grouped into three somewhat broader categories: *sarx* as expressions of physical commonality (usages 1 through 3); *sarx* as an expression of collective values (usages 4 and 5); and *sarx* as opposition to God (usages 6 through 8).

The following examples are drawn from Romans and Paul's Corinthian correspondence, and they are organized by Paul's eight ways of using *sarx*. In each, the italicized words show what the text literally says, and the bracketed words show my interpretation.

Examples of ***sarx*** *as a synonym for one's personal body*

Rom 2:28: "For it is not the Jew in appearance who is the real one [i.e., the real Jew] nor the circumcision in the *flesh* [body] that is real . . . ."

1 Cor 6:16: "Do you not know that he who joins himself to a prostitute becomes one *flesh* [body] with her? For, as it is written, 'The two shall become one *flesh* [body].'"

2 Cor 4:11: For while we live we are always being given up to death for Jesus' sake, so that the life of Jesus may be manifested in our mortal *flesh* [bodies].

An example of ***sarx*** *used to indicate the unity of one's kindred or tribe*

Rom 11:14: ". . . if, somehow, I might provoke my *flesh* [kindred] to jealousy and save some of them.

Examples of ***sarx*** *used to indicate humanity (as opposed to supernatural beings)*

Rom 3:20: ". . . since by works of the Law no *flesh* [human] will be cleared when standing before him, for through the Law only comes identification of sin."

1 Cor 1:29: ". . . so that no *flesh* [human] might boast in the presence of God."

Examples of ***sarx*** *used to indicate the standards of this world in contrast to the standards of the spiritual world*

Rom 1:3: ". . . concerning his son, the one born of the seed of David *according to the flesh* [by the standards of this world] . . . ."

Rom 4:1: "What shall we say then that Abraham, our forefather *according to the flesh* [according to the standards of this world], discovered?"

Rom 9:3: "For I have been longing that I myself might be an offering from Christ for the brothers [and sisters] of my kindred *according to the flesh* [according to the standards of this world]."

Rom 9:5: "Also to whom belong the patriarchs, and from whom is the Christ *according to the flesh* [according to the standards of this world]."

1 Cor 1:26: "For consider your call, brothers [and sisters]; not many of you were wise *according to the flesh* [according to the standards of this world], not many were powerful, not many were well born . . . ."

Examples of sarx *used to indicate a naturalistic worldview in contrast to a worldview that includes spiritual dimensions beyond the natural*

Rom 8:6: "For the mind of the *flesh* [naturalistic worldview] is death, but the mind of the Spirit is life and peace."

2 Cor 1:17: "Or did I decide what I decided *according to the flesh* [in a naturalistic way] in order that the answer from me might be both Yes Yes and No No?"

2 Cor 5:16: "From now on, therefore, we regard no one *according to the flesh* [in a naturalistic way]; even though we once regarded Christ *according to the flesh* [in a naturalistic way], we regard him thus no longer.

2 Cor 10:3: "For though we walk *in the flesh* [in the natural world] we are not carrying on war *according to the flesh* [in a naturalistic way]."

An example of sarx *used as shorthand for inappropriate desires or conduct*

Rom 6:19: "I speak in a down-to-earth manner because of the *weakness* [strength] of your *flesh* [inappropriate desires]."

Examples of sarx *used to name the self in rebellion against God*

Rom 7:5: "For when we were in the *flesh* [in rebellion against God], the sinful passions were energized in our members through the Law, bearing the fruit of death."

Rom 7:18: "For I know that good does not live in me, that is in my *flesh* [self in rebellion against God]. For the desire is present with me, but actually doing good is not."

Rom 7:25: "For I myself serve as a slave, on the one hand, to the Law of God with my mind, and on the other hand, to the law of sin with my *flesh* [self in rebellion against God]."

Rom 8:8: "And those living *in the flesh* [in rebellion against God] are not able to please God."

Rom 8:9: "You are not *in the flesh* [in rebellion against God] but in the Spirit, if the Spirit of God lives in you. But if anyone does not have the Spirit of Christ, this person is not his."

An example of **sarx** *personified as an agent of evil*

Rom 8:12: "So then, brothers [and sisters], we have obligations, not to the *flesh* [here personified as an agent of evil], [that is] to live according to the *flesh* [in rebellion against God] . . . ."

THE COMPLEXITY OF PAUL'S USE OF *SARX*

As an example of the complex ways in which Paul uses *sarx*, notice how in the following two verses the word is used in four different ways:

Rom 8:3-4: "[Knowing] the powerlessness of the Law because it was weakened by the *flesh* [inappropriate desires], for the removal of sin God condemned sin in the *flesh* [body] by sending his own son in the likeness of sinful *flesh* [humanity], in order that the just decree of the Law might be fulfilled in us who walk not *by the flesh* [with a naturalistic worldview] but by the Spirit."

A FINAL THOUGHT

It is important not to think "the flesh" means simply "the body." That mistaken notion was one of the factors that led the Gnostics astray. Paul often contrasts Spirit with flesh, but this usually is not a contrast between immaterial Spirit and material bodies. Instead, it often is a contrast between worldviews. In such cases, "the flesh" stands for a reductionistic, naturalistic worldview devoid of any spiritual consideration. In contrast "the Spirit" represents a worldview open to the work of the Holy Spirit, while also recognizing the natural dimension. Paul does not have a negative view of the body. If he did, he would not emphasize the importance of the resurrection of the body, which commits him to the eternal value of the body (although in changed form).

ROMANS 8

TRANSLATION: ROM 8:1–8

THE SPIRIT CAN DO WHAT THE LAW CANNOT

¹So there is now no condemnation to those in Christ Jesus ²for the Law of the Spirit of life in Christ Jesus has freed you from the Law of sin and death. ³What was impossible for the Law to do since through the flesh it was weak—by sending his own son in the likeness of sinful flesh and as a sin offering, God condemned sin in the flesh ⁴in order that the just decree of the Law might be fulfilled in us who walk not by the flesh but by the Spirit. ⁵For those who live [governed] by the flesh think the things of the flesh, but those [who live governed] by the Spirit [think] the things of the Spirit. ⁶For the mind of the flesh is death, but the mind of the Spirit is life and peace. ⁷Therefore the mind of the flesh is hostility to God, for it will not be subject to the Law of God, nor is it able [to be so]. ⁸And those living in the flesh are not able to please God.

COMMENTARY

Vss. 1–2: The word "condemnation" is often wrongly understood to imply psychological condemnation. It is not that those in Christ Jesus do not have to live with an angry God wagging his finger at them. It is also not talking about psychological self-condemnation. One should picture Paul's declaration within the context of the court. A person who is in Christ has been declared to be in the right; the charges against her are moot. Whereas the "those" of vs. 1 is plural, the pronoun "you" in vs. 2 is singular.

Vss. 1 and 2 should be read together. For the assertion in vs. 1, that there is no condemnation, is based on the truth expressed in vs. 2, that realizing the Law points to Christ Jesus frees a person from Sin's attacks launched from its beachhead, the Law. Some understand the Greek word *nomos* in vs. 2 to mean "pattern" or "principle" rather than as a reference to the Law of Moses. But Paul is not setting up a new principle over against the Law of Moses. Instead, he is contrasting two ways of looking at the same Law of Moses, one of which sees the Law pointing directly to Jesus.

Vss. 3–4: The beginning of vs. 3 recapitulates what Paul has already explained in vss. 7–25 of the previous chapter: because Sin uses the flesh as a beachhead, the Law is unable to accomplish what it points out as being necessary. But God has accomplished that necessary thing by sending his son both in human flesh and as a sin offering. In this way Sin, which Paul continues to anthropomorphize, is "condemned" as the criminal it is. The result of all this is that "the just decree of the Law" is "fulfilled." The sacrifice of Jesus as a perpetual "sin offering" is central to bringing about this just decree, but the condemnation of the proper offender—Sin—plays a role as well.

"As a sin offering" translates *peri hamartias* (literally "concerning sin"), which seems to function as an idiom. This idiom is peculiar to the use of *peri* with *hamartia*.[1] In the LXX *peri* is repeatedly used with *hamartia* in a way that does not occur with other sacrifices. Sometimes in such contexts *peri* translates the Hebrew *'al* ("concerning"), but more often it translates *le* ("for"). While in such situations *hamartia* often clearly means "a sin offering" rather than "sin," in other situations it is unclear where "for sin" leaves off and "as a sin offering" begins. Moule concurs with translating *hamartia* here as "sin offering."[2]

Vs. 3 stresses the importance of God's son having come "in the likeness of sinful flesh." As the fourth-century theologian and bishop Gregory of Nazianzus states, "For that which He has not assumed He has not healed; but that which is united to His Godhead is also saved."[3] By this he means that if Christ had not taken up any part of the human configuration, that part would not have been healed in any human. If Christ had not assumed human flesh, no human's flesh would have been restored. Further on in the chapter, in vs. 29, Paul will declare that God's children have been appointed to be "copies of his son's image." His point is that receiving the image of Christ more than compensates for the marring of the *imago dei* in humankind caused by sin. As an additional exposition on the importance of Christ having assumed human flesh, Gregory writes, "[As an heir of Adam] I had a share in the image,

---

1. BAG, s.v. "peri."
2. Moule, *Idiom Book*, 63.
3. Gregory of Nazianzus, *Letter 101.5 (to Cledonius)*, 440.

and I did not keep it. He [Christ] shared in my flesh in order both that the image might be saved, and that flesh might be made immortal."[4]

Paul's use in vs. 4 of the verb "to walk" meaning "the way one conducts his life" is a commonplace in Jewish literature. A binary alternative is suggested: either one conducts his life by the flesh (devoid of the influence of the Spirit), or one conducts his life guided by the Spirit.

Vss. 5–7: What governs a person will affect her thinking and her mind. It also affects one's ultimate destiny, since "the mind of the flesh" is both "death" and "hostility to God."

In classical Greek *echthra* ("hostility") is a noun, but in *Koinē* Greek this same form can also serve as a feminine adjective (meaning "hostile"). However, since here *echthra* modifies *phronēma* ("mind"), which is neuter, it cannot be an adjective. Accordingly, it should be construed as a noun.

Vs. 8: Paul asserts that "those living in the flesh are not able to please God," even though he hardly needs to mention this given what he has already stated. If "the mind of the flesh is hostility to God," it should seem obvious that people exhibiting such hostility will not please God. However, those living in the flesh may think they are pleasing God since in their blindness they do not recognize their hostility toward God. Such blindness was central to Paul's own pre-Christian story.

TRANSLATION: ROM 8:9–17

BY THE SPIRIT WE ARE ALIVE AND CO-HEIRS WITH CHRIST

[9]You are not in the flesh but in the Spirit, if the Spirit of God lives in you. But if anyone does not have the Spirit of Christ, this person is not his. [10]But if Christ is in you, on the one hand, your body is dead on account of sin, but on the other hand, your spirit is alive on account of righteousness. [11]But if the Spirit of the one who raised Jesus from the dead lives in you, the one who raised Christ from the dead will also make your mortal bodies alive by his Spirit who lives in you.

[12]So then, brothers [and sisters], we are debtors, not to the flesh, [that is] to live according to the flesh. [13]For if you live according to the flesh, you are going to die. But if by the Spirit you put to death the activities of the body, you will live. [14]For as many as are led by the Spirit of God, these are the children of God. [15]For you have not received a spirit of slavery leading again

---

4. Gregory of Nazianzus, *Oration 38*, 13. This quotation was also referenced in relation to Rom 5:12.

to fear, but you have received a Spirit of sonship by which we cry out, "Abba Father!" ¹⁶The Spirit himself testifies with our spirit that we are children of God. ¹⁷But if we are children, we are also heirs: on the one hand, heirs of God and, on the other hand, co-heirs with Christ, since we suffer together with him in order that we might also be glorified with him.

COMMENTARY

Vs. 9: This verse emphasizes the vital importance of the Spirit in the Christian life. *For a more extensive discussion of this topic, see the excursus titled "The Indispensable Spirit."*

The way Paul uses the words "flesh" and "Spirit" can be confusing, but this verse adds some clarity. Having "flesh," i.e., a body, is not determinative in the way that having the Spirit of God is determinative. Those having flesh may either be "in the flesh" or "in the Spirit." What determines which of these alternatives properly describes a person is whether or not the Spirit of God lives within them. Thus, the two alternatives are 1) only having flesh (i.e., a body), or 2) having flesh plus the Spirit of God within.

In the first half of this verse the Spirit is called "the Spirit of God" (*pneuma theou*). In the second half of the verse, the Spirit is called "the Spirit of Christ" (*pneuma christou*). Does the genitive relationship of these two phrases indicate that the Spirt comes "from God" and "from Christ"? Although it is not the only possibility, this is perfectly plausible, and it accords well with Western Theology.

In contrast, the Eastern Church has historically been opposed to the idea that the Spirit "proceeds from" Christ. The Niceno-Constantinopolitan Creed of 381 affirmed that the Spirit "proceeds from the Father," based on the text of John 15:26. However, by the eighth century, some in the West had expanded the Creed to say the Spirit "proceeds from the Father and the Son," based on statements such as the one found in this verse. In Latin the phrase "and the Son" is *filioque*, and consequently, this debate is often called the *Filioque* Controversy.

The Eastern Church acknowledges "the monarchy of the Father," who sits at the apex of a triangle with the Son and the Spirit representing the triangle's other corners. In terms of their ontology, all three persons of the Godhead are equal: they are all fully God. But in terms of function, they have different roles. The role of the Father includes his monarchy.

The complaint of the Eastern Church is that saying the Spirit "proceeds" from both the Father and the Son means that the Spirit has two origins, and it ruins the symmetry of the Trinity. Furthermore, saying the Spirit proceeds from the Son makes Pneumatology a subset of Christology. It is important that the theology of the Son and the theology of the Spirit each have their own proper and separate grounding. In contrast, in the theology of the West one of the principal roles of the Spirit is to point to Christ.

While the Eastern Church has a robust theology of the Spirit, it should surprise no one that the Pentecostal Movement emerged in the West. For Pentecostals, the work of the Spirit is closely related to the work of Christ. One of Pentecostalism's distinctive emphases is that Christ is the one who baptizes in the Holy Spirit. In Luke 3:16 John the Baptist says, "I baptize in water, but . . . he [Jesus] will baptize you in the Holy Spirit and in fire." And in Luke 24:49 just before he ascends into heaven, Jesus says, "I am sending the promise of my Father upon you."

Two identifying marks of Pentecostalism are 1) "Jesus piety," a very Christocentric approach to its teaching and proclamation, and 2) a strong emphasis on the importance of the presence and power of the Holy Spirit. These twin emphases are not thought to conflict at all.

Vss. 10–11: There is a very trinitarian quality to these verses. Christ, the Spirit, and "the one who raised Jesus from the dead" (God the Father) are all mentioned.[5] Vs. 10 describes the duality of the present existence, with the body trapped in its mortality due to the disruption of sin, while the human spirit is alive. The Greek *men . . . de* construction implies the "on the one hand . . . on the other hand" English construction found in the translation.

Vs. 11 points to the resolution of the present duality in the future. The promise is that one who restored life to Jesus (God the Father) will "also" (*kai*) "make alive" (*zōopoieō*) the mortal bodies of those indwelt by Christ. Notice that the verb *zōopoieō* is placed in the future tense. This promise will be accomplished by God's Spirit who also indwells the believer. This indwelling of both Christ and the Spirit provides an internal witness and assurance of what will happen in the future. While Paul can describe this experience of being indwelt by both Christ and the Spirit, in a practical sense this indwelling is experienced as something unified. Wright speaks of "a fluidity between the indwelling Messiah and the spirit."[6] This indistinguishable experience of Christ and the Spirit may explain, at least in part, why in vs. 9 Paul uses the phrase "the Spirit of Christ."

Vss. 12–13: "We are debtors": the Greek word *opheiletēs* is not limited to financial debts. In fact, the clause could be translated "We have obligations." Roman society was built on a vast network of obligations of many

---

5. In the NT Jesus is never said to raise himself or "to resurrect"; he is always raised by God (used absolutely), or this is implied by use of the divine passive.

6. Wright, *Paul and the Faithfulness of God*, 858–59.

kinds. Receiving certain honors required reciprocation with public gifts. Appointments were made with the expectation of loyalty, understood as a kind of obligation. Freed slaves and adoptees had perpetual obligations to their patrons. And breeching obligations resulted in shame and a loss of honor. Virtually everyone in Rome had various kinds of obligations.

Paul's point is that based on one's past behavior, it might appear that a person had obligations to serve the flesh, but she has no such obligations. The flesh has never done anyone any favors, so there is no conceivable way that the flesh could be a person's patron. Instead that person should accept the aid of the Holy Spirit in putting to death the "activities of the body," as vs. 13 words it. At this point, it would seem more natural for Paul to write "the activities of the flesh" (*tas praxeis tēs sarkos*) than "the activities of the body" (*tas praxeis tou sōmatos*). In fact, some manuscripts do read this way, and perhaps they were changed to accommodate this expectation. However, the textual evidence makes "the flesh" unlikely to be original.

Vss. 14–17: The theme of these verses is "sonship." As vs. 14 explains, those who are led by the Spirit are the sons and daughters of God. Those indwelt by the Spirit do not need to fear a cruel or capricious master; they have the access reserved for children. The cry, "Abba Father!" is derived from the prayer-life of Jesus, and it highlights an intimacy unusual in Second Temple Judaism. *For more about this, see the excursus, "The Indispensable Spirit."* Since those led by the Spirit are God's children, they are also God's heirs (vs. 17), and they are destined to stand alongside Christ as co-heirs. When Paul writes in 1 Cor 6:2, "Or do you not know that the saints will judge the world?" he likely draws on the idea that as co-heirs with Christ, the saints will share in ruling the kingdom of God.

This special status as children of God is restricted to those who are led by the Spirit. The popular idea that every human is a child of God has no place in Paul's theology. All people are valuable and created in God's image, but many live in hostility to God (vs. 7) and have not received "a Spirit of sonship" (vs. 15).

In vs. 16 "the Spirit himself" might be translated "the Spirit itself" since both the noun *pneuma* ("Spirit") and the reflexive pronoun *auto* are neuter. However, throughout this passage the Spirit is treated as a person with personal characteristics.

Vs. 17 raises the expectation that, linked to Christ as co-heirs, God's children will suffer with Jesus. This is reminiscent of Paul's comment in Gal 6:17 that "in his body I bear the marks [*stigmata*] of Jesus." It also calls to mind the words of Jesus, "If anyone wants to come after me, let him deny himself and let him take up his cross and follow me" (Matt 16:24).

TRANSLATION: ROM 8:18–25

SUFFERING, WE WAIT IN HOPE OF A NEW AGE

[18]For I reckon that the sufferings of the present time are not equal to the coming glory to be revealed for us. [19]For the expectancy of creation anticipates the revelation of the sons of God. [20]For creation has been subjected to futility, not willingly but on account of subjection, in hope [21]that the creation itself will also be freed from the slavery of decay in order to experience the freedom of the glory of the children of God. [22]For we know that the entire creation has been groaning and travailing inwardly until now. [23]Not only that, but we ourselves who have the first-fruits of the Spirit, we too groan while anticipating sonship, the redemption of our bodies. [24]For with this hope we have been saved. But hope that is seen is not hope. For who hopes in what he sees? [25]But if we hope in what we do not see, we will anticipate with patience.

COMMENTARY

Vs. 18: This verse introduces the two themes that will dominate the eight verses that make up this paragraph (vss. 18–25): "suffering"; and the coming completion of what is now present in partial form. What is coming will be glorious, and it will more than compensate for the present sufferings.

Although the precise wording differs, Paul's contrast of present sufferings with future glory in this verse call to mind the similar images found in 2 Cor 4:17: "For at the moment the slightness of our tribulation is preparing us for an eternal weight of glory that is beyond measure...."[7]

Vs. 19: The word *apokaradokia*, which I have translated "expectancy," occurs only here and in Phil 1:20 in the New Testament. Paul is the first person on record to use the noun *apokaradokia*, although the cognate verb appears occasionally in earlier literature. While the word implies eager expectation, it does not necessarily imply expectation of childbirth. In Philippians it refers to Paul's expectation that he will not be put to shame despite being imprisoned.

On the other hand, the expectation of childbirth probably figures in this word's formulation. The prefix *apo* means "from" or "apart from," and *kara* is a poetic word for "head." Combined with *dokia*, a noun form related

---

7. Although similar, Paul's contrast in Romans does not contain the artful Semitism "weight of glory" found in 2 Corinthians. The Hebrew verb *kaved* ("to be heavy") is cognate with *kavod* ("glory").

to the verb *dokeō* ("to think" or "to seem"), it suggests anticipation of a head "crowning" and coming out, as a newborn baby emerges from its mother.

Whether or not this word by itself implies expectancy of childbirth, the paragraph certainly does. Creation is about to give birth to a new world order. Included in that new world order will be "the revelation of the sons of God." This phrase should probably be regarded as a continuation of the birthing imagery.

Paul's language is surprising since the Spirit already testifies to those whom he indwells that they are sons and daughters of God. This revelation points to something beyond the current experience of the Roman believers. In the Old Testament the phrase "sons of God" sometimes refers to angelic beings (e.g., Gen 6:2, 4; Deut 32:8 in the Dead Sea Scroll 4QDeut^j; Ps 29:1; Job 1:6, 2:1). However, given Paul's stress on "sonship" and the indwelling Spirit marking people as the children of God, that meaning is unlikely here.

Vss. 20–22: Paul suggests that the destiny of creation depends on the destiny of the sons of God who will receive glory. This is the reverse of the modern secularist view that humans—even the whole of humanity—are insignificant specks at the mercy of the natural order. Instead, the natural order was created as a home for humanity and the future of the natural order is linked to, and dependent upon, the future of humanity.

These sons who in the future will receive glory are the same children in whom the Spirit currently dwells and has made heirs. Furthermore, when vs. 17 said these heirs are also co-heirs with Christ who will be glorified with him, this was simply another way of describing "the glory of the children of God" mentioned in vs. 21.

The word "children" does not translate *huioi* ("sons") but rather is a plural of the neuter noun *teknon*, which refers to a child of either sex. The phrase "the freedom of the glory of the children of God" is an example of Paul's fondness for piling up genitives (roughly equivalent to "possessives"). Paul does this here to emphasize the wonderful blessedness of this coming state.

As the excursus titled "The Indispensable Spirit" points out, in Paul's view creation's subjection to "futility" and "the slavery of decay" has been a long-term problem; it is not a recent event related to the "birth pangs of the Messiah," as in later rabbinic speculation. Paul does use the image of a new world on the cusp of being born, but nature's futility is not a recent arrival.

In vs. 22 two verbs are prefixed with *syn*: *systenazō* ("to groan inwardly") and *synōdinō* ("to suffer pain inwardly"). These verbs could imply that many things "groan and travail together." However, the noun "creation" (*ktisis*) is in the singular, and it is awkward to describe a single thing doing things "together." A better solution is to understand the *syn* prefixed to these words to point to action happening inwardly. In this way these words differ from the verb *sympaschō* in vs. 17, which was translated "to suffer together."

Paul uses the nonverbal sound of groaning to tie together the struggle of creation awaiting its deliverance (vs. 22) with the groaning of humanity awaiting its deliverance (vs. 23). Ultimately, he will explain that the Spirit also groans when assisting humanity as it struggles with its current weakness (vs. 26).

Vs. 23: "Not only" is a frequent expression in Romans. Besides using it here, Paul also uses it in 1:32, 5:3, 5:11, 9:10, 9:24, and 13:5.

The contrast between the present partial experience of God's blessings and the future glorious and complete fulfillment of these blessings is highlighted by use of the image of "first-fruits." First-fruits were the initial phase of the harvest that anticipated the bulk of the crop which came in later. The "first-fruits of the Spirit," an artistic metaphor for the present-day availability of the Spirit, marks the onset of the eschatological harvest.

Despite this reception of the Spirit, the vexation of not yet having experienced the full blessing awaiting God's children also produces "groaning." Paul describes the full blessing as both "sonship" (*huiothesia*) and "the redemption of our bodies."

Vss. 24–25: Paul is aware that hope implies absence. It is tied to an unseen future, but this does not mean it is uncertain. The clause "we will anticipate" could also be translated "we will await." Either translation might cause pause since the verb (*apekdechomai*) is in the present tense. However, this is a "present of anticipation" in which the present tense is used instead of the future "in statements of what is immediate, likely, certain, or threatening."[8] Some call this a "futuristic present," and an example of it is found in Rev 22:20: "I will come quickly." There the verb *erchomai* is in the present tense and literally means "I come."

TRANSLATION: ROM 8:26–30

THE SPIRIT HELPS US AS WE WAIT

[26]Similarly, the Spirit helps us with our weakness. For how else could we pray concerning what by necessity we do not know? But rather the Spirit himself more than intercedes with inarticulate groanings. [27]For the one examining hearts [God] knows what the thinking of the Spirit is, since he [the Spirit] intercedes for the saints according to the will of God.

---

8. Smyth, *Greek Grammar* §1879.

²⁸And we know that for those loving God, for those called according to his plan, all things work together for good. ²⁹[And we know] that those he foresaw he also appointed beforehand to be copies of his son's image, in order for him to be the firstborn among many brothers [and sisters]. ³⁰Those he appointed beforehand are the same people he also calls. And those he calls are the same people he also makes right. And those he makes right are the same people he glorifies.

COMMENTARY

Vs. 26: The word "similarly" invites the question: Which things are being compared? Previously, the Spirit has been described as helping "us" during the period of suffering that precedes the coming of glory. In other words, the Spirit helps with difficulties that are external to us. In a like manner, the Spirit also helps with our "weaknesses," i.e., those problems that are internal to us.

I have translated *synantilambanomai* as "helps us," even though the "us" is not explicitly stated. The *syn* prefix often indicates cooperation, and here suggests that the Spirit assists the one praying.

"Our weakness" certainly includes limited knowledge but may include more. The circumstances of life often require prayer for "what by necessity we do not know." This lack of knowledge sometimes precludes effective prayer with the mind. Perhaps our weakness also includes lapses or failures to anticipate the glorious future with patience, as described in the previous verse.

As in vs. 16, I have translated *auto to pneuma* as "the Spirit himself," although there is an argument that it ought to be translated "the Spirit itself." Because *pneuma* is neuter, the reflexive pronoun *auto* is also neuter. However, since the Spirit is depicted as acting in a personal way, personalizing the translation seems appropriate.

In the second half of vs. 26 the expression *to ti* appears. It is a neuter interrogative pronoun used with the definite article. It implies a question, but the precise nature of the question is unclear. Is it "why should we pray . . . ," "what should we pray . . . ," or "how else could we pray . . . ."? I have opted for the last option based mainly on the context.

The expression "concerning what" translates *katho*, which is a contraction of *kata* ("according to") and the relative pronoun *ho* ("which") that introduces the following clause ("by necessity we do not know"). To avoid excessive wordiness, I have translated *katho* plus the following clause: "concerning what by necessity we do not know."

In vs. 22 Paul states that the creation groans. In verse 23 he states that "we," the praying believers, groan. In this verse he adds that the Spirit also groans inarticulately. Likely this is a reference to the praying person speaking in tongues as enabled by the Spirit. The cries of pain associated with childbirth are inarticulate, i.e., not composed of words, but they are still vocal and meaningful at an emotional level. Similarly, prayer involving speaking in tongues is inarticulate but meaningful in some noncognitive way.

The words "more than intercedes" are an attempt to translate the verb *hyperentygchanō*. Without the prefix *hyper* (which means "above," "beyond," or can function as an intensifier), *entygchanō* ("to intercede" or "to entreat") appears twice more in this chapter (in vss. 27 and 34) and also in Rom 11:2. Luther points out that in the chapter 11 reference, *entygchanō* is used to describe Elijah pleading "with God against Israel."[9]

The word "groan" (*stenagmos*) is used in a wide variety of contexts. It can mean "a groan," "a moan," or "a sigh." Usually, it is an expression of pain or distress. Aristophanes uses it in conjunction with the pain of hemorrhoids, and Sophocles uses it to portray the suffering of Thebes when beset by a plague.

The "groans" or "groanings" are described as being "inarticulate" (*alalētos*). This is often translated "too deep for words" or "unutterable" or some other expression implying that no sound is made. The resulting oxymoron "unuttered groans" is unlikely to be the concept Paul wants to convey. This is particularly true since *alalētos* has a range of possible meanings, from "mute" to "nonverbal" to "unpronounceable." Here the groans or sighs are vocal, but they are not verbal language understandable by human hearers.

Some may object to the translation "inarticulate" believing that God the Holy Spirit will not speak inarticulately or incoherently, and the fault instead lies with the hearers who are unable to discern whatever meaning the Spirit intends. Therefore, this speech may not be understood, but it is not inarticulate. Yet 1 Corinthians 14 makes clear that the practice of speaking in tongues in a church founded by Paul included no expectation that the tongues would be understood without interpretation. The closest Paul comes to indicating an expectation of understandable glossolalia is in 1 Cor 13:1: "If I speak in the tongues of men and of angels . . . ," which presumably indicates real languages. This certainly suggests that Paul knows of some who regard understandable glossolalia as a possibility, but for him it is a hypothetical case of unusual ecstasy, not a normal expectation, and even such ecstasy would not eliminate the need for those in such ecstasy to treat others with love. Likely Paul has heard of the xenolalia ("speaking in a known human language one has not learned") that marked the first Pentecost after Christ's resurrection. Nevertheless, he does not consider that

---

9. Luther, *Lectures on Romans*, *Glossa*, ad loc. Rom 11:2.

kind of manifestation to be normative. I do not think Paul denies the possibility of xenolalia; it just is not what he *expects* to occur in his churches.

Many people believe glossolalia in Paul's churches must involve real language since it is supposed to be interpreted, which they understand to mean *translated*. However, neither the noun "interpretation" (*hermēneia*; 1 Cor 12:10; 14:26) nor the related verb "to interpret" (*diermēneuō*; 1 Cor 12:30; 14:5, 13, 27) imply "translation." Moreover, a single interpretation might explain two or three utterances in tongues (1 Cor 14:27), apparently precluding exact translation. If Paul had meant to say "translate," Greek contains a perfectly serviceable verb (*methermēneuō*) that indicates precisely this.

Vs. 27: The clause "the one examining hearts" refers to God the Father who knows not only what is in the heart of the person praying but also knows the thoughts of the Spirit, who shares these thoughts through intercession. This intercession is both "for the saints" and "according to the will of God," assuring appropriate and effective intercession. Also, as the verses that follow will explain, God's will is to effectuate a plan he devised long ago.

The idea that the Spirit intercedes with God the Father may seem to diminish the status of the Spirit to something less than fully divine. But this is no more the case than when Jesus the Son prays to God the Father. The doctrine of the Trinity, which was only spelled out in detail centuries after the time of Paul, posits an essential equality (equality of being) between the persons of the godhead, but allows for a functional subordination of the Son and the Spirit to the Father.

An illustration of this differentiation between essential equality and functional subordination is provided by marriage: My wife is every bit as fully human as I am—this relates to her essence or being—but I have a leadership role in our marriage that she does not—this relates to a subordination in function. Thus, our marriage involves both essential equality and functional subordination.

Vss. 28–31: These four verses highlight the relationship of those who are "called" to Christ himself. They are meant to be many brothers and sisters to Christ the firstborn. They have also been appointed beforehand to be copies of Christ's image. Except when describing apostles being called into their special roles, whenever Paul writes of "calling," he means calling to follow Christ.

Vs. 28: This verse is one of the most inspiring and well-known verses in Romans. Its power stems from the wonderful promise it contains. But why does Paul feel the need to encourage his readers this way? He has repeatedly mentioned suffering, evidently because they have been experiencing suffering, and meaningless suffering is much harder to bear than purposeful suffering. This is true even if how things fit together for good is not immediately clear.

Beloved as it is, this verse also presents an important text-critical problem. Despite the important text critical issues associated with this verse, in practical terms whichever way the issue is resolved will change the meaning of the verse very little.

Composed of a single sentence, the verse can be broken into four parts: 1) an introductory clause "We know that"; 2) one dependent clause specifying for whom the promise is operative ("for those loving God"); 3) another dependent clause also specifying for whom the promise is operative ("for those called according to his plan"); and 4) a clause containing the gist of the promise. The text-critical problem concerns only the fourth element, the clause containing the gist of the promise.

Before considering the details of the text-critical problem, I should point out that the two dependent clauses (parts 2 and 3 above) are overlapping, almost tautological. It is hard to contemplate a person called to follow Christ who does not also love God.

The texts printed in the Nestle-Aland and United Bible Society editions of the Greek New Testament present the gist of the promise as "all things work together for good."[10] The neuter plural form *panta* ("all things") serves as the subject of a third-person, singular verb (lexical form *synergeō*), which means "to work together." A peculiarity of Greek grammar is that neuter plural subjects must be used with verbs in the singular. Since it follows this rule, the clause is grammatically correct.[11] However, in P[46], the most important single manuscript of Paul's letters, two differences appear: 1) the neuter plural form *panta* is replaced with a neuter singular form *pan*; and 2) *ho theos* ("God") is inserted. With these changes incorporated, the clause then reads, "God works everything together for good."[12]

Two arguments suggest that, despite its importance, P[46] likely has not preserved the original text at this point. First, the reading P[46] presents stands against almost the entirety of the rest of the manuscript tradition. Therefore, this reading is likely a peculiarity of this single manuscript. One would expect an original reading to have spread more widely across the

10. Currently the texts printed in the Nestle-Aland edition and the United Bible Society edition of the New Testament are identical. Only their apparatuses differ.

11. In Classical Greek this requirement is absolute. In the *Koinē* Greek of the New Testament, this is no longer an absolute requirement but still is the best form.

12. As a reminder to the reader, the letter P indicates that the manuscript being designated is written on papyrus, an early form of paper. In general, the earliest manuscripts of the New Testament that have survived were written on this medium and were preserved in arid climates.

distribution of manuscripts. Second, the *syn* prefix of *synergeō* makes more sense with a plural subject. It indicates that multiple things work *together*.

However, even if "all things work together for good" is the correct reading, this hardly writes God out of the picture. This promise is "for those loving God" who are also "called according to his plan." Either God directly works everything together or he works indirectly as the puppeteer orchestrating the "all things" marionette to ensure they "work together for good."

Vss. 29-30: The link between these verses and the preceding verse is the idea of calling. Vs. 28 proclaims, "For those *called* according to his plan, all things work together for good." Vs. 30 asserts that "those [whom] he appointed beforehand are the same people he also *calls*." The appointment of "those he appointed beforehand" is to be "copies of his son's image." And continuing to work backwards, they are also "those [whom] he foresaw" (vs. 29). The overall point is that God has a plan, and these various steps—foreseeing, appointing, and calling—are all components of this plan. Furthermore, the execution of this plan provides assurance that "for those called according to his plan, all things work together for good."

In Rom 1:4 Paul uses the verb *horizō* with the meaning "to declare." Here the same verb is used except that *pro* ("beforehand") is prefixed to it. Based on this evidence from earlier in the letter, one might argue that *proorizō* should be translated "declared beforehand" rather than "appointed beforehand." However, to declare a person's status beforehand amounts to appointing that person to this status. Each one God foresaw coming to faith, he also appointed as a copy (*symmorphos*, literally a person "having the same shape") of Christ's image, qualifying him or her to be Christ's brother or sister.

The great mystery is what God's foresight implies. This word "to foresee" (*proginōskō*) can also be translated "to foreknow," a translation often colored with overtones of individual election. Does this word imply antecedent determination of one's status by God? Or does it simply mean that God looks into the future and therefore knows what will ultimately happen, and who will end up being saved?

Proginōskō sometimes refers to earlier knowledge obtained from a source who has tipped the person off. But far and away its most common meanings are "to foresee" or "to foretell," by shrewd calculation of where events are headed or by intuition. God, of course, does not need to be tipped off, nor does he have to surmise or guess at the truth. Still, the point here is not about eternal decrees of election defining which individuals will be saved and which will be damned. It has to do with God's plan of salvation for mankind. He foresaw a great family. Paul's point here is that believers, those called according to God's purpose, both Jews and gentiles, are appointed or ordained to resemble Jesus, the bearer of the true image of humanity. Those called according to his plan will not remain unchanged.

Paul's use of the word "chosen" (*eklektos*) in vs. 33 suggests to some that Paul is discussing individual election. However, his clear teaching in 1 Cor 10:1–13 is that God's people can be "overthrown" if they fall into idolatry and sexual sin suggests that God's foresight includes his knowledge of future events, not just eternal decrees. As 1 Cor 10:12 says, "Therefore, let the one thinking he stands take heed lest he should fall."

The last clauses of vs. 30 also mention two more steps in God's plan: making right (often translated "justifying"); and glorifying. This means that Paul mentions five steps in God's plan—foreseeing, appointing, calling, making right, and glorifying—of which "calling," Paul's point of entry into this discussion, is the middle term.

Paul's discussion of God's plan, including the five steps of this plan, explain that God is at work to accomplish his purpose. Much like his assertion that for the believer "all things work together for good," this discussion is meant to reassure the Roman believers, who are suffering, that God stands with them and is guiding their steps.

TRANSLATION: ROM 8:31–39

GOD IS ON OUR SIDE, AND NOTHING CAN SEPARATE US FROM HIS LOVE

³¹What shall we say then about these things? If God is for us, who [can stand] against us? ³²He who did not spare his own son, but handed him over for the benefit of us all, how will he not graciously give us all things along with him? ³³Who will accuse God's chosen? God is the one declaring us in the right. ³⁴Who is the condemner? Christ Jesus, the one who died but was raised and is at the right hand of God, he intercedes on our behalf. ³⁵Who will separate us from the love of Christ? Tribulation? Distress? Persecution? Famine? Nakedness? Danger? The sword? ³⁶Just as it is written,

> Because of you we are being put to death all day long.
> We have been reckoned as sheep for slaughter.

³⁷But despite all these things, we achieve overwhelming victory through the one who loved us. ³⁸For I am convinced that not death, or life, or angels, or rulers, or the present, or the things to come, or powers, ³⁹or heights, or depths, or any other created thing will be able to separate us from the love of God, the love that is in Christ Jesus our Lord.

COMMENTARY

Vss. 31–32: Once again Paul uses the expression "What shall we say then" to refocus his argument. While in vss. 2–27 Paul used the word *pneuma* ("Spirit") 21 times, he does not mention that word through the remainder of the chapter. Instead, the focus is on God's devoted support of his "chosen" and their invulnerability to attack from outside. As he says, "If God is for us, who [can stand] against us?"

Throughout his letters, Paul repeatedly emphasizes, as he does here, that God gave up his son "for the benefit of" (*hyper*) his people. This is the ultimate assurance of God's commitment.

Paul's rhetorical question, "How will he not graciously give us all things along with him?" is reminiscent of his expansive promise in 1 Cor 3:21–23: "All things are yours, whether Paul or Apollos or Cephas, whether the world or life or death, whether things present or things future; all are yours! And you are Christ's and Christ is God's."

Vss. 33–34: These verses use the language of the courtroom. Accusations and lawsuits may come, but they will come to naught because God, the great judge, is the one declaring his people to be in the right. Furthermore, Christ Jesus, who is at the right hand of God, "intercedes on our behalf," much as the intercession of the Spirit is described in vss. 26 and 27.

Vss. 35–36: The chief problem for the interpreter of these verses is how to relate the Old Testament quotation in vs. 36 to vs. 35. Psalm 44 (Psalm 43 in the LXX) is a psalm of complaint. It starts off by recounting the wonderful ways the Lord won victories for Israel during its conquest of Canaan, driving out their enemies before them and giving them the land. But then it appeared that God cast Israel off and did not continue to bless its armies. As a result, Israel has been shamed and abased before the surrounding peoples. The Psalmists (the sons of Korah, according to the superscription) claim the people of Israel are not to blame for this state of affairs; they have remained faithful to the covenant and have not worshipped other gods.

In the verse Paul quotes (Ps 43:23 in the LXX; Ps 44:23 in the MT; Ps 44:22 in the English), God is blamed: "*Because of you* we are being put to death all day long. We have been reckoned as sheep for slaughter." Paul's wording exactly mirrors what is found in the LXX. How does this bolster Paul's contention that nothing can separate the believer from the love of Christ?

Paul seems to argue that the afflictions Christians experience in the present day are nothing new. God's people have a long history of suffering, but this does not mean God has abandoned them. The Messiah has come! Furthermore, suffering is not an indicator of unfaithfulness. The psalm argues as much. Present-day distress, persecution, famine, nakedness, and danger may even seem to pale in comparison with the Psalmists' complaint of being put to death all day long and being reckoned as sheep lined up for slaughter. Paul's argument is that if the Israelites could suffer unjustly and not lose faith, you who have experienced the indwelling of both the Spirit and Christ, should be unwavering in the face of any challenge.

Vss. 37–39: Paul does not deny that he and other Christians experience suffering. Nevertheless, they are achieving, or even have achieved—the tense of the verb is aorist (roughly "past")—an overwhelming victory. This verb *hypernikaō* ("to achieve overwhelming victory") is an intensified version of the verb *nikaō*, that means "to win a victory." It is often translated "more than conquerors," but I prefer to avoid transforming the verb into a noun.

Vss. 38 and 39 contain a list of ten hypothetical obstacles that might separate the believer from God's love. In the Greek these ten items are marked off from each other by the conjunction *oute* (literally "and not"). However, in English the standard convention is to negate the first item in a list and the following items in the list will also be negated. It is considered incorrect to negate each item in the list by pairing it up with either "not" or "nor." So, although the translation might not seem it indicate this, be assured that in the Greek each of the ten items is specifically negated.

Through Paul's use of cascading repetition, the chapter concludes with this soaring affirmation:

> I am convinced that not death, or life, or angels, or rulers, or the present, or the things to come, or powers, or heights, or depths, or any other created thing will be able to separate us from the love of God, the love that is in Christ Jesus our Lord.

This, of course, is a poetic way of saying that nothing in the entire universe can sever us from God's love!

Excursus: The Indispensable Spirit

SPIRIT AND SONSHIP

The word "Spirit" (*pneuma*) occurs 21 times in Romans 8. In all the other chapters of Romans combined, it occurs 13 times for an average of less than once per chapter. Furthermore, Paul positions this profusion of comments about the Spirit as the culmination of the grand theological exposition making up the first eight chapters of Romans, after which he switches to his distillation of God's redemptive plan for his people (chapters 9 through

11). Therefore, Paul's discussion of life in the Spirit, and through the Spirit, found in chapter 8 is presented as a climax to the first half of his epistle.

While much of chapter 6 had been addressed to gentile believers at Rome and much of chapter 7 had been addressed to Jewish believers, chapter 8 is addressed to all believers: "to those in Christ Jesus," as he states in vs. 1. In fact, Paul forcefully makes the point that having the Spirit in one's life defines who is and who is not a Christ-follower. Possessing the Spirit is a *sine qua non* of Christian identity. Paul expresses this both positively and negatively in vs. 9. Positively, he writes, "You are not in the flesh but in the Spirit, if the Spirit of God lives in you." Negatively, he declares: "If anyone does not have the Spirit of Christ, this person is not his." Life in the Spirit is not optional for anyone who follows Christ.

The presence of the Spirit in one's life is closely linked to "sonship" or "adoption" (both being translations of *huiothesia*). The English word "sonship" is slightly problematic since *huiothesia* includes both sons and daughters, but the English word "adoption" is also problematic since Jesus Christ, like his followers, has "sonship" but his sonship is not through adoption; Jesus is a naturally born son. In an apparent attempt to overcome difficulty with the word "sonship," the first complete English translation of the Bible, published in 1535 by Miles Coverdale, translated *huiothesia* in Rom 8:23 as "childship" (spelled "childshippe"), although in Rom 8:15 the Coverdale version translated it "adoption" (spelled "adopcion"). The word "childship" never became popular, perhaps because it could refer to "childhood" in addition to indicating one's status as the child of a particular parent. Today the term is considered archaic.

While *huiothesia* only appears twice in Romans 8, with *huios* ("son") appearing five times more, it is a very important concept. The presence of the Spirit marks a person as God's child. As vss. 14 and 15 declare, "For as many as are led by the Spirit of God, these are the children of God. For you have not received a spirit of slavery leading again to fear, but you have received a Spirit of sonship [*huiothesia*] by which we cry out, 'Abba, Father!'" Furthermore, Gal 4:6 suggests that sonship comes first, qualifying a person to receive the Spirit: "*Since* you are sons, God has sent the Spirit of his son into our hearts, crying, 'Abba, Father!'"

Paul frequently describes the followers of Christ as being "in" him. Being "in Christ" implies that like Christ such people are sons of God—although through adoption and not with the only begotten (*monogenēs*) status of Jesus—and therefore they receive the Spirit of God's son.[13] Awareness of this presence of the Spirit—what John Calvin called "the sure guarantee and seal of their adoption"[14]—is a constant testimony to God's children of their special status before him.

THE CRY "ABBA"

The cry, "Abba," is especially notable, and it leads us back to Jesus, who used this address in his prayer life. 'Abba' appears to be an Aramaic word literally meaning "the Father," but it likely came to mean "my Father," perhaps even "Daddy," after the standard form for "my father" ('avi) fell out of use.[15] Whether it meant "the Father" or "my Father," the word goes back to the earthly ministry of Jesus and the earliest period of the church. Only words that were deeply imbedded in the worship of the earliest church had the emotional impact required for preservation in their original Aramaic or Hebrew forms within the alien environment of Greek Christian worship and literature. Other examples of Aramaic or Hebrew words that survived in a Greek context include "Amen," "Hallelujah," "Cephas," and "Maranatha."[16]

In 1898 the German scholar Gustaf Dalman published *Die Worte Jesu*, which appeared in an English version (*The Words of Jesus*) four years later. In this book Dalman contrasted the way Jesus addressed God with the way the Jewish literature of the Intertestamental Period, the Targumim (translations of the Hebrew scriptures into Aramaic), and the Mishnah (the earliest part of the Talmud) showed God being addressed. He concluded Jesus was much more familiar—very literally claiming God as family—when addressing God than his contemporaries were. After Dalman's death, his student Joachim Jeremias continued exploring this extraordinary way Jesus addressed God in prayer.

It was well-known to the Jews that God was the Father of the Israelite nation. In Deut 32:6 when speaking of God, Moses asks the rhetorical question: "Is he not your father who acquired you, who made you, and

---

13. I do not mean to imply that *monogenēs* is a Pauline term or concept. It is not. But Paul certainly does not imply that Christ followers are identical to Jesus in every way.

14. Calvin, *Institutes of the Christian Religion* 3.2.12.

15. See Dalman, *Words of Jesus*, 192.

16. In the first century Aramaic and Hebrew were often not clearly differentiated. Aramaic documents contained many Hebrew loanwords and Hebrew documents often contained Aramaic loanwords.

established you?" In Exod 4:22 the Lord instructs Moses to tell Pharaoh, "Israel is my first-born son." Nevertheless, when Jews spoke of God, he was referenced obliquely, not personally and directly. Heaven, the abode of God, was often used as a circumlocution to avoid naming God directly. The common reference in Matthew's Gospel to "the kingdom of heaven" rather than "the kingdom of God" is an example of such a circumlocution. When Jews prayed, it was normal to address God as "our Father" rather than "my Father." Very commonly God was described as "our heavenly Father" to distinguish him from an earthly father.

Jesus prayed in Gethsemane before his arrest, using the words, "Abba, Father, all things are possible for you. Take this cup from me. But not what I want, let what you want be done" (Mark 14:36). The immediacy with which Jesus addressed God as "Abba" was likely one factor leading to the formal charge of blasphemy and ultimately to his crucifixion. In so many ways, the leaders of the nation felt Jesus claimed too much. Moreover, he also taught his disciples to pray as he did. The pattern for prayer he sets in Luke 11:2–4, begins: "Father [*pater*, apparently translating *'abba'*], may your name be sanctified . . . ."[17]

A FULLER REALIZATION OF SONSHIP

While the presence of the Spirit in one's life provides assurance of being a child of God, this present reality is also pictured as a foreshadowing of a more complete realization of this sonship. We may be sons, and we may have the first-fruits of the Spirit, but we "groan while anticipating sonship" (vs. 23), suggesting this sonship is not yet complete. And as this verse goes on to explain, the believers' sonship will only be completed when their bodies are redeemed.

Some within the Pentecostal/Charismatic tradition may be aware of a teaching known as "The Manifest Sons of God" based on Rom 8:19. This teaching was featured in the revival movement known as "The New Order of the Latter Rain." *For more on this subject, consult the excursus titled "The New Order of the Latter Rain and Romans."*

---

17. Dalman seems dismissive of Matthew's version of the Lord's Prayer (Matt 6:9–13), addressed as it is to "our Father in heaven." He apparently believes Luke's version reflects the original form of Jesus's prayer, with Matthew's form being assimilated to prevailing Jewish norms.

BIRTH PANGS OF THE MESSIAH?

Paul says our bodies groan while awaiting sonship in the fullest measure. But it is not only our bodies that "groan" while awaiting this full expression of sonship; the entire creation groans in anticipation of "the revelation of the sons of God." These groanings can be understood as the birth pangs of a new age being born, and many claim Paul is tapping into the Israelite/Jewish tradition of "the birth pangs of the Messiah" (*chevle mashiach*). Determining whether or not Paul has in mind a "birth pangs of the Messiah" tradition is a complex issue, and where one lands depends on the definitions employed.

Throughout the Old Testament and the Intertestamental Literature there are numerous accounts of judgments and tribulations to come, some of which use the image of birth pangs (Hebrew singular *chevel*; Greek singular *ōdin*) or pain like birth pangs, to express the trauma of those periods of suffering (e.g., Isa 13:8; 26:17; 66:7; Jer 13:21; 22:23). However, by itself use of "birth pangs" imagery does not indicate participation in "the birth pangs of the Messiah" tradition. The full expression *chevle mashiach* does not appear until the Amoraic period of rabbinic literature (roughly AD 250 to 450), and despite its name, this phrase refers to birth pangs suffered by the earth as a new age/world is being born. It never refers to sufferings experienced by the messiah himself. These birth pangs are related to the messiah in the sense that the appearance of the messiah marks a transitional era, a liminal period between "this age" and "the age to come." It is during this transitional period that the earth experiences turmoil likened to childbirth. Furthermore, the onset of these birth pangs is sudden.

Outside of Romans 8, the most striking description of eschatological birth pangs in the New Testament occurs in the Olivet discourse of Jesus (Matt 24:1–36; Mark 13:1–37; and Luke 21:5–36), where famines, earthquakes, and perhaps other events, are described as "the beginning of birth pangs." Surprisingly, the Lucan version of the Olivet discourse does not reference "birth pangs," even though one would expect *ōdines* in vs. 11. It may be that there the phrase "the beginning of birth pangs" found in Matt 24:8 and Mark 13:8 has been replaced by "there will be both dreadful sights and great signs from heaven."

In all three of the Synoptic Gospels, Jesus's discussion of end-time events follows his prediction that the Jerusalem temple will be destroyed, accompanied by a question from the disciples about the timing of that destruction and the signs pointing to it. While in Mark and Luke, the question is framed in more general terms, in Matthew the question is specific: "Tell us, when will these things occur, and what is the sign of your coming and of the consummation of the age?"

While the phrase "birth pangs of the Messiah" is not specifically found in the Olivet discourse, three converging factors suggest this is an early expression of that theme: 1) the word "birth pangs" appears; 2) these pangs are associated with convulsions of the earth that resemble childbirth, especially "earthquakes"; and 3) the association of these events with the arrival of a messianic figure.

At first glance, Rom 8:18–27 seems similarly to function as an expression of the "birth pangs of the Messiah" theme. The unusual verb *synōdinō* ("travailing inwardly" or "travailing with") appears in vs. 22. This is the only occurrence of this verb in the New Testament, although the same verb without the *syn* prefix occurs three times. This verb is cognate with the noun *ōdin* ("birth pang"). That the earth is experiencing this pain is indicated by use of the word *ktisis* ("creation"), which appears four times in vss. 19–22. The earth's turmoil is further pictured by the expressions "subjected to futility" and "the slavery of decay," both in vs. 21. Reference to a messiah figure might be found in the multiple references to the Spirit, which as vs. 9 informs the reader, is "the Spirit of Christ."

However, there is a significant difference between what is said in Romans 8 and the standard conception of "the birth pangs of the Messiah." The subjection to futility and the slavery to decay, which characterize the creation, are not newly emergent and linked to the beginning of a messianic age; they are longstanding problems in need of repair. While the beginning of creation's futility is not explicitly explored, it is implied that this dysfunction is as old as the mortality of the human body. In other words, the futility of creation, like the loss of immortality, should be traced back to the sin of Adam and Eve in the Garden. Perhaps we should hear echoes of the cursing of the ground (Hebrew *ha'adamah*) pronounced in Gen 3:17–19. Given its sad state, creation "looks forward" to "the revealing of the sons of God," who apparently will have redeemed bodies, because the whole of creation will be swept along in redemption with these bodies.

These verses depict a tension between the way things are at present and a coming transformation. As the first-fruits of that transformation, the Spirit living within provides assurance to the believer that what has begun will be brought to consummation. But Paul acknowledges that living with this tension also requires hope for what is not yet seen.

INARTICULATE GROANINGS

Just as the presence of the Spirit provides assurance of sonship to the believer, the presence of the Spirit also provides assurance that the transformation of creation, including the physical transformation of believers' bodies, will happen. But for believers, the Spirit does more than serve as a sign. The Spirit actively assists them in prayer, by compensating when they pray without full knowledge of specific situations. This is accomplished "with inarticulate groanings" (*stenagmois alalētois*). While some have argued that the Spirit's groanings take place in a heavenly dimension separate from the prayer life of believers, most scholars understand this to be a reference to speaking in tongues. The Spirit does not accomplish this work apart from the believer's prayer, but rather through the believer's prayer, transcending the believer's normal limitations.

Both the word "groanings" (*stenagmos*) and the word "inarticulate" (*alalētos*) point to the incomprehensible nature of these utterances. Perhaps babies learning to speak can illustrate what Paul implies: they become vocal before they become verbal. To say this differently, babies make sounds before they use words. Similarly, Paul here seems to point to vocal, non-verbal prayer. For a more complete discussion of these words and what they imply, see the commentary on Rom 8:26.

Paul implies that what is uttered by the individual and seems to humans (including the speaker) to be "inarticulate groanings," in fact has cognitive meaning to the Holy Spirit. Could it be that the Spirit, who understands the entirety of the situation at hand, has crafted a prayer that is fully comprehensible to him but somehow is incomprehensible to person articulating it? This points to prayer functioning in a realm that is noncognitive and that defies analytical description. Paul's description also raises other questions: Are the "inarticulate groanings" described in Romans 8 the same phenomena as the public articulation in tongues mentioned in 1 Corinthians that he expects to be interpreted? In addition, are these "inarticulate groanings" the same as what happens when someone speaks in tongues privately (1 Cor 14:18–19, 28)?

The answers to these questions are not as clear as we might like. Paul suggests that he can pray with his spirit, which differs from praying with his mind (1 Cor 14:14–15) and both are good. But in 1 Corinthians 14 he does not explain how the Holy Spirit interfaces with his spirit when his spirit prays. Perhaps Romans 8 fills in this blank: When we pray, the Holy Spirit is active in our prayer. Rom 8:26 explains that the Spirit helps us pray by supplying us with inarticulate groanings and by interceding on our behalf. In some sense, this prayer is a cooperative process.

The term "speaking in tongues" can be confusing because not everyone means the same thing by this expression. Some make a sharp distinction between xenolalia or xenoglossy ("speaking in a foreign language one has not learned") and glossolalia ("speaking in tongues") understood to be gibberish. This sharp distinction has never made a great deal of sense to me since in Acts 2 communication in known human languages is implied, but Acts 2:4 describes this as speaking "in other tongues" (*heterais glōssais*), a rough approximation of the expression "speaking in tongues."

Paul apparently did not expect xenolalia (speaking in a known language) in the churches he founded.[18] He teaches that public utterances in tongues should be interpreted, since without interpretation they would not be understood (1 Cor 14:13–19). In fact, he calls uninterpreted utterances "mysteries" (1 Cor 14:2). Does this mean that this sort of speaking in tongues which can be "interpreted" differs from the "inarticulate groanings" of Rom 8:26? Not necessarily. Paul's word "to interpret" (*diermēneuō*) is different from the word "to translate" (*methermēneuō*). Interpretations of tongues in Pauline churches likely addressed the context of what was happening without being exact translations. Paul implies that it was "in order" for up to three utterances in tongues to be interpreted with one (general) interpretation (1 Cor 14:27).

As a lifelong Pentecostal, I have encountered situations that left the congregation puzzled about what had just happened. Perhaps one such situation illustrates what I mean by the difference between "interpretation" and "translation." Frequently a message in tongues will be given in a public service, and it will be followed by an interpretation that is either much shorter or much longer than the message it supposedly interprets. One may last a few seconds and the other may go one for one or two minutes. If interpretation means translation, this seems very problematic. However, if interpretation has a looser meaning, if it could involve a summary or a discussion of the context of the larger issue at hand, then such a disparity in length should not be so disconcerting. If an interpretation might explain two or

---

18. Paul mentions "the tongues of men and of angels," by which he might mean "the languages of men and of angels" (1 Cor 13:1). It is also possible that the rather confusing discussion in 1 Cor 14:20–25 of whether tongues or prophecy is meant to serve as a "sign for unbelievers" was provoked by expectations of xenolalia. The story of xenolalia on the Day of Pentecost may have spread to Corinth and created an expectation of similar events in their own context.

three messages in tongues rather than translate a single message, even less correlation in length should be expected.

According to 1 Cor 14:14, when praying in tongues one's mind is "unfruitful." However, Paul does not wish to set mindful prayer over against prayer "with one's spirit," so he recommends praying both with one's mind and with one's spirit (1 Cor 14:15). How does this praying with one's spirit relate to the Spirit's intercession described in Romans 8?

The way in which the Holy Spirit interacts with a person's own spirit is not clearly spelled out. Probably such an explanation, if offered, would be impossible for humans to grasp. Nevertheless, a linkage is implied. The phrase "inarticulate groanings" of Rom 8:26 suggests vocalizing what sounds like gibberish with the Holy Spirit enabling these sounds through use of the human vocal apparatus. While this speech is spiritually significant, it is also inarticulate and noncognitive. A similar divine-human interaction is described in Acts 2:4. As that verse puts it, "they began to speak in tongues *as the Spirit gave them utterance*." The difference is that the speech described in Acts 2:4 consisted of understandable human language while this is not the case in Romans 8.

In Romans 8 Paul does not mention praying with the mind alongside the intercession of the Spirit. The situation he addresses makes informed prayer with the mind impossible because salient facts are unknown. No doubt, to the extent one is able, praying with the mind would be appropriate but of limited value.

In this chapter Paul makes another important point somewhat indirectly. After highlighting that God's children groan as they await the redemption of their bodies (vs. 23) and that creation groans as it awaits being freed from the slavery of decay (vs. 21), Paul also describes the Spirit groaning. Unlike the first two instances, the Spirit is not awaiting some future blessing for itself. Rather it groans in support of the saints (vss. 26–27). This way the selfless, giving nature of the Spirit is highlighted.

PAUL'S PNEUMATOLOGY AND LUKE'S PNEUMATOLOGY: A COMPARISON

Two of the most distinctive doctrines of classical Pentecostal theology are 1) the expectation of an experience usually called "baptism in the Holy Spirit," which is both separate from, and subsequent to, the experience of salvation, and 2) the idea that speaking in tongues serves as evidence that someone has been baptized in the Holy Spirit.[19] Both doctrines are based largely on the way the Spirit is presented in the book of Acts.

Since the publication of Hermann Gunkel's book *Die Wirkungen des heiligen Geistes* (English title: *The Influence of the Holy Spirit*) in 1888, it has been recognized that the book of Acts presents the work of the Spirit differently than Paul does. In Acts the Spirit is not involved in making people followers of Christ but rather the Spirit empowers those who are already Christ followers for prophetic witness. As Acts 1:8 says, "But you shall receive power after the Holy Spirit comes upon you, and you will be my witnesses in both Jerusalem and in all Judea, and in Samaria, and to the end of the earth." Furthermore, outward signs, especially those involving inspired speech such as speaking in tongues, mark the presence of the Spirit. A pattern is set in Acts 2, where both tongues of fire and speaking in tongues are presented as visible evidence of the Spirit's presence. Perhaps most clearly, in Acts 10:44–46 the narrator—who presumably represents the viewpoint of Luke, the author of Acts—asserts that speaking in tongues serves as outward evidence that the Spirit has been "poured out":

> While Peter was speaking these words, the Holy Spirit fell on all who heard the message. And the believers from the circumcision who came with Peter were amazed that the gift of the Holy Spirit had also been poured out on the gentiles. For they heard them speaking in tongues and magnifying God.

While Paul accepts that the Spirit can confer spiritual gifts on those who are already in Christ—he provides lists of such gifts in both Romans 12 and 1 Corinthians 12—in Romans 8 he more fundamentally insists that the internal presence of the Spirit is a necessary component of one's identity in Christ. This is an important difference from the presentation found in Acts.

Another way to express this difference is that Acts presents a quasi-sacramental view of speaking in tongues, while Paul does not. Instead, Paul focuses on the intrinsic value of speaking in tongues, prophecy, words of

---

19. While "baptism in the Holy Spirit" is used as a technical term in Pentecostal circles, this exact phrase never occurs in the New Testament. In fact, there is not one single technical term used to express the Spirit's empowering. Instead, a number of expressions are used to identify this experience: "baptized in the Spirit" (Acts 1:5; 11:16), being "filled with the Spirit" (Acts 2:4; 4:8,31; 9:17; 13:9,52), being "full of the Spirit" (Acts 6:3,5; 7:55; 11:24), "receiving the gift of the Holy Spirit" (Acts 2:38), and being "clothed with power from on high" (Luke 24:49).

wisdom, etc. themselves.[20] In Acts, the primary importance of speaking in tongues is that this outward sign points beyond itself to an internal change which has already occurred. Speaking in tongues, and perhaps prophecy, function as signs of a prior experience of empowering for witness by the Holy Spirit.

The idea of a sacrament is often connected with the Latin expression *sacramentum est invisibilis gratiae visibilis forma* ("A sacrament is the visible form of an invisible grace"), a formula that appears at least as early as the eleventh century. Often this idea is expressed more popularly as, "A sacrament is an outward sign of an inward work of grace." I have described the pneumatology of Acts as being only "quasi-sacramental" rather than fully sacramental in order not to claim too much, since some contend that sacraments only pertain to graces indicating salvation (i.e., baptism and the Lord's Supper). Acts presents neither the empowering for witness often called "baptism in the Spirit" nor speaking in tongues as salvific, but as gracious gifts from God, nonetheless. In fact, Acts 10:45 specifically refers to "the gift [*dōrea*] of the Holy Spirit."

So how should the contemporary believer deal with these divergent presentations of the Spirit's work, both of which appear in the New Testament? First, I think it is important to recognize that different presentations do not have to imply contradiction. Teachers and preachers in the contemporary church often have distinctive emphases. One teacher may habitually discuss evangelism and missions, while another may habitually discuss end-times, and still another may habitually discuss how the church should relate to the larger society and culture. They may have different messages, but this does not mean their teaching is contradictory.

Pentecostals have regularly insisted that Paul's and Luke's separate teachings about the Spirit are both inspired and correct. Each simply focuses on a different aspect of the Spirit's work. In Romans 8 Paul focuses on the internal and invisible work of the Spirit that accompanies the beginning of life in Christ, although elsewhere he also discusses additional giftings that may come later in one's spiritual life. On the other hand, in Acts Luke focuses on visible manifestations that demonstrate added power bestowed on the believer. It is quite easy to harmonize the two by asserting that the Spirit begins to dwell in the believer from the moment of her conversion,

---

20. I would like credit my brother, Robert P. Menzies, for this observation that Paul places more intrinsic value on the activity of speaking in tongues itself than does Acts. He offered this observation in a private phone conversation in October 2023.

marking that person as a Christ-follower, but that the Spirit can also later endue that same person with greater power for witness demonstrated by manifestations of inspired speech. Both components are important in a full presentation of the New Testament's pneumatology.

Excursus: The New Order of the Latter Rain and Romans

AN OVERVIEW OF LATTER RAIN

The "New Order of the Latter Rain," also known simply as "the New Order" or "Latter Rain" (hereafter "Latter Rain"), was a movement with a flurry of momentum in the late 1940s and early 1950s. It included both churches and para-church structures and drew support primarily from Pentecostals. As a movement it overlapped with the contemporaneous Healing Revival that featured such figures as William Branham, Oral Roberts, and T. L. Osborn. Richard Riss describes it as "only one of many aspects of the Evangelical Awakening during 1947–1952."[21]

Although Latter Rain had an impact in the United Sates and other English-speaking countries, its influence in Canada, especially western Canada, was strongest. It drew much of its imagery and language from the Pentecostal Revival of the first decade of the twentieth century, although with added embellishments. It also claimed to mark an advancement beyond that earlier revival. Latter Rain had an important impact on several leaders of the Charismatic Movement of the 1960s and 1970s (which had important forerunners in the 1950s). Latter Rain also has influenced Kingdom Now theology and the New Apostolic Movement.

One might plausibly ask why Latter Rain is being discussed in a commentary on Romans. A thorough discussion of Latter Rain would not be appropriate, but since some Latter Rain teachings grew out of Romans 8, it seems appropriate to explain these elements of Latter Rain teaching, given the intended audience of this commentary. The history and impact of Latter Rain is available elsewhere, and it will not be considered here.

---

21. Riss, *Latter Rain Movement of 1948*, 33.

The central focus of Latter Rain was a new understanding of ecclesiology. Furthermore, since eschatology and ecclesiology generally go hand-in-hand, there was an eschatological element in Latter Rain theology as well.

The name "Latter Rain" comes from Joel 2:23, which speaks of both the former rain and the latter rain. These images are of the natural blessing of the agricultural cycle, but they were understood to represent spiritual blessings as well, with the latter rain representing the greater measure of blessing of the two. Five verses later, in Joel 2:28–32, the verses that Peter used as the scriptural text for his Pentecost sermon appear. The Pentecostal Movement of the beginning of the twentieth century understood the blessing it received to be the "latter rain" prophesied by Joel, succeeding the former rain of the apostolic age. In contrast, the Latter Rain teachers of the 1940s and 1950s considered the eruption of Pentecostalism at the beginning of the twentieth century to be the "former rain," while Joel's prophecy of a "latter rain" was being fulfilled during their era forty years later.

Israel's three great festivals—Passover and the Feast of Unleavened Bread, the Feast of Weeks or Pentecost, and the Feast of Booths or Tabernacles—were also used to illustrate a progressive outpouring of spiritual power. The events recounted in Acts fulfilled the Feast of Unleavened Bread. The great Azusa Street Revival and the events associated with it fulfilled the Feast of Pentecost. And the events unfolding in the 1940s and 1950s were to represent the Feast of Tabernacles, the greatest celebration of the three. Just as the Feast of Tabernacles celebrated the culmination of the annual agricultural harvest, Latter Rain was to usher in God's great harvest of souls just before the rapture of the church and the second coming of Christ.

In addition, just as the Pentecostal Revival of the early twentieth century had restored the gifts of tongues and the interpretation of tongues to the church, Latter Rain was to restore the gift of apostleship and especially the gift of prophecy to the church. When Eph 2:20 declares that the church "was built on the foundation of the apostles and prophets," in Latter Rain circles this was often, although not always, viewed as a continuing phenomenon, so that present-day apostles and prophets serve as the church's foundation. Some extremists within Latter Rain considered their prophetic messages to be equally authoritative as scripture.

Ephesians 4 pictures the body of Christ organized in a way that seemed very different from the way most had heretofore experienced everyday church life in the twentieth century. This disconnect suggested that a more biblical model was needed. The five-fold "ascension gifts" were not fully deployed, and the leaders of the church did not properly equip all the saints for "the work of the ministry," leaving the church lifeless and powerless. The proliferation of denominations displayed a lack of "unity of the faith," which according to Eph 4:13 should characterize the church, and this was judged to result from sectarian disputes labeled as "denominationalism." In short, the church did not function as the body portrayed in Ephesians.

According to Latter Rain teaching, when the church did begin to function properly tremendous things would happen. A great and invincible army of righteous and powerful warriors would arise. Called "Joel's army," based on the description of an army in Joel 2:1–11, it would help prepare the way for the great harvest of the Feast of Tabernacles and then the return of Christ. This army represented a church loosed from denominational control and activated by the proper exercise of spiritual gifts.

Ordination by denominations or the districts of denominations were generally held to be invalid. In part, this was due to a rejection of the validity of denominations as non-biblical entities. In part, this was due to the widespread failure of denominations to ordain leaders in the way approved under Latter Rain teaching. Proper ordinations required those laying hands on an individual to name the specific ascension gift to which he or she was being ordained as hands were applied. This naming one of the gifts mentioned in Eph 4:11 was not a normal part of denominational ordinations, rendering these ordinations invalid in the eyes of Latter Rain leaders. This rejection of their ordinations led, of course, to widespread suspicion of Latter Rain among denominational leaders.

ROMANS 8 AND LATTER RAIN

Overlapping with the concept of Joel's army was the doctrine of "the manifestation of the sons of God" (Rom 8:19). According to the teaching of many within Latter Rain, these "manifest sons of God" were to be revealed prior to the rapture of the church.

Paul wrote his letter to people who had received "the first-fruits of the Spirit," and were awaiting a further blessing (Rom 8:23). In the same verse, Paul goes on to link the full reception of sonship (or adoption) with "the redemption of our bodies." This suggested to those in Latter Rain that it was possible, prior to Christ's return, to receive redeemed bodies that were impervious to disease and even to death.

Rom 8:19 personifies creation and pictures it eagerly awaiting "the revelation" (or "the manifestation") "of the sons of God" in the expectation that its release from "futility" (*mataiotēs*) will come at that time. However, nothing in this passage suggests that either the revelation of the sons of God or creation's release from futility will precede the second coming of Christ. In fact, elsewhere in the New Testament such cosmic events are linked with Christ's second coming (Matt 24:29–31//Mark 13:24–27//Luke 21:25–28).

Apparently, the reason some Latter Rain teachers anticipated "the manifestation of the sons of God" prior to the return of Christ was that they read Romans 8 in conjunction with Joel 2:1–11. If Joel prophesied the rise of an end-time army of saints, "Joel's army" in their parlance, then one might see why they connected these two ideas. However, the army pictured in Joel 2 is not described in positive terms; the language describes threatening judgment. Most scholars understand this army to be a metaphorical continuation of the plague of locusts described in Joel 1. Conversely, it might be that the locusts metaphorically picture the invasion of an army, although neither the Babylonians nor the Assyrians are mentioned. In either case, the image is menacing. This is not a picture of an army of righteous warriors bestowing blessings.

Romans 8 uses two similar but different expressions: "the sons [*huioi*] of God", found in vss. 14 and 19 with slight variations; and "the children [*tekna*] of God," found in vss. 16, 17, and 21 also with slight variations. While *huios* (the singular of *huioi*) means "son" and can be used irrespective of the son's age, *teknon* (the singular of *tekna*) means a pre-pubescent person whether male or female. The word is neuter in gender. When plural in form, "sons" (*huioi*) can include both "sons and daughters."

It is not clear why Paul switches back and forth between the two expressions. Maybe it is simply for stylistic variation. The expression *ta tekna tou theou* ("the children of God") never appears in the LXX. However, *toi huioi tou theou* ("the sons of God") appears several times: Gen 6:2, 4; Deut 32:43;[22] Ps 29:1 [Ps 28:1 in the LXX]; Ps 89:6 [Ps 88:7 in the LXX]; Wisdom of Solomon 5:5; Psalms of Solomon 17:27. Although it may refer to heavenly or angelic beings in a few places (Gen 6:2, 4; Deut 32:43; Ps 89:6), elsewhere it refers to those in right relationship with God (Ps 29:1; Wisdom of Solomon 5:5; Psalms of Solomon 17:27). This latter meaning is likely what Paul intends in Romans 8.

---

22. The Song of Moses (Deut 32:1–43) and particularly vs. 43, is quite different in the Masoretic Hebrew text and in the Greek LXX. The expressions "sons of God" does not appear in either the Masoretic text or in most English translations.

A SHORT ROMANS 9

TRANSLATION: ROM 9:1–5

ANGUISH FOR MY FELLOW ISRAELITES

¹I speak the truth in Christ; I do not lie, my conscience bearing witness to me by the Holy Spirit, ²that I have great sadness and unremitting anguish in my heart. ³For I have been longing that I myself might be accursed from Christ for the brothers [and sisters] of my kindred in the natural. ⁴They are Israelites, to whom belong sonship and glory and the covenants and the giving of the Law and the system of worship and the promises. ⁵Also, to whom belong the patriarchs, and from whom is the Christ in the natural. May God be forever blessed over all else. Amen.

COMMENTARY

Vss. 1–5: In these verses Paul discusses his personal anguish for the Jews who have not yet accepted Jesus as the Messiah of Israel. They are (largely) his genetic kindred—I translate the literal phrase "according to the flesh" (*kata sarka*) as "natural"—and share the same heritage as he does. This heritage stems from the patriarchs and the Sinai covenant. Why does he choose to unburden himself in this way?

In Christian circles most of the opposition to Paul and his gospel has come from believing Jews, some of whom understand him to be a traitor to his Jewish heritage and dismissive of Israel's special role as God's chosen people. As Paul begins a three-chapter discussion of how God has been at work creating a people for himself, he takes pains to emphasize that he cherishes his Jewish identity and empathizes with his unbelieving Jewish brothers and sisters. In short, he addresses the issues that divide the Jewish community from a place of love.

Vs. 1: Paul has already used the word "conscience" (*syneidēsis*) in 2:15, and he will use it again in 13:5. Here he invokes it as a somewhat independent witness to his personal pain over the failure of so many of his fellow Jews to accept Jesus as the Messiah. Outside of Judaism, earlier Greek literature had largely portrayed conscience as an external entity. In the LXX text of Eccl 10:20 *syneidēsis* appears as one's internal thoughts, but not as a moral compass. In the writings of Philo of Alexandria, Paul's slightly older contemporary, *syneidēsis* functions sometimes as an external judge and sometimes as an internal moral voice.[1] In this verse, Paul pictures conscience as an external witness apprehended internally through the Holy Spirit's influence. Although it is involved in moral evaluation, here conscience does not function as a moral compass.

Vs. 3: "I have been longing" (*ēuchomēn*): As an imperfect, this verb describes a continuing process. The translation sometimes offered, "I could wish," is inaccurate since this verb is in the indicative mood, not the subjunctive. Paul's longing is not hypothetical; it has been real and ongoing.

In Rom 12:1 Paul exhorts his readers: "Present your bodies as a living sacrifice" to God. The Greek he uses there is *thusia*, a rather standard word for sacrifice. This is relevant because in this verse Paul is offering to sacrifice himself and his eternal prospects for the redemption of his unbelieving kinsmen. This calls to mind the offer of Moses that God would "blot" him from the book [of life] in exchange for forgiving Israel's idolatry (Exod 32:32).

The word used here, which I have translated "accursed," is *anathema*. In secular Greek it usually means "a curse," and sometimes "something cursed." However, in the LXX it regularly translates the Hebrew *cherem* ("devoted thing," "things under the ban") and this background probably is in play here. During the conquest of Canaan, cities placed under the *cherem* were completely destroyed. Like Moses, Paul is willing to exchange not only his eternal beatitude but his continuing existence in exchange for the salvation of his unbelieving kinsmen.

Vss. 4-5: "They are Israelites": Paul wants to make clear he does not dismiss the heritage of Jews who do not accept Jesus as Messiah, as he has apparently been accused of doing. While he accepts that they are Israelites

---

1. Rather brilliantly Jacob Milgram finds the origin of conscience as an interior moral voice not in Hellenic antecedents but rather in careful exegesis of the Bible. For instance, in Lev 6:5 (Lev 5:24 in the MT) Philo understands the biblical phrase *beyom 'ashmato* (literally "in the day of his guilt") to mean "[when] convicted inwardly by his conscience" (Philo, *Special Laws* 1.235). Milgrom, "Response by Dr. Jacob Milgrom," 16.

and heirs of many of the blessings Israelites enjoy, he does not say they will ultimately be saved apart from Messiah Jesus. Most remarkably, Paul says that to them belong "sonship," "the glory," and "the promises." Exod 4:22 famously calls Israel "my first-born son," and while more commonly we read of "the glory of the Lord" or "the glory of the God of Israel," on occasion "the glory of Israel" is mentioned (e.g., Mic 1:15; see also Isa 4:2, 17:3). And, of course, the Old Testament is replete with promises to Israel. But Paul will quickly qualify his grand assertions in the verses that follow. In typical rabbinic fashion, he starts by making a broad general statement and then limiting its reach. While in rabbinic style such limitation is often indicated by pointing out exceptions, here it is not so much exceptions as clarifications that restrict the scope of the general principle.

The translation mentions "the covenants" following the reading of the Nestle-Aland and United Bible Society Greek texts. But it should be noted that the singular form "the covenant" has approximately equal manuscript support.

One important assertion is that the Christ (Messiah), when considered "in the flesh" or "in the natural" (*to kata sarka*; literally, "according to the flesh") is from Israel, which is largely unbelieving. Israel had been assigned a mission to redeem the world, and this mission remains in effect despite the Israelites' unbelief. Moreover, it is the Christ who leads the way in fulfilling this redemptive mission on behalf of Israel.

The expression *to kata sarka* is a bit unusual. The definite article *to* is neuter and does not agree in gender with *ho Christos* ("the Christ"). The use of the article in this way forcefully asserts the adverbial character of the expression, and it limits Christ's connection with Israel only to natural descent. Considering the totality of Paul's teaching, this implies that Jesus is also Christ to the gentiles but on a different, although equally valid, basis. Blass, Debrunner, and Funk suggest translating *to kata sarka* as "insofar as the physical is concerned."[2]

There is also an important textual issue in vs. 5, although it does not involve alternative wording but rather questions about punctuation. Punctuation is an especially problematic issue because the earliest Greek manuscripts did not supply punctuation and because after punctuation came into use many copyists felt free to emend punctuation as they saw fit. The issue here is whether the last clause of vs. 5 should be construed with "Christ in the natural" or should stand independently as a doxology to God (as my translation suggests). If the former path is taken, the verse would read: "Also to whom belong the patriarchs, and from whom is the Christ in

---

2. Bl-D-F §266 (2). See also Moule, *Idiom Book*, 58 and 111.

the natural, who is God over all. May he be blessed forever. Amen." While Paul does not often do this, in Titus 2:13 he calls Jesus Christ "God" (*theos*), so a similar statement here is not impossible.

TRANSLATION: ROM 9:6–13

NOT ALL DESCENDANTS OF THE PATRIARCHS ARE "ISRAEL"

⁶It is not the case that the word of God has failed. For not all coming from Israel are Israel. ⁷And it is not the case that all his children are the seed of Abraham, but rather: "Through Isaac will your seed be called." ⁸This is to say, it is not the natural children who are the children of God, but rather the children of the promise are reckoned as seed. ⁹For this is the word of promise: "At this time [next year], I will come, and Sarah will have a son."

¹⁰Not only this, but Rebecca also, after sharing the bed of one man, Isaac our father¹¹—when they had not yet been born or done anything good or bad in order that God's purpose with respect to choosing might continue, ¹²not by works but rather by calling—it was said to her, "The older shall serve the younger," ¹³as it is written, "Jacob I loved, but Esau I hated."

COMMENTARY

Vs. 6: The words "has failed" translate a perfect tense form of *ekpiptō*, which literally means "to fall out." *For a discussion of what would constitute the word of God failing, see the excursus "Guidance from Israel's History."*

Rendered literally, "not all coming from Israel are Israel" would be "not all coming from Israel they [are] Israel." The linking verb "are" is not present, only implied. Some interpreters suggest that Paul knew no Hebrew, but that contention is belied by the occasional appearance of Semitisms in his writing. The Greek word *houtoi* is probably a rendering of the Hebrew *hem*. Both *houtoi* and *hem* mean "they," but unlike *houtoi*, *hem* can function as a so-called "binder" and substitute for the verb "are," which seems to be what Paul is trying to accomplish here. Apparently, Paul unconsciously is thinking in Hebrew and writing in Greek. While what he writes is unusual Greek, it would have been understood by his readers.

Vs. 7: "Seed": The noun *sperma* ("seed") is singular in form, but it functions as a collective. This is clear since the "singular" noun serves as the subject of a verb in a plural form: *eisin* ("are"). *Sperma*, of course, here means "descendants."

In his quotation, Paul uses the precise language of Gen 21:12: "For through [literally "in"] Isaac shall your seed be called." The word "called" (from *kaleō* "to call") is often translated "reckoned" or "named" both in Gen 21:12 and in Rom 9:7. But being "called" implies more than that the line of promise is "reckoned" or "named" through Isaac. It also conveys missional significance. To say this differently, along with the promise comes a mission.

Within Judaism there has long been an awareness that Israel's special calling involves not only blessings but also a mission and responsibilities. These responsibilities constitute a burden that can be difficult to bear. As Tevye in the musical "Fiddler on the Roof" says, "Dear God, . . . I know, I know we are the chosen people. But once in a while, can't you choose someone else?"[3]

In Paul's letters, references to someone being called refer primarily to a person being called to become part of God's people. In a very real way, Gen 21:12 is the root of this theology of calling.

Vs. 8: This distinction between "natural children," literally "children according to the flesh," and "children of the promise" plays a central role in Paul's theology. It explains how descendants of Jacob can be excluded from the remnant; it also explains how gentiles who are not physical descendants of Jacob can be included. For his Jewish readers who did not already understand this, Paul's point would have been jarring and turned upside down the sense of pride and blessing they felt from being "naturally" Jewish. *For a more complete discussion of this, see the excursus "Guidance from Israel's History."*

Vs. 9: Paul explains at least part of what he understands to be "the promise" by paraphrasing Gen 18:10. While the promise was made by one of the three visitors Abraham and Sarah receive, Genesis suggests that these visitors are angels (messengers) from the Lord. The account begins: "And the Lord appeared to [Abraham] at the oaks of Mamre," and then proceeds to discuss the visit of the three men.

Vs. 10: The expression *ou monon de* ("not only") is typically Pauline. It is found here as well as in Rom 5:3; 5:11; and 8:23. Sometimes Paul uses the slightly shorter phrase *ou monon* found in Rom 1:32; 9:24; and 13:5.

The translation "sharing the bed" requires some explanation. The Greek word *koitē* usually means "bed," although it can refer to an act of "sexual intercourse." Here "the bed of one man" emphasizes that Jacob and Esau had not only the same mother, but also the same father. The word "sharing" is not a literal translation, but it gets the point across. Literally, the text reads, "having the bed of one man, Isaac our father."

---

3. "Fiddler on the Roof," Act 1, Scene 5.

Genesis repeatedly emphasizes the differences between Jacob and Esau, both physically and temperamentally, despite being twins. Although this characterization was not used in the ancient world, using the vocabulary of modern medicine, it is clear Jacob and Esau were fraternal rather than identical twins.

Vss. 11–12: In these verses Paul does not suggest God chose the patriarch Jacob for salvation and his brother Esau for damnation. Instead, he explains that God's choice of a covenant people was a sovereign act completely independent of any merit one twin might have had over the other. Paul points out that at the time God's choice was made, there was no track record for God to judge. God simply chose for his special people to be traced through Jacob and not through Esau. As a result, although they were biological descendants of Abraham and Isaac, the Edomites (Esau's descendants) were gentiles.

Paul uses the word "calling" (a participle of the verb *kaleō*, "to call") in vs. 11 to continue his emphasis begun in vs. 7 on the missional aspect of being chosen. What was true of Isaac being chosen over Ishmael is also true of Jacob being chosen over Esau. Paul then amplifies this by quoting Gen 25:23: "The older shall serve the younger." In the Greek, this statement is worded to emphasize the greater honor of the elder brother. It could be translated: "The greater shall server the lesser." The dynamics are roughly the same in the wording of the MT.

Vs. 13: The quotation found in this verse is from Mal 1:2–3, and in what is quoted it agrees word-for-word with the LXX although Paul's quotation does not describe the calamities that will befall Edom, as does the LXX.

In its context in Malachi, the references to Jacob and Esau are not really to these individuals but rather to the nations of Israel (really Judah at this point) and Edom, represented by the founding fathers of each. However, this is appropriate because Paul's principal point is that God chose the nation of Israel rather than the nation of Edom.

The name "Edom" is a variation on the Hebrew word *'adom*, which means "red." In the Bible, the color red is associated with Esau in three ways. First, Gen. 25:25, which narrates the birth of the twins, says, "The first came out reddish (*'admoni*)." Second, Gen. 25:30 explains that Esau was also called "Edom" (*'edom*) because he sold his birthright to his brother Jacob for some of "the red stuff" (*ha'adom*) Jacob had prepared, thought to be red lentil stew. Third, the identification of Esau with the name Edom is found in Gen 36:1, 8, and 19, in what are probably glosses added to the text of Genesis well after its original composition. Gen 36:8 also informs the reader that Esau settled in the hill country of Seir. This is significant because Mt. Seir was located in Edom.

The biblical portrait of the deteriorating relationship between the nations of Israel and Judah, on the one hand, and Edom, on the other, is very sad. Early on, the Edomites are favored as relatives, but particularly after the destruction of Solomon's temple by the Babylonians with Edom's aid (see Psalm 137:7) Edom becomes Judah's enemy. The most extreme picture of this is found in Isa. 63:1–6, where Yahweh himself is pictured returning from battle against Edom, covered with blood and looking like someone who in the wine-making process has "trampled out the vintage," to use the language of "The Battle Hymn of the Republic." This scene in Isaiah 63 probably describes the Nabatean conquest of Edom.

TRANSLATION: ROM 9:14–29

IS GOD UNJUST TO EXCLUDE SOME AND INCLUDE OTHERS?

[14]What shall we say then? There is not a charge of injustice against God, is there? Absolutely not! [15]For he said to Moses, "I will have mercy on whomever I want to have mercy, and I will have compassion on whomever I want to have compassion." [16]Therefore it is not by desiring or running the race, but by God's mercy. [17]For the Scripture says to Pharaoh, "For this very thing I aroused you in order that I might show my power to you and in order that my name might be proclaimed in all the earth. [18]So then he has mercy on whom he desires, and he hardens whom he desires.

[19]Then you will say to me: "So why does he still find fault? For who can stand up against what he wants?" [20]O Man, consider instead: Who are you to talk back to God? The thing being shaped will not say to the one shaping it, "Why did you make me like this?" will it? [21]Or does the potter not have the right to make from the same lump of clay, on the one hand, an article for honorable use and, on the other hand, an article for dishonorable use? [22]And if God, who desired to demonstrate his wrath and to reveal his power, with much patience produced objects of wrath crafted for destruction, [23][and] so that he might reveal the riches of his own glory upon objects of mercy which he had prepared for glory, what is that to you?

[24]We whom he called are not only from the Jews but also from the gentiles, [25]as indeed it says in Hosea:

> I will call Not-My-People, My-People
> And Not-Loved, Beloved.

²⁶ And it will be in the place where it was said to them, "You are Not-My-People,"

there they will be called children of the living God.

²⁷ And Isaiah cries out on Israel's behalf:

Should the number of the children of Israel be as the sand of the sea, only the remnant will be saved. ²⁸ For by finishing things up and by cutting them short, the Lord will accomplish his word upon the earth.

²⁹ And as Isaiah foretold,

Unless the Lord Sabaoth had left us a seed, we would have become as Sodom, and we would have been named as Gomorrah.

COMMENTARY

Vs. 14: Once more we encounter the question, "What shall we say then?" which does not change the subject under discuss, but rather refocuses it. *For more about this, see the comment on 3:9.*

This question is followed by a second question, which I have translated in the form, "There is not . . . , is there?" This form is how in English we signal that a negative answer is expected. That a negative answer to a question is expected in Greek is indicated by use of the negative particle *mē*, as occurs here. Furthermore, when the answer to a question is already known, this means it is a rhetorical question. Paul's point is that God cannot be charged with injustice.

At this point, as so often is the case in Paul's letters, he engages in diatribe. While in popular usage, a diatribe means "a bitter attack," in more technical usage, it refers to "an argument against an imaginary opponent." While the opponent may be imaginary or unnamed, the opponent's argument is very real. Based on his past experience, Paul is sure someone will object that God is being unjust when he chooses one person or nationality rather than another simply because he wills to do so. Paul then completely dismisses this objection from his imaginary opponent.

Vs. 15: In this verse Paul quotes Exod 33:19, matching the LXX text word-for-word. The quotation is made up of two parallel main clauses with each containing a main verb in the future tense and each main clause also containing a direct object comprised of a "more vivid future conditional relative clause."⁴ These relative clauses use the particle *an* along with verbs in the subjunctive mood. There is a tentativeness to the subjunctive that is hard to express in English. Using the future tense ("on whom I will have mercy") does not capture it. Translating with "on whomever I want to have mercy" is not strictly speaking literal, but it does capture some of the subjunctive's tentativeness. When Paul revisits this topic in vs. 18, he does not again use this "more vivid future conditional relative clause" construction.

Vs. 16: The grammar of this verse is unusual. The verse contains three participles, but there is no main (finite) verb, and grammatically this verse seems quite independent of both the verse preceding and the verse following. It could be construed as a genitive absolute, but it is probably better to assume an implied verb "it is" (*estin*).

The participle *thelontos* (from *thelō*) can mean either "desiring/wanting" or "willing." But Paul much more frequently uses it in the sense of "desiring" or "wanting." The participle *trechontos* (from *trechō*) literally means running, as in a race. Clearly it is used here metaphorically, assuming the common characterization of life as a race. Paul's point is that living a good life (or even desiring to live a good life) will not earn special standing before God.

A possible translation is, "Therefore, it is not the one desiring or the one running the race but God having mercy." Brooks and Winbery propose a more accurate option, employing what they call "an ablative of means"—actually three ablatives of means.⁵ This results in the translation, ". . . not by desiring or by running the race, but by God mercying." Of course, "God mercying" is intolerable English, so in the proposed translation this has been changed to "by God's mercy." Perhaps the difference in meaning between the two options is slight, but there is a difference. The first option focuses on who is the agent of choosing; the second focuses on the means by which a person or nation is chosen.

Vs. 17: The quotation is from Exod 9:16. The LXX reads similarly, but not identically. It has *dietērēthēs* ("you have been preserved") where Romans has *exēgeira* ("I aroused"), and *ischyn* ("strength") where Romans has *dynamin* ("power"). The MT has *he'emadtika ba'bur har'otka 'eth-kochi* ("I have caused you to stand in order to show you my might").

In the context of Exodus, God is instructing Moses what to say to Pharaoh. Moses is to make the point he could already have destroyed Pharaoh and the Egyptian people by plague, but he has not. Whether Pharaoh has been preserved or aroused, he is there because God wants him there.

4. Smyth, *Greek Grammar* §2565.
5. Brooks and Winbery, *Syntax of New Testament Greek*, 26.

Did God desire to show his power "to you [Pharaoh]," "in you [Pharaoh]," or "by you [Pharaoh]"? All are grammatically possible, but arousing Pharaoh to demonstrate divine power to him makes the best sense, so I have translated "to you." Pharaoh was given fair warning.

Vs. 18: "He has mercy on": As in vss. 15 and 16, the text expresses God's mercy through use of a verb. Literally, it says, "God mercies," which is unacceptable English.

"He hardens": The Greek verb *sklērynō* means "to harden," and Paul's use of it is based on his Greek text of Ex. 4:21. But while the LXX uses *sklērynō*, the Hebrew verb apparently lying behind it, as the MT attests, is *chazaq*, which can mean "to grow hard or rigid" but often means "to strengthen." For example, in Deuteronomy the charge is given several times to "strengthen" Joshua (1:38; 3:28; 31:7, 23) using the Hebrew verb *chazaq* and the Greek verbs *ischyō* or *katischyō*. The related adjective *chazaq* is often used with the nouns "hand" and "arm" in the expressions "strong hand" or "strong arm." But when the verb *chazaq* is used with "heart" (*lev*) it seems to be considered an idiom, and the translators of the LXX rendered it as "he *hardened* the heart of . . . ."

But hardening the heart of someone, or for that matter strengthening someone, does not imply determining their decisions or their actions. It seems rather to confirm them in the orientations they have already assumed. Hardening and strengthening are about promoting continuity, not change.

Vs. 19: The diatribe continues. Paul's imaginary opponent objects that, if life is a chessboard and we are all pawns in God's hands, how can God "find fault" (*memphomai*) with anything we do?

Paul chooses not to contest the logic behind this objection. Instead, he contests the standing of his imaginary opponent and his right to put God on trial. Based on Paul's failure to engage with the objection itself, some presume that Paul accepts the theory of God's "meticulous sovereignty" over the universe. This theory holds that God directly causes everything that happens to happen, and that human choices that seem free are in fact determined by God. Furthermore, those who accept God's meticulous sovereignty believe this puts them on Paul's side of the argument rather than Paul's opponent's side.

But does Paul's contention that God is free to extend mercy and to harden as he wills commit him to a view of meticulous sovereignty? He does not say that God chooses between mercy and hardening for every person. He simply says that God extends mercy "on whom he desires" and hardens "whom he desires." As Paul recounts Israel's story, he mentions God's extension of mercy and his hardening only upon key figures representing entire peoples. While God's power over each person's eternal destiny is a fearful thing, in truth we do not need to be afraid. If our identity is "in Christ," we are assured that we will receive mercy.

Vs. 20: "O Man": In keeping with the translation of 2:1 and 2:3 and a history of rendering it this way, I have translated *ō anthrōpe* as "O Man," even though "O Human Being" would be more accurate. Functionally, it probably means something like, "You poor person!" Paul is expressing mock pity on his imaginary opponent. This means he is expressing pity for those who feel entitled to make themselves God's judge. *For more about this formulation, see the excursus titled "O Man."*

This verse contains a question followed by a second question with a third question embedded within the second question. As in vs. 14, the second question uses the negative particle *mē*, implying that the answer to this question must be negative. Again, when the answer to a question is already known, this makes it a rhetorical question. Paul's point is that an object in a potter's hand never complains, "Why did you make me like this?"

Vs. 21: Paul continues to depict sharp contrasts, but in this verse the contrasting language changes subtly. The opposition of "mercy"/"hardening" in vs. 17 gives way to "honor"/"dishonor." The question in this verse uses the negative *ouk* rather than *mē*, so it does not automatically demand a negative response. Nevertheless, Paul expects his imaginary opponent (and the reader) to affirm that the potter has the right to make items both for honorable and items for dishonorable use. The potter is free to make both fine tableware and chamber pots. It is her choice.

Vss. 22–23: These verses contain an elaborate protasis ("if" part) of a conditional sentence, while the apodosis (the "then" part)—"What is that to you?"—is implied but not stated. There is also the question of how to understand the *kai* ("and") at the beginning of vs. 23. Conceivably it serves as an intensifier, but it may also simply divide the protasis into two parts.[6] The "and" is placed in square brackets to highlight the ambiguity of whether or not it should be translated into English.

The verb "produced" (an aorist form of the very irregular verb *pherō*) usually means something like "carried," but the context makes that unlikely here. Although less common, it can mean "produced," which makes perfect sense in this context.

The verb *gnōrizō* (translated "to reveal") appears once in vs. 22 and once in vs. 23. Both occurrences are part of another rhetorical question Paul uses against his imaginary opponent. Paul's point is that God's right to choose and to harden must be weighed not only in the context of how this affects the individuals chosen or hardened, but it must also take into

---

6. For a discussion of *kai* as an intensifier, see Smyth, *Greek Grammar* §2881.

account the impact of his choosing and hardening on subsequent generations. It is not only Isaac and Ishmael, Jacob and Esau, and Pharaoh who have been affected by God's choices, it is all of humanity.

Vs. 24: After a brief exchange with his imaginary opponent precluding charges of injustice against God, including when God hardened Pharaoh's heart, Paul returns to the matter raised earlier in vss. 10–13 of God having called Jacob/Israel, and therefore his having called the people of Israel. In this verse Paul adds a zinger to this discussion of calling: "We whom he called are not only from the Jews but also from the gentiles." This inclusion of gentiles in the calling of Israel was already implied in vs. 8 and it foreshadows his contention in chapter 11 that gentiles will be grafted into the olive tree that represents Israel, and furthermore, that "all Israel" includes gentiles.

Vss. 25–26: Paul's quotation of Hosea is a composite. The material in vs. 25 is from Hosea 2:23 (2:25 in the LXX), and the wording in the LXX is slightly different. The material in vs. 26 is from Hosea 1:10 (2:1 in the LXX), and the LXX wording is identical to that found here.

The book of Hosea famously records God's command to Hosea the prophet "to take for yourself a wife of adulteries and children of adulteries for the land is extremely adulterous rather than being faithful to the Lord" (Hos 1:2). This he does by marrying Gomer, who has three children, the paternity of which is unclear. Thus, Hosea's family life serves as a prophetic sign-act illustrating Israel's faithlessness.

The symbolic names of Hosea and his wife Gomer's third child, a son named "Not-my-People," and their daughter "Not-Loved" illustrate the Lord's rejection of his people Israel and Judah because of their faithlessness just as Hosea rejects Gomer and her children. But this rejection is not the end of the story. Later Hosea woos Gomer, and she returns to him as a faithful wife. She also brings with her the children that Hosea had rejected, and he also accepts them. In the book of Hosea, the dynamics are focused entirely on the Lord's relationship with Israel and Judah.

Paul interprets Hosea creatively. He concludes that when the Lord called Israel "Not-my-People" and when he called Judah "Not-Loved," they became gentile nations. They had been rejected and cut off from the covenant. Then when Hosea successfully woos Gomer, a figure for the Lord successfully wooing Israel and Judah, these gentile nations again become part of God's chosen people. This provides a precedent for the Lord's acceptance of other gentiles into his chosen people.

Vss. 27–29: These verses contain a chain of quotations from the book of Isaiah. Perhaps the first of these quotations is the most important since it contains the statement "only the remnant will be saved," which is foundational to Paul's remnant theology.

In vs. 27 the quotation is from Isa. 10:22. It varies slightly from the wording of the LXX.

In vs. 28 Paul paraphrases Isa. 28:22. Paul's use of the verb *synteleō* ("to finish" or "to accomplish"), coupled with the verb *syntemnō* ("to cut short"), give a strong eschatological flavor to this chain of quotations. *Synteleō* is the same word Jesus uses in his Olivet Discourse (Mark 13:4: "What is the sign when these things to come *will be accomplished*?").

In vs. 29 Paul quotes the LXX of Isa 1:9 exactly, except for omitting its opening *kai* ("and"). In the context of Isaiah, a scene of devastation is being described, and *sperma* ("seed") is often understood to mean a few "survivors" left to carry on Israel's line. But Paul no doubt sees in this word a reference to Jesus as either Abraham's seed, as in Gal 3:16, or as Jacob/Israel's seed.

"Lord Sabaoth" combines the English "Lord" with a transliteration of the Hebrew word *tsebaʼot* meaning "of hosts" or "of [heavenly] armies." I have translated it this way because the Greek of both Rom 9:29 and the LXX of Isa 1:9 combines the Greek word for "Lord" (*kyrios*) with a transliteration of the Hebrew word into Greek characters (*sabaōth*). (This transmission through a Greek intermediary results in a slightly different spelling for the transliterated word.) An interesting question is why the LXX translator chose to transliterate *tsebaʼot* rather than to translate it.

This writing of a Hebrew word using Greek letters may suggest that in in the first century in both Jewish and Christian circles, even within a Greek context, this Hebrew word (*tsebaʼot*) was used in worship. Furthermore, in the present day this word still finds a place in worship in the English-speaking world. The second stanza of Martin Luther's great hymn *A Mighty Fortress* contains the line, "Lord Sabaoth his name," which approximates the wording of the German original.

A LONG ROMANS 10

TRANSLATION: ROM 9:30—10:4

WHY HAVE SOME GENTILES BEEN INCLUDED AND SOME JEWS EXCLUDED?

³⁰What shall we say then? That the gentiles, by not pursuing [the Law of] righteousness received a right relationship [with God]—the right relationship of faith—³¹but Israel by pursuing "the Law of righteousness" did not attain the Law's purpose. ³²Why? Because they pursued it not by faith, but as though by works. They stumbled on the stone of stumbling, ³³as it is written:

> See, I have set in Zion a stone of stumbling and a rock of offense,
> and the one believing in him will not be put to shame.

¹Brothers [and sisters], the desire of my heart and my plea to God on their behalf is for their salvation. ²I bear witness for them that they have zeal for God but not with discernment. ³For by ignoring God's righteousness and seeking to establish their own, they did not submit to the righteousness of God. ⁴For in relation to righteousness, Christ is the end of the Law for everyone who believes.

COMMENTARY

Vss. 30–31: In vs. 30 Paul once again asks, "What shall we say then?"¹ As we have noted, Paul uses this question to refocus the current discussion. Here he uses it to allow himself an opportunity to express a conclusion to the exposition that has filled chapter 9.

---

1. For more about this question, see the comment on 3:9.

In these two verses the word *dikaiosynē* appears four times; twice I have translated it as "righteousness" and twice I have translated it as "right relationship." I have done this to point out the word's ambiguity. "Righteousness" was often considered behavior that meets a measurable standard, as judged by the Law of Moses. This is also why I have inserted the bracketed words "[the Law of]" in vs. 30. They are not stated, but they are implied. This kind of *dikaiosynē* would have been impossible for Abraham to achieve because the Law did not exist in his day. In contrast, Paul insists that *dikaiosynē* means a right relationship with God. This was the kind of *dikaiosynē* God reckoned to Abraham and the kind of *dikaiosynē* believing gentiles could experience apart from the Law.

Scare quotes did not exist in ancient Greek, but this does not mean that common sayings were never quoted. I have enclosed "the Law of righteousness" in scare quotes because I believe Paul is quoting a common expression, and he is quoting it ironically. He does not mean "the Law that brings righteousness," but rather "the Law that claims to bring righteousness."

Other translations often render "the Law of righteousness" non-literally. The RSV renders it "the righteousness which is based on law." This is an attempt to distinguish a bankrupt approach to *dikaiosynē* from proper *dikaiosynē*. I am not attacking this translation, even if I am attempting to present the ambiguity inherent in *dikaiosynē* in a slightly different way.

Paul's point is that if the nature of *dikaiosynē* is misunderstood, pursuit of it will be futile. In fact, *dikaiosynē* is one of those things that cannot effectively be pursued directly. It is a byproduct of trust in God as revealed in Jesus Christ. *Dikaiosynē* is not about a status we achieve; it is about our standing before God as he determines it. When gentiles believe in Jesus as the one God sent to rescue them and to be their savior, God makes their standing with him right, as Paul's gospel proclaims.

Unfortunately, Israel—not all of it, but much of it—chose a different path. They tried to obtain *dikaiosynē* directly and on their own terms. They made the issue focus completely on themselves. By scrupulously following the many regulations in the Law of Moses, they hoped to qualify as being *dikaios* ("righteous") in their own eyes and in the eyes of others. Because of this, "they did not attain the Law's purpose [*eis nomon ouk ephthasen*]."

What was the Law's purpose, one might ask? It was to identify what pleases God, and what does not please God. But it was also to lead to life, something that without faith in Christ and without the Holy Spirit in one's life the Law was helpless to achieve. By attempting to use the Law as a guide, many Jews tried to please God through their own efforts, and Paul contends that this sabotages the faith that leads to God's declaration of right standing. Another way to put this is that many Jews trusted in their own ability to follow the rules laid out in the Law of Moses and by so doing to live rather than seeking acceptance by God based on their faith in him as the one who brought life to a dead Jesus, and who will also bring life to them.

Some have attempted to blame Israel as uniquely faithless or uniquely prone to self-justification. But this sort of antisemitic blame-shifting demonstrates the very wickedness to which every human is prone. The idols that tempt each of us may differ, and the points in which we take unwarranted pride may differ, but the basic dynamics are universal. God may have chosen Israel as the first direct recipients of his special revelation, but everything contained in that revelation indicts all of humanity and offers hope to all as well.

A few interpreters translate *eis nomon ouk ephthasen*, not as "they did not attain the Law's purpose" but rather "they did not attain the [requirements of] the Law," suggesting that they did not follow the rules of the Law perfectly. I find such a translation difficult to square with Paul's overall critique of the Law.

Vss. 32–33: In vss. 14–29 Paul responded to the charge that God might be unjust by excluding some and including others. Here the question is slightly different: Why does God include some *gentiles* while excluding some *Jews*? In response to the question that he himself has raised—an indicator that Paul is using the rhetorical device called "diatribe"—Paul maintains that some gentiles have exhibited faith while some Jews have not.

The question "Why? [*dia ti*]" might be translated more literally "On account of what?" but the implication is the same. The words that immediately follow have no verb, so usually the verb "to pursue" (*diōkō*), found in vs. 31, is supplied as a continuation of the same discussion. This raises the most important exegetical question of the verse: What should we assume the implied object of "pursued" to be? Did Israel pursue "righteousness" not by faith but as though by works? Or did Israel pursue "the Law's purpose" not by faith but as though by works? Either is possible, but in the immediate context Paul seems focused on the Law. To those using the eyes of faith, the Law points beyond itself to Christ.

The particle *hōs*, which I have translated "as though," suggests that many Jews thought they were pursuing the Law's purpose by works, though in truth they were not. Smyth notes that *hōs* can shift the focus of action to what was intended from what actually happened.[2]

The Old Testament quotation in vs. 33 conflates Isa 28:16 and Isa 8:14. The first source makes clear it is the temple (or possibly the temple mount) that is being discussed. The latter source is perhaps the more important one

---

2. Smyth, *Greek Grammar* §2996.

since it mentions the "stone of stumbling." In that verse the MT and the LXX read somewhat differently. The MT suggest that the Lord will become both "a sanctuary/holy place" and "a stone of stumbling." The LXX suggests "if you have believed" the Lord will be "a sanctuary/holy place," but if not, he will be "a stone of stumbling." It is unclear how the Hebrew text used by the translators of the LXX read.

Paul clearly understood both Isa 28:16 and Isa 8:14 to speak of the temple. But because Jesus spoke of his body as a replacement for the Second Temple/Herod's Temple, as noted in the Olivet Discourse (Matt 24:1–3// Mark 13:1–2//Luke 21:5–6) and in John 2:19–21, Paul regards these verses as prophecies about the body of Jesus. Paul was particularly influenced by the LXX version of Isa 8:14, in which belief or lack of belief will determine whether the (crucified and resurrected) body of Jesus is, on the one hand, "a sanctuary" and blessing or, on the other hand, "a stone of stumbling," tripping a person up. Read this way, this verse teaches that a person's response to the proclamation of the crucifixion and resurrection of Jesus determines whether or not that person is included in the people of God.

There is a question about whether part of the quotation of Isa 8:14 should be translated "the one trusting in it" or "the one trusting in him." Since the pronoun *autō* ("him" or "it") is either masculine or neuter, its antecedent cannot be "rock" (*petra*), which is feminine. In could be "stone" (*lithos*), which is masculine. However, since in Isaiah 8 the antecedent is "the Lord" (*kyrios*), which Paul may also understand to refer to Jesus, *autō* more likely means "him." This is confirmed by Rom 10:11, in which Paul quotes this passage again. There *autō* almost certainly means "him."

Vs. 1: The address to "Brothers [and sisters]," which in Greek takes the form of the vocative *adelphoi*, could mark the beginning of a new topic. However, Paul has already been discussing the unbelief of many Jews, and in a sense Rom 10:1–4 continues this discussion.

Paul declares his heartfelt desire for the salvation of his fellow Jews. He also shares that he pleads to God on their behalf. While certainly these claims are true, one wonders if Paul has been accused of being hardhearted to his kindred and abandoning them in favor of more receptive gentiles. Christians today might ask themselves a similar question: Is adequate attention currently given to presenting the gospel to the Jewish community?

Vs. 2: The word "zeal" (*zēlos*) is a loaded, even inflammatory, term evoking great emotion. It is often used in a positive sense, as apparently is the case here. The Lord himself has zeal (e.g., English Isa 9:7; MT and LXX Isa 9:6), but sometimes this zeal is scarily linked to his anger (e.g., English and MT Ps. 79:5; LXX 78:5). The word *zēlos* can also be translated "jealousy," and the choice of which English word to use in translation hinges largely on whether the emotion associated with the zeal/jealousy implies self-interest or the interest of another. The Lord is a jealous God, interested in protecting his prerogatives. Zeal for the Lord is depicted as being very good, although sometimes with an ugly side. Prov 6:34 illustrates the dark side of *zēlos* (*qin'ah* is the equivalent in the Hebrew): "For jealousy brings the wrath of a man, and he will not spare in the day of vengeance."

Zeal for the Lord came to be associated with violence, and a willingness to kill or be killed to defend God's honor. The two most famous stories of zeal are that of Phineas and that of Mattathias. Num 25:1–14 tells the story of how the sons of Israel "began to play the harlot" with the daughters of Moab and "to sacrifice to their gods," particularly the Baal of Peor. When Moses commanded that those men who had been so engaged be killed, one of them, named Zimri the son of Salu, ostentatiously took a Moabite woman into his tent. Phineas saw this, went into the inner compartment of the tent, and ran his spear right through both Zimri and the Midianite woman, who were *in flagrante*. The Lord turned back his wrath from upon the people because Phineas "was zealous with my zeal" (Num 25:11).

The story of Mattathias concerns a precursor to the armed resistance to the Seleucid (Syrian Hellenistic dynasty) rule over Judah called the Maccabean Revolt. The story takes place during the second century BC, and it is recounted in 1 Maccabees 2.

Mattathias was a priest who lived in the village of Modin, who had five sons, and who was outraged that the temple in Jerusalem had been defiled by the Seleucid overlords of the Jewish people. Certain Seleucid officers (literally "men from the king") came to Modin, built an altar for pagan sacrifice, and commanded Mattathias and the other Jews of Modin to sacrifice on the altar. When one of the Jews came to offer sacrifice, Mattathias slew him on the altar and then he also slew "the king's man." Then before he and his sons fled into the mountains, Mattathias cried out in a loud voice, "Everyone who is zealous for the Law and stands on the covenant, let him follow me!" (1 Macc 2:27).

At the time Paul was writing Romans, some people claimed to be "zealots," those who were willing to take up arms in defense of Judaism. It is unclear whether these people had yet coalesced into an organized party capable of making war on the Romans. However, less than a decade later there was an active Zealot party in Judah.

When Paul says that the unbelieving Jews he knows "have zeal for God," he is complimenting them on their passion and commitment. However, they lack "discernment" (*epignōsis*). In vs 3 he elaborates on this, suggesting that this deficiency involves an active choice of their will. The charge that these unbelieving Jews lack "discernment" resembles his contention in 2

Cor 3:14, also leveled at unbelieving Jews, that "their understandings have been hardened, for until the present day when the old covenant is read, the same veil remains."

Vs. 3: Many translations render the beginning of vs. 3 something like, "Being ignorant of God's righteousness." The verb *agnoeō* can mean either "to be ignorant" or "to ignore," and obviously this common translation chooses the first option. But this is not the best solution because, as the last part of the verse indicates, "they did not submit to the righteousness of God." To submit implies knowledge of what is required. It is not that they are ignorant; it is that they ignore what has been presented to them and choose another path. The problem is not that they do not understand the gospel message, a message that reflects God's righteousness; they reject it.

One might ponder: What was so insulting about God's righteousness that so many Jews chose the path of rejection? This is not completely clear, but likely it had to do with the contention of Paul's gospel that gentiles have the same access to God they did as observant Jews. They found this insulting, and consequently they chose to obey the Law (as they read it) rather than to submit to God's plan that centered on Jesus. But beyond denying them a privileged place, God's offered decree did not imply the merit of intrinsic goodness. Remember, righteousness is about legal status, not character. Therefore, they could not glory in their goodness. This was also offensive to them.

"To establish" translates an infinitive of *histēmi* ("to stand" or "to make stand"). It is a righteousness of their own they want to establish. Paul considers meticulous observation of the commandments to mask arrogance. These very religious individuals profess submission to God, but Paul claims they resist true submission. One suspects that memories of his own pre-Christian experience have informed his depiction of this unwillingness to submit to God.

Vss. 3–4: These verses form an important crux, and in the twenty-first century after all the ink that has been spilled over their meaning through the past half millennium, one must basically read them, on the one hand, with Calvin, or on the other hand with N. T. Wright. While variations on these two options are no doubt possible, these two heavyweights define the basic fork in the road.

Calvin lays out what later became the standard Protestant position. While he acknowledges that the phrase "the righteousness of God" refers in part to the personal righteousness of God, his greater emphasis is on the righteousness that comes from God and is imputed to the believer. Concerning "God's righteousness" in this verse he says,

... it is, undoubtedly, called the divine righteousness, because it is a gift from the Most High ... No human being, desirous to be justified in himself, can possibly be subject to the righteousness of God. Is it not a sense of our own utter destitution, which compels us to seek for righteousness from another? Men ... are clothed with the divine righteousness by faith, because Christ's righteousness is imputed.[3]

In contrast, Wright will have none of this:

> There should be no question, here or elsewhere, of 'the righteousness of God' being seen as the righteous status which humans receive from God, though that continues to be assumed here and there. When Paul speaks of 'God's righteousness' in 10.3 as something of which Paul's unbelieving Jewish contemporaries were 'ignorant', he is, I suggest, invoking the entire train of thought from 9.6 forward. It was that strange narrative of God's elective purposes which raised the question of God's righteousness in the first place (9.14, *mē adikia para tō theō*, 'is there injustice with God'), and Paul answered the question with more of the same narrative. When we put together the 'ignorance' motif in 10.3 with the material toward the end of the chapter, and ask what Paul supposed these people were ignorant *of*, it is clear: (a) that they were ignorant of what God had been doing in their history, in other words, of the way in which the purpose of election had actually been working out not just through the choice of Abraham but also through the narrowing down of his offspring to an exiled remnant; and (b), exactly cognate with that, they were ignorant of the fact that the crucified Jesus was Messiah.[4]

In a sense Wright has refurbished the standard view of "the righteousness of God" that predated Luther and Calvin, namely, that this phrase refers to God's personal righteousness. His departure from that earlier Catholic view comes with his rejection that the verb *dikaioō* (traditionally "to justify" but in Wright's view "to declare in the right") means "to impart personal righteousness to the individual."

Perhaps Wright's approach can be embellished slightly in the interest of clarity. Functionally, in this verse "God's righteousness" means "God's

---

3. Calvin, *Commentary on Romans*, ad loc. Rom 10:3.
4. Wright, *Paul and the Faithfulness of God*, 1168.

righteous way." It is his personal righteousness expressed in his dealings with humanity.

Calvin understood the contrast Paul makes to be between two approaches to achieving human righteousness. Wright, I think rightly, understands the contrast to be between God's plan and a human plan arrogantly imposed on God.

Vs. 4: Arguments about the meaning of "the end of the Law" have been highly charged. Like the English noun "end," the Greek noun *telos* can mean either "termination" or "goal." It is also possible that here *telos* means both, with Christ being the goal toward which the Law aimed, but that once that goal was reached, the Law, having accomplished its mission, was no longer relevant in the same way it had been before.

Paul specifies the context in which Christ marks the *telos* of the Law in two ways. Christ is the *telos* of the Law first "in relation to righteousness" (*eis dikaiosynēn*), and second this *telos* is limited to "everyone who believes." Paul's point is that those who believe in Christ have exercised the faith of Abraham, that is, they believe in a God who "brings the dead to life" (Rom 4:17). As in Abraham's case, God reckons righteousness to them, and therefore a quest for righteousness through the Law becomes irrelevant. This is the case for both Jews and for gentiles.

While Paul's primary emphasis is on the goal for which the Law was given, the Law's status as the primary pointer to what God desires has come to an end for those who believe in Christ because for them what God desires is made most clear in the teaching and ministry of Jesus Christ. This will be made clearer in vss. 5–13. Paul also returns to this theme in Rom 13:8–10. In vs. 8 of that passage, Paul writes: ". . . the person loving the other person has fulfilled the Law . . . ."

Some claim there is a conflict between this verse and Matt 5:17–20. Vs. 17 of this passage in Matthew reads: "Do not think that I have come to destroy the Law or the prophets; I have not come to destroy but rather to fulfill." But the "end" (*telos*) that Paul associates with the Law is only "in relation to righteousness." Furthermore, it is not a destruction of the Law. As just stated, Rom 13:8 says that when loving someone else, a person "has fulfilled the Law." Paul also says that the command to love each other "recapitulates" the commands found in the Law (Rom 13:9). While Paul quotes the command, "You shall love your neighbor as yourself" once in Romans (13:9) and once in Galatians (5:14), this saying appears three times in Matthew's Gospel (5:43; 19:19; and 22:39). Love is the culmination and recapitulation of the Law for Matthew as well as for Paul.

TRANSLATION: ROM 10:5–13

RIGHT STANDING BEFORE GOD COMES FROM CALLING ON JESUS

[5]For Moses writes concerning the righteousness from the Law: "The person doing these things will live by them." [6]But the righteousness that comes from faith says this: "You should not say in your heart, 'Who will ascend into heaven?" That is to bring Christ down [from heaven]. [7]Or, "Who will descend into the abyss?" That is to bring Christ up from the dead. [8]Rather, what does it say? "The word is near you, in your mouth and in your heart." That is the word of faith we proclaim. [9]For, if you confess with your mouth that Jesus is Lord and believe in your heart that God raised him from the dead, you will be saved. [10]With the heart one believes resulting in righteousness, and with the mouth one confesses resulting in salvation. [11]For the Scripture says: "Everyone believing in him will not be put to shame." [12]For there is no difference between Jew and Greek, for the same one is Lord of all, enriching all who call upon him. [13]For "everyone who calls on the name of the Lord will be saved."

COMMENTARY

Vss. 5–8: The argument contained in these verses builds upon, and assumes, the declaration of vs. 4, that in relationship to righteousness and for those who believe, "Christ is the end of the Law."

Paul proceeds to contrast two visions of righteousness. In vs. 5 he quotes Lev 18:5: "The man doing these things will live by them." The context of Leviticus specifies that "these things" are God's "decrees" and "commandments," and Paul points to the focus on "doing."

In vss.6–8 Paul paraphrases Deut 30:11–14, combined with an allusion to Deut 9:4. He is not offering an interpretation of what Moses meant when he spoke those words to the people of Israel; he is using those words to make his own point.

In Deuteronomy 30 Moses addresses the people of Israel. In verse 6 of that chapter, he announces God's great promise: "The Lord your God will circumcise your heart and the heart of your descendants, to love the Lord your God with all your heart and with all your soul, in order that you may live." He goes on to forestall the objections of those who might scoff in vss. 11–14:

> For this commandment which I command you today, it is not unfathomable, nor is it far from you. It is not in heaven above, that someone might say, "Who will ascend into heaven for us and get it for us; and that after hearing it we might do it?" Neither is it beyond the sea, that someone might say, "Who will cross over beyond the sea for us and get it for us, and announce it to us that we might do it?" The word is very near you, in your mouth, and in your heart, and in your hands to do.

The emphasis is on the accessibility of the Law; no heroic measures are necessary to know what God wants.

Within Judaism Deuteronomy 30 was a very well-known passage of scripture, and when Paul paraphrases it, most of his Jewish readers would immediately have caught the reference. They would also have recognized the way he had transformed it from a homily on the accessibility of "the commandment" (i.e., the Law) to one on the accessibility of the gospel message concerning Christ. In his paraphrase, Paul eliminates the references to "the commandment" and introduces two references to Christ, more or less in place of the expurgated words. This suggests that Christ fulfills the role Moses had promised the Law would fill, and that Christ, who was no longer physically present, was nevertheless easily accessible through the message of Paul's gospel. The upshot of this is that the arrival of Christ ended the old role Moses had granted to the Law.

To adapt the imagery to fit Christ more clearly, Paul jettisons Moses's reference to crossing the sea, substituting going down to "the abyss" (*abyssos*), "the place of the dead." This, of course, is a reference to the period between Christ's death and his resurrection.

The allusion to Deut 9:4 comes when Paul says in vs. 6, "You should not say in your heart." This wording is not found in Deuteronomy 30, but twice something similar is implied. While the wording is terse, in the translation of Deut 30:11–14 above, I have rendered it "someone might say." While the fact that Paul borrows this short clause from Deut 9:4 in itself is not very significant, what may be more significant is the thrust of the entirety of the verse, which Paul apparently had in mind as he wrote Romans 10. The LXX text of Deut 9:4 reads:

> You should not say in your heart, after the Lord your God has consumed these nations from before you, "It is because of my righteousness that the Lord has led me in to inherit this good land"; but rather it is because of the wickedness of these nations that the Lord is destroying them before you."

This verse is interesting in that it both asserts that Israel is no more righteous than other peoples and that God is using them to punish particularly wicked nations. This might suggest that Israel is less wicked that those the Lord will destroy, but even that is not sure. Remember the complaint of Habakkuk: "Why do you look upon rebels? You are silent when the wicked swallows up the one more righteous than he" (Hab 1:13).

Returning to Romans, Paul's critique of his fellow Jews who refused to believe in Jesus is that "seeking to establish a righteousness of their own, they did not submit to the righteousness of God." This echoes the "my righteousness" of Deut 9:4. God's impending judgment on the wickedness of many gentiles, as described in Romans 1, apparently caused many of Paul's fellow Jews to glory in their moral superiority. This prideful elevation of themselves made it difficult to accept gentiles coming to faith in Jesus. In this way they stubbornly refused to submit to the righteousness of God, a righteousness that would accept gentiles on an equal basis.

If God would reckon righteousness to gentiles who knew little to nothing of the Law of Moses, then this extraordinary turn of events spelled the end of the Law with respect to righteousness even for Jews. If a person was reckoned righteous by faith in Christ, then what additional sort of righteousness could the Law add?

Vss. 9–10: The confession "Jesus is Lord" or "Jesus Christ is Lord" is the earliest Christian confession. It is found here as well as in 2 Cor 12:3 and Phil 2:11. (Also see 2 Cor 4:5 for a similar statement.)

In modern western society, the heart is often associated primarily with one's emotions, but Paul thinks of it differently. Here he talks about believing with one's heart, but elsewhere he speaks of desires and knowledge coming from the heart. But, yes, the heart is also where emotions (specifically "anguish") and secrets are kept (Rom 9:2; 1 Cor 14:25). In short, the heart is an image for the innermost, most authentic faculties of a person. This means that "to believe in your heart" means more than superficial mental affirmation or a transient emotional assent; it is a commitment from one's core.

I have a Jewish friend who has often been asked by evangelicals, "Are you saved?" His standard response is "Saved from what?" to which he rarely got a cogent reply. When Paul writes about being "saved," he means "saved from the coming divine judgment which is already underway." (This is made particularly clear in Rom 5:9.)

Wright has pointed out that there are only three passages in Romans in which Paul brings together the ideas of "justification" and "salvation."[5] These passages are Rom 1:16–17, 5:9–10, and 10:9–11. He also notes that

---

5. Wright, *Paul and the Faithfulness of God*, 887.

in contemporary preaching justification and salvation are seen as near synonyms, while Paul kept them more separate. In both observations he is correct. The primary difference is that justification has to do with one's current status before God, and salvation points more to avoidance of eschatological judgment.

Vs. 11: The quotation is from Isa. 28:16. It has already been quoted in Rom 9:33, just eleven verses earlier. In 9:33 Paul's emphasis was on the body of Christ as a new temple and as a touchstone dividing between those who believe in a God who brings life out of death, and those who do not. In other words, the focus was on Jesus's resurrected body as the object of belief. Here the focus is on the dynamic of belief, for belief leads to justification, to salvation, and it is available to Jew and gentile alike.

Vss. 12–13: The fact that there is only one Lord means that both Jews and gentiles must come to the same Lord, and there can be no difference between Jews and gentiles in this matter. Paul's assertion that this Lord "enriches (*plouteō*) all who call upon him," calls to mind 2 Cor 8:9 in which the incarnation of Christ is depicted in terms of Christ leaving the riches of heaven so that by his assumption of poverty "you might become rich."

Normally the verb *plouteō* means "to be rich" not "to enrich." However, Greek does not have a causative verb meaning "to enrich," so Paul used the material available to him, adding the preposition *eis* ("into") to express that the wealth is distributed.

The quotation in vs. 13 exactly matches the LXX of Joel 3:5 (=English Joel 2:32) and also functions as the climactic verse of Peter's Pentecost sermon in Acts 2:21. In Joel this material is part of a vision of the future in which God will pour his Spirit out on "all flesh"—for Paul a reference to both Jews and gentiles—and in Peter's sermon it is an announcement that this future Joel prophesied has, in fact, come to pass.

TRANSLATION: ROM 10:14–21

WE SPREAD THE GOSPEL, BUT SOME WILL NOT ACCEPT IT

[14]So, how can they call on the one they have not believed? And how can they believe someone of whom they have not heard? And how can they hear without someone announcing a message? [15]And how can they announce a message unless they are sent? It is just as it is written: "How welcome are the feet of those announcing good news."

¹⁶But not all obey the gospel. For Isaiah says: "Lord, who has believed our message?" ¹⁷So, faith [comes] from a message, and the message comes through a word about Christ. ¹⁸But I ask: Have they not heard? Indeed, they have!

> Their speech has gone out into all the earth
> and their words to the ends of the world.

¹⁹But I ask: Did Israel not know? First, Moses says:

> I will make you jealous by what is not a nation;
> by a foolish nation I will anger you.

²⁰And Isaiah is forthright and says:

> I was found by those not seeking me;
>   I became conspicuous to those not asking [for me].

²¹And to Israel he says:

> All day long I have stretched out my hands
>   to an unbelieving and disputatious people.

COMMENTARY

Vss. 14–15: In these verses Paul asks a series of rhetorical questions, the cumulative impact of which is powerful. His questions list a cascade of effects requiring causes. Vs. 14 starts with allusions to Isa 65:12 and Isa 66:4 where the Lord wistfully recalls his calling out to Israel, entreaties that were not answered.

In vs. 15 the quotation of Isa 52:7 is not an exact match to either the MT or the LXX. There is a strong chance Paul's text differed somewhat from both strains of Isaiah that have survived. The adjective *ōraios*, which I have translated "welcome," literally means "to be in season" or "to be fresh." "Welcome" is a bit of a harmonization of the MT ("lovely"), the LXX ("a season"), and the text of Romans ("fresh"), being a comprehensive term that includes all three aspects.

Vs. 16: The striking expression "obey the gospel" also occurs in 2 Thess 1:8. The similar phrase "obedience of faith" occurs in Rom 1:5 and 16:26. These locutions indicate that for Paul faith is more than mental assent; it involves a change in how a person lives her life.

Paul's quotation of Isa 53:1 exactly matches the wording in the LXX. In Isaiah this plaintive cry comes just before a detailed account of the sufferings of the Servant of the Lord, which the earliest Christians read as predictive of the sufferings of Christ. Paul likens the failure of Israel to heed the prophetic message in the book of Isaiah to the contemporary problem of many Jews rejecting the gospel message he proclaims. The Greek word for "message" is *akoē*, which is related to the verb *akouō* ("to hear"), and Paul uses the noun in vs. 17 and the related verb in vs. 18 to further his argument.

Vs. 17: The word "message" (*akoē*) appears twice in this verse, the first time without a definite article and the second time with the definite article. The first part of the verse posits a generalization: Faith requires a message to believe in. The second part of the verse specifies "the message" (*hē akoē*) Paul proclaims that leads to faith in Christ. The phrase "a word about Christ" is literally "a word of Christ" (*rhēmatos Christou*). This translation treats *Christou* as an objective genitive, but it is possible that it is a subjective genitive or a genitive of source meaning "a word from Christ."

There is a question about whether the text Paul wrote was *rhēmatos Christou* ("word of Christ") or *rhēmatos Theou* ("word of God"). While the later alternative is unlikely to be original, Metzger's Textual Commentary explains the rationale in support of it: "The expression *rhema Christou* occurs only here in the New Testament, whereas *rhema theou* is a more familiar expression (Luke 3.2; John 3.34; Eph 6.17; Heb 6.5; 11.3)."[6]

Vss. 18–19: Each of these verses begins with *alla legō*. Normally, this would be translated "But I say." However, since in each case this opening clause is followed by a question, the translation "But I ask" seems more appropriate.

In vss. 14 and 15 Paul asked rhetorical questions. Here he shifts into diatribe mode with an imaginary interlocutor asking questions Paul chooses to answer. In vs. 18 the question is: "Have they not heard?" Paul's emphatic one-word response in Greek (*menounge*) requires more words in English: "Indeed, they have!" He then cites scriptural evidence to support this contention, quoting from the psalm that famously begins: "The heavens declare the glory of God." Paul provides an exact quotation of the LXX text of Ps. 18:5 (English Ps. 19:4; MT Ps. 19:5). The psalm argues that the heavens by their orderly and beneficial operation declare God's glory without using words or speech, yet they speak clearly and profoundly.

But to whom does the word "they" refer in Paul's question? Who does Paul say has heard? Much depends on which type of parallelism Paul employs between vss. 18 and 19. It could be synthetic parallelism with vs. 19

---

6. Metzger, *Textual Commentary*, ad loc. Rom 10:17.

both echoing the idea found in vs. 18 and also advancing it. However, more likely it is a kind of antithetic parallelism with vs. 18 discussing gentiles and vs. 19 discussing Israel. If so, this alternating pattern is continued in vs. 20, which discusses gentiles, and vs. 21, which discusses Israel.

But if vs. 18 relates to the gentiles, as I think it does, how does "the glory of God" that is declared by the heavens relate to Christ or the message about Christ? Does Paul understand "the glory of God" to be a cipher for "Christ." This would mean that the heavens declare Christ.

Elsewhere Paul closely associates "the glory of God" with Christ, but is that what he is doing here? The phrase "the glory of Christ" appears in 2 Cor 4:4, and "the glory of God" is linked with Christ in 2 Cor 4:6. But there is a particularity to Christ, who has been forever joined to humanity through his incarnation, so it is hard to understand exactly how a message about Christ could be learned from observation of the heavens, as the existence of God the Father or even the Holy Spirit might be.

A simpler solution is to conclude that Paul has borrowed the words of the psalm, separating them from their original context. He uses biblical language to highlight his contention that the gospel has been proclaimed throughout the world. But this widespread proclamation has come about by word of mouth, not through the speechless voice of the heavens.

The exact nuance of the question raised in vs. 19, "Did Israel not know?" may at first seem unclear. The verb *ginōskō* can mean "to know" or "to understand." So, does Paul ask, "Has Israel been exposed to the gospel?" or "Was Israel able to understand the gospel?" If vs. 19 parallels vs. 18, then the first alternative is probably correct; the "know" of vs. 19 better matches "heard" of vs. 18.

In vs. 19 the quotation that forms Paul's response to the question of his imaginary interlocutor has been taken from Deut 32:21, which is a supremely important verse for Paul. He mentions "jealousy" again in 11:11 and 11:14, and the idea contained in Deut 32:21 forms the foundation of his distinctive ministry. By evangelizing gentiles, Paul makes his unbelieving fellow Jews "jealous" and hopefully provokes them to faith. In this way, he ministers to Jews and gentiles alike. To Jews, his ministry is usually indirect; to gentiles, his ministry is direct.

Vss. 20–21: The quotation found in these verses is from Isa 65:1–2. Paul has rearranged the word order found in the LXX, but this does not really change the material's meaning.

Since in antiquity there were no chapter and verse numbers associated with scriptural texts, often part of a passage was cited to reference the larger passage. In such cases, if the larger passage is not consulted, then significant points may be lost to the reader. (Similarly, in today's world we often cite a song by singing a line or two of it, and then discuss the meaning of the entire song.) This may be one such situation. In Isa 65:1, appended to "I became conspicuous to those not seeking me" and "I was found by those not asking for me" is the additional comment: "I said, 'Here I am,' to a nation/gentile that had not called my name."

In the context of Isaiah 65 "those not seeking me" and "those not asking for me" seem to be Israelites and Judahites rather than gentiles. But the reference to "a nation/gentile" (Hebrew *goy*; Greek *ethnos*) in the part of Isa 65:1 that Paul does not quote may have signaled to the apostle that gentiles are under discussion. In any case, those who were not seeking God—whether Israelite or gentile—surprisingly found him.

In vs. 21 Paul quotes Isa 65:2 to suggest that the disbelief of his fellow Jews is not without precedent. In the book of Isaiah, the Lord had castigated similar unbelief.

ROMANS 11

TRANSLATION: ROM 11:1–10

HAS GOD THRUST ISRAEL ASIDE?

¹Therefore I ask: Has God thrust his people aside? Absolutely not! For I am an Israelite, from the seed of Abraham, of the tribe of Benjamin. ²"God has not thrust aside his people," whom he foreknew. Or do you not know that the Scripture says something about Elijah, that he appealed to God against Israel? ³"Lord, they killed your prophets, they destroyed your altars, I alone am left, and they are seeking [to take] my life." ⁴But what does the [divine] response say to him? "I have kept for myself seven thousand men who have not bent the knee to Baal." ⁵In the same way at the present time, in accordance with [God's] choice, a remnant has come to exist by grace. ⁶But if it is by grace, it is no longer from works since [if that were true] grace would no longer be grace.

⁷What shall we say then? That what Israel strives for, it has not attained, but [God's] choice has attained it. The rest became hardened. ⁸As it is written:

> God gave them a spirit of stupor,
> eyes unable to see and ears unable to hear,
> unto the present day.

⁹And David says:

> Let their table be for [baiting] snares and for [feeding] wild animals,
> and for [baiting] traps and for their own recompense.
> ¹⁰Let their eyes be darkened so they cannot see.
> Bend their backs continually.

COMMENTARY

Vs. 1: In this verse Paul recites his credentials but not to amass enough authority to be persuasive. Instead, these credentials serve to establish his Jewish identity. Before listing his *bona fides*, he has asked, "Has God thrust his people aside?" again voicing the question of an imaginary interlocutor. His response to this question is, in effect: "Look at me. I'm clearly an Israelite, but I have not been thrust aside."

The verb *apōtheō* ("thrust aside") can also be translated "to reject." It is a compound of the preposition *apo* ("from") and the verb *ōtheō* ("to push"). I have chosen the translation "thrust aside" because the underlying charge is that God has thrust aside Israel to make room for the gentiles.

To those who knew his personal story, his claim to be "of the tribe of Benjamin" might have been especially impactful. They would know that the Hebrew name Paul had been given at birth was *Sha'ul* ("Saul"), and very likely he was named after Israel's first king, who was also from the tribe of Benjamin.

Vss. 2–4: Vs. 2 contains a paraphrase of Ps 94:14 in the English and MT (Ps. 93:14 in the LXX). More precisely the psalm reads: "The Lord will not thrust aside his people." To the paraphrase, Paul adds, "whom he foreknew." The verb *proginōskō* literally means "to know beforehand," although it can also be translated "to foresee." Paul clearly believes God knows Israel's future because he is in charge of it. That "the Lord will not thrust aside his people" is the primary pillar of "remnant theology."

With Paul's discussion of Elijah, Paul begins an important exposition of the remnant theology that undergirds Romans 9–11. Elijah's appeal to God against Israel is found in 1 Kgs 19:10 and 14. It takes place during the reign of King Ahab of Israel and his wife Jezebel, a daughter of the king of Tyre. Both were devoted worshippers of Baal.

The story is gripping, in part because it comes on the heels of Elijah's extraordinary contest with 450 prophets of Baal and 400 prophets of Asherah, in which Yahweh ("the Lord") sends down fire from heaven. After this spectacular demonstration of the Lord's supremacy, the people all yell, "The Lord, he is God." Then at Elijah's command, the people kill all the prophets of Baal.

This slaughter angers Jezebel greatly and she threatens Elijah's life. In the face of this danger, he flees to Mount Horeb, and while living in a cave there, the Lord speaks to him, asking why he was hiding. He replies that despite having been very zealous for the Lord, "I alone am left, and they seek to take my life" (1 Kgs 19:10).

The Lord responds with specific instructions that will unleash violence upon both Syria and the northern kingdom of Israel, killing most of their warriors. But the Lord also promises, "I will leave in Israel seven thousand, all who have not bowed the knee to Baal" (1 Kgs 19:18), which Paul paraphrases in vs. 4.

In vs. 3 the word translated "life" is literally "soul" (*psychē*), which corresponds to the Hebrew *nephesh*. Paul also uses *psychē* in the sense of "life" in 16:4, although in 2:9 and 13:1 it means "person."

Vs. 5: The word *eklogē* ("choice") appears here and in vs. 7, but its meaning differs slightly in these verses. Here the accent is on the act of choosing; in vs.7, by metonymy, it refers to the people who have been chosen.

The phrase "by grace" (lexical form *charis*) employs a genitive construction. This genitive is used with *ginomai* ("to become"; "to be"; or "to be born") a "verb of beginning."[1] It is the coming into existence of the remnant that is "by grace." Without that grace there would be no remnant. This is personal for Paul because he understands himself to be included within this remnant.

Vs. 6: Paul consistently contends that grace cannot be earned. In other words, what is received by grace and what is earned are mutually exclusive categories. Therefore, if God's chosen were chosen "by grace," their status cannot have been earned, even in part. People do not become "chosen" by their works.

This suggests Paul does not consider remaining faithful to the Lord/ faithful to the covenant to constitute "works." Not bowing the knee to Baal was not a work, but rather an expression of faith and loyalty.

Vs. 7: Once again, Paul uses the question, "What shall we say then?" to refocus the topic under discussion. He continues to discuss the remnant, but he turns the focus to why the majority of Israel is not part of the remnant. For more about Paul's use of this question, see the comment on 3:9.

The verb *epizētei* ("strives for") is a present indicative, indicating that from Paul's perspective Israel's striving is ongoing. When Paul says "Israel" here, he means the majority of Israel, but not all of it. Their mistake has been to try to earn the status of being chosen. They have done this by assiduously observing the Law in order to curry favor with God. Having lived the earlier part of his life this way, Paul understands that this amounts 1) to trying to establish "their own righteousness" (Rom 10:3); and 2) to a lack of belief in God's goodness and faithfulness. Paul also describes this lack of faith by using the verb *pōroō* ("to harden"; "to callus").

---

1. Smyth, *Greek Grammar* §1348.

The verb *pōroō* appears once in the LXX (Job 17:7), where it describes the dimming of sight. Besides in this verse, Paul uses it in 2 Cor 3:14, where the word describes "minds" being hardened. It is also used three times in the New Testament by authors other than Paul. In each of these cases it describes hardened "hearts."

It is interesting that in Rom 9:18 Paul uses the word *sklērynō*, not *pōroō*, when he says, "[God] hardens whom he desires." In the LXX *sklērynō* is used much more frequently to describe what happens to hearts than is *pōroō*. If a distinction is to be made between the two verbs, perhaps *sklērynō* emphasizes hardening in the sense of "making obtuse" or even "making obstinate," and *pōroō* suggests the dimming of eyes that comes with their hardening and loss of flexibility to focus. Therefore, Paul may be emphasizing the blindness of his kindred rather than headstrong disobedience.

The context makes clear that God's "choice" (*eklogē*) here refers to "the people who have been chosen." The word *eklogē* refers to "the act of choosing," but it serves as a metonym for the people defined by that choosing. This people includes both a few Jews and a larger company of gentiles.

Vs. 8: Paul's paraphrase draws mainly from Deut 29:3 (English 29:4), but the phrase "spirit of stupor" comes from Isa 29:10. The word *katanuxis* ("stupor") appears to be related to the noun *nuxis* ("stabbing"; "pricking"), but I suspect instead it is related to *nux* ("night"). Some support for this comes from Isa 29:10, where the LXX has this word and the equivalent in the MT is *tardemah* ("deep sleep"). The prefix *kata* can serve as an intensifier, so this word probably refers to the stupor associated with being awakened from a very deep sleep.

The phrase "unto the present day" is part of Deut 29:4. Paul suggests that Israel's chronic insensibility about which Moses complained has not gotten any better in his own time.

Vss. 9–10: In these verses Paul quotes, with minor differences, the LXX of Ps. 68:23 (English 69:22; MT 69:23). This psalm famously is an imprecatory psalm, and the verse quoted expresses the desire of a suffering person (David?) for those who have hurt him to be repaid in kind.

The image is of a table in a home that has been laid waste and therefore the table no longer feeds its owners. The food on it is spoiled and good only for baiting snares and traps. In addition, wild animals enter and eat the spoiled food.

The reason Paul moves from the paraphrase of Deut 29:4 in vs. 8 to the quotation of this psalm in these verses is the catch-word association of "eyes" (the plural of *ophthalmos*). In vs. 8 they are "unable to see." In vs. 10 they are "darkened."

The translation "continually" for *dia pantos* (literally "through everything") is supported by Liddell and Scott.[2]

TRANSLATION: ROM 11:11–24

ISRAEL MAY HAVE STUMBLED, BUT IT REMAINS THE "ROOT" OF GOD'S PEOPLE

[11]Therefore I ask: They did not stumble so they would fall down, did they? Absolutely not! Still, by their trespass salvation came to the gentiles in order to provoke [Jews] to jealousy. [12]But if their trespass is gain for the world and their failure is gain for the gentiles, how much more will their fullness be. [13]But I say to you gentiles, as much as I am an apostle to gentiles, I would attribute glory to my ministry [14]if, somehow, I might provoke my kindred to jealousy and save some of them. [15]For if their rejection is an exchange for the world, what is their acceptance except life from the dead? [16]If the first fruits are holy, so is all the dough. And if the root is holy, so are the branches.

[17]But if some of the branches have been broken away, and you being a wild olive grafted into [the branches] have come to share in the abundance from the root of the olive tree, [18]do not boast against the branches. But if you do boast, remember you are not supporting the root, rather the root supports you. [19]Then you will say in response: The branches were broken away in order that I might be grafted in. [20]Well enough: They were broken away in unbelief, but you, who have stood in faith, do not think arrogant thoughts; rather be afraid. [21]For if God did not spare the natural branches, he will not by any means spare you. [22]Observe therefore the kindness and the excision of God: on the one hand excision for those who fall, and on the other hand for you the kindness of God, if you should remain in his kindness. Otherwise, you will be cut off. [23]And if those [branches] should not remain in unbelief, they will be grafted in. For God is able to graft them in again. [24]For if you could be cut away from the wild olive tree to which you belonged by nature and then contrary to nature you were grafted into a domesticated olive tree, how much more will those natural branches be grafted into the same olive tree.

---

2. Liddell and Scott, *Greek-English Lexicon*, s.v. "dia," A.II.1.

COMMENTARY

Vs. 11: The question Paul asks in this verse—"They did not stumble so they would fall down"—uses the negative *mē* with a verb (*piptō*; "fall" or "fall down") in the subjunctive mood. This requires a negative answer, which the "did they?" appended at the end of the question tries to express. Although voicing an answer to this question is really unnecessary, Paul nevertheless writes the answer with the written equivalent of a shout: "Absolutely not!" (*mē genoito*).

The question contains within it a purpose clause: "so they would fall down." Such a hypothetical falling would have implied a decisive end to a present status or a possible future status as God's people. Paul maintains hope: they have stumbled, but all is not lost.

This verse is the only place Paul uses the verb *ptaiō* ("to stumble"). Elsewhere he uses *koptō* or *proskoptō* when he wants a verb meaning "to stumble." The meanings of the verbs are very similar, yet there might be some difference in nuance. *Koptō* and *proskptō* perhaps imply "striking one's foot against something" while *ptaiō* may imply "making a misstep."

Paul suggests that the trespass of the Jews provided the occasion for the gospel to come to the gentiles. But what exactly does this mean?

Dispensationalists have a ready answer to this question. The inclusion of the gentiles would never have taken place if Israel had not rejected Jesus when he first came.

They contend that God's original plan (Plan A) stipulated that during Jesus's first advent Israel would acclaim him as Messiah and to install him as king on a physical throne in Jerusalem. From this throne, he would rule the entire world. In short, the Triumphal Entry started down the right path, but somehow it got derailed. When Israel did not recognize Jesus as their king, God put into place a new plan (Plan B) in which the church was created for the gentiles. Later, at the moment of a secret rapture ("snatching up") of the church, "the times of the gentiles"—also known as "the church age"—would come to an end. Then would come a seven-year Great Tribulation, followed by the Return or Second Advent of Christ and the beginning of a millennium during which Jesus would rule as king over the entire world from a throne in Jerusalem. With the beginning of the millennium, comes the resumption of Plan A, which had been paused. Thus, what God had planned for Israel in Plan A will take place, only on a delayed schedule.

According to this dispensationalist scheme the mainly gentile church was inserted into the divine timeline as a parenthesis. Due to Israel's "trespass," i.e., their rejection of Jesus, God's dealing with his people was put on hold and the gentiles received a great benefit.

But is this what Paul means when he writes, "By [Israel's] trespass salvation came to the gentiles"? Probably not. More likely Paul's statement is an extension of the belief of the earliest Christians, and in fact the belief of Jesus himself, that both the crucified body of Jesus and the church, which Paul calls "the body of Christ," are replacements for the Jerusalem temple.[3] By gaining access through faith in Jesus to this new temple—what we may call the third and everlasting temple—gentiles can now worship God although previously access had been prohibited to them and they were blocked from temple worship.

Paul observes that Israel's trespass brought salvation to the gentiles. But he also hopes that this salvation gentiles experience will provoke Israel to jealousy and their own salvation. This idea is of paramount importance to Paul and serves as a foundation of his distinctive ministry. It is rooted firmly in the words of Deut 32:21: "I will provoke [Israel] to jealousy with those who are not a people." In its original context, it is not clear to whom Moses refers. This may be part of why Paul considers this a prediction reserved for the distant future. Moses's statement takes the form of a threat issued in response to the idolatry of Israel. Similarly, Paul sees the salvation of the gentiles as a response to Israel's unbelief.

Vs. 12: This verse takes the form of an *a fortiori* ("how much more") argument. On the one hand, Paul considers the present "trespass" (*paraptōma*) and "failure" (*hēttēma*) of Israel, and on the other hand, he considers their future "fullness" (*plērōma*), concluding that the results of the latter situation will be far better. While here Paul discusses the *plērōma* of Israel, in vs. 25 he will discuss the *plērōma* of the gentiles. Wright notes the similarity of the *a fortiori* structure of this verse to the "christological summary" found in Rom 5:10.[4]

The noun I have translated "gain" (*ploutos*) appears twice in this verse, and it literally means "riches" or "wealth." Since it is used metaphorically, the more abstract "gain" seems a fitting rendering.

Paul contrasts "gain" with "failure" (*hēttēma*). The origins of this word are murky. It was not used in secular Greek, and it only appears once before

---

3. In discussions about Judaism and Christianity the word "replacement" often provokes considerable anger. The classic "replacement theory" suggests that the church replaced Israel. Sometimes the destruction of the Second Temple shortly after the birth (or renewal) of the church on the day of Pentecost has been offered as evidence of this. But what I am suggesting, following others before me, is that (the body of) Jesus replaces the Jerusalem Temple. Furthermore, since Jesus was a Jew and the Messiah of Israel, he does not replace Israel but rather fulfills Israel's unfinished calling.

4. Wright, *Paul and the Faithfulness of God*, 1198.

Paul, in the LXX of Isa. 31:8 where it describes something bad that will happen to "young men" in a context of battle. The MT of the verse says these young men will be taken as a tax of *courvée* ("conscript") laborers, but this meaning is not found in Greek usage. In the only other place Paul uses this word (1 Cor 6:7), it means "defeat" or "failure" in a moral or spiritual sense.

Vss. 13–14: Paul points out to his gentile readers that while he mainly ministers among gentiles, he is hopeful of his ministry bearing fruit among Jews as well, and he would relish this outcome. The verb he uses to describe what might happen among the Jews is *parazēloō* ("provoke to jealousy"), which based on its use in other Greek literature might also be translated "stimulate [them] to emulation." However, the sense in which Paul uses this verb elsewhere makes clear that "provoke to jealousy" is the proper sense. For example, in 1 Cor 10:22 he asks, "Shall we provoke the Lord to jealousy?" Rendering this verse with the alternative meaning results in nonsense: "Shall we stimulate the Lord to emulation?"

Lying behind Paul's reference to jealousy, as in his similar reference in vs. 11, stands Deut 32:21.

Vs. 15: This verse contrasts "rejection" (*apobolē*) with "acceptance" (*proslēmpsis*). Literally, *apobolē* refers to "something cast away," and *proslēmpsis* refers to "something received to oneself."

The phrase "reconciliation of the world" (*katallagē kosmou*) is probably better translated "an exchange for the world." The rationale for this preference is not lexical, since *katallagē* can mean either "exchange" or "reconciliation." In the context, however, "exchange" makes more sense. Since most of the world is gentile, when Paul writes "the world" (*kosmos*), he means "the gentile world," and he thinks of the exchange of the smaller Israel for the larger gentile world as a good deal. Looking back, the death and resurrection of Christ has resulted in both the loss of Israel from God's household and the addition of gentiles to God's household.

But Paul does not stop there: he hopes that, following this exchange, Israel will also be accepted and added back into the household of God. Many interpreters understand Paul's reference to "life from the dead" to suggest that the acceptance of Israel in some way facilitates the hoped-for general resurrection of all believers. But it is more likely that Paul's image portrays the transformation of dead Israel into a vibrantly alive Israel. In other words, Israel's acceptance will be like a resurrection.

Vs. 16: Paul's reference to the "dough" (*phyrama*) and the "first fruits" (*aparchē*) of it come from the LXX text of Num 15:20–21. There, the combined phrase "first fruits of the dough" (*aparchēn phyramatos*) occurs. Through this image Paul says to the Jewish believers in Rome: "If you and I are holy, so are all the other Jews who will become believers."

The image of the "root" (*rhiza*) and "branches" (*klados* in the singular) makes much the same point, but in addition it introduces the basic image that Paul will turn into a short allegory in the following verses.

Vs 17–18: In this allegory, the figure with the clearest symbolic meaning is the "wild olive" (*agrielaios*; literally the "field olive"). This stock taken from a wild olive tree to be grafted into the "olive tree" (*elaia*), also called the "domesticated olive tree" (*kallielaios*; literally "the good olive tree"), represents the believing gentiles. The "branches" (*klados* in the singular) apparently represent Jews. Since "branches" is plural, perhaps each branch represents one Jew.

It is somewhat more difficult to determine the meaning of the "root" (*rhiza*) and the "abundance" (*piotēs*; literally "oil" or "fat"). Probably we should identify the root with "the remnant" or "true Israel." (Is there a difference between the two?) The root is a particularly apt image for a hidden righteous remnant. The foliage and its fruit may be cut off above ground, so the plant is not seen, but if a root is left in the ground, there is hope for future flourishing. This is the image of the "root" found in 2 Kgs 19:30–31// Isa 37:31–32 and in the second-century BC apocryphal work 1 Esdras (3 Esdras in the Latin Vulgate) 8:78–89.

However, many dispensationalists would object to characterizing the root in this way, since this would imply that gentiles can be grafted into the remnant or "true Israel." Ryrie contends that the root represents "the place of privilege," first occupied by the Jews and then later occupied by the gentiles—but not simultaneously![5] The "abundance" provided by the root represents spiritual blessings, although exactly which blessings is not made clear.

The basic idea of the noun *piotēs*, "oil" or "fat" is often extended metaphorically. The word is often used in the LXX to speak of "the fat [abundance] of the land." Because olives were such an important source of oil, this noun can function as a metonym for "[olive] oil" (e.g., in the LXX of Judg 9:9), which is similar to how the word functions here.

The thrust of this allegory appears to be directed toward gentiles who are in danger of arrogantly claiming superiority over the Jewish community, many of whom have been "broken away." Many more gentiles are coming to belief in Christ than Jews. Paul bluntly commands: "Do not boast against the branches!" which of course really means, "Gentiles, do not boast against the Jews!"

Paul's warning to those who boast that "the root supports you" implies that the root is Israel—"true Israel" or "the remnant" to be sure, but Israel

---

5. Ryrie, *Ryrie Study Bible*, ad loc. Rom 11:17–24.

nonetheless. He suggests that the gentile believers should not boast against Israel because in a real sense they are rooted in and nourished by Israel.

Vss. 19–21: In these verses Paul fleshes out the rebuttal some gentile believers might make in response to the warning of vs. 18, followed by his response to that rebuttal. Once again Paul utilizes the device of diatribe, an argument with an imaginary (although very plausible) interlocutor.

The rebuttal consists of the premise: If they were broken off to make room for me, then I must be more important than they are. Paul's response amounts to this: Arrogance and taking God's grace for granted is what caused the branches (i.e., the unbelieving Jews) to be broken off. If you gentiles assume a similarly arrogant posture, also taking God' grace for granted, you too will be broken off. Arrogance has no place in a believer's life. Instead, live in humility. awe and fear before God's majesty.

The phrase "arrogant thoughts" (*hypsēla*, the plural of *hypsēlon*) means "high things" or "the [mountain] heights." The implication here as in Rom 12:16 is that these "high things" would be thought about oneself. The contrast here is with fearing God. In Rom 12:16 such thoughts are contrasted with humility.

The word "natural" translates a Greek phrase *kata physin* (literally "according to nature"). Paul does not use "nature" as a scientific term, but rather phenomenologically. It describes what one expects to find in the normal course of events: Olive trees have olive branches.

The verb "spare" (*pheidomai*) appears twice in vs. 21. In Romans it appears only one other time, in 8:32 where it speaks of God not sparing his own son.

Vs. 22: In this verse "kindness" (*chrēstotēs*) and "excision" (*apotomia*) are contrasted, but both are affirmed as characteristics or activities of God. *Apotomia* is often translated "severity," perhaps to render it as a characteristic like *chrēstotēs*. However, it seems to designate an action. Literally it means "a cutting away." Perhaps the translation "excision" is overly stuffy, but it is a very literal rendering of the Greek. The only two times *apotomia* appears in the New Testament are both in this verse.

The noun *chrēstotēs*, in contrast, is a characteristically Pauline word. He is the only New Testament author to use it, and he uses it ten times. It appears three times in this verse alone. It is difficult to decide if "kindness" or "goodness" is the better translation.

The phrase "those who fall" might also be translated "those who have fallen." The participle is in the aorist tense, the significance of which is often ambiguous. In either case, the verb "fall" (*piptō*) here implies falling from a state of grace to a state of impending wrath.

The exact force of the clause "if you should remain in his kindness" in unclear. Does Paul offer a near tautology (You will experience the kindness of God if you continue to experience his kindness)? Or is he giving an exhortation to continue to honor God's kindness (You will experience the kindness of God if you choose to continue in his kindness)? The latter option seems much more likely to be correct.

The word *epei* translated here "otherwise" can have either a temporal or a causal force depending on the context. If its force here were temporal, it would mean "At that time you will be cut off," surely a strange coda to the promise of God's kindness. No doubt the causal rendering ("otherwise") is correct.

Vs. 23: In this verse Paul slips slightly from his pure narration of the allegory to direct discussion of the allegory's figurative meaning. The clause "if those [branches] should not remain in unbelief" does not really discuss branches but rather people. It is possible, however, that this clause should be translated, "if those [people] should not remain in unbelief," since both "branches" (*kladoi*, the plural of *klados*) and an implied "people" (*anthrōpoi*, the plural of *anthrōpos*) are masculine. But even if Paul is discussing "those people" the verse remains a mixture of figure and symbolic meaning, since the verse goes on to discuss grafting them—either branches or people—back into the tree.

Paul's point is that neither the situation of the believing gentiles nor the situation of the unbelieving Jews is fixed in stone. Arrogant gentiles who quit believing will be excised from the root. Unbelieving Jews who come to accept Jesus as the Messiah of Israel will be grafted back into the root.

Vs. 24: Once again Paul employs an *a fortiori* argument, and it is aimed directly at the gentiles who are in danger of becoming arrogant. If branches from a wild olive tree can be grafted into the root of a domesticated olive tree, one stock into a different stock, how much more easily can a branch from a domesticated olive tree be grafted into the root of a domesticated olive tree, the same stock into the same stock. Furthermore, the *a fortiori* character of this argument only makes sense if the symbolic equivalent of the root is Israel, with Jew being grafted back into Israel. This exegetical point inflicts a very serious blow to the dispensationalist contention that Israel and the church represent entirely different peoples of God and must always be kept separate. Both Jews and gentiles can be grafted into Israel.

TRANSLATION: ROM 11:25–36

GOD WILL USE GENTILES TO BRING JEWS BACK TO HIMSELF

²⁵For I do not want you to be ignorant of this mystery, brothers [and sisters], so you may not be "wise" in your own estimations, for a partial hardening has happened to Israel until the full number of gentiles can come in, ²⁶and in this way "All Israel will be saved," as it is written:

> The Redeemer will come out of Zion,
> he will turn ungodliness away from Jacob.
> ²⁷And this [will be] my covenant with them,
> when I would cancel their sins.

²⁸On the one hand, respecting the gospel [they are] enemies for your sake, but on the other hand, respecting [God's] choice [they are] beloved for the sake of the patriarchs. ²⁹For the gracious gifts and the calling of God are unwavering. ³⁰Just as you once disobeyed God, but now you have been shown mercy by their disobedience, ³¹so too now they have disobeyed in order that by the mercy you have received they also may receive mercy. ³²For God confined all people in disobedience in order that he might have mercy on all.

> ³³Oh, the depth of wealth
> and wisdom and insight of God!
> How unsearchable are his judgments
> and untraceable are his ways!
> ³⁴Who has known the mind of the Lord?
> Or who has become his advisor?
> ³⁵Or who has given to him first
> so that he will be repaid by him?
> ³⁶For all things are from him, and through him, and for him.
> To him be the glory forever. Amen.

COMMENTARY

Vss. 25–36: This passage forms the climax to Paul's discussion of the relationship of Israel and the gentiles in God's Plan for the Ages that fills chapters

9–11. In vs. 25 Paul describes it as a "mystery" (*mystērion*) by which he does not mean something unknowable but rather something that has previously been hidden but he is now revealing. This means that *mystērion* here is not the antonym of "revelation" but instead is a near synonym of it. Presently Paul's readers are ignorant, or at least may be ignorant, of this mystery, namely, that a partial hardening has come upon Israel and that a way of salvation has been opened to the gentiles. If both believing Jew and believing gentile understand their distinctive parts in God's plan, then hopefully neither group will consider itself to be wiser than the other.

Vss. 25–26: In vss. 11–24 Paul has already directed his remarks primarily to gentiles, whom he believes are in danger of arrogantly claiming a position over their Jewish brothers and sisters. These gentiles continue to be the main group Paul addresses, although his exposition of the mystery is relevant to Jews as well as gentiles. The fact that in vs. 26 Paul likely quotes a Pharisaic slogan suggests his message is aimed at Jews as well as gentiles.

The phrase I have translated "wise in your own estimations" (*par' heautois phronimoi*) employs an idiom that is at least as old as the LXX translation of Prov 3:7 (first-century BC?). "Wise" should probably be enclosed in scare quotes, since this word is suggested sarcastically and is not found in the Greek text. Although not specifically mentioned, Prov 3:7 makes clear that the word "wise" is implied. The MT of that verse specifically includes the word "wise," while the idiom the LXX employs only suggests it. It is this same idiom that Paul employs here. It involves use of the noun *phronimos* with the preposition *para* and an object of the preposition in the dative case. Here *phronimoi* is a plural form of *phronimos*, *par'* is an abbreviated form of *para*, and *heautois* ("ourselves," "yourselves," or "themselves") is in the dative case. Paul employs this same idiom in Rom 12:16.

An important matter of interpretation is how the expressions "partial"/"in part" (*apo merous*), "full number"/"fullness" (*plērōma*), and "all" (*pas*) are used. Should the meaning of one of these expressions influence our understanding of the meaning of another? For instance, Krister Stendahl has argued that the hardening "in part" of Israel is a temporary phenomenon and that the "all Israel" that will be saved is an eschatological pronouncement, both of which relate to the Jewish people alone. According to Stendahl, Paul intends "in part" to contrast with "all."[6]

Similarly, the "full number" or "fullness" of the gentiles could be seen to balance "all Israel," particularly if "all Israel" is thought to consist of Jews alone rather that a mixture of Jews and gentiles. Such a parallel might

---

6. Glen Menzies, "N.T. Wright's Reading of Paul," 90.

suggest that God is trying to save both a full complement of Jews and a full complement of gentiles.

The expression "partial" (*apo merous*) is used in conjunction with the noun "hardening" (*pōrōsis*), and it could mean "for a time," as N.T. Wright suggests.[7] However, it more likely means "to a limited degree." Since some Jews such as Paul have become believers, the hardening is not complete.

Prior to Paul's use of *pōrōsis* here, it was a term limited to use in medical literature. It usually referred to the callouses that grow on broken bones where they mend. This is a positive hardening or strengthening of what is broken, in contrast to Paul's less concrete and more negative use of the term. In the two other places in the New Testament where the word occurs (Mark 3:5; Eph 4:18), it refers to "hardness of heart." However, as the comment on vs. 7 concerning the cognate verb of *pōrōsis*, i.e., *pōroō* ("to harden") suggests, it is possible that the image of hardening concerns the dimming of the eyes through their loss of flexibility to focus. If this is the case, then the "hardening" Paul describes implies blindness more than headstrong disobedience.

The word *plērōma*, that I have translated "full number" can have several shades of meaning, all of which revolve around the idea of "fullness" or "filling up." More literally, it means "the fullness of the gentiles," and it should be seen in some way as a parallel to Paul's reference to the "fullness" of Israel in vs. 12. In vs. 12 this "fullness" is contrasted with Israel's "trespass" and "failure." This suggests that Israel's "fullness" will happen in the future, and it will mark a newfound state of spiritual success. Perhaps it designates a specific number of believing Jews, although this is not necessarily so. Whatever *plērōma* means in vs. 12, in vs. 25 this word cannot indicate a reversal of failure, since among the gentiles evangelistic success is already underway. Despite this success, the gentiles' "fullness" has not yet appeared. Just as Paul envisions Israel's "fullness" occurring in the future, he also envisions the gentiles' "fullness" as a future event. Nevertheless, in these instances the same word *plērōma* apparently means two different things.

Most translations extend the partial hardening of Israel "until [the full number of gentiles] *will* come in." I have translated this somewhat differently: "until [the full number of gentiles] *can* come in." The reason I prefer "can" is that Paul places the verb "come in" (*eiserchomai*) in the subjunctive mood, indicating some sort of contingency. It is also important to point out that the tense of the verb "come in" is aorist; it is not future. While the aorist can be described as most similar to the past tense when considering the various tenses of the English language, it often functions as a sort of default

---

7. Wright, *Paul and the Faithfulness of God*, 1231.

tense when there is no desire to indicate the time or aspect of a verb. When the subjunctive mood is used, the tense of the verb is usually not significant.

Achri, the Greek word translated "until," is an adverb that in some instances, such as in this verse, is used as an "improper preposition." It can anticipate a future moment in time, but it can also indicate reaching a particular degree or measure. Does "until" here indicate reaching a particular point in time, or reaching a particular number of gentiles? Perhaps this is a distinction without a difference, but given the quantitative connotations of *plērōma*, the ascent to a particular number of gentiles seems more likely.

For dispensationalists, vss. 25 and 26 are a very important. Vs. 12 has already indicated that Israel will have its own "fullness," which seems to indicate an important advance over its present "failure." Presumably, the "partial hardening" Paul mentions here is equivalent to, or at least similar to, the "failure" of vs. 12. Furthermore, this partial hardening (and failure) will continue "until the full number of gentiles can come in." After that time is reached, or after that count of gentiles is reached, the hardening of Israel will diminish or disappear, and at some point it must disappear, if Israel is to experience its own "fullness." This suggests that a great end-time revival among Jews will come after God's blessing on the gentiles has been fully poured out.

Dispensationalism fills in a few additional details about these events. The rapture of the church removes the believing gentiles from the earth, constituting the end of "the times of the gentiles" (Luke 21:24), and the great revival among the Jews will take place during the millennium.

But is this dispensationalist schema what Paul intends to teach? Likely, it is not. Many people misconstrue what *achri* ("until") implies in the clause "until the full number of gentiles can come in." It does not necessarily mean "until and only until" God's target for the gentiles is reached. It might mean "until and possibly beyond" when the target is reached. When "the full number of gentiles have come in" does not necessarily imply that Israel will immediately be "unhardened" and a massive wave of Jewish conversions to faith in Christ will commence.[8] It certainly does not imply that this full number of believing gentiles will immediately be removed from the scene. How would they be able to provoke Israel to jealousy if they are not present?

The question about the precise significance of *achri* ("until") in this context reminds me of a story that has been repeated many times. A state or a city decides it wants a highway or a bridge constructed in a certain place, but it does not have the funds to build the highway or bridge. So, it decides

---

8. The unusual expression "unhardened" is N.T. Wright's coinage. Wright, *Paul and the Faithfulness of God*, 1239.

that assessing a toll is the solution. Money will be borrowed. The project will be built. Tolls will then pay off the loan. The matter is taken to the people or to a legislative body with the assertion that "we will collect tolls until the loan is paid off." After a few years, when sufficient tolls have come in to pay the construction bill plus interest, and the toll could be discontinued, the government decides to continue to collect tolls since money is rolling in so well. The defense for this is this: "We promised to collect tolls until the debt was paid off. We did not promise to discontinue charging tolls at that time."

I do not want to suggest that either Paul or God is like a conniving politician, but I do want to suggest that the word "until" can be slippery. Paul may write that Israel will undergo a partial hardening until there is a sufficient number of believing gentiles to make Israel jealous—if that is what "the fullness of the gentiles" means—but that does not mean that the partial hardening will end at precisely that time. The hardening will not end before the fullness of the gentiles is reached, but it may well continue beyond that point. So, in the present day, nearly two millennia after Paul writes to the Romans, the question presents itself: Has the "fullness" or "full number" of the gentiles been reached? The answer to that question is unknowable. We know that the target had not been reached in Paul's day. We do not know if it has been reached in our day or if it still lies in the future.

Vs. 26: The expression "in this way" translates the adverb *houtōs*, which usually describes the manner in which something occurs. Other locutions that could translate *houtōs* are "thus," "so," "that is how," "in this way," or "even on this supposition."[9] Occasionally it is used to express an inference ("therefore"), and usually it should be construed more with what follows that what precedes.

It seems Paul wants to affirm the popular slogan "All Israel will be saved," but he wants to stipulate the precisely how this will occur—through the inclusion of both Jews and gentiles.

Although there is no certainty about this, the slogan "All Israel will be saved" seems likely to be an early form of the dictum "All Israel has a share in the world to come" found in *m.Sanh.* 10.1.[10] Although the Mishnah was not compiled until around AD 250, it contains traditions that go back at least to the second century AD and probably to the first century AD. While on its face it appears to suggest that every Jew will receive eschatological blessings, this is not what it means in the context of tractate Sanhedrin. In good rabbinic fashion, after setting forth the general statement, Sanhedrin

---

9. Liddell and Scott, *Greek-English Lexicon*, s.v. "houtōs."

10. *Kol Yisrael yesh lahem cheleq ba'olam haba'*. Some editions print "of the world to come" (*la'olam haba'*).

goes on to list at least fifteen groups who appear to be "Israel" but who will not inherit the world to come. *For more about this, see the excursus "All Israel will be saved."*

Similarly, Paul does not anticipate that all who claim to be Jews will inherit the world to come. However, the entirety of "true Israel," what could also be called "the remnant," will receive this inheritance. But Paul also insists that there will be believing gentiles within the "true Israel" he speaks of in vs. 26, although without using that specific verbiage.

Why does Paul use the word "all"? It seems confusing, since neither his wording nor the wording of tractate *Sanhedrin* means to indicate that every last person who claims to be a Jew will be saved. One answer is that the traditional wording of the dictum used the word "all." Then a great deal of discussion went into clarifying how the general principle needed to be limited. For Paul, I think the importance of the word "all" was that the expansive term "all Israel" could accommodate the inclusion of gentiles. Because believing gentiles were added to believing Jews, the term "all" was appropriate, even though not every person of Jewish lineage was included.

If an interpreter (such as Luther) wanted to insist that Paul intends for "all Israel" to include only Jews—contrary to the exegesis I have outlined— then probably the adverb *houtōs*, which I have translated "in this way" should instead be translated "even on this supposition."[11] In this case, Paul would be suggesting that even though a partial hardening has come on Israel this does not negate the expectation/slogan that "all Israel will be saved."

Vss. 26–27: Material from the LXX of Isa. 59:20–21 is reproduced in vs. 26 and the first line of vs. 27. The most significant difference between the two texts is that Paul writes "from [*ek*] Zion" whereas the LXX has "for the sake of [*heneken*] Zion," a reading echoed by the MT. The origin of the second line is unclear, but it may be a paraphrase of part of Exod 34:9, part of the dialogue between Moses and God before Moses descends from Mt. Sinai with the second set of stone tablets.

The point of the quotation is to affirm that the partial hardening of Israel will not last forever; despite Israel's current sorry state, God has promised to turn away their ungodliness and to cancel their sin.

Vs. 28: Two seemingly contradictory things are both true, and Paul communicates them using a *men/de* ("on the one hand"/"on the other hand") construction. The unbelieving Jews are enemies of the gospel, but they are beloved of God. They are enemies "for your [pl.] sake," and they are beloved "for the sake of the patriarchs." The reason for God's love of the unbelieving

---

11. On "even on this supposition" as a possible translation, see Liddell and Scott, *Greek-English Lexicon*, s.v. "houtōs," I.1.

Jews is easy enough to understand. God had a special relationship with the patriarchs and these unbelieving Jews are physical descendants of these patriarchs. That these unbelieving Jews are enemies of the gospel is also easy to understand; they reject the gospel and lobby against it, and Paul is writing to some who have borne the brunt of this hostility.

Paul's use of the word "enemies" highlights how disruptive the introduction of the message of Jesus was within the Jewish community. It was so disruptive that the Roman government considered it necessary to intervene, first forbidding public meetings (Cassius Dio, *History*, 60:6.6) and then exiling a significant number of Jewish leaders (Acts 18:1–4; Suetonius, *Claudius* 25; Paul Orosius, *History Against the Pagans* 7:6, 15–16). These exiled Jews were apparently believers in Jesus rather than the main faction of the Jews who rejected him. This is attested by the fact that Priscilla and Aquila were included among the ranks of the exiles.

When Paul uses the second person plural in "for your sake," the gentiles are clearly in view. Similarly, when he uses the third person plurals "their" in vs. 30 and "they" in vs. 31, Paul designates the Jews. These verses are a discussion of salvation history, but they are also a warning against haughtiness directed to the gentiles.

Vs. 29: The Greek word I have translated "unwavering" is *ametamelētos*. Literally, it means "without regret" or "lacking regret." It has often been translated "irrevocable," although this suggests something more than the "lacking regret" the word implies. Something is "irrevocable" when it is objectively impossible to change. "Lacking regret" in contrast speaks to someone's subject evaluation of a past decision or event, whether that decision or event can be changed or cannot be changed.

In the only other place where Paul uses this word it bears the sense of "without regret." In 2 Cor 7:10, he writes, "Godly grief . . . brings no regret." This also accords with the way the word is used in *1 Clement* (2.7; 54.4; and 58.2). *Ametamelētos* is used three times by Dionysius of Halicarnassus, who lived a generation or two before Paul. Twice it is used with the meaning "lacking regrets" (*Roman Antiquities* 8.56.1; and 11.13.2). Once it is used with the meaning "without fear of changing one's mind" (*Roman Antiquities* 2.35.4).

An important question is who might regret "the gifts and calling of God." Is it God who might regret giving them (or even change his mind about having given them)? Or is it the recipients of those gifts who might regret having received them? While the latter option is not impossible—1Clement 54.4 similarly suggests that "those who live as citizens of the commonwealth of God" will not regret it—it is much more likely that the former option is correct. God will not regret deploying his gifts and calling.

It seems that vs. 29 is an answer to the unexpressed question implicit in vs. 28: If the patriarchs were beloved by God, has God now rejected their descendants, who are antagonistic to the gospel of God? Paul's point is that God still loves those who have become enemies of the gospel, and he desires for them to repent and accept the grace he offers through Jesus the Christ. While Paul says they are beloved of God, nothing he says suggests that they will be saved apart from faith in Jesus.

Vss. 30–31: In these verses Paul argues that God's plan includes both Jews and gentiles, each having been disobedient but then afterward being offered God's mercy. Paul's gospel, with its offer of salvation to the gentiles, is no Plan B; the salvation of the gentiles has always been part of God's purpose. And the Jews who have stumbled have not fallen away from the continuing offer of God's mercy, as vs. 11 already informed the reader.

For Paul, the fates of both Jews and gentiles are inextricably intertwined because they are intertwined in God's eternal plan. The Jew/gentile divide may be binary, but these two groups are not intended to be binary opposites but rather complementary expressions of a greater unity. Paul will later express this greater unity in Eph 2:15 using the phrase "one new human being."

The verb "disobey" (*apeithō*) and its associated noun "disobedience" (*apeitheia*) play key roles in this verse. The verb *peithō* usually is translated "persuade" or "cause to believe" in the active voice and "obey" in the passive voice, but this hard and fast distinction between the two shades of meaning is not always appropriate. Here the alpha privative has been prefixed to a passive form of the verb (*a* + *peithō*, thus *apeithō*), negating its normal meaning. The English word "apathy" comes from the Greek noun used in these verses that usually means "unbelief" or "disobedience." This may lend some insight to the connection between "unbelief" (*apeitheia* stated more energetically) or "lack of an active belief" (*apeitheia* stated more inertly) and the "disobedience" that is associated with it.

Vs. 32: When Paul says that God "confined all people" in disobedience, he is plowing new ground. No one before him used the verb *sygkleiō* to make such a sweeping statement about all humanity. The basic meaning of the verb *sygkleiō* is "to shut" or "to shut up" and in the LXX it usually translates some form of the Hebrew verb *sagar*, "to shut." *Sygkleiō* is often used quite literally to refer to the shutting of doors, of eyes, of mouths, or the closing of wombs. The word can refer to being "isolated," either voluntarily or involuntarily, or to being "shunned" (i.e., being isolated socially). In the context of fishing, it can mean "to net." In military contexts it often refers to one military force "hemming in" another military force or "laying siege" to a city. Sometimes it is used to describe the confinement of individuals or groups, but it does not mean "to imprison" in the ordinary judicial sense, but rather refers to more makeshift or temporary confinements.

In this verse *sygkleiō* is often translated "consigned," which seems to be something of a weasel-word. Normally "consigned" means to transfer something to someone, but this is not the normal meaning of *sygkleiō*. The issue, of course, is that the verse could be understood to mean that if God "shut up" all people into disobedience/unbelief, he caused or at least promoted this disobedience/unbelief. Doing something like this seems unbecoming of God.

Apeitheia ("disobedience" or "unbelief") serves as the object of the proposition *eis*. While this preposition can imply other things, here it most likely has a local meaning with "disobedience" serving as a surrogate for a holding pen. Remember that *sygkleiō* typically implies shutting up on a short-term basis rather than long-term imprisonment. The image is of God shutting people up in a temporary holding pen of disobedience until they can be "mercied." This holding pen of disobedience is not a place where those confined are made disobedient. It is a place where they are stored in their already disobedient and helpless state.

The clause "he might have mercy on" translates a single Greek word: *eleēsē*, an aorist subjunctive form of *eleeō* ("to show mercy" or more literally "to mercy," which is an odd locution in English). The point is that all people are held temporarily in a disobedient state in order for God to reveal his mercy to them. Whether or not each individual will accept God's mercy when it is made available is beyond the scope of Paul's discussion.

Vss. 33–35: Perhaps these verses should be described as a florilegium or a catena ("chain"), linking passages contrasting the majesty of God with human limitations. But it is also possible that Paul is here quoting a hymn sung in early Christian worship. Of course, these are not mutually exclusive alternatives.

Vs. 33: Paul seems to be quoting something in this verse, but his source is unclear. There are similarities to 1 Sam 2:10 (the Song of Hannah) and to Job 5:9. While there are also similarities to the *Syriac Apocalypse of Baruch* 14:8–9, this work was not composed until well after Paul's death.

"Oh": While many would print "O" here since the Greek has Ō, it seems best in contemporary English to restrict "O" to use as a sign of the vocative case, and to use "Oh" for interjections such as this one. Perhaps it goes without saying that the interjection is onomatopoetic, evoking a gasp of wonder. (For more about this subject, see the excursus called "O Man.")

Paul ascribes both "wisdom" and "insight" to God. The noun *gnōsis* is usually translated "knowledge," but Paul frequently uses it to mean "insight," implying a perspective not shared by the public. This is especially evident in 1 Corinthians, where the word *gnōsis* figures more prominently than in Romans. Paul's point here is that God's insight far surpasses the generally received knowledge of humanity.

Paul spells the adjective I have translated "unsearchable" according to the standard Hellenistic convention (*anexeraunētēs*), while the classical spelling had been *anexereutēs*. An *ereutēs* was a tax collector (i.e., one who searched out who should pay). The *an* prefix negates the word's meaning and the *ex* ("out") prefix makes it more emphatic, thus implying "un-search-out-able," or more conventionally "unsearchable." The point is that God's judgments are beyond human comprehension.

The word I have translated "untraceable" resembles "unsearchable." The adjective *anexichniastos* is built on the noun *ichnion*, which means a "footprint" or a "track." To this noun are added two prefixes: *ex* ("out") which intensifies its meaning, and *an*, which negates its meaning. Thus, the word means "un-track-out-able." Since English has no word "untrackable" or the like, the near equivalent "untraceable" has been employed. While the English words "unsearchable" and "untraceable" have similarities, they are not as similar in sound and construction as the Greek words *anexeraunētēs* and *anexichniastos* that Paul employs. Unlike its mate *anexeraunētēs*, *anexichniastos* appears in the LXX four times.

Vs. 34: In this verse Paul's quotation closely matches the LXX text of Isa 40:13. Interestingly, the LXX's "mind of the Lord" diverges from the MT's "Spirit of the Lord." Paul also quotes Isa 40:13 in 1 Cor 2:16, there also following the LXX text.

Vs. 35: In this verse Paul again appears to quote some preexistent text, but his source is unclear. He may be paraphrasing either Job 35:7 or Job 41:3.

The translation contains two words not based on Greek equivalents: "first" and "so." These have been added to make clear that the hypothetical figure pays first with the purpose of obtaining an obligation he might later be cash. The verb *antapodidōmi* ("to repay") is composed of three parts: *anti* ("in place of"); *apo* ("from"); and the verb *didōmi* ("to give"). The future passive form (here *antapodothēsetai*) does not by itself ordinarily express purpose. However, the context clearly requires this meaning, and the syntax is likely influenced by Hebrew, in which the imperfect (roughly Hebrew's "future" tense) is often used in purpose clauses.

The point of the verse is that God is always the one giving, never receiving, and he is never in anyone's debt. This has profound implications for worship. Christians rightfully offer worship to God because we owe it to him, but regardless of what we might give him, he is never in our debt.

Vs. 36: This chapter ends with a doxology (i.e., an ascription of glory [Greek *doxa*] to God). The first line of this doxology is wonderfully succinct but also expansive, describing the relationship of "all things" to God. He is their source, he is their sustainer, and he provides their purpose. This material resembles that found in 1 Cor 8:6.

This doxology concludes with "Amen," as is common with doxologies and other expressions of praise particularly in the New Testament and in the books of the Old Testament Apocrypha. Variously described as an adverb or a particle, "Amen" in both Greek and English is a transliteration of a Hebrew expression which means "truly" or "surely." It occurs five times in Romans.

Excursus: Guidance from Israel's History

Chapters 9 through 11 of Romans feature the longest discussion of a single topic in the letter. While these chapters retell parts of Israel's history, they do not exactly form a synopsis of that history. Instead, this discussion offers guidance into Paul understanding of how God's promises to the patriarchs were being fulfilled in his own time. In the background of this discussion stands the dynamic of large numbers of gentiles coming to faith in comparison with a relatively small number of Jews. Paul insists that the inclusion of the gentiles does not diminish the status of Israel as God's chosen people; it enhances this status by making Israel the vehicle for the salvation of all the families of the earth.

CHILDREN OF THE PROMISE

A key principle is stated in Rom 9:8: "It is not the natural children who are the children of God, but rather the children of the promise are reckoned as descendants." In certain ways the concept of "children of the promise" is broader than the concept of "natural children," and in other ways it is narrower. The category of "children of the promise" is broader in that it can include gentiles. From a narrower perspective it implies that, as Rom 9:6 says, "not all coming from Israel are Israel." This principle has deep roots in the Old Testament concept of the "remnant."

Remnant theology is built on two pillars: 1) there will always be heirs of the promises made to the patriarchs; and 2) many who might be thought to qualify as heirs of the promises do not in fact qualify. In Rom 9:6 Paul says, "It is not the case that the word of God has failed." Presumably, if all the heirs of the promises made to the patriarchs were to be wiped away from the face of the earth, then the word of God would have failed. But this is not what has happened: the promises are being fulfilled, but they do not have to be fulfilled to the maximum extent conceivable.

It is the second pillar of remnant theology that has provoked the most controversy, and in large part Paul offers chapters 9 through 11 as his discussion of this important subject. While this is not certain, it seems likely that many in the Jewish community—both those who accepted Jesus as the Messiah of Israel and those who did not—expressed their hope using a slogan that Paul quotes in Rom 11:26: "All Israel will be saved." Paul does not reject this slogan, but he insists that it must be qualified properly if it is to be accepted.

Clearly, some Jews understood this slogan to mean that "all coming from Israel are Israel" (the inverse of Paul's statement in Rom 9:6), and therefore all descendants of Israel (Jacob) would ultimately be saved. Perhaps some even believed that every descendant of Abraham would ultimately be saved.

Paul acknowledges that in some sense the Jews who do not accept Jesus as Messiah are still part of Israel. In Rom 9:4 he says, "They are Israelites," and then he lists the many blessings they have received, including "sonship" (*huiothesia*). However, Paul resolutely rejects the idea that descendants of Jacob will be saved without faith in Christ. Therefore, the slogan "All Israel will be saved" cannot mean that one's physical ancestry by itself determines his or her eternal destiny.

Paul explains that the descendants of Ishmael, although they are biological offspring of Abraham, are not children of the promise and therefore are excluded from the chosen people (Rom 9:7). Similarly, although the twins Jacob and Esau were born of the same father and mother, the promise was only passed to Jacob (Israel) and his descendants, so Esau and his line are excluded (Rom 9:10–13). Furthermore, since "not all coming from Israel are Israel," even within the line of Jacob there is further limitation.

In fact, during the time of Elijah (the ninth century BC) the remnant numbered roughly seven thousand men and presumably a commensurate number of women and children (Rom 11:2–4; 1Kgs 19:18), which must have constituted only a small fraction of Israel's population. And on what basis were the remnant distinguished from the rest? These were the ones who had not bowed down to Baal or worshipped him (Rom 11:4; 1 Kgs 19:18). In other words, those numbered among the remnant had remained faithful to the Lord, unlike so many others in Israel.

In Rom 11:16–24, when discussing the olive tree which serves as a symbol of God's people Israel, Paul emphasizes that the number of branches is not fixed ineluctably, but instead is subject to both pruning and grafting—subtraction and addition—in response to varying levels of faith. Vs. 20 provides contrasting situations. Negatively, branches "were broken away in unbelief." In contrast, Paul's readers are addressed positively as "you who have stood in faith." Furthermore, if those branches that have previously been broken off "should not remain in unbelief," they will be grafted back in (vs. 23). Clearly faith is a requirement for inclusion in God's chosen people.

Some interpreters will object to this portrayal of Paul's remnant theology, insisting that it places too much weight on the human response of faith and not enough emphasis on God's sovereign choice. In Rom 9:11 Paul describes how Jacob came to be favored over Esau. This happened "when [the twins] had not yet been born or done anything good or bad in order that God's purpose with respect to choosing [his people] might continue." Furthermore, this election of one over the other happened "not by works but rather by calling." Rom 9:16 is even more explicit: "It is not by desiring or running [the race], but by God's mercy." The participle of *thelō* that I have translated "desiring" might also be translated "willing." And "running" is a common metaphor indicating the way a person conducts his life. In essence, Paul's point is that Jacob was chosen over Esau not on the basis of any superior desires, choices, or behaviors. He was not chosen because he had any greater merit than Esau. He was chosen simply because God picked him.

So how is this emphasis on God's prerogative to choose independently of any human desire, thought, or behavior compatible with Paul's contention that the remnant is characterized by faithfulness? Is there not a tremendous inconsistency built into the argument of Romans 9 through 11?

Not at all. Paul's argument is thoroughly consistent if one recognizes a fundamental distinction he assumes but does not articulate clearly. This is the distinction between 1) God's choosing of a special people for himself, and 2) determining who are and who are not included in that people. Until God has selected a special people, and until he has established a covenant relationship with that people, it did not make sense to evaluate who had remained faithful and who had not. Until there is a covenant, there is no standard by which faithfulness or a lack thereof might be judged.

Furthermore, when Paul speaks of Jacob and Esau, he is really speaking of nations. This presumption echoes God's declaration to Rebekah recorded in Gen 25:23: "Two nations are in your womb." Yes, there was an individual named Jacob/Israel, but when Paul speaks of God choosing Jacob, he is really speaking of God choosing the nation of Israel. When Paul speaks of God rejecting Esau in favor of his younger brother Jacob, he is really speaking of God rejecting the nation of Edom in favor of the nation of Israel. God's selection of Abraham, Isaac, and Jacob as the line through whom the promises and the blessings would pass was the unconditioned choice of the sovereign God. As Paul puts it, Israel and the nation held within his loins were selected "not by works but by calling" (Rom 9:12).

However, things changed at Sinai and thereafter. When God formalized his choice of the nation of Israel as his people, he also established standards by which his people were to live. That was the point of the Law. This is not to suggest that it had been impossible to live by faith or to live faithfully prior to the giving of the Law—Abraham's life is a testimony to this—but at Mount Sinai the expectations became clearer. The tragedy of Israel's story is that although they had been given the Law, the faithful were so few—a mere remnant—because while the Law set a high standard, it did not empower those under the Law to keep it faithfully. This is why "not all coming from Israel are Israel," and why the remnant, which we may call "true Israel," was often so small.

In Paul's day the remnant was also quite small. Paul contended that his Jewish kindred must express faith in Jesus the Messiah of Israel if they were to remain faithful to God. Faithfulness to the covenant obligations found in the Law were not enough. Some had expressed faith in the Messiah, but many others had not, and this caused Paul great sorrow (Rom 9:2). But the joy of his heart was that many gentiles were also coming to faith in the Messiah, and through the Messiah of Israel these non-Israelites were being grafted into the olive tree that represents true Israel. God had promised that in Abraham "all the nations/gentiles of the earth will be blessed" (Gen 18:18; 22:18), and this was coming to pass!

As mentioned above Paul states in Rom 9:8: "It is not the natural children who are the children of God, but rather the children of the promise are reckoned as descendants." While I have underscored how "children of the promise" can define a narrower pool than "natural children," it is also true that "children of promise" can define a wider pool. Paul clearly understood the gentiles he saw coming to faith in Christ as the prime examples of "children of promise" who would have been excluded had the category been limited to "natural children." That these gentiles were "children of the promise" was the ideological anchor of his entire mission to the gentiles.

THE GRACIOUS GIFTS AND THE CALLING OF GOD

I mentioned above that some interpreters would object to the way I describe Paul's remnant theology. Many of these same people will also point to Rom 11:29 as a refutation of my explanation of Paul's ideas on this issue.

As I translate it, Rom 11:29 reads: "For the gracious gifts and the calling of God are unwavering." The Greek adjective I have translated "unwavering" is *ametamelētos*. This word is composed of three parts: *a*, commonly called the alpha privative, which negates the word's meaning; *meta*, which means "after"; and *melētos*, a form related to the verb *melō*, which means "to think about something" or "to care for something." It implies that some decision a person has made will not later have to be reconsidered, or that the person will not later waver or become regretful about the original decision.

My translation differs somewhat from the standard translations. The Revised Standard Version renders it: "For the gifts and the calling of God are irrevocable." The King James Version famously rendered it: "For the gifts and calling of God are without repentance." The KJV translation was largely based on the use of similar words, *metameleia*, *metamelō*, and *metamelomai* in the LXX. These words often mean "to change one's mind," i.e., "to repent," or "to regret." The RSV translation follows the same line of thought but with a harder edge. If something is "without repentance," then it cannot be changed. If it cannot be changed, it is "irrevocable." However, I think these translations are mistaken and based on misleading evidence. It is better to determine the meaning of a word by the way that specific word is used rather than by the way similar words are used.

Besides Rom 11:29, Paul uses *ametamelētos* in only one other place: 2 Cor 7:10. There he writes, "For godly grief produces a repentance that leads to salvation and brings no wavering," or perhaps, "For godly grief . . . brings no regret." It cannot reasonably mean "For godly grief . . . is irrevocable" or "For godly grief . . . is without repentance." While, on the one hand, wavering about something or regretting something and, on the other hand, something being irrevocable or without repentance are similar in certain respects, they are not identical. Decisions are often regretted or questioned even though it is possible to undo them. It is also true that some irrevocable decisions are not regretted or subjected to second thoughts.

Diodorus Siculus uses *ametamelētos* with the meaning "unwavering" (*Historical Library* 10.16.3). The historian Dionysius of Halicarnassus uses *ametamelētos* twice where "unwavering" works well (*Roman Antiquities* 8.56; 11.13) and once where "without regret" works better (*Roman Antiquities*

2.35). The pseudonymous *Tablet of Cebes*, dating from the first or second century AD, uses *bebaios* in conjunction with *ametamelētos* to mean "firm and unwavering" (32.3).[12] Clement of Rome consistently uses the word to mean "unwavering" (*1 Clement* 2:7, 54.4 and 58.2), and he uses the related adverb *ametamelētōs* to mean "unwaveringly" (*1 Clement* 58.2).

In addition to the lexical evidence, it is important to consider context. Rom 11:29, the verse that contains *ametamelētos*, appears sandwiched between two short expositions about unbelieving Jews. Before his statement about the gifts and calling of God, Paul asserts the seemingly contradictory statements that the same unbelieving Jews are both "enemies of God" because of their opposition to the gospel and "beloved [of God] for the sake of the patriarchs." These enemies apparently are Jews who reject Jesus and are hostile to those Jews who accept him as their Messiah.

Then following his statement about the gifts and calling of God, Paul asserts that God's plan is for everyone to be disobedient first prior to receiving mercy and salvation. Thus, the opposition of these unbelieving Jews neither surprises him nor phases him. He reminds the believing Jews of Rome that once they did not believe, but now they have received God's mercy. In the same way, he hopes that those unbelieving Jews who at present act as enemies will one day also receive God's mercy. Paul himself has been both an enemy of the gospel and a proponent of the gospel, so he knows what it is like to be an insider of both groups.

So, what is Paul's point when he asserts that "the gracious gifts and the calling of God are *ametamelētos*"? Does he mean they are "irrevocable"? Are they "without regret"? Or are they "unwavering"?

One clue is Paul's use of the word "calling" (*klēsis*). This brings to mind his reference to Jacob being chosen not on the basis of any works or any desire but rather only because of God's calling (Rom 9:12, 16). It also reminds the reader of his quotation of Gen 21:12 in Rom 9:7: "Through [literally "in"] Isaac will your seed be called." As Paul reads this text, with the promise comes a *calling*, or perhaps *an identity*. (People are *called* by a name, and a name provides *an identity*.) This has implications for the unbelieving Jews of Paul's day.

Paul argues that because the unbelieving Jews who persecute the believing Jews of Rome are physical descendants of Jacob (and the other patriarchs), despite their behavior, they are beloved by God. The reason for this is

---

12. Dionysius of Halicarnasus also pairs *bebaios* ("firm") with *ametamelētos* in *Roman Antiquities* 8.56, suggesting that this paring ("firm and unwavering") was common and perhaps idiomatic.

that when God grants gifts, and when he calls a people he thereby gives them an identity. Moreover, he does so without wavering. This does not mean that such unbelieving Jews are descendants of the promise and are grafted into the olive tree, but it does mean that they remain Jews. Furthermore, God has a special interest in them, and they remain called to the mission God had previously given them however much or little they understand that mission.

I do not deny that the word "calling" has some soteriological significance in Rom 11:29, but this does not exhaust its meaning there. In large part the word "calling" here is aspirational in the sense that it reflects God's aspirations for his gifts and his calling. The whole of Romans 9 through 11 emphasizes that God's plan for the redemption of all humanity relies on the special mission God has assigned the descendants of Abraham, Isaac, and Jacob, in other words, the people of Israel. More particularly, the word "calling" in Rom 11:29 speaks to continuing Jewish identity, but it also carries a missiological significance. The gentiles who are flooding into the church would not be coming without Israel, and certainly the remnant within Israel has received God's grace through this same mission. God's gracious gifts are unwavering, and his calling of Israel to be "a light to the gentiles/nations" (Isa 42:6; 60:3) is unwavering as well, despite the unbelief of many Jews. Remarkably, the fact that many Jews have "disobeyed God" has provided a special opportunity for gentiles to come to faith and receive God's mercy (Rom 11:30).[13]

It is unclear precisely how Paul views the disobedience of the Jews providing this special opportunity for the gentiles. In one sense, it seems that the obedience or disobedience of one people (Israel) would have no impact on the standing of another people (the gentiles). But Paul is clear in his affirmation that Jewish disobedience proved to be a blessing to the gentiles. It also seems clear that for Paul the intersection of the destinies of these two peoples occurred at the cross. Based on these two points of clarity, the following explanation seems likely. The widespread rejection of Jesus by the people of Israel led to his crucifixion. And his actual crucifixion was carried out by gentiles—specifically Roman soldiers. This shared responsibility for the execution of Israel's Messiah put both peoples in exactly the same place before God. Consequently, both required a *teshuvah* (Hebrew for "conversion"), a complete reversal of direction, to stand in right relationship with the Crucified One and the God who raised him up from the dead. For each people their collective rejection of Jesus requires a change of heart accomplished by faith.[14] This was the silver

---

13. I would like to thank my brother, Robert P. Menzies, for encouraging me to stress the missiological significance of the word "calling" in Rom 11:29.

14. I would like to thank my friend Michael A. Stone for pushing me to explain

lining in the faithlessness of Israel: it placed gentiles in exactly the same position as the sons of Israel themselves.

Furthermore, as has already been stated, the crucifixion of Jesus led to the resurrection of his body, which became a new temple through which those "in Christ" have access to God.

ALTERNATE INTERPRETATIONS

I have argued that the physical descendants of Jacob/Israel who continue to reject Christ will not be saved. Two groups dispute this point. Both argue that these unbelieving Jews must necessarily be saved in the end because they are "beloved" and because God's calling is "irrevocable." If these Jews were called when they were in Jacob's loins, they remain called and ultimately will be saved.

However, these two groups differ about the grounds on which these unbelieving Jews will ultimately be saved. The first group believes that unbelieving Jews will be given a second chance following the rapture of the church. Immediately after the rapture, there will be a great, worldwide revival in which all unbelieving Jews will come to believe. I do not believe such a revival is Paul's expectation, but a great end-time revival of this sort would not be inconsistent with the rest of his argument.

However, a second group of interpreters suggest that unbelieving Jews will receive God's mercy without faith in Christ. Instead, they are included simply based on physical descent from the patriarchs. I regard this as unacceptable. It would make a hash of Paul's argument that those branches that have been broken off the vine will only be grafted back in if they do not remain in unbelief (Rom 11:23).

Excursus: All Israel will be saved

Rom 11:25–26 reads as follows: "^{25}For I do not want you to be ignorant of this mystery, brothers [and sisters], so you may not be wise in your own estimations, for a partial hardening has occurred in Israel until the full number of gentiles can come in, and in this way "All Israel will be saved . . . ."

---

this point with greater clarity.

With these verses Paul's discussion of God's promise and calling to both Israel and the gentiles that stretches over chapters 9 through 11 reaches a climax. Consequently, these verses are important, but they are also somewhat unclear, and they have had a significant impact on the development of Christian theology.

PRELIMINARY COMMENTS

Paul calls the matter he discusses in these verses and those that follow a "mystery" (*mystērion*). When he uses this term, it normally does not mean something currently hidden, but rather something that was hidden in the past but now has been revealed. In this way, "mystery" is a near synonym to "revelation." Such mysteries regularly have to do with the advent of Christ and the transition to a new stage of salvation-history that Christ's coming signaled. However, it is not clear exactly what is contained in this mystery. Is it 1) the grafting of wild olive branches into the domesticated olive tree he has just discussed, which could also be described as "the coming in" of gentiles, or 2) the partial hardening that has occurred in Israel, or 3) that "all Israel will be saved"? Possibly, more than one of these elements is combined in this mystery. Option 1 seems most likely to be correct.

A second consideration is that Paul's motivation for explaining this mystery is to avoid having one group of believers in Rome become conccited and consider themselves better than another group of believers in Rome. Since the fundamental division in Roman Christianity is between Jewish believers and gentile believers, it is likely that Paul is worried about Jewish believers arraying themselves against the gentile believers or *vice versa*. Both problems are possibilities. However, Paul seems already to have tipped his hand about which group is in greater danger of arrogantly arraying themselves against the other. In vss. 18–21 Paul has already warned the gentile believers against boasting about displacing their Jewish brothers. Possibly the issue is that gentile believers have started to dominate leadership in the Christian community and have become dismissive of Jewish concerns.

Paul's illustration of the olive tree is instructive in three ways. First, the "root" is Israel, more exactly the "righteous remnant" of Israel.[15] This is made clear when Paul calls the branches representing Israel "branches by nature" (*tōn kata physin kladōn*) in vs. 21, and through his use of a similar

---

15. For more about the image of the root as a remnant, see the comments on Rom 11:17–18.

construction in vs. 24 implying the same thing. If the natural branches represent Israel, then the root is part of that same tree.

Paul often uses the word "nature" (*physis*) to mean "what is expected" or "the normal course of things." Israel is the olive tree (*elaia*) in vss. 17 and 24, and the domesticated olive tree (literally the "good olive tree"; *kallielaios*) in vs. 24. In contrast, branches from the wild olive tree (literally the "field olive tree"; *agrielaios*) represent the gentile believers in vss. 17 and 24. When these branches are grafted in, it is "contrary to nature" (*para physin*; vs. 24).

Second, Paul makes clear that both the natural branches and the contrary-to-nature branches receive the benefits provided by the root. The word used here, *piotēs*, literally means "fatness." If the root is Israel, then gentiles are grafted into Israel. They are not proselytes; they come in as gentiles. This seems to echo Paul's assertion in Rom 10:12 that "there is no difference between Jew and Greek."

Third, the criterion that determines whether one qualifies to be grafted in is belief. Vs. 23 makes clear that the natural branches that have been broken off will only be grafted back in if they do not remain in unbelief.

The impression left is that Jewish believers have the honor of seniority, but not greater privilege. (Israel was publicly declared God's "chosen" before the gentiles, but this does not mean it is presently more chosen than believing gentiles.) Both Jewish believers and gentile believers draw nourishment from being rooted in Israel. This, in part, is why Paul deemphasizes the role of the Law for Jews who are in Christ. Gentiles do not have to observe the Law of Moses because they were never part of the covenant made at Sinai. It would seem odd to require Jews to live by this standard when they already receive the nourishment of the root apart from the Law, just as the gentiles do.

M.SANHEDRIN, CHAPTER 10

I have long been intrigued by the similarity of the clause from Rom 11:26, "All Israel will be saved," with the opening statement of chapter 10 of the tractate Sanhedrin in the Mishnah, the oldest part of the Talmud: "All Israel has a share in the world to come."[16] Both seem to promise participation in the future resurrection of the dead. While the Mishnah was completed and committed to writing about AD 250, it contains many traditions from much earlier, some dating back to the time of Paul. Many of the Mishnah's sayings

---

16. *Kol Yisrael yesh lahem cheleq ba'olam haba'*. Some editions print "of the world to come" (*la'olam haba'*).

contain a chain of authorities who passed them along (often in the format: Rabbi X said in the name of Rabbi Y, who spoke in the name of Rabbi Z), although these chains of oral transmission are often unreliable. This specific dictum lists no chain of authorities who passed it down, but there is extensive discussion about it in the following pages of the Mishnah, and some of the earliest rabbis mentioned in these discussions are Rabbi Akiba and Rabbi Jose the Galilean, both from the early decades of the second century. On the basis of this evidence, I suspect that this saying dates from at least the second century, if not the first century AD.

"All Israel will be saved" could be a line Paul composed himself. But Paul uses it as if it is an important and respected principle within Judaism, just as at a later time "All Israel has a share in the world to come" functioned within Judaism. In fact, I suspect "All Israel will be saved" is a slogan that some first-century Jews used, and Paul then quotes. If this is the case, ultimately, this slogan found its way into *m.Sanhedrin* 10.1 in a slightly revised form. This slogan would have passed through the traditions of the Pharisees, the only sect of Jews besides the Messianists who survived the First Jewish War. At one time Paul had been a card-carrying Pharisee so he knew Pharisaism very well. In fact, he is the only Pharisee or former Pharisee from the first century whose writings have survived to the present day.[17]

On its face, "All Israel has a share in the world to come" seems to promise that every Jew without exception will receive the eschatological blessing of resurrection. However, reading the material following this statement suggests this assertion is not as comprehensive as it first appears. It is typical rabbinic style to proclaim a general principle and then to list all of the exceptions to it, and this is what happens in *m.Sanhedrin* 10.1. The general principle that "all Israel has a share in the world to come" is announced, and then at least fifteen groups are listed as exceptions. These include those who deny the Torah teaches resurrection of the dead, those who deny the Torah is of heavenly origin, Epicureans, and people who read heretical books (like

---

17. All of Paul's writings that have survived were written when he was an ex-Pharisee. While Paul never ceased to be a Jew, he clearly was no longer representative of Pharisaism. Flavius Josephus is sometimes proposed as a first-century Pharisee whose writings have survived. However, Josephus was clearly just a dabbler in the various sects within Judaism, and it is unclear how well acquainted he was with the distinctives of the Pharisees.

Romans?). The point is that all *true* Israel has a share in the world to come, but various Jews have excluded themselves from *true* Israel.[18]

One exegetical question is whether Paul similarly means *true* Israel when he asserts that "all Israel will be saved." He has already made clear that only believing Jews will have their branch grafted back into the olive tree, and apparently believing Jews means Jews who put their faith in Jesus the Messiah. Furthermore, in Rom 9:6 he says, "For not all coming from Israel are Israel." This indicates that the "all Israel" of 11:26 does not include Jews who reject Jesus.

ARE SOME GENTILES PART OF "ALL ISRAEL"?

A second major exegetical question is this: Are some gentiles part of "all Israel"? Paul's illustration of the olive tree indicates that branches representing gentiles who believe in Jesus will be grafted into the olive tree, and thus into *true* Israel. Similarly, in Rom 9:24 Paul states, "We whom he called are not only from the Jews but also from the gentiles. . . ."

Additionally, in Romans 2 Paul has already discussed the question: Who is a real Jew? He asks the rhetorical question: "If the uncircumcised man keeps the requirements of the Law, will not his uncircumcision be reckoned as circumcision?" (Rom 2:26). In this verse Paul does not suggest that "[keeping] the requirements of the Law" is accomplished by following the Law's many rules since the Law was given as part of a covenant made with Israel, not the gentiles. Instead, "[keeping] the requirements of the Law" was accomplished by trusting in the God who brings life to what is dead. Paul then caps off his discussion of who the real Jew is with this summary: "For it is not the Jew in appearance who is the real one nor the circumcision appearing in the flesh that is real, but the Jew in what is hidden, and the circumcision of the heart, in the Spirit not in the letter" (Rom 2:28–29). This implies that Paul believes some "Jews in what is hidden" are gentiles circumcised in the heart. Furthermore, these gentiles are included in the "all Israel" of Rom 11:26.

---

18. I must acknowledge that "true Israel" is not an expression Paul uses, although perhaps a similar idea is implied by his charge in 1 Cor 10:18, "Consider Israel according to the flesh." Surely, this implies an analogous "Israel according to the Spirit," which includes a different set of people. This and other Pauline expressions have resulted in "true Israel" long being used in Christian theology. Note the title of Marcel Simon's book *Verus Israel* ("True Israel" translated into Latin).

Another hint that Paul includes gentiles in "all Israel" is found in Rom 9:24. After discussing God's choosing of Jacob/Israel over Esau in Rom 9:10–13, which he frames in terms of God's "calling," he then dismisses a potential objection that God is unjust. In Rom 9:24 Paul resumes his discussion of God's "calling," explaining: "We whom he called are not only from the Jews but also from the gentiles." In this passage, found in Romans 9, Paul anticipates what he will write in Romans 11, namely that gentiles are included in true Israel, or as he puts it in Rom 11:26, "all Israel."

FOUR VIEWS

Over the last half-millennium there have been four main approaches to this important but enigmatic text. I have named these approaches: 1) Calvin's View; 2) Luther's View; 3) the Dispensationalist View; and 4) the Dual Covenant View. While Luther preceded Calvin by a generation, I have placed Calvin's View and the Dispensationalist View at opposing ends of this discussion because they are far apart theologically. The Dual Covenant View is listed last both because it is farthest removed from Calvin's View and also because this places it next to the Dispensationalist View with which it has some affinities.

Calvin's View

Calvin is quite explicit in his view that "all Israel" does not consist only of Jews. His comments are worth repeating at length, in part because they reveal a point on which he has been roundly criticized:

> *And so all Israel*—Many expositors make this passage relate to the Jewish people, as if the meaning of Paul was, "that religion should be renewed among the Israelites, as before;" but I extend the sense of the word Israel to the whole people of God, and thus interpret it, "When the Gentiles shall have entered into the church, and the Jews, at the same time, shall betake themselves to the obedience of faith, and forsake their present revolt from the Saviour of the lost, the salvation of the whole Israel of God, which must be collected from both, will thus be completed, and in such a manner that the descendants of the father of the faithful, as being the first-born in the family of God, shall enjoy the preeminence." I consider this exposition

> to agree better with the context, because Paul was desirous to point out here the consummation of the kingdom of Christ, which was by no means limited to the Jews, but comprehends the whole world. And, in the same manner, (Gal 6:16) he denominates the church, which consisted equally of Jews and Gentiles, the Israel of God, and opposes a people, thus collected from a scattered and wasted state, to the carnal children of Abraham, who had departed from the faith.[19]

To understand Calvin's comments fully, the reader must be aware of two things. First, Calvin understands the "church" not to have been born during the earthly ministry of Jesus or on the day of Pentecost, but to have already existed throughout much of Old Testament history. The LXX regularly translated "assembly" (Heb. *qahal*) with the Greek *ekklēsia* ("assembly," "church"), so Calvin thought of the church as an Israelite institution. This is a marked difference from the Dispensationalist View that the church is very much a New Testament institution and separate from Israel.

Second, Calvin reads Gal 6:15–16 in a particular way:

> For neither circumcision is anything nor uncircumcision, but a new creation [is what matters]. And as many as order their lives by this rule, may peace and mercy be upon them, that is, upon the Israel of God.

This is a grammatically plausible understanding of these verses, but it is not the only option. The last phrase of vs. 16 could also be translated: "and upon the Israel of God." Calvin's translation understands those who regard the new creation as of paramount importance—both Jewish believers and gentile believers—to be "the Israel of God." An alternative reading suggests there are two separate groups: 1) those who regard the new creation as paramount (i.e., only gentile believers?); and 2) "the Israel of God" (i.e., the Jewish people).

The Greek word *kai* appears three times in vs. 16. These two options understand the force of the third occurrence of that word differently. Calvin understands this *kai* epexigetically, that is to say, that this *kai* further clarifies what is already in view. The second option understands this *kai* conjunctively or adjunctively, indicating that an additional group is being added, hence the rendering above "and," rather than "that is." The King James translation

---

19. Calvin, *Commentary on Romans*, ad loc. 11:26.

took this second course, translating the last part of the verse: "and upon the Israel of God."

Calvin's perspective is that the old Israel was defined by means of fleshly descent from Abraham. Furthermore, old Israel had "departed from the faith." In contrast, the new "Israel of God" was made up of both believing Jews and believing gentiles organized into one church. In contemporary theology, this is often styled "replacement theology," suggesting that the church replaced Israel. There is a certain force to this analysis, but it also ignores the fact that Calvin often wrote of "the church" in the Old Testament. Calvin emphasized continuity between the Old Testament and the New Testament to a greater degree than, say, Luther did. But Calvin did believe that with the coming of Christ, Judaism or Israelite religion—as distinct from believing Jews in the church—retained no continuing part in salvation-history. For the thoroughgoing Calvinist, what today some call "national Israel" is a historical curiosity but not a theological reality.

Luther's View

In contrast to Calvin's view, Luther understands "all Israel" to refer exclusively to Jews. On the other hand, it does not refer to every last Jew; it refers to the "mass" (*massa*) of Jews. His interpretation is influenced by the Vulgate translation of 11:16, which departs a little in meaning from the Greek. It reads, *quod si delibatio sancta est et massa et si radix sancta et rami*, which I translate as "But if the sample is holy, so also is the lump (*massa*), and if the root is holy, so also are the branches." This means that some Jews will perish, but on the whole, they will be saved. Luther writes:

> For this entire text has the purpose of persuading his people to return. Therefore in order that the apostle may be understood correctly, we must understand that his remarks extend over the whole mass of the Jewish people and refers to the good among them, both past, present, and future. Although some among them are lost, yet the mass of them must be respected because of the elect. . . . Therefore he uses the term "mass," so that he may show that he is speaking not of individual people but of the entire race, in which are many unholy people.[20]

---

20. Luther, *Lectures on Romans: Scholia*, ad loc. Rom 11:26 (in Corollary).

Commenting on 11:25–26, Luther endorses the idea that "at the end of the world" the Jews "will return to the faith." While he asserts that by itself, this passage would convince few of this spectacular future development, when it is compounded with Luke 21:23–24, the argument becomes more convincing. He quotes Jesus saying in those verses,

> For great distress shall be upon the earth, and wrath upon this people; and they will fall by the edge of the sword and be led captive among all nations; and Jerusalem will be trodden down by the Gentiles, until the times of the Gentiles are fulfilled.

Luther then judges Luke's clause "until the times of the gentiles are fulfilled" to mean precisely the same thing as "until the full number of gentiles come in" found in Rom 11:25.[21] The linkage of these two passages of scripture has since become a commonplace in Protestant exegesis. However, this does not mean it is correct.[22]

This portion of Luther's *Lectures on Romans* (9:1—16:27) was prepared and delivered during the summer of 1516, which was very early in his career—in fact before the Reformation had even begun.[23] Sadly, by the end of his career Luther was much more pessimistic about the ultimate fate of the Jews. His *The Jews and their Lies*, published in 1543, three years before his death, is an angry and vicious antisemitic screed. Although he acknowledges that Jesus said, "Salvation is from the Jews" (John 4:22), he gives no hint of his earlier expectation of end-time salvation of the mass of Israel.

---

21. Luther, *Lectures on Romans: Scholia*, ad loc. Rom 11:25.

22. Luke 21:24 foretells three things: 1) Many Jews will die by the sword; 2) Many Jews will be led captive into exile; and 3) Jerusalem will be overrun by gentiles until their (the gentiles') time is over. None of these conditions speak to a spiritual blessing of gentiles or the completion of such a spiritual blessing as is implied in Rom 11:25–26.

Some Dispensationalists understand the budding described in the parable of the fig tree (Matt 24:32–33//Mark 13:28–29//Luke 21:29–31) to point to a restoration of Israel following the "the fulfillment of the times of the gentiles," seeing the fig as a symbol of Israel. In fact, Luke may himself have been familiar with such an interpretation. If so, however, he seems inclined to dispel it. In his version of the parable, Jesus tells his audience to look not just at the "fig tree" but rather at "the fig tree and all the trees," minimizing the focus on the fig/Israel. Thanks to my brother Robert P. Menzies for this observation shared in a private email on Oct. 2, 2023.

23. The date of Luther's work is supplied by Hilton Oswald on p. x of the "General Introduction" to Luther's *Lectures on Romans: Glosses and Scholia*.

Scholars debate whether Luther's change-of-mind was gradual or abrupt, and when it began. It seems likely that as the Reformation progressed, and as what he believed to be a purer form of the gospel became widely proclaimed, he expected a great movement of Jews into the church. When this did not happen, he became bitter and resentful.

The Dispensationalist View

Since a fuller account of Dispensationalism is presented in the excursus called "Dispensationalism," the full outline of this theory of salvation-history ("God's plan for the ages"), will not be presented here. It is enough to say that the Dispensationalist explanation of Rom 11:26 is very similar to Luther's, although presented with greater vigor and detail. "All Israel will be saved" refers exclusively to Jews. It predicts an end-time revival of Jewish people that will take place at the second coming of Christ (which is distinguished from a preceding rapture of the church). As was the case with Luther, Rom 11:26 is coordinated with Luke 21:23–24 that mentions the fulfillment of "the times of the gentiles," but it is also coordinated with other verses as well (e.g. Rev 19:11–16 and Ezek 20:33–44).

"Dual-Covenant Theology," a Response to "Replacement Theology"

In the wake of the holocaust and the Nazi extermination of six million Jews, a great deal of attention has been focused on elements within Christianity that either facilitated this horror in and by Germany, a nominally Christian country, or at least precluded more robust opposition to it. Two factors that seemingly came into play were Luther's *zwei-Reiche-Lehre* ("two kingdoms doctrine") and Calvin's so-called "replacement theology." While Rom 13:1–7 may have had some impact on Luther's formulation of the former, the following discussion is primarily concerned with the second factor, "replacement theology."

The term "replacement theology" has become an epithet of reproach, and it has often been associated with Calvin's view of Romans 11 and those influenced by it.[24] A related term is "supersessionism," which is often regarded as a synonym for replacement theology." In many ways, both terms are unhelpful since they include a wide variety of views and are often used

---

24. This is not to deny that forms of replacement theology existed long before Calvin's time. Examples may be found as early as the second century.

to insult rather than to clarify. Furthermore, unless a person is committed to extreme pluralism—the idea that all paths to God are equally valid—it seems to go without saying that any proponent of a particular religion will consider his chosen belief to describe spiritual reality most accurately. This implies that other religions miss the mark in some way. If "replacement theology" or "supersessionism" is to mean anything useful at all, it must mean something different from this.

As already mentioned, it is probably inaccurate to characterize Calvin as suggesting that "the church" replaced Israel, since he considered the church to have been an Old Testament institution prior to Christ reframing it as a New Covenant institution. In this sense, the congregation (*qahal* in the MT; *ekklēsia* in the LXX) of Israel constituted the church long before gentile believers became part of it. Those within Israel who accepted Jesus as Israel's messiah remained in the church. They were joined by gentiles who also accepted Jesus as Israel's messiah and as their savior.

Paul did not conceive of Judaism (membership in Israel), on the one hand, and faith in Jesus Christ, on the other hand, as mutually exclusive alternatives. He himself was both a Jew and a believer in Christ. Although he would not have used such anachronistic terms, he would have viewed pitting Judaism and faith in Christ against each other in this way as a category mistake. To be a Jew is to be part of a *people*; it is not strictly speaking an ethnic, a cultural, or a religious category although aspects of all three are sometimes implied. In contrast, Christianity is a *religion*; ethnicity has no part in defining its boundaries. Therefore, one did not have to give up her Jewish identity to become a follower of Christ.

The central problem was that for much of church history, there was no realistic way to live simultaneously as both a Jew and a follower of Jesus. Within a century of the writing of Romans, this possibility which had been very much alive in the middle of the first century began to disappear. The church life that came to prevail allowed no room for Jews to continue to live as Jews while also following Christ. Unfortunately, they were forced at the same time to become religious converts *to* Christianity and both cultural and religious converts *from* Judaism. This transformation might be described as a problem of Christian culture that ended up having serious theological consequences. To most Christians, Judaism came to be regarded as an alternative religion much like paganism or Zoroastrianism/Mithraism, and it was treated antagonistically. To be sure, Judaism reciprocated in this animosity. Many Jews refused to acknowledge that Christians worshipped the same God as they did.

The transition from Paul's acceptance of both Jews and gentiles in the church, including observance of Torah by Jewish believers, to a pattern less accommodating of Jewish practices and Jewish identity began in the first half of the second century, if not earlier.

An example of a non-Pauline pattern is found in the *Epistle of Barnabas*, which considers the covenant received at Sinai to be lost (*apōlesan*).[25] It states this covenant was broken and lost "in order that the covenant of the beloved Jesus might be sealed in our heart."[26] Although God had offered the covenant to Israel after a miraculous deliverance from slavery in Egypt, due to their idolatry "after such extraordinary signs and wonders were done in Israel, even then they were abandoned. . . ."[27]

But what was lost by faithless Israel has accrued to the benefit of the author's community. He suggests that the blessings apparently promised to Israel instead point to blessings for his contemporaries who follow Christ:

> Observe, then, that we have been created anew, just as he [God] says once more in another prophet: 'Behold,' says the Lord, 'I will take away from these (that is to say, from those whom the Spirit of the Lord foresaw) their stony hearts, and put in hearts of flesh,' [Ezek. 11:19] because he [God] was about to be manifested in the flesh and to dwell in us. For the dwelling place of our heart, my brothers, is a holy temple dedicated to the Lord. . . . Therefore, we are the ones [i.e., instead of the children of Israel] whom he brought into the good land.[28]

This truly is a "replacement theology," since Israel is thought to have been entirely abandoned by God to make room for the church. Furthermore, Israel's story is emptied of meaning outside of its blessings being reinterpreted as blessing for the church, and its failures serving as warnings to the church. Past salvation history is reduced to an elaborate parable.

People may justifiably quibble over whether the *Epistle of Barnabas* is antisemitic. In contrast, there is little doubt that Melito of Sardis's *Homily on the Passion* crosses that line. Written much later in the second century than the *Epistle of Barnabas*, it too makes considerable use of Old Testament scripture but always in a way that foreshadows the Christian era and

---

25. *Barn.* 4.6 and reiterated in 4.8.
26. *Barn.* 4.8.
27. *Barn.* 4.14.
28. *Barn.* 6.14–16.

minimizes the importance of God's past dealings with Israel. Even more disturbing is the blame it casts on Israel for the crucifixion of Jesus:

> Why, O Israel, hast though done this strange wrong? . . . Is it not written, "Thou shalt not shed innocent blood lest thou die an evil death?"[29]
>
> Come, he says, Israel, thou hast slain the Lord. Why? because he must need die? . . . Thou errest, O Israel, in reasoning falsely upon the slaying of the Lord. He must need suffer, but not through thee. . . . Thus, O Israel, shouldst thou have cried to God: "O Master, even though thy son must suffer, and this is thy will, let him suffer, but not at my hand; let him suffer at the hand of the Gentiles, let him be judged by the uncircumcised, let him be nailed to the cross by the oppressor's hand, but not by me." But thou, O Israel, didst not raise thy cry thus to God, nor didst thou clear thyself of blame in the sight of thy master. . . .[30]

Given Melito's plea that the Jews should have extracted themselves from the situation and let Jesus suffer at the hand of gentiles, how strange it is that he includes in his recitation of charges against Israel several actions that the gospels clearly attribute to the Roman authorities, i.e., to gentiles:

> Thou didst put a scarlet robe upon his body and thorns upon his head. Thou didst bind the beautiful hands with which he shaped thee from the earth; and his beautiful mouth, the mouth that fed thee with life, thou hast fed with gall, and thou hast slain thy Lord in the great feast.[31]

And then Melito reaches his crescendo, charging Israel, and Israel alone, with deicide:

> And so he is raised upon a high cross, and a title is set upon it making known him who was slain. Who was he? Painful it is to tell, more terrible not to tell. Hear ye, and tremble before him who made heavens and earth tremble. He who hung the

---

29. This is an apparent allusion to Matt 27:4 and Deut 27:25.

30. Melito of Sardis, *Homily on the Passion* 12, lines 73–77; translation in Bonner, *Homily on the Passion*, 176–77.

31. Melito of Sardis, *Homily on the Passion,* 13, line 79; translation in Bonner, *Homily on the Passion*, 177.

earth in its place is hanged, he who fixed the heavens is fixed upon the cross, he who made all things fast is made fast upon the tree, the Master has been insulted, God has been murdered, the King of Israel has been slain by an Israelitish hand.[32]

Perhaps all of humanity is guilty of deicide, but certainly the people of Israel are not uniquely culpable.

While possibly no one in the second century exceeded the anti-Jewish vitriol of Melito, in scope his attempt to distance Christianity from Judaism and the Jewish people was perhaps surpassed by Marcion of Sinope, who after moving from Pontus to Rome taught a version of the faith proclaiming that the God of Jesus and of Paul was a different deity than the one depicted in the Jewish scriptures. Marcion also created his own version of a New Testament that consisted of an edited version of Luke and ten letters of Paul (including an Epistle to the Laodiceans and lacking the pastoral epistles). Neither this gospel nor the letters included any quotations from the Old Testament. While the church pulled back from Marcion's extremism, other versions of replacement theology continued to flourish and in fact often occupied the church's mainstream until the second half of the twentieth century. In this manner, a central theme of Paul's gospel was marginalized and sidelined—that Jews were welcome in the church as Jews so long as they trusted in and worshipped Jesus.

In recognition of the problems with replacement theology and in response to the manifest evil of the holocaust, a different approach has been embraced by many main-line (and liberal) theologians. Called "dual covenant theology," it teaches that God has established two tracks of salvation: Judaism; and Christianity. Jews who are faithful to their traditions will be saved without belief in Jesus as Israel's messiah. Believers in Jesus, whether of Jewish or gentile background, constitute the church, and they will be saved by faith in Jesus. Since both streams believe in Yahweh (the Lord), the God of Israel, both streams will be saved. The biblical justification for this is centered on the supposition that Rom 11:26 foretells a future salvation of "all Israel," a designation that does not require belief in Jesus as Israel's messiah. Thus, the religion of Judaism is as legitimate in God's eyes as Christianity.

Of course, the problem with this line of argumentation is that it conflicts with the views of Paul, especially what he teaches in Romans 11. There he distinguishes between the remnant and those branches that have been

---

32. Melito of Sardis, *Homily on the Passion*, 16, lines 95–96; translation in Bonner, *Homily on the Passion*, 179.

broken off. "All Israel" does not mean every person who claims to be a Jew. It designates the entire *remnant*; it means all of *true* Israel (i.e., those who believe in Christ).

There are similarities between dual covenant theology and Dispensationalism in that both teach separate paths of salvation for Israel and the church. But whereas Dispensationalism teaches that Jews must believe in Jesus to be part of the "all Israel" that will be saved, dual covenant theology does not.

If Paul had accepted such a view, it is hard to understand his lament that his fellow Jews who do not believe in Christ are unenlightened, have not submitted to God's righteousness, and are not headed toward salvation (Rom 10:1–3). Furthermore, this causes him sorrow and anguish to the point that he wishes he could sacrifice himself to bring them into right relationship with God (Rom 9:1–3).

WHAT IS THE ROLE OF ISRAEL TODAY?

Paul believed the Jews and the gentiles of his day had different ways of "being in the world," as the expression goes. They held different values, followed different habits, had different collective histories, anticipated different futures, and held different views of God/the gods. Of course, any given Jew was not identical to every other Jew. And the diversity among gentiles was even greater since the word "gentile" defines one's identity negatively as "not a Jew" rather than positively as something concrete and precise. Still, despite their limitations, the categories were meaningful. They were also largely binary. One was either a Jew or one was a gentile.

So, it is noteworthy that Paul uses the word "gentile" (*ethnos*) in two distinct senses. Most commonly he uses the term in its normal sense designating a "non-Jew." But he also uses it to mean something like "pagan" or "heathen." While believing gentiles remain gentiles in the first sense of the term, they are no longer "gentiles" in the second sense of the term. They remained non-Jews, but they were no longer "pagan" or "heathen." In this way, Paul fractures the binary nature of the Jew/gentile distinction. He tells gentile converts that they are not "gentile sinners" (literally "sinners from the gentiles"; Gal 2:15). They are not "gentiles who do not know God" (1 Thess 4:5). They "must no longer live as the gentiles live" (Eph 4:17).

Paul did not similarly charge believers not to live like Jews. It would have made no sense for him to say, "You may be a Jew, but now that you follow

Jesus, you must not live as a Jew." He might have said, "Live better than most Jews actually live." He might also have warned, "Do not think through the Law you can earn righteousness apart from God's grace." Furthermore, he certainly would have said, "Have faith in Jesus the Messiah." But he would not have said, "Reject the values and lifestyle divinely revealed to Israel."

In this way, Paul's attitude toward Jews and gentiles was neither equivalent nor symmetrical. In my comment to 3:19 I mentioned Barth's comparison of Judaism to "the empty canal," a dry riverbed that points to what used to flow but does so no longer. While this image is often perceived to be negative, even antisemitic, it also carries a positive implication. This image certainly elevates Judaism over gentile paganism since paganism never had a flowing canal at all. But Barth's image is incomplete. Judaism continues to proclaim many truths about God in a way that paganism does not and never has. Despite these positive dimensions, Paul did not consider Judaism to be a full conduit of salvation apart from faith in Jesus, the Messiah of Israel. Some of God's grace remains visible in contemporary Judaism, and this is more than simply that they are historical successors of ancient Israel.

Barth wrote his commentary after the Zionist project had begun but before the establishment of the modern state of Israel. Following 1948, many Christians have seen the emergence of the state of Israel as a fulfillment of prophecy and as evidence that God continues to deal with Israel as a people of God separate from the church. Dispensationalists await a mass conversion of Jews to faith in Christ at his second coming, an eschatological event that will result in "all Israel [being] saved." While I do not believe this Dispensationalist approach is what Paul teaches, Jews continue to come to faith in Christ, often while emphatically maintaining their Jewish identities, and personally I am unwilling to preclude the possibility that God continues to work with Israel in some mysterious way I do not understand. I hope and pray for a great end-time revival among the Jewish people, but I am not convinced there is prophetic assurance this will happen.

Excursus: Dispensationalism

PRELIMINARY THOUGHTS

It is hard to know how to categorize Dispensationalism. It may fairly be described as a theological framework or a hermeneutical method. Perhaps it is best characterized as an attempt to systematize salvation-history, or to use a more popular turn-of-phrase, "God's plan for the ages." Whatever Dispensationalism is, why would a discussion of it belong in a commentary on Romans?

The truth is that in many commentaries on Romans, such a discussion would seem out of place. This is because in some branches of Christianity Dispensationalism has had little influence and is little understood. But this commentary is aimed at a particular audience, Pentecostals and Charismatics. Dispensationalism has had such a major impact on this audience, particularly the classical Pentecostal wing of it, that I think it is important to acknowledge the elephant in the room. Romans contains material that is very important to any account of Dispensationalism. And whether framed in Dispensationalist terms or not, Paul's discussion of God's election of his chosen people in chapters 9–11, and especially in 11:25–26, should be of intense interest to anyone interested in salvation-history and Israel's role in it.

While the author of this commentary does not consider himself a Dispensationalist, he thinks it is important to explain Dispensationalism accurately and fairly. However, this discussion will of necessity be limited and incomplete. Hopefully, despite these constraints, it will still be useful.

THE NAME "DISPENSATIONALISM"

Dispensationalism is poorly named. While dispensations are part of its system, dividing salvation-history into different eras is hardly unique to dispensationalism. Also, dispensations are not the core of Dispensationalism. What is central to Dispensationalism is keeping Israel and the church separate and distinct. Related to this is Dispensationalism's insistence that all the Old Testament promises to Israel must be fulfilled literally. Dispensationalism was birthed in large part by frustration that most Protestants "spiritualized" many of the Old Testament prophecies and promises, claiming such prophecies and promises have already been fulfilled or that they would be fulfilled in some non-literal way.[33] To state this differently, literal fulfillment of prophecy is a key principle of Dispensationalism.

---

33. As an example of this, Bible expositors from the Reformed tradition often lean on 2 Cor 1:20: ". . . for as many promises of God as there are, receive the Yes in him [i.e., in Christ], and therefore through him receive from us the Amen, to the glory of God." This, they argue, means that all the promises given in the Old Testament have already been fulfilled in Christ, even though it is far from clear this

Dispensationalism comes in several variations, and this complicates discussion of it. While numerous varieties might be considered, I believe there are three main forms of Dispensationalism which include the more minor variations under their umbrellas. It is these three forms we will discuss: Classical Dispensationalism; Revised Dispensationalism; and Progressive Dispensationalism.

CLASSICAL DISPENSATIONALISM

While its proponents claim Dispensationalism is taught in the Bible, and they point to examples of chiliasm (millennialism) in the ancient church as forerunners to modern Dispensationalism, modern Dispensationalism began in the nineteenth century with the teaching of John Nelson Darby, an Anglo-Irish leader of the Plymouth Brethren. While his work was mainly centered in Ireland and England, Darby made seven trips to the United States and Canada between the years 1862 and 1877, spending a total of about seven years in North America.[34]

After the Civil War, Dispensationalism became firmly rooted in North America, and prominent leaders emerged on the continent: James Hall Brookes, Adoniram Judson Gordon, and Arno C. Gaebelien being among them. The most influential proponent would turn out to be Cyrus I. Scofield, an American Congregationalist minister, who was exposed to Dispensationalism by James Hall Brookes.

Scofield's chief contribution was to prepare the notes for *The Scofield Study Bible*, published in 1909 by Oxford University Press. A second, revised edition of this study Bible appeared in 1917. After "Revised Dispensationalism" made its appearance, beginning in the 1950s, the earlier form of Dispensationalism taught by Darby, Scofield, and their associates came to be known as "Classical Dispensationalism."

Classical Dispensationalism not only taught that God had two separate people which should not be confused—Israel and the church—but also that the redemptive futures of these two peoples are different. To say this differently, the ages during which these peoples would flourish spiritually to their greatest extent are different. The great age of salvation for the gentiles is the church age. The same is not true for Jews, although there will be some believing Jews (i.e., the remnant) in that period. Throughout the Old

---

is what Paul means.

34. Ice, *Short History of Dispensationalism*, 7.

Testament period there was always a "spiritual Israel" constituting a subset of the larger people of Israel, namely "the remnant" of Israel. In addition, there will be a great spiritual awakening among the Jews during the great tribulation. As *The Scofield Study Bible* explains,

> In the history of Israel a "remnant" may be discerned, a spiritual Israel within the national Israel. . . . At the advent of our Lord, John the Baptist, Simeon, Anna, and "them that looked for redemption in Jerusalem" (Lk. 2.38), were the remnant. During the church age the remnant is composed of believing Jews (Rom. 11.4, 5). But the chief interest in the remnant is prophetic. During the great tribulation, a remnant out of all Israel will turn to Jesus as Messiah, and will become His witnesses after the removal of the church (Rev. 7.3–8). Some of these will undergo martyrdom (Rev. 6.9–11), some will be spared to enter the millennial kingdom (Zech. 12.6—13.9). Many of the Psalms express prophetically the joys and sorrows of the tribulation remnant.[35]

Because God had two peoples which should not be confused, it was crucial to identify which passages of scripture related to Israel and which related to the church. 2 Tim 2:15 became a key verse used to articulate this principle. As the King James Version put it: "Study to shew thyself approved unto God, a workman that needeth not to be ashamed, rightly dividing the word of truth." "Rightly dividing" literally meant to divide between verses concerning Israel and verses concerning the church.

Beyond this fundamental distinction between Israel and the church, of great significance to Dispensationalism is the nature and timing of the kingdom, or more precisely, the (earthly) kingdom of heaven. At the present time many (most?) Christians believe that "the kingdom of God" and "the kingdom of heaven" refer to the same thing, and that this kingdom has already been inaugurated.[36] It is present but in an incomplete way, and it will be consummated following the return of Christ.

---

35. *Scofield Study Bible*, ad loc. Romans 11, note 1.

36. The explanation usually given for use of these two synonymous phrases is as follows: In the phrase "kingdom of heaven," the word "heaven" is a metonym for God. Because heaven is regarded as the abode of God, referring to "heaven" is an indirect way of referring to God himself. To show reverence for God, Jews often but not always preferred referring to God indirectly. This less direct phrase "the kingdom of heaven" only appears in Matthew's Gospel.

This is not the view of Classical Dispensationalism, which distinguishes between "the kingdom of God" and "the kingdom of heaven." "The kingdom of God" refers to God's rule throughout the ages. This rule is a present reality. In contrast, at this time "the kingdom of heaven" is entirely a future hope. For this reason, Dispensationalism is often said to embrace "futurist eschatology" rather than "inaugurated eschatology." Additionally, the kingdom of heaven can also be described as "David's kingdom" or "the kingdom of the Messiah."

The foundation of the messianic hope is the promise God gave to David in 2 Samuel 7 that he would build a "house" (or "dynasty") for him and give to him and to his descendants an "eternal kingdom." According to Classical Dispensationalism, Jesus does not yet rule as an earthly king, so the kingdom of heaven is not yet a present reality, although it could have been. John the Baptist proclaimed that the kingdom of heaven was "at hand" (Matt 3:2), as did Jesus (Matt 4:17). However, because during his earthly ministry Jesus did not come in triumphant glory, the Jewish people largely rejected him.[37] As a result, the coming of the kingdom of heaven was postponed. What could have been an immediate blessing was deferred to the millennium. This allowed the church age, which was unknown to the Old Testament prophets, to occur. In a sense, the Jews' rejection of Jesus as their messiah at his first coming became a great blessing for the gentiles. Had the coming of the kingdom not been postponed, the church of the New Testament would not have been born.

One of several important differences between Dispensationalism and the Covenant Theology of John Calvin concerns when the church began. Calvin noted that the in the LXX, a Greek translation of the Old Testament, the word *ekklēsia* ("assembly" or "church") often appeared, usually as a translation of the Hebrew *qahal* ("assembly"). For this reason, Calvin was accustomed to write of "the church of the Old Testament." In contrast, Dispensationalists teach that the church began when the Spirit was poured out on the day of Pentecost. Understandably, this also coincides with the beginning of "the church age."

Despite the postponement of the kingdom, Dispensationalists affirm that the fulfillment of God's promises will never be thwarted by human limitations or indifference. And because divine prophecy will always come to pass, one day Jesus as the anointed son of David will become the earthly king of Israel, and he will reign over the entire world from a throne in Jerusalem. This rule of Jesus will take place during the thousand-year

---

37. About this rejection, see *Scofield Study Bible*, ad loc. Matthew 3, note 2.

period usually called the "millennium," which is mentioned in Revelation 20. This millennium will follow the rapture ("snatching up") of the saints, a seven-year Great Tribulation, and the second coming (or return) of Christ with his saints in triumph over the forces of evil. At the second coming, all the Jews on earth will recognize Jesus as their Messiah, "and so all Israel will be saved" (Rom 11:26).

Darby and his followers were quite taken with the prophecies found in the Old Testament, many of which they believed pointed to Israel's future, the coming of Israel's Messiah, and ultimately the Messiah's rule over the entire earth in the period of great blessing just described. They did not, however, observe similar Old Testament prophecies about the coming of a largely gentile church. Therefore, they concluded that God's timeline of salvation centered around Israel, God's chosen people. The church age, which stretches from the day of Pentecost until when the church will be removed from the earth at the rapture, is an interruption to God's timeline for Israel's salvation. Sometimes this interruption in God's dealings with Israel is described as a "parenthesis."

The "rapture of the church" is a hallmark doctrine of Dispensationalism. Dispensationalists distinguish the catching up ("rapture") of the saints as an event separate from and preceding the second coming of Christ. It is at this rapture that the saints will receive the resurrected bodies described in 1 Corinthians 15.[38] Sometimes called a "secret" rapture to distinguish it from the very public and triumphant second coming of Christ, this rapture is vividly described in 1 Thess 4:15–17. One reason Dispensationalists found it important to separate this rapture from the second coming was to get the church out of the way so that fulfillment of the remaining sequence of Old Testament prophecies concerning Israel could resume.

Another reason was the direction of the saints' movement implied in 1 Thess 4:16–17. First, the dead in Christ will "rise" and then those who are still alive will be "snatched . . . to meet the Lord in the air." The Greek verb "snatched" (*harpazō*) was translated in the Vulgate with the Latin *rapio* or perhaps its biform *rapto*, from which the word "rapture" derives. The image is of a bird of prey (i.e., a "raptor") seizing an animal.

There is no doubt that a sudden and jarring transition is described. But why are the saints snatched into the air? Are they to join the Lord as they

---

38. Those who do not embrace Dispensationalism generally regard the "snatching up" ("rapture") of the church and the second coming of Christ to be the same event. They also believe it is at this time that the saints (composed of both Jews and gentiles) will receive their resurrected bodies.

commence a journey to heaven, as Dispensationalists envision? Or is it the older view that this is an *adventus* (literally a "coming to"), the ceremonial escorting of a dignitary on the final leg of his journey to his destination. In this case the dignitary is *Jesus*, on the last leg of his journey to *earth*.

The *adventus* was a well-known ritual in the ancient world. The triumphal entry of Jesus into Jerusalem is one example of an *adventus*. Another is pictured in Acts 28:15–16 as Paul is escorted into Rome by the Christians of the area. However, many Dispensationalists found the idea of rising to meet the Lord in the air only to return immediately to earth difficult to accept. Instead, Dispensationalists believed those in the church, both those who had already died and those still alive, would join Christ in the clouds to be escorted to heaven.

A third reason Dispensationalism embraced a secret rapture is that, based on 1 Thess 1:10 and Rev 3:10, its proponents believed the church would not go through the great tribulation mentioned in Matt 24:21 and Mark 13:19.[39] 1 Thess 1:10 describes Jesus as "the one rescuing us from the coming wrath," and Rev 3:10 promises to the church of Philadelphia "I will keep you from the hour of trial which is coming on the whole world."

Entwined with the theory of a secret rapture separate from the second coming is the idea that the great tribulation will be a seven-year period sandwiched between the rapture of the church and the second coming. While the Olivet Discourse of Jesus describes this tribulation, the length of this event is indicated by Daniel 9:25–27. In the prophecy of 70 weeks of years, the first 69 weeks run consecutively, but the seventieth week seems detached from the other weeks. This seventieth week will come sometime after the Messiah is cut off, and this cutting off refers to the crucifixion of Jesus. According to Dispensational theory, the 69 weeks are detached from the seventieth week because the progression of prophetic events relating to Israel is interrupted by the insertion of the church age into God's original plan. According to Dispensationalist theory, this seventieth week of years marks out the great tribulation. Because it involves exactly one week of years, the great tribulation will last exactly seven years.

---

39. In Luke 21:23, "great distress" or "great necessity" (*anangkē megalē*) appears rather than "great tribulation" (*thlipsis megalē*) as in Matt 24:21 and "tribulation" (*thlipsis*) as in Mark 13:19. In Luke, Jerusalem is also depicted as being "trampled by gentiles until the times of the gentiles are fulfilled." While many believe Luke 21 pictures the trampling of Jerusalem by the Romans during the First Jewish War (AD 68–70), for Dispensationalists these events will take place during the great tribulation that follows the rapture of the church.

An important aspect of the Great Tribulation is that it will provide subjects over whom Jesus the Messiah will reign in his millennial kingdom. The raptured saints are gone, and while they will return with Christ at his second coming, they will come to reign with him, not to be reigned over. During the Tribulation, there will be gentiles who refused to believe in Christ prior to the rapture, but in the face of the evil imposed by the Antichrist—a figure who will take power during that awful period—some of these gentiles will have a change of heart and will begin to believe. In addition, either during the Tribulation or at the second coming of Christ, there will be a massive Jewish embrace of Jesus as the Messiah of Israel. These two groups will constitute the people over whom Christ and the raptured saints will rule during the millennium.

One difficulty attending this view is that during the millennium there will be both people with resurrected bodies and people in natural bodies on the earth. Those reigning with Christ will have resurrected bodies. Those reigned over will have natural bodies and they will continue to reproduce. Those with natural bodies and their offspring may also continue in unbelief.

The book of Revelation is especially important in Dispensationalist thinking. Unlike many who understand the narration in the Revelation to employ recursive cycles to present the same events multiple times in multiple ways, Dispensationalists generally believe the narrative of the Revelation unfolds sequentially—at least in chapters 4 through 22—foretelling a sequence of events in the order they will occur. The rapture is usually located at 4:1, where a voice like a trumpet says, "Come up here!"[40] In reference to this, *The Scofield Study Bible* comments, "This call seems clearly to indicate the fulfillment of 1 Thes. 4.14–17 [i.e., the "rapture"]. The word 'church' does not again occur in the Revelation till all is fulfilled."[41] Then the following chapters up through chapter 18 describe events of the great tribulation. Chapter 19 describes "the marriage supper of the Lamb" and the second coming. At this second coming of Christ in triumph, many Jews will accept him as their Anointed King and be saved.[42]

---

40. Most non-Dispensationalists understand the command "Come up here!" to be instruct to John to ascend into heaven—whether bodily or in a vision is unclear—to behold God's throne and other aspect of heaven. This is in keeping with the pattern of literature such as Daniel, Ezekiel, and 1 Enoch in which glimpses of heaven are revealed.

41. *Scofield Study Bible*, ad loc. Rev 4:1, note 2.

42. Christ's second coming is usually portrayed as a moment of judgment that closes out the opportunity for conversion. Somewhat problematically, for

It is finally in Revelation 20, according to Dispensationalism, that the culmination of the prophetic hope for the kingdom promised to David arrives. During "the millennium," as the thousand-year period mentioned there is called, Jesus sits on a throne and physically rules as the king of Israel and as the true successor to David.[43] Despite the fact that the millennium lasts one thousand years, the rule begun during that period commences "an eternal kingdom" in fulfillment of God's promise to David recorded in 2 Samuel 7.

THE CHURCH AS A "PARENTHESIS"

As we have already seen, in dispensationalist thought the "Church Age" is considered an interruption of God's redemptive interaction with Israel. It is a "parenthesis" inserted into God's Plan for the Ages (i.e., salvation history) during which salvation is offered to the gentiles through the gospel. This inclusion of the gentiles (God's Plan B) would never have taken place if Israel had accepted Jesus as their messiah and king at his first coming (God's Plan A).

The foundation of this dispensationalist idea is that "[Israel's] failure is gain for the gentiles" (Rom 11:12). This "failure," or "stumbl[ing]," as Paul describes it in the previous verse, refers to the widespread rejection of Jesus by the Jewish community. The "gain for the gentiles" is the insertion of the Church Age into salvation history through which many gentiles have been saved.

A key question concerns whether this is what Paul intends to teach in Rom 11:11–12. I contend it is not. When Paul says, "by [Israel's] trespass salvation came to the gentiles" (Rom 11:11), he suggests that their lack of support for Jesus led to his crucifixion—conducted by the Romans, to be sure—which in an extraordinary way facilitated the body of Christ becoming a new temple. Jesus himself had mysteriously identified his body with the Jerusalem temple (Matt 24:2//Mark 13:2//Luke 21:6; see also John 2:18–21). And Paul describes the church as "the body of Christ" (e.g., Rom 12:5; 1 Cor 12:27; Eph 4:12) and as a "temple" (1 Cor 3:16; 2 Cor 6:16; Eph 2:19–22). Gentiles, who had been denied access to the Jerusalem temple

---

Dispensationalism in addition to being a time of judgment the second coming must simultaneously function as a moment of salvation of a great multitude of Jews.

43. Dispensationalists often make much of the fact that "one thousand years" is mentioned seven times in Revelation 20, once each in vss. 2–8.

through the death of Jesus are granted access to this new temple, as Isaiah had prophesied would take place (Isa 56:6–8). This is the "gain for the gentiles" to which Paul alludes in Rom 11:11–12.

PECULIARITIES OF DISPENSATIONALISM

One peculiarity of Classical Dispensationalism is its thesis that the Sermon on the Mount is not intended as instruction for the church age. Instead, it is a handbook for life during the millennium. During the church age it would set an impractically high standard of behavior since this world is so beset with sin and evil. After the millennium comes and the world is governed righteously, only then will the high moral standard of the Sermon on the Mount be attainable.

Another peculiarity of Classical Dispensationalism is that Israel's acceptance of the Law as part of the Mosaic Covenant is considered to have been a mistake. *The Scofield Study Bible* terms it "rash," because it ended the more favorable Dispensation of Promise that had begun with Abraham.[44]

According to Classical Dispensationalism, the three covenants of promise (the Abrahamic Covenant, the Davidic Covenant, and the New Covenant) are unconditional. More strikingly, these covenants do not represent promises to the church, but only to Israel. This is difficult to square with New Testament teaching. For instance, Romans 4 makes clear that many gentiles are heirs of Abraham and receive blessings promised to him. Even the promise of "the land," found among other places in Gen 13:15, is pronounced on Abraham's children including his gentile children (Rom 4:13–17).

It also seems odd that while Jesus celebrates "the new covenant in my blood" at the Last Supper (Luke 22:20; 1 Cor 11:25), and this is re-enacted whenever the church celebrates the Lord's Supper, according to Dispensationalist teaching the new covenant pertains only to Israel. To deal with this problem, sometimes two new covenants are hypothesized: one for Israel; and another for the church.

---

44. *Scofield Study Bible*, ad loc. Gen 12:1, note 1. Scofield makes clear that while the Dispensation of Promise ended when the Dispensation of Law began, the unconditional Abrahamic Covenant remained in effect.

REVISED DISPENSATIONALISM

The term Revised Dispensationalism refers to the variety of dispensationalism articulated by important figures such as Charles Ryrie, John Walvoord, and Dwight Pentecost, beginning about 1950. It maintained the essential features of Classical Dispensationalism, while jettisoning some troublesome aspects of the earlier teaching. It also represents a reinvigoration of dispensational interest in "physical Israel," prompted by the establishment of the modern state of Israel in 1948.[45]

The following notes from the *Ryrie Study Bible* reflects the editor's essential continuity with Classical Dispensationalism:

> The [Davidic] covenant did not guarantee uninterrupted rule by David's family (and, in fact, the Babylonian Exile interrupted it), but it did promise that the right to rule would always remain with David's dynasty. Jesus Christ is the ultimate fulfillment of these promises (Luke 1:31–33) and, although at this present time He is not ruling from the throne of David (Heb. 12:2), at His second coming He will assume this throne.[46]
>
> [The] *kingdom of heaven* . . . the rule of heaven over the earth. The Jewish people of Christ's day were looking for this messianic or Davidic kingdom to be established on this earth, and this is what John proclaimed as being "at hand." The requirement that the people must repent in order for the kingdom to be established was new and became a stumbling block to them. The rejection of Christ by the people delayed its establishment until the second coming of Christ (25:31).[47]

---

45. The following comment is typical of the idea that the formation of the modern state of Israel correlates with prophecy. In a note to Rom 11:15, the *Ryrie Study Bible* remarks: "When the Lord returns, the Jewish people will be regathered, judged, restored to favor, and redeemed (v. 26)." However, the establishment of the state of Israel also created some problems for dispensationalists. Schofield had taught that "the times of the gentiles" would only end with the onset of the millennium: "The Times of the Gentiles is that long period beginning with the Babylonian captivity of Judah, under Nebuchadnezzar, and to be brought to an end by the destruction of Gentile world-power by the "stone cut out without hands" (Dan. 2.34, 35, 44), i.e. the coming of the Lord in glory (Rev. 19.11, 21), until which time Jerusalem is politically subject to Gentile rule (Lk. 21.24)." *Scofield Study Bible*, ad loc. Rev 16:10.

46. *Ryrie Study Bible*, ad loc. 2 Sam 7:12–16.

47. *Ryrie Study Bible*, ad loc. Matt 3:2.

On the other hand, Ryrie breaks from Classical Dispensationalism in important ways. He does not distinguish "the kingdom of God" from "the kingdom of heaven." He also acknowledges that the parables of the kingdom of heaven found in Matt 13 "present truths about the kingdom *in this present day*" (emphasis added). However, he claims these truths are called

> 'mysteries' (v.11) because they were not revealed in the OT, and they are revealed by Christ only to those who are properly related to him (vv. 11–13 and Mark 4:11–12). . . . Jesus now turns to instructing His disciples about the present dispensation (a mystery, Eph 3:5–6) between the first and second comings of the Lord.[48]

To state this differently, these parables about the kingdom of heaven relate to the church and the church age, something Scofield would never have accepted.

Ryrie also acknowledged that the Sermon on the Mount was instructive for present-day life. He writes the following:

> The Sermon on the Mount does not present the way of salvation but the way of righteous living for those who are in God's family, contrasting the new Way with the "old one" of the scribes and the Pharisees. For the Jews of Christ's day this message was a detailed explanation of "Repent" (3:2; 4:17). It was also an elaboration of the spirit of the law (5;17, 21–22, 27–28). For all of us it is a detailed revelation of the righteousness of God, and its principles are applicable to the children of God today.[49]

He also backpedals from Scofield's contention that the new covenant pertains only to Israel. He identifies "the New Testament" with "the New Covenant" mentioned in Luke 22:20, and then he explicitly states that "[t]he message of the New Testament centers on" (1) Jesus, and "(2) the people (the church) who have received His salvation."[50]

Interestingly, the *Ryrie Study Bible* nowhere mentions Scofield's contention that Israel's acceptance of the Mosaic Law as part of the covenant at Sinai was a mistake. Ryrie does not criticize Scofield; he simply avoids the matter altogether.

---

48. *Ryrie Study Bible,* ad loc. Matt 13:3.
49. *Ryrie Study Bible,* ad loc. Matt 5:1.
50. Ryrie, "Introduction to the New Testament," 1498.

The *Ryrie Study Bible* does not explicitly restate Scofield's contention that the three "covenants of promise" (the Abrahamic, the Davidic, and the New) were unconditional, although this is probably implied. Furthermore, these differ from the conditional Mosaic covenant.[51] But whereas Classical Dispensationalism believed these covenants pertained only to Israel, Revised Dispensationalism recognizes that the new covenant relates to the church. "The Old Testament primarily records God's dealings with Israel on the basis of the covenant given though Moses at Mount Sinai, while the New Testament describes the new arrangement of God with men through Christ on the basis of the *new covenant* . . ." (emphasis added).[52]

PROGRESSIVE DISPENSATIONALISM (AND THE THEOLOGY OF GEORGE ELDON LADD)

The origin of Progressive Dispensationalism can be traced to the Evangelical Theological Society's Dispensational Study Group which began meeting in November of 1986. At the 1991 meeting of the Evangelical Theological Society, the label "progressive dispensationalism" was introduced.[53] Its leading figures have been Craig Blaising, Darrell Bock, Robert Saucy, and Gerry Breshears.

In my opinion, Progressive Dispensationalism is very similar to the Historic Premillennialism of my former professor George Eldon Ladd. During Ladd's lifetime—he died in 1982—he was considered a leading critic of Dispensationalism, yet today his teaching is largely embraced by Progressive Dispensationalists. In large part, this is an acknowledgment that Ladd's criticisms were perceptive. Furthermore, those who framed this new form of Dispensationalism were charitable with open minds willing to follow the biblical evidence wherever it took them. I remember a roughly two-hour discussion I had with Craig Blaising nearly thirty years ago. I asked many questions and pointed out how similar his explanation of Progressive Dispensationalism was to Ladd's theology. He did not dispute this contention. When I asked him why he and his colleagues continued to call this "Dispensationalism," he acknowledged that many felt there was value in the name, even if what it represented had shifted a great deal.

---

51. *Ryrie Study Bible*, ad loc. Jer 31:31–34.
52. Ryrie, "Introduction to the New Testament," 1498.
53. Kober, "Problematic Development," unnumbered.

Since Ladd died before the advent of Progressive Dispensationalism, we have no record of his own evaluation of the movement. While I think he would have found the name perplexing, otherwise I believe he would have endorsed it heartily. Progressive Dispensationalists themselves do not all agree on every theological point, and no doubt Ladd would have quibbled over minor points with some within the Progressive Dispensationalist camp. Nevertheless, I find it difficult to describe how Ladd's theology differs in any significant way from the main contours of Progressive Dispensationalism.

Ladd understood the New Testament to teach an inaugurated eschatology of the kingdom of God. He rejected the Classical Dispensationalist teaching that the kingdom referred exclusively to a physical kingdom and was entirely future. He often used pithy expressions to express his view. "We live in the already, but not yet." "We live between the times." One of his books was titled *The Presence of the Future*.

One of Ladd's favorite verses pointing to the kingdom as a present reality was Luke 11:20 (//Matt 12:28): "But if I cast out the demons by the finger of God, then the kingdom of God has come upon you." Another favorite was Luke 17:21: ". . . for behold, the kingdom of God is in your midst."[54]

But there also remained a future aspect to the kingdom of God. In teaching the disciples how to pray, Jesus instructed them to say, "May your kingdom come; may your will be done on earth as it is in heaven" (Matt 6:10//Luke 11:2). Furthermore, in Acts 1:6 the disciples ask Jesus, "Lord, are you at this time restoring the kingdom to Israel?" implying that in their view the kingdom had not yet been fully restored.

Ladd felt the tension between the initial presence of the kingdom and the future consummation of the kingdom was expressed by two parables of the kingdom found in Matthew 13. The parable of the mustard seed contrasted the small beginning of the kingdom with its eventual large size. The parable of the leaven contrasted the pinch of leaven that would ultimately fill the entire loaf, suggesting that the small, barely noticeable presence of the kingdom would one day fill the entire world. Ladd also believed there remained a future role for Israel, and he considered the establishment of the modern state of Israel to be prophetically significant.

---

54. By this Jesus meant that his personal presence was a manifestation of the kingdom of God. In contrast, some translate this "The kingdom of God is within you," but this is contextually improbable. Jesus was speaking with Pharisees, and it is unlikely he would have suggested the kingdom was "within" these critics of his teaching.

Given the similarities between Progressive Dispensationalism and Ladd's Historic Premillennialism, some dispensationalists dismiss it as a departure from true dispensationalism. Since I largely follow Ladd's view of the kingdom, that is a matter for others to judge.

PROBLEMS WITH CLASSICAL AND REVISED DISPENSATIONALISM

Since, as I have argued, Progressive Dispensationalism is very similar to Historic Premillennialism (my own position), the following brief critique of Dispensationalism is directed at Classical Dispensationalism and Revised Dispensationalism. The point of this critique is not to demean Dispensationalists, who should generally be praised for their careful study of scripture and their commitment to its authority; it is simply to suggest there is a better way to systematize how salvation-history is presented in scripture.

One of the limitations of Dispensationalism is the rigid separation it seeks to maintain between the church and Israel. While the church may or may not be called "Israel" in only two disputed passages (Gal 6:16 and Rom 11:26), there are three places where gentile individuals in the church are clearly included among "the true circumcision" or called "a Jew in what is hidden": Rom 2:28–29; Phil 3:3; and Col 2:11.

Furthermore, Paul sometimes tells converted gentiles not to live like "the gentiles," implying that they are no longer fully members of this category (e.g., 1 Cor 5:1; 12:2; Eph 4:17; 1 Thess 4:5). This means that sometimes when Paul uses the word *ethnē* (the plural of the word *ethnos*), he means "gentiles" (focusing on their non-Jewish identity) and at other times he means "pagans" (focusing on their polytheistic religion and lifestyle). Such latter instances imply these converted gentiles have become either functionally equivalent to Jews or "a new race"—neither Jew nor gentile—as some fathers of the early church suggested.[55] (Eventually Christians gave

---

55. It is unclear who first made this suggestion. It may have been the anonymous author who wrote *The Epistle to Diognetus* (1.1). He considered being a member of this race praiseworthy. It may also have been the Aristides who wrote an apology sometime in the second century. The Greek version of the text lists Christians as one of three races; the Syriac text lists Christians as one of four races (in chapter 2). Tertullian is also aware of the idea, which is used to vilify the Christians. He defends against this insult (*To the Nations* 1.8). Clement of Alexandria uses the term *tertium genus* ("third race"), but he does not oppose it to Jews and Greeks, but rather uses the

up on the idea they were a separate race since there is nothing racial about Christianity.)

Similarly, Gal 3:28 says when speaking of the church, "... there is neither Jew nor Greek." See also the similar statements in 1 Cor 12:13 and Col 3:11. Dispensationalists acknowledge that Jews who believe in Jesus can become part of the church, so such statements are not necessarily devastating to their system. Nevertheless, these passages suggest an erasure of boundaries between believing gentiles and believing Jews, which is inconvenient for Dispensationalists. Even more emphatically, Eph 2:15 speaks of Christ by dying on the cross creating "in himself one new man in place of the two," an apparent present-day abrogation of the distinction between Jews and gentiles that is essential to dispensational thought. This emphasis is reaffirmed in the following chapter when Paul calls believing gentiles "fellow heirs" (a plural of *sygklēronomos*), "fellow body members" (a plural of *syssōmos*), and "fellow interest-holders" (a plural of *symmetochos*) with Israel (Eph 3:6).[56]

Finally, in many places the New Testament describes the spread of the gospel as a fulfillment of Old Testament prophecy. Citing passages from Romans alone produces the following list: Rom 1:17; 4:17; 8:36; 9:33; 10:15; 15:9; 15:10; 15:11; 15:12; and 15:21. While in these passages the covenant with David is not specifically referenced, the same cannot be said of the quotation of Amos 9:11 found in Acts 15:16. There the success of the gentile mission is described as "rebuilding the fallen tabernacle of David."

STRENGTHS OF DISPENSATIONALISM

While the problems with Dispensationalism are manifold, it is not without its strengths. Its distinctive explanation of salvation-history began as a protest. It reacted against the idea that the gentile embrace of the gospel fulfilled many Old Testament promises made to Israel. Perhaps the most egregious example of what offended Dispensationalists was the interpretation of 2 Cor 1:20 offered by Covenant theologians: "For all the promises of God in him [Christ] are yea, and in him Amen, unto the glory of God by us" (KJV). This meant, according to Covenant theology, that all the Old Testament promises had already been fulfilled; none remained yet to be fulfilled.

However, in the context of 2 Corinthians 1 Paul is clearly not explaining the timeframe of prophetic fulfillment. Instead, he is rebutting charges

---

three categories of "called," "chosen," and "race" (*Stromata* 3.10).

56. Israel is not specifically mentioned, but the idea is implied.

that he has waffled on certain past commitments he had made. He asserts that God is always faithful, and that God has anointed him for the ministry he pursues. Therefore, he suggests that if the Corinthians trust God, and if they accept his apostolic role, they should quit complaining. Clearly, the Dispensationalists had a legitimate complaint about the exegesis offered by the Covenant theologians.

Another strength of Dispensationalism is its recognition of Paul's reluctance to call Jesus "king" (*basileus*) or to say that Jesus "rules" (literally "kings," *basileuō*) at the present time. The one passage from Paul's letters in which he may affirm something like this is 1 Cor 15:25, but whether the kingly rule of Jesus refers to the present, to the future, or to both is unclear.

There seems to be some variety in the way the New Testament authors present this matter. Hebrews affirms the present kingship of Jesus rather openly. In contrast to the less exalted role of the angels, ". . . respecting the Son he [God] says, 'Your throne O God is forever and ever, and the scepter of uprightness is the scepter of your kingdom'" (Heb 1:8). Furthermore, looking back God's son is said to have already assumed this throne "after making purification for sins" (Heb 1:3). Perhaps no more overt reference to the present kingly reign of Jesus appears until the middle of the second century when *The Martyrdom of Polycarp* dates the execution of the great bishop of Smyrna "when Philip of Tralles was high priest during the proconsulship of Statius Quadratus, but while Jesus Christ was reigning as King [*basileuontos*] forever."[57]

Similarly, but more coyly, Matthew's Gospel portrays Jesus as a present king, but one not recognized as such. Early in the gospel the magi ask, "Where is the one born king of the Jews?" (Matt 2:2). At his trial before the Sanhedrin, the high priest commands Jesus, "I adjure you by the living God that you tell us if you are the Christ, the son of God" (Matt 26:63). This is followed by another mocking command: "Prophesy to us, you Christ!" (Matt 26:68). Later, the Roman soldiers mocked Jesus by putting a crown of thorns on his head, and as they knelt before him feigning adulation, they saluted derisively, "Hail, king of the Jews!" (Matt 27:27–29). The sign attached to the cross on which Jesus died stated, "This is Jesus, the king of the Jews." Using these vignettes, Matthew artistically delivers his message that those who mocked Jesus, although they did so unwittingly, spoke the truth more clearly than Jesus's own disciples.

In Matthew 26 the way the members of the Sanhedrin use the word "Christ" (*Christos* in the Greek) raises the question of this term's specific

---

57. *Mart. Pol.* 21.1.

force. A translation of the Hebrew *meshiach* ("Anointed One"), this word as used by the Sanhedrin functions as a virtual synonym for "king." And this is not surprising since in ancient Israel and Judah kings were anointed. While the title "Christ" could imply that a person is designated to become king at a later time, in Matthew it means he is already king.

In John 12:13 at the Triumphal Entry of Jesus into Jerusalem, the crowd calls him "the King of Israel." However, this cry is anticipatory of something they expect to happen, not yet a present reality. Moreover, soon the fickle crowd turns on Jesus.

As we have seen, Paul is reluctant to call Jesus "king." But he is not reluctant to call him "Christ," and he also frequently calls him "Lord" (*kyrios*). Perhaps the distinction implied by Paul's preference for the titles "Christ" and "Lord" is that while at present Jesus rules, he does not yet rule as an earthly monarch—a key point of Dispensationalism.

DISPENSATIONALISM AND PENTECOSTALISM

The charge is often made that Dispensationalism is inherently cessationist (i.e., it affirms that the miraculous and oral gifts of the Spirit, at a minimum, ceased to be operative when the last apostle died or when the last book of the New Testament was written). This charge is unfounded. While many Dispensationalists have been cessationists, there is nothing inherently cessationist in dispensational teaching. The apostles lived during the church age just as we today live during the church age. If miraculous and oral gifts of the Spirit operated at the time of the Twelve and of Paul, such gifts should operate in the church of today as well.[58] And, of course, cessationism is often linked to the covenant theology of the Reformed tradition, which on some issues, particularly the future of Israel and the shape of salvation-history, stands as the polar opposite of Dispensationalism.

However, there is another issue which highlights a true incompatibility between Dispensationalism and Pentecostalism, despite the incontrovertible fact that many people have claimed to be both Dispensationalists and Pentecostals. Dispensationalism holds to an entirely futurist eschatology, denying that the kingdom has yet begun to function. In contrast, today the majority of evangelicals (including Pentecostals) embrace inaugurated eschatology. This is the idea that the kingdom has begun in a limited and

---

58. This was carefully explained to me by Craig Blaising in a personal conversation nearly thirty years ago.

somewhat hidden form, but that eventually it will come in full power and visibility. As already noted, Jesus' parables of the mustard seed (Matt 13:31–32//Mark 4:30–32//Luke 13:18–19) and the leaven (Matt 13:33//Luke 13:20–21) vividly picture the contrasts between small beginnings and large endings. Despite its small beginning, the kingdom that once was almost imperceptible will one day fill the entire world.

Why does it matter if a person holds a futurist or inaugurated eschatology? If the kingdom is entirely in the future, then kingdom power, the power that will one day turn the world upside down and right every wrong, is not available today for healing, for the casting out of demons, or for miracles. If, however, the kingdom has already begun and God's people are to be heralds of the glory that is to come, then ministry not only in word but also in signs and wonders becomes possible. My old professor George Eldon Ladd used to talk about living in the "already but not yet." The kingdom is already here, but it is not yet consummated. That is the tension of Christian life before the second coming of Christ.

ROMANS 12

TRANSLATION: ROM 12:1–21

BEHAVIOR APPROPRIATE TO GOD'S PEOPLE

¹Therefore, I urge you, brothers [and sisters], by God's mercies to present your bodies as a living sacrifice, holy and acceptable to God, your figurative temple service. ²Do not be conformed to this age but be transformed by the renewal of the mind in order to ascertain what is the good, well pleasing, and perfect will of God.

³For by the grace given to me, I speak to everyone present among you, not to think of yourselves more highly than is necessary, but for proper thinking in each case to consider that God has distributed a measure of faith [to him or to her]. ⁴For just as the body has many members but all the members do not have the same function, ⁵so we many are one body in Christ, and individually its members belong to each other. ⁶We have different spiritual gifts according to the grace given to us: whether prophecy, in proportion to one's faith; ⁷or service by [his or her] serving; or the one teaching by [his or her] teaching; ⁸or the exhorter by exhorting; the giver by [his or her] sincerity; the leader by [his or her] devotion; the merciful by [his or her] cheerfulness.

⁹Let love be genuine. Abhor evil. Seek the good. ¹⁰Show affection to each other in a brotherly way. Prefer each other in honor. ¹¹Do not be slow to express devotion. Boil with the Spirit. Serve the Lord. ¹²Rejoice in hope. Be patient in difficulty. Persevere in prayer. ¹³Share the needs of the saints. Seek out opportunities for hospitality. ¹⁴Bless those who persecute you; bless and do not curse them. ¹⁵Rejoice with those rejoicing. Weep with those weeping. ¹⁶Have a consistent attitude with one another. Do not take pride in elite matters but rather associate with humble people. Do not be wise in your own estimations. ¹⁷Repay nobody evil for evil. Presume good when

dealing with all people. ¹⁸Be at peace with everyone, if matters outside your control make this possible. ¹⁹Do not avenge yourselves, beloved, but rather leave room for the wrath [of God], for it is written: "'Vengeance is mine; I will repay,' says the Lord." ²⁰But "If your enemy should be hungry, feed him; if he should be thirsty, give him drink. For by doing this, you will pile coals of fire on his head." ²¹Do not be conquered by the Evil One, but rather conquer evil with good.

COMMENTARY

Vs. 1: In Rom 11:36 Paul concluded his long exposition of God's plan for Israel and the gentiles with a doxology punctuated by a final "Amen." Consequently, the first verse of chapter 12 constitutes something of a new beginning. In fact, from 12:1 through 15:6 Paul deals with more practical concerns than he has previously. Often this material is described as paraenesis (Greek *parainesis*), which means "exhortation." While exhortations are found in this material, it also contains instruction, so perhaps this long section would be better described as ethical instruction and encouragement.

The abrupt transition from the end of chapter 11 to the beginning of chapter 12 makes Paul's use of the inferential conjunction *oun* ("therefore") at the beginning of 12:1 somewhat puzzling. This reminds me of the old preacher's saw, "When you see a 'therefore,' you need to ask what it is there for." To rephrase this slightly: On which prior comments exactly, does Paul base the exhortation that follows?

Herbert Smyth states that inferential *oun* "signifies that something *follows* from what precedes. [It] marks a transition to a new thought . . . ."[1] Probably the fact that *oun* marks a transition is Paul's chief motivation for using it here. As he launches into a new topic, the basis for his opening exhortation may be, on the one hand, general rather than specific. He may be saying, "Therefore, in the light of everything I have written so far, I urge you . . . ." On the other hand, he may have in mind a more particular idea, such as the soaring affirmation that God stands at the center of all things found in the doxology that concludes chapter 11. This exaltation of God serves as a fitting foundation for Paul's depiction at the beginning of chapter 12 of corporate worship in the church as a sacrificial offering to God.

It is "by the mercies of God" that Paul urges his readers. In the Old Testament this word for "mercy" (Greek *oiktirmos*) is frequently associated with God, and he is often called "merciful" (*oiktirmōn*). Rather than simply urging his readers under his own authority, Paul chooses to claim God's

1. Smyth, *Greek Grammar* §2964.

authority, and rather than stating flatly "I urge you by God," he chooses a less direct and therefore more reverential way of invoking God's authority. This indirect referencing of God is an expression of Paul's Jewish heritage and ethos. To write "I urge you . . . by God's mercies" is functionally very similar to writing "I urge you in God's name."

Why does Paul speak of "your bodies"? In part it may be because bodies are often sacrificed. It may also be that Paul uses the word "body" (*sōma*) as a metonym for "self." Certainly, the gist of Paul's exhortation is that the Roman believers present *themselves* to God as a "living sacrifice."

Paul thinks of the church as a temple made up of humans filled with the Spirit of God (1 Cor 3:16; 2 Cor 6:16; Eph 2:19-22). Its worship of God fills the place that the sacrificial service of the Jerusalem temple held under the old covenant prior to the coming of Christ. Therefore, Paul feels free to discuss Christian life using sacrificial imagery. However, the Law had expressly forbidden human sacrifice (Deut 18:10), so lest anyone misunderstand, Paul makes clear that "living sacrifices" are to be offered. This also comports with his belief that the ministry of the old covenant kills, and the ministry of the new covenant brings life (2 Cor 3:6-8). Despite the Law's prohibition of human sacrifice, these sacrifices Paul enjoins are "holy" and "acceptable to God."

The notion of non-physical sacrifice would not have been completely foreign to the Jewish believers in Rome. The LXX text of Ps 49:13-14 (English and MT, 50:13-14) contains this marvelous statement: "I do not eat the meat of bulls, and I do not drink the blood of rams. Sacrifice to God the sacrifice of praise and return to the Most High your prayers."

The phrase "figurative temple service" translates *tēn logikēn latreian*, which is more commonly translated as "spiritual worship" or "reasonable service." The Greek does not contain a word meaning "temple," but *latreia* ("service" or "worship") can be used of the priestly service at the Jerusalem temple and that is likely what is referenced here. One might ask why I did not simply translate this "figurative worship" or "figurative service." "Service" is too general since it could refer to many kinds of service. And "worship" in the sense of oral praise is not very concrete so it is not clear what "figurative worship" would mean. The temple service/worship involved concrete activity, and consequently Paul's phrase "*figurative* temple service" probably is a way of referring to oral worship.

The word *latreia* is flexible and therefore also vague. It can refer to "worship" or "a system of worship." Sometimes it refers to a specific religious rite, often involving sacrifices of various kinds. Often *latreia* is best translated "the act of making an offering." It can refer to "religious service" such as that performed by priests, but it also often refers to "service" or "labor" in secular contexts. In the context of this verse, the earlier reference to a "living sacrifice" in vs. 1 suggests the word's meaning is not only religious but also associated with sacrifice, specifically sacrifice in the Jerusalem temple.

One problem with the English word "offering" is that it can mean either "the thing offered" or "the act of offering." The same is not true of *latreia*. It refers to the act, not the thing offered. Whether one chooses to translate the word as "offering" or "service" does not matter a great deal so long as one is clear that it refers to an act, not a sacrificial victim.

The adjective *logikos* ("logical," "spiritual," or "figurative") is as flexible and vague as *latreia*, although it is a less commonly used word. If one were to consider only secular Greek literature, it would be judged to mean "logical" or "reasonable." However, in the only other occurrence of the word in the New Testament, it means "figurative." 1 Pet 2:2 reads: "As newborn babies, desire figurative pure milk in order that by it you may grow into salvation . . . ." "Logical" would not make much sense in this context. *Logikos* is often translated "spiritual," but when this is done, it generally misleads the reader, who thinks it is related to the Spirit (*pneuma*) in some way. Here "spiritual," when translating *logikos*, means "spiritual" in contrast to literal, i.e., "figurative."

Another significant point concerns Paul's use of singulars and plurals in this verse. When he speaks of the actions of the congregation using second-person verbs and second-person possessive pronouns ("*you* present"; "*your* bodies"; "*your* figurative temple service") these are all plural. But the "sacrifice" offered and "the temple service" undertaken are both given singular forms. This suggests that when the church meets together, it collectively is a temple, and its collective praise constitutes a single sacrificial offering.

Vs. 2: The English words "conformed" and "transformed" make an elegant poetic pair because they are formed from the same Latin root, and they rhyme. Unfortunately, the Greek words that lie behind them—*syschēmatizō* and *metamorphoō*—do not resemble each other in the same way. As its English cousins "scheme," "schema," and "schematic" suggest, *schēmatizō* describes the way something is formed or organized, and with the *syn* prefix (or in this case the *sys* prefix due to assimilation), it indicates organization "with" or "like" something. "Do not be conformed" captures this meaning quite well.

The Greek word *metamorphōsis*, the noun cognate with the verb *metamorphoō*, has entered English with both its pronunciation and its meaning remaining intact. This provides an excellent "hook" by which to explain *metamorphoō* to the person studying Romans in English. Just as "metamorphosis" means "transformation," *metamorphoō* means "to transform." Since in this verse the verb form is both an imperative and in the passive voice, Paul's command is "Be transformed."

Paul's readers are urged not to be conformed "to this age" (*tō aiōni toutō*). The word *aiōn* can also be translated "world." Basically, it refers to the way the world is arranged in a particular age. Change the age and the world is changed. The expression "this age" calls to mind the way both Jesus and rabbinic literature bisect time into "this age" and "the age to come." (For more about this, see the comments to Rom 1:18.) For Paul, "this age" is pejorative, implying that it is under the dominion of sin and darkness. Paul urges his readers not to settle for the values of this age, but rather to be transformed so as to live the life of "the age to come" proleptically, that is, foreshadowing the full appearance of the coming age.

Paul tells his readers that the transformation of which he writes will come by "the renewal of the mind," and the purpose of this renewal of the mind is "to ascertain" the will of God. Here "to ascertain" translates the infinitive of *dokimazō*, which is sometimes translated "to judge" but means "to judge by testing" not "to decree some verdict." While Paul expects his readers to fill in some of the steps in his logic, he implies that a renewed mind will be able to discern God's will and thereby guide the person to live in accordance with, and in anticipation of, the full flowering of "the age to come." Although the wording is different, the idea is basically the same as in Phil 3:20: "For we have our citizenship in heaven, from which we await a savior, the Lord Jesus Christ." This means that believers live as "foreigners" or "aliens" in this present evil age.

The phrase "the renewal of the mind" is often translated "the renewal *of your* mind" or "the renewing *of your* mind." This is based on a textual variant in which *hymōn* ("of your [pl.]") has been added. No doubt some scribe thought the addition made the passage read better, but two factors assure that this longer reading is not original. First, the manuscript evidence strongly favors the shorter reading. Second, if "of your" were originally in the text, there would be no reason to remove it, whereas its addition is more easily imagined. Nevertheless, whether *hymōn* was or was not originally in the text, this changes the meaning very little.

Vss. 3–7: In these verses Paul discusses the nature of the body of Christ and how its members are to relate to each other. This discussion is much briefer than the similar discussion in 1 Corinthians 12. Paul expresses concern that some believers in Rome have behaved arrogantly, but he gives no details about the reason for his concern. Not clearly stated but implied nonetheless, is a distinction between natural human abilities and gifts distributed by God.

Paul begins his exhortation by asserting his own divinely given authority in the gentlest of terms: "by the grace given to me." This is an example of use of the "divine passive," which is frequent in both early Jewish and early Christian writing. The blunter way of stating the same thing would have been to say, "by the authority God gave me . . . ."

Vs. 3: Four places in this verse some form of the Greek verb *phroneō* ("to think") appears. Twice it appears without anything prefixed to it. Once it appears with the proposition *hyper* prefixed, and once it appears with a shortened form of the adjective *sōs* ("safe" or "well, healthy") prefixed. Clearly the differing nuances implied by these variations are important to the point Paul wants to get across.

"To think [of themselves] more highly" translates the verb *hyperphroneō*. Paul charges his readers not to think of themselves more highly than "is necessary [*dei*] to think [*phroneō*]." In my translation this particular "to think" is omitted, since in English it seems redundant. Instead of thinking in this egotistical way, Paul's readers are urged "to think properly" (*sōphroneō*). Literally, *sōphroneō* means "to think sanely" or "to think with a right mind" as opposed to being deranged, but here "to think properly" conveys the right nuance.

When Paul warns the Roman believers not to think too highly of themselves, his basic point is easily understood, but the exact justification for this warning is more difficult to discern. Paul's readers are to think properly when they consider each person in their community, either on the one hand, because God has distributed "a measure of faith" (*metron pisteōs*) to each of these other individuals, or on the other hand, because God has distributed "a measure of faith" to the very people doing the assessing. Does God distribute "the measure of faith" to others ("to him or to her"), or does God distribute it to those Paul challenges to assess properly ("to you")? The NIV avoids choosing between these options by translating very non-literally: "Be honest in your evaluation of yourselves, measuring yourselves by the faith God has given us." This implies that "a measure of faith" is distributed both to the assessor and the people being assessed, which probably is in fact correct, but it may also go beyond what Paul says and obscure the thrust of his argument.

An issue relevant to this discussion is whether *hekastō* ("for each person," "to each person," or "in each case") should be construed with the infinitive *phronein* that precedes it, which is my preference, or with the dependent clause that follows it. If the former option is chosen, the best sense is rendered by understanding *hekastō* to mean "in each case," as my translation reflects. The latter course was chosen by the KJV translators: "according as God hath dealt *to every man* [i.e, 'to each'] the measure of faith." The chief obstacle with this latter option is that *hekastō* is positioned before the start of the dependent clause, which commences with *hōs*. While in Greek the position of word is not nearly as important in conveying meaning as it is in English, it is not altogether irrelevant. Placing *hekastō* before the apparent beginning of the dependent clause suggests that it should not be considered part of the dependent clause.

It is also unclear whether "a measure of faith" (*metron pisteōs*) means some minimum measure of faith that God has supplied to all, or if it is a measure that varies from individual to individual. The phrase "according to the proportion of faith" (*kata tēn analogian tēs pisteōs*) found in vs. 6 might suggest the latter option is correct i.e., that Paul has a variable measure in mind.

Vss. 4–5: These verses contain a more compressed version of Paul's famous discussion in 1 Corinthians 12 comparing the church to a human body. While the body has many parts, which have differing functions, still it is one body. The same is true of the church. It has many members, but it is one body. There is unity in this diversity, and the basis of this unity is Christ. While one might consider Paul's discussions of the body merely to be an extended metaphor, he seems to regard it as more than a manner of speaking. For Paul the church as the body of Christ is a mystical reality. It is not *like* a body; it *is* the body of Christ (1 Cor 12:27).

This, of course, raises the question broached in the introduction of why Paul does not address his epistle to "the church in Rome." Whether because of geography—the Christians of Rome may no longer all live in proximity to each other—or because of cultural and ethnic divisions, or because of leadership squabbles, in Rome there likely was more than one church. Nevertheless, Paul tells his readers they belong to one body. There is only one Christ, so there can be only one body of Christ, fractured though it may be.

"So we many are one body in Christ": At this point Paul has never been to Rome, yet by his use of the word "we," he claims to belong to the same body as the Roman believers. And although the city of Rome was large, and relative to other places in the world the Christian population of Rome may have been large, Paul's use of the word "many" (*hoi polloi*) in vs. 5 likewise suggests that he is referring to Christians from all over the world.

Despite this sense of a universal body of Christ, the members of this body belong to each other. By belonging to Christ, members of the body of Christ belong to each other. This means that they have responsibilities to serve each other, to care for each other, and not to harm each other. This teaching sets the stage for the practical and ethical instruction that will dominate the last five chapters of his letter.

I have translated the phrase *kath' heis* as "individually." It is composed of two words. The first is an aspirated form of the preposition *kata*, which normally means "against" when preceding a noun in the genitive case, and "on account of" when preceding a noun in the accusative case. The second word is the number "one," expressed in the masculine gender and the nominative case. Strictly speaking, this is a violation of the rules of Greek grammar since the preposition *kata* supposedly only precedes nouns in genitive or accusative cases. Its use with a noun in the nominative case appears to be a grammatical monstrosity. A more euphemistic way to describe this situation is to call this expression an "idiom." The English word "idiom" comes from the Greek word *idiōma*, which politely means "a peculiarity." The word "idiom" has come to mean an expression that cannot be explained by the normal meaning of its constituent words. "Under the weather" is a good example of such an idiom. While *kath' heis* is problematic grammatically, there is enough evidence of its use to demonstrate that when it makes an appearance, it means "individually."[2]

The phrase "its members" of vs. 5 requires some comment. A neuter singular definite article (*to*) governs the clause that fills the second half of vs. 5. This shows that the "members" described in this clause are members of the noun *sōma* ("body") of the preceding clause, which is also a neuter singular. While this verse exhibits no neuter singular demonstrative pronoun—the normal way "its" is expressed—the tie between the definite article (*to*) and its antecedent (*sōma*) here functions equivalently.

Vss. 6–8: In these verses Paul lists seven gracious gifts (*charismata*). Given Paul's teaching in 1 Cor 12 that such *charismata* are manifestations of the Spirit, it is surprising that the Spirit is not mentioned in these verses. In 1 Corinthians 12 Paul provides three lists of gifts: in 1 Cor 12:8–10; in 1 Cor 12:28; and in 1 Cor 12:29–30. Of the thirteen gifts mentioned in one or more of these lists, only two also figure in this list in Romans 12: prophecy; and teaching. Particularly surprising is the absence of a reference to apostles or apostleship, which heads Paul's lists in 1 Cor 12:28 and 12:29–30. The other five gifts mentioned here are not mentioned in Paul's other lists of gifts. Although some early Pentecostals spoke of "the nine gifts of the Spirit" treating the list in 1 Cor 12:8–10 as privileged or normative, comparison with Paul's other lists of gifts demonstrates that none of his lists is normative or comprehensive; all are "for instance" lists.

In 1 Corinthians 12 and 14 two Greek words are sometimes translated "spiritual gifts": *charismata* (literally "gracious gifts"); and *pneumatika* (literally "spirituals"). While the precise relationship between these two

---

2. Bl-D-F §305; Moule, *Idiom-Book*, 60 note 1.

designations is not clear, almost certainly *charismata* make up a broader category of which the *pneumatika* constitute a subset. Not only this, but prophecy seems clearly to qualify as both a *charisma* ("gracious gift"; 1 Cor 12:10) and a *pneumatikon* ("spiritual"; 1 Cor 14:1). My own view is that the *pneumatika* are made up of oral gifts including prophecy, tongues, the interpretation of tongues, the word of wisdom, and the word of knowledge, and possibly the discerning of spirits, but this judgment is only what I might call "informed conjecture."

In 1 Cor 12:9 "faith" (*pistis*) is listed as a discrete *charisma*, while in Rom 12:6 it is associated obliquely with prophecy.

As Paul works through his list of gifts, he appends a short tagline to each gift. Although the tagline for prophecy seems to differ from the others, in general each tagline appears to indicate the sign or "grace" by which the associated gift becomes evident. For example, the person gifted as a teacher will be observed teaching, and the leader will be identified by his or her devotion to the work at hand.

However, not every Bible expositor has understood these verses in this way. Calvin taught that these taglines indicated boundary markers which limited those gifted with one gift from straying into the arena of another gift. As he puts it: "Every member of the church who shall keep his attention fixed on this [gift] as the mark to be aimed at, will confine himself within his own proper limits."[3] He also warns: "Since particular gifts are determined by their own boundaries, the mere declining from such fixed limits contributes to their corruption."[4]

His translation of vss. 6-8, reads as follows:

> Having then gifts differing according to the grace that is given to us, whether prophecy, let us prophesy according to the proportion of faith; Or ministry, let us wait on our ministering; or he that teacheth, on teaching; Or he that exhorteth, on exhortation; he that giveth, let him do it with simplicity; he that ruleth, with diligence; he that showeth mercy, with cheerfulness.[5]

It is important to note that in the translation above, the exhortation "let us prophesy . . ."—placed in the tagline appended to "prophecy"—and the exhortation "let us wait on . . ."—placed in the tagline appended to "ministry," but which also governs the grammatical construction of all the

---

3. Calvin, *Commentary on Romans*, ad loc. 12:4-8.
4. Calvin, *Commentary on Romans*, ad loc. 12:4-8.
5. Calvin, *Commentary on Romans*, ad loc. 12:4-8.

remaining taglines—do not occur in the Greek text. Nevertheless, Calvin's expansive translation which adds "let us prophesy" to "according to the proportion of faith" seems plausible. However, his expansion "let us wait on," by which I understand him to mean, "let us concentrate our attention on," is an unjustified imposition upon the text, seemingly drawn from thin air. Still, learning how Calvin translates these verses helps the reader of his commentary to understand why Calvin is so insistent on the importance of not straying from one's area of gifting.

Vs. 6: Despite my translation suggesting that this verse begins a new sentence, in the Greek it does not. Greek tolerates run-on sentences that are not acceptable in contemporary English, so I have split a long complex sentence in two. The "we" in this sentence refers to the same people as the "we many" of vs. 5.

I have translated *charismata*, the plural of *charisma*, as "spiritual gifts" since that is customary based on the word's close association with the Holy Spirit in 1 Corinthians 12. However, here it might be more appropriate to translate this word "gracious gifts," since it is built on the foundation of the word "grace" (*charis*). This is especially the case in this verse since these gifts are possessed due to "the grace [*charis*] given to us." In Paul's usage here, the words *charis* and *charisma* are essentially synonyms. If there is a difference, it is that *charis* focuses on the gracious act of giving while *charisma* focuses more on the gift given. Furthermore, these gifts differ from one another. They are all given graciously, but this does not mean that everyone receives the same gift. Also, it is implied that it is God who gives these gracious gifts. In other words, the passive verb "given" is a "divine passive" with God implied to be the active agent.

As previously mentioned, seven *charismata* are listed. Each of the first four is introduced by the word *eite*, which often means approximately what "or" does in English. I have translated the first occurrence of *eite* as "whether" and the other three occurrences as "or." *Eite* can also mean "next," and it would be possible to translate vss. 6–8 as, "first prophecy . . . next service . . . next the teacher . . . etc." Apparently, to avoid sounding overly repetitious, Paul dispenses with using *eite* when listing the last three *charismata*.

The most intriguing *charisma* Paul discusses is "prophecy," the first in his list. It is intriguing largely because of the enigmatic comment he makes about it. For each of the other *charismata* a short tagline is appended, apparently describing the evidence showing a person possesses this gift: "service by [his or her] serving; or the teacher by [his or her] teaching; or the exhorter by exhorting; the giver by [his or her] sincerity; the leader by [his or her] devotion; the merciful by [his or her] cheerfulness." Does the same pattern hold for Paul's tagline about prophecy? Apparently not.

This tagline is "according to the analogy of [the] faith," or perhaps "according to the proportion of [one's] faith." Especially since the beginning of the Protestant Reformation considerable ink has been spilled over the meaning of this phrase.

Luther and Calvin had distinctive perspectives on what "according to the proportion of" might mean. Luther thought Paul's point was that prophecy should be given based on faith, as opposed to reason or conjecture. Prophecy was not merely prognostication based on human devices.[6] Calvin thought prophecy originally referred to foretelling, but that with the close of the apostolic age and the completion of the New Testament canon, such foretelling was no longer needed. He believed prophecy had acquired by his own day "an extended sense" of referring to the interpretation of scripture.[7] He reached this conclusion by equating "the faith" of the phrase "the analogy of [the] faith" with the truth acquired through the interpretation of scripture. While these are interesting observations, it is unlikely either captures Paul's point. *For further reflection on the interpretations of Luther and Calvin, see the excursus titled "Rom 12:6 and 'The Analogy of Faith.'"*

But what did Paul mean by "according to the analogy of [the] faith" or "according to the proportion of [one's] faith"? Implicit within this question are two cruxes: 1) What is the meaning of *analogia*? and 2) What is the meaning of *pistis* ("faith")?

The Greek word *analogia* has two basic meanings. It can mean "proportion," or it can mean "analogy." An analogy is a literary device that compares two seemingly unrelated things based on some apparent point of similarity. For instance, in Rom 9:19–24 Paul draws an analogy between God, the shaper of humanity, and a potter, who shapes clay. His point is that what is shaped has no practical or moral say in how it is shaped; the prerogative lies entirely with God and the potter, both of whom are "shapers."

So, what does *analogia* mean in this context? On the one hand, if the context were a treatise on mathematics, it would certainly mean "proportion" or "ratio." But even in more general contexts it can also mean "proportion." And on the other hand, if the context were an analysis of a piece of literature, *analogia* would very likely mean "analogy." But even in more general contexts it can be used to point out how one thing is like another thing. Since Romans is neither a treatise on mathematics nor a piece of literary criticism but is more general in nature, both options remain possibilities.

The Greek word *pistis* has several possible meanings. In this context three rather conventional possibilities immediately come to mind. First, it

---

6. Starling, "Analogy of Faith," 9–10.
7. Calvin, *Commentary on Romans*, ad loc. 12:6.

can mean "faithfulness." Second, it can mean faith as the object of what is believed. The Latin expression for this is *fides quae creditor* ("the faith that is believed," i.e., "the Faith"). Third, it can mean the subjective activity of believing. The Latin expression for this is *fides qua creditor* ("the faith by which it is believed"). So, to this point three possible meanings have been offered: "faithfulness" (the first option), faith as an object of belief (the second option), or the subjective act of believing (the third option)?

But I think two additional possibilities should also be considered, even though they are less frequently discussed. *Pistis* might mean not the object or proposition that is believed, or the act of believing, but rather the *basis* for believing a proposition. In this case it would mean something very similar to "evidence," and brings to mind the explanation of *pistis* offered in Heb 11:1" "the substance things being hoped for, the evidence of actions not seen." This would be a fourth option.

One more additional possibility is that *pistis* might mean "the ability to believe." It is not exactly the act of believing, although it is similar. Instead, it is a capacity for belief. This would be a fifth option.

One hint about the meaning of *pistis* in vs. 6 is the use of this word in vs. 3. There Paul says it is distributed by God. Also, by using the phrase "measure of faith," he suggests that having or not having faith is unlike a light switch, either fully on or fully off. People receive a certain amount of faith from God. The amount is more than none and less than all. This "measure of faith" is unlike the expression "all faith" (*pasan tēn pistin*) Paul uses, perhaps somewhat facetiously, in 1 Cor 13:2. Paul's willingness to quantify faith, even vaguely, suggests that in this verse *analogia* means something like "proportion."

But how do "prophecy" and "faith" relate? Although he was not completely consistent in this regard, Calvin generally presented faith in this verse as meaning "the Faith" (the second option above).[8] No doubt part of the reason for this is that in this verse Paul uses the definite article with *pistis*, and therefore "the Faith" is a possible translation. However, the definite article is often used with abstract nouns such as *pistis*, and Paul quite frequently uses the definite article with *pistis* even when it manifestly does not refer to "the Faith" (e.g., Rom 4:9: "For we say, 'To Abraham, his faith was reckoned as right standing.'"

But Calvin leveraged the idea of "the Faith" even further. He understood the boundaries of "the Faith" to be defined by scripture and therefore he believed "prophecy" in this verse meant simply the interpretation and

---

8. Starling, "Analogy of Faith," 10.

exposition of scripture.[9] In his view, the gist of the verse was that prophecy must accord with the teaching of scripture, including New Testament scripture (which was only in the process of being written). There are several significant problems with Calvin's interpretation. *For a more detailed discussion of this, see the excursus "Rom 12:6 and 'The Analogy of Faith.'"*

Not only is "the Faith," that is, faith as the object of what is believed not the best option for *pistis* in this context; it is an option we can safely exclude. One does not speak of degrees, proportions, or ratios of "the Faith." Similarly, it likely does not mean "the basis of faith," i.e., evidence leading to faith (the fourth option above). One does not speak of degrees or proportions of evidence.

In this context it is also unlikely that *pistis* means "faithfulness" (the first option above). While Paul might suggest that prophecy should be entrusted to those who have proven themselves to be faithful, in vs. 3 Paul has just spoken of God's distribution of "a measure of faith." Faithfulness is something demonstrated by one's conduct rather than a blessing that is received.

This leaves two candidates for the meaning of *pistis*, and they are very similar to each other. Either subjective faith, the act of believing (the third option above) is correct, or one's capacity for belief (the fifth option above) is correct.

Paul implies that prophecy requires a degree of faith. If a person begins to prophesy, this requires faith that God will fill her mouth with the proper message. Thus, prophecy will come in proportion to a person's trust in God (as an action) or in proportion to a person's capacity to exercise such belief. However, again we face the challenge that the *pistis* of which Paul writes in vs. 3 seems to be distributed to the individual by God. 1 Cor 12:9 lists "faith" (*pistis*) as a distinct gift of the Spirit, so in some sense it can be given. Based on such evidence, it is more likely that what is given is "a capacity for faith" than the specific act of exercising faith.

Thus, Paul's point is that some are given the gracious gift of prophecy, but that this gift functions in proportion to the capacity to exercise faith God also gives these individuals. Those with a greater capacity for faith will prophesy more fully or perhaps more often. Those with a lesser capacity for faith will prophesy less fully or less often.

For Paul prophecy is an extemporaneous utterance inspired by the Spirit; it is not simply the interpretation of scripture. As a safeguard, the content of prophecy must be judged (1 Cor 14:29). Paul does not specify whether prophecy involves foretelling (describing future events) or

---

9. Starling, "Analogy of Faith." 5–7, 10.

forthtelling (declaring God's perspective on something) or both. If this prophecy resembles Old Testament prophecy, it will be predominantly forthtelling, but New Testament examples (Acts 11:28; 21:10–11) suggest that it might sometimes also include foretelling. Furthermore, it might also involve knowledge of things that would not be known in the natural, even if they do not pertain to the future. In 1 Corinthians 12 and 14 the boundaries between "prophecy" on the one hand, and "the word of knowledge," "the word of wisdom," and "a revelation" are not clear. Perhaps it is unnecessary to make rigid distinctions between these gifts.

Vs. 8: The word I have translated "exhorter" is a participial form of the verb meaning "to call," "to beseech," or "to comfort" (*parakaleō*). A noun related to this verb, *paraklētos*, is used in both John's Gospel and in 1 John to refer to the Holy Spirit. This noun is variously translated as "comforter," "counselor," or "advocate."

While in this context the participle could conceivably refer to "the one comforting," in the other passages in Romans where *parakaleō* occurs, it means "to appeal to" or "to urge." Thus, here it more likely refers to the person who urges people to embrace the Christian faith or to live it more fully. Long ago, when I first received ministerial credentials (from the South Texas District of the Assemblies of God), I was credentialed as "an exhorter." No doubt this classification was derived from this verse.

It is difficult to decide whether "the giver" is characterized by his "sincerity," his "simplicity," or his "generosity." The noun *haplotēs* is related to, and probably derived from, the adjective *haploos*, which means "singleness" and is often contrasted with *diploos*, "twofold." Paul may be stressing that the giver expresses single-mindedness by living out his or her values with deeds, or he may be stressing that gifts should be given not in a manipulative or self-aggrandizing way, but rather with a focus of the need being met.

"The leader" is characterized by his or her *spoudē*, which I have somewhat tentatively translated as "devotion." The word can also mean "haste," "effort," "zeal," or "esteem." If this word refers to "esteem," it is the esteem in which others hold the leader. In contrast, the other possible meanings would describe something about the leader himself or herself. A problem with translating this word as "zeal" is that it could be confusing. Elsewhere in Romans Paul uses the word *zēlos*, which traditionally has been translated "zeal." *Spoudē* also appears in vs. 11, so consult that vs. for additional comments.

Vss. 9–19: From the beginning of vs. 9 through the midpoint of vs. 19, which is to say ten-and-a-half verses, finite verbs are found only in vs. 14. The many clauses of the other verses contain participles and infinitives. This sort of verbless Greek is common in classical writers such as Herodotus and Thucydides, but in general it is less common in writers of Hellenistic (*Koinē*) Greek. It is also unusual but not unparalleled in Paul's writings. For example, Eph 1:15-23 contains only four finite verbs, one of which is in a quotation.

To translate these verses into acceptable English, these participles and infinitives must be converted into finite verbs. The question is whether they should be construed as indicatives or imperatives (command forms). Since the finite verbs in vs. 14 are imperatives, I have chosen to render this mass of participles and infinitives as imperatives as well. The result is a collection of many short, somewhat choppy, sentences.

It is widely understood that in Greek participles associated with imperatives often bear imperatival force. A famous illustration of this is the Great Commission, found in Matthew 28:19-20. Literally it reads: "Therefore, as you are going, make disciples of all nations, baptizing them into the name of the Father and the Son and the Holy Spirit, teaching them to keep everything as I have commanded you." Only one verb in these verses is an imperative: "make disciples." Nevertheless, many English versions translate this material with between two and four English imperatives. A translation with four imperatives would read: "Therefore, go, make disciples of all nations. Baptize them into the name of the Father and the Son and the Holy Spirit. Teach them to keep everything as I have commanded you."

If the participles and infinitives of Rom 12:9-12 were translated with English indicatives, this passage would read:

> Love is genuine. You who abhor evil, who are attached to good, who are affectionate with each other in a brotherly way, who prefer each other in honor, who are not slow to express devotion, are boiling with the Spirit, serving the Lord as a slave, rejoicing in hope, enduring in difficulty, persevering in prayer....

Paul's point in these verses seems self-evident. It is to encourage proper ethical behavior. However, it may also be to set an ethical foundation before discussing the difficult issue that will be raised at the beginning of chapter 13 of how as Christian believers to view the pagan governments of the city of Rome and the Roman Empire. One might also hear echoes of the Beatitudes of Jesus (Matt 5:3-12) in these verses.

Vs. 9: The word translated "genuine" (*anypokritos*) literally means "unhypocritical." This statement about love may be considered a generalization of the numerous exhortations that follows.

Vs. 10: In his book *The Four Loves*, C.S. Lewis described four Greek words that conveyed different aspects of love: affection or family love (*storgē*); friendship (*philia*); romance (*eros*); and charity (*agape*). Of these, only *storgē* does not appear in the New Testament, and in the LXX it only appears in the books of the Maccabees.[10] However, surprisingly this verse contains a variant form of *storgē* (*storgos*) in a compound formed with *philia*. The resulting combination (*philostorgos*) must mean something like "brotherly affection," indicating friendship that borders on a family relationship.

Vs. 11: In Greek the admonition "Do not be slow to express devotion" is a play on words. The adjective *okneros* means "slow" or "hesitant." In contrast, the noun *spoudē*, which already appeared in vs. 8, has a variety of possible meanings, one of which is "haste." While both here and in vs. 8 *spoudē* probably means something like "devotion," to an ear trained in Greek the idea of "haste" or "speed" would nevertheless lurk in the background. While the formulation "Do not be slow to make haste" results in nonsense, its echo gives Paul's admonition to exhibit "devotion" a lively turn.

The Greek word for "spirit" or "Spirit" is *pneuma*, which can also mean "wind," and in scripture the unpredictability, movement and power of the wind sometimes is used to describe the Spirit (e.g., "the wind blows where it wishes" of John 3:8 and "the rushing mighty wind" of Acts 2:2). But it is also striking how often liquid images are used in the New Testament to describe the Spirit and the Spirit's work. The Spirit is "poured out" (Acts 2:17, 18, 33). People are "baptized in" or "baptized by" the Spirit (e.g., Acts 1:5; 1 Cor 12:13) or they are "filled with" (e.g., Luke 1:15; Acts 2:4; 4:8; 13:9) or "full of" the Spirit (e.g., Luke 4:1; Acts 6:3, 5, 8). People are "made to drink" of the Spirit (1 Cor 12:13). This verse provides an image that combines both the liquid and gaseous pictures of the Spirit. Paul charges his readers to "boil [*zeō*] with the Spirit." His point is that an energetic presence of the Spirit should be visible in one's life.

Vs. 13: The verb translated "share" is *koinōneō*, which is related to the noun *koinōnia* ("fellowship" or "communion"). The *koin–* part of these words focuses on "commonality." While the degree of sharing in the earliest Christian communities varied from "[having] all things in common" (Acts 2:44) to "bear[ing] one another's burdens" (Gal 6:2), the fact that people were in communion with each other implied the obligation to care for one another. Within the community of saints no one was to starve, lack shelter,

---

10. That the New Testament does not mention *storgē* does not discredit it as irrelevant or a sham. In fact, Lewis calls it "the humblest and most widely diffused of loves." He even muses that animals might be capable of such love, and because of its wide distribution, Lewis honors "affection" by considering it before the other loves. Lewis, *Four Loves*, 41.

or suffer sickness alone. Care for those within the community took priority over the needs of those outside the community.

Vss. 14–15: Vs. 14 echoes the teaching of Jesus later recorded in Matt 5:11. While the words are not the same, the last half of vs. 15 also echoes the sentiment of Matt 5:4.

Vs. 16: This verse is made up of three sentences. The key to the meaning of the first sentence is the phrase *eis allēlous*. The reciprocal pronoun *allēlōn* means "each other," and *allēlous* is its accusative (plural) form.[11] The preposition *eis* often expresses purpose, but here a "local" use makes the most sense.[12] What I have translated "have a consistent attitude" literally reads "thinking the same thing." Paul's point is to project the same attitude and ideas no matter who is present. The RSV translates this first sentence "Live in harmony with one another," but Paul's point is not to avoid conflict but rather to avoid being double-minded or two-faced.

The same point is reinforced and extended in the verse's second sentence. The Roman Empire was very class conscious, and the danger was that some would gravitate toward those capable of discussing matters of importance to the higher classes (*ta hypsēla*, "the high things"), while ignoring those of a humbler station (*tois tapeinois*, "the humble people"). The participle of *synapagō* is functionally equivalent to *symperipheromai*, which means "to associate with."[13] Not only does Paul not want anyone to be two-faced, he wants everyone to be included and to feel included.

The third sentence of this verse contains an idiom which Paul has previously used in Rom 11:25. For more detail about this idiom, see the comments to that verse.

Vs. 17: The phrase "evil for evil" translates *kakon anti kakou*, which also appears in 1 Thess 5:15 and 1 Pet 3:9. In each case it appears in conjunction with a form of the verb *apodidōmi* ("to repay"). The inverse of this expression, "evil for good," appears several times in the LXX, where it regularly translates the Hebrew expression *ra'ah tachat tovah* ("evil in place of good"; e.g., Ps 38:21 [LXX 37:21]; 109:5 [LXX 108:5]; Prov 17:13; Jer 18:20).

The verb "presume" translates *pronoeō*, which literally means "to think beforehand." The improper preposition—an adjective used as a preposition—*enōpion*, literally means "facing," but can mean "before" or "in the

---

11. The lexical form of this pronoun is the genitive plural since this word never occurs in either nominative or singular forms.

12. For the ("local") meaning "in the presence of," see Smyth, *Greek Grammar* §1686 a.

13. On this equivalency, see Liddell-Scott, *Greek-English Lexicon*, s.v. "synapagō."

presence of . . . ." Paul's point is that when dealing with everyone, absent evidence to the contrary, believers should be gracious and not suspicious.

Vs. 19: The participle *ekdikountes* (literally "avenging") should be translated as an imperative coordinated with the imperative form of the main verb that follows. The expression "leave room for" is intended as a more common rendering of what is literally stated: "give a place for." This place is to be reserved for "wrath"—clearly meaning the wrath of God. A parallel construction is found in Eph. 4:27. Using a negative formulation, this verse reads: "Give no place to the devil."

The quotation is probably a paraphrase of Deut. 32:35 (LXX), which reads: "in the day of vengeance I will repay." However, several OT passages contain similar material, and R. H. Charles suggested Paul paraphrases *The Testament of Gad* 6.7. This text reads: "But even if he [your enemy] is devoid of shame and persists in his wickedness, forgive him from the heart and leave vengeance to God [*kai dos tō theō tēn ekdikēsin*]."[14]

While those following Christ should seek justice, God has established spheres of authority, and the boundaries of those spheres should not be crossed. It is not the believer's role to punish others for the sins they have committed.

But if this is so, then how can church discipline be administered? The answer is simple. It is not the prerogative for individual believers to punish. But when a church exercises discipline, this is not an individual action. In fact, to preserve the sanctity of the body, the church's discipline is performed as an agent of God.[15]

Vs. 20: The quotation is from Prov 25:21–22. It is almost identical to the text of the LXX.

Despite Paul's meticulous quotation of Proverbs, this verse contains something of a puzzle. It appears to contain an idiom—an expression that means something other than what its words literally say—and this idiom is unknown in Greek literature.

Furthermore, the wording of this idiom differs in the MT from the LXX text Paul quotes. In the MT of vs. 22, the idiom reads "for you snatch coals/sparks [from] on his head." This seems to depict what would seem without question to be a good deed. Sparks have flown and landed on someone's

---

14. The translation is that of James H. Charlesworth, *Old Testament Pseudepigrapha*, 1:816. The Greek text is from R. H. Charles, *Greek Versions of the Testaments of the Twelve Patriarchs*, 168.

15. I would like to thank Timothy Dresselhaus for pushing me to discuss how this passage relates to church discipline.

head, and apparently that someone is an enemy. Despite his enemy status, "you" choose to brush those sparks off his head.

In the LXX the text reads differently. A clause is prefixed to the idiom, and the meaning of the idiom's verb diverges considerably: "For doing this [good thing], you will heap coals of fire on his head." It is not nearly so obvious that heaping burning coals on someone's head is helpful to that person. In fact, I once heard a sermon on this passage in which the preacher suggested that doing something kind is often the best way to get back at an enemy. He argued that heaping burning coals on someone's head was a figure of speech meaning to get back at, or to punish, one's enemy. Doing good deeds can embarrass and humiliate those who do not deserve them, and supposedly Paul's point was that embarrassing one's enemies in this way is a clever response. This preacher seemed unfazed that only three verses earlier Paul had charged his readers, "Repay no one evil for evil."

Fortunately, few sermons are so misguided. On the theory that the context calls for a good deed rather than retribution, some interpreters have suggested that despite first appearances piling coals on an enemy's head was in reality a service to him. Carrying coals in a basket on one's head was a customary way transporting fire from one location to another, and getting assistance with loading those coals was a great help. Personally, I find this analysis somewhat farfetched.

Others have argued that "to heap coals of fire on a person's head" is an idiom meaning "to provoke remorse" or perhaps "to get the person's attention." While such a suggestion might explain the Greek version of this verse, it does not account for the nearly opposite meaning of the Hebrew version.

While no conclusive solution to this puzzle is available, I would like to offer what I consider a plausible conjecture to explain the evidence we find. First, I believe the MT preserves the original wording of the expression. Snatching burning sparks from an enemy's head is a good deed like the two examples that precede it: feeding one's enemy when he is hungry; and giving one's enemy water to drink when he is thirsty. However, this third good deed comes with an additional blessing. If you snatch the sparks away, "the Lord will pay you" for this service to your enemy.

Next, unfortunately, the Hebrew undergirding this portion of Proverbs was corrupted by a copyist's mistake. In some manuscript the participle *choteh* (from the verb *chatah*, "to snatch") was misread or miswritten as the participle *chopeh* (from *chapah*, "to cover"). A single letter was changed. The resulting form would have been somewhat plausible since the verb *chapah* usually refers to covering one's head or face (e.g., 2 Sam 15:30; Jer 14:3; 14:4; Esth 7:8). Then, when some unknown sage translated this Hebrew text into the LXX version of Proverbs, he used the Greek verb *sōreuō* ("to heap") to translate the Hebrew participle *chopeh*. While this choice did not suite the context perfectly, it reflected what he saw in his Hebrew manuscript.

Subsequently, when Jews read Proverbs 25 in Greek, they noticed that the context required a good deed to be performed for one's enemy. This meant that heaping burning coals on someone's head must indicate some positive action. Since this made little sense when interpreted literally, they understood the expression to be an idiom—inexplicable on its face, but meaningful nonetheless—and in this way an idiom was accidentally born. Furthermore, this is how Paul understood this peculiar expression, as an idiom meaning to assist one's enemy in some way. The precise nuance Paul intended is unclear. Maybe he understood the idiom to mean "to provoke remorse." Maybe he understood it to mean "to get the person's attention." Maybe he meant something else. About this and so many things, "now we see through a glass darkly" (1 Cor 13:12, KJV) and with this we must remain content for the time being.

Vs. 21: The phrase *hypo tou kakou* in this verse is usually translated "by evil," understanding *tou kakou* to designate an abstract noun ("evil"), much as *to kakon* ("evil") does at the end of the verse. However, there is a grammatical problem with such a translation. When *hypo* is used with the genitive, as is the case here, it expresses "agency" and requires a personal agent, not an impersonal instrument. For this reason, it is better to translate "by the Evil One" rather than "by evil."

While it is possible Paul has composed this verse unprompted by any earlier writing, it is also possible he has been influenced by *The Testament of Benjamin* 4.3. This text reads: "If they [sinners] should not take counsel for good concerning him [the good man], by doing good he may conquer evil. Being watched by God, he may love those wronging [him] as he loves his own life."[16] For both Paul and the author of *The Testament of Benjamin*, overcoming evil does not mean exacting retribution but rather standing firm for goodness in the face of wicked attacks, even at the cost of one's life.

---

16. For the Greek text, consult Charles, *Greek Versions of the Testaments of the Twelve Patriarchs*, 219. The translation is my own.

Excursus: Rom 12:6 and "The Analogy of Faith"

THE CONNECTION WITH ROMANS

An expression frequently invoked in Protestant hermeneutics is "the analogy of faith," often written in its Latin form *analogia fidei*. When asked what this expression means, one of two answers in usually given, or sometimes both. The first explanation is that it means "scripture interprets scripture." The second explanation is slightly more detailed. It is that the expression means "clearer passages of scripture should be used to explain obscurer passages." These explanations tend to confuse inquirers since to most of them there is no evident connection between the phrase "the analogy of faith" and either explanation.

While the connection between the phrase and its supposed explanations is hardly self-evident, there is a connection, at least historically. "The analogy of faith" is one way of translating a Greek phrase found in Rom 12:6: *tēn analogian tēs pisteōs*. John Calvin believed Paul intended this phrase to teach a hermeneutical principle mandated by Paul, and he stated this explicitly: it is a principle "to which Paul requires all interpretation of Scripture to conform."[17] Earlier Martin Luther had suggested a similar idea, but he was less clear and less emphatic about the matter. While discussion of the principle of "the analogy of faith" began with the exegesis of a biblical phrase, soon this discussion took on a life of its own and became separated from the exegesis of Rom 12:6. Despite being severed from its biblical root, discussion of this principle has continued under the name derived from Romans.

This excursus is not about what Paul meant by *tēn analogian tēs pisteōs*. For that, the commentary discussion of Rom 12:6 should be consulted. This excursus will instead provide an overview of how a theological principle emerged from the text of Romans, and how it became a commonplace in Protestant thought. The focus will be on Martin Luther and John Calvin, and when "the Reformers" are referenced, this term will primarily refer to them.[18]

In Romans 12 Paul mentions "the analogy of faith" as he briefly discusses "prophecy." This discussion occurs within a larger lesson about how differing gracious gifts (*charismata*) are situated in the one body of Christ. In Rom 12:6–8 seven gifts are listed, the first of which is prophecy

---

17. Calvin, *Institutes*, 4.17.32.

18. The general shape of this excursus is greatly indebted to David Starling's very helpful article titled "The Analogy of Faith in the Theology of Luther and Calvin."

(*propheteia*). To each of the gifts mentioned, Paul adds a tagline. For the other gifts these taglines describe how people might recognize each gift in action. But to "prophecy" the apostle appends a more cryptic tagline: "according to the analogy of the faith," or perhaps "according to the proportion of [one's] faith."

THE REFORMATION CONTEXT

The great issue raised by the Reformers was the matter of authority. Roman Catholicism claimed an unbroken succession of Catholic bishops going back to a first generation of bishops who had been ordained by the apostles. These first bishops then ordained the next generation of bishops, who ordained the third generation, and so on. Through this succession of bishops, the church exercised its teaching office (*magisterium*) and thereby determined what was proper doctrine. The most important reformers, all of whom besides Luther had been trained as Renaissance humanists, found this claim to be problematic. Trained in the study of ancient documents, they quickly became aware that the teaching of the New Testament differed profoundly from what was taught by the contemporary church.

As Jackson Spielvogel explains, the European intellectuals of the mid-fourteenth to the mid-sixteenth century called their age an "age of rebirth."[19] By this they meant a rebirth of civilization, seeing the classical civilizations of ancient Greece and Rome as the foundation on which to build anew. This implied that the intervening period extending from the fall of Rome up until the beginning of this rebirth had been inferior, marked by civilizational decline, and in need of a Renaissance (which means "rebirth"). As the Renaissance began in Italy, it was the Italian scholar Francesco Petrarch who in the 1330s first described this intervening period as "dark" in comparison with the earlier "light" period of ancient civilization. From this image, the now standard expression "Dark Ages" emerged when in 1602 the Italian Caesar Baronius first used the Latin expression *saeculum obsurum* ("dark age") to refer to this retrograde period.[20]

The first person to apply to the writing of history this tripartite model of antiquity, followed by a dark intermediate period, and culminating in a modern rebirth of civilization was Lorenzo Bruni, whose *History of the Florentine People* was compiled between 1415 and 1444. Bruni believed the

---

19. Spielvogel, *Western Civilization*, 332.
20. Baronius, *Annales Ecclesiastici* 10.647.

golden age of antiquity ended when Rome fell, and the succeeding the dark period ended when the Italian city-states were able to overthrow the shackles of the largely Germanic Holy Roman Empire. While modern historians date the transition from the Middle Ages to modernity somewhat later than Bruni, his tripartite division of history has largely been embraced.

In a very real sense, the Reformation was a logical extension of this Renaissance view of history into the religious sphere. If secular history had a golden age, so did the church. The church's golden age was when it was led by the apostles (i.e., in the first century) and during which it received "the faith once for all delivered to the saints" (Jude 3). In the minds of some early Protestants, this golden age also included the next four centuries. During this period apostolic teaching still gleamed brightly as the truths implicit in the faith were elaborated by the creeds of the first four ecumenical councils. Not coincidentally, this theological golden age ended at roughly the same time as the Roman Empire "fell."

Just as the golden age of Greek and Roman civilization was followed by a dark age of civilizational decline, the golden age of the church was followed by a religious dark age, which continued for roughly a millennium. In the same manner as the glories of ancient Rome had highlighted the benighted state of contemporary civilization, to the Reformers the winsomeness and power of the early church highlighted the corruption and fecklessness of the medieval church. By comparing the teaching of the apostles as recorded in the New Testament with the teaching of the contemporary (Catholic) church, it became clear that the continuous line of bishops that the Catholic church so prized had failed to preserve with purity the faith the apostles had taught. This calamitous discovery called for a different test by which congregations could rightly claim to be "apostolic." Rather than relying on a continuous line of teachers supposedly to assure conformity with apostolic teaching, the Reformers insisted that what the church taught should always be tested against the writings of the apostles, i.e., the New Testament. Any church teaching the same doctrine as the apostles could rightly claim to be apostolic.

AN ANCHOR FOR PROPER INTERPRETATION

Unsurprisingly, the Catholic bishops rejected the Reformers' dismissal of the twin doctrines of apostolic succession and the church's *magisterium* because this amounted to a rejection their authority. They argued that their dispute with the Reformers was not over the authority of scripture, which they also embraced; it was over the *interpretation* of scripture. Without an objective authority—namely, the teaching authority (*magisterium*) they exercised—to judge between competing interpretations, the scriptures by themselves were unable to provide sure guidance.

Calvin was certainly aware of this critique. He noted: "Indeed, our adversaries cry out that we falsely make the Word of God our pretext, and wickedly corrupt it."[21] In the face of this challenge, it became important for the Reformers to identify a hermeneutical principle that would validate their interpretation of scripture as being correct and a solid foundation for their theological assertions. Calvin claimed to find this principle in "the analogy of faith." He states: "When Paul wished all prophecy to be made to accord with the analogy of faith, he set forth a very clear rule to test all interpretation of Scripture. Now, if this interpretation be measured by this rule of faith, victory is in our hand."[22]

Indeed, the Catholic position pushed the hermeneutical challenge too far. While no book interprets itself, it was wrong to assert that scripture is meaningless apart from the *magisterium* of the church. Many passages are exceedingly clear when given a fair reading, even if some other passages are not so clear. In the face of the difficulty raised by obscure passages of scripture, the Reformers found it expedient to start with what was clear and use the guidance gathered from this exegesis to elucidate what was less clear. This principle of moving from passages of greater clarity to those of lesser clarity was based on the belief that all scripture was inspired by God and therefore taught a consistent message. This is where "faith," or more precisely "the Faith" as a unified body of truth, comes in. The Reformers believed the clearest parts of the apostolic teaching recorded in the New Testament was a surer guide than a discredited *magisterium* that clearly had failed to preserve in the church the teaching of the apostles.

The Reformers' line of reasoning makes sense, but is it Paul's point in Rom 12:6? Calvin seems overeager to find a hermeneutical anchor in scripture itself, and consequently he overinterprets his text. Regarding the quotations listed above, notice the ease with which Calvin transforms "the analogy of faith" into "the rule of faith." Notice too that "prophecy" is transformed into "interpretation." This is because Calvin understood prophecy in his day to be limited to the interpretation of scripture. In another place, Calvin explains his understanding of prophecy more fully:

---

21. Calvin, *Institutes*, "Prefatory Address to King Francis," section 2.
22. Calvin, *Institutes*, "Prefatory Address to King Francis," section 2.

> But I prefer the opinion of those commentators, who take the word ["prophecy"] in a more extended sense, and apply it to the particular gift of explaining revelation according as anyone executes with skill and dexterity the office of an interpreter in declaring the will of God. Prophecy, therefore, at this period, is nothing else in the Christian church than the proper understanding of Scripture, and a peculiar faculty of explaining the same, since all the ancient prophecies, and all the oracles of God, were contained in Christ and his gospel.[23]

While Calvin limits "prophecy" in his own day to the interpretation of scripture, he also recognizes that it functioned differently "in the church at its commencement." It designated "the power of prediction," and Calvin grudgingly acknowledges that in his day some continue to understand the word in that sense.[24] However, he believes that all the ancient prophecies and oracles have been fulfilled in Christ, no doubt based in part on his flawed exegesis of 2 Cor 1:20, which suggested that all Old Testament prophecies had been fulfilled in Christ, and consequently in this age of fulfillment no more prophecies are needed. Therefore, if prophecy is to have any continuing relevance to the church, he judges that this will have to be through "a more extended sense," namely the interpretation of God's will, which is the interpretation of scripture.

While Calvinists often accuse Pentecostals of deriving their theology from experience rather than scripture, here Calvin is guilty of that error. He sees no miraculous or oral gifts at work in the church of his day, so he concludes from this that it was God's will for such gifts to end at the close of the apostolic age. Nothing in scripture suggests that these gifts will cease before Christ's second coming, but here Calvin's interpretation of scripture is bound by his own experience.

It is somewhat surprising that Calvin is willing to grant prophecy this "more extended sense" since in general he is anxious about people straying beyond the boundaries of their giftedness. Calvin seems to conclude that if no new revelation is forthcoming then the interpretation of previously delivered revelation must fill that void.

Calvin does not seem to consider prophecy to be "forthtelling," despite the demonstrable fact that so much of Old Testament prophecy was

---

23. Calvin, *Commentary on Romans*, ad loc. 12:6.
24. Calvin, *Commentary on Romans*, ad loc. 12:6.

precisely that. Likely, he is reluctant to explain prophecy this way because one of the other gifts Paul lists is "the exhorter," whose role was forthtelling.

Calvin was more inclined than Luther to use the analogy of faith as a tool to fashion—Calvin would probably say "to discern"—a logically consistent body of doctrine. For this reason, sixteenth-century Lutherans sometimes accused Calvinists of excessive rationalism. David Starling offers vivid examples of the divergent ways the analogy of faith was used by Luther and Calvin. At the Marburg Colloquy (1529), Huldrych Zwingli repeatedly protested the "absurdity" of the Lutheran position on the Lord's Supper.[25] Luther held that Christ's body was ubiquitous, i.e., able to be in many places at the same time, so it could simultaneously be physically present whenever and wherever communion was celebrated. As Starling explains:

> Luther replies with 'the analogy of faith . . . according to the definition of faith in Hebrews 11:1.' His appeal is not here to 'the Faith', but to the believing faith of Hebrews 11:1, the faith that 'looks upon the body [of Christ] as present [in the sacrament] and upon the body which is in heaven.' It is (as in his Romans commentary) essentially an argument against rationalism: 'I am not concerned about what is contrary to nature but only about what is contrary to faith.'[26]

Thirty years after the Marburg Colloquy, Calvin resumed this controversy with the Lutherans. He took the place of the late Huldrych Zwingli, with Joachim Westphal taking the place of the late Martin Luther. Excerpts of this discussion are recorded in the Institutes.[27]

Calvin considered the Lutheran charge that he and his followers were mere rationalists to be slanderous. He writes:

> . . . [the Lutherans] boast that we are so bound to human reason that we attribute no more to the power of God than the order of nature allows and common sense dictates. From such wicked slanders I appeal to the very doctrine I have taught, which shows clearly enough that I do not at all measure this

---

25. Starling, *Analogy of Faith*, 12. Starling cites Luther's comments from the Marburg Colloquy, *LW*, 38.57–59.

26. Starling, *Analogy of Faith*, 12. Starling cites Luther's comments from the Marburg Colloquy, *LW*, 38.57–59.

27. Calvin's *Institutes* 4.17.20–34 contains extensive material gathered from Westphal's writings and from the dialogue between Westphal and Calvin. See also Starling, *Analogy of Faith*, 12 n.30.

mystery with the measure of human reason, or subject it to the laws of nature.[28]

Furthermore, he issues this rejoinder based on the analogy of faith:

> ... I reject their teaching of the mixture, or transfusion, of Christ's flesh with our soul. For it is enough for us that, from the substance of his flesh Christ breathes life into our souls—indeed, pours forth his very life into us—even though Christ's flesh itself does not enter into us. Besides, there is no doubt that the analogy of faith, to which Paul requires all interpretation of Scripture to conform [Rom 12:3, 6], in this case remarkably supports my view. Let those who so cry out against plain truth see to what standard of faith they are conforming themselves. He who does not confess that Jesus Christ came in the flesh is not of God (I John 4:2-3). These men, although they cover it up or do not notice it, deprive him of his flesh.[29]

Calvin's point is that the doctrine of the ubiquity of Christ's body empties out the doctrine of the incarnation of Christ, making his body unlike other bodies and more of a spiritual entity. For Calvin, the analogy of faith requires consistency between the meaning of every passage of scripture. Therefore, when the bread is consumed during the Lord's Supper, it cannot be the consumption of the physical body of Christ because this would require it to be ubiquitous and therefore mean that Christ's body was not a fully human body. This would violate the meaning of other texts of scripture.[30]

Although Calvin regards the primary significance of the analogy of faith to be its requirement that scripture not contradict itself, in practice he also uses Rom 12:6 to justify the use of analogical reasoning in biblical interpretation. When arguing in favor of infant baptism, he uses the practice of the circumcision of infants as a model for the baptism of infants. This is because he regards baptism to be analogous to circumcision. He states:

---

28. Calvin, *Institutes*, 4.17.24.

29. Calvin, *Institutes*, 4.17.31.

30. My point is not here to take sides in this debate, but rather to point out the divergent views of Luther and Calvin about how the analogy of faith should be deployed. While I lean toward Calvin's theory of Christ's spiritual presence in communion, I find his unwillingness to recognize Christ's post-resurrection body as a "spiritual body" (1 Cor 15:44) surprising.

> We therefore conclude that, apart from the difference in the visible ceremony, whatever belongs to circumcision pertains likewise to baptism. To this anagogic [mystically anticipatory] relationship and comparison we are guided by the rule of the apostle, which bids us examine all Scriptural interpretation according to the proportion of faith [*ad proportionem fidei*].[31]

Calvin believed that aspects of Old Testament worship and sacrifice prefigured Christian practices. He used the adjective "anagogic" to describe this relationship between anticipatory practices and their later fulfillment in the bright light of the New Covenant, but he also believed they were analogical. Besides circumcision, he also believed the death of Christ was anticipated in the Old Testament sacrifices of expiation or propitiation. In fact, these sacrifices would have had no effect before God if they had not pointed forward to the true sacrifice which was accomplished by Christ.[32]

In his view, the faith-filled interpreter will see the analogical relationship between circumcision and baptism. It is a relationship of anticipation and fulfillment, but it may also be properly spoken of as an analogical relationship of the kind Paul affirms in Rom 12:6.

ANALYSIS

Calvin considered Paul's phrase "the analogy of faith" to define a hermeneutical rule. However, the way Calvin invokes that rule demonstrates that he was in search of a rule for his own time, not trying to explicate a principle used and championed by Paul. While Calvin acknowledges that during the apostolic age prophecy was more than the interpretation of scripture, he nevertheless treats the analogy of faith only as a principle for interpreting scripture, not as a guide for the exercise of first-century prophecy. For this reason, his interpretation is profoundly ahistorical. Furthermore, when he speaks of the interpretation of scripture, he seems to have in mind the interpretation of both the books of the Old Testament and the New despite the fact that many New Testament books had not yet been written, the whole of the New Testament had not yet been gathered into a collection, and the collection that would eventually emerge had not yet been recognized by the church. All of this shows that Calvin's ruminations on the analogy of faith, whatever their merits, have little to do with the teaching of Paul.

---

31. Calvin, *Institutes*, 4.16.4.
32. Calvin, *Institutes*, 4.18.13.

Although the analogy of faith as explained by both Luther and Calvin reflect their own ideas rather than those of Paul, this does not mean those ideas are without merit. The doctrine of the inspiration of scripture by the Holy Spirit suggests that the various books it contains will, when read properly, contribute to a unified and consistent whole and will not contradict each other.

The danger of such a hermeneutical principle is that, if not monitored carefully, it can promote a flat view of scripture whereby portions of one book are intertwined with portions of another book or other books without regard for date or context. In this way the scriptures are not treated as true literature but rather as ciphers meant to be harmonized. Such an approach robs the authors of the Bible of their own distinctive voices.

An approach that is more sensitive to the individuality of these authors interprets each book of the Bible in terms of its timeframe and its context, and only after analyzing each individual message, and compiling and clarifying the distinctive contribution of each author, gathers the contributions of all into one comprehensive whole. Such an approach honors the role of the Spirit's inspiration but also avoids harmonistic and ahistorical readings of the biblical texts.

But what about the idea that the clearer portions of scripture must guide those that are less clear? In some sense, this is a general principle of all literary interpretation, both biblical and non-biblical. Individual words are first understood by their most common usages, and then extensions to those usages are acknowledged when contexts require. An author's meaning in a particular passage is best assessed by what he writes about the same subject in other places, but when there are no other places to consult, then what other writers of similar historical situation have to say about the matter must be consulted. This is a matter of reasoned interpretation; it is not a matter of some special apostolic revelation.

A pearl is a thing of beauty that grows from an injury, an irritant that provokes the oyster's defenses to create something magnificent. Although, the discussion of Paul's phrase "the analogy of faith" started with poor exegesis, that unpromising beginning grew into a long and fruitful consideration of the principles of biblical interpretation. It is analogous to a pearl.

ROMANS 13

TRANSLATION: ROM 13:1–7

SUBJECT YOURSELVES TO THE GOVERNING AUTHORITIES

¹Let every person be subject to the governing authorities. Since there is no authority unless it is given by God, those that exist have been put in place by God. ²So the person resisting it opposes the authority set in place by God, and those having resisted will themselves receive judgment. ³For rulers are not a cause of fear for good activity, but rather for bad. Do you want not to fear authority? Do good, and you will receive praise from that authority, ⁴for he is the servant of God to you for good. But if you should do evil, be afraid, for he does not bear the sword without purpose. Indeed, he is an avenging servant of God intending wrath to the one practicing evil. ⁵This is why it is necessary to be subject: not only on account of this wrath but also on account of conscience. ⁶Because of this also pay your tributes since [rulers] are ministers of God attending to this very thing. ⁷Pay all your obligations: to the one owed tribute, tribute; to the one owed tax, tax; to the one owed reverence, reverence; to the one owed honor, honor.

COMMENTARY

Vss. 1–7: These verses trouble many who read them. Experience suggests that governments do not always behave in benign, let alone beneficial, ways. Yet Paul insists that rulers are both *diakonoi* ("servants"/"ministers") and *leitourgoi* ("ministers"/"religious functionaries") of God. This noncombative approach should largely be understood within the framework of Paul's division of spheres of authority. In Rom 12:19 he makes clear that the administration of recompense and vengeance must be left to God. In contrast, believers are to return good for evil (Rom 12:17). *For more about this, see the excursus titled "The Governing Authorities."*

Vs. 1: The Greek word *exousia* ("authority") used in this verse should be distinguished from the word *dynamis* ("power"). Generally, *exousia* refers to rights or powers that have been delegated to someone; it implies that authorization has been received. In contrast, the power of *dynamis* is intrinsic power. One apparent exception to this distinction occurs in Acts 1:8 ("But you shall receive *dynamis* when the Holy Spirit has come upon you . . . .") However, this is only an apparent exception, not a real one. Despite the suggestion that *dynamis* will be received, implying it is something external, this is not the point. What will be received is not merely a new authorization, but a new internal capacity for effective influence, a new boldness and intrinsic power. Thus, Acts 1:8 uses *dynamis* in its normal sense.

The authorities (*exousiai*, plural of *exousia*) are people or governmental entities that have received their authority from above. They are agents empowered to speak on behalf of the City of Rome or the Roman Empire (which were separate entities, although both were headed by the same individual). Paul will quickly point out that ultimately the authority of the City of Rome and the Roman Empire come from God, not from human machinations or creativity.

The word translated "governing" is a participle of the verb *hyperechō*, which means "to stand out" or "to excel." For this reason, some translations speak of "the *prevailing* authorities." However, those authorities that are at the pinnacle by prevailing in the struggle for leadership are the ones that end up governing, so there is no real difference. Paul presumes that the Roman Christians had no say in which authorities would prevail because that was the reality.

Vs. 2: "The person resisting": One wonders why Paul felt the need to discuss the topic of resistance to the government. Since he does not relate his motivation, contemporary readers can only surmise his reason from the historical context. If some Jewish-Christian leaders such as Priscilla and Aquila had previously been exiled from Rome, this would suggest a history of trouble with the authorities. Paul seems eager to discourage more such trouble. (For more about past trouble with the authorities see, "The Origins of the Jewish and Christian Communities in Rome" in the introductory portion of this commentary.) It is also possible that the Zealot movement which was organizing in Judea would have been on the minds of Jews even as far away as Rome.

Furthermore, in vss. 18 and 19 of the previous chapter Paul has instructed his readers to strive for peace and to leave retribution and score-settling to God. Paul never suggests that believers can set this world right. That role is reserved for God alone and this transformation remains for the future. In fact, those resisting Rome will find themselves in the uncomfortable position of resisting God himself.

Vss. 3–4: In vs. 3 Paul switches from discussing "authorities" to "rulers" (a participial form of the verb *archō*, "to rule") and then back again to "authority." This toggling back-and-forth is probably simply to avoid excessive repetition. He somewhat optimistically suggests that rulers are only to be feared by those who behave badly, and he states that "it [the government] is the servant of God to you for good." Over the centuries considerable debate has ensued over how Christians should respond when the governing authorities do not seem to be working "for good." *For more about this see the excursus titled, "The Impact of Rom 13:1–7 on Western History."*

Vs. 4 twice refers to the Roman authority as God's servant (*diakonos*). In the second reference, it is called "the avenging servant of God." In this phrase the adjective "avenging" (*ekdikos*) calls to mind Rom 12:19 where Paul's readers receive the prohibition, "Do not avenge yourselves," and where they are reminded in a paraphrase of Deut 32:35 that God reserves vengeance for himself. In the prohibition, a participial form of the verb *ekdikeō* is used, and in the paraphrase of Deut 32:35 the noun *ekdikēsis* appears. Both are closely related to the adjective *ekdikos* of this verse. Paul's point is that sometimes God's vengeance is executed through governmental authorities that serve as his agents.

The adverb *eikē*, translated here "without purpose," can mean "randomly," "in vain," or "perhaps "indiscriminately." Since Paul follows this negative statement with the positive assertion that this governmental authority serves God's purposes, the initial denial that it is not "without purpose" makes good sense.

The grammar of the verse suggest that it is the servant who "intends wrath" rather than God. However, this subtle grammatical distinction may not mark a meaningful difference since as God's agent the servant's wrath may also be God's wrath. Furthermore, as indicated in the comment to 2:18, we should again heed Käsemann's exhortation not to interpret "wrath" psychologically. It is a near synonym to "punishment."

Vs. 5: Through use of a characteristic expression ("not only") Paul offers two arguments in support of his instruction to be subject to governmental authorities. The first is that those who do not subject themselves to governmental authority are likely to experience punishment. The second is grounded in "conscience" (*syneidēsis*). As in 2:15 conscience is viewed as an external testimony that is apprehended internally. Paul suggests there is a moral obligation to be subject to the governmental authorities, and here conscience seems to be something like a moral compass. While the Holy Spirit is not mentioned in this verse, it is possible that as in 9:1 Paul adduces a role for the Spirit in the reception of conscience's testimony.

The expression "not only" (*ou monon*) appears many times in Paul's writings and appears in Romans at 1:32 and 9:24. The slightly longer phrase *ou monon de*, which means virtually the same thing, appears in Rom 5:3; 5;11; 8:23; and 9:10.

Vs. 6-7: There is considerable confusion about the meaning of the Greek terms *phoros* (roughly "tribute") and *telos* ("tax"). Due to the nature of the evidence, these words can be discussed only in terms of probabilities and generalities. One problem is that the assessments levied in the provinces differed from those levied in Italy and in the city of Rome. Another difficulty is that the types and amounts of these assessments differed over time. A third problem is that we do not completely understand the social location of most Roman Christians, other than to suggest that there was considerable diversity. Peter Lampe tersely summarizes the situation: "We do not know which taxes applied to the Roman Christians."[1]

With that note of caution in mind, the following seems the most likely reconstruction. Rome had no income tax and no sales tax, but it had direct assessments such as the head tax and property taxes. These were collected by Roman government or military officials, which is why they are called "direct" taxes. Rome also had taxes on many financial transactions including excise taxes on products brought into the city of Rome. These latter taxes were aimed primarily at those in business. These "indirect taxes" were collected by publicans, who were private businessmen. They contracted with the government for the right to gather a percentage of certain business transactions, and they often overcharged making them unpopular. (Note the pejorative connotations of the famous phrase "publicans and sinners" in Mark 2:15-16 and Luke 15:1.) The Roman historian Tacitus explains that in AD 58, the year when Romans was most likely written, there was so much popular frustration over the indirect taxes (*vectigalia*) raised by publicans that Nero considered abolishing all such taxes. His advisors talked him out of this, arguing that abolition of the indirect taxes would lead to pressure also to abolish direct taxes such as the "tribute" (*tributum*). This, the advisors argued, would lead to the collapse of the empire.[2]

Likely many of the Christians were *peregrini* ("foreigners") and as such probably the *phoros* ("tribute"), a direct tax made up of the head tax and the property tax, applied to them. The *telos*, which refers to ("indirect")

---

1. Lampe, *From Paul to Valentinus*, 80.
2. Tacitus, *Annals* 13.50-51.

transaction taxes including excise taxes, likely applied only to the minority of Roman Christians who engaged in business.

The word translated "reverence" (*phobos*) often means "fear." It was a societal norm that rulers of various sorts and generals were to be treated with such reverence or fear. The word *timē* is customarily translated "honor." However, this word meant more than simply an attitude of respect; it also included certain prerogatives associate with office and/or station in life.

Because the word *phoros* ("tribute") is located so close to *phobos* ("reverence"), and because the words sound much alike, one wonders if Paul positions these words in this way as an act of literary artistry.

The expression "ministers of God" seems nearly identical to "servant of God" in vs. 4, but there is a difference. Rather than the *diakonos* of vs. 4, here the word translated "minister" is the plural of *leitourgos*. There is a whiff of the upper class about this word. While this word often refers to those who conduct ritual religious service, it is also used of upper-class Romans who are asked to provide a civic service, often financial in nature. In other words, secular *leitourgoi* are benefactors. However, since Paul says they are "ministers of God," he likely is invoking the image of service in the Jerusalem temple. He implies that when Roman authorities collect taxes, this is akin to priests offering sacrifices at the Jerusalem temple, and believers should not shirk their obligations.

Excursus: The Governing Authorities

THE PROBLEM

Rom 13:1–7 is something of a puzzle. It appears to be a full-throated appeal for obedience to the Roman Empire as a divinely appointed institution. Furthermore, when vs. 4 mentions "the sword," it alludes to the *jus gladii* ("the law of the sword"), the term by which Rome designated the right to impose capital punishment. There is some question about whether in the 50s of the first century the Roman right to execute was largely theoretical or a practical reality regularly put into practice. During the late republic, which ended in 27 BC, the death penalty was rarely inflicted within the city of Rome, at least upon its citizens. Those who were convicted of capital crimes were allowed to flee the city in a sort of self-imposed exile. This was usually followed by the imposition of a "bill of outlawry,"[3] technically called "inter-

---

3. This term is used by Peter Garnsey. See Garnsey, "Why Penalties Became Harsher," 143.

diction from fire and water," which converted the self-imposed exile to an imposed and formal decree of exile. Anyone in the city who assisted the exiled person by giving fire (e.g., by cooking) or water (e.g., by providing food and drink) himself became subject to criminal charges. The extent of capital punishment inflicted upon non-citizens during this period is unclear.[4]

However, in the city of Rome the executions of the mid-60s under Nero are legendary. These involved both citizens and non-citizens, with Paul and Peter representing both categories. The question is whether the transition from milder jurisprudence to a harsher form was gradual or sudden. A more sudden transition in the 60s might help explain Paul's rather generous description of the role of government as he writes in the 50s.

In any case, in Rom 13:1–7 Paul suggests that Rome administers the *jus gladii* thoughtfully and justly. Ironically, less than a decade after expressing such thoughts, Paul himself will be executed by Rome.

It is also a struggle to reconcile this passage with Paul's comments elsewhere. While he does not often discuss governmental authority, two passages stand out: 1Cor 2:6–10; and 1 Cor 6:1–8.[5] 1 Cor 2:7–8 reads: "But we speak the wisdom of God hidden away in a mystery, which God foreordained before the ages for our glory, which none of the rulers of this age knew. For if they had known, they would not have crucified the Lord of glory." Is Paul here blaming the Romans for the execution of Jesus and chalking it up to their ignorance? This is one plausible interpretation. In contrast, other commentators argue that "the rulers of this age" refers to demons, not to human rulers. Still others suggest that this is a distinction

---

4. Garnsey, "Why Penalties Became Harsher," 143–44.

5. A third passage may also be relevant, since it may suggest that martyrdom by burning is on Paul's mind. However, this is the case only if one of the two main textual variants for this verse is accepted. In 1 Cor 13:1–3 Paul offers up several impressive examples of piety, but in each he suggests that without love these amount to nothing at all. One of these examples appears in 1 Cor 13:3. There the text reads either "if I should give my body that I may be burned [*kauthēsomai*]" or "if I should give my body that I may boast [*kauchēsomai*]." While the first option is the more traditional reading, on text critical grounds the second option is more likely to be original. While the first option might suggest that Paul considers martyrdom by burning a current threat, it is more likely that sometime after Nero began executing Christians in this way a copyist substituted "that I may be burned" in place of the original "that I may boast." One additional question is what the second option might have meant before being altered. Perhaps it implied either martyrdom or imprisonment, but in comparatively colorless terms. About these matters see Fee, *First Epistle to the Corinthians*, 629 n. 18, 633–35.

without a major difference since demonic forces stood behind the execution of Jesus by Roman soldiers.

In 1 Cor 2:8 the word "rulers" reflects a participial form of the verb *archō* ("to rule"), which is also true of the word translated "rulers" in Rom 13:3. Commenting on 1 Cor 2:8, Fee argues this participle refers to the Romans who crucified Jesus, and possibly other earthly leaders as well. He bases this on "the linguistic evidence, the context, and Pauline theology."[6]

Those who argue that the participle of 1 Cor 2:8 refers to demons understand this participle to be equivalent to the noun *archē* ("principality" or "rule"), which seems to be a type of fallen angel or demon that is regularly listed with other types of fallen angels or demons: the *exousia* ("authority"); the *dynamis* ("power"); and the *kyriotēs* ("dominion"). Paul uses the word *archē* in this way in the following passages: Rom 8:38; 1 Cor 15:24; Eph 1:21, 3:10, 6:12; Col 1:16, 2:10 (possibly), and 2:15. However, Paul can also use *archē* in other ways, e.g., to refer to someone in church leadership (Titus 3:1).

Even if Paul is saying demonic forces were behind the crucifixion of Jesus and that it was demons who did not know what they were doing, the Romans still would have been complicit in this demonic scheme. Furthermore, would a lack of understanding have eliminated Roman culpability? Certainly not. But perhaps Paul echoes the sentiment of Jesus, who while hanging from the cross, prayed, "Father, forgive them for they do not know what they are doing"?[7] While the Romans were guilty of a grave offense, in an amazing twist this very evil was also used by God to make their redemption possible!

Whatever the measure of culpability attributed to the Roman executioners of Jesus, that is not precisely the issue at hand. Paul certainly knew that the Roman government was capable of injustice, cruelty, and acts designed to terrorize subject populations into abject submission. This mistrust of Rome was almost an article of faith among the Jews of Judea, despite the existence of some collaborators in their midst (e.g., the Herodians; and publicans such as Zacchaeus). While Paul was a diaspora Jew, he had plenty

---

6. Fee, *First Epistle to the Corinthians*, 103–4.

7. While these words may not have been in the earliest manuscripts of Luke's Gospel, as the United Bible Societies' editorial committee judged, "the logion . . . bears self-evident tokens of its dominical origin" and likely was incorporated into the text "by unknown copyists relatively early in the transmission of the Third Gospel." Metzger, *Textual Commentary*, ad loc. Luke 23:34.

of contact with the Jews of Judea and would have been aware of, if not convinced by, their widespread antipathy to Roman rule.

We encounter a somewhat different situation in 1 Cor 6:1–8. There Paul castigates a person who has sued a fellow believer in gentile court. This is probably not a Roman court as such, but rather a local Corinthian or Achaian court. Nevertheless, it is not a Christian "court" or even a Jewish court.

In general, Rome accepted the principle of "the personality of Law." The Romans recognized that not every people group embraced the same legal theories and traditions as they held. Rather than imposing Roman law concerning lesser disputes involving money, contracts, or family matters upon all the peoples they conquered, the Romans preferred to let local or ethnic courts adjudicate such disagreements. Within Jewish communities, Jewish courts usually handled their disputes. Despite such flexibility concerning lesser matters, when it came to capital punishment, Rome reserved for itself the exclusive right to execute (the *ius gladii* mentioned above).[8] Rome also would step in when a matter seemed to affect public order.

In 1 Cor 6:4 Paul asks the Corinthian church rather accusatorily, "If then you have such cases, why do you lay them before those who are least esteemed by the church?" These are not the words of a man who has high regard for gentile decision-making, including that of gentile magistrates.

The tension between these passages and Rom 13:1–7 is such that some have argued the latter cannot be an authentic part of Romans.[9] However, there is no manuscript evidence to support this theory, and to excise this problematic passage is to cut the Gordian knot, not to untie it. Additionally, in Rom 12:17 and 19 Paul makes statements that seem to anticipate the troublesome question he will discuss in 13:1–7. Thus, this passage fits well into its literary context in Romans and must be original.

WAYS TO RESOLVE THE TENSION

There are three ways to deal with the tension I have described. The first is to harmonize the texts as much as possible since they do not deal with precisely the same situations. The second is to assert as has often been done that Rom 13:1–7 speaks only of moral governments. For a more extended

---

8. The fact that occasionally subject peoples took "the law of the sword" into their own hands does not negate the fact that this violated Roman policy.

9. Jewett lists seven scholars known to him who regard Rom 13:1–7 as an interpolation. Nevertheless, he argues for the passage's authenticity. Jewett, *Romans*, 783 n.17, 784.

discussion of this approach, see the excursus titled "The impact of Rom 13:1–7 on Western History." The third approach assumes that Rom 13:1–7 does not teach general principles but rather speaks to the specific situation of Rome in the late 50s of the first century. Each of these three ways brings difficulties, so the best choice is not obvious.

THE HARMONIZATION APPROACH

First, we will discuss the "Harmonization" approach. It is not particularly difficult to harmonize Paul's teaching in 1 Cor 6:1–8 with his teaching in Rom 13:1–7 since it is possible to be subject to the government, obey at least most of the law, and to pay one's taxes without also choosing to resort to pagan law courts when settling differences. Paul may not think highly of many magistrates and still accept that God has placed a measure of authority into their hands.

It is also possible that Paul considered the Roman authorities to be clueless dupes who were manipulated by demonic forces when they crucified Jesus. A person holding this view would have to say that when Paul calls the governing authorities "God's servant for good," this does not mean unalloyed good, but only a preponderance of good. In other words, the good of providing stability to society outweighed the evil of Rome's brutality (including the crucifixion of Jesus). However, some will find even this limited affirmation of governmental goodness difficult to swallow.

THE MORAL GOVERNMENT ONLY APPROACH

The second approach does not seek to minimize Paul's assertion that the governing authorities are "God's servant for good." Instead, it highlights it, suggesting this description means Paul's discussion is not about all prevailing authorities but only those that are moral and execute their offices morally. This might be called the "Moral Government Only" approach. Against this interpretation is the rather emphatic and apparently universal character of Paul's command, "Let every person be subject . . . ." Paul seems to announce a general rule, applicable to all. Thus, this interpretation risks reading into the text what one wants to see.

THE CONTEXT IS KEY APPROACH

Like the second approach, the third approach seeks to limit the scope of Paul's command, making it less general. But it does this, not by presuming Paul speaks only about moral governments, but rather by addressing the immediate context of the people to whom he writes. Were he to write at a different time or to people in a different situation, he would express a different opinion. Perhaps this approach could be called the "Context is Key" approach.

It is apparent that in the past the Jewish believers in Rome had run afoul of the Roman authorities. Their expulsion under Claudius says as much. (On this see, "The Origins of the Jewish and Christian Communities in Rome" in the introductory portion of this commentary.) Even after it became possible for those Jews who had been exiled to return, they may have continued to be branded as subversive or problematic by the larger population. Consequently, it is possible that the gentile believers in Rome did not want to be tarred with the same brush as their Jewish brothers and sisters, and this tension kept the two groups apart. To put this differently, this residual stigma may have produced and/or prolonged hostility between the Christian Jews and Christian gentiles in Rome.

In contrast, the Jewish Christian community likely felt ill-at-ease and doubly or triply wronged. Since the commotion that resulted for some in exile from Rome was about "Chrestus,"[10] i.e., a misunderstanding of "Christus" ("Christ"), it seems their Jewish brothers and sisters who rejected Christ had also rejected his followers and loudly or violently confronted them. This was the first wrong they suffered. Then the Roman authorities had wrongly expelled them from the city or even from all of Italy. This was the second wrong. Finally, they felt wronged by their gentile Christian brothers and sisters who preferred not to associate with them after their return from exile. Potentially, this was a third wrong.

While the scenario just described is rather speculative, it could explain Paul's otherwise perplexing support of the Roman authorities and their legal system. In the Roman Empire Jews were widely regarded as being of questionable loyalty. They were exempt from compulsory military service since they refused to fight on the Sabbath. Their homeland was at the edge of the territory governed by Rome and very near to Rome's enemy, Parthia, the

---

10. "Since the Jews constantly made disturbances at the instigation of Chrestus, he [the Emperor Claudius] expelled them from Rome" (Suetonius, *Lives of the Caesars, Claudius* 25.4).

area formerly known as Babylonia and then Persia. In fact, during the first century there were more Jews living in Parthia than in Judea and Galilee combined. In other words, Jews were often suspected of forming a "fifth column," antagonistic to the interests of the Empire.

While Paul was known as the apostle to the gentiles, he was also a Jew and therefore a potential troublemaker. Perhaps he wrote a positive account of the Roman government to avoid stirring up more trouble. This would not imply he was being dishonest. He simply emphasized one side of the matter in view of the pastoral needs of the Roman context. When previously he had written to the Corinthian church, he had emphasized the other side of the matter since its members were too prone to trust Roman authorities.

SPHERES OF AUTHORITY

Whichever of the three approaches to this passage one chooses to take, one thing is clear: Paul does not encourage his readers to resort to violence. In Rom 12:17 and 19 Paul has indicated his opposition to believers engaging in retaliation. They are not to lash out at those who mistreat them. Punishment is to be left to God and to his agents, which in this case are governmental authorities. Ultimately at issue is the very large question of how the kingdom of God will be fully expressed. Do believers struggle and fight for justice by punishing injustice? Do they build the kingdom in this world by forcibly imposing the values of heaven? I think not.

Paul, like the other New Testament writers, instead insists that the transformation this world requires will only come when God, "the judge of all the earth" (Gen 18:25), brings it about. In the meantime, believers yearn for the return of Christ and a transformed world. With his first coming, Jesus brought the kingdom in a partial form, for which his people rejoice. But his people also long for the consummation of that kingdom—its full expression—which will come to pass at Christ's second advent. In the interim, believers may prophetically point to the values of a future world (presently stored up in heaven) but they may not presume to implement the justice and righteousness of that coming world on their own.

Excursus: The Impact of Rom 13:1-7 on Western History[11]

INTRODUCTION

There is a cluster of biblical texts, in which Rom 13:1-7 figures prominently, that has often been used to define the theoretical basis for the power of secular governments and the limits of that power. The texts in this cluster have had a greater impact on the development of western history than either the Magna Carta or the United States Constitution. Besides Rom 13:1-7, texts that have often figured in such discussions include the following: Exod 22:28 (22:27 in the MT and LXX); Deut 17:14-17; Ps 105:15 (104:15 in the LXX); Prov 8:15; Jer 1:10; Matt 16:18-19; 26:52; Luke 22:38; John 18:35; 1 Cor 2:15; Titus 3:1; and 1 Pet 2:17. In addition, the pattern of Israelite monarchy with its anointed kings has often been viewed as a political model to be emulated. Even today, evidence of this model can be seen in the "unction" (anointing) of the monarchs of the United Kingdom as part of their coronation rituals.

While Rom 13:1-7 seemingly provides a theoretical foundation for governmental authority, it also is an important touchstone for several related topics. These include whether kings rule by "divine right," what obligations a ruler might have, what constitutes a just war, and what is the best form of government.[12]

While it goes without saying that the Bible has been regarded as an authoritative source for church government, during the Middle Ages and the Early Modern Period it was also often considered an important sourcebook concerning secular government. The boundaries of these two spheres, the religious and the temporal, were often contested, sometimes with dramatic results (e.g., when King Henry VIII of England refused to accept the supremacy of the Catholic pope over the English monarchy, leading to

---

11. In this excursus "western" history is understood primarily in terms of cultural development rather than geography. While Australia cannot reasonably be construed to be in the West geographically, it certainly shares in western history. Furthermore, this brief essay cannot pretend to treat all the West evenhandedly. Particularly in its discussion of the modern period, it certainly focuses mainly on the English-speaking world.

12. The divine right of kings was often supported by Ps 105:15 (104:15 in the LXX) "Do not touch my anointed." Also commonly cited in support of this was 1 Sam 24:1-7 (24:2-8 in the MT and LXX), which recounts how David refused to kill Saul, even though Saul was trying to kill him, because Saul was the Lord's anointed.

the establishment of a separate Anglican Church). In these disputes Rom 13:1–7 was often used as a weapon, sometimes by the opposing sides at the same time.

THE DISTINCTION BETWEEN THE SECULAR AND THE RELIGIOUS SPHERES

The idea that the religious sphere is distinct from the temporal (or secular) sphere may seem axiomatic to most people in the English-speaking world, especially to those in the United States with its disestablishment of religion. But this distinction has not been recognized throughout much of human history, and it is still not recognized in much of the contemporary world (e.g., in those nations of the Muslim world in where *sharia* law has been institutionalized by the government). For instance, religion and government were thoroughly comingled in the (pagan) Roman Empire. One great difference between the Roman Empire and the Holy Roman Empire that succeeded it, was the still-developing distinction between spiritual and temporal powers in the latter. In fact, the introduction of this fundamental paradigm of a distinction between the sacred and the secular should be regarded as a signal contribution of the Judeo-Christian tradition.

This distinction was a long time in the making. A very early expression of it may be seen in ancient Israel's twin poles of authority vested in the persons of the high-priest and the king. It was also manifest in the distinctive roles of the tribe of Levi (from which priests and Levites came) and the tribe of Judah (from which King David and his successors came). But this distinction was not consistently observed. For instance, during the Maccabean period the same person sometimes held both the role of high priest and the role of king (e.g., Jonathan [Apphus] the Maccabee).

Paul assumes this distinction in Rom 13:1–7, but the impact of this assumption had little immediate effect on larger society. This is because there was no real opportunity for Christianity to be comingled with the secular government before the Peace of the Church (313). Even then, it was not until after Christianity became the official religion of the Empire during the rule of Theodosius I (379–95) that exploration of the boundaries between the Christian religion and a Christian state became possible.

The year in which Theodosius died also marked the beginning of the episcopacy of Augustine of Hippo, which extended from 395 to 430. His great work *The City of God* (written sometime between 410 and 426) postulates a fundamental difference between the purposes and struggles of the earthly city (*civitas terrena*) and God's eternal purposes for the City of God (*civitas Dei*). The church is involved in both arenas, and it attempts to mediate between God's goals both eternal and spiritual and the struggles of fallen men to construct a better civilization in a fallen and transitory world. Augustine is important because, although in his view the City of God is always superior to the earthly city, both are real and important.[13] Furthermore, the overall thrust of his thought implies a fundamental distinction between the religious and secular spheres.

THE PAPAL CLAIM TO TEMPORAL SUPREMACY

It is difficult to separate the political history and the ecclesiastical history of the Middle Ages. Much of this period was characterized by quarrels over matters of jurisdiction and supremacy, mainly between emperors and kings, on the one hand, and popes and bishops, on the other hand. Citing Rom 13:1, emperors and kings often argued that "there is no authority unless it is given by God," and that "those authorities that exist have been put in place by God." This, they contended, implied that they had received their authority directly from God and without the involvement of any intermediary agent such a pope.

Popes generally held a different view. The papal bull (apostolic decree) *Unam sanctam*, issued in 1302 by Pope Boniface VIII, expresses this perspective. Its principal points can be summarized as follows:

- There is neither salvation nor the remission of sins outside the one holy Catholic Church [*unam sanctam ecclesiam catholicam*], which is itself the apostolic church.

- The church is a mystical body, of which Christ is the head, and in which there is one Lord, one faith, and one baptism.

- The one and only church has one body and one head, not two heads like some monster. The one head is Christ and Christ's vicar, Peter, and subsequently Peter's successor [the current pope].

- When the Lord said to Peter, "Feed my sheep," the word "my" is general, not referring singularly to these sheep or to those sheep. Therefore,

---

13. While Augustine was greatly impacted by Neoplatonism, his stress on the importance and reality of human history marked a significant departure from the Platonic tradition.

we must understand that he committed all the sheep to himself, and if the Greeks or others are not committed to Peter and his successors, they are not the sheep of Christ. They should confess, as it says in John: "They will be one flock [with] one shepherd" (John 10:16).

- The two swords [mentioned in Luke 22:38] are powers, one spiritual and one temporal.
- When Jesus commands Peter, "Turn your sword into its place [sheath]" (Matt 26:52; see also John 18:10), Peter had previously been exercising the temporal power [of armed conflict, when he confronted those arresting Jesus with his sword].
- Each sword, then, is in the power of the church—the spiritual sword and the material—but the first is indeed for the church, while the second is only under the authority of the church; the first is executed by the priest, the second is executed by the hand of kings and soldiers, but at the behest and tolerance of the priest.
- Therefore, the second sword must be under the first sword, and the temporal authority must be subject to the spiritual authority. When the Apostle says, "There is no power unless it is given by God, for the things that exist are ordained by God" (Rom 13:1), he had this ordering in mind [i.e., that God gives it through the hand of his vicar]. For this judgment accords with the general principle that the spiritual surpasses every earthly power in both dignity and nobility. Furthermore, the prediction of the prophet Jeremiah concerning the church and ecclesiastical power has been fulfilled: "Behold, I have set you [Jeremiah, a priest representing spiritual authority] this day over nations and kingdoms [secular powers]" (Jer 1:10).
- Therefore, if the earthly power deviates, he will be judged by the spiritual power, and if a lesser spiritual authority deviates, he will be judged by his superior. But the supreme spiritual authority [i.e., the pope] is judged by God alone; he cannot be judged by man. For the apostle testifies: "A spiritual man judges all things, but he himself is judged by no one" (I Cor 2:15).
- Now this authority, though given to a man, and exercised by a man, is not a human, but rather a divine power, given by the divine mouth to Peter and to his successors.

- Whoever, therefore, resists this power ordained by God, resists what is ordained by God. Furthermore, we declare, say, and define that every human creature is subject to the Roman Pontiff, and that this subjection is absolutely necessary for salvation.[14]

It is somewhat surprising that *Unam Sanctum* does not also argue for supreme papal authority in both the spiritual and the temporal realms from the narration of the giving "the keys of the kingdom" to Peter (Matt 16:19). In 1245 Boniface's predecessor Pope Innocent IV had argued in this way. He believed the plural form "keys" hinted that Jesus gave Peter two keys: a temporal key; and a spiritual key.[15]

Given the fanciful exegesis that undergirds both Boniface's argument from the two swords and Innocent's argument from the keys, it is not surprising that their position was often challenged. While Paul acknowledges that God has placed the sword in the ruler's hand, it is difficult to find biblical support for the idea that the exercise of temporal authority by a ruler is always subject to the approval of a pope or any other religious authority.

LUTHER'S TEACHING OF TWO KINGDOMS

Not surprisingly, Luther is one of the figures who disputed papal claims to supreme temporal authority, even if, as Boniface VIII suggested, the pope does not directly exercise that authority himself. Simply put, Luther denies Boniface's claim that there are two swords, one spiritual and the other temporal. Luther recognizes only the temporal sword that Paul discusses in Romans 13.

However, he does believe in two kinds of righteousness. As he explains, there is "the righteousness that makes men good in the sight of God. Only faith in Jesus Christ can do that; and it is granted and given us by the grace of God alone, without any works or merits of our own . . . ."[16] The purpose of the church and its preachers is to promote this sort of righteousness by

---

14. This summary is based on the text of Boniface VIII's papal bull *Unam Sanctam* as printed in Mirbt, *Quellen sur Geschichte des Papsttums*, 162–64.

15. See Innocent IV, *Unterordnung der weltlichen Gewalt unter die königliche und priesterliche des Statthalters Christi* (*Subordination of secular power to the royal and priestly power of the vicar of Christ*) in Mirbt, *Quellen sur Geschichte des Papsttums*, 156. This decree was issued in 1245 during a turbulent dispute with the Holy Roman Emperor Frederick II.

16. Luther, *Whether Soldiers, Too, Can be Saved*, 95.

means of God's word. The other kind of righteousness, external righteousness, is the sort that rulers and secular governments seek to compel through laws and courts and ultimately with the sword. Although secular authorities have different ends and means than the church and preachers, they too operate as agents of God.

In his typically colorful and forthright manner Luther clearly expresses this distinction:

> The office of the sword is in itself right and is a divine and useful ordinance, which God does not want us to despise, but to fear, honor, and obey, under penalty of punishment, as St. Paul says in Romans 13. For God has established two kinds of government among men. The one is spiritual; it has no sword but it has the word, by means of which men are to become good and righteous, so that with this righteousness they may attain eternal life. He administers this righteousness through the word, which he has committed to the preachers. The other kind is worldly government, which works through the sword so that those who do not want to be good and righteous to eternal life may be forced to become good and righteous in the eye of the world. He administers this righteousness through the sword. And although God will not reward this kind of righteousness with eternal life, nonetheless, he still wishes peace to be maintained among men and rewards them with temporal blessings. He gives rulers much more property, honor, and power than he gives to others so that they may serve him by administering his temporal righteousness. Thus God himself is the founder, lord, master, protector, and rewarder of both kinds of righteousness. There is no human ordinance or authority in either, but each is a divine thing entirely.[17]

In Luther's view the Christian understanding of the basis of secular government differs fundamentally from the perspective of pagans or the irreligious. They considered government a creation of men. Since they were expressions of human initiative, governments could be established or removed rather easily. However, if God's hand is behind a specific ruler or government, rebellion becomes an insolent thing for it is rebellion against God.[18]

---

17. Luther, *Whether Soldiers, Too, Can be Saved*, 99–100.
18. Luther, *Whether Soldiers, Too, Can be Saved*, 104.

Luther held a high view of the ruler's "office." He writes: "... every lord and prince is bound to protect his people and to preserve the peace for them. That is his office; that is why he has the sword, Romans 13 [:4]."[19] But he was also a realist and recognized that many who hold that office seem unworthy of it. Nevertheless, those ruled must be careful not to resort to vengeance or to assume an authority not given to them. As he explains, Christians who have been wronged are warned against retribution by God, "... 'Vengeance is mine' [Rom. 12:19], and again, 'Judge not' (Matthew 7 [:1]."[20]

If one sovereign's rule was overturned by another ruler, Luther was inclined to see the hand of God at work in this. He thought God often punishes wicked rulers through their conquest by other rulers. And while he deplored the unjust violence some princes employed, he despised popular revolutions and eruptions of the mob even more. He thought it no more right for many to take justice into their hands, than for a single person to do so against his neighbor. Both instances would violate the legal principle, "No man ought to judge his own case."[21]

Some of his arguments against insurrection are prudential in nature. He asks: "What is the difference ... between ... a raging tyrant and a dangerous war as far as the many good and innocent people who perish in it are concerned? Indeed, a wicked tyrant is more tolerable than a bad war ...."[22] He also suggests that if the mob is able to depose the ruler, the result is many rulers: "Now, it is better to suffer wrong from one tyrant, that is, from the ruler, than from unnumbered tyrants, that is, from the mob."[23]

Some have alleged that Luther's stout defense of rulers was self-serving. As papal forces sought to hunt him down, Luther was often protected by state rulers, most notably Frederick III ("the Wise"), Elector of Saxony. It is unlikely Luther was insincere in his exegesis, but there is little doubt that Frederick benefitted from Luther's attacks on claims of unrestrained papal authority, just as Luther benefited from Frederick's protection.

A perennial criticism of Luther's Two Kingdoms Teaching (*zwei Reiche Lehre*) is that it implies Christians should participate in evil instigated by a ruler. The defense often offered against accusations of war crimes is "I was just following orders." Similarly, after the end of World War II many German Lutherans who had participated in atrocities defended themselves

19. Luther, *Whether Soldiers, Too, Can be Saved*, 121.
20. Luther, *Whether Soldiers, Too, Can be Saved*, 113.
21. Luther, *Whether Soldiers, Too, Can be Saved*, 108.
22. Luther, *Whether Soldiers, Too, Can be Saved*, 109.
23. Luther, *Whether Soldiers, Too, Can be Saved*, 106.

by saying, "I did not do this as a Christian, but as a German under orders. In personal matters I try to follow Christ, but when Germany charts a course, because I'm a Christian I'm obligated to obey governmental authority."

This, however, is a misreading of Luther's teaching. He sets stringent guidelines for how a Christian prince should conduct himself. He must not rebel against someone in authority over him, such as an emperor. He must not initiate war with other princes. If his land is attacked, he should try to negotiate peace, if that is possible. However, in many instances war becomes unavoidable and is morally necessary for the protection of the people a ruler leads. In such cases, Luther believed in just war.[24]

The rub comes when a ruler does not care about moral niceties. Are his subjects required to fight for the ruler and for their country, even when the ruler is leading badly? Luther addresses this predicament:

> What if a prince is in the wrong? Are his people bound to follow him then too? Answer: No, for it is no one's duty to do wrong; we must obey God (who desires the right) rather than men [Acts 5:29]. What if the subjects do not know whether their prince is in the right or not? Answer: So long as they do not know, and cannot with all possible diligence find out, they may obey him without peril to their souls. For in such a case one must apply the law of Moses in Exodus 21 [:13], where he writes that a murderer who has unknowingly and unintentionally killed a man shall through flight to a city of refuge and by judgment of a court be declared acquitted. Whichever side then suffers defeat, whether it be in the right or in the wrong, must accept it as a punishment from God. Whichever side fights and wins in such ignorance, however, must regard its battle as though someone fell from a roof and killed another, and leave the matter to God.[25]

Luther does not want to sanction committing evil simply because a ruler orders it done. But there is a tension here. If a ruler's orders may be disobeyed, perhaps repeatedly or even incessantly, at what point does refusal to obey become rebellion against the ruler and amount to insurrection? Luther seems to consider active insurrection against a ruler always to be wrong

---

24. The responsibilities of the ruler are discussed at length, including when a ruler may justly wage war, in Luther's *Temporal Authority*, 118–25.

25. Luther, *Temporal Authority*, 125–26. In effect, Luther judges wrongful killing when the moral situation is unclear to the perpetrator to be a kind of accident.

because it constitutes rebellion against that which has been instituted by God. On the other hand, he seems to condone noncooperation and the soft rebellion of disobedience.

CLAIMS THAT GOD ALLOWS TYRANTS TO BE DEPOSED OR KILLED

Not all protestants shared Luther's interpretation of Rom 13:1–7. A generation later, a slight break with him is seen in Calvin's *Commentary on Romans*. There Calvin writes: "For, although tyrannies, unjust despotisms, and usurpations, being full of anarchy, are not to be considered as regular governments, yet the very right of empire and of dominion is appointed by God for the safety of the human race."[26] Whereas Calvin cracked the door open to rebellion against unjust rulers, many of his followers swung it wide open. Of special note in this regard are John Knox, the founder of the Kirk (the Church of Scotland), and the English poet and polemicist John Milton.

These writers in the Reformed tradition were firm in their conviction that the Bible was the written word of God so they could not simply dismiss Rom 13:1–7. Nevertheless, their exegesis of other portions of scripture colored the way they understood this passage. Generally, they continued down the path laid out by Calvin, namely, that Paul's description in Rom 13:1 only applied to just governments. Since "he [the ruling authority] is the servant of God to you for good" (Rom 13:4), Paul could not have intended to include rulers who did not foster good in society as authorities "given by God."

These writers buttressed this basic argument with additional evidence drawn from the history of Israel's monarchy. They noted that several times kings were killed, apparently with divine approbation. Judg 3:15–30 recounts the story of how the left-handed Ehud was able surreptitiously to stab Eglon king of Moab to death and then muster the warriors of Israel into battle, winning a great victory over the Moabite forces. Judg 4:17–22 describes how Jael, the wife of Heber the Kenite, sheltered Sisera, a Canaanite general, who was fleeing Israelite forces. As Sisera lay down resting in her tent, Jael used a mallet to drive a tent-peg through the temple of his skull. While Sisera was not a monarch, he was nearly so.

A similar story is described in Judith 13, where a beautiful Jewish widow, Judith, gets the great Assyrian general Holofernes drunk and

---

26. Calvin, *Commentary on Romans*, ad loc. Rom 13:1.

alone.²⁷ As he lies in his bed, Judith uses his own sword to cut off his head. Again, although Holofernes was not a monarch, his death was a challenge to royal authority.

The deaths of two kings and a queen are described in 2 Kings 9. After Ahab king of Israel married the Phoenician princess Jezebel, he began to suppress Yahweh worship and inculcate devotion to Baal. This policy was continued by their son Joram, who followed Ahab as king. In the wake of this multi-generational idolatry, Jehu personally shot an arrow through the back of Joram king of Israel who was fleeing in his chariot. A fleeing Ahaziah king of Judah, who had been in league with Joram, was also shot, although not personally by Jehu. In addition, on Jehu's command, Jezebel, the mother of Joram, was thrown out a window and her body was devoured by dogs. After this, Jehu became the king of Israel. While he was not much more righteous than those he killed, many have seen Jehu's killing of Joram, Ahaziah, and Jezebel as God's hand at work.

The rejection by the ten northern tribes of rule by Rehoboam in favor of Jeroboam (1 Kgs 11:26—12:24) was also considered justification for the rejection of unwise or immoral monarchs. So too was the rejection of the rule of Antiochus Epiphanes, the Syrian who intentionally defiled the Jerusalem temple (1 Macc 1:20—2:70).

Although he was not killed, Samuel was deposed as a judge over Israel in favor of rule by a king. This decision was made due to the bad behavior of his sons, whom he had also made judges (1 Sam 8:1–7). Many Reformation scholars also understood this as a biblical warrant for the removal of any ruler who did not fulfill the obligations of his office.

This passage (1 Samuel 8) was sometimes used to support the theory that governmental authority was founded not only on divine authority but also on human covenants. According to 1 Samuel 8, Israel first received its king after the elders of Israel requested a king, since they wanted to be like the nations surrounding them.²⁸ Through the instrument of Samuel,

---

27. The book of Judith is found in the Apocrypha, those books of the LXX that were originally written in Greek and not translated from the Hebrew.

28. In a comment on Hosea 13:11, which seems equally apt here, Luther points to Aesop's fable about the frogs who insisted on having a king. When their wish was granted and a stork became their king, the stork quickly gobbled the frogs up. Luther, *Temporal Authority*, 114 and 114 n. 84. While it is questionable whether there ever was an historical Aesop, collections of many fables attributed to him circulated widely. The earliest form of this fable (#44 in the Perry Index) appears in Phaedrus' collection in Latin from the first century AD, although there the role of the stork is attributed to a water snake. See Phaedrus (edition of Perry), *Fables*, Book 1, Fable 2.

God communicated his reluctant acquiescence to this proposal with the accompanying insight that Samuel should not consider the request a personal rejection of his rule but rather a rejection of their God (1 Sam 8:7–8). Nevertheless, the account suggests that the Israelite monarchy was founded at the initiative of human leaders. The implication is that if humans instituted the monarchy, they could also undo it or modify it.

The observation that proper monarchy is based on covenants, and therefore the consent of those who will be ruled, is also derived from other passages of scripture. David was made king after concluding a covenant with the elders of Israel (2 Sam 5:3; 1 Chr 11:3).

Similarly, after the six-year reign of the female usurper Athaliah, followed by her execution, the rightful heir, the child Joash (or Jehoash), is installed as king of Judah. At that point Jehoiada the Priest apparently negotiated a covenant on the child's behalf with the people of Israel (2 Kgs 11:17).

Deut 17:14–17 seemingly addresses the issue of who selects a monarch: God; or the people. Both those who affirm the former answer and those who affirm the latter, have claimed this passage, for it cuts both ways. This passage predicts that after Israel has lived in the land promised to it for some time, the people will choose to be ruled by a king. God acquiesces, but he also charges them: "You will appoint over yourselves a king whom the Lord your God will choose for you. You will appoint a king over yourselves from among your brothers; you are not permitted to take upon yourselves a foreign man who is not your brother." The question is this: How much leeway is allowed to the people in this choice? On the one hand they are "to appoint," and the candidates eligible to be chosen are restricted to their kinsmen. These parameters suggest a measure of freedom in this choice. On the other, this person is described as someone "whom the Lord your God will choose for you." This suggests no freedom of choice at all.

The position that the right to govern is based on human contracts developed later than the idea that kings rule by virtue of divine decree. In part, this later development was promoted inadvertently by the practice of requiring monarchs to agree to limitations on their power through coronation oaths. However much or little thought was given to these oaths, the reality is that as the Middle Ages progressed, the imposition of oaths increased. This development raised two natural questions: What is the force of such oaths? and What should be done if the monarch does not abide by them?

John Milton very reasonably points out the incompatibility of the practice of requiring oaths with the idea that the monarch rules based exclusively on divine authority:

> . . . to say Kings are accountable to none but God, is the overturning of all Law and goverment [sic]. For if they may refuse to give account, then all covnants [sic] made with them at Coronation; all Oathes are in vaine, and meer mockeries, all Lawes which they sweare to keep, [are] made to no purpose . . . .²⁹

If it is proper to require rulers to adhere to the oaths they swear, and thus to recognize a covenantal basis for monarchy, then the answer to the second question follows from the affirmative answer to the first question. If a monarch steadfastly refuses to honor his oaths, then he must be deposed (or perhaps executed).

While at first coronation oaths were negotiated, after a while they became more-or-less standardized (although always subject to revision). Importantly, it is only a short step from a standardized oath or covenant to an implied covenant, conceived of as imposing duties upon both the ruler and the ruled. This implied covenant, most notably associated with the names Thomas Hobbes, John Locke, and Jean-Jacques Rousseau, came to be called "the social contract."

THE MEANING OF TYRANNY

The word "tyrant" is very old, and the meaning of this word plays an important role in assessing whether a king's rule is legitimate or not. For this reason, its meaning is important to consider even though the word does not appear in Romans 13. N. S. Gill cites Victor Parker's assertion that Archilochus of Paros, a poet from the mid-seventh century BC, was the first person in the written record to use the Greek word *tyrannos* ("tyrant").[30] Parker also asserts that initially this word served as a synonym for *basileus* ("king"). However, within about half a century it also began to be used in a more pejorative manner.[31]

While the negative connotation came to dominate, the more ambivalent usage as a rough equivalent to "king" continued. This can be seen in the one appearance of the word in the New Testament. In Acts 19:9 reference is made to "the hall of Tyrannos" or perhaps "the school of Tyrannos."

---

29. Milton, *Tenure of Kings and Magistrates*, 13.11–17.

30. Gill ("Classical Definition of a Tyrant," unnumbered. Parker, "*Tyrannos*," 149–52.

31. Parker, "*Tyrannos*," 152–57.

This building was evidently identified by its owner, whose name would have functioned much as "King" or "Rex" do in the modern English-speaking world. Since parents normally do not give their children derogatory names, it must be assumed that *tyrannos* could continue to convey a positive or at least a neutral sense.[32]

In antiquity the most extensive discussion of tyranny is found in Aristotle's treatise *Politics*. Aristotle describes three main types of government, and he asserts that each comes with both advantages and disadvantages. These are royalty (or kingly rule), aristocracy (i.e., "rule by the best"), and constitutional government (which he sometimes calls "polity"). Each also has a characteristic deformation or perversion of its true form. He writes:

> Of the above-mentioned forms, the perversions are as follows: of royalty, tyranny; of aristocracy, oligarchy; of constitutional government, democracy. For tyranny is a kind of monarchy which has in view the interest of the monarch only; oligarchy has in view the interest of the wealthy; democracy, of the needy: none of them [has in mind] the common good of all.[33]

Of these three perversions Aristotle most disliked tyranny, which he called "the worst of governments."[34] He also says tyranny "has all the vices both of democracy and oligarchy."[35]

While in outward appearance, tyranny resembles monarchy, it is ruined by the motivations of the tyrant, and these motivations are revealed by the selfishness with which he conducts the state's affairs. Aristotle explains:

> Whereas a tyrant . . . has no regard to any public interest, except as conducive to his private ends; his aim is pleasure, the aim of a king, honor. Wherefore also in their desires they differ; the tyrant is desirous of riches, the king, of what brings honor. And the guards of a king are citizens, but of a tyrant mercenaries.[36]

---

32. *Tyrannos* and its cognates *tyranneō*, *tyrannis*, and *tyrannikos* appear frequently in the LXX, but mainly in the later books that were originally composed in Greek rather than translated from Hebrew (i.e., books of the Apocrypha).

33. Aristotle, *Politics* 3.7. Aristotle's great complaint with democracy is that the masses, who own no property and pay little or no taxes, should not manage what costs them little or nothing.

34. Aristotle, *Politics* 4.2.

35. Aristotle, *Politics* 5.10.

36. Aristotle, *Politics* 5.10.

Until the Enlightenment, Aristotle's view of tyranny largely prevailed. However, as to an increasing degree monarchs were understood to be bound by the responsibilities of their office and by oaths they had sworn to uphold, the definition of tyranny evolved. It was not enough that this king or that king did not seek to enrich himself or luxuriate in wonton pleasures. Instead, holding power unchecked by other wings of government became the new definition of tyranny. The thought, apparently, was that if one king does not demean his office, the next one probably will. If there was potential for kingly misconduct, then at some point surely it would occur.

A decisive figure in this new perspective was Montesquieu, who in his famous book *The Spirit of the Laws* (1748) challenged Aristotle's analysis of the forms and perversions of governments. Rather than focusing on the single center from which power flows, whether from a king, an aristocratic class, or a constitution, Montesquieu stressed the importance of checks-and-balances. His ideal was a "separation of powers," namely separation of the government's legislative, executive, and judicial powers. If it became impossible for all authority to be concentrated in the hands of one individual, or a single group, then what he called "despotism" could be averted.

The United Kingdom never fully embraced these ideas. The monarch is the official head of state, and the (king or queen's) Prime Minister serves as both the functional head of the executive branch and as the leader of the legislative branch. There is also an independent judiciary.

In contrast, Montesquieu's ideas became deeply woven into both the *Constitution of the United States* (ratified in 1788) and France's *Declaration of the Rights of Man and the Citizen* (1789). In the U. S. Constitution, Article I describes the powers and responsibilities of the legislative branch of the government, Article II describes the powers and responsibilities of the executive branch, and Article III describes the powers and responsibilities of the judicial branch.

The governments of Canada and Australia resemble that of the United Kingdom in that the Prime Minister, who heads up the executive branch, also leads the legislative branch. The government of South Africa is slightly different in that the President serves as the chief executive. While he or she must be a member of the National Assembly when elected, the newly elected President must immediately resign from the National Assembly. In New Zealand the Governor-General is appointed by the monarch of the United Kingdom and serves as the functional chief executive. New Zealand also has a parliament.

The Enlightenment's new understanding of "tyranny" as a concentration of power rather than the misuse of power grew out of Montesquieu's thought and it is clearly stated by James Madison in *The Federalist*, No. 47:

> The accumulation of all powers, legislative, executive, and judiciary, in the same hands, whether of one, a few, or many, and whether hereditary, selfappointed [sic], or elective, may justly be pronounced the very definition of tyranny.[37]

This is a significant departure from the Calvinist stipulation that when Romans 13 calls the ruler "the servant of God" this assumes that the ruler labors "for good." Tyranny, an unjust form of government that can rightly be thrown off, has become defined in terms of a structure conducive to evil rather than the moral bankruptcy of rulers. The governmental framework prescribed by Montesquieu and Madison also seems to assume that government is founded by men rather than by God.

A CONCLUSION OF SORTS

Just as Western Civilization has been founded on the twin pillars of the Graeco-Roman tradition and the Judeo-Christian tradition, the modern democratic politics that prevails in the West is an amalgam of biblical insights into government combined with classical and Enlightenment political theory. If Paul were to observe the political outlook of many Christians today, one wonders how faithful he would judge his readers to have been in implementing and preserving the ideas he presented in Romans 13. Would he have accepted the distinction made by Milton and others that tyrants did not function as servants of God? Would he instead have condoned disobedience to tyrannical rulers but not active rebellion against them, as Luther's thinking suggests? It seems the church will continue to struggle with how to live under lesser rulers until the King of Kings rules this earth completely.

Perhaps the principle from Romans 13:1–7 that modern Christianity has done best to observe is the distinction between the two spheres, the spiritual and the secular, the ecclesiastical and the governmental, that Paul's words imply.

---

37. *The Federalist*, also known asl *The Federalist Papers*, consisted of 85 essays published in 1787 and 1788 as the form of the U.S. Constitution was being debated. The authors of the various essays were Alexander Hamilton, John Jay, and James Madison.

TRANSLATION: ROM 13:8–14

LOVE ONE ANOTHER AND PUT ON THE ARMOR OF LIGHT

⁸Owe nothing to anyone except to love one another. For the person loving the other person has fulfilled the Law, ⁹since the commandments, "You shall not commit adultery," "You shall not murder," "You shall not steal," "You shall not covet," and any other commandment, is recapitulated in this saying, "You shall love your neighbor as yourself." ¹⁰Love for one's neighbor does not do harm; therefore, love is the full expression of the Law.

¹¹And I say this, you know the time, that the hour has already come for you to awaken from your sleep, for now our salvation is nearer than when we believed. ¹²The night is far spent; the day is at hand. Therefore, let us put away the works of darkness and put on the armor of light ¹³so that in the day we may conduct ourselves properly, not in lewd and drunken parties, not in sexual and sensual activities, not in conflict and jealousy. ¹⁴But rather clothe yourselves in the Lord Jesus Christ, and do not make plans to entertain the desires of the flesh.

COMMENTARY

Vss. 8–10: In vs. 8 Paul rather deftly transitions away from his discussion of governing authorities. Roman life was built on seemingly unending obligations, only some of which were financial. In vs.7 he had charged his readers "Pay all your obligations," and in vs. 8 he says essentially the same thing viewed from a different perspective: "Owe nothing to anyone." If obligations are paid, they are no longer owed. In a sense, this is an oversimplification since some obligations were recurring. For instance, a freed slave was obligated to greet his patron every morning for the remainder of his life as a token of his gratitude. But the point is clear.

The sole exception to Paul's rule against owing anything is that "to love [*agapaō*] one another" is a perpetual obligation. With this, he turns the focus to behavior within the Christian community.

According to vs. 8, the one who loves "has fulfilled the Law." The reason for this is explained in vs. 9: the command to love one's neighbor recapitulates (*anakephalaioō*) the various other commandments. This interesting word "recapitulates," from *ana* ("re" or "again" or "up") and *kephalē* ("head"), calls to mind the *Anakephalaiosis* ("Recapitulation"), perhaps written by Epiphanius of Salamis or perhaps by someone else. This book is a short restatement of the chief points made in Epiphanius' *Panarion* ("Bread Basket"), a manual of heresies and in what ways they err. In the same way, Paul suggests that the command to love one's neighbor is a short restatement of the behavioral commands of the Law of Moses.

My translation of *ei tis hetera entolē* as "any other commandment" requires some comment. The most obvious translation of *ei tis* would be "if some" or maybe "perhaps some." However, "any" fits the context better, and Liddell-Scott, the standard lexicon of classical Greek, documents other instances where *ei tis* means something of this sort.[38]

The command "You shall love your neighbor as yourself" comes from Lev 19:18, although it is a pillar of the teaching of Jesus, appearing in Matt 22:39//Mark 12:31//Luke 10:27 and also again in Matt 5:43–44 and 19:19. Furthermore, Matt 22:40 perhaps goes even further than Paul's description of the requirement to love "recapitulating" the Law; it says, "On these two commandments [to love God and to love one's neighbor] hangs the whole Law and the Prophets." According to Matthew, these commandments are not just a restatement of the Law but their fundamental essence.

The command to love one's neighbor also appears in Gal 5:14.

Vss. 11–14: In the New Testament there is often a connection between eschatology and exhortations about behavior. This is certainly the case in these verses. The impending punishment that Paul calls "the wrath of God" in Rom 1:18 is described as being near and Paul intends his warning to sober the minds of those involved in "the works of darkness."

This passage led to one of the most famous conversions in history—perhaps second only in fame to Paul's own conversion. Augustine, the future bishop of Hippo in North Africa, relates the story in his book *Confessions*. It took place in Milan, the largest city in Italy at that time. His mother Monica was a Christian and she prayed for him regularly. In addition, he had heard Ambrose, the bishop of Milan, preach, and he was moved by the sermons he heard. But Augustine was living a very sensual life and he doubted he could live chastely. He describes the extreme conviction he felt at that time in his life as "a severe mercy."[39] He knew God would have to change him if he were to live a life pleasing before the Almighty, and he doubted this was possible.

In the midst of this struggle, which was accompanied by many tears, Augustine heard the voices of children playing a game at the house next door, although he could not see them. They were saying "Tolle lege, tolle lege" ("take up and read, take up and read") repeatedly. He was confounded by this, since he had never encountered a game in which these words figured.

---

38. Liddell and Scott, *Greek-English Lexicon*, s.v. "ei," VII.3.e.
39. Augustine, *Confessions*, 8.11.

He concluded it might be a sign from God. His friend Alypius was not far away, so he went to him and obtained a New Testament from his friend. He then dropped the book open, seemingly at random, and found the words of Rom 13:13–14: "Not in rioting and drunkenness, not in lewdness and wantonness, not in strife and envying; but put on the Lord Jesus Christ, and make not provision for the flesh, to fulfill the lusts thereof." He took this as a sign from God and at that point, "all the gloom of doubt vanished away," as he put it.[40] He was converted and on April 24, 387 he was baptized along with his friend Alypius and his son Adeodatus (the Latin equivalent of "Theodore").

Vs. 11: "And I say this" is an implied expansion of *kai touto*, which literally means "and this."[41]

Vs. 12: The image of "putting on" (*endyō*), usually implying putting on clothes, is one of Paul's favorite ways of expressing spiritual transformation. While *endyō* only occurs in this verse and in vs. 14 in Romans, it occurs eleven other places in the Pauline corpus.

The word translated "armor" (a plural of *hoplon*) could also be translated "weapons." Paul uses the same word in Rom 6:13 in his antithetical expressions "weapons of unrighteousness" and "weapons of righteousness."

---

40. The climax of his conversion account appears in his *Confessions*, Book 8, Chapter 12.

41. Bl-D-F §480.5 suggests this is an elliptical statement, leaving out an implied *legō* ("I say").

A LONG ROMANS 14

TRANSLATION: ROM 14:1—15:6

WELCOME OTHERS EVEN WHEN THEY HOLD DIFFERENT OPINIONS

¹Welcome the person who is weak in the faith, but not for divisions over differing opinions. ²On the one hand is the person who has faith to eat anything, but on the other hand, the weak person eats only vegetables. ³Let the one eating not despise the one who does not eat. Let the one not eating not judge the one eating, for God has accepted him. ⁴Who are you to condemn the servant of another? It is before his own lord that he stands or falls. And he will stand, for the Lord is able to make him stand.

⁵On the one hand there is the person who judges one day better than another, and on the other hand there is the person who judges every day the same. Let each person be fully convinced in his own mind. ⁶The person thinking something with respect to a day, thinks this in honor of the Lord. The person eating something, eats in honor of the Lord. ⁷For no one of us lives for himself alone, and no one dies for himself alone. ⁸For both, if we should live, we live for the Lord, and also if we should die, we die for the Lord. Therefore, if we should live or if we should die, we belong to the Lord. ⁹Indeed for this, Christ died and lives again in order that he might rule over both the living and the dead.

¹⁰Why do you condemn your brother? Or why do you despise your brother? For we will all stand at the judgment seat of God, ¹¹for it is written, "'As I live,' says the Lord, 'every knee will bow, and every tongue will confess to God.'" ¹²Therefore, each of us will give an account of himself to God.

¹³Therefore, let us no longer condemn one another, but instead determine this: Do not put a snare or a stumbling block in a someone's way. ¹⁴I know and have been persuaded by the Lord Jesus that nothing is profane

in itself. However, if a person considers something to be profane, then it is profane. ¹⁵For if on account of food your brother suffers pain, you are no longer conducting yourself according to love. ¹⁶So do not let the good you do be besmirched. ¹⁷For the kingdom of God is not eating and drinking but rather righteousness and peace and joy in the Holy Spirit, ¹⁸for the one serving Christ in this manner is pleasing to God and respected by other people. ¹⁹Therefore, let us pursue things promoting peace and things building each other up. ²⁰Do not destroy the work of God for the sake of food. Everything is clean, but it may cause harm to the person who eats and in so doing stumbles. ²¹It is good not to eat meat or to drink wine or to do anything by which your brother stumbles. ²²Do you have a matter of faith unique to you? Keep it before God. Happy is the person who does not condemn himself in what he approves. ²³And the person who distinguishes between kinds of food, if he should eat, he is condemned, for his action is not from faith. Anything that does not come from faith is sin.

¹We who are strong are obligated to bear the weaknesses of those who are not strong and not to please ourselves. ²Let each of us please his neighbor, working for his good, for building him up. ³For indeed Christ did not please himself, but as it is written, "The reproaches of the those reproaching You fell upon me." ⁴For everything written beforehand was written for our instruction, in order that through the perseverance and through the encouragement taught in the scriptures we might have hope. ⁵May the God of perseverance and encouragement cause you to think the same way about each other in the manner of Christ Jesus, ⁶in order that in solidarity, with one voice, you may glorify the God and Father of our Lord Jesus Christ.

COMMENTARY

Vss. 14:1—15:6: This passage discusses a division between two groups of believers in Rome called "the weak" and "the strong." While Paul identifies with the strong and to some extent argues the case for that way of thinking, he is less concerned with which group is right or which group is ascendant and more concerned with the way the two groups treat each other. While knowledge and insight are both valuable, if they are deployed without love, they can destroy rather than build up.

This issue is not a Jew versus gentile dispute; there are Jews and gentiles among both the weak and the strong. Although idolatry is not mentioned in this passage, based on information from 1 Corinthians the dispute likely centered on different approaches to avoiding idolatry. It seems the approach of the weak followed typical Jewish guidelines for avoiding not only meat and wine as it was being used in pagan temples and/or sacrificial ritual, but also avoiding meat or wine that had been owned by non-Christian gentiles, who were assumed to be idolaters. This second requirement meant that the origin and subsequent chain of custody of meat and wine needed to be tracked. If these things were not known, the food must be rejected. The practical outcome of this was that many of the weak in Rome ate only vegetables.

The strong rejected the notion that the individual histories of pieces of meat and bottles of wine could render them profane. They avoided eating in pagan temples and active participation in sacrificial acts but ate the meat and the wine they purchased in the public markets without determining the details of their provenance.

Another issue dividing the weak and the strong was over whether some days were special or all days were basically the same. Not much detail is given about this, but likely this involved the question of whether to observe sabbaths, new moon observances, and the festivals outlined in the Law of Moses. *For a more detailed discussion of these matters, see the excursus called "The Weak and the Strong."*

Vs. 1: Many take the expression "weak in (the) faith" to indicate weak commitment. However, both the use of the definite article with "faith" (*hē pistis*) and the context suggest the weakness is in the content of "the faith" these individuals believe. Paul is describing a limited command of foundational doctrine, not limited commitment. Such believers are to be welcomed, but not if they mean to provoke divisions over "opinions." Differences of opinions suggest that the content of their faith is the issue, not the intensity of their belief.

Vs. 2: It should probably be assumed that "the weak person" is weak in faith. As already mentioned, those who eat only vegetables likely fear that meat or wine previously owned by a gentile was "profane" by virtue of this fact. In contrast, Paul believed Jews and gentiles stood on the same footing before God. Unregenerate gentiles defiled food no more than did unregenerate Jews, which is to say not at all. Since the weak in the faith did not understand this, according to Paul's perspective, they were weak in their understanding of the implications of his gospel message.

Vss. 3–4: Paul contends that both the weak and the strong are members of the believing community. If God has accepted them, what right does any human have to exclude them? It is acceptable to disagree about nonessential beliefs, but not to exclude because of that disagreement.

In v. 4 Paul relates an illustration, which might even be termed a short parable. He points out that slaves are only accountable to their own masters, not to others. The word Paul uses to designate a master is *kyrios*, which means "lord" or "master." But perhaps we should see in this word a double-entendre since *kyrios* can also mean "the Lord," and Paul's point is that the foremost responsibility of each individual is to her lord, i.e., to the Lord Jesus (or possibly to the Lord God).

Vs. 5: "On the one hand . . . on the other hand": these alternatives are expressed by the *men . . . de* construction. The phrase "one day better than another" translates *hēmeron par' hēmeron* (literally "day beside day").[1]

The verb *plērophoreisthō* ("to be fully convinced") is composed of two parts *plēroō* ("to be full") and *pherō* (literally "to bear"). However, *pherō* is a very flexible word, especially when compounded with other words, as in this case. It can mean "to have an opinion," which is pertinent here.[2] The point is in this situation is "to have a full opinion." Paul uses a third-person imperative form, suggesting the translation, "Let each be fully convinced" or "Let each have a full opinion." Individual believers have freedom about this issue, which suggests that Christian groups which force conformity regarding sabbath observance or the so-called "Puritan sabbath" (Sundays) are out-of-step with Paul's instruction.

Vss. 6–9: Paul continues his discussion of differing attitudes toward special days. He points out that both groups conduct themselves in a way they believe honors the Lord. He continues in a manner that would appeal to Roman Catholic interpreters, whose understanding of "the communion of the saints"[3] includes both the saints militant and the saints triumphant (i.e., those saints who are still alive and those saints who have already died). Paul's point is that the Lord has a claim on believers in this life, at death, and after death. In every situation, believers belong to the Lord, and they have obligations to him.

The phrase translated "in honor of the Lord" appears twice in vs. 6. Literally the text reads "in the Lord," but this rather vague construction should probably be understood as a "dative of advantage," suggesting "for the Lord" or "in honor of the Lord."[4]

In vs. 7 the word "alone" is twice implied but not explicitly expressed. Vs. 9 grounds Christ's rulership over both the living and the dead in his own participation in human life and human death.

---

1. On this use of *para* to express comparison and contrast, see Moule, *Idiom Book*, 51.

2. Liddell and Scott, *Greek-English Lexicon*, s.v. "pherō," B.II.3.

3. Although this phrase does not appear in the New Testament, it appears in the Apostles' Creed and in other subsequent creeds.

4. Bl-D-F, §188.2

Vss. 10–12: This paragraph begins by asking why some condemn or despise their brothers. Then these verses emphasize the unavoidability of eschatological judgment. There is a question, however, about the point Paul is making. Is he saying that there is no need to condemn or despise others because they will each be judged by God, or is he warning those who condemn and despise others that they themselves will be judged by God? Perhaps both options are true.

The oath formula "As I live . . . ." is common in the Old Testament, appearing in Isa 49:18, Jer 22:24, Ezek 5:11, and elsewhere. The Lord swears by himself, since there is no greater being by which to swear. That "every knee will bow, and every tongue confess to God" comes from Isa 45:23. Paul may also have in mind the next two verses of Isaiah, which continue the theme of the Lord's supremacy. An expanded form of Isa 45:23 is also found in Phil 2:10–11.

Vs. 13: The verb *krinō* ("to judge") appears twice in this verse, but with different nuances. In the first clause, Paul admonishes his readers not to "condemn" one another—a meaning that falls within the range of meanings of *krinō*—and then he proposes an alternative, using *krinō* in the more neutral sense of "determining" something. Rather than condemning one another as they have been doing, they are to make it a principle to avoid putting a snare or a stumbling block in a fellow believer's way. The word "snare" (*proskomma*) is an allusion to Exod 23:33 and 34:12. The phrase "stumbling block" (*skandalon*) alludes to Lev 19:14 and other verses. Under the guise of upholding one part of the Law (i.e., prohibitions against idolatry), they have been violating another part of it (i.e., the command to love one's neighbor).

Vs. 14: The point Paul makes in this verse is foundational to his ethics. It also highlights his sense of freedom in Christ. Objects are neither pure nor profane in themselves. Objects have no moral sensibility. Instead, what matters is how objects are used by people, who do exercise morality and are morally responsible. This is why a person's convictions matter, whether those convictions are shared by others or not. When a person considers using an object in a way that would violate her convictions, then in that moment it is as if to her that object itself is profane. In vs. 23 Paul will underline this idea with the bold assertion "Anything that does not come from faith is sin."

Vs. 15: Here Paul gives a name to this controlling principle of his ethics: "love" (*agapē*). It is sometimes claimed that *agapē* is a divine love that only God can exhibit, but this is false. Paul clearly expects believers to exercise this type of love. This *agapē* is not an emotion or an urge, but rather controls how a person treats other people. If someone injures another person and causes that person to stumble, this is not the Christian way.

Vs. 16: The word I have translated "besmirched" could also be translated "blasphemed" since the Greek verb is *blasphēmeō*. Perhaps "the good" mentioned in this verse should be put in scare quotes since seemingly it is considered good by the person doing it, but others denounce it, apparently with justification.

Vss. 17–21: In these verses Paul continues his argument that building others up is more important than mundane matters such as what a person eats or drinks. In fact, focusing on these peripheral matters can be not only distracting but destructive. The better alternative of building others up and promoting peace is kingdom work. The phrase "the kingdom of God," which appears so often in the Gospels, makes its only appearance in Romans in vs. 17, although it occurs often elsewhere in Paul's writings.

Vs. 19 presents a question of text criticism. Is the reading "Let us pursue" (a hortatory subjunctive) or "we are pursuing" (an indicative) original? While the manuscript evidence is slightly stronger for the latter, the context favors the former.

The translation I have offered for vs. 20 is not strictly literal, although I think it expresses Paul's point accurately. Translated very literally, it would read: "Do not destroy the work of God for the sake of food. Everything is clean, but bad to the man eating on account of stumbling." One issue is whether the adjective *kakos* should be translated by "harm" or its more basic meaning "bad." I have chosen the former alternative since it suits the context best.

Vss. 22–23: There is some doubt about whether the opening clause of vs. 22 should be understood as a statement ("Your faith which you have") or as a question ("Do you have [a matter of] faith?"). Involved in this issue is also a text critical problem. While it is absent from most manuscripts, several very important manuscripts include the relative pronoun *hēn* ("which") in this clause. If this pronoun is included, the clause must be interpreted as a statement. If it is absent, it may be translated either as a statement or as a question. I have chosen to omit the pronoun and to translate the clause as a question largely because I think a question fits the context better.

In the phrase "a matter of faith unique to you," the word "faith" (*pistis*) refers to what is believed rather than the act of believing. This justifies the translation of that word as "a matter of faith." The phrase "unique to you" is an attempt to render *kata seauton*. This is the only occurrence of this expression (with *seauton* in the accusative case) in all the New Testament and the LXX. The translation "unique to you" fits the context well, but literally the phrase means approximately "according to yourself."

Paul has a strong sense of liberty in Christ. He recognizes that individuals may have distinctive ways of understanding what it means to follow Christ that they know will not sit well with others. In such situations, he encourages believers to avoid raising unnecessary issues before the community.

Paul's statement "Happy [or "blessed"] is the person not condemning himself by what he approves" is a beatitude. While beatitudes—blessings that begin with the word *makarios* ("happy" or "blessed")—are most often associated with the distinctive blessings of Jesus in the Sermon on the Mount (Matt 5:3–12) and the associated material in Luke's Gospel (Luke 6:30–22), in fact there are also many beatitudes in the Old Testament. Paul's beatitude is roughly the inverse of the woes pronounced by Jesus against hypocrites in Matt 23:23–29.

In vs. 23 the definite article *ho* ("the") and a participle from the verb *diakrinō* appear together: *ho diakrinomenos*. I translate this, "the person making distinctions [between different types of food and drink]." In contrast the RSV translates "he who doubts." Why the difference? My translation focuses on the larger controversy Paul addresses, whether, on the one hand, a person should make distinctions between which kinds of food and drink are permissible to consume and which are not, or, on the other hand, not to make such distinctions. In contrast, the RSV takes its clue from the end of the verse where "faith" is mentioned. The RSV translators understood "he who doubts" to be the person who lacks faith. While both approaches try to pay attention to the context, one factor that favors my translation is that *diakrinō* much more often means "to make distinctions" than "to doubt."

Vs. 23 also contains a Greek play on words that cannot be easily simulated in English. Two verbs built on the base verb *krinō* ("to judge") are juxtaposed. Paul uses participles of both the verb *diakrinō* ("to make distinctions") and the verb *katakrinō* ("to condemn") which share the same root and which sound alike. If a person thinks making distinctions about food and drink is important, and then eats what he judges to be impermissible, he has condemned himself as a hypocrite. Paul's maxim "Anything that does not come from faith is sin" should be understood as a generalized condemnation of hypocrisy, an example of which he has just provided.

"Anything that does not come from faith is sin" is a powerful maxim, and much of its power comes from its general and wide-ranging character. However, it also introduces a subjective element into ethical deliberations and as a result is easily abused. The subjective element enters because individuals do not all have the same personal convictions or the same dictates from their individual consciences. Another problem arises when people assume that the inverse of Paul's maxim is also true: Whatever comes from faith is not sin. However, logically this is not necessarily true, especially when different definitions of faith are confused. Does faith mean 1) the act of believing, 2) the content of belief, or 3) a state in which a person rests? In vs. 23 Paul probably has definition 1 or perhaps a combination of definitions 1 and 2 in mind. When definition 3 is substituted, problems often arise. It is not uncommon for people to justify living in sexual sin by claiming that a relationship arose in a context of belief and therefore is not incompatible with Christian faith. Perhaps it was because of such potential problems that Calvin insisted on identifying the "faith" mentioned in this verse as objective content: "To condemn whatever is not of faith is a rejection of everything that has not the support and approval of the word of God."[5]

Chapter 15, vss. 1–2: While in some sense Paul has never left it, here Paul explicitly resumes his discussion of the weak and the strong he introduced in 14:1. He notes that the strong have a special responsibility to "bear the weaknesses" of the weak. Furthermore, bearing those weaknesses will involve some personal discomfort since the priority should be on pleasing one's neighbor rather than oneself.

Vs. 3: This verse begins with the dual conjunction *kai gar* that I have translated "for indeed." Smyth suggests that this combination can mean "and indeed," but the combination is common in the New Testament, and it usually has an inferential force.[6]

The quotation is from Ps. 69:9 (MT 69:10; LXX 68:10). This is a "messianic" psalm, and in the fledgling church it was understood to be a prophetic narrative of the career of Jesus. An earlier portion of the verse is quoted in John 2:17. Here Paul uses the selflessness of Christ to inspire his readers to live more selflessly.

Vs. 4: This verse is not the only place where Paul argues that the Old Testament was written and recorded for those in the new age inaugurated by the death and resurrection of Christ. He makes essentially the same point in 1 Cor 9:9–10.

Vss. 5–6: The phrase "God of perseverance and encouragement" suggests that God is the source of these qualities. "Perseverance" and "encouragement" are echoes of the identical words in the preceding verse. The word "perseverance" suggests that the Roman believers are experiencing difficulty, probably difficulty engendered by disunity and squabbling. The word "encouragement" suggests they are struggling with despondency. Paul hopes that the example of Christ, who suffered much more than they have, will impel them forward in unity and with a united voice as they glorify God.

---

5. Calvin, *Commentary on Romans*, ad loc. Rom 14:23.
6. Smyth, *Greek Grammar* §2814.

Excursus: The Weak and the Strong

THE TERMS "THE WEAK" AND "THE STRONG"

A major issue affecting the interpretation of Romans chapter 14 and the beginning of chapter 15 is Paul's use of the categories "the weak" and "the strong." These designations almost certainly are not Paul's own creation but rather were so well known to his readers that Paul was able to use them without offering any definition or explanation. Whether one calls these technical terms or nicknames, they seem to describe not only divergent identities but also to suggest associated standards of behavior.

The interpretive situation is complicated by the fact that Paul had already written about "the weak" in an earlier letter to the Corinthian believers (1 Cor 8:7–10; 9:22) using very similar although not identical terminology. If someone were to interpret Paul's comments in 1 Corinthians without consideration of what he writes in Romans, the interpreter would conclude that the weak/strong divide was located predominately within the Corinthian church's large gentile community. In contrast, if someone were to interpret Paul's comments in Romans without consideration of what he writes in 1 Corinthians, this person would likely conclude the weak/strong divide was primarily an issue among the Jewish believers of Rome. (Of course, Rome had a much larger Jewish population than did Corinth, so that is an important variable.) Thus, we are left with a puzzle.

In Rom 14:1 and 2 the Greek word Paul uses that is normally translated "weak" is a participle of the Greek verb *astheneō*. In Rom 15:1 a similar word "weaknesses" (a plural of the noun *asthenēma*) is also used. Another word he uses (in 15:1) is *adynatoi*, which literally means "not strong" or "unable" but could also be translated "weak."

In 1 Corinthians 8 and 9 Paul uses the adjective *asthenēs* ("weak") five times. Three times he uses it substantivally (i.e., functioning roughly as a noun). Twice he uses it adjectivally. The fact that Paul uses the adjective in 1 Corinthians rather than a participle of a cognate verb as in Romans is interesting to observe but probably not a significant difference.

Of greater significance is that if both 1 Corinthians and Romans describe the same divisive issue, this means it was more than simply a local matter. Believers in both the East and the West were bedeviled by this faultline.

While Paul explicitly identifies himself as a member of "the strong" in Rom 15:1, the same identification is implied by 1 Cor 9:22. There he claims to have crossed boundaries by becoming weak to gain the weak. There is not a corresponding statement about ministry to the strong since no magnanimity was required for ministry among his own group.[7]

Taken at face value, the nickname "the weak" seems pejorative. However, there is nothing in either Romans or 1 Corinthians that suggests this appellation was rejected by those it identified. This dynamic reminds me of an illustration from American football. In his college days, my brother Bob was a defensive back for the Evangel University football team. His position was known as either "weak safety" or "free safety." It was called "weak safety" because this defensive player lined up across from the "weak side" of the offensive line—the one with a split end rather than a tight end (i.e., the side with fewer blockers in case of a running play). Our grandma used to get mad when the announcer would say something like, "The tackle was made by the weak safety Robert Menzies." Grandma thought the announcer was insulting Bob, when of course he was not. Nevertheless, when Bob identified his position, he usually claimed to be a "free safety," not wanting to be called a "weak safety." Some of the same dynamics are apparent in Paul's discussions of the weak and the strong. The nickname "weak," as used in Romans and 1 Corinthians, seems to function as a technical term rather than an insult. Nevertheless, it is doubtful that the weak chose this appellation for themselves.

WERE "THE WEAK" BELIEVERS?

A question of substantial importance is whether or not "the weak" were believers. Most scholars believe they were, but a few claim they are not. In my opinion, the idea that the weak were all unbelievers can be quickly dismissed for two reasons. First, in 1 Cor 9:22 Paul says, "To the weak I became weak in order that I might gain the weak." While Paul was certainly willing to modify his lifestyle to spread his gospel more effectively, he would not have been willing to become an unbeliever to reach a target audience. Second, in Rom 14:1 Paul speaks of those who are "weak in faith." He does not say they are without faith (or without the faith, i.e., the content of Christian belief). They have faith, but it is weak in some way. This suggests that they are believers.

---

7. However, it is possible to object to my logic here since Paul also says in this same passage (vs. 20) that he "became as a Jew to the Jews" even though he was a Jew himself.

WHAT IS THE CONTEXT OF THE WEAK/STRONG DIVISION?

More difficult is the question already mentioned as to whether the weak/strong division arose within, on the one hand, a Jewish context or, on the other hand, a gentile context. Most scholars opt for the former alternative, but a significant minority opt for the latter. It is also probable that this division began in either a Jewish or a gentile context, but then spread to the other sector of the believing community as well so that ultimately it involved both Jewish and gentile believers.

Before engaging fully in this debate, it is important to explore some terminology from the secular Roman world. When Paul refers to "the weak," some contend he has in mind an equivalent Latin term, probably either *tenuiores* ("the weak" or "the poor") or *proleterii* ("the working poor"). (The English word "tenuous" is related to the former term; the Marxist term "proletariat" is related to the second term.) This Latin connection would be especially relevant if the categories of "weak" and "strong" refer to distinctions made within the larger gentile society.

In the Roman world, the *tenuiores* were poor, owning little and just holding on, but they were not the abject poor who owned nothing at all or nearly nothing. These abject poor were called *capite censi* ("counted by head") because at census time they were counted but no property was attributed to them.[8] Despite their relatively low standing, Roman policy recognized that the *tenuiores* were a valuable part of society, and some effort was made to keep them satisfied, if not happy, since their labor was important to a well-functioning economy. Emblematic of this interest was the grain dole (*cura Annonae*).

Over the past twenty-five years a great deal of attention has been paid to *collegia tenuiorum* ("associations of the poor") since this terminology suggests publicly recognized groupings of "weak" or "poor" people, perhaps not unlike the groups Paul mentions in this passage. The earliest surviving reference to a *collegium tenuiorum* ("association of the poor") is in a legal digest of the Roman jurist Marcian from the early third-century AD (Justinian, *Digesta* 47.22.3.2).[9] Marcian's digest is found embedded in the

---

8. This distinction between *proletarii* and the *capite censi* is explained by the second-century writer Aulus Gellius 16.10.10–11 (*Attic Nights of Aulus Gellius*, Vol. III, pp. 168–69 in the Loeb edition), which is quoted by Reasoner, *Strong and the Weak*, 50–51.

9. Some have hypothesized that Pliny the Younger alludes to *collegia tenuiorum*

second portion of Justinian's sixth-century *Corpus Juris Civilis* ("Body of Civil Law"), which includes three collections: the Code, the Digests, and the Institutes. The point of Justinian's *Corpus* was to summarize and to systematize the great mass of earlier laws and enactments of various kinds into a coherent whole. Marcian's digest itself almost certainly distills earlier legal enactments, so Roman regulation of *collegia tenuiorum* ("associations of the poor") goes back to the second century AD or possibly even to the first century AD.

It Is clear the Roman Imperial government feared the social power of private associations and generally tried to suppress them. The only category of *collegia* ("associations") that received a pass was the *collegia tenuiorum* since these *collegia* were deemed to serve a useful purpose. By pooling their resources through these associations, the poor were able to achieve results which they would not have been able to achieve individually. The most well-known of these *collegia tenuiorum* provided funeral services to the poor. The full range of purposes for which *collegia tenuiorum* were established is unknown.

Since empire-wide persecutions of Christian churches began about the time that Marcian's digest was written, it is conceivable that at the end of the second century or the beginning of the third century the Roman government came to recognize Christian churches as *collegia* that should be suppressed.[10] However, that discussion would take us well beyond the purview of Paul's letter to the Romans.

In Romans 14 and 15 two issues are intermingled: the differences between the weak and the strong; and Paul's exhortations to be respectful and accepting of those on the other side of this issue. Paul clearly uses material drawn from the Old Testament as well as the example of Christ's life to instruct his readers about how they should treat those from the other group. However, it is important not to use the apostle's admonitions to be accepting of others as evidence for identifying what divides the weak from the strong; these are two separate matters.

---

in a letter he wrote to Emperor Trajan early in the second century (Pliny, *Epistula*, Book 10, Letter 93). However, while this letter does refer to "the poor" (*tenues*), it refers to a "fund" or "collection" (*collatio*) for them, not *collegia*.

10. The persecution under Nero was limited to the city of Rome. The persecution under Domitian occurred only regionally, in Asia Minor. Thus, neither of these persecutions was empire-wide. The first empire-wide persecution was likely under Septimius Severus (AD 193–211).

Even if Paul's exhortations to respect and accept those in the other camp are eliminated from the pool of evidence, several details might suggest the dispute arose in a specifically Jewish or Jewish-Christian context:

1. Some eat anything; others eat only vegetables. Does this reflect an aversion to eating meat that has not been slaughtered according to proper Jewish ritual and/or meat that is tainted by association with idolatry?[11] Quite possibly. It is also true that vegetarianism such as that practiced by the exemplary Jew Daniel (Dan 1:8–16) was recognized within Judaism as a commendable form of asceticism.

2. Rom 14:21 also suggests that drinking wine was a point of contention. Probably it was those who chose to eat only vegetables who also abstained from drinking wine. Like their vegetarianism, this abstinence might have been related to standards of Jewish ritual purity. The Mishnah (the earliest part of the Talmud) considers wine to be tainted by idolatry if it has belonged to a gentile or if a gentile has benefited from its production.[12] The assumption is that gentiles are idolaters and therefore the wine has been tainted by idolatry. This evidence does not mean such a strict standard prevailed during the first century, but it is a possibility.

3. Some treat certain days as special; others treat every day the same. Does this refer to disagreement over Jewish observances such as keeping the sabbath, new moon observances, or holidays prescribed in the Torah?

4. The words "snare" (Greek *proskomma*; Rom 14:13, 20; 1 Cor 8:9), "stumbling block" (*skandalon*; Rom 14:13), and especially "profane"

---

11. While there were ritual standards in Paul's day, these should not be confused with the standards that became more-or-less fixed during the Middle Ages. According to these standards, if meat had been previously owned by a gentile, it was considered ritually impure. Gentiles were assumed to be idolaters and therefore the meat was considered contaminated by idolatry. While it is not certain that such a standard was observed in the middle of the first century, Peter's refusal to eat with gentiles mentioned in Gal 2:12 was likely based on a desire to avoid consuming *eidōlothuta* ("food offered to idols"), understood in precisely these terms.

I am purposefully avoiding the Hebrew word *kashrut* ("*kosher* standards") since this term implies a more fully developed system than was in use in Paul's day.

12. This is stated in *m.Abod. Zar.* 2.3. The Mishnah was compiled around AD 250 from Jewish oral tradition, and *Abodah Zarah* is the tractate that deals primarily with idolatry.

Again, I have avoided using the word *kashrut* ("*kosher* standards") because the rules today known as *kashrut* were not fixed until well into the Middle Ages.

(*koinos*; Rom 14:14) seem to reference the Torah, suggesting this is a dispute between Jews. *Proskomma* reflects Exod 23:33 and 34:12. *Skandalon* appears many times in the Old Testament, but most famously in Lev 19:14: "Do not put a stumbling block in front of the blind." *Koinos*, here as in Acts 10:14, is a technical term referring to Lev 10:10: "You shall distinguish between the holy and the profane (Hebrew *chol*), between the unclean and the clean." While the LXX does not translate *chol* with *koinos*, *koinos* later came to be seen as an equivalent to *chol*. The matter of what constituted "profane things" was of such importance that an entire tractate of the Mishnah was devoted to this topic (Tractate *Chullin*).

In contrast, certain factors suggest the locus of this dispute could fit within the social matrix of the Roman world:

1. Roman society was preoccupied with various distinctions in social status. Class was an important distinction, with the senatorial and equestrian classes located at the apex of society. There was also one's legal status: freeborn, freedman, or slave. Whether a person was a citizen or not, and whether he was a foreigner (*peregrinus*) also factored into one's pedigree. Of course, the amount of wealth and property one possessed was also a factor.

2. Latin literature of the period frequently refers to *tenuiores* (a flexible term which can mean "the poor," "the weak," or even "the infirm"). A few other words—*proletarii* (roughly "working poor"), *infirmi* ("weaker ones"), and *invalidi* ("physically weak people") bear similar meanings. Similarly, the words *potentes* (singular *potens*) and *vires* (singular *vis*) can be used to mean "the strong."[13]

3. Later Roman legal literature mentions *collegia tenuiorum* ("associations of the poor"), although it is unclear whether these associations existed as early as the 50s of the first century.

4. Vegetarianism was honored in ancient Rome as something of a throwback to the city's early period which was less prosperous than during the early empire (i.e., Paul's time). Because meat was costly, poor people were more likely to be vegetarian than the wealthy. Some Roman literature celebrated "the simple life" of the Roman forefathers, including vegetarianism. An example is Horace's ridicule of gourmet eating

---

13. Mark Reasoner presents an excellent discussion of these words in *Strong and the Weak*, 45–58.

and celebration of "plain food" (*victus tenuis*) found in *Carmina*, Book 2, Satire 2, lines 53 and 70.[14] Furthermore, it is known that an advocate of vegetarianism was active in Rome during the 50s. His name was Musonius Rufus.[15]

5. The Romans observed certain holidays on which business was not transacted.[16] The fact that some Roman believers treated some days as special, and others treated every day the same, could reference divergent attitudes toward Roman holidays.

6. The fact that "the weak" are mentioned in 1 Corinthians 8, a passage discussing disagreements between gentile believers about whether it was permissible to eat in pagan temples as had been their custom prior to becoming Christian, suggests this is not a purely Jewish-Christian issue.

If one examines the material from 1 Corinthians and the material from Romans looking for areas of overlap, the issue of eating stands out and seems to lie at the center of the dispute. According to 1 Corinthians, the question underlying the debate about food was "What constitutes idolatry?" Idolatry is not explicitly mentioned in Romans 14 and 15, but it is not hard to imagine that the same issue might lie behind the vegetarianism and rejection of wine mentioned there.

FOOD AND IDOLATRY

"Offerings to idols" (*eidōlothuton* in the singular; *eidōlothuta* in the plural), or at least what might possibly be considered "offerings to idols," is discussed in three passages in 1 Corinthians: 1 Cor 8:1-13; 10:14-22; and 10:23-33. Although the Greek word *eidōlothuton* literally means "something offered to an idol" and does not specifically mention food, such offerings normally consisted of food. As a result, this word is often translated "food offered to idols." This term is pejorative and was used by Jews and Christians rather than non-Christian pagans. Pagans would not have called their gods "idols."

---

14. Horace also uses the phrase "plain table" (*mensa tenuis*) in *Carmina*, Book 2, Ode 16, line 14.

15. On Roman vegetarianism, see Reasoner, *Strong and the Weak*, 74-84. Reasoner quotes a fragment (now called "On Food") that has survived of Musonius Rufus' writings (pp. 83-84).

16. For a discussion of the Romans' great interest in calendars and days, see Reasoner, *Strong and the Weak*, 142-44.

The pagan term *hierothuton* ("sacred offering"), from which *eidōlothuton* is derived, occurs once in the New Testament, in 1 Cor 10:28.

These three passages in 1 Corinthians discuss offerings to idols, or what some considered such offerings. 1 Cor 8:1–13 presents the argument of some believers in Corinth that it was perfectly fine to eat in pagan temples since the pagan gods the idols represent did not really exist. Then 1 Cor 10:14–22 discusses people who both eat in pagan temples and participate in Christian communion. These are probably the same people discussed in 1 Cor 8:1–13. As Paul explains it, communion is "participation in the blood of Christ" (vs. 16), and while the pagan gods are not real, idol worship is not just empty ritual. Demons are involved in such worship, and a person cannot reasonably participate both in communion with demons and in Christian communion. The final passage is 1 Cor 10:23–33. There Paul discusses whether meat bought in the public market is tainted by idolatry and consequently should not be eaten. In effect, the question raised by this third passage is this: Is meat of unknown background to be considered *eidōlothuta* ("offerings to idols")?

Paul's comments about "offerings to idols" in 1 Corinthians suggest there were three groups of people in the Corinthian church holding three different positions. These are "the weak," "the strong" (which Paul never specifically names in 1 Corinthians), and a third unnamed group we will call "the pagan-temple Christians." This contrasts with the situation in Rome in which only "the weak" and "the strong" are present.

The third group, "the pagan-temple Christians," is that group discussed in 1 Cor 8:1–13 and 1 Cor 10:14–22. The gist of their argument is that because idols are not really gods, Christians have nothing to fear from such idols. Furthermore, avoiding pagan temples was inconvenient. In the Roman world, restaurants as known in the modern West did not exist. There were a few *taberni* ("inns") that catered to travelers on major roads, but people usually ate in private homes or in pagan temples. Some gentiles in Corinth who became believers had been accustomed to eating with their friends in these temples. They found it difficult to discontinue this practice, and they had trouble understanding what harm was in it since they no longer believed the pagan gods existed. In fact, they offered their insight as a mark of superior thinking.[17]

---

17. While Paul rejects this argument, it shows that already by the middle of the first century what would later become the central pagan critique of Christianity has already made an early appearance. The three main pagan critics of Christianity in antiquity, Celsus, Porphyry, and Julian the Apostate, all argued the same basic way:

Paul offers a counterargument. Unfortunately, the Greek text is somewhat uncertain at this point. The standard critical editions of the Greek read as follows for 1 Cor 8:2–3: "If anyone thinks he knows (something), he does not yet know as he ought to know; but if anyone loves (God), this one is known (by God)." Gordon Fee argues rather persuasively that the earliest witnesses from Africa (P[46] and Clement of Alexandria) record the original form of the text, which omits the words placed in parentheses. Making these adjustments, the text then reads: "If anyone thinks he has arrived at knowledge, he does not yet know as he ought to know; but if anyone loves, this one truly knows."[18] If Fee is correct, and I think he is, this completely changes the point and sharpens its connection with the issue at hand. Paul contends that having a lofty-sounding argument is not enough if it harms others. A person's knowledge must be shaped by the demands of love! Paul says pretty much the same thing in Rom 14:13–23.

Furthermore, Paul spells out the way in which "the pagan-temple Christians" do not exercise love. They may be convinced in their own minds that since these pagan gods do not really exist, it is fine to sit in a temple and eat food offered to theses "gods." But others with what Paul calls "a weak conscience" might see "the pagan-temple Christians" do this and misunderstand their actions to mean that they have reverted to their old habits of pagan worship. Alternatively, entering pagan temples may make it appear to others that their Christian faith simply means little to them. In either case, when those with weak consciences observe this apparent lapse of faith, their consciences will be defiled (vs.7) with devastating results.

It is possible that here "conscience" (*syneidēsis*) would be better translated "convictions." This would mean that some with "weak convictions" might be vulnerable. This possibility will be discussed in greater detail below.

Paul is not soft on idolatry. Everything he wrote suggests he found "offerings to idols" to be completely unacceptable. In this regard, he was

---

If you Christians really believed our pagan gods did not exist, you would not be afraid of them and you would not be afraid to enter our temples. Your unwillingness to come into our temples betrays your knowledge that some great power is at work. Such critiques, of course, miss Paul's acknowledgment that demons are at work in the temples, but not gods.

In a different vein, to illustrate the difficulty avoiding pagan temples implied, I once asked a group of students at a Christian university if their commitment to Christ would be affected if being a Christian meant they could never eat in a restaurant. They were shocked at the question, and in such a situation many seemed unsure where they would come down on the matter.

18. Fee, *First Epistle to the Corinthians*, 367. The translations are Fee's.

entirely within the mainstream of early Christianity. Nowhere in the New Testament, or for that matter in the Apostolic Fathers, is consuming "offerings to idols" considered acceptable. This does not mean, however, that Paul defined "offerings to idols" the same way every other Jew or Christian defined this term.

Most strikingly his definition differed from that of traditional Judaism. For Paul, what was unsavory and clearly idolatrous was an act performed before an idol and therefore in the service of this idol. Such an act could be as simple as eating food in a pagan temple since such eating was regarded as a sacrifice. The food itself was not contaminated. If it were carried away and someone ate it in a context unconnected to idol worship, Paul would not consider this to be idolatry. That is why a believer did not need to inquire about the history of a piece of meat sold in the public market (1 Cor 10:25).

This marked a very clear departure from Paul's Pharisaic past. For most Jews, and especially for Pharisees, "food offered to idols" was any food that had ever been associated with idolatry in any way. Even if a Jew bought meat in a public market for his family's use, its pedigree had to be ascertained. Its source was essential, as was inquiry about the chain of custody through which it had been passed. If there were any questions about ritual contamination by association with idolatry or any other kind of pollution, the food in question must be rejected. At a later period, and possibly in Paul's time, previous ownership by a gentile (who is presumed to be an idolater) automatically contaminated food.

Paul could not have accepted this last line of argumentation. He would not have agreed with the assumption that all gentiles should be considered idolaters. Such an acknowledgment would have completely undercut his mission to integrate gentiles into the church, which was the primary focus of his ministry.

Rom 14:2 suggests that "the person who is weak in faith" will only eat vegetables. Why might this be the case? If the context were a town with only a very small Jewish community, the reason for such fastidiousness would be obvious. Such a town might not have a *shochet*, a ritual slaughterer. Without a *shochet*, ritually correct meat would not have been available. But this was Rome, a major city with a robust Jewish community. Since ritually correct meat would have been available, why might some believers in Rome have felt the need to avoid eating meat?

There is no clear answer to this question, but two possibilities suggest themselves. The first is cost. Ritually correct meat likely was expensive. Meat generally is more expensive than vegetables, and ritually correct meat would have been in shorter supply than regular meat and therefore pricier.

The second and more important possibility is that ritually correct meat may have been available in Rome, but not to Jewish Christians. Perhaps the Jewish community that rejected faith in Jesus, particularly its *shochetim* ("ritual slaughterers"), was unwilling to transact business with Jewish Christians. They were treated as *minim* ("heretics"), and therefore they were excluded from polite Jewish society. Such shunning would have made ritually correct meat unavailable to the Jewish Christian community.

THE ROLES OF CONSCIENCE AND FAITH

We have seen that one characteristic of "the weak" is having a "weak conscience." The English word "conscience" comes from the Latin *conscientia*, which is composed of two parts: *con* meaning "with"; and *scientia* meaning "knowledge. This in turn, is a rather literal translation of the Greek word *syneidēsis*, which is also made of two parts: *syn* meaning "with" and *eidēsis* meaning "knowledge." In general, both *conscientia* and *syneidēsis* bore two distinctive shades of meaning, which may be roughly expressed by two English words derived from *conscientia*: "consciousness"; and "conscience." Both have to do with self-knowledge, but the former reflects awareness of one's own thinking processes, while the latter reflects awareness of one's own moral standards.

In the middle of the first century the word "conscience" was not widely used, and little consensus about its meaning or meanings had yet emerged. Nevertheless, it was an important category in Paul's thought. Furthermore, it is somewhat problematically for the modern interpreter that he uses the word in ways that suggest multiple shades of meaning.

In some instances (e.g., Rom 2:15; 9:1; 2 Cor 1:2) conscience, while located within oneself, seems to be an external (or quasi-external) witness that a person can call upon to testify on his behalf. To illustrate this meaning, Rom 9:1 says, "I speak the truth in Christ; I do not lie, my conscience bearing witness to me by the Holy Spirit, that . . . ."

But conscience is not a fully reliable moral compass or an immutable point of reference. Conscience is malleable. It can be shaped by internal attitudes or decisions. Consciences can be "good" (*agathos*; 1 Tim 1:5; 1:19), and they can be "pure" or "clear" (*katharos*; 1 Tim 3:9; 2 Tim 1:3). Conscience can also be "defiled" (1 Cor 8:7), "wounded" (1 Cor 8:12), "seared" (1 Tim

4:2), "corrupted" (Titus 1:15), and "rejected" (1 Tim 1:19). Because of these negative possibilities, conscience must be protected. This point is woven throughout Paul's teaching about conscience.

Paul also takes for granted that one person's conscience is not identical to another person's conscience. This is especially clear in 1 Cor 10:28–29, where he gives guidance about protecting someone's conscience, and then specifies whose conscience he has in mind. In a sense, conscience both shapes the morality of the individual and is also shaped by the individual's morality.

In several verses (Rom 13:5; 1 Cor 8:7, 10, 12; 10:25, 27, 28, 29; 1 Tim 1:5, 19; 3:9; 2 Tim 1:3) a person could substitute either the word "conviction" or the word "convictions" for the word "conscience" without loss of cogency. Thinking of conscience somewhat like "convictions" helps conceptualize what Paul means by "weak" and "strong." It is easy to visualize someone with weak convictions being more easily led astray. In contrast, someone with strong convictions would be less apt to stray.

It is not as easy to understand what Paul means by having "weak faith." Does he describe believing weakly? Or does he describe weak foundational beliefs?[19] In my experience, upon encountering the expression "weak in faith" most people interpret that to mean "believing weakly." However, the context of Rom 14:1, where the phrase "weak in faith" appears, suggests that the weakness involved has to do with the content of someone's beliefs, not intensity of belief. Paul encourages the larger Christian community to welcome the person who is "weak in faith," but not if this welcoming leads to "divisions over differing opinions." This possible undesirable outcome suggests that the problem is weak knowledge about God, about Jesus, or perhaps about Paul's gospel. Such people with more limited understanding are not less valuable to God and they are not to be shunned, but it is hard to construe being "weak in faith" as a compliment or even as a merely neutral description.

THE ORIGIN OF THE IDEAS OF THE STRONG

In Rom 14:14 Paul makes a striking declaration: "I know and have been persuaded by the Lord Jesus that nothing is profane [Greek *koinos*; literally "common"] in itself." But what does Paul mean by "profane in itself"? Probably he suggests that uncleanness does not inhere in food or wine, or any other physical object. Idolatry is an outward expression of inward

---

19. Theologians have long recognized a distinction between *fides qua creditor* ("faith by which someone believes")—faith as an action—and *fides quae creditur* ("the faith which is believed")—the content believed.

wickedness and confusion. Since food and wine have no rationality or intentionality of their own, uncleanness cannot inhere in them. Uncleanness is a matter of the human heart. In this, Paul the Jew has departed from traditional Jewish teaching.

Even more striking than Paul's recalibration of the Jewish theory of uncleanness, is whom he recognizes as the author of this insight. He says he has "been persuaded" that nothing is profane in itself "by the Lord Jesus Christ."[20] He does not specify whether he received this by private communication from the Lord, or if it came through oral tradition of Jesus's teachings. The clearest parallel of such a teaching by Jesus that we have is found in Matt 15:10–11 (// Mark 7:14–15). There Jesus says, "Hear and understand, what enters into the mouth does not defile the person, but what comes out of the mouth, this defiles the person." Both times where I have translated the Greek with "defile," the underlying verb is *koinoō*, which literally means "to make common." This verb is closely related to the adjective *koinos* ("common" or "profane") which Paul uses in Rom 14:14.

Thus, Paul implies that Jesus is the originator of the position championed by "the strong." Nevertheless, the ethic of love suggests that the strong should not insist other believers accept this insight despite its dominical authority. God will also accept those who do not understand all the implications of the new age ushered in by the death and resurrection of Jesus.

PROFILES OF THE WEAK AND THE STRONG

Any attempt to sketch profiles of the weak and the strong with any degree of certitude is impossible. Nevertheless, attempting such profiles seems a useful endeavor.

Both Jews and gentiles are found in both groups—the weak and the strong—although in Corinth there may have been few Jews in either camp, since the Corinthian church was largely gentile. The central rift involved differing perspectives on how to keep separate from idolatry. It is likely that the standard Jewish perspective served as the baseline for "the weak," and

---

20. I will acknowledge that it is possible Paul is expressing a slightly different idea: "I know and am persuaded before the Lord Jesus Christ that . . . ." This would involve taking the dative as a "dative of interest" rather than a "dative of the agent." (About the dative of the agent, see Smyth, *Greek Grammar* §1488.) There would be no doubt that Paul intended to express agency if he had used the more conventional *hypo* with the genitive to express this. Nevertheless, it seems most natural to the context for Paul to express by whom he has been persuaded.

that a reassessment of that baseline instigated by the teaching of Jesus and the revelation of the inclusion of the gentiles in the church informed the revised theory of the strong, including Paul.

If these generalizations are true, then the primary issue involved the status of meat and wine of uncertain provenance. Such meat and wine were unacceptable to the weak but were acceptable to the strong. Nevertheless, the strong were not to despise the weak because of their (excessive) scrupulousness, and the weak were not to condemn the strong as idolaters. While both groups had to work at accepting those in the other group, Paul suggests that the strong have a special responsibility to the weak. They are to "bear the weaknesses of those who are not strong" (Rom 15:1).

There were also differing opinions about whether some days were special or all days were the same. While this was a secondary issue, it too probably pitted a standard Jewish perspective about sabbaths, new moons, and the holidays described in the Bible against a Christian reconsideration of such things in the new era of salvation. It is unclear if calendrical issues were in play in Corinth since they are not mentioned in Paul's Corinthian correspondence.

When Paul describes some in Corinth as having "weak consciences," this might better be construed as having "weak convictions." They are not completely clear in their minds as to what constitutes idolatry and what does not, and therefore, they might be easily led astray by perceived inconsistency among fellow believers. They can also be described as "weak in faith." This is probably a way of stating that they have a weaker theological foundation than those well-versed in Paul's gospel and its many implications.

While several important terms in Roman society implied pecking orders of weaker and stronger, it is unlikely that categories from the larger Roman society formed the basis of the designations "the weak" and "the strong." Instead, these terms identified groups within the Christian community.

APPLICATION TODAY

The principles Paul underlines about disagreements over conduct are as applicable today as they were in the middle of the first century. Churches are filled with groups that unite around some behavior or principle that divides their group from another group that disagrees. Often these lines of demarcation have a moral shading to them, but that by itself does not justify condemning others. Which political party to support; whether consumption of alcohol is acceptable; whether tattoos are appropriate; whether or not certain styles of dress (e.g., shorts, halter-tops) can be worn in church; use of jazz bands or rock-and-roll music in worship; should the church be lit brightly or dimmed: these are all issues that challenge congregational unity today. When sorting such issues out, it is important to remember believers' consciences are not all the same, that causing someone else to violate her own conscience is unloving (14:15), and that whatever does not come from faith is sin (14:23).

Of course, there are non-negotiable fundamentals of the faith that cannot be compromised, but there is a common human tendency to elevate marginal matters to an unjustified prominence. The principles Paul teaches can serve as an antidote to much self-centeredness and folly.

A SHORT ROMANS 15

TRANSLATION: ROM 15:7–21

THE NATURE OF PAUL'S MINISTRY

⁷Welcome one another, therefore, just as Christ has welcomed you, to the glory of God! ⁸For I maintain Christ was born a minister of circumcision in defense of God's truth, in order to confirm the promises to the patriarchs, ⁹and in order for the gentiles to glorify God for his mercy, just as it is written: "On account of this I will confess you among the gentiles and I will sing your name." ¹⁰And again it says: "Be glad, gentiles, along with his people!" ¹¹And again: "All gentiles, praise the Lord, and let all the peoples extol him!" ¹²And again Isaiah says: "The root of Jesse will come, that is, the one arising to rule the gentiles. The gentiles will hope in him." ¹³May the God of hope fill you with all joy and peace as you believe so that you, by the power of the Holy Spirit, increase in hope.

¹⁴Concerning you, my brothers, I myself am convinced that you yourselves also are full of goodness having been filled with all knowledge, power, and ability to hold each other accountable. ¹⁵I have written to you more boldly than normal in part as reminders to you because of the grace given to me by God ¹⁶to be a minister of Christ Jesus to the gentiles, doing the priestly work of presenting the gospel of God in order that the offering of the gentiles might become acceptable, when sanctified by the Holy Spirit. ¹⁷Therefore, the boast I have in Christ Jesus is bringing the gentiles to God: ¹⁸For I will only dare to speak about what Christ has accomplished through me to bring about the obedience of the gentiles, in word and in deed, ¹⁹by the power of signs and wonders, by the power of the Spirit of God, so that I have fully proclaimed the gospel of Christ, from Jerusalem as far around as Illyricum, ²⁰and by this fulfilling my ambition to preach the gospel where Christ is not named in order that I may not build on another's foundation,

[21]rather as it is written, "It was not announced concerning him to those who will see, and those who did not hear will understand."

COMMENTARY

Vss. 7–21: With these verses Paul begins to close his letter. While this passage is not a summary of the letter he has written, it includes a summation of how he understands his ministry to the present point in his career.

Vs. 7: In this verse Paul commands his readers to welcome one another in a way that is reminiscent of 14:1. Just as 14:1 marked the beginning of a new section of the letter, this verse also marks a new beginning. Whereas divided groups were charged to welcome each other in 14:1, namely the strong and the weak, it is possible here too that division is implied by Paul's command to welcome each other. If Paul is indeed alluding to the need for reconciliation, the division is between Jews and gentiles. This distinction has often reappeared in this epistle suggesting it is the most basic faultline among the believers of Rome.

The imperative that is translated "welcome" (lexical form: *proslambanō*) could also be translated "receive." Paul's readers are encouraged to welcome each other in imitation of Christ, who has previously welcomed/received them all.

Vss. 8–12: These verses assert that both God's plan for the Jews and his plan for the gentiles are anchored in Christ. More specifically, they articulate a two-fold reason for the incarnation of Christ: "to confirm the promises to the patriarchs"; and "in order for the gentiles to glorify God for his mercy." The incarnation is also characterized as being "for the sake of" (*hyper* with the genitive) God's truth, which I have rendered "in defense of the God's truth."[1] A catena ("chain") of four Old Testament citations then unfolds. These citations buttress Paul's contention that it is part of the divine plan for the gentiles to glorify God alongside Israel.

The quotation in vs. 9 exactly reproduces the LXX of Ps 17:50 (English 18:49; MT 18:50) and 2 Sam 22:50. Since there were no chapters and verses in Paul's time, it is possible that he quotes this verse as a citation meant to include the following verse as well (in both the Psalm and in 2 Samuel 22): "I will magnify the saving acts of his king and the effecting of mercy to his Anointed, to David and to his Seed forever." If so, there can be little doubt that Paul understood the references to "his Anointed" and to "his Seed" as pointers to Jesus Christ.

---

1. In support of translating *hyper* "in defense of," see Smyth, *Greek Grammar* §1697.1(b).

The quotation in vs. 10 exactly reproduces a middle portion of the LXX text of Deut 32:43. In this verse the LXX text differs substantially from the MT and most English translations. There are strong reasons to believe the LXX preserves a form closer to the original than the MT. As is also the case in Deut 32:8, the LXX here discusses "the angels of God" in a way that was offensive to the Masoretes, who edited out what offended them. The LXX text of this verse also mentions "the sons of God," which was often considered a synonym for the angels of God, and this too was eliminated in the MT. What interested Paul in this verse was the command to the gentiles to be glad along with "his [i.e., God's] people." The implication is that God's blessings flow to gentiles as well as Israelites.

The quotation in vs. 11 is from Ps 117:1 (116:1 in the LXX). The quotation in vs. 12 exactly reproduces the LXX text of Isa 11:10, but with the omission of the introductory formula "in that day." The LXX hews close to the MT except that it prints "in him shall the gentiles hope [*elpizō*]" where the MT prints "the gentiles shall seek toward him." The word *kai*, in both Romans and in the LXX of Isaiah, which is usually translated "and," should not be translated that way here. It links "the root of Jesse" with "the one arising to rule the gentiles" exepigetically (i.e., with both clauses describing the same thing), and I have translated it "that is." Paul understands "the one arising to rule the gentiles" to be Jesus the Christ, and he sees in this passage a prediction of future gentile faith.

Vs. 13: Paul concludes his brief exhortation to "welcome" one another with a blessing. It is linked with the previous verse by use of the catchword "hope" (*elpis*) which appears twice in this verse. This noun "hope" (*elpis*) is closely related to the verb "to hope" (*elpizō*) from the previous verse. Paul's blessing is built on the triad of joy, peace, and hope.

Vss. 14–15: Aware that he has discussed difficult matters, Paul tries to soften the blow by assuring the Roman believers he thinks highly of them. His language is somewhat florid, using the intensive pronoun "I myself" (*autos ego* plus the inflection of the verb) for himself and the intensive pronoun "you yourselves" (*autoi* plus the infection of the verb) as he makes his point.

Paul uses the comparative form of the adjective *tolmēros* ("bold")—*tolmēroteron*—as a comparative adverb ("more boldly"). He does not specifically mention to what the comparison refers, but it is implied that he has written more boldly "than normal." He has written his difficult comments "in part" (*apo merous*) as "reminders" (using a participle of the verb *epanamimnēskō*, which only occurs here in the entire New Testament). This implies that perhaps they already knew and were practicing some of what he has written. He is being diplomatic, not wanting to offend anyone unnecessarily.

Vss. 16–17: In these verses Paul highlights that the focus of his ministry is bringing "the gospel of God" to the gentiles. Since much of what he has written is relevant to Jews as well, he is not trying to slight them. But the special "grace" (*charis*) that has been given him by God is to be a minister (*leitourgos*) of Christ Jesus to the gentiles. The exact nuance of *charis* is difficult to discern. In Gal 2:9 Paul uses almost the same language to describe the "grace," in the sense of a mission, that "had been given" to him. Often, he uses *charis* more-or-less as a synonym for "gift," and surely that factors in here. But does this imply simply the gift of this assignment, that he has been entrusted with this important task, or is it the gift of the assignment plus a special enabling? Likely he means the latter.

The word *leitourgos* is built on the words *laos* ("people") and *ourgos* ("work") suggesting "work for the benefit of the people." It usually meant "a person who performed a civic function" such as a public official. However, it could be used of a person who performed a ritual function in a religion. Given Paul's background and identity, this word probably evoked the image of a priest in the Jerusalem temple.

Paul also writes that he is "doing the priestly work [using a participle of the verb *hierourgeō*] of presenting the gospel of God." His heavy use of priestly language here and in 1 Cor 9:13–14 is one of the reasons that presbyters in the early church came to be called "priests." Paul was "of the tribe of Benjamin," as Phil 3:5 states, and therefore not a priest according to the normal conventions of Judaism. Paul probably intends this priestly imagery as metaphor and a correlate to his image of the gentiles as an "offering" (*prosphora*), yet one wonders how the Jewish believers in Rome processed this claim. Paul uses a similar metaphor in Phil 2:17, where he mentions "the sacrifice [*thusia*] and offering [*leitourgia*] of your faith."

If the foregoing comments have not already made this clear, Paul means "the offering of the gentiles" he mentions in vs. 16 to imply that the gentiles themselves are the offering; it is not that the gentiles bring some other offering to God. He, of course, does not mean that these gentiles who comprise this offering will die. Rather they are to be "living sacrifices," as in Rom 12:1.

As part of this imagery, Paul notes that this sacrifice of his gentile converts is "sanctified by the Holy Spirit." This is reminiscent of the guilt offering, about which Lev. 7:6 says, "It is most holy." Leviticus chapters 4–7 describe the sin offering, among other offerings, and the guilt offering. Lev 7:7 states that "the guilt offering is like the sin offering." Both were voluntary, which is to say, they were not required by decrees of a court. Rather, a person who feared he had sinned could choose to deal with that offense by way of the sin offering or the guilt offering, perhaps not always with clarity about which offering was needed. Paul's image is particularly apt because his gentile converts each voluntarily had chosen to seek atonement through the sacrifice of Christ, and each had experienced (initial) sanctification by the Holy Spirit as part of her salvation experience.

There is a question in vs. 17 concerning what Paul means by the neuter plural definite article *ta*. Many suggest his only boast is "the things [I have accomplished] for God" since *ta* often means "the things." However, in this case it seems more likely his boast is "[bringing] the gentiles to God." The word "gentile" (*ethnos*) is neuter, and *ta* could be understood to mean roughly "them," pointing back to "the gentiles" as an antecedent noun. Supporting this translation is the fact that "to" is a more standard translation of the preposition *pros* than "for." In either case a verb must be supplied.

Vss. 18–19: To make vs. 18 read more smoothly, I have rendered positively what Paul states using a double negative. Literally he writes: "For I will not dare to speak of the things Christ did not accomplish through me to bring about the obedience of the gentiles, in word and in deed." The word "only" is implied but not written.

The intriguing phrase "the obedience of the gentiles" resembles the phrase "obedience of faith" which bookends the letter, appearing in 1:5 and 16:26. Paul uses these phrases as shorthand expressions summarizing his mission, much as he uses the noun "gospel." These phrases have an apologetic character. While they accurately describe his mission, the "grace" God gave him, they also rebut the charge that he is antinomian. He not only preaches obedience to Jews, he also preaches obedience to gentiles, although it is not obedience to the Law of Moses. The charge against Paul of being anti-Law is discussed in Acts 21:21.

The emphasis of vs. 19 is that God's ministry is not merely a matter of words but also "power" (*dynamis*). This expression "power of"—*dynamis* coupled with a noun in the genitive case—appears twice in the verse, but with slightly different senses. The "power of signs and wonders" underlines Paul's ministry through deeds, already mentioned in the previous verse. This power Paul speaks of was *expressed* through "signs and wonders." Furthermore, this phrase "signs and wonders" highlights the miraculous nature of these deeds. Apparently, such miracles confirmed to those who witnessed them that Paul had a message from God.

The expression "power of" also bears a second sense. "Power of the Holy Spirit" indicates the *source* of the power. It could also be translated "power *from* the Holy Spirit." While Paul's readers could not have possessed copies of the book of Acts for it had not yet been written, they may have been aware of a tradition in which Jesus promised his disciples *dynamis* after they had received the Holy Spirit (Acts 1:8).

It is unclear whether the original Greek text read simply "Spirit," "Holy Spirit" or "Spirit of God." The bare reading "Spirit" is supported by one excellent witness, but only one. The other options are more widely supported. The fact that P[46], the earliest witness to Paul's letter collection, reads "Spirit of God" tips the choice that direction.[2]

In vs. 19 Paul describes the extent of his missionary travels to the current point of his career. Jerusalem was the eastern-most point and Illyricum the western-most point in which he had proclaimed the gospel. Illyricum was a Roman province when Paul wrote Romans, but within two decades it would be reorganized and renamed Dalmatia. Illyricum roughly corresponds with the coastal portion of present-day Croatia.

Paul's expression "from Jerusalem *as far around as* Illyricum" is artful. Unfortunately, no account of his expedition into Illyricum has survived. The Mediterranean Sea was the geographical anchor of the Roman world, especially when it came to travel. Paul pictured the Mediterranean as resembling an oval stretching from the southeast to the northwest. His travels had taken him from the eastern edge of this oval westward across much of the northern edge of the oval. The description "as far around as Illyricum" is both apt and helpful.

Vss. 20–21: Here Paul explains his ambition to spread the gospel in virgin territory, so to speak. He prefers going to areas where Christ is unknown and to make converts and to plant churches where he does not have to contend with other preachers. In 1 Cor 3:10 Paul reflects on having "laid a foundation" by planting the church in Corinth, after which Apollos built on that foundation. Laying the original foundation is the role he prefers.

The phrase "by this" translates the adverb *houtōs* (literally "thus"). The participle that follows *philotimoumenon* (lexical form *philotimeomai*) could be translated various ways: "making something an ambition"; "fulfilling an ambition"; "desiring the honor of something"; etc. Paul's point is that as Christianity sweeps westward, he desires to stay on the forefront of this expanding frontier in order always to venture where Christ has not been named. However, there is a certain irony in the fact that even while Paul is explaining this to people who live west of anywhere he has ministered, they were actually first taught about Christ by someone else.

The quotation in vs. 21 agrees perfectly with a portion of the LXX text of Isa 52:15. This material is from one of Isaiah's Servant Songs. As is sometimes the case, Paul may here quote a short piece of text with a larger

---

2. Metzger. *Textual Commentary, ad. loc.* Rom 15:19.

passage in mind. The beginning of Isa 52:15, a portion which Paul does not quote, reads: "Thus many gentiles will be amazed at him; even kings will hold their mouths." Paul understands these statements in Isaiah as predictions that are being fulfilled before his eyes. Gentiles, who did not originally share in the instruction given to Israel, nevertheless are amazed by Jesus, the Suffering Servant, and are seeing and understanding about him.

TRANSLATION: ROM 15:22–33

PAUL'S TRAVEL PLANS

[22]Since I have been hindered many times from coming to you [23]and now no longer have room in these regions, after many years of delay I have a great desire to come to you. [24]Whenever I should go to Spain, I hope to see you while passing through and to be helped along there by you, if first I may be filled with the joy of your company for a while. [25]But now I am going to Jerusalem to serve the saints. [26]For Macedonia and Achaia were pleased to collect some common funds for the poor of the saints in Jerusalem. [27]Indeed, the gentiles were pleased and are in debt to them: for if the gentiles came to share in their spiritual things, the gentiles also owe the Jerusalem saints to serve them with material things. [28]For this reason, after completing and putting my seal on this benefit to them, I will leave by way of you for Spain. [29]And I know that when I come to you, I will come with the fullness of Christ's blessing. [30]I urge you, brothers, through our Lord Jesus Christ and through the love that comes from the Spirit to fight with me in your prayers to God for me, [31]that I may be delivered from the unbelievers in Judea and that my ministry in Jerusalem may be acceptable to the saints, [32]so that when I come to you joyfully through the will of God I may refresh you. [33]May the God who produces peace be with you all. Amen.

COMMENTARY

Vss. 22–33: It is quite common for Paul to discuss his travel plans toward the close of a letter. To discuss his plans was especially important in this case, since he had never been to Rome, and it was far away, especially if one calculates the distance from Jerusalem rather than from the environs of Corinth. Also, the fact that he planned to take an intermediate trip before visiting Rome meant he needed to warn his letter's recipients not to expect him too soon. The modern reader is able to see a certain amount of irony in this passage since we know that Paul's trip to Rome was delayed by his arrest and imprisonment, matters his original readers could not have known.

Vss. 22–23: These verses are part apology, part explanation of his current situation. Paul expresses some frustration at often having been hindered from visiting Rome. Apparently, for many years he has desired to come but has been unable to do so. Nevertheless, he assures his readers of his great desire to visit them. The reference to "many years" suggests the Christian community in Rome had been in existence for considerable time.

Paul also explains that he has exhausted "room in these regions," probably meaning the province of Achaia (the area around Corinth) from which he writes and northward into Macedonia and perhaps into Illyricum. This, of course, does not mean that there is no opportunity to spread the gospel in these regions, but rather that they are no longer places where Christ has not been named. In keeping with his ambition explained in vs. 20, Paul wants to move into new territories. Beyond this basic point, there may also be an element of hyperbole in his statement.

Vs. 24: Paul shares the name of the new area where he wants to minister: Spain, at the western edge of Europe. One of Paul's purposes for writing Romans was to solicit support for his planned mission to Spain. He hopes to spend time with the Roman believers and get to know them, but then also to have them help him travel to Spain with supplies or funds.

The translation "being filled with the joy of your company" is not strictly literal, but it conveys what is implied. Literally, the clause reads "that I may be filled with you [plural]," but this implies the joy of time spent together. The time spent together will be "for a while" (*apo merous*). Usually *apo merous* means "in part," as it does in vs. 15, but here it refers to a period of time.

Although nothing is said about the matter, one wonders if Paul also hoped to learn or to improve his Latin while in Rome. While Latin was used throughout the Empire in military and governmental circles, in Spain it was also the language of everyday life. In Spain Paul would need to be able to speak Latin, but he was probably not yet fluent. Latin had not been the language of everyday life anywhere he had lived previously. So Rome presented him with a real opportunity. While Greek was the standard language of Christian worship in Rome during the first century, the capital of the Empire would have afforded many opportunities to use and learn Latin in other settings.

Vss. 25–28: In these verses Paul explains his plans to visit Jerusalem and to deliver the contribution that the mainly gentile Pauline churches of Macedonia and Achaia have collected for their Jewish brothers and sisters in Jerusalem. The great faultline that threatened the unity of the first-century church was the Jewish-gentile divide, and the greatest pastoral concern of Paul's life was to keep unity between these two groups. The great project he conducted to further this aim was collecting "common funds" for the poor among the saints of Jerusalem. "Common funds" translates *koinonia*, a word that elsewhere is commonly translated "communion," "fellowship," "partnership," and "participation." Raising these funds had dominated what is often called Paul's "third missionary journey."

This collection was intended "for the poor of the saints in Jerusalem." The genitive case used in the phrase "of the saints" is a partitive genitive, implying that some of the Jerusalem saints were poor and some were not. This reinforces what is implied in Acts, namely, that the holding of "all things in common" by the Jerusalem community did not last.

It is interesting how Paul frames the moral dimension of this project. He does not present it as charity for the poor saints of Jerusalem. Instead, he presents it as the repayment of a debt. As he explains in vs. 27: "If the gentiles came to share in their spiritual things, the gentiles also owe the Jerusalem saints to serve them with material things." In other words: The Jewish believers shared what they had with the gentile believers, and likewise the gentile believers should share with the Jewish believers what they have.

The phrase "their spiritual things" (*pneumatikois autōn*; literally "their spirituals") could also be translated "their spiritual gifts." In 1 Corinthians 14 this expression apparently denotes a narrower grouping of *charismata*, probably limited to oral gifts such as prophecy, speaking in tongues, and the interpretation of tongues. Here the phrase is contrasted with "material things" (*tois sarkikois*; literally "fleshly things") and probably does not bear such a specific sense. Paul makes a similar contrast between "spiritual things" and "bodily things" in 1 Cor 9:11.

In vs. 28 Paul more-or-less restates what he has already stated in vs. 24. After delivering the collection for the poor, he will leave Jerusalem for Spain, but he will stop on the way in Rome.

Vss. 29–32: Ever aware he is the slave of Christ, in vs. 29 Paul asserts that he has Christ's blessing. Christ for him was not a figure from the past, but rather a living companion, his master and guide. To paraphrase James Denney slightly, "When Paul thinks of Christ, he does not look back, he looks up."[3]

In vs. 30 what is translated "the love that comes from the Spirit" in the Greek literally reads "the love of the Spirit." This translation construes the genitive relationship as a "genitive of source." Paul's point is not that the

---

3. Denney, *Second Epistle to the Corinthians*, 140.

Spirit loves; his point is that the Spirit supplies the love that will motivate the Roman believers to conduct spiritual warfare on Paul's behalf.

The infinitive phrase "to fight with me" (*sunagōnisasthai moi*) evokes either the image of cooperation in military combat or the image of cooperation in athletic competition. In either case a struggle is involved, and the task requires joint effort rather than individual effort alone.

In vs. 31 Paul expresses a two-fold prayer agenda. His first point—"that I may be delivered from the unbelievers in Judea"—seems prescient in light of the forthcoming uproar in Jerusalem that resulted in his imprisonment (Acts 21). This prescience reminds me of Martin Luther King, Jr.'s famous "I've Been to the Mountaintop" address delivered in Memphis' Mason Temple, a historic Pentecostal church and landmark, the night before he was assassinated. In that great speech Dr. King warned his audience that like Moses he might not get "to the promised land" with the people he led.

The second point on Paul's prayer agenda is that his "ministry in Jerusalem may be acceptable to the saints." Paul had invested a huge amount of time and effort into gathering the collection for the poor among the saints of Jerusalem. The fact that he is not completely sure this gift will be accepted and appreciated shows the fragility of Jewish support in Jerusalem for Paul's gentile mission and for his gospel. He was engaged in high stakes diplomacy!

There is something very normal and human about Paul's wish that things might go well in Jerusalem so that when he arrives in Rome he will be in a joyful mood and will be able to share his delight with them, or as he puts it in vs. 32, that he may "refresh them" (*sunanapauomai hymin*). It is not completely clear whether this verb implies something Paul will do *for* the Roman believers or *with* them. If the latter option is taken, then the translation would be "so that . . . I may relax with you."

Vs. 33: The blessing recorded in this verse, concluding with the liturgical "Amen," marks a decisive break in the letter. If the form of the letter suggested by P[46] is correct, then this verse is followed immediately by a doxology and then several short sections that conform to standard letter-writing conventions or to Paul's personal conventions for closing a letter, or to both.

DOXOLOGY

TRANSLATION: ROM 16:25–27

DOXOLOGY

[25]To the one who is able to strengthen you, according to my gospel and the proclamation of Jesus Christ, according to the revelation of the mystery kept quiet for time immemorial, [26]but now has been displayed through both scriptures and prophetic sayings according to the decree of the eternal God for the obedience of faith made known to all the gentiles. [27]To the only wise God through Jesus Christ, to whom is the glory forever. Amen.

COMMENTARY

Vss. 25–27: As will be evident to the reader, in this commentary these verses are not placed in their conventional location. Placing them here follows their position in P[46], the most important single manuscript of Paul's epistles. While the reasons for this decision go beyond the evidence of this one manuscript, it is certainly an important witness. *For a fuller discussion of what goes where, see the Introduction to this commentary in the section titled "The Ending of Romans." For a more detailed discussion of the reasons for reordering the text in the way I have, see "Appendix 1: The Ending of Romans."*

The reader will also notice that this passage has a pronounced liturgical character. The use of the word "glory" (Greek *doxa*) in vs. 27 marks it as a "doxology." In fact, the word *doxa* appears at the end of this passage, and it set off as the climax of the passage by being the passage's only noun standing in the nominative case.

Another doxology appears in Rom 11:36. Furthermore, doxologies bear similarities to "benedictions," which are marked by use of the words "blessing" or "blessed," and benedictions appear in Romans at 1:25 and 9:5. Both doxologies and benedictions frequently, but not always, conclude with the liturgical word "Amen," which is a transliteration of an ancient Hebrew (and Aramaic) word that also appeared in transliterated form in subsequent Greek and Latin translations of the Bible. In accordance with this convention, vs. 27 concludes with "Amen."

Another mark of the poetic/liturgical form of these verses is that they lack a main (finite) verb. Instead, they are comprised of a series of phrases and clauses governed by participles.

The structure of this passage is shaped largely by three parallel elliptical phrases: "to the one who is able . . ."; "to the only wise God"; and "to whom . . . ." Each phrase describes the recipient to whom praise is addressed while omitting an overt mention of this praise, implying, for instance, "This praise is . . . to the only wise God."

While this passage is designed to honor God by giving him glory, it also highlights the eternal nature of God's plan, which was long kept secret but is now has been revealed and is being executed. The expressions "for time immemorial" (*chronois aiōniois*) and "the decree of the eternal God" (*epitagēn tou aiōniou theou*) describe this vividly.

Vs.25: It has been traditional to translate the beginning of this verse, "Now to him who is able . . . ," and this is fine, if these words are properly understood. The word "now" translates no specific Greek word. Moreover, in this context it has no temporal meaning as "now" normally indicates. "Now" is offered strictly to mark emphasis. Therefore, it is neither required nor missed by its absence from the translation.

The parallel expressions "my gospel" and "the proclamation of Jesus Christ" are interesting. Seemingly, these express similar but not identical concepts. The Roman believers to whom Paul writes have certainly been exposed to the proclamation of Jesus Christ, but it is less clear that prior to receiving this letter they have been exposed to what Paul calls "my gospel." Certainly, Paul's gospel is a proclamation of Jesus Christ, but it includes additional features, particularly concerning the inclusion of gentiles in God's plan.

By praising God as "one who is able to strengthen you," and tying together the noncontroversial "proclamation of Jesus Christ" with the relatively more controversial gospel he teaches, Paul hits a unifying note as he moves toward the end of his letter.

Paul indicates that the revelation of a long-hidden secret lies at the base of both his gospel and, in fact, any proclamation about Jesus as the Christ. It is hard to escape the conclusion that the Christian message is "apocalyptic" in nature, even if the genre of Paul's writing (i.e., letters) would not normally be classified as "apocalyptic." Paul claims to embrace Israel's hope revealed through God's long relationship with his covenant people, but he acknowledges that God's actions in and through Jesus are surprising and unforeseen. Nevertheless, they are true.

Vs. 26: This verse explains that "the revelation of the mystery" has "now" taken place. What previously had been shrouded in mystery has forthrightly been put on display.

The translation "through both prophetic sayings and writings" relies on giving full force to the Greek conjunction *te*, which is ignored in most translations. This is somewhat understandable since the use of *te* here is uncommon although not unprecedented. Most often when *te* is used, it is paired with *kai* to mean "both . . . and." Here, however, it is not used in this common way. Appearing as it does in the middle of a prepositional phrase, it likely coordinates elements within that phrase.[1] While *graphōn prophētikōn* is usually construed as a single category—"prophetic writings" or "prophetic scriptures"—the conjunctive particle *te* that precedes *graphōn prophētikōn* suggests Paul has two categories in mind: "scriptures" (or "writings"); and "prophetic sayings." While "prophetic" is an adjective, it sometimes is used without an explicit noun it modifies. In such cases, it usually refers to prophetic sayings.

This display of the mystery has occurred "according to the decree of the eternal God," and it is "for the obedience of faith for all gentiles." Paul's linkage of God's eternal decree with the inclusion of the gentiles is no accident. This linkage forestalls the grumbling of some Jews who sneeringly suggest that Paul's gospel implies that the unchanging God recently changed his mind by including gentiles who until recently had been excluded.

The very interesting phrase "the obedience of faith" appears one other time in Romans, in 1:5. The two occurrences of this expression, one near the beginning of the book and one toward the end of the book, function as bookends encapsulating the book's message. Both Jews and gentiles can and must obey God through expressing faith in Jesus, if they are to please God. Paul considers the obedience of faith to be part of the mystery he has discussed and part of the decree of the eternal God. Planned from time immemorial, that plan has only recently been activated and made known. Of course, Paul's gentile mission stands front and center in this plan.

Vs. 27: Two of the three parallel phrases that provide structure to this passage occur in this verse, and since they are only sparsely augmented, they are much shorter than the first. "To the only wise God" is more than a statement of monotheism; it points to God's surpassing wisdom. With

---

1. Smyth, *Greek Grammar* §2983 discusses the use of *te* both following prepositions and to join closely associated words.

three consecutive words—"only" (or perhaps "preeminent"), "wise", and God—each in the dative case, together they could be translated "to the pre-eminent-in-wisdom God."[2] God's superior wisdom is an important theme in Paul's letters. Consider, for example, his quotation of Is. 29:14 (LXX) in 1 Cor 1:19: "I will destroy the wisdom of the wise," and his pronouncement in the following verse, "Has not God exposed as foolish the wisdom of the world?"

---

2. On *monos* sometimes implying "preeminence," see Liddell and Scott, *Greek-English Lexicon*, s.v. "monos," II.4.

ROMANS 16

TRANSLATION: ROM 16:1–16

GREETINGS TO CHRISTIAN LEADERS IN ROME

¹I introduce to you Phoebe our sister, who is also a deacon of the church in Cenchreae, ²so that you receive her in the Lord in a manner worthy of the saints and that you provide her with the things she might need: She herself has become the patroness of many and of me myself. ³Greet Prisca and Aquila my fellow workers in Christ Jesus, ⁴who put their own neck under threat of the sword for my life, to whom not only I but also all the churches of the gentiles give thanks, ⁵and also greet the church that meets in their home.

Greet Epaenetus my beloved, who is the "first fruit" of Asia in Christ. ⁶Greet Mary, who has worked a great deal among you. ⁷Greet Andronicus and Junia, my kindred and my fellow prisoners who are notable among the apostles, who also were in Christ before me. ⁸Greet Ampliatus my beloved in the Lord. ⁹Greet Urbanus our fellow worker in Christ and Stachys my beloved. ¹⁰Greet Apelles, who is tried-and-true in Christ. Greet those from the household of Aristobulus. ¹¹Greet Herodion my kinsman. Greet those from the household of Narcissus who are in the Lord. ¹²Greet Tryphaena and Tryphosa, who have labored diligently in the Lord. Greet Persis the beloved, who has labored much in the Lord. ¹³Greet Rufus who has been chosen by the Lord and his mother, who is also my mother. ¹⁴Greet Asyncritus, Phlegon, Hermes, Patrobas, Hermas, and the brothers who are with them. ¹⁵Greet Philologus and Julia, Nereus and his sister, and Olympas and all the saints with them. ¹⁶Greet one another with a holy kiss. All the churches of Christ greet you.

COMMENTARY

Vss. 1–16: In the past I have on occasion referred to Romans 16 somewhat dismissively as "the chapter that no one reads." This is because it is dominated by greetings to people contemporary readers largely know little about. To the casual reader, this makes this chapter seem uninteresting.

However, my interest in this chapter has grown immeasurably over the years. Because of the many names included in it, along with characterizations of many of the people named, this chapter provides a window into the sociology of a Christian community in the middle of the first century unlike anything else in the New Testament. This makes it invaluable.

To a certain extent, this more sociological approach to Romans 16 was begun in the 1860s by the British scholar J. B. Lightfoot, who read this material carefully against the backdrop of Greek and Latin literature and inscriptions. More recently, Peter Lampe has demonstrated in magnificent fashion how careful reading of the Romans 16 material can be combined with the statistical analysis of databases of inscriptional evidence. The result was his 1987 (first) German edition of the book later translated as *From Paul to Valentinus: Christians at Rome in the First Two Centuries*. His work inaugurated a growing shift in how Romans 16 is perceived and studied.

Before examining this material in some depth, it is important to discuss certain matters of vocabulary. As mentioned near the outset of this commentary, Paul never refers to a unified "church of Rome," which is surprising given the way he addresses Christian communities in other cities. Paul does, however, refer to a "church" (*ekklēsia*) that meets in the home (*oikos*) of Prisca and Aquila. Because *oikos* often means "house," this reference has led to the widespread contemporary use of the expression "house church," which is used with varying connotations and nuances. In relation to the People's Republic of China, "house church" is often nearly synonymously with the expression "underground church," marking a contrast with "registered churches" or "Three-Self" churches, which are recognized by the Chinese government. For the purposes of this commentary, this sense of the term "house church" is not helpful. In the 50s of the first century there was no "registered" alternative, and Christianity was not yet being suppressed in the way that would begin only a few years later.

Sometimes "house church" is used to describe a rather informal gathering of people without much structure surrounding it. This sort of church meets in someone's home rather than a special building used primarily for church functions. This, of course, comes close to describing the groups mentioned in Romans 16. In the discussion below, I will occasionally use the term "house church." When I do, I mean the term in this sense. The term really means a "home church" since whether the group met in a shop, a tenement of an *insula* (a Latin term meaning roughly "an apartment building") or a *domus* (Latin for "house") is irrelevant.

Some might consider this similar in meaning to the expression "small group," as it is widely used in Christian circles today. Often, "small group" suggests a subset of a larger unified congregation, sometimes temporary in duration and largely social in nature. This term might have some utility when discussing groups mentioned in Romans 16, except that it is unclear how these groups understood themselves in relation to each other. The fact that in his letter Paul addresses them all does not necessarily mean they considered themselves to be part of a larger whole. In fact, Paul may go out of his way to address these various groups and their leaders to assure them that his letter is meant for them.

Because of his location in Corinth, Paul is unable to greet the individuals he names in person. Therefore, he asks the recipients of his letter to greet various individuals and groups on his behalf. He does this by using imperatives ("Greet such-and-such."). Of course, many of those whom Paul wants greeted will also become the recipients of his letter when it is read publicly (probably in several different sittings), so to some degree the situation is artificial: they will be greeting themselves. But his requests are certainly not pointless. Paul starts the passage by commending to them Phoebe, whom they have not previously met. He asks those he writes to "receive" her, even though she is a stranger to them. This implies not only greeting her but also extending her every courtesy. He then proceeds to have them issue numerous other greetings on his behalf.

Paul directs his Roman readers to greet for him twenty-four individuals by name. Two other individuals are designated by a relative's name (Rufus's mother and Nereus's sister). In addition, five groups are mentioned: 1) the church (*ekklēsia*) that meets in the home (*oikos*) of Prisca and Aquila; 2) those of the household of Aristobulus; 3) those of the household of Narcissus who are in the Lord; 4) the brothers (and sisters?) with Asyncritus, Phlegon, Hermes, Patrobas, and Hermas; and 5) all the saints with Philologus, Julia, Nereus, Nereus's sister, and Olympas.

The first group clearly refers to members of a house church that meets at the home of Prisca and Aquila. The second and third groups are associated with heads of households. These households may include family members related by blood but likely also include slaves owned by head of the household. Former slaves of this individual may also be included. In ancient Rome, slaves, freedmen, and freedwomen could all be considered part of a person's household.

Lampe makes the important grammatical point that for two groups, those associated with Aristobulus and those associated with Narcissus, the Christians who are to be greeted do not include the entirety of the household. If Paul had wanted to indicate the entire household of Aristobulus he would have written *hoi Aristoboulou* (literally, "the people of Aristobulus"). Instead, he writes, *hoi ek tōn Aristobulou* (literally, "the people from those of Aristobulus"). The same is also true of those in Narcissus's household. Furthermore, neither Aristobulus nor Narcissus is to be greeted because neither was a believer.

For some reason Paul reemphasizes that he means to greet only the Christian part of the household of Narcissus by adding the qualifying clause "who are in the Lord." He does not make the same addition when mentioning the household of Aristobulus.[1]

The last two groups mentioned by Paul raise an important question: What does it mean to be "with" the brothers or saints he lists? While it might refer to some other type of association, given the context it seems most likely to mean something like "associated with them in a house church."

Because Paul starts his list of people to greet with Prisca and Aquila and the house church they host, we know that at least part of Paul's list refers to house church leaders and participants. Can we therefore assume the two references to certain individuals and the groups "with" them also speak of house church leaders and participants? This is likely, but not certain. In these cases, the word *oikos* (meaning either "house" or "home") is not used, but this may be because these churches do not meet in a home. They may meet in a workshop or even outside. Or they may not have a permanent gathering point at all. Also, likely they do not have a host or hosts analogous to Prisca and Aquila.

If the first group mentioned consists of a house church, and it is presumed that the fourth and fifth groups also consist of house churches, then what should we make of the second and third groups? It is likely both groups consisted of slaves or former slaves of the head of their household. This also suggests that they all worked together. Both those from the household of Aristobulus and those from the household of Narcissus functioned as churches connected by their natural associations. They worshipped together within the parameters available to them.

Apparently, neither Aristobulus nor Narcissus were believers. The fact that Paul does not greet them when he greets those who were "from" their households implies they themselves were not part of the Christian

---

1. Lampe, "Roman Christians" 222; *Paul to Valentinus*, 165.

community. Nevertheless, both were likely prominent figures in Roman society since they headed up households of some size.

All considered, we have plausible evidence pointing to at least five "house churches." This leads to a follow-up question: How should we think of the fourteen individuals who are not expressly connected with any of these five groups: Epaenetus; Mary; Andronicus and Junia; Ampliatus; Urbanus; Stachys; Apelles; Herodion; Tryphaena and Tryphosa; Persis; Rufus; and Rufus's mother. I suspect that several of the persons mentioned just prior to "those from the household of Aristobulus" are leaders of that group, and several others mentioned just prior to "those from the household of Narcissus" are leaders of that group. This would reduce the number of people not connected with any of the five groups by perhaps half a dozen. To account for those eight to fourteen unconnected individuals that remain, Lampe suggests that there may have been seven house churches or more rather than the minimum of five that seem clearly indicated.[2]

Of the 24 named individuals in the first sixteen verses of this chapter, it is somewhat surprising that only five or six—Aquila, Andronicus, Junia, Herodion, probably Prisca, and possibly Mary—can be identified with any confidence as Jewish believers. Since tensions between Jewish believers and gentile believers seem an ever-present undercurrent in this letter, one might have expected more. Nevertheless, if these named individuals are leaders, then roughly one quarter (6 of 24) are Jews, which is not an insignificant share. Somewhat more difficult to evaluate is the number of Jewish-Christian house churches, as opposed to gentile-Christian house churches, or mixed house churches. If not only Aquila but also Prisca is a Jew, then the house church in their house is likely Jewish-Christian. If the Jews Andronicus and Junia lead a house church—as apostles, they might—it likely would be a house church made up largely of Jews. Beyond this, there is little to say.

The genders of the 24 named individuals plus the two specified by family relationships (Rufus's mother and Nereus's sister) prove interesting, particularly if these individuals constitute the leadership of the believing community in Rome. Of these 26 individuals, 9 are women—Julia, Junia, Mary, Nereus's sister, Persis, Prisca, Rufus's mother, Tryphaena, and Tryphosa—who constitute more than a third of the total. In addition, Paul discussed the active engagement in ministry of six of these nine women (only the activities of Julia, Rufus's mother, and Nereus's sister remain undescribed). In comparison, Paul describes the activities of only three, or

---

2. Lampe, *Paul to Valentinus*, 359. However, Chrys C. Caragounis dismisses Lampe's suggestion as a "Vermutung" (German for "supposition"). See Caragounis, "From Obscurity to Prominence," 256.

possibly five, of the 17 men listed: Aquila, Andronicus, and Urbanus; and perhaps also Apelles and Rufus.[3] Since the ministry activity of two-thirds of the women is mentioned compared with the ministry activity of less than a third of the men, it is hard to dismiss the significant leadership roles of women. To make this point differently, it appears that Prisca the house church host and Junia the apostle, while special in their own ways, were not complete aberrations. Women played important leadership roles among the believers in Rome.

Vss. 1–2: Paul begins this section of his letter introducing Phoebe and urging the believers of Rome to extend to her appropriate hospitality. The verb he uses, *synistēmi*, could also be translated "I commend," and his introduction amounts to a forceful commendation. The other times Paul uses this verb in Romans (3:5; 5:8), it basically means "to show." (In my translations of these passages, I use the similar English verbs "to highlight" and "to demonstrate.") By introducing Phoebe to the Roman believers, he is showing her to them.

While Paul does not state this explicitly, it is nearly certain that Phoebe has delivered his letter to Rome. She may be described as his *messenger*. It would be quite some coincidence if Phoebe, this person from the environs of Corinth showed up in Rome just as Paul's letter happened to arrive, containing as it does a commendation of her and an exhortation to care for her in a way that marks her as Paul's associate. Some things are so obvious they do not require saying.

William Doty notes that in the late Hellenistic era it was common for an author to write politely and in generalities within a letter and to entrust his real message to the messenger. This was often done because of political intrigue and the fear of having committed dangerous ideas to writing.[4] That is not likely to be the case with Romans since Paul expresses himself forthrightly in his letter. But that such behavior was common illustrates the point that letter-carriers often did more than deliver the mail, and the way Paul charges the Roman believers to care for her suggests she was expected to stay for a while and to be available to answer their questions about what he has written.

Doty further explains the role of Paul's messengers:

> ... I often have the sense that Paul, who made such a point of indicating his trust in the carriers (co-workers), did not think of his written letters as exhausting what he wished to

---

3. This analysis is similar but not identical to that of Lampe, "Roman Christians," 222–23.

4. Doty, *Letters in Primitive Christianity*, 45.

communicate. He thought of his associates, especially those commissioned to carry his letters, as able to extend his own teachings. I wonder if the Pauline letters may not be seen as the essential part of the messages Paul had to convey, pressed into brief compass as a basis for elaboration by the carriers. The subsequent reading of the letters in the primitive Christian communities would then have been the occasions for full exposition and expansion of the sketch of material in the letters.[5]

Paul notes that besides being a "sister," i.e., a fellow believer, Phoebe is also a "deacon"—not a deaconess, as some have proposed—of the church at Cenchreae, a port city just east of Corinth. She is a proven church leader. It is noteworthy that while Phoebe is called a deacon rather than a deaconess, she is called a "patroness" rather than a patron. Both patrons and patronesses were known in the Roman world although their roles may have differed since women generally could not hold public offices. In contrast, there seems to have been a unified office of ministry in the church for both sexes: the deacon. *For a fuller discussion of the significance of the title "deacon," see the excursus called "The Women of Romans 16."*

Some translations have rendered *prostatis* with the colorless "helper." Instead, it is a technical term and a Latinism, the rough equivalent of the Latin *patrona* ("patron," or more accurately "patroness" since it is feminine in form).[6] This suggests that she has been a financial supporter, and Paul notes that she has become "a patroness of many and of me myself." Clearly, Phoebe is a person of substantial means, and it may well be that she paid her own way to deliver Paul's letter to Rome. She may also have hired Tertius, Paul's amanuensis, to assist his writing, and paid for writing materials. Jewett also points out that by calling Phoebe his "patroness," in the class-oriented society of Rome, Paul has marked her as his social superior, and someone to whom he is obligated.[7]

Vss. 3–5a: Paul directs his readers to greet Prisca and Aquila—Prisca being a shortened form of Priscilla—who are described as fellow workers in Christ Jesus. No doubt this is true, but according to Acts 18:3–4 for a time in Corinth they were also fellow-workers in the tent-making business. Translated literally, Paul says that these colleagues "put their neck under for my life." This elliptical statement implies it was a sword their collective neck was under. While this colorful expression is probably metaphorical and did not literally involve potential beheading, Paul makes clear that they risked

---

5. Doty, *Letters in Primitive Christianity*, 45–46.
6. Bl-D-F §5.3.
7. Jewett, *Romans*, 947.

a great deal, possibly their lives, for him. The exact situation Paul alludes to is unknown to contemporary readers, although Prisca and Aquila may have related it to their friends in Rome. In 1 Cor 15:32 Paul says that he "fought with beasts at Ephesus," an event the details of which are also unclear. Here, too, Paul probably speaks metaphorically about some terrible struggle he had with governmental authorities. Since Prisca and Aquila lived in Ephesus for a time, it is possible that both accounts relate to the same event and that when Paul's life was on the line Prisca and Aquila risked a great deal to save him.

Three divergent explanations have been given for the name Aquila (*Akylas* in Greek). It may be a transliteration of the Latin word for "eagle" (*aquila*). It might also be based on the Greek word for "acorn" (*akylos*). A third option connects it with Rome's noble Acilius family. Which explanation seems strongest depends in large part on how one reconstructs Aquila's biography. *For more about Aquila (and Prisca), see the excursus titled "The Women of Romans 16."*

In Rom 11:13 Paul has already claimed the title of "apostle of the gentiles." Given this role, Paul feels the liberty to speak not only for himself but also for "all the churches of the gentiles" in charging the Roman believers to thank Prisca and Aquila, and to greet the church that meets in their house.

Vs. 5b–c: Paul calls Epaenetus both "beloved" and "the 'first fruit' of Asia." This latter designation means he was the first gentile converted to following Christ, and leaving paganism, in the Roman province of Asia. Paul would not have considered Jews who came to follow Jesus as converts in the same way. His use of first-fruits terminology reaffirms his belief that gentile believers constituted a metaphorical sacrificial "offering" which he presents to God (Rom 15:16). Since Epaenetus was originally from Asia, almost certainly from Ephesus, Paul must have met him there, and the term of affection "beloved" suggests they were close. Epaenetus also likely first became acquainted with Prisca and Aquila while they all still lived in the East. This long-standing association likely accounts for why Paul names him immediately after Prisca and Aquila.

Lampe remarks that Paul's comments about Epaenetus imply nothing about the level of his Christian activity in Rome.[8] While this is true, in this case silence about this matter should not be taken as an affront. Given his past associations, it would not be surprising if he participated in the church that met in Prisca and Aquila's house, although evidently not as a leader.

The name Epaenetus (*Epainetos*) is Greek, meaning roughly "praised" or "praiseworthy." Most people with Greek names living in Rome were

---

8. Lampe, *From Paul to Valentinus*, 166 n. 40.

either slaves or freedmen, but this was not always the case. Although an immigrant to Rome, the circumstances of his migration are unknown.

Vs. 6: It is unclear whether the woman mentioned in this verse was named Mary (*Maria*) or Mariam (*Mariam*). The manuscript evidence is about equally divided. Even if the name is Mary, there is the further question whether it should be understood as a Latin name or a Hebrew variation of Miriam. According to Lampe, it is likely a Latin name, the feminine form of the Roman *nomen gentilicium* Marius.[9] In this case, she would be a gentile. In contrast, if her name is either "Mariam" or a variation of it also written as *Maria*, she would likely be a Jew. The mother of Jesus was clearly a Jew, having been given the name of the sister of Moses. In the LXX this name is *Mariam*. The Gospels are divided in how they report her name. Although English translations rather uniformly call her "Mary," and *Maria* is the name by which she is called in Matthew and Mark, in Luke she is called *Mariam*.

I have decided to call her "Mary" in my translation despite the fact that I consider *Mariam* the more difficult reading.[10] Considering that the manuscripts of the New Testament were transmitted through the centuries in a largely gentile environment, it seems more likely that a scribe would change *Mariam* to *Maria*, from the more exotic to the more common, than vice-versa. Even in the Jewish inscriptions from Rome studied by Harry Leon, the name Maria appears several times but not the name Mariam.[11] However, there is a major problem with calling her Mariam and thus treating this woman as a Jew: Paul does not call her his "kin," as he seems to do in this passage whenever the designation is fitting.

Paul's comment that Mary "has worked a great deal among you" is warm, but not based on first-hand knowledge. A source has reported this to him. The verb Paul uses, *kopiaō* ("to toil," "to work hard"), is a favorite of his for expressing effort in ministry. He also uses it twice in vs. 12.

Vs. 7: Andronicus (*Andronikos*) and Junia (*Iounia*) are likely married to each other. They are also his "kinsmen" (the plural of *suggenēs*), by which Paul means fellow Jews, and they like him have been imprisoned. Almost certainly they were imprisoned for the gospel or why else would Paul bring this up as a badge of honor?

---

9. Lampe, *From Paul to Valentinus*, 175–76. He also considers it likely she was a slave, a freedwoman, or a descendant of a slave. On this, see Lampe, *Roman Christians*, 228.

10. Text critics often prefer the *lectio difficilior* ("more difficult reading") since it is unlikely that a scribe purposefully changed a text to read that way. However, there are limits. Sometimes difficult readings are really impossible readings.

11. Leon considers *Maria* to be a Semitic name. Leon, *Jews of Ancient Rome*, 105.

Paul calls them "apostles," and he notes that they "were in Christ before me." If they had become believers in Christ before Paul, this must have happened very early in the Christian story. Certainly, it happened before the proclamation about Jesus had spread to Europe. This early date coupled with their Jewish identity suggests they likely became believers while in Judea and later emigrated to Rome. When Paul calls them "apostles," he may be signaling that they were instrumental in bringing the message of Jesus to Rome. That they suffered in prison may also be a factor. *For more about Andronicus and Junia, see the excursus titled "The Women of Romans 16."*

Vss. 8–10: In these verses Paul greets four individuals and one group. It seems Paul knew each of these individuals from when they earlier lived in the East. Paul does not associate them with any particular house church, and Paul may not know with whom they are currently fellowshipping.

The first individual is Ampliatus, who despite having a Latin name, was likely a slave or a freedman since he bore a name that during the reign of Augustus was created for slaves and continued afterward to be so used.[12] Paul calls him "my beloved," so they had a personal relationship. This marks him as someone from the East who migrated to Rome.

The name Urbanus (Greek *Ourbanos*) is Latin and means "city-dweller." Paul calls him "our fellow worker." If he has worked with Paul, this marks him as being from the East, yet his Latin name suggests he likely was freeborn.[13] Why is he called "our" fellow worker when Paul calls Prisca and Aquila "my" fellow workers? This is unclear. He may have worked with Paul in the East and the Roman believers in the West, but the same was also true of Prisca and Aquila.

It is unclear whether Stachys was a slave, a freedman, or freeborn. His name is Greek, and it means "a kernel of grain," or when applied to human offspring, "progeny." Other than this use as a name, the word appears four times in the New Testament (Matt 12:1; Mark 2:23, 4:28; and Luke 6:1). Paul calls Stachys "my beloved," marking him as another person from the East with whom he has a personal relationship.

Paul describes Apelles (Greek *Apellēs*) as "tried and true" (*dokimon*). Paul must know him from the East and have worked with him to be able to describe him in this way. His name is Greek, and he likely was named after the great fourth-century BC painter Apelles of Kos discussed by Pliny the Elder.[14] It is known that slaves were sometimes named after famous artists (e.g., Praxiteles, Zeuxis, Phidias, and Themison), so this suggests the

---

12. Lampe, *From Paul to Valentinus*, 173.
13. Lampe, *From Paul to Valentinus*, 167–68.
14. Pliny the Elder, *Natural History* 35.36.79–97.

possibility of a slave background. Nevertheless, it is impossible to know if Apelles had a slave background or not.[15]

As previously mentioned, Paul instructs his readers to greet a group of believers from the household of Aristobulus (Greek *Aristoboulos*). This Aristobulus did not have Roman roots of long standing.[16] There had been a line of Judean rulers and high priests named Aristobulus that began with Aristobulus I, who ruled for only a year (c. 104–3 BC). Josephus credits him with being the first Hasmonean king.[17] Although their origin was in the East, a strong linkage with Rome developed. An Aristobulus who is usually called Aristobulus Minor was educated in Rome, along with his brothers Agrippa I and Herod of Chalcis as well as the future Emperor Claudius. Aristobulus Minor lived out the remainder of his days as a private person (*idiōtēs*), presumably in Rome, but it is uncertain if he would still have been alive when Romans was written.[18] This may not be an impediment to the theory since Lightfoot contends that "[w]hen the slaves of a household passed into the hands of a new master, by cession or inheritance or confiscation, they continued to be designated by the name of their former proprietor."[19]

The name Aristobulus is Greek and means something like "best advising." Furthermore, as Lampe perceptively notes, this Aristobulus mentioned by Paul may have inadvertently had a hand in introducing Christianity to Rome and for that matter to the European continent. He writes:

> Aristobulus, who may have been a member of King Herod's household, emigrated to Rome. If he brought his Christian slave with him from the East, then *we have come upon one of the channels through which Christianity infiltrated the capital* [emphasis retained].[20]

Vs. 11: In this verse Paul directs his readers to greet Herodion (Greek *Hērōidiōn*), whose name indicates some connection with Herod or Herod's family. The fact that this name is listed immediately after "those from the

---

15. Lampe, *From Paul to Valentinus*, 179.

16. As Lampe puts it, "The master Aristobulus was hardly an autochthonous Roman. The masculine form of his name appears only twice in CIL 6 (17577, 29104); the feminine form, 'Aristobula,' once." Lampe, *From Paul to Valentinus*, 165.

17. Josephus, *Antiquities* 13.11.1 (Loeb numbering 13.301).

18. Lightfoot, *Epistle to the Philippians*, 174–75. Although there is some confusion about the family tree, Josephus attests that Aristobulus Minor remained a private person. See *Jewish War* 2.11.6 (2.221 in the Loeb numbering).

19. Lightfoot, *Epistle to the Philippians*, 175.

20. Lampe, *From Paul to Valentinus*, 165.

household of Aristobulus" may not be a coincidence. Whether consciously or unconsciously, in his mind Paul may have linked the names Aristobulus and Herod since Aristobulus IV was Herod's son and the family trees became interconnected.[21]

The specific form of the name *Hērōidiōn* is unusual, and no other person of that name is known to have lived in Rome. Even the more usual name Herodianus was rare in Rome, likely because it was originally a Semitic (Hebrew or Edomite/Idumean) name. However, the Herod family definitely had a Roman connection. During a trip to Rome, the first-century BC figure Herod I (the Great) was declared "king of the Jews" by the Roman Senate in 40 or 39 BC This king served as a client of the Roman Empire and founded the Herodian dynasty. There is also a slight possibility that Herod became the patron or sponsor of a synagogue in Rome.[22]

Paul calls Herodion "my kinsman," which means he was a fellow Jew, and which accords with his Semitic name. A Latin inscription records that a certain slave named Coetus had been the possession of a Herod and subsequently became the property of the Emperor Augustus. Lampe suggests that the Herodion Paul mentions was likely a slave with a similar history of having been owned by Herod at one time.[23]

Narcissus, the other head of a household that contains Christians, was likely a Roman native. Numerous people with this name are known, with some living in the same timeframe as Paul, and some owning slaves.[24] Suetonius, Cassius Dio, and Seneca mention a very wealthy and powerful freedman of Claudius by this name,[25] and Cassius Dio mentions another Narcissus from the reign of Nero.[26] Lampe considers it possible that the

---

21. Murphy-O'Connor, *Paul: A Critical Life*, 146.

22. A broken inscription (JIWE 2.292 = CIJ 173) may read "Synagogue of the Herodians." However, this transcription and translation is not assured and furthermore the inscription is from the third or fourth century. The argument that the synagogue must have been founded in the first century is based on the theory that Herod himself sponsored it. For a recent evaluation of this theory, see Burnett, "Reconsidering the Number of First Century C.E. Synagogues in Rome."

23. Lampe, *From Paul to Valentinus*, 177.

24. Lampe has done impressive research on Narcissus, and Jewett has supplemented this with additional information. See Lampe, *From Paul to Valentinus* 165 and Jewett, *Romans* 967.

25. Suetonius, *Claudius* 28. Cassius Dio, *Roman History* 60.19.2. Seneca, *Naturalis quaestiones* 4.15. These citations are from Cancik and Schneider, *Brill's New Pauly*, 9:507 (s.v. "Narcissus").

26. Cassius Dio, *Roman History* 64.3.

Narcissus Paul mentions was himself a freedman.[27] Nothing in Roman law or society prevented freedmen from owning slaves themselves.

Some scholars consider it likely that Claudius's freedman is the Narcissus in view here, largely because of his power and wealth. If this identification is correct, it is likely his household was quite large. However, there may be a problem with this identification: This Narcissus died in AD 54 and at that time his vast fortune was absorbed into imperial hands.[28] In other words, this Narcissus was dead before Paul wrote his letter. Still, if Lightfoot's observation noted above with respect to the household of Aristobulus is correct, then even after Narcissus's death, the slaves of his household might have continued to be known by the name of their former master. In fact, Jerome Murphy-O'Connor asserts there is inscriptional evidence that *Narcissisiani* (the Latin equivalent of "the household of Narcissus") passed into the possession of Emperor Nero.[29]

Vs. 12: It is Jewett's conjecture that Tryphaena (*Tryphaina*) and Tryphosa (*Tryphōsa*) were sisters since their names are linked by "and" (*kai*) and their names are so similar. In Greek Tryphosa means "luscious." Jewett calls Tryphaena "a Greek slave name" and reports that it means "dainty." Their names are well established in Roman inscriptions and papyri from Lydia and Egypt.[30] Lampe also considers it probable that they had slave backgrounds.[31]

As was the case with Mary, Paul says Tryphaena and Tryphosa "labored diligently" (*kopiaō*). This labor certainly involved ministerial activity or Christian service since Paul qualifies it as being "in the Lord."

Another person who "labored . . . in the Lord" is Persis (*Persis*) and Paul quantifies her work: she labored "much" (*polla*). Persis means "Persian," which implies an ethnic identity although such ascriptions may be based on guesswork and are not always reliable.[32] Nevertheless, such an ethnic name suggests she was a slave and a transplant. Had she remained in Persia (contemporary Parthia) among other Persians, the name would not make much sense.

Vs. 13: In this verse Paul charges his readers to greet two people: Rufus; and Rufus' mother. Rufus is a Latin name meaning "redhead." It was

---

27. Lampe, *From Paul to Valentinus*, 165.

28. Cancik and Schneider, *Brill's New Pauly*, 9:507 (s.v. "Narcissus").

29. The inscriptions are *CIL* 3.3973 and 6.15640. Murphy-O'Connor, *Paul: A Critical Life*, 326 note 16.

30. Jewett, *Romans*, 968.

31. Lampe, *From Paul to Valentinus*, 179–80, 183–84.

32. Lampe, *From Paul to Valentinus*, 174–75.

a cognomen often given to people with red hair. Based on his name and no obvious indicators of enslavement, Rufus was likely freeborn.

Paul commends him as "chosen [*eklektos*] in the Lord," the meaning of which is not clear to modern readers. In one sense, all believers may be described as "elect." If this is Paul's intended meaning, then this is more-or-less equivalent to calling him a "brother." However, because in the military calling someone "elect" or "select" indicated an honor setting an individual apart from the majority, some have wanted to understand Paul's phrase to mean something like "eminent" or "special." Similar usages are supposedly found in Jewish or Christian literature: "the chosen lady" of 2 John 1, which likely refers to a local church; "Rhaius [or possibly Gaius] Agathopus, a chosen man" in Ignatius, *Philippians* 11.1; and "special grace of faith" (*tēs pisteōs eklektē charis*) in the LXX's *Wisdom* 3.14.

Another matter of debate is whether this Rufus is the same person mentioned in Mark 15:21, in which Simon of Cyrene is described as "the father of Alexander and Rufus." Since Rufus was a common name, at first glance this identification seems far-fetched. However, two considerations increase its likelihood. First, the statement in Mark presupposes that book's intended audience will know who Alexander and Rufus are and that their names will add interest or relevance to the story. Normally people who are extraneous to a narrative would not be mentioned. Second, there is a long tradition connecting the Second Gospel with Rome, as the place where a young Mark, who was himself not an apostle, heard the apostle Peter recount many stories and sayings about Jesus. Mark then used these to compose his Gospel. At the beginning of the second century Papias of Hierapolis reports this basic story but without noting any clear connection with Rome. Irenaeus, writing his *Against Heresies* in the 170s or 180s, likewise notes that Mark wrote his Gospel based on the teaching of Peter but without mentioning Rome.[33] However, at the end of the second century or the beginning of the third, Clement of Alexandria explicitly states that it was in Rome that Peter's "sayings" were offered, which Mark then used to write his Gospel.[34]

If Mark had been around when Peter taught at Rome, he may have known the Christian community at Rome well enough to know it was familiar with Rufus. Therefore, as he composed his Gospel, perhaps while he remained in Rome, he chose to highlight a connection in the passion

---

33. Irenaeus, *Against Heresies* 3.1.1.

34. While Clement of Alexandria's book *Hypotyposeis* ("Outlines") in which this is made clear has not survived independently, Eusebius of Caesarea has preserved several quotations from it. In this context, the relevant passage is Eusebius, *Ecclesiastical History* 6.14.6.

narrative with one of their own. Based on this reasoning, Lightfoot judiciously observes that there is "at least fair ground for identifying the Rufus of St. Paul with the Rufus of St. Mark."[35]

Vs. 14: Of the five names listed in this verse, only Phlegon and Hermas may or may not have been slaves or freedmen based on analyses of their names. The other three were almost certainly slaves or former slaves.[36] Given the way Paul links them together with a group of unnamed individuals, it seems likely they comprised a house church with the named individuals constituting its leadership. The named people are all male, and probably the unnamed people are male as well since they are called "brothers." But it is unclear whether this refers only to males or a mixed group of "brothers and sisters." (In Hellenistic Greek masculine labels can designate mixed-gender groups.) Furthermore, it seems possible that this entire group of males worked together in some strenuous enterprise of their master or masters. In modern western society, congregations are usually organized along geographic lines rather than commonalities based on work or interests. If things were organized more in line with early Roman practice, we might have congregations such as the Smithfield meatcutters' church, the Pulte construction workers' church, or the fly fishermen of the Yellowstone River church, but without formal names.

Vs. 15: In this verse Paul names four more individuals plus the sister of one of the named persons. These then are linked with another group of unnamed individuals described as "saints." This too likely refers to a house church, although clearly in this case the church includes both men and women. In this case too, the named individuals are presumably the leaders of this house church.

It is probable that Philologus (*Philologos*) and Julia (*Ioulia*) were married since their names are linked with *kai* ("and"). While Julia is a Latin name, she is likely a freedwoman of someone who was a member of the very powerful *gens Iulia* (the clan of Julius Caesar). The alternative is that she is an aristocratic noblewoman. However, this is unlikely since Philologus, whose name is Greek, was likely a freedman, and noble women married freeborn noble men. In the inscriptional databases, Julia is also by far the most common of the Romans 16 names. Only a small fraction of the women so named in these inscriptions could have been noble freeborn women.

Nereus (*Nereus*) was a slave or a freedman, and his sister likely had a slave background as well. Nereus was named for a Greek sea god that

---

35. Lightfoot, *Epistle to the Philippians*, 176.

36. The name Patrobas is either shortened form of Patrobios ("[I have received] life from [my] father") or a nickname of much the same nature. See Bl-D-F §125.

Homer called "the old man of the sea," and it was common for slaves to be named after gods.[37]

The name Olympas (*Olympas*) is Greek and likely a shortened form of *Olympiodōpos* ("gift of Olympus"). In the first century this was always the name of slaves or freedmen.[38]

Vs. 16: The charge, "Greet one another with a holy kiss," is somewhat formulaic, although not always used as Paul moves toward the close of a letter. Exactly the same words appear in 1 Cor 16:12 and 2 Cor 13:12. Only slightly different is 1 Thes 5:26. This is not to say that this exhortation was uniquely Paul's. 1 Peter closes with a charge to greet each other with a "kiss of love." Since kissing normally takes place mainly between family and friends, in a context of some disunity a charge to kiss one another may be a subtle way of saying: "Settle your differences."[39]

After charging his readers to greet so many people, as a kind of reciprocation Paul makes an announcement: "All the churches of Christ greet you." This is certainly hyperbole since Paul cannot have had a full understanding of Christian developments in Africa or in Parthia. However, as in vs. 4, Paul takes upon himself the role of spokesman for others.

Excursus: The Women of Romans 16

In the following essay, the roles of three women discussed in Rom 16:1–16 will be examined in some detail: Phoebe, Junia, and Prisca. But these three are not the only women whose roles in the church Paul highlights in this passage. Mary, Tryphaena, Tryphosa, Persis, Rufus's mother, Julia, and Nereas's sister—a total of ten—are singled out. This compares with seventeen men who are similarly singled out. If these individuals comprise the Christian leadership (broadly defined) in Rome, and if Phoebe is excluded from the list since she was not a resident of Rome, this means that nine of these twenty-six leaders—more than a third—were women. It is hard to avoid the implication that women were entrusted with great responsibility among the Christians of Rome.

---

37. Homer, *Iliad* 18.35.
38. Lampe, *From Paul to Valentinus*, 179.
39. Jewett, *Romans*, 974.

CHURCH LEADERSHIP AND THE EXAMPLE OF PHOEBE

In the contemporary context, most Classical Pentecostal groups allow women to serve as ministers, unlike many non-Pentecostal evangelical denominations. The situation is more mixed among charismatics. Catholic and Eastern Orthodox charismatics do not recognize female priests, although the two Protestant groups that have the largest charismatic populations (Anglicans and Lutherans) generally do credential female clergy. More Baptist and Reformed charismatics do not. It is hard to generalize about independent charismatics. These observations highlight the continuing controversy surrounding women ministers in contemporary Christianity.

The biblical basis for authorizing women as ministers is a complex and fraught matter, and this commentary is not an appropriate venue for a full consideration of the biblical evidence. However, Romans contains considerable material that is pertinent to this issue and therefore some consideration of this matter is necessary. In general, the evidence of Romans strongly supports formal ministry by females. *For additional information about two relevant passages from other letters of Paul, see Appendix 2: Comments on 1 Cor 14:34–35 and 1 Tim 2:11–15.*

Of course, a question of central importance in this discussion is this: What is meant by ministry? If it simply means "service" then no Christian group of which I am aware would deny that women can be ministers in that sense. The issue at stake is whether women should be allowed 1) to teach a general population that includes adult males, or 2) to have a leadership role over a general population that includes adult males. Generally, even those groups that do not allow women to serve as formal clergy have allowed women to teach and to lead other women and to teach and have authority over children and adolescents.

Also complicating this discussion is the fact that the churches pictured in the New Testament were often organized quite differently from contemporary churches. For instance, no one associated "church" with a building, as is common today. Christians met in homes, shops, or other structures built for other uses.

And leadership structures differed too. Let me explain somewhat whimsically. If a Martian came to earth and spied on church activities in the United States in order to report to his superiors on Mars about what he observed, he might relay back something like this:

These churches are led by pastors. They have senior pastors, lead pastors, associate pastors, preaching pastors, youth pastors, worship pastors, teaching pastors, executive pastors, pastors of evangelism, pastors of missions and outreach, etc. That book they read all the time surely must say a lot about pastors.

The fact is that it does not. In the New Testament the word "pastor" translates the Greek word *poimēn*, which literally means a "shepherd," and this word is used in three ways. First, it can refer to a literal "shepherd" who supervises and cares for sheep. Second, it can be used metaphorically, which is to say, it describes behaving like a shepherd through caring for people just as a literal shepherd cares for his sheep. An example is John 10:12. There the behavior of the hireling is contrasted with that of a shepherd: "The hireling, not being a shepherd, is not the one to whom the sheep belong. He sees the wolf coming, he leaves the sheep, and he flees." The third use of *poimēn* is as an official title, meaning "pastor." This third usage only occurs once in the entire New Testament, in Eph. 4:11: "And he [Jesus] gave apostles, prophets, evangelists, pastors and teachers . . . ."[40] So, why is it that a term that appears only once in the New Testament has become so central in contemporary church life? Why are there "teaching pastors" rather than "teachers"? Why are there "pastors of evangelism" rather than "evangelists"? Why does every church leader have to be called some kind of pastor?

Setting the Context: Overseers, Elders, and Deacons

Of course, there are other titles for leaders found in the New Testament beyond pastors. Perhaps the most obvious are the "overseer" (*episkopos*, also called "bishop"), the "elder" (*presbyteros*,[41] also called "presbyter"), and the "deacon" (*diakonos*, also called "minister" or "servant").

In Rom 16:1 Phoebe is called "a deacon of the church in Cenchreae." Since Phoebe is also called "our sister," there can be no doubt she was female. Several translations call her a "servant" of the church in Cenchrea, but this is a tendentious translation designed to deny to Phoebe the status of a

---

40. It might be argued that in John 10:11 *poimēn* also is used as a title. There Jesus calls himself "the good shepherd." But as the context makes clear, this quasi-title is used to point out the shepherd-like care Jesus will show for his followers: "The good shepherd gives his life for the sheep."

41. Literally *presbyteros* means "older man." It is a comparative form of the adjective *presbys* ("old man").

formal title. Where a man is referred to the same way, he will be called either a "deacon" or a "minister." Taken in context—in this verse Paul is making a formal introduction—*diakonos* here should be translated as a title, not as a description. While the English words "deacon" and "minister" often are used as titles, "servant" is not. Even more prejudicially, in other translations Phoebe is called a "deaconess," even though when that title does emerge later in church history it is spelled differently than in this verse.[42]

The Traditional Paradigm

Some who oppose allowing women to serve in church leadership roles will acknowledge that Phoebe was a "deacon." However, they will oppose ordaining women because they claim in the New Testament no woman is ever called either an "overseer" or an "elder," and both are considered higher titles than "deacon."

This argument presumes the theory of "the two-fold order" of leadership in the New Testament. Those who hold this theory usually also believe that sometime in the second century (at least in the East) the two-fold order of leadership was supplanted by "the three-fold order."

When examining the New Testament evidence, a good place to begin is Phil 1:1. This verse refers to "saints," "overseers," and "deacons" in the church at Philippi. The "saints" are generally understood to be the church's laity, while the "overseers" and "deacons" are understood to be its leaders. Notice that "elders" are not mentioned in this verse (Phil 1:1), while they are mentioned elsewhere in the New Testament. Notice too that the word "overseers" is plural, suggesting there was not one top leader.

To account for the absence of "elders" in Phil 1:1, a theory emerged that in the New Testament the words "overseers" and "elders" referred to the same people. They were twin titles that were interchangeable. So, there were two orders of leaders: first, the "overseers" (*episkopoi*)/"elders" (*presbyteroi*) who were the senior leaders; and second, the "deacons" (*diakonoi*), who were junior leaders.

There is some biblical evidence in favor of this theory. In Titus 1:5–6 Paul recounts how he had charged Titus to appoint "elders" in the various towns of Crete. Then two verses later Paul mentions "overseers," along with a list of qualifications for such "overseers."

---

42. An example is the Revised Standard Version, according to which Rom 16:1 reads: "I commend to you our sister Phoebe, a deaconess of the church at Cenchreae."

How are these two terms to be understood in relation to one another? Are they synonyms? Or does Paul have two different categories in mind?

According to Titus 1:5–6 each "elder" is to be "blameless, a one-woman man, having children who are believers, not charged with recklessness or unruliness." Then, in Titus 1:7–9 Paul lists several additional qualifications for "overseers." Is he supplementing the list of qualifications he has just given since he considers "elders" and "overseers" to be synonymous terms? Or is he implying a distinction? Is he suggesting that all elders (both deacons and overseers) must meet the standards of the first list, but overseers must also meet the standards of the second list? Either interpretation is possible.

Another passage often taken to support the traditional two-fold order is Paul's farewell address given to the Ephesian elders in Acts 20:17–38. Acts 20:17 reports that Paul summoned the "elders" from Ephesus to meet with him in Miletus. Then in vs. 28 Paul says: "Watch yourselves and the entire flock, to which the Holy Spirit appointed you overseers to shepherd the church of God which he secured though his own blood." While Paul does use the plural form of the noun "overseer" (*episkopos*) here, given the pastoral imagery of this verse he is likely using that word in a general sense rather than as a formal title. Shepherds oversee their flock.

Some have noted additional support for the two-fold order from the second-century literature. In the collection of books known as The Apostolic Fathers there is a letter written by Polycarp, a leader of the church at Smyrna, that is addressed to the church at Philippi. There is also another letter written to Polycarp by Ignatius, a leader of the church located in Antioch on Syria's Orontes River. In the letter that Polycarp wrote, he styles himself an "elder" (*presbyteros*). The letter begins: "Polycarp and the elders with him to the church of God that sojourns at Philippi." In contrast, in Ignatius's letter to him, Polycarp is called an "overseer" (*episkopos*). This letter begins: "Ignatius, who is also called Theophoros ["God-bearer"], to Polycarp, overseer of the church of the Smyrnaeans . . . ." It seems that Polycarp could reasonably be addressed with two different titles.

However, sometime in the second century this earlier "two-fold order" gradually began to give way to a "three-fold order." The title of "overseer" (*episkopos*)—also known as "bishop"—was separated from, and elevated over, the title of "elder" (*presbyteros*). No longer did the same people hold both titles; some were overseers and others were elders.

To this was also joined another innovation. A new limitation was imposed: there could be only one "overseer" per city. This idea has come to be known as "the monarchical episcopacy," since it meant that one man was fully in charge of all the Christians in each city. While this new pattern gained traction relatively quickly in the East, it took considerably more time to take hold in the West.

Both innovations—the development of the three-fold order and the development of the monarchical episcopacy—are associated in some manner with Ignatius, the monarchical bishop (*episkopos*) of the church at Antioch who has already been mentioned. (Notice that Ignatius was eager to address Polycarp as an "overseer," not one of a group of elders.)

A Different Paradigm

Having explained this standard theory of the evolution of the two-fold order into the three-fold order in some detail, I will now explain why I think this standard theory is wrong. I will also explain how this relates to our understanding of the role of Phoebe and the contemporary debate about whether women should serve as church leaders.

1 Tim 3:1–7 lists the qualifications to be expected in an "overseer" (*episkopos*). Similarly, 1 Tim 3:8–13 lists the qualifications expected in a "deacon" (*diakonos*). Surprisingly, there is no similar list of qualifications expected of an "elder" (*presbyteros*). It is equally surprising that Paul unabashedly uses the term "elder" in this letter (e.g., 5:17, 19) even though he lists no qualifications for such an office. Why does he do this? Well, I think it is because the word "elder" (*presbyteros*) is a more general term than either "overseer" or "deacon." It incorporates both categories. A person who is an "overseer" is also an "elder." And a person who is a "deacon" is also an "elder." In Phil 1:1 Paul does not mention "elders" because he has already mentioned the component categories of "overseers" and "deacons" and therefore to list qualifications for "elders" would be redundant. While Ignatius addresses Polycarp as an "overseer" to distinguish him from a deacon, Polycarp modestly calls himself an "elder" to include himself among the other elders of Smyrna, some of whom are "overseers" and some of whom are "deacons."

Similarly, in *Didache* 15.1 the author instructs his readers "to ordain for yourselves overseers and deacons" with no mention of elders. Likely this is because the term "elder" (*presbyteros*) was more general than either "overseer" or "deacon" and included both, in precisely the same way as these words are used in 1 Timothy.[43]

---

43. On the other hand, Polycarp, in *Phil.* 5.2 and 6.1, lists qualifications for both

This theory accounts for the evidence on which the traditional two-fold order is built, but it also accounts better for the evidence from 1 Timothy and the *Didache*.[44]

Furthermore, if this theory is correct, then Phoebe was both a "deacon" (*diakonos*) and an "elder" (*presbyteros*). This also means it is not true that no female elders are mentioned in the New Testament, even if that specific appellation is not specifically applied to her.

Phoebe the Letter Carrier and Patroness

We should also be careful not to minimize the important role Paul gave to Phoebe. It is very probable that she carried Paul's epistle to Rome. She was also likely charged with clarifying points Paul's readers did not understand.

Paul also calls Phoebe his "patroness." Apparently, she was a person of considerable means. She may, in fact, have bankrolled Paul's project of writing Romans (perhaps by hiring the amanuensis Tertius and buying writing materials), and she may have paid her own way to deliver the letter. *For more about Phoebe, see the comments to Rom 16:1–2.*

A FEMALE APOSTLE?

If the claim that Phoebe was an "elder" is shocking to some, the claim that a female apostle is mentioned in Romans 16 might seem a greater shock. But in Rom 16:7 Paul writes: "Greet Andronicus and Junia, my kindred and my fellow prisoners who are notable among the apostles, who also were in Christ before me." The first key question, of course, is whether Junia (Greek *Iounia*) was a female or a male.

There is substantial evidence that this person was female. The name as I have presented it—Junia (*Iounia*)—is female. This is a matter of Greek orthography. But conceivably the name could be Junias (*Iounias*), which would indicate a male name. The text of Romans does not make this clear because in Rom 16:7 the name is placed in the accusative case with the form

---

deacons and for elders, but not for overseers. This may suggest that he simply prefers the title "elder" (*presbyteros*) to overseer (*episkopos*).

44. I want to make clear that I did not originate this theory. The credit belongs to Gordon Fee, although perhaps I have extended his argument a bit. See Fee, *1 and 2 Timothy, Titus*, 78.

Iounian, which would be the correct form for either *Iounia* or *Iounias*.[45] So why am I insistent this is a female name? It is because the epigraphic evidence (evidence from inscriptions) suggests that while *Junia* was a relatively common name in the ancient Roman world, *Junias* was not a name at all.[46] The male name complementing *Junia* was *Junius*, and several prominent Romans bearing that name are known. Furthermore, the Greek rendering of the Latin name *Junius* would be *Iounios*. Some have suggested that *Junias* was an abridged form of *Junianus*, a well attested name, but there is no evidence for this either.[47]

A second key question concerns what is meant by the clause "who are notable among the apostles" (*hoitines eisin episēmoi en tois apostolois*). *Hoitines* is an indefinite relative pronoun in form and in classical Greek usage would mean "whoever." But in the New Testament the definite relative and the indefinite relative pronouns were no longer clearly distinguished; thus, the translation "who."[48]

The adjective *episēmos* (the singular of *episēmoi*) originally meant "marked with a sign or symbol," as a shield might be marked. By extension this came to mean "notable," i.e., marked not physically but in some other way. Another possible translation would be "remarkable." But how does this adjective relate to "among the apostles." The two options seem to be 1) that they are apostles and are particularly notable ones, or 2) that they are considered notable by the apostles but they themselves are not apostles.

While both translations are grammatically possible, the first option seems more straightforward and likely. For the second option to be correct, Paul would have to know the consensus view of the apostles concerning

---

45. Technically, the accent would distinguish between the masculine and feminine names of the accusative form *Iunian*. If the name were masculine, a circumflex accent should appear on the ultima. If the name is feminine, an acute accent should appear on the penult. The problem is that accents were not added to New Testament manuscripts until the ninth century. So, at best evaluating the accents in manuscripts would tell us how the text was understood in the ninth century; it would not indicate what Paul wrote. On this, see Wallace, "Junia Among the Apostles."

46. Lampe reports that *Iunia* appears over 250 times in the *Corpus Inscriptionum Latinarum*, and while *Iunianus* appears 21 times, the abbreviated form *Iunias* never appears. Lampe, *From Paul to Valentius*, 176.

47. Lampe offers this succinct assessment: "In antiquity the name "Junia" was widespread, while "Junias" (a possible short form of "Junianus," cf. Bl-D-R §125⁶) is attested nowhere." The section corresponding to Bl-D-R §125 (6) in Bl-D-F is §125 (1, 2). See Lampe, *From Paul to Valentinus*, 165 n. 39.

48. Bl-D-F §293.

these two individuals, but it is not as if the apostles had annual conventions in which such matters might be discussed. It is not even clear what kind of apostles would be involved in arriving at such a consensus. Except in Galatians 2, where Paul apparently discusses the decision of the so-called Jerusalem Council (Acts 15), I do not know of any place where Paul discusses the collective views of apostles. Even in Galatians 2, he reports on the apostles' consensus grudgingly.

Since Andronicus and Junia are mentioned together, it seems likely they are married, and they minister together. Despite their names being Greek and Latin respectively, they are Jewish since Paul calls them "his kindred." Apparently, they presently live in Rome. They came to faith in Christ before Paul, which suggests that they came to faith in the East, perhaps in Israel, before Christianity had spread to the West. Did they help bring the faith to Rome? Might this be why Paul calls them apostles?

Paul also calls them his "fellow prisoners." While this could mean that they were imprisoned in the same place and at the same time as Paul, more likely it simply means that they too have been imprisoned for the faith. Did that happen in conjunction with the disturbances that led Claudius to expel Jews—probably Jewish Christians—from Rome? Concerning these very interesting individuals, we have more questions than answers.

PRISCA (AND AQUILA)

Paul mentions Prisca three times, each time in greetings to Aquila and her or in greetings from Aquila and her (Rom 16:3; 1 Cor 16:19; 2 Tim 4:19). In Rom 16:3 Paul calls them his "fellow workers" and states that she and her husband "risked their neck" for him (Rom 16:4). Apparently, they liked to host house churches because both in Rom 16:5 and in 1 Cor 16:19 such churches are mentioned, one in Rome and the other apparently in Ephesus. In Acts a couple named Priscilla and Aquila is also mentioned three times (Acts 18:2, 18, 26), and this is almost certainly the same couple, Prisca being a shortened form of Priscilla. The name Prisca (or Priscilla) is Latin, and Aquila is likely Latin.

The account in Acts 18 provides more information about this couple than does Paul's brief citations: 1) Aquila was a Jew; 2) Aquila was originally from Pontus, a region in the northeast of Asia Minor facing the Black Sea;[49] 3) the couple had recently arrived in Corinth from Italy, having been

---

49. Pontus is not far from the area of ancient Persia, which contained a large

expelled by Claudius; 4) Paul lived with them for a while; 5) they, like Paul, were "tentmakers," and Paul worked with them in tentmaking while he lived with them; 6) they sailed with Paul from Corinth to Ephesus; and 7) in Ephesus they were able to explain "the way of God" more accurately to Apollos, who apparently did not know about Christian baptism, but only "the baptism of John."

By the time Paul writes Romans, they have apparently returned to Rome, where, as in Ephesus, they host a church which meets in their house (Rom 16:5). Later, they apparently return east, moving back to Ephesus (2 Tim 4:19). The fact that they can move around the Roman world rather freely implies they are freeborn.

One unusual matter associated with Prisca/Priscilla and Aquila is that in four of the six times they are mentioned in the New Testament, Prisca/Priscilla's name is listed first (in Acts 18:18, 26; Rom 16:3; 2 Tim 4:19). Customarily husbands were listed before wives. An explanation commonly offered is that Prisca was of higher social standing than her husband. Another explanation is that she was more prominent in ministry.

Two individuals offer fascinating but quite different reconstructions of the lives this extraordinary couple. The German scholar Peter Lampe and the late American scholar Robert Jewett were friends, and both spent time engaged in research at the University of Heidelberg where Lampe was a regular professor and Jewett served in various visiting roles. Despite these shared experiences, they painted radically different pictures of the lives of Priscilla and Aquila.

Jewett's reconstruction is intriguing, very creative, and highly romantic. He contends that this couple was a most improbable match, Prisca being a daughter of a prominent Roman family and Aquila being a slave from Pontus (in northern Asia Minor) whom Prisca purchases, frees, and then marries. Key anchors of this theory are the association of the noble Roman Acilius family with Christianity and the hypothesis that Rome's Catacomb of Priscilla was named after the biblical Prisca/Priscilla. Neither anchor is securely moored.

The Catacomb of Priscilla is one of the most significant catacombs in Rome. Sometimes called "the queen of the catacombs," it is located near the second milestone of the Via Salaria, a road heading northeast out of Rome. During the second through the fourth centuries it was used for Christian burials, including for the burials of bishops of Rome (i.e., popes). It was originally excavated as a quarry, before being repurposed for burials and

---

Jewish population. Some apparently relocated southwest to Pontus.

religious ceremonies. At the end of the first century AD, the site apparently belonged to a Roman senator named Manius Acilius Glabrio, who served as a consul in AD 91.[50] This Glabrio built what Jewett describes as a "country estate" above the excavations below.[51] Furthermore, by the end of his life, Glabrio was apparently a Christian. Suetonius reports Domitian had him killed while he was in exile. The true but unofficial reasons for his execution are outlined by Cassius Dio, namely "atheism" and "drift[ing] into Jewish ways," although the official pretext was Glabrio's unseemly gladiatorial combat with an animal.[52]

While Christian burials were not taking place in the catacomb in the middle of the first century, when the biblical Prisca/Priscilla was alive, it is not impossible that by then the Acilius family already owned the site. The date of its acquisition is unknown. It is also unclear when a member of the Acilius family first became Christian or whether any member of the Acilius Glabrio family by the name of Prisca/Priscilla lived during the middle of the first century AD.

An inscription indicates that Glabrio's wife was named Priscilla, with her full name being Arria L.f. Plaria Vera Priscilla.[53] An important question is whether the Catacomb of Priscilla is named for the Priscilla mentioned in the New Testament or for Glabrio's wife, who lived a generation or so later. The latter option is the conventional view, but Jewett argues for the former.

A key element of Jewett's reconstruction is Aquila's name. Jewett contends that the Greek form *Akylas* is a transcription of the Latin *Acilia*, the feminine form of *Acilius*. If Prisca's father had a *nomen gentilicium* of *Acilius*, then it would have been customary for a daughter's *nomen* (i.e., Prisca's *nomen*) to be *Acilia*. If at some point Prisca owned Aquila and then freed him, she would have become his "patroness" and both her *nomen* and the initial "*L*," standing for *Libertus* ("freedman"), would have become part of his name. It seems the Christian community used simple one-word names as an egalitarian gesture, almost certainly because slaves usually only had a

---

50. This Manius Acilius Glabrio is not to be confused with his son of the same name, who served as consul in AD 124.

51. Jewett, *Romans*, 955.

52. Such fighting, if it truly happened, was considered beneath the dignity of a senator. Suetonius's report in *Domitian* 10.2 is confirmed by Juvenal, *Satire IV*, 94–96. Cassius Dio, *Roman History* in John Xiphilinus's epitome of Book LXVII, 14.1–3.

53. This inscription is CIL VI, 6333. This name suggests that Glabrio's wife was a *liberta* ("freedwoman").

single name—as "property" they were not accorded a *nomen gentilicium*—and slaves made up a large part of the Christian community. Therefore, it would not be surprising if Aquila as a freedman, went by his newly acquired *nomen gentilicium* as the single name he used in the Christian community.

Many scholars reject the idea that Aquila's name was based on a connection with the *Acilius* family. The Latin word *aquila* means "eagle," and it was common for Jews to assume designations for animals as personal names. (This interpretation likely explains why the standard English form of the name is "Aquila.") Another option hews more closely to the Greek from of the name (*akylas*): *Akylos* means "acorn" in Greek. However, it is hard to explain the shift in the final vowel that this explanation would require. In this explanation's favor is the inherently greater probability that a Jew from Pontus would have a Greek name than a Latin one.

As creative as Jewett's reconstruction is, it is improbable for three reasons. First, if Prisca were a Roman citizen and, in fact, a scion of a senatorial-class family, it is unlikely she would have been exiled from Rome with the Jewish-Christian troublemakers during the imperium of Claudius. On the other hand, perhaps her husband Aquila was exiled, and she was unwilling to remain in Rome without him.

Second, it is unlikely a senatorial-class Roman would be skilled as a tentmaker. Again, it might be objected that Aquila was the tentmaker of the family, but Acts 18:3 specifically says, "*they* were tentmakers by trade."

Third, Roman law did not allow senatorial-class women to marry slaves or freedmen.[54] Concubinage (*contubernium*) was allowed between upper class individuals and slaves or freedpersons, but marriage (*conubium* or *manus*) was not. The problem was especially acute if the potential husband was a slave or freedman. This is because *manus* (literally "hand") brings the wife under the authority (i.e., "the hand") of the husband, and this would contravene the social hierarchy of the classes. To state this differently, it would put the freedman's patron under his authority.

However, we know that almost precisely such contraventions of Roman law took place in the Roman church during the early third century. An anonymous treatise titled the *Refutatio*, which is widely, although not securely, attributed to Hippolytus, contains a screed against Callistus, the bishop of Rome. The *Refutatio*'s author seems to have instigated a church split, claiming Callistus permitted and even encouraged moral laxity.

---

54. The foundation of this restriction was Augustus' decree, promulgated in 18 BC, of the *Lex Julia de maritandis ordinibus* ("Julian Law concerning marriage orders").

Reading between the lines, it seems that Callistus permitted church marriages between Christians of disparate classes, even when such unions violated Roman law. Apparently, in the church there was a surplus of noble women over available noble men, so some noble women desired unions that were not recognized by law. Such marriages, the *Refutatio*'s author contends, were contemptable and inexcusable. He also alleges that the noble women involved often sought to avoid procreation through contraception and abortion:

> When women from the noble class were unmarried and in the heat of their youthful passion desired to marry and yet were unwilling to give up their class through a legal marriage, he [Callistus] allowed them to choose a partner, whether slave or free, and to consider him to be their husband without a legal marriage. From that time on the alleged believing women began to resort to contraceptive methods and to corset themselves in order to cause abortions, because, on account of their lineage and their enormous wealth, they did not wish to have a child from a slave or from a commoner.[55]

At this time most of the Roman church—in defiance of the position articulated in the *Refutatio* related above—considered the classist regulations of Roman society to be incompatible with Christian moral teaching. The Roman church apparently also felt secure enough to act upon that conviction. We do not know if in the first century the Roman church was as daring. However, if Jewett's reconstruction of events related to Prisca and Aquila is correct, then the church in Rome did recognize a marriage between a senatorial-class woman and a freed slave.

In contrast to Jewett's reconstruction, Lampe considers it more likely that Aquila was a freeborn Jew from Pontus who somehow ended up in Rome. Lampe thinks it likely his name was Latin (and meant "eagle"). In Rome he met Prisca, who likely was also a Jew. She had no connection to the Acilius family or to the later Catacomb of Priscilla. Even if she had not been a Jew, at marriage she would have come under her husband's authority and thereafter would have been treated as a Jew. Together they were exiled under Claudius. This suggests they were not Roman citizens.

While they were neither wealthy nor from the upper classes—they were tentmakers, tradesmen, after all—it is likely they were freeborn. Their

---

55. Hippolytus, *Refutatio* 9.12.24 (according to the translation of Lampe, *From Paul to Valentinus*, 119). See also the Greek edition of Marcovich.

ability to travel freely meant they were not obligated to honor a patron on a regular basis as they would have been if they were former slaves. Although both in Ephesus and in Rome they hosted a "church" in their home, the language used does not require that they owned houses. In fact, it is likely they did not have the resources necessary to own a house. Priscilla and Aquila's tentmaking business that employed Paul probably was not very lucrative since Paul writes that during his time in Corinth he had been "in need." Nevertheless, he did not burden his fellow believers for relief (2 Cor 11:9). Furthermore, Priscilla and Aquila's home in Corinth apparently was too small to use for preaching (and perhaps for his housing) since Paul found it necessary to use the home of Titius Justus, although its location next to the synagogue likely also figured into this decision (Acts 18:7).[56]

The nature of Priscilla and Aquila's relationship with Paul is interesting to contemplate. Certainly, the three of them were friends and associates-in-ministry. But they were not Paul's converts; they had already become baptized believers while in Rome, prior to their expulsion under Claudius. This is confirmed by Paul's report omitting them from the list of people he baptized in the early days of his time in Corinth.[57]

Furthermore, they were not only associates-in-ministry, they were also important cogs in Paul's missionary program. Lampe suggests that Paul used Priscilla and Aquila as forerunners or "vanguards" of his missionary activity.[58] When Paul decided to travel from Corinth to Syria, he took Priscilla and Aquila with him, but dropped them off at Ephesus, to give guidance to the fledgling Christian community there until he could join them himself (Acts 18:18–19). It is also possible or even probable that, to prepare for the trip Paul planned to make to Rome, at some time before he wrote his letter, Priscilla and Aquila had returned to Rome. In any case, much of the information Paul knows about the Christians in Rome likely came from correspondence with them.

---

56. Lampe, *From Paul to Valentinus*, 191. Paul probably not only preached in this home but also lived there since in Rom 16:23 Gaius was his "host." Furthermore, on the basis of both Acts 18:7 and Rom 16:23, Edgar J. Goodspeed has proposed that the homeowner's full name was Gaius Titius Justus. See Goodspeed, "Gaius Titius Justus," 382.

57. In 1 Cor 1:14–16 Paul claims that to the best of his recollection that he only baptized Crispus, Gaius, and the household of Stephanas. Although the passage implies that others were also baptized, Paul seems to have performed the earliest baptisms himself and Priscilla and Aquila would have been baptized quite early, if they had required baptism.

58. "Vanguard" is Lampe's precise word. Lampe, *From Paul to Valentinus*, 193.

I have indicated that I regard Lampe's biographical reconstruction to be more persuasive than Jewett's. And this is not a trivial matter since the example of Priscilla and Aquila affects an issue about which the New Testament says surprisingly little: Within the Christian community was it possible for Jews and non-Jews to marry? On the one hand, if Jewett is correct about Aquila being a Jew and Priscilla being a gentile, then this couple provides a clear example of such a "mixed marriage" within the Christian community. If, on the other hand Lampe is right that both Priscilla and Aquila were Jews, then their marriage does not speak to this issue at all.

While it would be helpful to have clearer information on this subject, Paul hints at his attitude in 1 Cor 7:39. When discussing a widow's freedom to remarry, he limits her marital prerogative in only one way: that she remarry "in the Lord." This fundamental identity defined by allegiance to Christ transcends the divide between Jews and gentiles.

THE CUMULATIVE TESTIMONY OF ROMANS 16 ABOUT WOMEN

The evidence of Romans 16 is not as clear as one might desire. While Phoebe's role as a patroness and letter-carrier is clear enough, that Junia was an apostle is only likely, not certain. It is even less likely that Prisca was a freeborn woman of a senatorial-class family who chose to marry a Jewish slave, and then purchased his freedom and married him. Nevertheless, she and her husband led a church in their home. Furthermore, in Rom 16:1–16 Paul charges the believers of Rome to greet an additional seven women: Mary, Tryphaena, Tryphosa, Persis, Rufus's mother, Julia, and Nereus's sister. While the roles of all these women are not clearly defined, the cumulative weight of the evidence demonstrates the importance of women in both Paul's ministry and in Rome.

TRANSLATION: ROM 16:17–19

WARNINGS AND A GOOD REPORT

[17]I encourage you, brothers, to watch out for those causing dissensions and placing obstacles in the way of what you were taught. [18]For such do not serve Christ our Lord but rather their own belly and deceive the hearts of

the naïve through sweet-talk and exuberance. ¹⁹For word of your obedience has reached all; therefore, I rejoice because of you. I want you to be wise with respect to good, harmless with respect to evil.

COMMENTARY

Vss. 17–18: The warning contained in these verses resembles Paul's warning in Phil 3:2 and 18–19. There too Paul warns against those who only present themselves as servants of Christ while serving themselves. The clearest similarity is the use of the word "belly" (*koilia*) in both Rom 16:18 and Phil 3:19. Likely these charlatans have not yet found their way to Rome. If they had, Paul would not have mentioned them only briefly and in his closing remarks. Instead, Paul knows of such people who are "making the rounds," and he wants the believers in Rome to be forewarned.

The word I have translated "sweet-talk" (*chrēstologia*) occurs only here in the New Testament and not at all in the LXX. The word I have translated "exuberance" (*eulogia*) is somewhat slippery. It can mean a "blessing" (e.g., Rom 15:29; 1 Cor 10:16). Somewhat differently, in 2 Cor 9:6 Paul notes the axiom: "He who sows sparingly will also reap sparingly, and he who sows bountifully [*ep' eulogiais*] will also reap bountifully [*ep' eulogiais*]." Both times *ep' eulogiais* could be translated rather literally as "with exuberance." Paul's picture is vivid. There are hucksters on the loose waiting to deceive those who are not watchful. No doubt the same it true today. Does the contemporary church so clearly warn about them?

Vs. 19: Paul's warnings of the previous two verses were not aimed at anyone currently in Rome. Instead, he offers a compliment tinged with a bit of hyperbole: "your obedience has reached all." While he does not make clear what sort of obedience he means, likely it is a reference to "the obedience of faith" (Rom 1:5; 16:26). Literally, Paul writes, "Your obedience has reached all," yet it is clear he means *word of* your obedience has reached all. And this brings him joy.

Paul's exhortation to be wise (*sophos*) but also to remain harmless (*akeraios*) echoes the teaching of Jesus. In Matt 10:16 we find as Jesus sends out the Twelve, "See, I send you out as sheep in the midst of wolves. Therefore, be shrewd (*phronimos*) as snakes and harmless (*akeraios*) as doves." Similarly, in Luke 10:3 as Jesus commissions the Seventy, he says, "See, I send you out as lambs in the midst of wolves."

The word *akeraios*, which appears in both Rom 16:19 and Matt 10:16 is often translated "innocent." However, literally it means "without horns," so "harmless" seems apt.

TRANSLATION: ROM 16:20

THE GRACE BENEDICTION

²⁰May the God of peace quickly crush Satan under your feet. May the grace of our Lord Jesus be with you.

COMMENTARY

Vs. 20: The endings of Paul's letters invariably contain a grace benediction. This verse contains the grace benediction of Romans. The juxtaposition of an image of peace with an image of violence is jarring—no doubt intentionally so. The crushing of Satan underfoot should be understood as an allusion to Gen 3:15.

The phrase "the God of peace" occasionally occurs toward the end of Paul's letters. Besides here, it occurs in 2 Cor 13:11 and 1 Thess 5:23.[59] The phrase also occurs in the body of Paul's letters in Rom 15:33, 1 Cor 14:33, and Phil 4:9. While it is interesting that Paul sometimes uses this expression toward the close of his letters, this pattern is not nearly as regular and formulaic as "peace from God" is in his opening greetings.

Rendered in a woodenly literal fashion, this verse begins, "The God of peace will crush . . . ," but here the future indicative expresses a wish: "*May the God of peace crush* . . . ." In classical Greek an optative form would have been used, but in Hellenistic Greek the optative has largely disappeared.[60] Furthermore, that this is the expression of a wish rather than a prediction is suggested by the sentiment that follows: "May the grace of our Lord Jesus be with you [plural]." Unlike the preceding sentence, this sentence contains no expressed verb; it is merely implied.

While Paul uses the name "Satan" regularly (ten times in addition to this occurrence), this is the only place where Satan occurs in Romans.

TRANSLATION: ROM 16:21–23

THE POSTSCRIPT

²¹Timothy my fellow-worker greets you, also Lucius, Jason and Sosipater, my kinsmen. ²²I, Tertius, the one writing this epistle in the Lord, greet

---

59. This phrase also appears at the end of Hebrews (13:20), which may partially account for why it has sometimes been included in the Pauline corpus.

60. Bl-D-F §384.

you. ²³Gaius my host greets you, as well as the whole church [of Corinth]. Erastus, Treasurer of the city [of Corinth], greets you, and Quartus, his brother, greets you.

COMMENTARY

Vss. 21–22: These verses raise a natural question: Why does Paul choose to send greetings from these particular people? Is it because those in Rome who have immigrated from the East might know them? This is a possibility. More likely, however, is Robert Jewett's suggestion that these are church dignitaries who happened to be present in Corinth at the time Paul concluded his letter. Two of these—Timothy and Sosipater—have come to Corinth with money their churches have collected for the saints of Jerusalem.[61] They are gathering as part of the delegation mentioned in Acts 20:4 that will deliver these funds. The rest of the delegation either has not yet arrived or will meet up with the group at some point in transit. The leaders Lucius and Jason are present for other reasons.

To contemporary readers of the New Testament, Timothy is one of Paul's best-known "fellow workers," as he is styled here. While he would have been known to some of those believers in Rome who had spent time in the East, Paul felt the need to explain his role to most of the others.

Of the three individuals who are mentioned next—Lucius, Jason, and Sosipater—at least the final two are called "kinsmen" and therefore are Jews. The grammar of the passage makes it unclear whether Lucius is also a Jew.

Lucius (*Loukios*) is a Latin name. Paul certainly knew the Lucius of Cyrene who was a prophet and/or a teacher of the church at Antioch, the church that had originally sent Paul out as a missionary (Acts 13:1). Since Cyrene, a city in what is present-day Libya, had a large Jewish presence, it is likely that this Lucius of Cyrene was a Jew like Barnabas, another of the prophets/teachers of Antioch. Nevertheless, because Antioch is so far from Corinth it seems unlikely that this Lucius was present with Paul in Corinth as he finished writing his letter.

The Jason discussed in Acts 17:5–7 is likely the person mentioned here. After Paul has preached in Thessalonica, upsetting both Jews and gentiles, "the house of Jason" is attacked (Acts 17:5), probably because Paul is inside. Furthermore, in Acts 17:7 Jason is accused of "harboring" (*hypodechomai*) Paul.

---

61. Sopater (*Sōpatros*), the name that appears in Acts 20:4, is a shortened form of Sosipater (*Sōsipatros*). On this, see Bauer, Arndt, and Gingrich, *Greek-English Lexicon*, s.v. "Sōsipatros."

It is possible that Jason, a representative of the church at Thessalonica, has come to inform Paul about the travel plans of Aristarchus and Secundus, who are slated to represent Thessalonica in the delegation to Jerusalem (Acts 20:4). Maybe they will arrive in a few days, or perhaps they will join Paul and the rest of the delegation at a different meeting point than Corinth.

Tertius is the amanuensis (professional scribe) who helped Paul write Romans. Whether he simply recorded what Paul dictated, or helped to revise Paul's drafts is unknown.

The name Tertius is Latin and means "third born." It was a common slave name, and it is possible that he was a slave belonging to Phoebe, Paul's patron. Slaves often functioned as amanuenses. If Phoebe financed the writing of Romans and carried the letter to Rome herself, it is possible that Tertius accompanied her on this journey. That Tertius was invited to send his greetings suggests he was a Christian, and perhaps also to introduce him to the believers in Rome. Jewett argues that amanuenses not only were professional writers but also professional readers, and that Tertius was tasked with reading the letter in Rome.[62]

Paul may not have always used amanuenses. The issue is confusing because it is not always clear what he means by "writing." Is it composing or composing and putting pen to papyrus? In some letters he says he wrote them (e.g., 2 Cor 13:10; Gal 6:11). In others, he claims only to have written a final greeting in his own hand. This was to authenticate the letter as being from him, much as a signature functions in the modern world (e.g., 1 Cor 16:21; Col 4:18; 2 Thess 3:17).

Vs.23: Gaius (*Gaïos*), whom Paul calls "my host" (*ho xenos mou*), also sends his greetings. It is tempting to try to associate him with the Gaius of Berea mentioned in Acts 20:4 (and in Acts 19:29) who was part of the previously mentioned delegation to Jerusalem. However, the Gaius referenced in this verse of Romans clearly lives in Corinth. Instead, he is the Gaius mentioned in 1 Cor 1:14, who was an early convert during Paul's ministry in Corinth and who was baptized by him. Furthermore, according to Acts, Gaius's home is where Paul preached and apparently lived after being expelled from Corinth's synagogue. Conveniently, his home was located next door to the synagogue (Acts 18:7). If this reconstruction is correct, then Gaius's full name was Gaius Titius Justus, with Gaius being his praenomen, Titius his nomen gentilicium, and Justus a cognomen.[63]

The word *xenos* can function as either a noun or an adjective. As an adjective, its basic meaning is "foreign." As a noun, it can mean "a foreigner,"

---

62. Jewett, *Romans*, 979.
63. Goodspeed, "Gaius Titius Justus," 382.

but it often means "a guest," i.e., someone who does not usually live in a place and is therefore "foreign." By association, it is less commonly used to refer to the "host" of a guest, which is how the word is used here.

Paul's readers are told that "the whole church" greets them. Almost certainly this refers to the whole church of Corinth, although some interpreters have suggested Paul extends a greeting from the church universal. In 1 Cor 14:23 Paul similarly refers to "the whole church" of Corinth. Murphy-O'Connor perceptively notes that these references to the whole church suggest that due to its size and space limitations often the entire church of Corinth did not meet together, although sometimes it did.[64] This greeting may have been extended through Gaius, one of the leaders of the church there, but more likely it was extended directly through Paul himself, the founder of that church.

Paul's delivery of a greeting from Erastus has generated considerable discussion. The name *Erastos* is Greek, meaning either "beloved" or "lovely." Although it is a proper noun, it is adjectival in form and is related to the noun *eros* ("love" or "physical attraction"). If Corinth had been the long-time home of the person Paul mentions in Romans, as seems nearly certain, his Greek name suggests he is likely a freedman, a transplant from elsewhere, or both.

While Corinth is in Greece, the city was refounded by Julius Caesar as a Roman colony in 44 BC after having lain almost completely uninhabited for a century.[65] This followed its destruction in 144 BC by Roman forces. At first, most of the inhabitants were Italian freedmen, who were attracted from nearby by the opportunities the new colony afforded.[66] It also became populated by Roman citizens, mainly retired army officers, who received estates as rewards for their military service. These factors made it a dynamic young city—about a century old when Paul wrote Romans—despite its long and storied Greek past that had been interrupted by its lengthy desolation. Its governance was Roman in form, and it had no historic, elite Greek families to lead it, as was the case elsewhere in Greece.

Much of the discussion about the Erastus in Romans has been generated by an inscription that mentions an individual named Erastus. The stone slabs into which the inscription is cut currently lie in the ground near a limestone pavement east of Corinth's theater although this was not their

---

64. Murphy-O'Connor, *Paul: A Critical Life*, 149.

65. Caesar's order that Corinth be built as a Roman colony in his own honor was his last major act before being assassinated. Despite his death, this order was faithfully executed.

66. Kent, *Corinth Vol. 8, Part 3: Inscriptions (1926–1950)*, 20.

original position. Furthermore, the decorative molding that remains on one of the slabs—this molding has been trimmed from a second slab, and the third slab is lost—indicates that originally these slabs formed an epistyle (a beam laid across the tops of columns) rather than signage resting in the ground.[67]

When the Erastus of the inscription is added to the three times an Erastus is mentioned in the New Testament (in this verse; in Acts 19:22; and in 2 Tim 4:20), a question arises: Do these citations all reference the same person?

Acts 19:20 describes Erastus as someone "serving" Paul whom Paul send outs on missionary assignments. Similarly, 2 Tim 4:20 explains that while Paul is imprisoned, rather than coming to his aid Erastus has remained at home in Corinth, either at Paul's bidding or because he is unable to leave. If Erastus held a position in the city government of Corinth as Rom 16:23 indicates, this might explain why he was unable to join his imprisoned mentor. However, at an earlier time apparently he had been free to conduct missionary activity outside of Corinth.

The title "*oikonomos* of the city" is difficult to translate. This is not because there are no options but rather because there are several possibilities. *Oikonomos* is a Greek word meaning approximately "steward." However, this was not Erastus's official title, which would have been worded in Latin. Clearly since Paul is writing in Greek, he has translated this title into the language in which he writes.

So, what was this Erastus' formal title? If Corinth's Erastus inscription were unknown, the leading candidates would be *arcarius* ("treasurer"; the term used in the Latin Vulgate of Rom 16:23), *actor* ("agent"), *dispensator* ("administrator"), and *vilicus* ("manager"), each of which refers to a low-level to mid-level employee. Other than *arcarius*, Cadbury considers these other terms to be inappropriate because they were "used of agents of the emperors or of private persons rather than of municipal appointees."[68] Whatever the main designation happened to be, it is likely either *ciuitatis* ("of the city") or *rei publicae* ("of public matters") was appended to it.

The inscription is incomplete, but enough remains to be useful. John Harvey Kent's transcription is "[praenomen nomen] Erastus pro aedilit[at]e s(ua) p(ecunia) stravit." He translates this as "[——] Erastus in return for his

---

67. This observation was made by Guy D. R. Sanders and communicated to me in an email dated October 20, 2024. Dr. Sanders is Director Emeritus of the Corinth Excavations.

68. Cadbury, "Erastus of Corinth," 51.

aedileship laid (the pavement) at his own expense."[69] Both the *praenomen* and the *nomen gentilicium* are missing. "Erastus" is this man's *cognomen*.

This Erastus was an *aedililis* ("magistrate"; English "aedile"), one of the four highest ranking officials of the city. Only the *duoviri* (literally "two men") were of higher rank. Like the *duoviri*, aediles were elected annually, and there were two of them. Thus, it was a relatively temporary position and was considered both an honor and a steppingstone to long-term membership in the city council (*dicuriones*).[70] Obligations came with the honor, often to provide the funding for athletic games. In this case, Erastus paid to lay a pavement in exchange for the honor of his aedileship. In Rome aediles were always freeborn citizens, but in Corinth there was greater flexibility and freedmen qualified as *duoviri* and aediles.[71]

Could Paul's title *oikonomos* be a translation of the Latin *aedililis*? Both Mason and Kent think so, but Henry Cadbury is skeptical because *aedililis* was normally translated into Greek as *agoranomos* ("clerk of the market").[72] Kent describes the responsibilities of Corinthian aediles in the following manner:

> Aediles were primarily city business managers, being responsible for the upkeep and welfare of city property such as streets, public buildings, and especially the market places (hence their Greek title *agoranomoi*), as well as the public revenue therefrom. They also served as judges, and it is probable that most of a colony's commercial and financial litigation was decided by them rather than by the *duoviri*.[73]

Thus, Kent considers the Greek term *oikonomos* to be properly descriptive of this role.

Lexically this seems possible. In large part one's answer to the question of whether *oikonomos* could equal aedile turns on whether she finds it reasonable that so prominent a figure as an aedile could be mentioned in the context of Romans 16.

---

69. Kent, *Corinth Vol. 8, Part 3: Inscriptions (1926–1950)*, 99–100 (Inscription 232).

70. Kent, *Corinth Vol. 8, Part 3: Inscriptions (1926–1950)*, 27.

71. Evidence of this is found in the inscription to Corinth's Babbius Monument in which the freedman Cnaeus Babbius Philonis describes himself as a *duovir*. See Sanders, et al. *Ancient Corinth Site Guide*, 60–61.

72. Mason, *Greek Terms for Roman Institutions*, s.v. *oikonomos*. Kent, *Corinth Vol. 8, Part 3: Inscriptions (1926–1950)*, 99–100. Cadbury, "Erastus of Corinth," 53–54.

73. Kent, *Corinth Vol. 8, Part 3: Inscriptions (1926–1950)*, 27.

Paul's attribution of a municipal title to Erastus is most unusual. In no other place does he describe a fellow Christian in this way. (Although he describes Luke's profession as "physician" in Col 4:14, this is not a municipal title.) For this reason, some have suggested that the Erastus of Rom 16:23 is not a believer; he sends greetings to the faithful in Rome for some other reason than bonds of Christian fellowship. However, it is hard to imagine what such a reason might be. Would a young striving politician from Corinth be eager to be mentioned in any letter to Rome regardless of its audience? Some have also suggested that a government official would necessarily be so entangled in pagan religious activity that this would preclude simultaneous Christian commitment. However, this is simply conjecture.

Furthermore, another question intrudes on this discussion. Did the Erastus of the inscription live during the middle of the first century AD when Paul's Erastus lived? The evidence is unclear.

Kent assumes that the inscription and the pavement east of the theater were built at roughly the same time. In addition, he declares: "the pavement was laid some time near the middle of the first century after Christ."[74] In contrast, Friesen considers this dating to be methodologically tainted. While Kent does not state this explicitly, seemingly he proposes this date based on Paul's reference to Erastus in Rom 16:23. The argument becomes circular if first the inscription and pavement are dated based on Paul's statement, and then the two Erastuses are identified as the same person based on the inscription's date.[75]

More recent evidence indicates that the pavement must have been laid no earlier than the rule of Hadrian (AD 117 to 138) and likely during the mid-to-late second or even the third century. While the pavement has not been fully excavated, a semi-circular area of latrines lying under the edge of the pavement has been excavated. In 1999, during these excavations a coin from the time of Hadrian was discovered "in the bottom stratum of earth above the latrine floor." The coin has not yet been published, but it is identified in the excavation/museum inventory as Coin 1999-224.[76]

Despite this late date for the pavement, the date of the Erastus inscription may be earlier. There might have been an earlier pavement that preceded the surviving one, or it is possible that an original first-century pavement was later extended to cover the former latrines. This would explain how

---

74. Kent, *Corinth Vol. 8, Part 3: Inscriptions (1926–1950)*, 99.

75. Friesen, "Wrong Erastus," 237.

76. The information about the excavation of the latrines, the quotation, and the coin identification are all from an email to me from Guy D. R. Sanders, dated October 20, 2024.

a coin from the time of Hadrian came to lie under part of the pavement. Such new information would also require a reassessment of the surviving pavement's date.

There are reasons to think the inscription may have been cut during the first century. The inscription's broad, deep grooves originally were filled with gold-plated copper inserts. This closely resembles the design of an inscription that decorated the architrave (vault above an opening) of Corinth's Temple E. If this inscription was cut during the first phase of the temple's construction, it can be dated to the first century AD.[77] While the construction of the inscription on Corinth's Babbius Monument differs from that of the Erastus inscription, the formulaic initials *S P* (short for *sua pecunia*; "[built with] his own money") also appear on this monument constructed in the first century AD. In fact, Kent lists this as one of six first-century inscriptions from Corinth (beyond the Erastus inscription) that use the *S P* formula or the slightly more elaborate initials *S P F C* (*sua pecunia facienda curauit*; "he organized building [this item] with his own money").[78] While use of this formula is not restricted to the first century, in Corinth it was more popular in that period than in the second or third centuries.

Quartus (Greek *Kuartos*) is a Latin name meaning "fourth born." Despite being Latin, it was commonly used for slaves (and therefore for freedmen as well).[79] The verb "greets" (*aspazetai*), in which Erastus is the subject, is singular, but a similar verb is implied for Quartus even though it remains unwritten.

Quartus is described as *ho adelphos* (literally "the brother"). This person is either a believer in some way associated with Erastus, or he is Erastus's biological brother. On the one hand, the translation "Quartus the brother [sends you greetings]" seems slightly odd since many other Christians have been mentioned in chapter 16 and Quartus would be the only one described by the singular *adelphos*, meaning "fellow believer." Also, would calling him a Christian brother help identify him in any meaningful way? Would he be the Christian Quartus as opposed to the non-Christian Quartus? On the other hand, if Paul intends to identify Erastus's biological brother it is odd that he does not call him *Kuartos ho adelphos autou* using the word "his"

---

77. These statements about the style of the Erastus inscription's cuttings as well as Temple E and its inscription are based on observations by Guy D. R. Sanders shared in an email to me dated October 21, 2024.

78. Kent, *Corinth Vol. 8, Part 3: Inscriptions (1926–1950)*, 21; 60 (inscr. 130); 73 (inscr. 155); 126–27 (inscr. 318); 128–29 (inscr. 322); 131–32 (inscr. 326); 134 (inscr. 333).

79. Jewett, *Romans*, 983.

(*autou*) as he does in vs.15 when identifying Nereas's sister. The construction without *autou* is grammatically possible, but unusual.[80]

TRANSLATION: ROM 16:24

THE INTERPOLATION

[[²⁴The grace of our Lord Jesus Christ be with you all. Amen.]]

COMMENTARY

This material is double bracketed because it is doubtful that it appeared in Romans as Paul originally wrote it. These words are missing in much of the manuscript tradition, and it seems redundant in light of the grace benediction contained in vs. 20. These words are identical to the *textus receptus* ("received text") form of 1 Cor 16:23 and may have been borrowed from that letter. *For more about these matters, see Appendix 1: "The Ending of Romans."*

---

80. As Jewett puts it, "the article often functions as a possessive in Greek." Jewett, *Romans*, 983.

APPENDIX 1:
THE ENDING OF ROMANS

MULTIPLE FORMS OF THE LETTER

As the main part of the commentary noted, the way Romans ends is perplexing. The manuscript tradition presents the final chapters of Romans in a variety of forms, with some manuscripts containing text which other manuscripts omit, and sometimes with the order of material being rearranged. While there are a few text-critical problems in the first fourteen chapters of Romans, these difficulties are very modest compared to the tangles and challenges posed by the various forms of the text that come after 14:23, the last verse of chapter 14 in modern printed Bibles.

Harry Gamble, Jr., suggests that three forms of Romans were known in antiquity: a fourteen-chapter version; a fifteen-chapter version; and a sixteen-chapter version. These descriptions may seem anachronistic since the books of the Bible had not yet been divided into chapters and verses in antiquity, but of course what Gamble speaks of are the portions of text now identified by such chapter designations.

Contemporary Bibles present Romans as a sixteen-chapter letter, and most scholars believe the letter Paul wrote to Roman believers contained all sixteen chapters. However, a significant minority of scholars, particularly in Germany, believe Romans originally had fifteen chapters and then the sixteenth chapter was appended later. However, before considering the fifteen-chapter theory, an earlier fourteen-chapter theory must be discussed.

THE FOURTEEN-CHAPTER LETTER THEORY

In his commentary on Romans, the third-century church father Origen discusses a fourteen-chapter version of Romans circulating in his day. He believed the second-century heretic Marcion, who was famous for editing out the passages in Paul's letters he did not like, had removed the last two chapters of Romans. Whether or not Marcion was the culprit—there is really no evidence pointing to anyone else—it does seem that the fourteen-chapter version came into existence when a longer version was shortened. The main argument that a longer version was shortened rather than a shorter version lengthened is this: Paul's discussion of whether some foods should be avoided and whether certain days should be considered special starts in chapter 14 but then continues through 15:6, as the apostle exhorts the strong to shoulder the load caused by the limitations of the weak. While inelegant pruning of Romans could account for a book that eliminates 15:1 and what follows, it seems very unlikely that someone jumped into the middle of an existing discussion, composed a continuation of that discussion, and then added more material discussing other topics.

T.W. Manson and Robert Jewett think Marcion wanted the letter to end with the punchline that "whatever does not come from faith is sin."[1] Marcion was rabidly opposed to the Law, so opposed in fact that he rejected the entire Old Testament, believing it depicts a different god than the one Paul served. He set faith against Law, always elevating faith. It is a puzzle why Marcion felt so free to edit Paul's writings since he claimed to be an ardent follower of Paul.[2]

THE TWO-EDITIONS THEORY

Although it is too complex a matter to detail fully here, Gamble argues that there is a connection between the fourteen-chapter version of Romans and the omissions in Codex Bornerianus of any reference to Rome in 1:7 and 1:15, making it unclear to whom the letter was addressed.[3] According to Gamble and others, Marcion wanted to convert Paul's letter to a specific group of believers in Rome into a manifesto of Paul's gospel aimed at a

---

1. Jewett, *Romans*, 1002. Manson, "Romans–and Others," 11.

2. The Marcionite urge recurs in the church from time to time. The latest manifestation is Andy Stanley's challenge for the church to "unhitch" from the old covenant and the Old Testament, which he understands as a "culprit" and "stumbling block" to faith. See Stanley, *Irresistible*, 278, 280, 315.

3. Gamble, *Textual History*, 29–33.

general audience. In addition to removing Paul's discussion in chapter 15 of his travel plans that included a stop in Rome and the many personal greetings of chapter 16, he also removed the specific passages in the book that identified it as a letter addressed to a single city.

THE FIFTEEN-CHAPTER-LETTER THEORY

It was common during the second half of the twentieth century for scholars, especially in Germany, to argue that originally Romans had only fifteen chapters. Although this view is less common today than a few decades ago, this view still has proponents. Furthermore, it is not so easily dispatched as the fourteen-chapter theory.

The main argument that Romans originally contained only fifteen chapters is the alleged improbability that Paul would have so many people to greet in far-away Rome, as chapter 16 records, when he had never visited the city. He greets twenty-four individuals by name plus people associated with four others mentioned by name. If chapter 16 had been originally penned as part of a letter to Ephesus, a city where Paul had lived for considerable time, this long list would seem more plausible. In addition, Paul asks the letter's recipients to "greet Epaenetus my beloved who was the 'first fruit' of Asia in Christ" (vs. 5), a description which might seem more relevant to an audience in Ephesus, the largest city in the province of Asia.

An additional argument is that 1 Cor 16:19 places Aquila and Prisca in Ephesus, Paul's location when he wrote 1 Corinthians. Furthermore, 2 Tim 4:19 seems to place them somewhere else, namely wherever Timothy is located when Paul writes to him. That place is not Rome for the following reason. Paul speaks of his bonds in 2 Tim 1:18. If Paul is shackled in Rome, as has traditionally been thought, then Timothy is not in Rome when Paul writes 2 Timothy. A letter such as this would not have been written if both the author and the recipient were in the same city. Timothy is also apparently not in Ephesus, judging from the references to Ephesus in 2 Tim 1:18 and 4:12. This means Prisca and Aquila would have been quite mobile. They are in Ephesus when Paul writes 1 Corinthians. Did they then move to Rome before Paul wrote Romans, and then on to somewhere else when Paul wrote 2 Timothy? Many scholars, of course, dismiss 2 Timothy along with 1 Timothy and Titus as the products of a writer who lived a generation or two after Paul.

However, the hypothesis that Romans 16 was originally intended for an Ephesian audience is not without problems. Since Ephesus is in Asia, would it make sense to inform the Ephesian believers that Epaenetus was "the 'first fruit' of Asia in Christ" (16:5)? They would surely already know this, although it could be this comment was offered not to inform but rather to honor Epaenetus. The explanation that Timothy is Paul's "fellow worker" (16:27) would also seem unnecessary since Timothy was well-known in Ephesus. Also, unless 2 Timothy is dismissed as ahistorical, this would still require Prisca and Aquila to have moved away from Ephesus before Paul writes 2 Timothy.

Furthermore, there is a defense against the charge that Paul could not have had personal relationships with so many people in far-away Rome. If personal information that could have been learned from others about the people Paul mentions in Romans 16 is distinguished from what had to be personal associations, then Paul only had to have a personal relationship with twelve individuals: Prisca, Aquila, Epaenetus, Andronicus, Junia, Urbanus, Rufus, Rufus's mother, Ampliatus, Stachys, Persis, and probably Apelles. Given the relative ease with which people transversed the Roman highways and the Mediterranean during the Empire, this list does not seem excessive.[4]

Peter Lampe has conducted extensive evaluations of the names listed in Romans 16 with inscriptional evidence from both Rome and Ephesus. It is his judgment that the Romans 16 names "correspond better with Rome than with Ephesus."[5]

Furthermore, if Romans originally did not contain chapter 16, it would not end with a grace benediction, as is the case in all Paul's other letters. To mitigate this problem, some have hypothesized that the original ending of Romans was removed in favor of chapter 16, which was originally intended for an Ephesian audience.

The greatest problems with the Ephesian hypothesis are how to explain both the creation of this chapter as a document addressed to Ephesus and its subsequent attachment to Romans. The main theory is that "chapter 16" was salvaged from an irretrievably damaged letter Paul wrote to the Ephesian believers, and then out of a desire to preserve every possible bit of Paul's writings, it was attached to his fifteen-chapter letter to the Romans. A second somewhat wilder hypothesis is that Paul wrote two forms of the same letter: one intended for Rome, that included the Rome-specific material in chapters 1 and 15, but not chapter 16; and a second letter sent to Ephesus that excluded the Rome specific material in chapters 1 and 15 but with the

---

4. This helpful list was developed by Peter Lampe. See Lampe, "Roman Christians," 220.

5. Lampe, *From Paul to Valentinus*, 157.

many greetings of chapter 16 appended. Later, the textual traditions of these two forms of the letter became conflated. Neither theory seems compelling.[6]

THE DOXOLOGY

If one concludes the letter originally had sixteen chapters, as seems likely, arriving at this conclusion does not end the discussion of how Romans ends. There remains the matter of the doxology (16:25–27), including questions about both its authenticity and its original location.

Bruce Metzger's *A Textual Commentary on the Greek New Testament* serves as a record of the judgments of the Editorial Committee that supervised the publication of the third edition of the United Bible Societies' Greek New Testament.[7] It includes a very helpful distillation of the main groupings of manuscript variations related to the ending of Romans, and especially the location of the doxology. The following table lists Metzger's six groupings, but rather than repeating the sigla of the various manuscripts cited in the *Textual Commentary*, I will assist the reader by characterizing the nature and importance of these manuscript groups.

a. 1:1—16:23+doxology: An impressive list of Alexandrian and Western witnesses of great importance

b. 1:1—14:23+doxology+15:1—16:23+doxology: Contains two Alexandrian witnesses of great importance and other manuscripts

c. 1:1—14:23+doxology+15:1—16:24:   Contains Alexandrian, Western, and Byzantine manuscripts of some importance

d. 1:1—16:24: Contains a few Western manuscripts of some importance

e. 1:1—15:33+doxology+16:1–23: Contains only one manuscript, P^{46}, the single most important manuscript of Paul's letters

f. 1:1—14:23+16:24+doxology: Contains only Latin (Western) manuscripts

If text critical decisions were made only on the weight of manuscript evidence, Metzger's group (a) would be the winner, with (e) perhaps running second. But the matter is not that simple. It is important not only to identify the most likely original reading but also to account for how the

---

6. For a more detailed defense of chapter 16 being an integral part of Romans from its beginning, see Lampe, *From Paul to Valentinus*, 153–64.

7. Metzger, *Textual Commentary*, ad loc. Rom 14:23.

variants arose. This is especially important for a situation in which the text seems to have been disturbed intentionally, such as the ending of Romans.

OBSERVATIONS:

1. Since in all his other letters Paul invariably concludes with a grace benediction, it is surprising that no manuscript ends with 16:20 (a grace benediction).

2. If vss. 21–23 were a later addition to the letter, this addition must have occurred very early since these verses are present in most of the manuscript tradition, missing only in the Latin manuscripts in which chapter 16 is not found (group f). These verses could have been appended to 16:20 by Paul himself as a sort of postscript, although this would constitute a deviation from his normal pattern. The manuscripts without chapter 16 (group f) cannot preserve the original form of the text since they do not contain a grace benediction, and therefore vss. 21–23 must have been contained in the archetype of the *Corpus Paulinum*.

3. If vs. 24 (a grace benediction) originally followed vss. 21–23, it is difficult to understand why it would have been eliminated (groups a, b, e) or moved to an earlier position (such as vs. 20b). While vs. 24 concludes the letter in some manuscripts (groups c, d), in many others it does not (groups a, b, e, f). This suggests that this verse was a later addition designed to make Romans follow Paul's normal pattern of ending with a grace benediction. Not only is the motivation for adding vs. 24 readily apparent, this form of the benediction is identical to the one found in 2 Thess. 3:18, which explains the source of this interpolated material. Even the final "amen" is present in many manuscripts of 2 Thess. 3:18.

4. There are five variations of where the doxology (now conventionally printed as Rom. 16:25–27) is found: 1) at the end of chapter 14 (groups c, f); 2) at the end of chapter 15 (group e); 3) at the end of chapter 16 (group a); 4) appearing twice, both at the end of chapter 14 and the end of chapter 16 (group b); and 5) not being found anywhere (group d). Paul is fond of doxologies, but normally they do not appear as the final element of a letter. Apparently, some editors felt that this doxology made a fine ending to the letter since in three of the six manuscript endings Metzger identifies, the doxology is the concluding element.

5. If the doxology is original—and this is a big if—its most likely position is at the end of chapter 15, as P^{46} suggests (= group e). If located at the

end of chapter 14, it would intrude into Paul's discussion of whether it was important to keep kosher and to observe certain days as being special, a discussion that extends through 15:6. Such an intrusion would mark this as a later interpolation. If it were originally at the end of chapter 16, it is hard to understand why it would have been relocated to the end of chapter 14 or to the end of chapter 15 unless entire chapters were being removed (which may be the case for group f).

6. Following this line of reasoning, P^{46} is most likely to represent the original text of the ending of Romans as it appeared in the archetype (original manuscript) of the *Corpus Paulinum*, and that conclusion will be reflected in the translation included with this commentary (1:1—15:33+doxology+16:1–23). While this arrangement is a departure from Paul's normal practice of concluding his letters with a grace benediction, it does contain a grace benediction in 16:20 followed by a postscript. Gamble notes that in Paul's letters the grace benediction functions much like the "final wish" in secular letters of the period, usually employing either the word *errōso* ("Farewell") or *euchomai* ("May you prosper").[8] He also notes that short postscripts following such a final wish are common.[9] It seems reasonable to consider 16:21–23 as just such a postscript. Employing a postscript is a departure from Paul's normal practice but not a radical departure.

---

8. Gamble, *Textual History*, 58, 65–67.
9. Gamble, *Textual History*, 64.

APPENDIX 2: COMMENTS ON 1 COR 14:34–35 AND 1 TIM 2:11–15

General Prefatory Comments

The two New Testament passages most often used to exclude women from ordained ministry and other leadership roles in the contemporary church are 1 Cor 14:34–35 and 1 Tim 2:11–15. The way these passages have been traditionally translated and interpreted bolsters this exclusionary practice. These translations and interpretations also limit the possibilities exegetes consider when interpreting other passages of Scripture. This is the reason for including this appendix in a commentary on Romans, for if a biblical "Overton window" excludes the possibility of women functioning as leaders in the first-century church, then of course one will not find such female church leaders in Romans 16 even if a straightforward reading suggests this possibility.

I prefer to keep the interpretive possibilities open a bit wider. When this is allowed, in numerous New Testament passages,[1] and even in passages in Paul's writings (including Romans 16),[2] women appear to exercise

---

1. Acts 18:26 describes Priscilla (and Aquila) teaching Apollos. She and Aquila also hosted a church in their house (Rom 16:3–5). Female "prophets" are mentioned in the New Testament, and prophecy implies a teaching role. Acts 2:17 states that "your daughters" will prophesy. Acts 21:8–9 mentions "four daughters of Philip" who prophesied.

2. In Rom 16:1 Paul describes Phoebe as "a minister [*diakonos*] of the church in Cenchraea." Some have translated this "servant," to deny the obvious implications of a leadership role at that church, but she brought Paul's letter to Rome and likely was entrusted with explaining anything in it that was confusing to its readers. In Rom 16:7 Paul calls Junia an apostle, which surely implies a leadership and teaching role.

teaching and leadership roles involving public speech. This suggests that a reconsideration of the traditional interpretations of 1 Cor 14:34–35 and 1 Tim 2:11–15 is warranted.

For many, widening the Overton window, as I propose, will require a drastic reconsideration of the meaning of these texts. Hopefully, such readers will find my interpretations offered below to be convincing.

1 Cor 14:34–35

The primary issue with these verses is not how they should be translated but rather if they belong in the text of 1 Corinthians at all. In other words, these verses present a significant text critical issue.[3]

TRANSLATION OF 1 COR 14:34–35 (RSV, 1971 EDITION)

[34][T]he women should keep silence in the churches. For they are not permitted to speak, but should be subordinate, as even the law says. [35]If there is anything they desire to know, let them ask their husbands at home. For it is shameful for a woman to speak in church.

COMMENTARY

Vss. 34–35: This discussion requiring women to keep silent in the church seems out of place, coming as it does in the middle of a discussion of how to maintain order when oral gifts of the Spirit are manifested. Paul's focus is on how to exercise gifts not on who may exercise gifts. Furthermore, notice how well 1 Cor 14:29–40 reads when these two verses are removed:

> [29]Let two or three prophets speak, and let the others weigh what is said. [30]If a revelation is made to another sitting by, let the first be silent. [31]For you can all prophesy one by one, so

---

Nympha hosted a church in her house (Col 4:15). While we do not know for sure the extent of her role, Paul speaks of her as if she is the leader of that church. In addition, Paul calls Prisca (Priscilla) a "co-worker" in Rom 16:3, and he says of Euodia and Syntyche that "they labored side-by-side in the gospel with me" (Phil 4:2–3).

3. I was introduced to this issue by reading Gordon Fee's commentary on 1 Corinthians, in which he makes a persuasive case for the inauthenticity of vss. 34–35. See Fee, *The First Epistle to the Corinthians* 699–708. Also of some importance is Metzger, *Textual Commentary*, ad loc. 1 Cor 14:34–35, although the committee report contained therein leans toward accepting the material as authentic.

that all may learn and all be encouraged; ³²and the spirits of prophets are subject to prophets. ³³For God is not a God of confusion but of peace, as in all the churches of the saints. ³⁶Or did the word of God originate with you? Or are you the only ones it has reached? ³⁷If anyone thinks that he is a prophet or spiritual, he should acknowledge that what I am writing to you is a command of the Lord. ³⁸If anyone does not recognize this, he is not recognized. ³⁹So, my brethren, earnestly desire to prophesy, and do not forbid speaking in tongues; ⁴⁰but all things should be done decently and in order.

Note: This translation of vss. 29–40 without vss. 34–35 assumes the phrase "as in all the churches of the saints" is part of vs. 33. Some translations (including the RSV cited above) construe this phrase, although it lies in vs. 33, to begin the first sentence of vs. 34. Grammatically, either option is plausible.

THE POSITION OF VSS. 34–35

While no extant manuscripts omit the material traditionally printed as vss. 34 and 35, several manuscripts, which were mainly written in the West, place this material at the end of the chapter (i.e., after verse 40) rather than following verse 33. In addition, one manuscript (Codex Fuldensis) prints this material in both places. Perhaps the easiest explanation for such uncertainty about the proper location of this material is that it was not originally composed by Paul but rather was originally composed as a note in a manuscript's margin by some unknown figure. Later, this note was mistakenly inserted into the text at two different points by two different scribes as they were making copies of Paul's letter.[4] Thinking this note to be a correction, they were unsure about where it belonged, and they made different guesses. These copies were then, in turn, reproduced by other scribes and in this way the marginal note came to be transmitted as if it had originally been penned by Paul. We might even say that the scribe who put this material at the close of the chapter (i.e., after vs. 40) did not so much decide where it belonged as simply stick it at the end of the literary section in which it appeared in a gesture of futility. While chapter divisions did not exist when this would

---

4. That marginal notes are sometimes mistakenly inserted into a text is well-known. For an example, see John Strugnell's comments on 1 Cor 4:6. Strugnell, "Plea for Conjectural Emendation," 555–58. For another example, see Elijah Hixson's comments on 2 Cor 8:5. Hixson, "When a Marginal Note Becomes the Text."

APPENDIX 2: COMMENTS ON 1 COR 14:34–35 AND 1 TIM 2:11–15

have happened, there is a major change in subject matter between chapters 14 and 15, so in any case, vs. 40 marked the end of the section.

Given the lack of any surviving manuscript that omits this material altogether, such an inadvertent insertion of a marginal note into the text must have occurred very early, probably within about fifty years of when Paul penned 1 Corinthians.[5] It was at roughly this fifty-year point that the *Corpus Paulinum*, the collection of Paul's letters into a single manuscript took place. Since all our surviving manuscripts of Paul's letters derive from this collection, any prior insertions into the text would have left no trace in the manuscript record.

Modern readers may have some difficulty imagining such a scenario since today the difference between a book's printed text and handwritten marginal notes is always obvious. But in antiquity all books were handwritten and all contained copyists' mistakes which required correction. Sometimes the copyists themselves fixed their own mistakes and sometimes later readers made such corrections (occasionally in error). If they were short, these corrections were usually made within the line or between lines. Longer corrections, however, often had to be added in a manuscript's margins. Since longer corrections needed to be positioned where room was available and this was not necessarily adjacent to where the error had occurred, sometimes readers found it difficult to know where in the text the correction should be placed.

However, in addition to corrections, ancient readers also made marginal notes, just as contemporary readers make marginal notes. While marginal notes today are never confused with the printed text, in antiquity marginal notes were frequently confused with corrections to the text. Thus, it was not uncommon for foreign material to become included in an ancient text accidentally.

---

5. Günther Zuntz has argued convincingly that all of Paul's letters (minus the pastoral epistles, but including Hebrews, erroneously thought to be by Paul) have essentially identical manuscript histories. This suggests that they were part of a collection of Paul's letters gathered into a common manuscript. Furthermore, the manuscript of collected letters must have been compiled early. Zuntz suggests the collection was made about fifty years after Paul wrote his letters (Zuntz, *Text of the Epistles* 278). Zuntz also argues that apart from the few isolated references to Paul's letter to the Romans found in manuscripts of 1 Clement, all surviving evidence of the wording of Paul's letters go back to a manuscript of this collection. To say this differently, none of these ten letters was propagated independently of the others. This also means that any errors introduced into the manuscript tradition prior to the gathering together of the collection of Paul's letters are beyond discovery and correction through normal text critical means.

If some ancient reader composed a marginal note about women as hypothesized above, what might have motivated him to do so? Generally, readers create marginal notes in response to something in the text that stimulates an idea. In verses 28 and 30 two situations are mentioned in which Paul teaches that someone ought to be silent: 1) if a person has a message in tongues but there is no one present able to interpret; and 2) if a person is uttering a prophecy and then another person begins uttering a prophecy before the first person is finished. As our hypothesized reader reads this, he may have wanted to note a third instance in which he thought there should be silence: if speakers or potential speakers were women! No doubt with pious intentions, this reader then placed his observation in in the margin of his manuscript. Ultimately, his note accidentally found its way into the standard text of Paul's letter.

One other argument suggests vss. 34 and 35 are inauthentic. They seem to contradict what Paul has written just three chapters earlier (in 1 Cor. 11:2–16). In that enigmatic passage Paul instructs the Corinthians about how women should manage their heads during times of public prayer. (Traditionally but perhaps inaccurately, this passage has been understood to require women to veil their heads.) In whatever way this difficult passage is interpreted, Paul makes clear that women may pray and prophesy in church settings if they present and comport themselves and their heads properly (whatever that propriety might imply). So how could Paul permit women to speak in church in chapter 11 and then deny them this privilege in chapter 14? Something seems amiss.

1 Tim 2:11–15

There is a significant question about whether or not the traditional translation of this passage is correct. One way to illustrate the problem is to compare a traditional translation with an alternative suggestion and to compare their relative advantages and disadvantages.

TRADITIONAL TRANSLATION (RSV, 1971 EDITION):

[11]Let a woman learn in silence with all submissiveness. [12]I permit no woman to teach or to have authority over men; she is to keep silent. [13]For Adam was formed first, then Eve; [14]and Adam was not deceived, but the woman was deceived and became a transgressor. [15]Yet woman will be saved through bearing children, if she continues in faith and love and holiness, with modesty.

APPENDIX 2: COMMENTS ON 1 COR 14:34–35 AND 1 TIM 2:11–15   453

AN ALTERNATIVE TRANSLATION

[11]Let the wife receive instruction peacefully in every situation. [12]I do not permit wives to lecture or to dominate her husband, but rather to be peaceful. [13]For Adam was formed first, and then Eve. [14]And Adam was not deceived, but his wife became deceived by transgression. [15]But he [Adam, i.e., humankind] will be saved through her childbearing, if they should remain in faith and love and holiness with self-control.

COMMENTARY

Vss. 11–15: The three verses preceding vss. 11–15 discuss how believing men and women or believing husbands and wives should comport themselves. These verses continue along that same line.

The great divide in interpretation has been between whether these verses set out standards for, on the one hand, who may teach and lead in a church setting or whether, on the other hand, they set out standards for instruction and authority within a marriage. What may be called the traditional view opts for the former approach, and what may be called the alternative view argues for the latter. My comments will show that I am firmly within the alternative camp but with my own exegetical twists.

Vss. 11–12: The phrase *en hēsychiai* ("peacefully") appears twice in these two verses. While some translate this phrase as "remaining quiet" or "in silence," the phrase does not necessarily exclude speaking, even though such a meaning is possible. An alternative is to translate this phrase "peacefully." Often such prepositional phrases function adverbially, as I propose here.

Liddell-Scott lists Thucydides *Peloponnesian War*, 3.12 (lines 4–5) as contrasting *en tē hēsychiai* ("at peace") with *en tō polemō* ("at war"). This suggests that *en hēsychiai* can imply the opposite of conflict; it does not have to imply silence. This is also the way the adjective *hesychios* functions in the phrase "peaceful life" in 1 Tim 2:2. Paul certainly is not imposing a vow of silence on everyone in the church.

As is the case in many languages, the Greek word for "woman" (*gynē*) is also the standard way to refer to a "wife." Similarly, the Greek word for "man" (*anēr*) is also the standard way of referring to a "husband." Upon examination of these verses, a question presents itself: Are we reading about, on the one hand, women and men or, on the other hand, wives and husbands?

The way *gynē* and *anēr* are presented in the Greek text of these verses is puzzling. One reference to a woman/wife is singular and another reference to women/wives is plural. In addition, one reference to a man/husband is singular. Why does Paul introduce this inconsistency in number?

The RSV text printed above plays fast and loose with the singulars and plurals of these words. In vs. 12 it prints "woman" where the Greek has women/wives. At the end of that same verse, the RSV prints "men" where the Greek has man/husband.

Likely Paul's goal is to teach generically, which accounts for the plural form women/wives at the beginning of vs. 12. But the singular "woman/wife" in vs. 11 and the singular "man/husband" toward the end of vs. 12 underline the one-on-one nature of the marital relationship. This combination of a plural with two singulars suggests that Paul is teaching generically about relationships in marriage.

Paul is not reluctant to exercise his apostolic authority. In vs. 12 he shares that he does not permit wives to do two things. The challenge is to determine what these two things are.

The first prohibition is for the wife "to teach," according to the conventional translation. However, the meaning of this verb (*didaskein*; lexical form *didaskō*) is not limited to classroom or formal teaching. In fact, usually it refers to informal instruction. And it can include instruction that is uninvited or unwelcome (e.g., Matt 21:23; John 9:34; LXX of Prov 1:23). In this context, when Paul speaks disapprovingly of what wives say to their husbands, I think an appropriate translation would be "I do not permit wives to *lecture* . . . ," or perhaps even, "I do not permit wives to *scold* . . . ."

Paul's second prohibition is for wives to "have authority over [men]," according to a common "traditional" translation. The Greek word used here is *authentein* (lexical form *authenteō*), which is notoriously difficult to translate because it was so seldom used. In fact, one difficulty in this regard is the problem of lexical circularity. Lexicographers use a theory about what 1 Tim 2:12 means to construct how this word is defined in their lexicons, and then exegetes use the meaning these lexicons provide to support that very theory. This means that the lexicographer's initial guess about the meaning of 1 Tim 2:12 without much else to go on receives formal "authentication" (pun intended) as the correct meaning.

Liddell and Scott's *Greek-English Lexicon* lists two meanings for *authenteō*: 1) "to have full power or authority over"; and 2) to "commit a murder."[6] Presumably we can dispense with the second meaning since it seems unlikely Paul would write, "I do not permit a wife . . . to murder her husband."

---

6. Liddell and Scott, *Greek-English Lexicon*, s.v. "authenteō."

There is a difference in nuance between the RSV translation "to have authority over" and my proposed (alternative) translation "to dominate," but this is a relatively minor issue in comparison with the larger issue of whether Paul is setting out rules for home life or church life. I think both translations are in keeping with what lexical evidence exists.

In the alternative translation my addition of the word "her" to the word "husband" may surprise some. I will acknowledge that a corresponding word does not appear in the Greek, although I contend that it is implied; I am not simply playing fast and loose with the Greek text. Blass, Debrunner, and Funk argue that "formulae" often omit definite articles where they would normally be expected. They specifically list vs. 12 as an example of such a formula where an article is implied. Furthermore, their comment suggests this missing article has the force of a possessive pronoun ("her").[7] If the word *andros* (the genitive singular of *anēr*) refers to a "husband" rather than a "man," surely the implication is that it is "her husband."

The Greek conjunction *alla* ("but rather") in vs. 12 implies a strong contrast between what has been stated before and what follows. If the phrase *en hēsychiai* ("peacefully") following this disjunctive conjunction implies peace of some sort, this would also imply that what precedes the conjunction depicts some sort of strife or conflict. Apparently, Paul has marital conflict in view. Oddly, the RSV dispenses with translating *alla* altogether. Perhaps this is because the RSV translators have chosen to translate *hēsychia* as "silence" rather than "peace" and a strong disjunction does not work well with this interpretation.

According to the traditional interpretation, the Greek phrase *en pasē hypotagē* should be translated as "in all submissiveness" or something similar. This is not an impossible construction, but it is awkward. Normally, when used with a singular noun the Greek adjective *pas* means "every." If Paul's objective were to express "complete" submissiveness, it would have been more usual to use a participle such as *peplēromenē* ("full"; lexical form *pimplēmi*) or *exērtismenē* ("complete"; lexical form *exartizō*) to express this.

I propose an alternative translation: "in every situation." My reasoning is that this fits the context better (while also being lexically defensible). The noun *hypotagē* is related to the verb *hypotassō*, which can be used in various ways having to do with ordering things. The basic meaning of the prefix *hypo* is "under," which suggests to some interpreters that this word group must mean "to subordinate" (suggesting a vertical hierarchy) or "to place behind" (suggesting a horizonal ordering). However, according to Liddell-Scott, the verb *hypotassō* can also mean simply "to assign," and participles

---

7. Bl-D-F §257.3.

of this verb when used in description of a list can indicate "the things that follow." Therefore, it is likely that the associated noun can also be used in a more general, non-subordinating way. A "situation" is a particular ordering of various factors, and when they are reordered, a different "situation" is created. The phrase "in every situation" implies "in whichever ordering of things should happen to occur."

Some may not find this proposal persuasive. Nevertheless, even if the more traditional rendering "in all submissiveness" were to be retained, it would not damage my primary theory about this passage, that it relates to husband-wife relationships.

The bottom line is that Paul is frustrated with discord between wives and husbands in the church at Ephesus, and evidently this has been caused largely by hectoring wives. There is no indication they are lecturing their husbands (or men in general) over matters of scriptural interpretation or Christian doctrine, but more likely are troubling them over more mundane family matters. To state this differently, there is no indication Paul forbids women to teach or exercise leadership in church settings.

Vss. 13–15: These verses contain a *midrash* on Genesis 3, which describes the disobedience of Adam and Eve and the fallout from that disobedience. The Genesis narrative contains blame-shifting and depicts tension between Adam and Eve, which make it rich ground for Paul to mine as he instructs about husband-wife relations.

The meaning of 1 Tim 2:13–15 has often been obscured by translators who are so interested in producing smooth-flowing English that they finesse what Paul actually writes. Notice that in the RSV the last clause of vs. 15 reads: "if she continues in faith and love and holiness, with modesty." The problem with this is that the verb of that clause (*meinōsin*; lexical form *menō*) is both plural and in the subjunctive mood. Thus, the clause is better translated "if they should remain . . . ." The subjunctive mood emphasizes a note of uncertainty about their future actions.

Paul presents Adam and Eve both, on the one hand, as historical characters and, on the other hand, as primal representatives of their countless sons and daughters. But what exactly do they represent? Does Adam represent all future men and Eve all future women? Or does Adam represent all future husbands and Eve represent all future wives? While Paul's argument starts with two concrete historical figures—Adam and Eve—he ends with people whose future faithfulness, love, and holiness remains an open question. Paul's promise of safety or salvation is qualified by his words: "if they should remain . . . ." Apparently, Paul includes many of his readers within this group.

Adam and Eve are introduced in vs. 13. This verse is rather straightforward and noncontroversial.

The Greek text of vs. 14 emphasizes a distinction—perhaps it should be called a play-on-words—that is difficult to duplicate in English. Adam is described as not having been "deceived" (lexical form *apataō*). In contrast, "his wife" is described as having been "strongly deceived," or perhaps "beguiled," using the same verb applied to Adam but intensified by the addition of a prepositional prefix (lexical form *exapataō*).

No doubt in pursuit of a smooth English, the RSV mistranslates *parabasei gegonen* as "became a transgressor." There are two problems with this. First, *parabasis* (the lexical form of *parabasei*) does not mean "transgressor"; it means "transgression."[8] Second, *gegonen* (lexical form *ginomai*, *gignomai* in Classical Greek), a verb in the perfect tense, should probably be construed with the participle *exapatētheisa*, forming a periphrastic participle meaning "became deceived."[9] This deception came "by transgression."

The formulation "Adam and his wife," rather than "Adam and Eve," echoes the LXX text of Gen 3:8. In Genesis the meaning is clear because a possessive pronoun (*autou*) modifies the word "woman/wife" (*gynē*). While 1 Tim 2:14 also probably refers to "his wife," this is less clear because of the absence of the possessive pronoun.

How does what Paul writes in vs. 14 address the situation in Ephesus? Genesis 3 narrates the first disagreement between the first couple. It describes how the wife coaxes her husband, perhaps even hectors him, into doing something wrong. This is an example of how not to conduct a marriage. Instead, Paul contends that in the home it is the husband who should give instruction and lead.

There is also ambiguity in the first part of vs. 15. In fact, there are two points of ambiguity. First, it is unclear who the subject of the main verb is. Second, the meaning of the main verb is unclear.

Grammatically the subject of the main verb could be either masculine or feminine. The subject must be singular in number, but the gender is unspecified. Choosing the former option would result in the translation: "He will be saved through her childbirth." The latter option would result in the translation: "She will be saved through childbirth." Normally, the reader would examine the preceding text, and she would assume the closest

---

8. I make this judgment with full awareness that based on this verse Bauer, Arndt, and Gingrich list "transgressor" as a possible meaning for *parabasis*. See Bauer, Arndt, and Gingrich, *Greek-English Lexicon*, s.v. "parabasis." I find this unlikely.

9. On the formation of periphrastic participles formed with forms of *gignomai*, see Smyth, *Greek Grammar* §1964.

antecedent noun in the nominative case is the implied subject. In this case that would be "the wife" (*hē gynē*) and the translation would be "She will be saved through childbirth." However, there is reason to believe that in this verse the normal pattern does not hold, and the implied subject is "Adam." If this is the case, then the translation would be "He will be saved through her childbirth."

The main verb (*sōthēsetai*; lexical form *sōzō*) is future passive in form and depending on the implied subject it means approximately either "she will be saved" or "he will be saved." But the key question is this: Saved from what? There are several possibilities. However, considering that this passage is a *midrash* on Genesis 3, it seems best to look for the answer to this question in Genesis.

The most basic meaning of the verb *sōzō* is to "save from death."[10] The drama of Genesis 3 centers around God's command to Adam and Eve not to eat from the Tree of the Knowledge of Good and Evil. Furthermore, God declares that if they do eat from it, they will surely die. Despite this declaration, after disobeying God's command they do not immediately fall down dead, although they become mortal, which is to say, they become liable to physical death.[11] In addition, in Romans 5 Paul suggests that the disobedience of Adam brought spiritual death on both himself and on his posterity.[12]

The imposition of mortality suggests a threat to the survival of the human race. Seemingly, this threat is answered in God's words to "the woman" found in Gen 3:16, which are usually construed as a curse but may also contain a blessing—the solution to this threat. Although she will suffer greatly in her labor, through childbirth the imposition of death will not mark the end of mankind.

As has already been stated, in 1 Tim 2:15 the implied subject of the verb *sōthēsetai* is unclear. However, if this implied subject is Adam, which in addition to being a personal name also means "humankind" in Hebrew, Paul's *midrash* makes a great deal of sense: "He [Adam=humankind] will be saved through her childbearing." This statement is then qualified: "if they [Adam's descendants] should remain in faith and love and holiness with

---

10. Liddell and Scott, *Greek-English Lexicon*, s.v. "*sōzō*."

11. This is the way the narrative is usually understood. However, there is some tension in the text. If Adam and Eve were not created mortal, then what possibility did the Tree of Life represent?

12. C.F.D. Moule has suggested an interesting but implausible interpretation of this verse. He understands *sōsthēsetai dia tēs teknogonias* to mean "she will be brought safely through childbirth." This makes reasonable sense of the Greek, but it is hard to understand how it would fit into Paul's argument. See Moule, *Idiom-Book*, 56 (under section C).

self-control." Thus, the first verb's subject in the singular implying Adam/humankind gives way to a second verb in the plural.

If an exegete would interpret this passage as teaching that women may never instruct or hold authority over men, it is difficult to see what the limiting principle would be. There is nothing in the passage that suggests this teaching relates only to authority in a church setting. Therefore, it would also suggest that, based on Christian principles, women in the business world could never supervise men. Such problems are avoided if the exegete follows the clues indicating that Paul's teaching regards marital relationships and homelife.

An Additional Note

The interpretation of these passages has often been considered crucial in a theological tug-of-war between "complementarian" and "egalitarian" positions, terms which are thought to define overarching principles of how the sexes relate to each other. The thought is that, on the one hand, complementarians consider the created order to involve fixed differences between males and females that will perdure at least until the full consummation of the kingdom of God. On the other hand, egalitarians believe that at least some of the domination of women by men throughout history is related the fall and the introduction of sin into the world, and that in Christ this consequence of sin may be at least partially surmounted. Furthermore, this division of theological perspectives would imply that the interpretation I have presented of this passage necessarily aligns me with egalitarianism.

I would like to register my objection to anyone taking this logical leap. While I do not think this text should be used to restrict women from teaching in churches or exercising authority in churches, this does not imply that I believe all differences between the sexes are the result of the fall or have been erased by the inauguration of the kingdom of God in the earthly ministry of Christ. Continuing differences between male and female seem implied by the complementarity illustrated in their sexual union, which often leads to reproduction, and I expect such differences to continue until the need for reproduction ceases in the eschaton. This book is not a treatise on the full range of issues related to human sexuality. Nevertheless, given issues raised in Romans 16, it seemed appropriate to make clear that I believe Paul was not averse to allowing women to take teaching and leadership roles in the church.

BIBLIOGRAPHY

1 Clement. "A Letter of the Romans to the Corinthians (I Clement)." In *The Apostolic Fathers*, 2nd ed., edited by Michael W. Holmes, et al., 23–101. Grand Rapids: Baker, 1992.

2 Clement. "An Ancient Christian Sermon (2 Clement)." In *The Apostolic Fathers*, 2nd ed., edited by Michael W. Holmes et al., 103–27. Grand Rapids: Baker, 1992.

1 Enoch. *The Ethiopic Version of The Book of Enoch*, Translated by R. H. Charles. Oxford: Clarendon,1906.

2 Baruch. 2 (Syriac Apocalypse of) Baruch. Translated by A. F. J. Klijn. In *The Old Testament Pseudepigrapha, Vol. 1*, edited by James H. Charlesworth, 615–52. New York: Doubleday, 1983.

4 Ezra. *The Fourth Book of Ezra*. Translated by Bruce M. Metzger. In *The Old Testament Pseudepigrapha, Vol. 1*, edited by James H. Charlesworth, 517–59. New York: Doubleday, 1983.

Aesop. Ben Edwin Perry, trans. and ed. *Babrius and Phaedrus*. Loeb Classical Library 436. Cambridge, MA: Harvard University Press, 1965.

Aland, Kurt, and Barbara Aland. *The Text of the New Testament: An Introduction to the Critical Editions and to the Theory and Practice of Modern Textual Criticism*. Translated by Errol F. Rhodes. 2nd ed. Grand Rapids: Eerdmans, 1989.

Ambrose of Milan. *On the Death of His Brother Satyrus (De Excessu Fratris Sui Satyri)*. In *Patrologia Latina*, Vol. 16, edited by J.-P. Migne, cols. 1345–1414. Paris: Garnier Frères, 1844–55.

Aristotle. *Politics*. Benjamin Jowett, ed. *The Politics of Aristotle*. 2 vols. Oxford: Clarendon, 1885.

Augustine of Hippo. *Confessions*. James J. O'Donnell, ed. *Augustine, Confessions, Vol. 1: Introduction and Text*. Oxford: Clarendon, 1992; J. G. Pilkington, trans. "The Confessions of St. Augustine." In *Nicene and Post-Nicene Fathers*. First Series. Vol. 1, 45–207. 1886. Reprint. Peabody, MA: Hendrickson, 1994.

(Pseudo-) Barnabas. "The Epistle of Barnabas." In *The Apostolic Fathers*, 2nd ed., edited by Michael W. Holmes et al., 271–327. Grand Rapids: Baker, 1992.

Barclay, John M. G. *Paul and the Gift*. Grand Rapids: Eerdmans, 2015.

Baronius, Caesar. *Annales Ecclesiastici*. 12 vols. Rome: Typis Leonardi Venturini, 1588–1607.

Barth, Karl. *The Epistle to the Romans*. Translated by Edwyn C. Hoskyns. London: Oxford University Press, 1933.

Barrett, C. K. *A Commentary on the Second Epistle to the Corinthians*. New York: Harper & Row, 1973.

Bates, Matthew W. *Salvation by Allegiance Alone: Rethinking Faith, Works, and the Gospel of Jesus the King*. Grand Rapids: Baker Academic, 2017.

Bauer, Walter, William F. Arndt, and F. Wilbur Gingrich. *A Greek-English Lexicon of the New Testament and Other Early Christian Literature*. 4th ed. Chicago: University of Chicago Press, 1957.

Binns, Michael. "Roman Personal Names." *Pompei in Pictures*. https://www.pompeiinpictures.com/pompeiinpictures/Ro/Roman%20Personal%20Names.htm.

Blass, Friedrich, et al. *A Greek Grammar of the New Testament and Other Early Christian Literature*. Chicago: University of Chicago Press, 1961.

Blass, F., A. Debrunner, and F. Rehkopf. *Grammatik der neutestamentlichen Griechisch*. 14th ed. Göttingen: Vandenhoeck & Ruprecht, 1976.

Brooks, James A., and Carlton L. Winbery. *Syntax of New Testament Greek*. Lanham, MD: University Press of America, 1979.

Brown, Francis, et al. *The Brown-Driver-Briggs Hebrew and English Lexicon with an Appendix Containing the Biblical Aramaic*. 1906. Reprint. Peabody, MA: Hendrickson, 2017.

Brown, Raymond E. *An Introduction to the New Testament*. The Anchor Bible Reference Library. New York: Doubleday, 1997.

Bruce, F. F. *Paul: Apostle of the Heart Set Free*. Grand Rapids: Eerdmans, 1977.

Burnett, D. Clint. "Reconsidering the Number of First Century C.E. Synagogues in Rome." *Ad Fontes: A Blog Dedicated to Studying the Jewish Apostle Paul in his Greco-Roman Context*, May 31, 2020. https://www.clintburnett.com/2020/05/31/reconsidering-the-number-of-supposed-first-century-ce-synagogues-in-rome/

Cadbury, Henry J. "Erastus of Corinth." *Journal of Biblical Literature* 50.2 (1931) 42–58.

Cagnat, René, ed. *Inscriptiones Graecae ad Res Romanas Pertinentes: Inscriptiones Asiae*. 3 vols. 1906–1927. Reprint. Chicago: Ares, 1975.

Calvin, John. *Acts of the Council of Trent with the Antidote*. Translated by Henry Beveridge. 1851. Reprint. https://www.monergism.com/thethreshold/sdg/calvin_trentantidote.html.

———. *Commentary on Romans*. Edited by Timothy George. Translated by Francis Sibson in 1834. Nashville: B&H Academic, 2022.

———. *Institutes of the Christian Religion*. Edited by John T. McNeil. Translated by Ford Lewis Battles. 2 vols. Philadelphia: Westminster, 1960.

Cancik, Hubert, et al. *Brill's New Pauly: Encyclopaedia of the Ancient World*. 15 vols. Leiden: Brill, 2002–10.

Caragounis, Chrys C. "From Obscurity to Prominence: The Development of the Roman Church between Romans and 1 Clement." In *Judaism and Christianity in First-Century Rome*, edited by Karl P. Donfried and Peter Richardson, 245–79. Grand Rapids: Eerdmans, 1998.

Catechism of the Catholic Church. New York: Doubleday, 1995.

Dahl, Nils Alstrup. *Jesus the Christ: The Historical Origins of Christological Doctrine*. Edited by Donald H. Juel. Minneapolis: Fortress, 1991.

Dalman, Gustaf. *The Words of Christ*. Translated by D. M. Kay. 1902. Reprint. Minneapolis: Klock & Klock Christian, 1981.

Denney, James. *The Second Epistle to the Corinthians*. The Expositor's Bible. London: Hodder & Stoughton, 1894.

Dessau, Hermann, ed. *Inscriptiones Latinae Selectae*. 3 vols. Berlin: Weidmann, 1892–1916.

Didache. "The Didache (The Teaching of the Twelve Apostles)." In *The Apostolic Fathers*, 2nd ed., edited by Michael W. Holmes et al., 246–69. Grand Rapids: Baker, 1992.

Dionysius of Halicarnassus. *Roman Antiquities*. 7 vols. Translated by Earnest Cary. Loeb Classical Library. Cambridge, MA: Harvard University Press, 1937–50.

Donfried, Karl P., ed. *The Romans Debate*. Rev. and exp. ed. Peabody, MA: Hendrickson, 1991.

Donfried, Karl P., and Peter Richardson, eds. *Judaism and Christianity in First-Century Rome*. Grand Rapids: Eerdmans, 1998.

Doty, William G. *Letters in Primitive Christianity*. Eugene, OR: Wipf & Stock, 1973.

Dunn, James D. G. *The Christ & The Spirit*, Vol. 1: *Christology*. Grand Rapids: Eerdmans, 1998.

———. *Romans 1–8*. Word Biblical Commentary 38A. Dallas: Word, 1988.

———. *Romans 9–16*. Word Biblical Commentary 38B. Dallas: Word, 1988.

Ellis, E. Earl. "'Spiritual' Gifts in the Pauline Community." *NTS* 20.2 (Jan. 1974) 128–44.

Fee, Gordon D. *1 and 2 Timothy, Titus*. New International Biblical Commentary. Rev. ed. Peabody, MA: Hendrickson, 1988.

———. *The First Epistle to the Corinthians*. The New International Commentary on the New Testament. Grand Rapids: Eerdmans, 1987.

———. *God's Empowering Presence: The Holy Spirit in the Letters of Paul.* Peabody, MA: Hendrickson, 1994.

"Fiddler on the Roof." Text by Joseph Stein. New York: Music Theatre International, 1964.

Friesen, Steven J. "The Wrong Erastus: Ideology, Archaeology, and Exegesis." In *Corinth in Context: Comparative Studies on Religion and Society*, edited by Steven J. Friesen et al., 231–56. Leiden: Brill, 2010.

Fuller, Daniel P. *Gospel and Law: Contrast or Continuum? The Hermeneutics of Dispensationalism and Covenant Theology.* Grand Rapids: Eerdmans, 1980.

Gamble, Harry, Jr. *The Textual History of the Letter to the Romans.* Studies and Documents 42. Grand Rapids: Eerdmans, 1977.

Garnsey, Peter. "Why Penalties Became Harsher: The Roman Case, Late Republic to Fourth Century Empire." *Natural Law Forum* 13 (1968) 141–62.

(Aulus) Gellius. *The Attic Nights of Aulus Gellius.* 3 vols. Edited and Translated by J. C. Rolfe. Loeb Classical Library. London: Heinnemann, 1927–28.

Gill, N. S. "The Classical Definition of a Tyrant." *ThoughtCo*, Aug. 27, 2020. https://thoughtco.com/tyrant-in-ancient-greece-118544.

Glare, P. G. W. *Oxford Latin Dictionary.* Oxford: Clarendon, 1982.

Goodrich, John K. "Erastus of Corinth (Romans 16.23): Responding to Recent Proposals on his Rank, Status, and Faith." *New Testament Studies* 57.4 (Sept. 2011) 583–93.

Goodspeed, Edgar J. "Gaius Titius Justus." *Journal of Biblical Literature* 69 (1950) 382–83.

Gregory of Nazianzus. *Letter 101 (to Cledonius).* Translated by Charles Gordon Browne and James Edward Swallow. In *Nicene and Post Nicene Fathers*, Second Series, Vol. 7, edited by Philip Schaff and Henry Wace, 439–43. 1894. Reprint. Peabody, MA: Hendrickson, 1994.

———. *Orationes (Orations).* In *Patrologia Graeca*, vol. 36, edited by J.-P. Migne, cols. 11–664. Paris: Imprimerie Catholique, 1857–66.

Grosart, Alexander B., ed. *The Complete Works of Richard Crashaw.* 2 vols. Blackburn, Lancashire: St. George's, 1873. https://www.gutenberg.org/files/38550/38550-h/38550-h.htm#FIDES_QUAE_SOLA_JUSTIFICAT.

Hermas. "The Shepherd of Hermas." In *The Apostolic Fathers*, 2nd ed., edited by Michael W. Holmes et al., 329–527. Grand Rapids: Baker, 1992.

Heppe, Heinrich. *Reformed Dogmatics: Set Out and Illustrated from the Sources.* Revised and edited by Ernst Bizer. Translated by G. T. Thomson. Grand Rapids: Baker, 1978.

Hippolytus. *Refutatio Omnium Haeresium.* Edited by Miroslav Marcovich. Patristische Texte und Studien 25. Berlin: de Gruyter, 1986.

Horace. *Q. Horati Flacci Carmina*. Edited by Fredericus Vollmer. Leipzig: Teubner, 1908; *Horace for English Readers*. Translated by E. C. Wickham. Oxford: Clarendon, 1903.

Hunter, David G. "2008 NAPS Presidential Address: The Significance of Ambrosiaster." *Journal of Early Christian Studies* 17:1 (2006) 1–26.

Ice, Thomas D., "A Short History of Dispensationalism." 2009. Liberty University Article Archives 37. https://digitalcommons.liberty.edu/pretrib_arch/37.

Ignatius of Antioch. "The Letters of Ignatius." In *The Apostolic Fathers*, 2nd ed., edited by Michael W. Holmes et al., 129–201. Grand Rapids: Baker, 1992.

Hixson, Elijah. "When a Marginal Note Becomes the Text." *Evangelical Textual Criticism*, Oct. 19, 2022. http://evangelicaltextualcriticism.blogspot.com/2022/10/when-marginal-note-becomes-text.html.

Jastrow, Marcus. *Dictionary of the Targumim, Talmud Bavli, Talmud Yerushalmi and Midrashic Literature*. 2nd ed. 1903. Reprint. New York: Judaica Treasury, 2004.

Jefford, Clayton N. *The Apostolic Fathers and the New Testament*. Peabody, MA: Hendrickson, 2006.

Jewett, Robert. *Romans: A Commentary*. Hermeneia. Minneapolis: Fortress, 2007.

Jipp, Joshua W. "Ancient, Modern, and Future Interpretations of Romans 1:3–4: Reception History and Biblical Interpretation." *Journal of Theological Interpretation* 3:2 (2009) 241–59.

Josephus. Translated by Henry St. J. Thackeray, et al. 10 vols. Loeb Classical Library. Cambridge: Harvard University Press, 1926–1965.

Justinian. *The Digests of Justinian*. Edited by Theodor Mommsen and Paul Krueger. Translated and edited by Alan Watson. Philadelphia: University of Pennsylvania Press, 1985.

Käsemann, Ernst. *Commentary on Romans*. Translated by Geoffrey W. Bromiley. Grand Rapids: Eerdmans, 1980.

Keener, Craig S. *Romans*. New Covenant Commentary Series 6. Eugene, OR: Cascade, 2009.

Kent, John Harvey. *Corinth: Results of Excavations Conducted by The American School of Classical Studies at Athens*, Vol. VIII, Part 3: *The Inscriptions 1926–1950*. Princeton: The American School of Classical Studies at Athens, 1966.

Kittel, Gerhard, ed. *Theological Dictionary of the New Testament*. 10 vols. Translated by Geoffrey Bromiley. Grand Rapids: Eerdmans, 1964–76.

Kober, Manfred. "The Problematic Development of Progressive Dispensationalism, Parts 1 & 2." *Faith Pulpit* (March–April, 1997). https://faith.edu/faith-news/the-problematic-development-of-progressive-dispensationalism-parts-1-2/.

Koester, Helmut. *Ancient Christian Gospels: Their History and Development*. Philadelphia: Trinity Press International, 1990.

———. *Introduction to the New Testament*, Vol. 2: *History and Literature of Early Christianity*. English ed. New York: De Gruyter, 1982.

Kornelis, Michael. "Peter Lombard and the Holy Eucharist: Resolving Three 'Augustines' into One." https://www.academia.edu/2541134/Peter_Lombard_and_the_Holy_Eucharist_resolving_three_Augustines_into_one.

Ladd, George Eldon. *A Theology of the New Testament*. Revised ed. Edited by Donald A. Hagner. Grand Rapids: Eerdmans, 1993.

Lampe, Peter. *From Paul to Valentinus: Christians at Rome in the First Two Centuries*. Translated by Michael Steinhauser. Edited by Marshall D. Johnson. Minneapolis: Fortress, 2003.

———. "The Roman Christians of Romans 16." In *The Romans Debate*, edited by Karl P. Donfried, rev. and exp. ed., 216–30. Peabody, MA: Hendrickson, 1991.

Leon, Harry J. *The Jews of Ancient Rome*. Updated ed. Peabody, MA: Hendrickson, 1990.

Lewis, C.S. *The Four Loves*. 1960. Reprint. Signature Book ed. San Francisco: HarperOne, 2017.

———. *Mere Christianity*. 1952. Reprint. Signature Book ed. New York: HarperOne, 2001.

Liberman, Anatoly. "A Missionary Imposition (or a Rambling Sermon on Miss/Mess/Mass and their Kin." *Word Origins . . . And How We Know Them*, Dec. 22, 2010. https://blog.oup.com/2010/12/mass/.

Liddell, Henry George, and Robert Scott, et al. *A Greek-English Lexicon, with a Revised Supplement*. 9th ed. Oxford: Clarendon, 1996.

Lightfoot, J. B. *Saint Paul's Epistle to the Philippians*. 8th ed. London: Macmillan, 1888.

Luther, Martin. *Against the Robbing and Murdering Hordes of Peasants*. In *Luther's Works*, Vol. 46. American ed. The Christian in Society III, edited by Robert C. Schultz and Helmut T. Lehmann, 45–55. Philadelphia, Fortress, 1967.

———. *Lectures on Romans: Glosses and Scholia*. Edited by Hilton C. Oswald. Translated by Walter G. Tillmanns and Jacob A. O. Preus. Luther's Works 25. Saint Louis: Concordia, 1972.

———. *Luther's Works*. American ed. Edited by Jaroslav Pelikan, Helmut T. Lehmann, and Christopher Boyd Brown. 75 vols. Philadelphia: Fortress, 1955–.

———. *Temporal Authority: To What Extent It Should be Obeyed*. In *Luther's Works*, Vol. 45. American ed. The Christian in Society II, edited by Walther L. Brandt and Helmut T. Lehmann, 75–129. Philadelphia: Muhlenberg, 1962.

———. *Whether Soldiers, Too, Can be Saved*. In *Luther's Works*, vol. 46. American ed. The Christian in Society III, edited by Robert C. Schultz and Helmut T. Lehmann, 87–137. Philadelphia, Fortress, 1967.
Manson, Thomas Walther. "St. Paul's Letter to the Romans–and Others." In *The Romans Debate*. Rev. and exp. ed., edited by Karl P. Donfried, 1–15, Peabody, MA: Hendrickson, 1991.
Mason, Hugh J. *Greek Terms for Roman Institutions*. American Studies in Papyrology 13. Toronto: A. M. Hakkert, 1974.
Mason, Steve. *Josephus, Judea, and Christian Origins: Methods and Categories*. Peabody, MA: Hendrickson, 2009.
Mauss, Marcel. "Essai sur le Don: Forme et Raison de l'Échange dans les Sociétés Archaïques." *Année Sociologique*, 30–186. English translation: Marcel Mauss. *The Gift*. Translated by W. D. Halle. London: Routledge, 1990.
McGrath, Alister E. *Iustitia Dei: A History of the Christian Doctrine of Justification*. 3rd ed. Cambridge: Cambridge University Press, 2005.
Melito of Sardis. *The Homily on the Passion*. Edited and translated by Campbell Bonner. Studies and Documents. Philadelphia: University of Pennsylvania Press, 1940.
Menzies, Glen W. "Assessing N.T. Wright's Reading of Paul through the Lens of Dispensationalism." In *Pentecostal Theology and the Theological Vision of N.T. Wright: A Conversation*, edited by Janet Meyer Everts and Jeffrey S. Lamp, 85–106. Cleveland, TN: CPT, 2015.
Menzies, Robert P. "Subsequence in the Pauline Epistles." *Pneuma* 39 (2017) 342–63.
Metzger, Bruce M. *The Text of the New Testament: Its Transmission, Corruption, and Restoration*. 2nd ed. Oxford: Clarendon, 1968.
———. *A Textual Commentary on the Greek New Testament*. United Bible Societies, 1971.
Michel, Otto. *Der Brief an die Römer*. Göttingen: Vandenhoeck & Ruprecht, 1957.
Milgrom, Jacob. "Response by Dr. Jacob Milgrom." In *The Idea of Conscience in Philo of Alexandria: Protocol of the Thirteenth Colloquy: 12 January, 1975*, edited by Richard T. Wallis, 16–18. Berkeley, CA: The Center for Hermeneutical Studies in Hellenistic and Modern Culture, 1975.
Mirbt, Carl. *Quellen sur Geschichte des Papsttums und des römischen Katholizismus*. 3rd ed. Tübingen: J. C. B. Mohr (Paul Siebeck), 1911.
Mishnah. *The Mishnah: A New Translation*. Translated by Jacob Neusner. New Haven: Yale University Press, 1988.
Mitford, T. B. "Notes on Some Published Inscriptions from Roman Cyprus." *The Annual of the British School at Athens* 42 (1947) 201–30.

Moule, C. F. D. *An Idiom-Book of New Testament Greek*. 2nd ed. Cambridge: Cambridge University Press, 1959.

Mowinckel, Sigmund. *He That Cometh*. Translated by G. W. Anderson. Nashville: Abingdon, 1954.

Murphy-O'Connor, Jerome. *Paul: A Critical Life*. Oxford: Clarendon, 1996.

———. *St. Paul's Corinth: Texts and Archaeology*. Collegeville, MN: Glazier, 1983.

Neusner, Jacob. "Mr. Sanders's Pharisees and Mine." *Bulletin for Biblical Research* 2 (1992) 143–69.

Pagels, Elaine. *Adam, Eve, and the Serpent*. New York: Random House, 1988.

———. "The Politics of Paradise: Augustine's Exegesis of Genesis 1–3 Versus That of John Chrysostom." *Harvard Theological Review* 78:1–2 (1985) 67–99.

Parker, Victor. "*Tyrannos*, The Semantics of a Political Concept from Archilochus to Aristotle." *Hermes* 126.2 (1998) 145–72.

Philo of Alexandria. *The Special Laws*. Translated by F. H. Colson. In *Philo*, vol. 7, 98–607. Loeb Classical Library. Cambridge, MA: Harvard University Press, 1937.

Pliny the Elder, *Natural History: C. Plini Secundi Naturalis Historiae Libri xxxvii*. Edited by Karl F. T. Mayhof. 5 vols. Leipzig: Teubner, 1892–1909.

Polycarp. "The Letter of Polycarp to the Philippians." In *The Apostolic Fathers*, 2nd ed., Michael W. Holmes et al., 222–45. Grand Rapids: Baker, 1992.

Reasoner, Mark. *Romans in Full Circle: A History of Interpretation*. Louisville: Westminster John Knox, 2005.

———. *The Strong and the Weak: Romans 14.1–15.13 in Context*. Society for New Testament Studies Monograph Series 103. Cambridge: Cambridge University Press, 1999.

Reid, James S. "Human Sacrifices at Rome and Other Notes on Roman Religion." *Journal of Roman Studies* 2 (1912) 34–52.

Riss, Richard. "The Latter Rain Movement of 1948." *Pneuma* 4 (Spring 1982) 32–45.

Rocca, Samuele. "In the Beginning; Jews as a Minority Group in the Middle and Late Republican Period." *Scripta Judaica Cracoviensia* 12 (2014) 7–24.

———. *In the Shadow of the Caesars: Jewish Life in Roman Italy*. Brill Reference Library of Judaism 74. Leiden: Brill, 2022.

Ryrie, Charles Caldwell. "Introduction to the New Testament." In *Ryrie Study Bible*, exp. ed., New American Standard, 1995 update, edited by Charles C. Ryrie, 1498–1503. Chicago: Moody, 1995.

———, ed. *Ryrie Study Bible*, exp. ed., New American Standard. 1995 update. Chicago: Moody, 1995.

Sanders, Guy, et al. *Ancient Corinth Site Guide*. 7th ed. Princeton: American School of Classical Studies at Athens, 2018.

Scofield, C. I., ed. *The Scofield Study Bible*. Facsimile ed. New York: Oxford University Press, 1917.
Segal, Alan F. *Paul the Convert: The Apostolate and Apostasy of Saul the Pharisee*. New Haven: Yale University Press, 1990.
Simon, Marcel. *Verus Israel: A Study of the Relations between Christians and Jews in the Roman Empire (AD 135–425)*. Translated by H. McKeating. Oxford: Oxford University Press, 1986.
Smyth, Herbert Weir. *Greek Grammar*. Revised by Gordon M. Messing. Cambridge, MA: Harvard University Press, 1956.
Spielvogel, Jackson J. *Western Civilization*. 9th ed. Stamford, CT: Cengage Learning, 2015.
Starling, David. "The Analogy of Faith in the Theology of Luther and Calvin." *The Reformed Theological Review* 72:1 (April 2013) 5–19.
Stendahl, Krister. "The Apostle Paul and the Introspective Conscious of the West." *Harvard Theological Review* 56 (1963) 199–215.
Stern, Gaius. "*Devotio* and Human Sacrifice in Archaic Italy and Rome." *Acta Classica* 63 (2020) 1–35.
Strugnell, John. "A Plea for Conjectural Emendation in the New Testament, with a Coda on 1 Cor 4:6." *Catholic Biblical Quarterly* 36 (1974) 543–58.
Suetonius, *Lives of the Caesars*. Translated by J. C. Rolfe. 2 vols. Loeb Classical Library. London: William Heinemann, 1914.
Tacitus. *The Annals of Tacitus, Books XI–XVI*. Translated by George Gilbert Ramsay. London: John Murray, 1909.
Testaments of the Twelve Patriarchs. R. H. Charles, ed. *The Greek Versions of the Testaments of the Twelve Patriarchs*. Oxford: Clarendon Press, 1908; James H. Charlesworth, ed. "Testaments of the Twelve Patriarchs." In *The Old Testament Pseudepigrapha*, vol. 1, 775–838. Garden City, NY: Doubleday, 1983.
Trobisch, David. *Paul's Letter Collection: Tracing the Origins*. Bolivar, MO: Quiet Waters, 1994.
Wallace, Daniel B. *Greek Grammar Beyond the Basics*. Grand Rapids: Zondervan, 1996.
———. "Junia Among the Apostles: The Double Identification Problem in Romans 16:7." *Bible.org*, June 24, 2004. https://bible.org/article/junia-among-apostles-double-identification-problem-romans-167.
Wright, N. T. *Justification: God's Plan and Paul's Vision*. Downers Grove, IL: IVP Academic, 2009.
———. *Paul and the Faithfulness of God*. 2 vols. Minneapolis: Fortress, 2013.
———. "The Paul of History and the Apostle of Faith: The Tyndale New Testament Lecture, 1978." *Tyndale Bulletin* 29 (1978) 61–88.
Zuntz, Günther. *The Text of the Epistles: A Disquisition Upon the Corpus Paulinum. The Schweich Lectures of the British Academy 1946*. London: Oxford University Press, 1953.

NAME INDEX

Some very commonly occurring names, such as Paul, Jesus, and Christ, are not included in this index. Also not included are supernatural figures (real or imagined), e.g., God, the Holy Spirit, Satan, the Snake, Baal, Zeus, Thor. Israel and Judah, when they represent a people, are not included. Because this is an index of people's names, an attempt has been made to distinguish individuals from books named after them, especially biblical books.

Abel, 173
Abelard, 67
Abihu, 108
Abraham, 4, 49, 54, 66, 76, 110, 117–25, 147, 180, 217–19, 226, 228, 233–34, 243, 265, 267, 270, 277–78, 295, 298, 316
Achaicus, 3
Acilius Glabrio, Manius, 425
Adam, 18, 62, 126, 129, 136–54, 166, 184, 204, 452–53, 456–59
Adeodatus, 362
Agathopus, Rhaius (Gaius), 413
Agrippa I, 410
Ahab, 244, 354
Ahaz, 66
Ahaziah, 354
Alexander (the son of Herod), 7
Alexander (the son of Simon of Cyrene), 413
Alypius, 362
Ambrose, 137–39, 361
Ambrosiaster, 137–38
Ampliatus, 400, 404, 409, 444
Andronicus, 8–9, 34, 400, 404–5, 408–9, 421, 423, 444
Antichrist, 293

Anna, 289
Anselm, 67–68, 105
Antiochus (king of Syria), 116
Antiochus Epiphanes, 354
Apelles, 400, 404–5, 409–10, 444
Apelles of Kos, 409
Apollos, 198, 391, 424, 448
Aquila, 3–5, 9–10, 156, 260, 335, 400–407, 409, 423–29, 443–44, 448
Aquinas, Thomas, 70, 71, 75
Archilochus of Paros, 356
Aristarchus, 433
Aristides, Aelius, 300
Aristobulus, 9, 400, 402–4, 410–12
Aristobulus I, 410
Aristobulus IV, 411
Aristobulus Minor, 410
Aristophanes, 152, 193
Aristotle, 45, 87, 357–58
Arndt, William F., 184, 432, 457
Arria Plaria Vera Priscilla, 425
Asyncritus, 400, 402
Athalia, 355
Augustine of Hippo, 121, 137–39, 143, 147, 151–54, 346–47, 361
Augustus, 6–7, 409–11, 426

NAME INDEX

Babbius Philonis, Cnaeus, 436
Barclay, John M. G., 24–28, 83, 158, 177
Barnabas, 17, 33, 432
Baronius, Caesar, 326
Barth, Karl, 2, 71, 72, 102, 103, 286
Bates, Matthew W., 98, 116
Bauer, Walter, 184, 432, 457
Benjamin, 243, 244, 389
Berengar of Tours, 121
Binns, Michael, 16
Blaising, Craig, 298, 303
Blass, Friedrich, 36, 89, 141, 158, 159, 216, 312, 362, 366, 406, 414, 422, 431, 455
Bock, Darrell, 298
Boniface VIII, 347, 349
Branham, William, 210
Breshears, Gerry, 298
Bridges, Matthew, 157
Brooks, James A., 222
Brooks, James Hall, 288
Brown, Francis, 55
Brown, Raymond, 1
Bruce, F. F., 4
Bruni, Lorenzo, 326–27
Burke, Kenneth, 25
Burnett, D. Clint, 411

Cadbury, Henry J., 435–36
Cagnat, René 32
Cain, 159, 173
Caligula (Gaius), 6
Callistus, 426–27
Calvin, John, 84, 174, 201, 232–34, 276–78, 280, 281, 290, 313–17, 325, 328–33, 353, 370
Cancik, Hubert, 411–12
Canute I, 174
Caragounis, Chrys C., 404
Cassius Dio, 10, 260, 411, 425
Cassius Longus, 6
Celsus, 378
Charles, R. H., 322, 324
Charlesworth, James H., 322
Chloe, 3
Chrysostom, John, 154
Cicero, Marcus Tullius, 16

Claudius, 9–10, 13–14, 32, 343, 410–12, 423–24, 426–28
Clement of Alexandria, 300–301, 379, 413
Clement of Rome, 17, 145, 269
Coetus, 411
Coverdale, Miles, 200
Crashaw, Richard, 21
Crassus, 6
Crispus, 428
Crum, Ellis J., 68

Dalman, Gustaf, 201–2
Damasus, 138
Darby, John Nelson, 288, 291
David, 30, 35, 40, 106, 117–18, 180, 243, 246, 290, 294, 296, 301, 345–46, 355, 387
Debrunner, Albert, 36, 89, 141, 158, 159, 216, 312, 362, 366, 406, 414, 422, 431, 455
Denney, James, 394
Descartes, René, 72
Dessau, Hermann, 32
Diodorus Siculus, 268
Dionysius of Halicarnassus, 260, 268–69
Domitian, 374, 425
Doty, William G., 405–6
Dresselhaus, Timothy, xvi, 68, 109, 322
Dunn, James D. G., 21, 35–36

Eco, Umberto, 148
Eglon king of Moab, 353
Ehud, 353
Elijah, 193, 243, 244, 265
Ellis, E. Earl, 43
Epaenetus, 9, 400, 404, 407, 443–44
Epiphanius of Salamis, 360–61
Erastus, 13, 32, 432, 434–38
Esau, 217–19, 225, 265–67, 276
Euodia, 448–49
Eusebius of Caesarea, 102, 413
Eve, 62, 126, 129, 139, 141, 148–54, 204, 452–53, 456–58

Fee, Gordon, 43, 339–40, 379, 421, 449
Ford, Gerald, 55
Fortunatus, 3

NAME INDEX 473

Francis (King), 328
Frederick II (Emperor), 349
Frederick III (Elector), 351
Friedrich, Gerhard, 39, 40
Friesen, Steven J., 13, 437
Fuller, Daniel, 110
Funk, Robert W., 36, 89, 141, 158, 159, 216, 312, 362, 366, 406, 414, 422, 431, 455

Gaebelien, Arno C., 288
Gaius, 32, 428, 432–34
Gallio, 13–14
Gamble, Harry, Jr., 441–42, 447
Garnsey, Peter, 338, 339
Gill, N. S., 356
Gingrich, F. Wilbur, 184, 432, 457
Gomer, 225
Goodspeed, Edgar J., 428, 433
Gordon, Adoniram Judson, 288
Gregory of Nazianzus, 139–40, 184–85
Gregory of Nyssa, 153–54
Grosart, Alexander B., 21
Gunkel, Hermann, 208

Habakkuk, 237
Hadrian, 437–38
Halle, W. D., 24
Hamilton, Alexander, 359
Hannah, 88, 262
Hays, Richard B., 21
Heber the Kenite, 353
Henry VIII, 345
Henry of Huntingdon, 174
Hermas, 400, 402, 414
Hermes, 400, 402
Herod the Great, 7, 106, 230, 410–11
Herod of Chalcis, 410
Herodion, 9, 400, 404, 410–11
Herodotus, 33, 318–19
Hesiod, 45
Hippolytus, 426–27
Hixson, Elijah, 450
Hobbes, Thomas, 356
Hodge, Charles, 110
Holofernes, 353–54
Homer, 38, 45, 414–15
Horace, 376–77

Hort, J. F. A., 136
Hosea, 225
Hunter, David G., 138

Ice, Thomas D., 288
Ignatius, 39, 413, 419–20
Innocent IV (Pope), 349
Irenaeus, 139, 413
Isaac, 38, 124, 217–19, 225, 267, 269–70
Isaiah, 221, 239, 295, 386
Ishmael, 219, 225, 265

Jacob (Israel), 38, 217–19, 225–26, 265–67, 269–71, 276
Jael, 353
Jason, 431–33
Jastrow, Marcus, 160
Jay, John, 359
Jehoiada, 355
Jehu, 354
Jeremias, Joachim, 201
Jeroboam, 354
Jerome, 31
Jesse, 386, 388
Jesus who is called Justus, 17
Jewett, Robert, 5, 162, 341, 406, 411–12, 415, 424–27, 429, 432–33, 438–39, 442
Jezebel, 244, 354
Joash (Jehoash), 355
John Mark, 17, 413–14
John the Baptist, 187, 289–90, 296, 424
John (the Revelator), 293
Jonathan the Maccabee, 346
Joram, 354
Joseph who is called Barsabbas and surnamed Justus, 17
Joseph who is surnamed Barnabas, 17
Josephus, 7–8, 106, 116, 274, 410
Joshua, 92, 223
Judith, 353–54
Julia, 400, 402, 404, 414–15, 429
Julian the Apostate, 378
Julius Caesar, 414, 434
Junia, 8–9, 34, 400, 404–5, 408–9, 415, 421–23, 429, 444, 448
Justinian, 373–74

Kant, Immanuel, 26, 81–82
Käsemann, Ernst, 73, 80, 336
Kent, John Harvey, 434–38
Keener, Craig, 10, 46, 48
King, Martin Luther, Jr., 395
Knox, John, 353
Koester, Helmut, 39, 40–42, 102
Korah, 108, 198
Kornelis, Michael, 121

Ladd, George Eldon, 74, 298–300, 304
Lampe, Peter, 5, 8–9, 17, 337, 401,
    403–5, 407–12, 415, 422, 424,
    427–29, 444–45
Leon, Harry, 408
Lewis, C. S., 81, 320
Liberman, Anatoly, 138
Liddell, Henry George, 48, 76, 247, 258,
    259, 321, 361, 366, 399, 453,
    454, 455–56, 458
Lightfoot, J. B., 401, 410, 412, 414
Locke, John, 356
Lucius, 431–32
Lucius of Cyrene, 432
Luke, 207–9, 279, 437
Luther, Martin, 2, 21–23, 37, 47, 59–62,
    67–68, 176–77, 193, 226, 233,
    259, 276, 278–80, 315, 325–26,
    330–31, 333, 349–54, 359

Madison, James, 359
Manasseh, 66
Manson, T. W., 442
Marcian (jurist), 373–74
Marcion of Sinope, 59, 284, 442
Mark, see John Mark
Mary, 400, 404, 408, 412, 415, 429
Mary (the virgin), 139
Mason, Hugh J., 436
Mason, Steve, 38, 40–42, 45
Mattathias, 231
Matthew, 234, 302, 361
Mauss, Marcel, 24
McDonnell, Kilian, xiii
Melito of Sardis, 282–84
Menzies, Glen, 255
Menzies, Robert P., xvi, 43, 209, 270,
    279, 372

Metzger, Bruce, 136, 240, 340, 391,
    445–46, 449
Michel, Otto, 4
Milgram, Jacob, 215
Milton, John, 353, 355–56, 359
Mirbt, Carl, 349
Mitford, T. B., 32
Moltmann, Jürgen, 62
Montesquieu, 358–59
Moses, 22, 50, 54, 62, 86–87, 92–93,
    95–96, 100, 102, 104, 108, 110,
    113, 118, 127–29, 131, 133, 136,
    142, 144, 153, 164, 167–69, 174–
    75, 177, 184, 201–2, 213, 215,
    220, 222, 228–29, 231, 235–37,
    239, 246, 249, 259, 273, 298,
    352, 361, 365, 390, 395, 408
Moule, C. F. D., 140–41, 184, 216, 312,
    366, 458
Mowinckel, Sigmund, 35
Murphy-O'Connor, Jerome, 13, 411–12,
    434
Musonius Rufus, 377

Nadab, 108
Narcissus, 400, 402–4, 411–12
Nebuchadnezzar, 296
Nereus, 400, 402, 404, 414–15, 429
Nero, 8, 9, 14, 337, 339, 374, 411–12
Neusner, Jacob, 23
Nixon, Richard, 55
Noah, 127, 130
Not-Loved (Lo-Ruchamah), 220, 225
Not-my-People (Lo-Ammi), 220–21,
    225
Nympha, 448–49

Olympas, 400, 402, 415
Onesimus, 142
Origen, 33, 102, 106, 148, 442
Orosius, Paul, 260
Osborn, T.L., 210
Oswald, Hilton, 279
Owen, John, 158

Pagels, Elaine, 147, 148, 153–54
Papias of Hierapolis, 413
Parker, Victor, 356

NAME INDEX 475

Patrobas, 400, 402, 414
Pelagius, 151
Pentecost, Dwight, 296
Persis, 400, 404, 412, 415, 429, 444
Peter, 9, 35, 42, 84, 164, 208, 211, 238, 339, 347–49, 375, 413
Petrarch, Francesco, 326
Pharaoh, 202, 220, 222–23, 225
Philemon, 142
Philip of Tralles, 302
Philo, 6, 7, 74, 148, 215
Philologus, 400, 402, 414
Phidias, 409
Phineas, 120, 231
Phlegon, 400, 402, 414
Phoebe, 3, 5, 400, 402, 405–6, 415–18, 420–21, 429, 433, 448–49
Plato, 45, 94, 152
Pliny the Elder, 409
Pliny the Younger, 373–74
Polycarp, 302, 419–21
Pompey, 6
Poppaea Sabina, 8
Porphyry, 378–79
Preisker, Herbert, 142
Praxiteles, 409
Prisca (Priscilla), 3–6, 9–10, 156, 260, 335, 400–407, 409, 415, 423–29, 443–44, 448–49
Ptolemy, king of Egypt, 116

Quartus, 432, 438

Reasoner, Mark, 102, 373, 376–77
Rebecca, 217
Rehoboam, 354
Riss, Richard, 210
Roberts, Oral, 210
Rocca, Samuele, 6–7
Rousseau, Jean-Jacques, 356
Rufus, 400, 402, 404–5, 412–15, 429, 444
Ryrie, Charles Caldwell, 251, 296–98

Salzer, Kean, xvi
Samuel, 38, 354–55
Sanders, Guy D. R., 435–38
Sanders, E. P., 21–25, 27
Sarah, 123–25, 217–18

Saucy, Robert, 298
Saul (King), 40, 244, 345
Schleiermacher, Friedrich, 71–72
Scofield, Cyrus I., 288–90, 293, 295–98
Scott, Robert, 48, 76, 247, 258, 259, 321, 361, 366, 399, 453, 454, 455–56, 458
Secundus, 433
Seneca, 13, 25–26, 411
Septimius Severus, 374
Sergius Paulus, 31–32
Silvanus (Silas), 4, 40
Simeon, 289
Simeon who is called Niger, 17
Simon, Marcel, 275
Simon of Cyrene, 413
Sisera, 353
Smyth, Herbert Weir, 36, 122, 140, 191, 222, 229, 245, 306, 321, 370, 383, 387, 398, 457
Solomon, 220
Sophocles, 193
Sosipater, 431–32
Spielvogel, Jackson, 326
Stachys, 400, 404, 409, 444
Stanley, Andy, 442
Starling, David, 315–17, 325, 330
Statius Quadratus, 302
Stendahl, Krister, 21, 255
Stephanas, 3, 428
Stone, Michael A., xvi, 89, 169, 270–271
Strugnell, John, 450
Suetonius, 10, 260, 343, 411, 425
Syntyche, 448–49

Tacitus, 8, 337
Teacher of Righteousness, 112
Tertius, 406, 421, 431, 433
Tertullian, 300
Tevye, 218
Themison, 409
Theodosius I, 346
Thring, Godfrey, 157
Thucydides, 318–19, 453
Timothy, 4, 40, 431–32, 443–44
Tiro, slave of Cicero, 16
Titius Justus, (Gaius?), 428, 433
Titus, 418

Trajan, 373–74
Tryphaena, 400, 404, 412, 415, 429
Tryphosa, 400, 404, 412, 415, 429
Turretin, Francis, 20
Tyrannos, 356

Urbanus, 400, 404–5, 409, 444

Wallace, Daniel B., 422
Walvoord, John, 296
Wesley, John, 130–31, 171, 176–77
Westphal, Joachim, 330
Winbery, Carlton L., 222

Wittgenstein, Ludwig, 51
Wright, N. T., 21, 47, 51–54, 60–65, 83, 125–26, 146, 168, 187, 232–34, 237, 249, 256–57

Zacchaeus, 340
Zahavy, Tzvee, 148
Zeuxis, 409
Zimri, 231
Zinzendorf, Nicolas Ludwig von, 176
Zuntz, Günther, 451
Zwingli, Huldrych, 330

ANCIENT AND MEDIEVAL SOURCES INDEX

The commentary is divided into discussions of specific sections of Romans. Scripture references for the passages currently under discussion are obvious and therefore are not included in this index (e.g., a reference to Rom 1:11 in the comments to Rom 1:8–13 will not be noted in the index below).

OLD TESTAMENT

Genesis

1—3	147, 151, 153–54
1:1—2:4a	151
1	151
1:22	151
1:28	151
2—3	147
2	151–53
2:7	84
2:16–17	149
2:17	149, 153
2:25	149
3	129, 141, 148–49, 151, 153, 456–58
3:1	149–50
3:4–5	149
3:7	150
3:8	150, 457
3:15	431
3:16	458
3:17–19	151, 204
3:19	151
3:21	150
4:6–7	159
4:7	126, 159, 173
6–9	127
6–8	130
6:2	190, 213
6:4	190, 213
6:5	108, 127
6:12–13	130
12	120
12:1	295
12:1–3	118, 125
12:7	76, 122
12:8	125
13	120
13:3–4	125
13:15	122, 295
14:14	119
15	54, 110, 120–21, 147
15:1	120
15:6	62, 118, 120–21
15:7	122
15:18–21	122–23
17	120, 147
17:8	122–23
17:11	121
18:10	218
18:18	267

Genesis (cont.)

18:25	344
19	130
19:24–26	108
21:12	218, 269
22	120
22:1	54
22:18	267
25:23	219, 266
25:25	219
25:30	219
33:18	93
36:1	219
36:8	219
36:19	219

Exodus

4:21	223
4:22	46, 202, 216
9:16	222
16:10	133
21:13	352
22:28	345
23:33	367, 376
24:16–17	133
32:14	107
32:28	108
32:32	215
33:19	221
34:9	56, 259
34:12	367, 376
34:15–16	88
40:35	133
20:17	88

Leviticus

4—7	389
4:3–12	107
4:22–26	107
4:27–35	105
4:29	105–6, 108
6:5	215
7:6	389
7:7	389
10:1–2	108
10:10	376
16	105
16:13	105–6
18:5	235
18:21	65
19:14	367, 376
19:18	361
20:2–5	65
20:13	78

Numbers

15:20–21	250
15:28	56
15:30–31	107
16:32	108
25:1–14	231
25:9	108
25:11	231
26:61–62	108
30:5	56
30:9	56
30:13	56

Deuteronomy

1:38	223
3:28	223
4:12–18	88
5:24	133
6:25	63
9:4	235–37
9:5	53, 96
12:31	65
17:14–17	345, 355
18:10	65, 307
19:10–11	65
27:25	283
29:4	246
29:19	56
30	167, 235, 236
30:6	235
30:11–14	235–36
30:19	167
31:7	223
31:23	223
32:6	201
32:8	190, 388
32:21	241, 249, 250
32:35	322, 336
32:43	213, 388

ANCIENT AND MEDIEVAL SOURCES INDEX 479

Judges
3:15–30	353
4:17–22	353
11:40	47

1 Samuel
2:10	88, 262
3:2–9	38
8	354
8:1–7	354
8:7–8	355
24:1–7	345

2 Samuel
4:10	39–40
5:3	355
7	290, 294
7:12–16	296
15:30	323
22:50	387

1 Kings
8:30	56
8:34	56
8:39	56
8:50	56
11:26—12:24	354
12:11	164
14:1–20	33
14:6	33
19:10	244
19:14	244
19:18	245, 265

2 Kings
5:18	56, 107
9	354
11:17	355
16:2–3	66
19:30–31	251
21:6	66
24:4	56, 107

1 Chronicles
11:3	355

2 Chronicles
6:21	56
6:25	56
6:27	56
6:30	56, 107
6:39	56
7:14	56
28:1–3	66

Esther
7:8	323

Job
1:6	190
2:1	190
5:9	262
17:7	246
35:7	263
41:3	263

Psalms
1:2	92
2:7	35
5:9	101
10:7	102
14	101
14:1–3	101
18:49	387
19:1–6	71
19:1	75, 133, 240
19:4	240
19:7	92
24:5	63
25:11	56, 107
29:1	190, 213
32:1–2	120
32:2	118, 121
33:5	63
36:1	102
38:21	321
44	198
44:22	198
50:6	98
50:13–14	307
51:4	98
53	101

Psalms (cont.)

53:2–4	101
57:5	133
57:11	133
65:4	107
69:9	370
69:22	246
78:38	107
79:5	230
89:6	213
90:4	149
94:4	244
103:3	56
103:6	63
105:15	345
106:30–31	120
106:37	66
109:5	321
116:11	98
117:1	388
119:18	92
137:7	220
140:3	101

Proverbs

1:23	454
3:7	255
6:34	231
8:15	345
17:13	321
25:21–22	322
25:22	322

Ecclesiastes

7:20	101
10:20	215

Isaiah

1:9	226
1:17	64
1:27	63
4:2	216
8	230
8:14	229–30
9:7	230
10:22	226
11:10	388
13:8	203
14:25	164
17:3	216
26:17	203
28:16	229–30, 238
28:17	63
28:22	226
29:10	246
29:14	399
31:8	249–50
37:31–32	251
40:13	263
41:8	119
42:6	270
45:23	367
49:18	367
50:8	64
52:7	39, 239
52:15	392
53	68
53:1	240
53:12	67–68
56:6–8	294–95
56:16	63
59:7–8	102
59:20–21	259
60:3	270
60:5	11–12
63	220
63:1–6	220
65	242
65:1–2	241
65:1	242
65:2	242
65:12	239
66:4	239
66:7	203
66:19	127

Jeremiah

1:10	345, 348
5:7	56
7:31	65
13:21	203
14:3	323
14:4	323
18:20	321

ANCIENT AND MEDIEVAL SOURCES INDEX

19:4–6	65	**Micah**	
22:23	203	1:15	216
22:24	367	7:9	64
31:31–34	298		
31:33	87	**Habakkuk**	
31:34	56	1:2	49
32:35	65	1:6	48–49
33:8	56	1:11	48
35:3	56	1:13	49, 237
50:20	56	2	49
		2:1	49
Lamentations		2:3	49
3:42	56, 107	2:4	48–49
Ezekiel		**Zechariah**	
5:11	367	12:6—13:9	289
11.19	282		
20:33–44	280	**Malachai**	
23:36–39	65	1:2–3	219

Daniel

1:8–16	375
2:34–35	296
2:44	296
9:19	56
9:25–27	292

APOCRYPHA

1 Esdras (3 Esdras in the Vulgate)

8:78–89	251

Hosea

1:2	225
1:10	225
2:23	225

Judith

13	353–54

Wisdom of Solomon

3.14	413
5:5	213
8:3	151
19:13	109

Joel

1	213
2	213
2:1–11	213
2:23	211
2:28–32	211
2:28	134
2:32	238

1 Maccabees

1:20—2:70	354
2	231
2:27	231

2 Maccabees 95

14:3	109
15:8	109

Amos

7:2	56
9:11	301

NEW TESTAMENT

Matthew

2:2	302
3	290
3:2	290, 296–97
4:17	290, 297
5:3–12	319, 369
5:11	321
5:17–20	234
5:17	297
5:21–22	297
5:27–29	88
5:27–28	297
5:43–44	361
5:43	234
6:9–13	202
6:10	299
7:1	351
10:5–23	33
10:16	430
12:1	409
12:28	299
12:32	74
13	297, 299
13:3	297
13:11–13	297
13:11	297
13:31–32	304
13:33	304
15:10–11	383
16:4	88
16:19	349
18:18–19	345
16:24	188
18:23	142
19:16–30	91
19:19	234, 361
21:23	454
22:39	234, 361
22:40	361
23:23–29	369
23:31	158
24:1–36	203
24:1–3	230
24:2	294
24:8	203
24:21	292
24:29–31	213
24:32–33	279
25:14–30	91
25:19	142
25:31	296
26	302–3
26:52	345, 348
26:59	107
26:63	302
27:4	283
27:27–29	302
28:19–20	319

Mark

1:1	39
2:23	409
3:2	296
3:5	256
4:28	409
4:11–12	297
4:30–32	304
5:1	297
7:14–15	383
10:17–31	91
10:30	74
12:31	361
13:1–37	203
13:1–2	230
13:2	294
13:4	226
13:8	203
13:10	39
13:19	292
13:24–27	213
13:28–29	279
14:9	39
14:36	202
14:55	107

Luke

1:15	320
1:31–33	296
2:38	289
3:2	240
3:16	187

ANCIENT AND MEDIEVAL SOURCES INDEX   483

4:1	320	15:26	186
6:1	409	18:10	348
9:1–6	33	18:35	345
10:1–12	33		
10:3	430	**Acts**	
10:27	361	1:5	208, 320
11:2–4	202	1:6	299
11:12	299	1:8	208, 335, 390–91
11:20	299	1:21–22	34
13:18–19	304	1:23	17
13:20–21	304	2	206, 208
17:21	299	2:2	320
18:13	106	2:4	206–8, 320
18:18–30	91	2:17	134, 320, 448
18:30	74	2:18	134, 320
20:34–36	74	2:21	238
21	292	2:33	320
21:5–36	203	2:38	208
21:5–6	230	2:44	320
21:6	294	4:8	208, 320
21:11	203	4:31	208
21:23–24	279–80	4:36	17
21:23	292	5:29	352
21:24	257, 279, 296	6:3	208, 320
21:25–28	213	6:5	208, 320
21:29–31	279	6:8	320
22:22	297	7:55	208
22:38	345, 348	9	171
23:24	340	9:17	208
24:13–35	40	10:1–4	230
24:44–49	40	10:11	230
24:46–47	40	10:14	376
24:49	187, 208	10:34	84
		10:42	57
John		10:44–46	208
1:17	147	10:45	134, 209
2:17	370	11:16	208
2:18–21	294	11:24	208
2:19–21	230	11:28	318
3:8	320	13:1	17, 432
3:34	240	13:7	32
4:22	279	13:9	208, 320
9:34	454	13:52	208
10:11	417	12:12	17
10:12	417	14:14	33
10:16	348	15	423
12:13	303	15:10	164

Acts (cont.)

15:16	301
15:23	30
15:37	17
17:5–7	432
17:5	432
17:7	432
18	3, 423
18:1–4	260
18:2	423
18:3–4	406
18:7	428, 433
18:12	13
18:18–19	428
18:18	14, 423–24
18:23	14
18:25–26	156
18:26	423, 424, 448
19:9	356
19:22	435
19:29	433
20:4	432–33
20:17–38	419
20:17	419
20:28	419
20:31	14
21	395
21:8–9	448
21:10–11	318
21:21	390
21:39	12
22:25–28	31
22:28	12
24:24–27	14
25—28	31
27:7	14
27:9	14
27:14	14
27:19	14
27:27	14
27:33	14
27:41	14
27:43–44	14
28:11	14
28:15–16	292
28:30	14

Romans

1	49, 72, 75, 93, 127, 130, 237, 444
1:1—16:24	445
1:1—16:23	445
1:1—15:33	29, 445, 447
1:1—14:23	445
1:1	12, 35
1:3	180
1:4	134, 196
1:5	239, 390, 398, 430
1:7	45
1:9	134
1:16–17	237
1:17–18	73
1:17	60, 72–73, 301
1:18–32	80, 81
1:18	125, 127, 309, 361
1:23	125
1:24	80
1:25	396–97
1:32	133, 191, 218, 337
2	75, 87, 93, 275
2:1	75, 90–91, 224
2:3	90, 224
2:5–11	28
2:5	73, 77, 127
2:6	112
2:9	46, 245
2:10	46
2:12–29	97
2:12	4, 95
2:14	93–94, 111
2:15	215, 381
2:16	40
2:17–24	5, 88
2:23	126
2:26	275
2:28–29	275, 300
2:28	180
2:29	86, 134
3	106
3:3	100
3:4	98, 156, 161
3:5	100, 405
3:6	98
3:9–20	97

3:9	5, 118, 156, 160, 221, 227, 245	5:18	125, 126, 143, 152
3:19	286	5:19	152
3:20	57, 83, 111, 180	5:20	12, 152, 160
3:21—4:25	2	5:21	143, 152
3:21–26	108–9, 129	6	134, 170, 172, 200
3:21	160	6:1–10	158
3:22	115	6:1	100, 156
3:23–25	129	6:2	98, 158, 161
3:24	58	6:4	58
3:25	58, 68–69, 109, 129	6:5	157
		6:6	156
3:27	112, 119	6:8	67
3:28	57–58, 111	6:9	159
3:30	57	6:14	147, 161, 172
4	49, 54, 66, 120, 147, 295	6:15	98, 147, 172
		6:17	45
4:1	5, 100, 156, 180	6:19	172, 181
4:2	57	6:21	141
4:3	62	7	134, 161, 171–72, 175–77, 200
4:5	55	7:1–6	170, 172
4:9	316	7:1	5, 109, 172
4:12	124	7:3	145
4:13–17	295	7:4	5, 165
4:13	62	7:5	166, 172–73, 181
4:15	126–27, 130, 142, 144	7:6	172, 173
		7:7–25	165, 167, 169–78, 184
4:17	162, 234, 301	7:7	98, 100, 156, 170, 177
4:20	76		
4:25	126	7:12	96
5	147, 458	7:13	98
5:1	57	7:14	96, 170
5:3	78, 191, 218, 337	7:18	181
5:6	68, 135	7:21	175
5:7	52	7:22	171
5:8	67, 405	7:23	175, 218
5:9–10	237	7:24	157
5:9	58, 237	7:25	145, 181
5:11	78, 133, 191, 218, 337	8	87, 134, 170, 172, 178, 199–200, 203–5, 207–8, 210, 213
5:12–21	143, 147–48, 152		
5:12–14	142, 166		
5:12	143, 152, 162	8:2–27	198
5:13	128, 146, 152	8:3–4	182
5:14	126, 129, 143, 152	8:3	10
5:15	126	8:5	178
5:16	126, 143, 146, 152	8:6	178, 181
5:17	62, 126, 143, 152		

Romans (*cont.*)

8:7	188
8:8	182
8:9	178, 182, 187, 200, 203
8:12	145, 182
8:14	200, 213
8:15	200
8:16	192, 213
8:17	213
8:18–27	204
8:18–25	189
8:19–22	204
8:19	202, 212–13
8:21	204, 207, 213
8:22	192, 204
8:23	78, 105, 133, 191–92, 200, 202, 207, 212, 337
8:26–27	207
8:26	191, 205–7
8:27	193
8:28	134, 196
8:30	57
8:31	100, 156
8:32–34	58
8:32	252
8:33	57
8:34	1193
8:36	301
8:38	340
9:1—16:27	279
9—11	147, 199–200, 244, 254–55, 264–66, 270, 272, 287
9	227, 276
9:1–3	285
9:1	337, 381
9:2	237, 267
9:3	180, 231
9:4–5	98
9:4	265
9:5	180, 396–97
9:6	233, 264, 275
9:7	38, 265, 269
9:8	225, 264, 267
9:10–13	225, 265, 276
9:10	78, 133, 191, 337
9:11	266
9:12	38, 112, 267, 269
9:14–29	229
9:14	98, 100, 156, 224, 233
9:15	223
9:16	56, 145, 223, 266, 269
9:17	224
9:18	222, 246
9:19–24	315
9:19	100, 156
9:20	80, 90–91
9:21	138
9:24	133, 191, 218, 276, 337
9:30—10:13	2
9:30	100, 156
9:31–32	62
9:31	229
9:33	238, 301
10	236
10:1–4	230
10:1–3	285
10:3	96, 245
10:4–5	62
10:5–13	234
10:9–11	237
10:11	230
10:14	240
10:15	240, 301
10:16	37
10:17	240
10:18	240
10:20	241
10:21	241
11	225, 276, 280. 284, 289, 306
11:1	98
11:2–4	265
11:2	193
11:3–4	289
11:4	265
11:6	112
11:7	245, 256
11:8	246
11:11–24	255
11:11–12	294–95

11:11	98, 126, 241, 250, 261, 294	13:4	338, 351, 353
11:12	126, 256–57, 294	13:5	133, 191, 215, 218, 382
11:13	5, 35	13:7	360
11:14	180, 241	13:8–10	234
11:15	296	13:8	234
11:16–24	266	13:9	234
11:16	138, 278	13:23	367
11:17–24	251	14	371, 377, 441–42, 446–47
11:17–18	272	14:1	370–72, 387
11:17	273	14:2	145, 371, 380
11:18–21	272	14:13–23	379
11:21	272–73	14:13	375–76
11:23	266, 271, 273	14:14	375–76, 382, 383
11:24	272–73	14:15	385
11:25–26	271, 279, 287	14:19	145
11:25	249, 279, 321	14:20	112, 375–76
11:26	136, 266, 275–76, 280, 284, 291, 296, 300	14:21	375
		14:23	xv, 29, 385, 441
11:27	87	15	36, 42–43, 371, 377, 442–44, 446
11:28	261	15:1—16:24	445
11:29	268–70	15:1—16:23	445
11:30	270	15:1	371, 384, 442
11:31	56	15:6	442, 447
11:33	90	15:7	42
11:36	306, 396	15:8	112
12:1—15:6	306	15:9	56, 301
12	208, 306, 312, 325	15:10	301
12:1–4	313	15:11	301
12:1	215, 306, 389	15:12	301
12:3	316–17, 331	15:15–32	11
12:5	294, 314	15:15–16	35
12:6–8	162, 314, 325	15:15	393
12:6	311, 313, 315, 317, 325, 328, 329, 331	15:16	407
12:8	43, 320	15:18	112
12:11	318	15:19	11, 391
12:16	252, 255	15:20	11, 393
12:17	335, 341, 344	15:21	301
12:19	334–36, 341, 344, 351	15:23–25	14
		15:23	11
13	349–50, 359	15:29	430
13:1–7	336, 338–39, 341–42, 345–46, 353, 359	15:33	431
		16	4, 9, 36, 400–402, 406–7, 409, 414–15, 421, 429, 436, 443–44, 448, 459
13:1	245, 347, 348, 353		
13:3	340		

Romans (cont.)

16:1–23	445, 447
16:1–16	415, 429
16:1–2	421
16:1	5, 417–18, 448–49
16:3–16	9
16:3	423–24, 448–49
16:4	5, 415
16:5	5, 424
16:7	8–9, 34, 421, 448–49
16:10	9
16:16	5
16:17–19	3
16:17	45
16:20	29, 439, 446–47
16:21–23	29, 446
16:23	5, 13, 32, 428
16:24	29, 445–46
16:25–27	29, 36, 445–46
16:25	4, 40
16:26	11, 239, 390, 430

1 Corinthians

1:2	5
1:11	3
1:13	67–68
1:14–16	428
1:14	433
1:18	46–47, 76
1:18–25	72, 76
1:19	399
1:21	72, 76
1:26	181
1:29	180
2:6–10	339
2:8	340
2:15	345, 348
2:16	263
3:10	391
3:12–15	28
3:16	89, 294, 307
3:17	89
3:21–23	198
3:27	112
4:5	88
4:6	450
4:8–13	88
5:1	300
5:2	78
5:9–10	100
6:1–8	339, 341–42
6:2	188
6:4	341
6:7	250
6:9–11	77
6:13	158
6:15	98
6:16	180
7:1	3
7:17–24	37
7:20	37
7:25	3
7:39	429
8:1–13	377–78
8:1	3
8:2–3	379
8:6	264
8:7–10	371
8:7	379, 381–82
8:9	375–76
8:10	382
8:12	87, 381–82
9:1	33, 112
9:11	394
9:13–14	389
9:19–23	59
9:20	160, 372
9:22	371, 372
10:1–13	197
10:12	197
10:14–22	377–78
10:16	430
10:18	275
10:20–21	66
10:22	250
10:23–33	377–78
10:25	380, 382
10:27	382
10:28–29	382
10:28	378, 382
10:29	382
11	452
11:2–16	452
11:14	86

ANCIENT AND MEDIEVAL SOURCES INDEX 489

12	162, 208, 309, 311–12, 314, 318
12:1	3
12:2	300
12:8–10	312
12:9	313
12:10	194, 313
12:13	301, 320
12:27	294, 311
12:28	312
12:29–30	312
12:30	194
13:1–3	339
13:1	193, 206
13:2	316
13:3	339
13:12	324
14	43, 193, 205, 312, 318, 394, 450–52
14:1	313
14:2	206
14:5	194
14:13–19	206
14:13	194
14:14–15	205
14:14	207
14:15	207
14:18–19	205
14:20–25	206
14:23	434
14:25	88, 237
14:26	194
14:27	194, 206
14:28	205, 452
14:29	317
14:30	452
14:33	431, 450
14:34–35	416, 448–50, 452
14:40	450–51
15	34, 143, 291, 450–51
15:1–11	41
15:3	42, 67
15:4	34
15:7	34
15:8	34
15:9	34
15:22	143
15:24	340
15:25	302
15:32	407
15:44	331
15:58	112
16:1	3
16:10	112
16:12	3, 100, 415
16:19	423, 443
16:21	433
16:23	439

2 Corinthians

1	301
1:2	381
1:17	181
1:20	287, 301, 329
2:3	40
2:16	47–48
3:1	34
3:6–8	307
3:14–18	167
3:14	231–32, 246
4:3	4
4:4	241
4:5	237
4:6	241
4:11	180
4:15	146–47
4:17	48, 189
5:4	140–41
5:10	57
5:14	67
5:16	181
5:21	60, 68
6:7	160
6:14	164
6:16	89, 294, 307
7:10	260, 268
8:9	36, 238
8:23	33
9:6	430
10:3	181
10:13	11
10:15–16	11
11:4	41
11:5	34

2 Corinthians (cont.)

11:6	34
11:9	428
11:13	34
12:3	237
13:10	433
13:11	431
13:12	415

Galatians

1	41
1:2	5
1:6	41
1:11–12	41
1:12	42
2	423
2:7	35, 42
2:9	389
2:12	375
2:15	285
2:16	58, 111, 115
2:17	57, 98
2:19–21	62
2:20	67
2:21	147
3	87
3:2	86–87, 111
3:5	111
3:8	4, 57
3:10	111
3:11	57
3:16	226
3:19	127
3:21–22	62
3:21	98
3:23	160
3:28	301
4:4–5	58
4:4	160
4:5	160
4:6	200
4:21	160
5:1	164
5:4	53, 147, 234
5:14	361
5:18	160
5:22–23	134

6:2	320
6:11	433
6:14	98
6:15–16	277
6:16	277, 300
6:17	188

Ephesians

1:15–23	319
1:21	340
2:15	261, 301
2:19–22	294, 307
2:19–20	34
2:20	211
3:5–6	297
3:6	301
3:10	340
4	212
4:11	212, 417
4:12	294
4:13	212
4:17	285, 300
4:18	256
4:27	322
4:28	43
5:2	67
5:25	67
6:12	340
6:17	240

Philippians

1:1	418, 420
1:20	189
2	36
2:6–7	36
2:11	237
2:17	389
2:25	33
3:2	430
3:3	300
3:4–6	167, 171, 178
3:5	389
3:8	167
3:9	47, 60, 62, 83
3:12	141
3:18–19	430

3:19 430
3:20 309
4:2–3 448–49
4:9 431
4:10 141

Colossians

1:16 340
2:5 115
2:10 340
2:11 300
2:15 340
2:20 58
3:11 301
4:11 17
4:14 437
4:15 448–49
4:18 433

1 Thessalonians

1:5 4, 40
1:10 292
2:8 43
4:5 285, 300
4:9 3
4:13 3
4:14–17 293
4:15–17 291
4:16–17 291
5:1 3
5:10 67
5:15 321
5:23 171, 431
5:26 415

2 Thessalonians

1:8 37, 239
2:14 4, 40
3:17 433
3:18 446

1 Timothy

1:5 381–82
1:19 381–82
2:11–15 416, 448–49, 452–53
3:1–7 420
3:8–13 420
3:9 381–82
4:2 381–82
5:17 420
5:19 420

2 Timothy

1:3 381–82
1:18 443
2:8 4, 40
2:15 289
4:1 57
4:8 57
4:12 443
4:19 423–24, 443
4:20 435

Titus

1:5–6 418–19
1:7–9 419
1:15 381–82
2:13 217
3:1 340, 345
3:5–6 134
3:5 157

Philemon

18 128, 142

Hebrews

1:3 302
1:8 302
2:17 106
6:5 240
9:28 67
11:1 316, 330
11:3 240
12:2 296
13:20 431

James

2:9 84
5:9 57

1 Peter

2:17	345
2:24	67–68
3:9	321
5:8	126–27

2 Peter

3:8	149

1 John

4:2–3	331

2 John

1	413

Jude

3	327

Revelation

3:10	292
4—22	293
4:1	293
6:9–11	289
7:3–8	289
16:10	296
19	293
19:11–16	280
19:11	296
19:12	157
19:21	296
20	294
20:2–8	294
22:20	191

JUDAIC WRITINGS

Dead Sea Scrolls

4Q82Minor Prophets^g	48
4QDeut^j	190
4QFlor (4Q174)	
1.7	111
4QMMT	112, 114
C 26–27	112
C 27	111
C 31–32	112

Pseudepigrapha

1 Enoch

71:15	74

4 Ezra

7:48–50	74
8:1	74

4 Maccabees

17:22	106
22:9	104–5

Apocalypse of Baruch (Syriac), aka 2 Baruch

14:8–9	262
15:7	74

Jubilees

4:30	149

Psalms of Solomon

17:27	213

The Testament of Benjamin

4.3	324

The Testament of Gad

6.7	322

Mishnah

	113

m.Aboth

1.1	92, 113, 160
3.5	160

m.Abodah Zarah

2.3	375

m.Chullin 376

m.Sanhedrin

10.1	258, 273–75

Josephus

Antiquities

12.47	116
12.147	116
13.11.1	410
16.182	106

17.324–31 (xii.1) 7
20.195 8
Jewish War
2.104 (ii,7) 7
2.221 (2.11.6) 410

Philo

Embassy to Gaius
23 (155–57) 7
Special Laws
1.235 215

GRAECO-ROMAN INSCRIPTIONS

Corpus Inscriptiones Latinarum 3
3973 412
Corpus Inscriptiones Latinarum 6
15640 412
17577 410
29104 410
Corpus Inscriptionum Iudaeae
173 411
Inscriptiones Graecae
IX, 1 , 61 128
Jewish Inscriptions of Westerns Europe
2.292 411

GRAECO-ROMAN WRITINGS

Aesop/Phaedrus

Fables
Perry #44 (Book 1, Fable 2) 354

Aristotle

Politics
3.7 357
3.13 87
4.2 357
5.10 357

Aulus Gellius

Attic Nights
Vol. III, pp. 168–69 (Loeb) 373

Cassius Dio

Roman History
60.6.6 10, 260
60.19.2 411
64.3 411
67 425

Diodorus Siculus

Historical Library
10.16.3 268

Dionysius of Halicarnassus

Roman Antiquities
2.35.4 260, 268–69
8.56.1 260, 268, 269
11.13.2 260, 268

Homer

Iliad
18.35 415

Horace

Carmina
Book 2, Ode 16, line 14 377
Book 2, Satire 2, lines 53, 70 376–77

Juvenal

Satire IV
94–96 425

Musonius Rufus

On Food 377

Plato

Gorgias
483, a, 4 94
Symposium
189c–193e 152

Pliny the Elder
Natural History
35.36.79–97   409

Pliny the Younger
Epistula
Book 10, Letter 93   374

Seneca
De Beneficiis   25
Letters
104:1   13
Naturalis Quaestiones
4.15   411

Suetonius
Lives of the Twelve Caesars
Claudius
25.4   10, 260, 343
28   411
Domitian
10.2   425

Tablet of Cebes
32.3   269

Tacitus
Annals
13.50–51   337
15.40   8

Thucydides
Peloponnesian War
3.12.4–5   453

EARLY CHRISTIAN WRITINGS

Apostles' Creed
    366

Apostolic Fathers
1 Clement   39
2.7   260, 269
5.7   46
31:2   120
32:3   120
35:1–2   145
54.4   260, 269
55.2   17–18
58.2   260, 269

Didache
15.1   420

Epistle of Barnabas   39
4.14   282
4.6   282
4.8   282
6.14–16   282

Ignatius of Antioch
Philippians
11.1   413

Martyrdom of Polycarp
21.1   302

Polycarp
Philippians
5.2   420–21
6.1   420–21

Aristides, Aelius
Apology (Greek text)
2   300

Augustine
Against Two Letters of the Pelagians
4.7   137
City of God   346–47
13.14   154
14.2   154
14.23   152
21.12   138–39
Confessions
8.11   361
8.12   362
10.29   151

Diverse Questions to Simplicianus
1.2.19   138

On the Merits and Forgiveness of Sins, and On the Baptism of Infants
3.1   137

Chrysostom

Homily to the People of Antioch
7.3   154

Clement of Alexandria

Hypotyposeis   413

Stromata
3.10   300–301

Epiphanius of Salamis

Anakephalaiosis   360

Panarion   360–61

Epistle to Diognetus

1.1   300

Eusebius of Caesarea

Ecclesiastical History
6.14.6   413

Gregory of Nazianzus

Letter 101 (to Cledonius)
5   184

Oration 38
13   139, 184–85

Oration 40 (Oration on Holy Baptism)
7   139–40

Gregory of Nyssa

On the Creation of Mankind
4.1   153

Hippolytus

Refutatio
9.12.24   427

Irenaeus

Against All Heresies
3.1.1   413
5.19   139

Melito of Sardis

Homily on the Passion   282
176–77 (in Bonner)   283
177 (in Bonner)   283
16.95–96 (179 in Bonner)   284

Orosius, Paul

History Against the Pagans
7:6   260
7:15–16   260

Tertullian

To the Nations
1.8   300

MEDIEVAL WRITINGS

Aquinas (Thomas)

Summa Theologiae
II, q. 4, art. 8, ad 2   70

Everyman   91

Boniface VIII (Pope)

Unam Sanctam   347–49

Innocent IV (Pope)

Subordination of secular power   349

Justinian

Corpus Juris Civilis   373–74

Digesta
47.22.3.2   373

www.ingramcontent.com/pod-product-compliance
Lightning Source LLC
Chambersburg PA
CBHW052111010526
44111CB00036B/1634